"Given the recent and continuing spate of major crises, this book should be read by every corporate executive, student of business, and EVERYONE connected with business."

Ian Mitroff, *University of California Berkeley, US*

THE ROUTLEDGE COMPANION TO RISK, CRISIS AND EMERGENCY MANAGEMENT

This volume provides a comprehensive, up-to-date overview of the latest management and organizational research related to risk, crisis, and emergency management. It is the first volume to present these separate, but related, disciplines together. Combined with a distinctly social and organizational science approach to the topics (as opposed to engineering or financial economics), the research presented here strengthens the intellectual foundations of the discipline while contributing to the development of the field.

The Routledge Companion to Risk, Crisis and Emergency Management promises to be a definitive treatise of the discipline today, with contributions from several key academics from around the world. It will prove a valuable reference for students, researchers, and practitioners seeking a broad, integrative view of risk and crisis management.

Robert P. Gephart, Jr. is Professor at the University of Alberta, School of Business. He has served as Associate Editor for *Organizational Research Methods*, and in 2015, received the Sage Career Achievement Award from the Research Methods Division of the Academy of Management.

C. Chet Miller is C.T. Bauer Professor of Organizational Studies at the University of Houston. His research focuses on the functioning and effects of executive teams, the design of strategic decision processes within firms, and the use of seemingly impossible organizational goals. His work has appeared in outlets such as *Harvard Business Review* and *Academy of Management Journal*.

Karin Svedberg Helgesson is Associate Professor in the Department of Management and Organization at the Stockholm School of Economics, Sweden. She has published several books, and her work has appeared in journals such as *Organization Studies* and the *Journal of Common Market Studies*.

ROUTLEDGE COMPANIONS IN BUSINESS, MANAGEMENT AND ACCOUNTING

Routledge Companions in Business, Management and Accounting are prestige reference works providing an overview of a whole subject area or sub-discipline. These books survey the state of the discipline including emerging and cutting edge areas. Providing a comprehensive, up-to-date, definitive work of reference, Routledge Companions can be cited as an authoritative source on the subject.

A key aspect of these Routledge Companions is their international scope and relevance. Edited by an array of highly regarded scholars, these volumes also benefit from teams of contributors which reflect an international range of perspectives.

Individually, Routledge Companions in Business, Management and Accounting provide an impactful one-stop-shop resource for each theme covered. Collectively, they represent a comprehensive learning and research resource for researchers, postgraduate students, and practitioners.

Published titles in this series include:

For more information about this series, please visit: www.routledge.com/Routledge-Companions-in-Business-Management-and-Accounting/book-series/RCBMA

THE ROUTLEDGE COMPANION TO RISK, CRISIS AND EMERGENCY MANAGEMENT

Edited by Robert P. Gephart, Jr., C. Chet Miller, and Karin Svedberg Helgesson

Routledge
Taylor & Francis Group

NEW YORK AND LONDON

First published 2019
by Routledge
605 Third Avenue, New York, NY 10017

and by Routledge
4 Park Square, Milton Park, Abingdon, Oxon OX14 4RN

First issued in paperback 2022

Routledge is an imprint of the Taylor & Francis Group, an informa business

Copyright © 2019 Taylor & Francis

Publisher's Note
The publisher has gone to great lengths to ensure the quality of this reprint but points out that some imperfections in the original copies may be apparent.

Library of Congress Cataloging-in-Publication Data
A catalog record has been requested for this book

Typeset in Bembo
by codeMantra

ISBN 13: 978-1-03-247598-1 (pbk)
ISBN 13: 978-1-138-20886-5 (hbk)

DOI: 10.4324/9781315458175

*To people who have experienced harm from organizational risks and crises
and to first responders who have given their lives in the process.
And as always, to Bev, Keith, and Laura with love.*
−Robert P. Gephart, Jr.

*To Laura, Martini, and Olive: The adventure would not be
the same without you.*
−C. Chet Miller

To Maj and Jerry who paved the way.
−Karin Svedberg Helgesson

CONTENTS

FIGURES

TABLES

PREFACE

The idea for this book emerged from an invitation from Sytze Kingma to help Arjen Boin and himself organize a sub-theme on risk and crisis management for the 2008 annual meeting of the European Group for Organization Studies (EGOS) in Amsterdam. The success of the session led to subsequent risk-related sub-themes at EGOS in Gothenburg, Sweden, and in 2011, and in Montreal, Canada, in 2013 with Sytze Kingma and Chet Miller as co-organizers. I was also pleased to help co-organize an EGOS risk session with Michael Power and Steve Maguire in Athens in 2015. Sharon Golan, then an editor at Taylor and Francis Publishers, supported the project from the outset and encouraged Chet and I to move forward with a third co-editor. Fortunately, Karin Svedberg Helgesson agreed to join in as co-editor.

Risks, crises, and emergencies are outcomes of the activities of enterprises and organizations that can and do produce both benefits and harms. A strong argument that risks have become ever more important in contemporary society is provided by Ulrich Beck in *Risk Society*. Beck explores the thesis that prior capitalist economies and societies were organized around a principle of wealth production. This created prosperity but also significant risks and harms as side effects of wealth production (e.g., ecological damage). As a result, economies and societies in the contemporary world became organized around a risk management principle that addresses the need to overcome the damages, harms, and hidden costs of unbridled wealth production.

The seemingly inexhaustible supply of risks, crises, emergencies, and disasters provided in society suggests we often know much less about preventing or managing risks, crises, and disasters than we might wish to know. And, even when there is actionable knowledge to prevent or manage technical aspects of crises, there is often a lack of political will to do so. Hence, there is great need to better understand the human, social, and organizational issues involved in detecting, managing, and remediating risks, crises, and emergency events.

This volume addresses this need for innovative theories, methods, and practices in the field. The volume reviews key issues, concepts, theories, and methods in the area of risk, crisis, and emergency management; offers numerous case examples of risk and crises; and explores organization change and development strategies to prevent, manage, and mitigate risks and crises. This volume results from, and seeks to share, many of the ideas and insights provided by our colleagues who participated in the EGOS risk sessions as well as other colleagues with whom we have shared rich conversations and interesting research on risks and crises. We hope that readers will find the chapters to be stimulating and meaningful sources of insight into the complex aspects of organizationally based risks, dangers, and harms. In any event, here at last, is the final product!

–Robert P. Gephart, Jr.
Edmonton, Alberta, Canada
May 4, 2018

ACKNOWLEDGMENTS

The editors of this volume wish to thank Sharon Golan, Erin Arata, Meredith Norwich, and Alston Slatton of Routledge for guidance and support for this project. We also thank Karl Weick, Michael Power, and Mark De Rond for useful suggestions.

Robert Gephart, Jr. This research was supported in part by funding from the Social Sciences and Humanities Research Council of Canada.

Karin Svedberg Helgesson The Ragnar Söderberg Foundation [Grant EF/12/10] helped provide editing time, and the possibility for the editors to meet up in Banff, Canada. I also wish to thank my colleagues Ulrika Mörth, Ebba Sjögren, Anna Nyberg, Pernilla Bolander, and Karin Fernler for professional support. Finally, I am grateful to CF, Alice, and Linus for bearing with me with love in the everyday.

AUTHORS

Cynthia Hardy & Steve Maguire The authors gratefully acknowledge funding support from the Australian Research Council (DP110101764) and the Social Sciences & Humanities Research Council of Canada (435-2014-0256).

Jan Hayes & Sarah Maslen This work was funded in part by the Energy Pipelines Co-operative Research Centre, supported through the Australian Government's Cooperative Research Centres Program. The cash and in-kind support from the Australian Pipelines and Gas Association Research and Standards Committee is gratefully acknowledged.

Henry Rothstein This chapter was informed by research funded under the *Open Research Area (ORA) for the Social Sciences* program by the Economic and Social Research Council (No. ES/K006169/1), the Agence Nationale de la Recherche (ANR, France), Deutsche Forschungsgemeinschaft (DFG, Germany), and the Nederlands Organisatie voor Wetenschappelijk Onderzoek (NWO, the Netherlands).

April D. Schantz & Juanita M. Woods Authors would like to extend an acknowledgment to colleague Anastasia Miller, for her helpful comments and feedback during early development of this chapter.

Cyrus B. Parks & Laura B. Cardinal The authors wish to thank Chet Miller for his thorough feedback during the editorial process, Leiser Silva for his support of early manuscript versions, and Vincent Giolito and the rest of the Error Management community at the Academy of Management 2016 meeting in Anaheim, CA.

CONTRIBUTORS

Mário Aquino Alves is an associate professor of Public Administration and Government at Fundação Getúlio Vargas, Escola de Administração de Empresas de São Paulo (FGV/EAESP), Brazil. His research interests include corporate political activity, civil society organizations, and political participation.

Mike Annett is an assistant professor of human resource management at MacEwan University's School of Business and an active human resource professional. His scholarship centers on workplace inclusion to better understand and resolve management and system difficulties in producing diverse and inclusive workforces. His industry experience includes roles directly addressing and minimizing human resource risks in government departments. Dr. Annett earned his PhD in Human Resource Management and Industrial Relations at the University of Alberta, and is designated as a chartered professional in Human Resources.

Thomas D. Beamish is professor of sociology at the University of California, Davis. His research interests and expertise includes a focus on Risks, Hazards, and Environment; Community Politics and Social Movements; Institutions, Organizations, and Economy; and Science, Technology, and Innovation Studies. As an environmental and organizational sociologist, and as a sociologist of risk, Professor Beamish's research has generated two books and many papers published in leading journals.

Fatma Umut Beşpınar is associate professor of sociology, Middle East Technical University in Ankara. She has an MS degree in sociology from METU and a PhD degree in Sociology, University of Texas at Austin, USA, 2007. Her areas of interest are work, family, and gender and women studies. She has published chapters in edited volumes such as *Women in the Middle East and North Africa: Agents of Change*, *The Routledge Handbook of Modern Turkey* and *Turkey and the Politics of National Identity: Social, Economic and Cultural Transformation*, and she has published articles in such journals as *New Technology, Work and Employment,* and *Work and Family.*

Kees (F.K.) Boersma is associate professor in the Department of Organization Sciences of the VU University Amsterdam. He completed his (awarded) PhD thesis at the Eindhoven

University of Technology. His current research is about organization networks and strategies in the context of safety, crisis management, and security. He is the group leader of AREA: Amsterdam Research on Emergency Administration, senior member of the Netherlands Institute of Governance (NIG), and senior editor of the *Journal of Contingencies and Crisis Management* (guest editor), *Organization Management Journal,* and the *International Journal of Emergency Services.*

David M. Boje is an international scholar with over 22 books and 140 journal articles, doing keynotes, visiting scholar lectures, and seminars in organizational storytelling research methods to faculty and doctoral students around the world. His contribution to organization research methods has applications to strategy-as-process, ensemble leadership, socio-economic interventions, and organizational systems disciplines. He is a Regents Professor of New Mexico State University, and Distinguished Achievement Professor, holds an honorary doctorate from Aalborg University, and is considered godfather of their Material Storytelling Lab.

Marc Bonnet is professor and executive dean at the Institut d'Administration des Entreprises, University Jean Moulin Lyon 3 in France, and Directeur adjoint de l'ISEOR. Groupe Management Socio-Economique (Centre iaelyon Magellan, Université Jean Moulin). He has undertaken extensive intervention research using the SEAM approach and published numerous scholarly articles on the results of this research.

Laura B. Cardinal is the SmartState Endowed Chair and Director for the Center for Innovation and Commercialization at the Darla Moore School of Business at the University of South Carolina. She earned her PhD from the University of Texas at Austin. Professor Cardinal sits on the Board of Governors of the Academy of Management. She has served on editorial boards of top journals in management, acted as an associate editor of the *Academy of Management Annals*, and sat on the Board of Directors of the Strategic Management Society. Her book, *Organizational Control* (with Sitkin and Bijlsma-Frankema), was published by Cambridge University Press.

Konstantinos Chalkias is a research fellow at Cass Business School, City University of London. His research interest resolves around the practices and strategic dynamics of organizations and markets. Drawing from social-practice theory, he studies how strategy is done inside organizations and how financial markets are constructed. He is also interested in theories of risk and risk management, with a recent focus on investigating the market mechanisms that transfer uninsurable risk into global financial markets to bridge the global insurance gap.

Tom Christensen is Professor in Public Administration and Policy at Department of Political Science, University of Oslo. He is also adjunct research professor at Uni Research Rokkan Centre, University of Bergen, and visiting professor at School of Public Administration and Policy, Renmin University. He has published extensively on institutional change and comparative public sector reforms, based on organization theory.

W. Timothy Coombs (PhD Purdue University) is a full professor in the Department of Communication at Texas A&M University. He is also an honorary professor in the Department of Business Communication at Aarhus University. He received the 2002 Jackson,

Jackson & Wagner Behavioral Science Prize from the Public Relations Society of America, and the 2013 Pathfinder Award from the Institute of Public Relations in recognition of his research contributions to the field and to practice. Dr. Coombs has worked with governments, corporations, and consulting firms in the USA, Asia, and Europe on ways to improve crisis communication efforts. He currently edits *Corporation Communication: An International Journal*.

Barbara Czarniawska is senior professor of Management Studies at Gothenburg Research Institute, University of Gothenburg, Sweden. She takes a feminist and processual perspective on organizing, recently exploring connections between popular culture and practice of management, and the organization of the news production. She is interested in in techniques of fieldwork and in the application of narratology to organization studies. Recent books in English: *A Theory of Organizing* (second edition, 2014), *Social Science Research from Field to Desk* (2014), and *A Research Agenda for Management and Organization Studies* (edited, 2016).

Henrik Dosdall is a post-doctoral researcher at Bielefeld University who takes a profound interest in the dynamics of the financial crisis of 2007. He publishes on this topic from a perspective informed by the sociology of risk and sociology of organizations. Further interests include economic sociology as well as financial markets in general.

Max Ganzin is an assistant professor at the University of Windsor, Canada. His research interests include entrepreneurship, in particular, the ways entrepreneurs cope with risk and uncertainty, and the ways they project positive future, as well as the question of whether entrepreneurial opportunities are discovered or created. Other interests include sensemaking, institutional work, institutional myths, and rhetorical history.

Robert P. Gephart, Jr. is full professor at the University of Alberta, School of Business and Chercheur associé, ISEOR, Magellan, IAE Lyon, Université Jean Moulin. His research has appeared in the *Administrative Science Quarterly*, the *Academy of Management Journal*, the *Journal of Management, Organization Studies, Organizational Research Methods, Qualitative Sociology,* and other journals. Dr. Gephart served as associate editor of the journal *Organizational Research Methods* for over ten years, and in 2015, received the Sage Career Achievement Award from the Research Method Division of the Academy of Management.

Paulo Cesar Vaz Guimarães is a Senior Officer of Public Policy and Governmental Management in the Ministry of Planning, Development, and Management, Brazil. His experience centers on administration, with an emphasis on public organizations, working mainly in organizational planning and management, environmental management, risk management, and social policies.

Markus Hällgren (markus.hallgren@umu.se) is a professor of management and organization at Umeå School of Business and Economics, Umeå University. His research interests involve everyday practice in extreme contexts. His work has been published in the *Academy of Management Annals, European Management Journal, Scandinavian Journal of Management,* and *International Journal of Project Management*.

Cynthia Hardy is a laureate professor in the Department of Management & Marketing at the University of Melbourne and Professor at Cardiff Business School. She received her PhD from the University of Warwick, UK. Her research interests revolve around discourse, power, and risk. She has published over 60 refereed journal articles and 10 books, including the *Handbook of Organization Studies*, which won the George R. Terry Book Award, and the *Handbook of Organizational Discourse,* which won the Outstanding Book at the Organizational Communication Division of the National Communication Association. She is co-founder of the International Centre for Research in Organizational Discourse, Strategy, and Change.

Debbie Harrison is a professor of Strategy at BI Norwegian Business School, Oslo, Norway. Her research interests are in the area of inter-organizational relationships and networks, and constructivist market studies. She is currently involved in projects about sustainability practices in networks, the micro-foundations of market regulation, networked innovation in project settings, and the roles of users in markets. She has co-published several books and articles regarding markets, networks, and relationships, with the articles appearing in journals such as *Research Policy, Journal of Management Studies*, and *Marketing Theory.* Harrison also teaches several courses focused on business networks and strategy.

Claes-Fredrik Helgesson is professor in Technology and Social Change at Linköping University, Sweden. He works in the fields of economic sociology and science and technology studies (STS), currently emphasizing the emerging field of valuation studies which is focused on valuation as a social practice. Helgesson is co-founder and co-editor-in-chief of *Valuation Studies*, an open access journal, which published its first issue in spring 2013. He is co-editor with Isabelle Dussauge and Francis Lee of "Value Practices in the Life Sciences and Medicine" (Oxford University Press, 2015).

Jan Hayes has over 30 years' experience in safety and risk management. Her current activities cover academia, consulting, and regulation. She holds an associate professor appointment at RMIT University where she is program leader for the social science research activities of the Energy Pipelines Co-operative Research Centre. Dr. Hayes has just completed seven years as a member of the Advisory Board of the National Offshore Petroleum Safety and Environmental Management Authority.

Karin Svedberg Helgesson is associate professor in the Department of Management and Organization at the Stockholm School of Economics, Sweden. Her research focuses on the interplay and changing boundaries between business and society, including questions of accountability, legitimacy, and risk management. She is currently working on a project analyzing the role of for-profit professionals in securitization. Another research interest is gender in organizations, with a view to the reproduction of (in)equality in elite organizations. Helgesson has published several books, and her work has appeared in journals such as *Organization Studies* and the *Journal of Common Market Studies*.

Christian Huber, a lecturer at the Helmut Schmidt University – University of the Federal Armed Forces in Hamburg, Germany – received his PhD from Innsbruck University in organization studies, management and economics. His research has been published in *Human Relations, Management Accounting Research, Critical Perspectives on Accounting, Journal of Management Inquiry*, and *the Journal of Business Ethics*.

Paula Jarzabkowski is a professor of strategic management at Cass Business School, City University of London. Her research focuses on strategy-as-practice in complex and pluralistic contexts such as regulated infrastructure firms, third-sector organizations and financial services, particularly insurance and reinsurance. She has conducted extensive, internationally comparative audio and video ethnographic studies in a range of business contexts. Her work has appeared in leading journals including *Academy of Management Journal, Journal of Management Studies, Organization Science, Organization Studies,* and *Strategic Management Journal.* Her most recent co-authored book, *Making a Market for Acts of God,* was published by OUP in 2015.

Sytze F. Kingma is senior lecturer in the sociology of organizations at the Department of Organization Sciences, VU University Amsterdam, the Netherlands. His research interests involve the confrontation between the material and virtual dimensions of organizational networks, and the way risk is implicated in organizational contexts. He has published extensively in the field of gambling and is the editor of *Global Gambling: Cultural Perspectives on Organized Gambling* (Routledge, 2010). Recently, he edited (together with Karen Dale and Varda Wasserman) "Organizational Space and Beyond. The Significance of Henri Lefebvre for Organization Studies" (Routledge, 2018). Overall, his publications deal with risk, responsibility, organizational space, and technology; most recent articles are about "third workspaces" and "new ways of working."

Per Lægreid is professor at the Department of Administration and Organization Theory, University of Bergen, and adjunct research professor at Uni Research Rokkan Centre. He has published extensively on institutional change and public sector reforms from a comparative perspective. He is currently leading an international comparative research project on Organizing for Societal Security and Crisis Management: Building Governance Capacity and Legitimacy.

Carole Lalonde is a full professor and director of the PhD and Master Research Program at the Faculty of Administrative Sciences, Laval University, Canada. She teaches change and crisis management, qualitative research and consulting practices at the graduate level. She obtained her PhD in 2003 from HEC-Montreal. Prof. Lalonde is the author of peer-reviewed articles on crisis management, consulting, and change management.

Agnieszka Latuszynska is a PhD student at Warwick Business School, University of Warwick. After obtaining an MSc degree in public health from the Medical University of Warsaw (Poland), she spent several years working at the Division of Contract Supervision and Audit of National Health Fund in Warsaw, Poland, being responsible for supervision of contracts with health care providers. Her dissertation work investigates the role of risk in different health care settings.

Loïc Le Dé is lecturer and program leader of Emergency and Disaster Management from the Faculty of Health and Environmental Sciences at Auckland University of Technology, New Zealand. His research focuses on disaster risk reduction, disaster management, migration and remittances, sustainable livelihoods, and participatory approaches and tools for disaster risk reduction.

Connor Lubojacky is a doctoral student in the Management Department at the University of Houston. He earned his MSc in Finance at the University of Edinburgh and his Bachelor's degree at the University of Texas at Dallas. His research interests include opportunity recognition, decision-making, and entrepreneurial orientation.

Steve Maguire (steve.maguire@mcgill.ca) is professor of strategy and organization at the Desautels Faculty of Management at McGill University. He received his PhD from HEC-Montréal. His research focuses on technological and institutional change driven by the emergence of new risks to human health and the environment, theorizing the role of non-market actors in shaping the adoption or abandonment of particular technologies. He has particular expertise on the organizing of risk and the management of chemical risks, serving in an advisory role to the government of Canada during 2007–2011, and working currently on research projects with scientists from Health Canada and Environment Canada.

Sarah Maslen is assistant professor of sociology at University of Canberra. Her research has focused on engineering decision-making and expertise practices, and the impact of incentive arrangements on major accident risk management. She is co-author of book *Risky Rewards* with Prof. Andrew Hopkins.

Rob Austin McKee is an assistant professor of leadership and entrepreneurship at the University of Houston–Downtown. He earned his PhD and MBA from the University of Houston. His research interests include decision-making, leadership, personality, and visceral states. His work has appeared in *Journal of Management, The Leadership Quarterly,* and *Business Horizons.* Rob is vice president for Business Development at Flexios, a medical device startup, working in the area of hand tendon repair. He is a former nuclear reactor operator for the United States Navy and an avid rock climber.

C. Chet Miller is the C.T. Bauer Professor of Organizational Studies at the University of Houston. He has worked with a number of organizations to improve their positioning and impact. In addition, he is an award-winning teacher and researcher. His published research focuses on the functioning and effects of executive teams, the design of strategic decision processes within firms, and the use of seemingly impossible organizational goals. His work has appeared in outlets such as *Harvard Business Review, Academy of Management Journal, Academy of Management Review, Strategic Management Journal,* and *Advances in Strategic Management.*

Rolf Nichelmann is an independent postdoctoral researcher at the Institute of Sociology at Dresden University of Technology. Previously, he worked as a senior lecturer at the Faculty of Sociology at Bielefeld University. His teaching and research interests include (1) issues at the intersection of legal dogmatics and legal sociology, (2) political sociology from a systems theoretical perspective with a current focus on public opinion and the politics-media interface, and (3) organizational theory.

Eivor Oborn is professor of healthcare management within the Entrepreneurship and Innovation Group and the Organizing Health Research Network at Warwick Business School. She is also a research fellow at Judge Business School, Cambridge University. Eivor is an honorary research associate in the Department of Bio-Surgery and Surgical Technology at Imperial College London, working in association with Lord Darzi. Her research interests include knowledge translation, multidisciplinary collaboration, organization theory and change, health service innovation, technology use, and health policy reform.

Maria Paola Ometto is a PhD candidate in Strategic Management and Organization at the University of Alberta. She holds a PhD in Public Administration and Government from Fundação Getúlio Vargas, Escola de Administração de Empresas de São Paulo (FGV/EAESP),

Brazil. Her research interests include institutional theory, social movements, communities, corporate political activity, and entrepreneurship.

Cyrus B. Parks is a doctoral student in strategic management at the C.T. Bauer College of Business at the University of Houston. He earned BS and MS degrees in environmental health engineering and worked in the chemical industry for two decades in roles ranging from environmental expert to production manager to Lean Six Sigma Master Black Belt. He is author of several environmental risk assessments and manufacturing site strategies, and he has led over 20 root cause investigations. His research lies at the intersection of ethical behavior and determinants of firm performance.

David Passenier obtained his master's in social research at the Vrije Universiteit Amsterdam, specializing in organization sciences. For his PhD, he studied risk and safety management in commercial aviation, focusing on pilots' improvisational work processes and deviant practices.

Christine M. Pearson is professor of global leadership, Thunderbird School of Global Management, Arizona State University. She is an expert on curtailing and containing dysfunctional behavior at work, from the dramatic sweep of organizational crises to the corrosive impact of low-intensity workplace incivility. Her research has appeared in outlets such as *Harvard Business Review, Sloan Management Review,* and *Academy of Management Review,* and has been reported by more than 600 newspapers and magazines, and international radio and television stations. She has more than two decades experience researching, consulting, and teaching globally, with students in 180 countries. Pearson is currently completing her seventh book, a contemporary view of global crisis leadership.

Charles Perrow is Emeritus Professor of Sociology at Yale University. The author of several books and many articles on organizations (e.g. *Complex Organizations, a Critical Essay, 3rd ed.,* 1984), he is primarily concerned with the impact of large organizations on society (*Organizing America: Wealth, Power, and the Origins of Corporate Capitalism,* 2002), and their catastrophic potentials (*Normal Accidents: Living with High-Risk Technologies* 1984, rev. ed. 1999, and *The Next Catastrophe: Reducing Our Vulnerabilities to Natural, Industrial, and Terrorist Disasters,* 2007). The 2011 edition covers the economic meltdown, the Gulf oil spill, and global warming. He also has published on the Fukushima disaster and its radiological consequences.

Trish Reay is a professor in strategic management and organization, School of Business, University of Alberta. She also holds a partial appointment in Entrepreneurship and Innovation at Warwick Business School. Her research interests include institutional and organizational change, professions and professionals, and organizational learning in the contexts of healthcare and family business. She is academic director for the Centre for Effective Business Management of Addiction Treatment at the University of Alberta, and currently serves as editor-in-chief of *Organization Studies.*

Henry Rothstein is a reader in risk and regulation, King's College London. His main research interests concern the institutional factors shaping risk governance regimes across policy domains and countries. His publications include *The Government of Risk* (with Christopher Hood and Robert Baldwin. OUP: 2001) and numerous articles in a wide range of academic journals, including *Economy and Society, Public Administration, Regulation and Governance* and *Socio-Economic Review*. Most recently he has led a three-year international comparative research project on the relationship between risk and regulation in the UK, France, Germany, and the Netherlands.

Linda Rouleau is professor of organization theory at the management department of HEC Montreal. Her research on identity, sensemaking, middle managers, and strategic change has been published in peer-reviewed journals such as *Academy of Management Review, Organization Science, Accounting, Organization and Society, Journal of Management Studies,* and *Human Relations*.

Lise H. Rykkja is associate professor at the Department of Administration and Organization Theory at the University of Bergen and adjunct research professor at the Uni Research Rokkan Centre, Norway. Her research concentrates on public administration and public policies based in a broad institutional and comparative perspective, focusing on organizing and coordinating for crisis management. Rykkja currently leads the Horizon 2020 TROPICO project: Transforming into Open, Innovative and Collaborative Governments.

Amandine Savall is an assistant professor at Université Jean Moulin Lyon 3 and researcher at ISEOR, Lyon, France. She examines management of international practices in family-owned businesses.

Henri Savall is Emeritus Professor at the University Jean Moulin Lyon 3 and the founder and president of the ISEOR Research Center in France. He holds two doctoral degrees in economic sciences and in management science and has authored and co-authored 53 books, 98 articles, and 300 conference papers. In 2017, Dr. Savall was appointed Chevalier of the Legion of Honor in France.

Kelly E. See is an Associate Professor of Management at the Business School of the University of Colorado Denver. She received her PhD from Duke University. Her current research falls into two main streams: how contextual factors affect the flow of input or advice through the organizational hierarchy, and the use of extreme goals in organizations. Her published work appears in leading management and disciplinary journals, including the *Academy of Management Review, Organization Science, Harvard Business Review, Organizational Behavior and Human Decision Processes, Journal of Personality and Social Psychology, Journal of Experimental Psychology, Personnel Psychology,* and *Operations Research*. Her research has won several awards and has been covered in a variety of media outlets, such as *Forbes, The Wall Street Journal, ABC News, FOX news,* and *INC*.

April D. Schantz is an assistant professor with the Usha Kundu, MD College of Health at University of West Florida, Pensacola, FL, USA. She completed her PhD in Industrial-Organizational Psychology with a Minor in Quantitative Methods at Florida International University. Her research focuses on attributes and processes of action- or performance-based teams and health and well-being outcomes for those employed in high stress industries. Her work has been published in the *Journal of Workplace Behavioral Health, Work & Stress,* and *The Industrial-Organizational Psychologist*. She is an active member of Academy of Management (Research Methods Division) and a campus representative for Consortium for the Advancement of Research Methods and Analysis (CARMA).

Tobias Scheytt is Professor of Management Accounting and Control at Helmut-Schmidt-University Hamburg, Germany. He studied business economics at Witten/Herdecke University, where he earned his PhD degree and his habilitation degree at Innsbruck University. His research that focuses on strategic control, quality, and risk management has been published in *Organization Studies, Journal of Management Studies, Management Accounting Research* and *Organizational Research Methods.*

Yossi Sheffi is the Elisha Gray II Professor of Engineering Systems and Director of the MIT Center for Transportation and Logistics (CTL). He is an expert in supply chain management and is the author of five books. Under his leadership, the CTL has launched many educational, research, and industry/ government outreach programs, including the MIT SCALE network, and the online Micromaster's program. Outside the institute, Dr. Sheffi has consulted with numerous organizations. He has also founded or co-founded five successful companies, all acquired by large enterprises. Dr. Sheffi has been recognized in numerous ways in academic and industry forums.

Sushma Shrestha is Shelter and Reconstruction Specialist in Plan International Nepal where she provides backstopping support and technical advice in formulating, planning, and implementing disaster recovery, reconstruction, and disaster risk reduction programs. She holds a PhD in environment science from the University of Auckland (New Zealand).

Sim B. Sitkin is the Michael W. Krzyzewski University Professor, Professor of Management and Public Policy, Faculty Director – Fuqua/Coach K Center on Leadership and Ethics, and Director – Behavioral Science and Policy Center at Duke University. He is a Fellow of the Academy of Management and the Society for Organizational Behavior. He is co-founder and co-president of the Behavioral Science and Policy Association. His research focuses on the effects of leadership and organizational control on trust, risk-taking, experimentation, learning, and innovation. His most recent books are *Organizational Control, The Six Domains of Leadership,* and *The Routledge Companion to Trust.*

Kathleen M. Sutcliffe is a Bloomberg Distinguished Professor at Johns Hopkins University with appointments in the Carey Business School, the School of Medicine, the School of Nursing, and the Armstrong Institute for Patient Safety. Professor Sutcliffe focuses her research on understanding how organizations and their members cope with uncertainty and unexpected surprises, and how organizations can be designed to be more reliable and resilient. She has published widely in management and organization theory and healthcare. In 2015, she received a distinguished scholar award from the MOC division of the Academy of Management.

Cagatay Topal teaches in the Department of Sociology at Middle East Technical University in Ankara. He has an MS degree in sociology from METU and a PhD degree in sociology from Queen's University at Kingston in Canada. Among his research interests are surveillance, sociological theory, and science and technology. He has published in several established journals, including *Social Text, European Societies,* and *International Sociology.*

Cagri Topal is a researcher/instructor in the Department of Business Administration at Middle East Technical University in Ankara. He has an MS degree in sociology from METU and a PhD degree in organizational analysis from the University of Alberta in Canada. Among his research interests are risk construction processes and micro processes of institutionalization. He has published in several organization-focused journals, including *Tamara: Journal of Critical Postmodern Organization Science*, *Organization Studies*, and *Journal of Management and Organization*.

Gail Whiteman is professor-in-residence at the World Business Council for Sustainable Development and the Rubin Chair and Director of the Pentland Centre for Sustainability in Business at Lancaster University, UK. Her research analyzes how actors make sense of complex problems and build resilience across scales given environmental pressures and social inequities. In collaboration with British Antarctic Survey, she is also the creator of the Arctic Basecamp at Davos, an innovative science communication and outreach event that calls for action from global leaders to address global risks from Arctic change.

Amanda Williams is a PhD candidate at Rotterdam School of Management, Erasmus University. Her research lies at the intersection of corporate sustainability and social-ecological resilience. The objective of her research is to understand how organizations impact the environment and how the environment in turn impacts organizations through feedback loops over time and space. Recently, she conducted research about corporate engagement with the UN Sustainable Development Goals.

Jeroen Wolbers Assistant Professor of Crisis Governance at the Crisis Research Center, Institute for Security & Global Affairs, Leiden University. His expertise lies in fast-response organizing on the topics of coordination, sensemaking, and decision-making, with a special focus on crisis management. His work is published in leading organization and crisis management journals. In his PhD thesis Jeroen studied coordination processes between emergency services on disaster sites. His thesis was selected for the top 3 dissertations worldwide in management science with the Grigor McClelland Award 2017, and he was awarded with the VU Faculty of Social Science Dissertation Award. Previously Jeroen was a postdoctoral researcher in the NWO project on Smart Disaster Governance at the VU University, where he performed fieldwork during the response to the Nepal Earthquakes in 2015, the refugee crisis in Europe, and multiple disaster exercises throughout the Netherlands. In 2018, Jeroen received a prestigious Veni grant from the Netherlands Organisation for Scientific Research (NWO) to study how frontline commanders can mitigate fragmentation in crisis response operations.

Juanita M. Woods, PMP, PgMP, PhD is an assistant professor of project management at the Mike Cottrell College of Business at the University of North Georgia in Gainsville, GA, USA. She focuses her research on bridging the disciplines of leadership, people development, and work teams after a successful career managing people, teams, and projects in the private sector. Dr. Woods is currently focused on building leadership capacity in the next generation of workplace leaders by engaging with management students and professionals in the private and public sector.

Véronique Zardet is a professor at the Institut d'Administration des Entreprises, University Jean Moulin Lyon 3, co-director of the Socio-Economic Management Masters program, and Director of the ISEOR Research Center. She holds two doctoral degrees in management sciences and was awarded (with Henri Savall) the Rossi Award from the Academy of Moral and Political Sciences.

George A. Zsidisin, PhD (Arizona State University), CPSM, CPM, is a professor of supply chain management at Virginia Commonwealth University. Professor Zsidisin has conducted extensive research in the field of purchasing and supply management, with a focus on how firms assess and manage supply disruptions and commodity price volatility in their supply chains. He has published over 70 research and practitioner articles and three books that have been extensively cited. He is one of the initial founding members of the *International Supply Chain Risk Management* (ISCRiM) network, Co-Editor Emeritus of the *Journal of Purchasing & Supply Management*, and Director of the Master of Supply Chain Management program at Virginia Commonwealth University.

PART I

An Introduction to Risk, Crisis and Emergency Management

1

INTRODUCTION TO RISK, CRISIS AND EMERGENCY MANAGEMENT IN ENTERPRISES AND ORGANIZATIONS[1]

Robert P. Gephart, Jr., Karin Svedberg Helgesson, and Max Ganzin

June 30, 2013, was another hot day in a demanding fire season in Arizona for the Granite Mountain (GM) Hotshot crew. The crew members were experienced but tired when they arrived at the Yarnell Fire Station early in the morning to assist with a nearby fire and had worked 28 out of 30 days fighting wildfires. After consulting with local officials, the crew had a look at the fire. The front of the fire was 1.5 miles long, but 45 minutes later, the fire had grown to 1,500 acres and was spreading rapidly. Additional air support was requested for the fire control operation, but a shortage of aircraft meant only two of four aircraft requested arrived by noon to coordinate the operation and drop fire retardant.

Brendan McDonough, a GM hotshot, was assigned to monitor the fire and warn the crew of danger. The other 18 crew members and their leader Eric set off to the anchor of the fire (McDonough, 2016, pp. 187–188). By 1.04 p.m., the fire was defeating all attempts at control. Soon thereafter, the fire status was increased to Type 1 TMT – the highest designation for fire, making the Yarnell fire the largest fire burning in Arizona.

When a thunderstorm rolled in, the wind reversed direction and the wind speed increased to 45–50 miles per hour due to the outflow winds, a situation that occurred in a previous fire that killed 14 firefighters. The Type 1 TMT fire designation was approved at 2.13, but the fire continued to be unstoppable, and the fire front grew to 3 miles in size. Then, the fire shifted suddenly and headed for the town of Yarnell.

At this time, the GM crew were positioned in a safe area near the fire (without the lookout McDonough), and they declined to redeploy to Yarnell. Then at 3.50 p.m., the GM crew learned the fire had turned toward Yarnell and would soon reach the GM vehicles. Eric, the GM crew leader, worked on an escape plan while he received a weather update. The fire line became increasingly unstable with tongues of flame heading in multiple directions as winds rose to 40–50 miles per hour.

McDonough abandoned his lookout position at 3.52 p.m. when the fire, "moving faster than anyone could remember" (p. 199), came within 300 yards of his position. McDonough thought the other crew members were safe. But by 3.54 p.m., the fire was beyond control and closing in on the GM crew. At 4.04 p.m., Eric radioed that the crew were using the escape route. The fire was 0% contained, and the town of Yarnell was engulfed in flames.

The GM crew reached a saddle on a ridge enroute to the safe area at 4.20 p.m. and then moved down into a box canyon near the safe area for reasons that are unclear. Suddenly the wind speed increased to 50 mph, the fire changed direction, and a 100-feet high wall of flame that the crew could not see ran up the canyon toward the crew.

By 4.39 p.m., the GM crew were the only crew left in the area. Eric called an air tanker requesting a fire-retardant drop. He confirmed the crew were now cut off from their escape route and was preparing to deploy their fire shelters. The fire, now over 70-feet high and over 3,000 degrees F in temperature, passed over the crew who no longer responded to radio calls.

When the medical response team's flight medic finally reached the deployment area by foot, he found the 19 bodies of the GM crew laid out on the ground in a horseshoe shape. The safe area they sought was only 600 yards away. Their radios were still working, but they were unable to survive a fire hot enough to melt uranium.

Introduction

This volume provides a comprehensive, broadly based and contemporary discussion of management and organizational research addressing risk, crisis and emergency management. Risk, in quantitative terms, is the probability of an event occurring multiplied by the magnitude of losses or gains involved in the event (Lupton, 1999). Historically, risk was essential to accessing opportunities and included both positive and negative outcomes. The meaning of risk has changed in late modernity, and it now refers to threats, hazards and dangers that are unquantifiable uncertainties with unknown probabilities of occurrence. And risks may require expertise for detection and/or mitigation.

Consider the GM example above. Wildfire management requires skilled workers trained in the technical challenges involved in controlling wildfires that by nature are unpredictable in their behavior. Firefighters at Yarnell faced numerous risks including the threat of incineration by the wildfire. The GM crew were early responders to a risky event that quickly escalated into a crisis. Organizational crises can thus be conceived as realized risks that involve major, unpredictable events that have the potential to produce extensive harms and where the aftermath of the events may "damage an organization and its employees, products, services, financial condition and reputation" (Barton, 1993, p. 2). The GM case shows the company's firefighters experienced a crisis because the risks they anticipated evolved into a crisis when the crew were unable to properly locate and monitor the boundaries of the fire. They then became trapped by the fire and lost their lives. The fire was part of a larger, preexisting crisis – the wildfire threatening the town of Yarnell. In addition, the management of emergencies by definition requires urgent efforts by individuals and organizations to address and remediate the immediate and local impacts of an emerging danger. In this case, local officials attempted to contact the GM crew and sent emergency workers to rescue the trapped workers. They were unsuccessful because the 19 workers had lost their lives due to the unanticipated intensity of the fire when they sought to protect themselves.

This example also shows how risk, crisis and emergency management can occur in close temporal and physical proximity as part of the triad of risk, crisis and emergency management processes explored in this volume. The current volume extends the conceptual boundaries of the risk, crisis and emergency management domain addressed in previous research. It encourages and assists readers to envision a broader perspective on risk that addresses risks and crises in emergency contexts, thus emphasizing the interactions between these three aspects and the need to examine and understand risk and crisis events in their naturally occurring contexts. To do so, the volume includes theoretical and conceptual reviews, original empirical research including case studies that illustrate the issues involved, as well as essays and opinion pieces that extend and inform management practice. Overall, the volume provides an important, stand-alone introduction to the field and an important and detailed resource for use in teaching, designing research and informing practice.

Following from this, the general purpose of the book is to offer an up-to-date and state-of-the-art understanding of risk, crisis and emergency management issues based on social science theories, concepts, methods and empirical findings. Practitioner insights are presented in actionable frameworks, practical essays, case descriptions and data from interviews included in the chapters. The book also contributes to the advancement of the field of risk and crisis management by integrating three interrelated streams or areas of scholarship and practice that often overlap but are seldom considered in the same volume: the areas of risk and risk management, industrial crisis management, and emergency and safety management. The book is therefore distinct because it seeks to be highly integrative across previously isolated areas. Further, it takes a strong social and organizational science view rather than emphasizing engineering practice or financial economics and incorporates advances from cultural studies of risk. Because many, if not most, of the existing general texts on risk, crisis or emergency management are becoming dated and do little to address all three of the interrelated features the current book will address, the book offers a uniquely up-to-date and integrated perspective on the field of risk and crisis studies.

The volume builds on the needs of the field initially outlined in part by Pearson, Roux-Dufort and Clair (2007). It strengthens the intellectual foundations of risk, crisis and emergency management, foundations that are not yet fully developed. It captures grounded perspectives based on evidence, research and practice rather than on speculation or armchair theorizing. It brings the contributions of organizational science and cultural studies of risk more fully into the field of crisis management and related areas. And it provides insights to help create more integrated, effective and practical approaches to anticipating, preventing, managing and recovering from crisis. To ensure the quality and timeliness of these contributions, the contributing authors are actively involved in the field of risk, crisis and emergency management. Many of the authors have undertaken extensive and recent research in the field, thus ensuring the scholarly quality and rigor of the book. Also, a number of authors have experience as risk, crisis and management consultants and practitioners. Finally, the specific issues addressed in the book were identified through an extensive review of recent and foundational scholarly research in the field of risk and crisis management. The parts of the volume are presented in terms of the general themes we found in the scholarly literature as well as the important features or components of scholarly research.

The Current Volume

Part I: Introduction

The first part of the volume provides an overview of the background, objectives, contents and contributions of the present volume.

Part II: Foundational Processes

The second part addresses common processes and essential aspects of risks and crises. It provides readers with information on the context of crisis management and research and addresses basic challenges in crisis management including recovery from disaster, communication and emergency response teams foundational to risk, crisis and emergency management scholarship.

Chapter 2, "Key Challenges in Crisis Management" by Wolbers and Boersma, addresses the role of the four c's of crisis management – cognition, communication, coordination and control. The focus is on the needs of first responders and the organizational challenges they face as they attempt to address the situation. The issues are illustrated with a description of the initial response to the February 2009 Turkish Airlines crash at Schiphol Airport that killed nine persons and wounded 86 others, and the authors discuss how these processes are essential but often problematic during the initial response operations. Based on the dilemmas observed, the authors suggest three themes for future research related to the four c's: the use of ad hoc teams in emergency management, the need to monitor and implement command tactics to ensure co-ordination, and developing and using a flexible information management process.

Chapter 3, "Post-disaster Recovery: Pathways for Fostering Disaster Risk Reduction" by Le Dé and Shrestha, examines the process of disaster recovery from a geographer's perspective. The authors emphasize the importance of recovery that reduces the risk of future disasters. Challenges to disaster risk reduction in the recovery process are noted, extensive examples of disaster recovery issues in developing and developed countries are provided, and the chapter discusses how to overcome the challenges of recovery to build back better.

Chapter 4, "Crisis Communication: The Best Evidence from Research" by Timothy Coombs, provides an overview of evidence-based knowledge generated through experimental research and content analysis in crisis communication. Coombs covers topics that are important to crisis managers: effectiveness of various crisis response strategies, timing of crisis communication, the use of news stories and social media, and the qualities that enhance the effectiveness of spokespersons. Coombs emphasizes the critical role crisis communication plays in crisis management and provides insights into effective ways to engage in crisis communication.

Chapter 5, "Collective Fit for Emergency Response Teams" by Schantz and Woods, develops a multilevel model of team-level fit in emergency response teams. The authors extend the individually focused concept of person-environment fit by developing the concept of collective fit as a meso-level property and explore how individual, environmental and contextual factors influence collective fit in emergency response teams. Because the work of emergency response teams saves lives, it is very important to understand the conditions of collective fit that leads to optimal functioning. The model can be used by emergency management leaders to strengthen the development of collective fit in emergency response teams.

Part III: Theoretical Viewpoints and Methods

The third part describes theoretical perspectives and methodological orientations that are commonly used in the field of crisis management research including newer and emerging approaches.

Chapter 6, "Risk, Crisis and Organizational Failure: Toward a Post-rationalist Theory" by Thomas Beamish, reviews the strengths and limits of prevailing rational sociological theories of risk and organizational failure to explore how normative processes that lie outside of rational actions lead to failure as theorized by institutional theorists. The chapter reviews sociological theories of organizational risk including normal accident theory and high reliability theory, noting strengths and limits of these theories. Beamish then offers a post-rational theory of risk and organizations that extends the institutional perspective on risks, crises and organizational failures in rationally planned to organizations to situations where nonrational factors including "normal" technological failures, informal normative processes and informal structures play a central role.

Chapter 7, "Risk Sensemaking" by Gephart and Ganzin, explores risk sensemaking as the primary agentive process in crisis and emergency management that involves noticing, interpreting, understanding and reacting to risks and crises. Sensemaking is foundational to understanding risks and crises because it addresses the active and agentive aspect of human conduct – noticing, interpreting and acting in the social world. The chapter describes and compares two important approaches to sensemaking about risk: (1) the sociological approach of ethnomethodology (Garfinkel, 1967) and (2) the cognitive approach of Karl Weick (1995, 2001). Examples of research using each approach are described, and guidance is provided for future research using the perspectives.

Chapter 8, "Qualitative and Quantitative Methods" by McKee, Lubojacky and Miller, explores questions of rigor and balance in the methods used in the field of crises, risks and emergency management through analyses of 139 unique and recent empirical studies. The authors primarily analyze five issues: the relative use of quantitative vs. qualitative approaches, preferences for theory-driven or phenomenon-driven underpinnings, the assortment of archival and more proximate data sources, emphases on real-time vs. retrospective vs. prospective data, and how the surfacing of victims' voices rather than only those of elites are handled. The chapter also probes the possible presence of publication bias and limited triangulation in the empirical studies analyzed. The authors conclude that, overall, the field is reasonably well balanced and rigorous. Still, they raise concerns relating to the underutilization of quantitative studies, an overabundance of theory-driven foundations, probable publication bias and limited triangulation.

Chapter 9, "Researching Extreme Contexts: Taking Stock of Research Methods on Extreme Contexts and Moving Forward" by Hällgren and Rouleau, explores research on extreme contexts where risks, crises and emergencies can occur. The researchers identified three time periods of extreme context research that they label emergence, expansion and consolidation. They then assess the methods sections from 120 papers published in top-tier journals in each period between 1980 and 2015 to uncover trends in methods and suggest opportunities for future research.

Chapter 10, "Local Translations of Operational Risk" by Barbara Czarniawska, extends the theoretical viewpoints in the volume by offering a translation perspective on risk management and highlighting its merits relative to a diffusion perspective. The chapter then provides a comparative analysis of the translation of a European financial regulation in two local national contexts, Sweden and Poland, and discusses how local translations are influenced by both present and past circumstances and how they differ from one another. The chapter finds that a widely shared belief in the value of quantifying risks is the main suggested remedy and preferred way to manage risk across the two contexts. This illustrates how vague formulations of risk, combined with sophisticated calculation techniques, take precedence over the complexity of actual practices.

Part IV: Types of Crises

The fourth part, Types of Crises, addresses a range of well-known and important forms of crises recently studied and that are highly salient today.

This discussion starts with Chapter 11, "The Co-evolution of Reputation Management, Governance Capacity, Legitimacy and Accountability in Crisis Management" by Christensen, Lægreid and Rykkja. The authors argue that principal-agency-centered models do not suffice as a basis for how to handle the complexities of crisis management that face extant governance systems. They call for a crisis management that is responsible, decisive and better able to act for the public good. They also present a road map for how to proceed. The authors argue that what needs to be better understood are the often ambiguous and hybrid interrelationships between governance capacity, accountability, governance, legitimacy and reputation management in crisis management. The authors then apply institutional and instrumental approaches to promote a more in-depth understanding of these relationships in crisis management.

Chapter 12, "Relative Risk Construction through Risk Boundaries and Rituals" by Topal, Topal and Bespinar, analyzes a mining disaster in the Turkish town of Soma from the employment context perspective. They argue that risk cannot be properly analyzed without consideration of the social-economic context of the organizations and employees. They identify three ritualistic contextual mechanisms that function as a boundary: (1) relative risk rationality embedded within unemployment intensity and lack of employment alternatives; (2) control over individual agency due to lack of effective labor unions, safety and job training; and (3) relational networks shaped by family needs and production pressures. Though their analysis, they found that the risk in the mine was constructed by the workers as relatively acceptable because of the alternative risk of unemployment.

Chapter 13, "Systemic Ecosystem Risks: Implications for Organization Studies" by Whiteman and Williams, addresses organizationally based planetary risks that pose a threat to our species. The role of organizations in producing ecosystem risks requires further exploration. The chapter thus poses a three-phase framework to help managers and sustainability personnel better identify and understand these planetary risks and the groupings of actors that produce these risks. The phases are building a planetary view of organization risk at several levels of scale, making sense of these risks, and building organizational and adaptive capacity to manage these risks.

Chapter 14, "Event Risks and Crises: Barriers to Learning" by Huber and Scheytt, explores risks and crises in public events and mass gatherings. They use the HOT framework developed by Shrivastava (1987) to systematically interpret the human, organizational and technical factors that influence the sources and scope of risk involved in public events. They address the potential to learn from these events as well as the barriers to learning that are due to event specificities. They illustrate their ideas by contrasting two public sports events: the successful 2012 Olympic Games in London and the 1996 Hillsborough soccer game where overcrowding led to a stampede of spectators with multiple deaths. The authors discuss how better integration of practitioner, regulatory and theoretical frameworks and ideas could help to better understand event risks and crises.

Chapter 15, "Bernácer's Topical Theory of Crisis and Unemployment" by Savall and Zardet, addresses contemporary and well-known neoliberal theories of economic crisis. The chapter then provides an introduction to the innovative macroeconomic theory of German Bernácer, a Spanish economist, and outlines Bernácer's basic theory of economic crises that arise due to the existence of speculative markets for goods that provide income without work, that is, unearned income. Unearned income does not require entrepreneurial risk, the creation of real value added, or sharing revenue from market speculation between economic and social stakeholders. Bernácer argued that the elimination of speculative markets would significantly contribute to the economic and social development necessary to overcome unemployment and help eliminate speculation, thereby preventing the recurring financial "bubbles" that frequently accompany global business cycles. The theory is applied to the territorial and state levels of governments. Recent experiments with economic ideas (e.g. that assume economies can still function at near-zero interest rates) are discussed.

Chapter 16, "Risk and Human Resource Management" by Mike Annett, examines risks related to the employment of people. Annett makes a systematic presentation of labor risk categories through real-life examples of organizational crises and illustrates how the concepts of risk and crisis apply to human resource management. He then theorizes organization change as both a risk-mitigating and risk-inciting activity and presents the concerns-based adoption model to help resolve labor's reluctance to change.

Part V: International Case Studies

The fifth part (International Case Studies) contributes crucial insights into risk, crisis and emergency management during events in specific industry domains in a wide range of national and cultural settings where crises have recently occurred. Each of the chapters includes a case study of risk and crisis management in a specific industry or profession – international sea freight, airlines, financial services, oil and gas, dairy and higher education – to illustrate the rich and detailed aspects of specific crises, highlight industry-specific concerns and practices and extend empirical knowledge of crises.

Chapter 17, "Invasive Species, Risk Management, and the Compliance Industry" by Harrison, Helgesson and Helgesson, outlines and illustrates the challenges arising from the common need to balance compliance risk and focal risk. The authors argue these types of risks are interrelated but do not necessarily fit well together, and this makes attempts at mitigation complex. The chapter further draws attention to the role of the supply side of risk management, and to what can be denoted as the compliance industry. Specifically, it discusses Daro Marine's (a pseudonym) attempt to develop a risk management solution for the risk of invasive species in international sea freight. The authors analyze how the balance shifted between mitigating focal risk and compliance risk during the product development process, and in different parts of the organization.

Chapter 18, "Tension in the Air: Behind the Scenes of Aviation Risk Management" by David Passenier, engages with the debate on whether irregularities are to be considered accidents waiting to happen, as implied by a Normal Accidents perspective, or be treated as part of normal risk management, as follows from ideas on High Reliability Organizations. Drawing on a set of vignettes from diverse qualitative field studies in commercial aviation, the author showcases how contrasting risk perceptions of safety-critical processes emerge among actors in airline companies. He further discusses how this promotes the emergence of a negotiated order that seeks to satisfy the contrasting risk perceptions. In conclusion, Passenier argues that by studying social tensions emerging in regular work settings, it is possible to get at a range of more nuanced risk management interpretations of irregularities.

Chapter 19, "The Risks of Financial Risk Management: The Case of Lehmann Brothers" by Dosdall and Nichelmann, demonstrates that risk management presents itself as an inescapably risky operation, and that risk reduction and risk escalation often go hand in hand. The authors analyze the regulatory interventions during the subprime crisis that created new risks for the regulators. They note that interventions that favor too-big-to-fail banks are prone to political risks and force a choice between economically opportune but politically detrimental decisions and politically opportune but economically detrimental decisions.

Chapter 20, "Blame and Litigation as Corporate Strategies towards Environmental Disaster: Shell in Brazil" by Alves, Ometto and Guimarães, describes two sites of environmental disasters in Brazil and presents a critical analysis of how they were handled by the multinational corporation implicated. The authors outline and analyze how this corporation did not walk the talk of its own policies on corporate, social and environmental responsibilities, but rather chose to focus on litigation and blame-shifting in order to minimize liability and reputational risk. They further show how these strategies exacerbated the incidents and turned critical events into disaster, resulting in catastrophic effects on individuals, communities and the environment.

Chapter 21, "Family Firms and Stakeholder Management: Crisis at Blue Bell Ice Cream" by Parks and Cardinal, examines the 2015 product contamination crisis at Blue Bell Creameries. The case study is based on the analysis of decades of archival data that revealed how owner-managers frame their decisions according to their view of power and control. Under increasing pressure caused in part by growing complexity, managers take decisive action to preserve tightly coupled relationships (with customers) while hoping to not overly damage loosely coupled ones (with employees).

Chapter 22, "Risky Double Spiral Sensemaking of Academic Capitalism" by David Boje, outlines a Deleuzian-Double-Spiral-Antenarrative theoretical framework for understanding the public research university, where double spiraling is related to a theory of storytelling. Through an auto-ethnographic approach, Boje explains how risky double spirals play out at a focal US public research university and also discusses the broader implications of this theoretical and methodological approach for conceptualizing the risks and crises facing other universities around the world.

Chapter 23, "Managing Risk in Healthcare Settings" by Latuszynska, Oborn and Reay, presents a framework to explain how different actors identify and manage risk in healthcare, and why they do so in different ways. The framework is based on a stakeholder approach and concepts that describe different perceptions of risk. The authors see provision of healthcare services as a large-scale multilayered risk management process and notice that stakeholders, including government, healthcare managers, physicians and patients, differ in their risk perceptions. They argue that the different risk regimes affect stakeholder views on value creation, which affect their risk perception.

Chapter 24 "Buncefield Stories: Organizational Learning and Remembering for Crisis Prevention" by Hayes and Maslen, follows accounts of the Buncefield fuel terminal explosion. Specifically, the authors examine the link between incident investigations and the production of stories in the Buncefield case. Stories tend to be overlooked in incident investigations, but deserve more attention, the authors argue. Notably, they show how shared stories of critical incidents and disasters forge vital links between the everyday and the disastrous and provide opportunities for learning how to improve safety in ways that go beyond imagined changes in technical standards.

Part V: Current and Emerging Issues in Risk and Crisis Management

This part features chapters that explore emerging concerns and trends in risk and crisis management research and practice including the role of space and time in crises, how to change organizations and improve their ability to effectively prevent or manage crises, the need for crisis management to go global and the effectiveness of risk and crisis management. These chapters also discuss how practitioners can better address the management of risks and crises.

The part begins with Chapter 25, "Spatial and Temporal Patterns in Global Enterprise Risk" by Yossi Sheffi. Sheffi provides a hands-on account of how risks associated with geographically dispersed supply chains arise and are managed. Drawing on multiple examples from businesses around the world, he analyzes the geographic risk footprint of a company, including deep-tier suppliers, customers, logistics networks and key natural resources. Sheffi further elaborates the three points in time that are particularly salient for the management of supply chain disruption (detection time, time to impact and time to recovery), and discusses how new technological advances can help improve monitoring.

Chapter 26, "The Development of Actionable Knowledge in Crisis Management" by Carole Lalonde, addresses how to create actionable knowledge that can change organizations and mitigate crises. Lalonde provides an overview of key organization development (OD) practices and then lays out principles for OD intervention research to help management practitioners adapt their organization to crisis contingencies. Lalonde previews literature on OD, early disaster management research in sociology and Danny Millers' organizational configuration framework as foundations for new principles of crisis management. The second part of the chapter provides a case study of a crisis in a long-term care facility that shows how researcher-practitioner collaboration in action research can use the new principles to create practices to empower crisis managers and enhance their effectiveness.

Chapter 27, "The Socio-Economic Approach to Management of Risks and Crises" by Bonnet, Savall, Savall and Zardet, addresses how the socio-economic approach (SEAM), an intervention research technique that uncovers hidden costs not on the balance sheet and converts these into value-added performance, can be used to prevent and reduce micro- and macro-financial crises. The approach is promising as a micro-level tool given that it has been successfully implemented in over 2,000 organizations. The chapter also applies SEAM to the macro-economic level to show how crises macro can be prevented and mitigated in innovative ways that harness hidden costs and provide prosperity to societies.

Chapter 28, "Why Crisis Management Must Go Global, and How to Begin" by Christine Pearson, provides practical suggestions on what to do to globalize crisis management. Pearson offers an overview of cross-cultural issues for crisis managers of global organizations. She gives very practical steps that can be taken to improve global crisis management programs including strengthening senior executive endorsement of cross-cultural crisis management, conducting a preliminary analysis of key stakeholders at locations across the organization and creating a global crisis management team. By raising the issue of importance of accounting for international contexts, Pearson differentiates global crisis management from more narrowly cast crisis management.

Part VII: Dialogue and Commentary on the Future of Risk, Crisis and Emergency Management

In this concluding part of the volume, we feature commentary by renowned risk scholars we invited to share their insights and views on the future of risk, crisis and emergency management. These chapters complement the other scholarly contributions in the volume by providing more additional dialogue and commentary on a range of new, emerging and important concerns.

In Chapter 29, "Making Markets for Uninsured Risk: Protection Gap Entities (PGEs) as Risk-Processing Organizations in Society," Jarzabkowski and Chalkias spotlight the widening gap between ensured and actual losses when crisis strikes, and the economic and social problems that occur as a result. They then discuss and problematize how society has aimed to deal with this protection gap through new forms of risk-processing organizations.

Chapter 30, "Risks of Addressing vs. Ignoring Our Biggest Societal Problems: When and How Moon Shots Make Sense" by Sitkin, Miller and See, calls attention to the grand problems our society is facing, including global poverty and safety, access to education, food, water and energy, climate sustainability and equality across people and countries. The authors suggest that contemporary organizational leaders have to complete the seemingly impossible tasks and help us cope with complexity and rapid change, rebuild trust in our societal institutions and help us learn how to collectively tackle today's challenges.

Chapter 31, "Managing for the Future: A Commentary on Crisis Management Research" by Kathleen Sutcliffe, brings attention to the process-centered perspective to studying organizational crisis management. Sutcliffe seeks to understand processes and dynamics relating to the sensing of risks and uncertainty and the foundations of organizational reliability and resilience. To emphasize the importance of these topics, she goes over some of the findings in the areas of organizational reliability, healthcare safety, and organizational adaptability and resilience.

Chapter 32, "From Risk Management to (Corporate) Social Responsibility" by Sytze Kingma, makes a conceptual connection between risk management research and corporate social responsibility research. Kingma argues that the concept of corporate social responsibility (CSR) that refers to the self-regulatory processes through which corporations meet their ethical obligations, is well suited for addressing the productive role of risk. CSR ideas help us with the anticipation, mitigation and prevention of negative externalities or consequences of organizational functioning. Kingma addresses three topics in connection with organizational risk-research on (corporate) responsibility: responsibility starts with an awareness and recognition of risks, the connection between risk and responsibility is best addressed with a process view of risk, and the connections between risk management and corporate responsibility involve the creation of new distinctions and interactions between managers and clients and other stakeholders.

Chapter 33, "Why We Need to Think More about National Political Philosophies of Risk Management" by Henry Rothstein, brings our attention to the importance of understanding different political philosophies about how the state manages risks. By bringing the examples of risk-based approaches to flood management in different countries such as the UK, France and Germany, Rothstein suggests that the differences in risk management are shaped by national ideas of how the state should act.

Chapter 34, "Supply Chain Risk: Transcending Research beyond Disruptions" by George A. Zsidisin, argues for a holistic perspective of supply chain risk. Zsidisin outlines the development of supply chain research which departs from a unilateral understanding of risk and concentration on threat of disruption to incorporation of cross-functional perspectives from Marketing, Management, Legal, Accounting, Finance and Information Systems. He brings examples of such research, which incorporates a greater focus on financial flows, including the topics of commodity price volatility and foreign exchange risk. A holistic perspective of supply chain risk can help businesses reduce supply chain risk exposure and improve business performance.

Chapter 35, "The Janus Faces of Risk" by Hardy and Maguire, draws upon the image of Janus, the Roman god of transitions, time and duality, to argue that risk is Janus-faced and even has multiple Janus faces. As part of the description of the risk faces, the authors argue that risk looks both to the past and to the future, is both real and objective, but also constructed and subjective, and poses a problem of whether risk is to be avoided or embraced. They conclude that risk is itself risky and suggest that researchers need to foreground the link between risk and power, and find ways to help organizations to manage a range of novel and systemic risks.

Finally, Chapter 36, "Effectiveness of Regulatory Agencies" by Charles Perrow, examines the questions of safety regulations by the government. Perrow looks into the work of regulatory agencies and raises concerns with their role in preventing serious accidents. He poses a question of whether the current efforts of Trump administration to reduce regulations in many areas of activity will lead to increase or decrease in the number of accidents in the future.

Note

1 Our colleague, Chet Miller, was a full partner in creating and editing this book. He, however, asked to be omitted from writing the opening chapter as he was facing excessive time demands in other professional areas.

References

Barton, L. 1993. *Crisis in organizations: Managing and communicating in the heat of chaos.* Cincinnati, OH: South-Western Publishing Co.

Garfinkel, H. 1967. *Studies in ethnomethodology.* Englewood Cliffs, NJ: Prentice Hall.

Lupton, D. 1999. *Risk.* London and New York: Routledge.

McDonough, B. & S. Talty. 2016. *Granite Mountain: The firsthand account of a tragic wildfire, its lone survivor, and the firefighters who made the ultimate sacrifice.* New York: Hachette Books.

Pearson, C., C. Roux-Dufort & J. Clair. 2008. *International handbook of organizational crisis management.* Thousand Oaks, CA: Sage Publications.

Shrivastava, P. 1987. *Bhopal: Anatomy of a crisis.* Cambridge, MA: Ballinger Publishing Company.

Weick, K. 1995. *Sensemaking in organizations.* Thousand Oaks, CA.: Sage Publications.

Weick, K. 2001. *Making sense of the organization.* Oxford, UK: Blackwell Publishers.

PART II

Foundational Processes

2

KEY CHALLENGES IN CRISIS MANAGEMENT

Jeroen Wolbers and Kees Boersma

Introduction: The Turkish Airlines Crash

Wednesday February 25, 2009. Thirty minutes into our interview with a field commander, he abruptly stopped talking when his pager alarm triggered. 'So… a VOS6', he stated, remarkably calm. '*A VOS6 is something serious…*'. He remained silent for about half a minute, after which he continued his explanation: '*VOS6 stands for aviation accident at Schiphol Airport. Category 6 means the plane has actually crashed and has between 50–250 persons on board. If you don't mind, it's probably best to end the interview*'. He excused himself and headed towards the crash site to assume his role of field commander.

We witnessed the start of the response to one of the largest aviation disasters in the Netherlands. Turkish Airlines Boeing 737–800, flight 1951, stalled on the final approach to runway 18R of Schiphol Airport. The pilots failed to respond adequately to a loss of airspeed caused by a defective radio altimeter, and the aircraft crashed into a field just short of the runway. Unfortunately, nine people including the three pilots lost their lives, and 86 people were injured, including 25 people who sustained serious injuries.

Months later, the first evaluation reports appeared, applauding the professionalism of the response operation. The public opinion about the response operation was positive, with the headline on the national newspaper noting '*No disaster after the disaster*' (NRC-Next, 2009). Although the media applauded the professionalism and promptness of the response operation, the public investigation reports of the Inspectorate of Justice and Safety (IoJS) and the Dutch Safety Board (DSB) noted some significant challenges. First, the emergency services had trouble locating the crash site. This led to a delay of 15 minutes before the first crews arrived on site. Second, the emergency services had difficulty determining the exact number of victims and the severity of their condition. Third, command centers were activated quickly but were deprived of information for several hours. These challenges are similar to the key challenges often experienced in crisis management operations worldwide. They relate directly to four critical processes in crisis management: cognition, communication, coordination, and control (Comfort, 2007).

The following sections review the crisis management literature on cognition, communication, coordination, and control and use insights from this literature to uncover the practical challenges experienced by crisis managers during the Turkish Airlines crash response operation. In doing so, we pose the following research question: *what is the role of cognition, communication, coordination, and control in crisis management?* To answer this question, we analyse what role these key processes play in crisis management operations, and develop a research agenda to enhance our understanding about the key challenges in crisis management.

The 4Cs of Crisis Management

Crisis management entails organizing the responses of stakeholders and then applying resources to an ambiguous environment in order to bring a disrupted system (an organization or a community) back into alignment (Sommer & Pearson, 2007). This definition of crisis stresses the disruption of a system that requires an intervention to restore the system back to its previous state. Further, crisis management studies often address the dynamics of a response operation and conceive of two broad types of crisis: crisis as an event, and crisis as a process (Williams et al., 2017). When crises are considered specific events, studies typically seek the triggers of the event and attempt to understand how the event disrupted organizational performance (Lagadec, 2007). Important studies have investigated catastrophic events like the Challenger disaster (Vaughan, 1999), the Mann Gulch Fire (Weick, 1993), and the Stockwell shooting in London (Cornelissen et al., 2014). The most frequently used definition of a crisis in these studies is '*a low-probability, high-impact situation that is perceived by critical stakeholders to threaten the viability of the organization*' (Pearson & Clair, 1998, p. 66).

In contrast to the view of crises as events stands a different set of studies that regard a crisis as a gradual process that develops as an organization drifts away from safe practice. There is an incubation phase before the inadequate practice leads to the triggering event that requires a response and resolution (Roux-Dufort, 2016). These studies thus argue that, rather than a sole focus on the triggering event, understanding crisis management requires knowledge of the evolution of a crisis (Turner, 1976). This shifts the primary focus in crisis management from accident investigation to understanding the organization and organizing processes in the production of a crisis (Roux-Dufort, 2016).

Organizing processes play a crucial role in crisis management and influence the capacity to mitigate the effects of crisis. Four key processes underlining organizing and the ability to manage a crisis are conceptualized as the '4Cs': *Cognition, Communication, Coordination,* and *Control* (Comfort, 2007). *Cognition* entails recognizing the degree of emerging risk and conceiving ways to act on that information. Crisis managers then face the challenge of *communicating* to update an emerging network of actors about the crisis and the response operation. The goal is to create a sufficient level of shared meaning to enable crisis managers from different organizations to understand what is going on and how they can contribute to the operation. Communication feeds into the process of *coordination* where interdependent actors engage in mutual adjustment of their actions to achieve a shared goal. To ensure all actions remain focused on the shared goal, commanders need to guide the process and retain *control*. Next, we discuss the '4Cs' of crisis management in detail and highlight the main debates in which they are discussed.

Cognition

Cognition involves recognizing the degree of emerging risk and developing the ability to act on that information (Comfort, 2007). To recognize a disruptive event, crisis managers need to clearly frame the setting and understand how the setting works. Managers must be able to recognize the characteristics of different types of crisis situations, and quickly manage to set up the response organization so they can react to the different types of crises.

An important concept that explains how the process of cognition shapes the work of frontline commanders is recognition-primed decision-making (Klein, 1993). Klein et al.'s (1986) study of fire-ground commanders noted that conscious deliberation of alternative solutions at the accident scene was rare. Instead, fire commanders classified the situation based on previous experience to generate the most suitable decision from their memory. Klein found that experienced leaders drew upon a repertoire of previous actions to create workable strategies that fit the existing context for action.

A more recent experimental study of frontline decision-making in the London Fire Brigade acknowledged that commanders primarily acted based on previous experience and intuition (Cohen-Hatton & Honey, 2015). However, the analysis also indicated that relying only on previous experience actually diminished the performance of frontline commanders because they were less sensitive to the specific operation, limiting their situational awareness.

Situational awareness, another key concept for crisis management that is often related to cognition, concerns 'the perception of elements in the environment within a volume of time and space, the comprehension of their meaning, and the projection of their status in the near future' (Endsley, 1995, p. 36). This definition shows it is possible to attain different levels of situational awareness. The first step is to perceive the status and attributes in the environment. In a fire, this step would involve attending to the specific characteristics of the building, the location of the fire, and the presence of people trapped inside. The second step in attaining situational awareness is to comprehend the situation by relating the situational attributes to the goals of the commander. In a fire, this means the frontline commander as-sesses the kinds of firefighting tactics necessary to deal with the severity of the fire, and the possibility of people trapped inside. The third step and level in situational awareness involves projection of the future status of the fire based on the knowledge of the dynamics of the situation. A fire commander could, for instance, notice that the color of the smoke is a cue to the imminent risk of a flashover. This might lead to a decision to cool the fire and smoke before attempting a rescue operation.

Situational awareness also supports judgments and skills that are embodied in the crafts-manship and proficiency of professionals (Faraj & Xiao, 2006). Cognition implicitly guides interactions between groups with a similar proficiency through anticipation and dynamic adjustment (Rico et al., 2008). For instance, when firefighters estimate the hose length for frontline teammates, they do not explicitly discuss the fact they will continuously adjust the length during the operation. Similarly, studies of high-reliability organizations point out how organizations operating in high-risk settings can achieve reliable performance through collective mind, which is conceptualized as a pattern of heedful interrelations of action (Weick & Roberts, 1993). Collective mind thus describes how actors are able to synchronize their actions with others by developing a detailed understanding of work in different parts of the organization. Situational awareness is needed to develop collective mind.

However, the concept of situational awareness does not entirely explain how the relation between cognition and action unfolds over time, according to the psychological literature on crisis sensemaking (Weick, 1995). Weickian sensemaking emphasizes how people create meaning through a cycle that interweaves interpretation and action (Weick, 1995). The sensemaking process starts when people's expectations are violated during attempts to de-velop a plausible explanation for what is going on (Sandberg & Tsoukas, 2015). To find out what is going on, people take action (enactment) and label and connect cues (selection), preserving how these labels fit into their personal cause map (retention) (Weick, 1979). This sensemaking cycle becomes sustainable over time when individuals interlock their behavior and create consensus on how a task ought to be carried out (Maitlis & Christianson, 2014).

The cycle of enactment, selection, and retention shows that sensemaking differs from situational awareness because sensemaking involves the active framing of events in order to develop understanding (Cornelissen et al., 2014). In other words, people play a crucial role in fabricating the very situation they are trying to comprehend because crisis managers create a frame to render sequences of events meaningful and to classify and predict the behavior of others (Cornelissen et al., 2014). Building substantial common ground is essential to ensuring crisis managers know what is expected of them (Weick & Roberts, 1993). The commitment to a frame is crucial for managing expectations. Yet, it might also entrap crisis managers and hinder their ability to perceive changes in their environment, thus resulting in the collapse of sensemaking if managers act based on a flawed understanding of the situation (Weick, 1993; Snook, 2000; Cornelissen et al., 2014).

In sum, the cognition literature highlights the importance of being sensitive to the environment when managing a crisis. A key insight is that frontline commanders are inclined to fall back on previous experience when the situation intensifies and tend to interpret cues using preexisting frames. The challenge with cognition is thus to be sensitive to changing circumstances and adapt the operation accordingly.

Communication

Communication, a second key challenge, can become problematic when response operations evolve into a distributed structure (Topper & Carley, 1999) where responders cannot see or hear what is happening in other locations (Netten & van Someren, 2011). Therefore, it is crucial for first responders to communicate to enhance their level of shared understanding. Many communication issues in crisis management involve the lack of intersubjectivity, the process through which one knows the subjective meanings of others (Schutz, 1973). Intersubjectivity plays out in various ways during crisis management, as numerous studies highlight issues with missing information, lack of a common vocabulary, and interoperability between information systems (Kapucu, 2006; Manoj & Baker, 2007; Bharosa et al., 2010; Netten & van Someren, 2011).

A key concept that describes the difficulties with information sharing in disasters is variable disjunction of information (Turner, 1976). Disasters scenes are difficult to monitor because unexpected events can rapidly trigger an escalation. Turner (1976) argued that each individual responder collects a slightly different set of information and develops a slightly different idea of what is happening and what needs to occur. The result is that information about the incident varies and additional effort needs to be invested to reduce this variability. Variable disjunction of information, however, cannot be dismissed as a lack of communication (Turner, 1976). Rather, the concept of variable disjunction stresses that when time is short and resources are limited, an imbalance can be created between the amount of information generated and the amount of information needed to fully describe the complexity of the situation. Thus, response operations with high complexity and continuous change make it necessary to be extremely selective in the use of communication (Turner, 1976).

The aforementioned point was acknowledged by Quarantelli (1997) in the ten criteria he proposed for evaluating the management of disasters. Information is one of the ten key issues in crisis management but is often confused with problems of information technology and interoperability of information systems. Instead, problems stem from what is being communicated, rather than from what means of communication is used. A major contributing factor in response operations is the fact that information flow moves through fixed channels following the chain-of-command. Moving through the entire chain-of-command can severely slow down communication and decision-making because information needs to flow from the bottom to the top of the command chain, and back again. Thus, it is important to differentiate between mini-second and many-second cycles in response operations (Chen et al., 2008). Mini-second cycles take place on-site when the response is reactive and the time window for action is small, requiring a more direct link between communication and action. Many-second cycles include communication to command centers that operate with a larger time window to deal with tactical and strategic management issues.

Reddy et al. (2009) note that a lack of common ground due to differences in terminology also plays a major part in communication of problems. Each of the emergency services (e.g. police, fire fighters) has distinct backgrounds, specialized operational expertise, and professional jargon. These can give emergency responders a unique and clear professional identity, but can also create misunderstandings between them (Comfort & Kapucu, 2006). For example, the professional cultures of different response organizations hinder them from sharing and interpreting disaster knowledge (Marincioni, 2007; Moynihan, 2012; Tsai & Chi, 2012). In contrast, some response organizations (e.g. the US Coast Guard) address this problem by training their members to understand the different professional languages used by many of the different stakeholders. This practice was a key success factor in the response of the US Coast Guard to hurricane Katrina (Morris et al., 2007).

Another important factor of effective communication in emerging response networks is trust. Personal relations are essential to communication networks since these networks are often organized according to existing (phone) contacts (Landgren & Nulden, 2007; Uhr et al., 2008). When these personal relations are missing, it becomes difficult to share information because responders from different organizations lack mutual trust (Manoj & Baker, 2007). Responders must then rely on swift trust generated by judging the quality of performance and role execution (Majchrzak et al., 2007).

In sum, communication is challenging in crisis situations because variable disjunction of information arises in a distributed response structure. Responders struggle to inform one another while dealing with diverging information flows, differences in terminology, and limited trust. To overcome these challenges, commanders need to adapt on scene by differentiating the information from mini-second and many-second cycles, translating the different terminology to others, and relying on swift trust. This is a key challenge because the time to act is generally limited, the situation can escalate quickly, and responders may be forced to assume that their communication to other stakeholders is adequate and accurately interpreted.

Coordination

Keeping the actions of involved units and organizations synchronized during a response operation is the third key challenge. Coordination concerns linking together different parts of an organization to accomplish a collective set of tasks (Van de Ven et al., 1976). Scholars have long assumed that organizations can be designed in ways that allow individuals to coordinate their actions. Designed coordination supposes that each coordination mechanism has certain information-processing capabilities that can be utilized in different kinds of environments (Lawrence & Lorch, 1982). In stable environments, coordination can indeed be achieved by using procedures that have a low information-processing capability. That is, procedures prescribe a specific way of working, but do not provide a means to transfer additional information. Standard operating procedures function by structuring the response operation in advance, allowing professionals to fall back upon well-thought-out plans of action, known to everybody in the organization (Okhuysen & Bechky, 2009). In this way, less time is needed in stressful and dynamic environments to structure the organizational response itself. This allows commanders to focus on other priorities in the first hectic moments of a response operation.

Studies on coordination in crisis management settings, focusing on trauma centers (Faraj & Xiao, 2006), emergency response (Wolbers et al., 2017), and police pursuits (Schakel et al., 2016), demonstrate that a rise in volatility makes it increasingly difficult to rely on designed coordination mechanisms because circumstances change more rapidly and unexpectedly. This shows the limits of the information-processing logic that presumes contingencies can be assessed beforehand, and that predefined coordination mechanisms work in the situation at hand (Faraj & Xiao, 2006). Yet, in dynamic situations, the environment is prone to change and predefined interdependencies differ in practice. Hence, classic coordination theories based on an information-processing logic do not fully incorporate the organizing dynamics needed for crisis management operations (Bigley & Roberts, 2001; Klein et al., 2006).

Recent studies illustrate that ongoing adaptation is required as fast-paced environments are often too unstable for aligning coordination mechanisms with predefined contingencies (Bigley & Roberts, 2001; Faraj & Xiao, 2006; Kellogg et al., 2006). In addition to standard operating procedures, mutual adaptation, improvisation, and ad-hoc networking are found to be important elements of coordination that enable first responders to adapt to changing circumstances at the disaster site (Kapucu, 2006; Comfort, 2007; Moynihan, 2009). In that respect, coordination in fast-response settings is much better characterized as 'a temporally unfolding and contextualized process of input regulation and interaction articulation to realize a collective performance' (Faraj & Xiao, 2006, p. 1157).

Studies that explore how coordination processes occur in crisis situations show that unambiguous command is needed for the timely direction of, yet flexibility and on-the-spot decision-making are required to adapt to a continuously changing situation (Bigley & Roberts, 2001; Comfort, 2007; Majchrzak et al., 2007; Moynihan, 2009). Coordination at the incident scene is thus a combination of designed and emergent coordination (Bigley & Roberts, 2001; Okhuysen & Bechky, 2009). The challenge of combining designed and emergent coordination means that coordination is no longer straightforward. As contingencies become more complex, locally situated adaptations are necessary to keep the operation in sync. While such adaptations create flexibility, they also increase ambiguity and diminish the predictability of the outcome of designed procedures that partly restrict coordination based on anticipation (Okhuysen & Bechky, 2009).

In sum, dynamic circumstances in crises often force frontline commanders to abandon designed coordination mechanisms and find ad-hoc solutions. The variability of this process depends largely on the specific requirements and dynamics of a crisis, since each new situation requires a different adaptation of structures. Therefore, coordination in crisis response settings requires commanders to keep adapting and informing other stakeholders of the how these adjustments impact work practices and procedures.

Control

The fourth key challenge in crisis management operations concerns keeping the operation and the involved units under control. Control, in this respect, is about the capacity to keep ongoing action focused on a shared goal. While the overarching goal of control is to get units to work in the same direction, the reputation of control is often rather authoritarian (Alberts & Hayes, 2003). This understanding comes from the early command and control doctrines that stressed a form of top-down command, in which subordinates receive rigid orders that leave little scope to exercise their own initiative (Shamir, 2010). This form of control, also known in military literature as 'Befehlstaktik' (Van Creveld, 1989), supposes that in times of crisis, a one-way directional command approach is beneficial because it increases the commanders' feeling of control. Likewise, in crisis management, for a long time the assumption prevailed that effective crisis management requires authoritarian command and control (Quarantelli, 1977). Directive command works in operations that are relatively stable and predictable, but as a crisis escalates, it turns out that commanders are often unable to retain control because of rapid developments and too many actors that become involved (Comfort, 2007).

A different doctrine proved necessary that could incorporate the capacity to adapt and increase the flexibility of units operating in the frontline. In military doctrine, this was established by the concept of 'Auftragstaktik' (Van Creveld, 1989). Auftragstaktik is based on a goal-oriented approach, in which subordinate leaders understand the intent of the orders, are given proper guidance and training to act independently, and act according to their perception of the commander's intent (Shamir, 2010). NATO incorporated this type of warfare with the concept of 'mission command', which became the leading command and control doctrine of modern Western armed forces (Keithly & Ferris, 1999).

The central principle of mission command is commanders' intent. When a commander gives direction by communicating his/her intent to subordinates, it helps them understand the larger context of their actions. This allows them to depart from the original plan in the heat of battle in a way that is consistent with the aims of the higher commander (Cowper, 2000). Commanders' intent is a specific operational methodology designed to prevent micromanagement and oversupervision of subordinates, while supporting initiative at the lowest possible level. The underlying idea is that frontline commanders are able to operate independently through self-synchronization under a shared goal frame. Self-synchronization pushes decision-making authority down to the lowest level within the organization by relaxing the traditional hierarchical approach to command and control. While the idea is clear in theory, in practice it turns out that developing a congruent mindset remains difficult. A study by Shattuck (1995) showed that in a simulation by the U.S. Army commanders, only 34% of the company commanders' decisions matched their battalion commander's intent.

The arrangement and use of control is a key issue in the field of safety management. Perrow (1999) found that too much control by tight-coupling leaves organizations vulnerable to failure. Tight-coupling means the organization is highly integrated, whereby actions in one unit have a direct effect on actions in another unit. Highly integrated units and dependence on the performance of other units make it easier for low probability, high-consequence failures to spread. Units that are loosely coupled are less dependent on each other and have less unitary designs, making them less vulnerable to cascading effects. While these characteristics are important for organizing safety in normal operations in high-reliability environments, crisis settings bring an additional factor into play. High-tempo operations often feature moments where loosely coupled systems suddenly become highly coupled systems (Weick, 1998). Snook's (2002) analysis of a friendly fire incident where two US Army Black Hawk helicopters were shot down by the US coalition force F-15s in Iraq demonstrates that operators were unable to imagine and assess how the previously loosely coupled systems would interact when they suddenly became tightly coupled (Snook, 2002). This led the coalition forces to overlook the fact that the two Black Hawks had already entered the area being scanned for enemies by the F-15s. When coupled with the policy of using different (unique) 'squawk codes' to recognize friendly units that had not been integrated properly in the two formerly loosely coupled systems, the Black Hawks' entry into restricted airspace resulted in catastrophe.

Loosely coupled systems are common in emergency response operations because frontline commanders tend to create separate pockets of control (Wolbers et al., 2017). The reason is that crisis managers act on multiple problems at once by delegating task execution to subordinates and engaging in parallel processing of information. The risk is that separate pockets of control can suddenly become tightly coupled when crisis managers encounter critical situations like explosion risks or hazardous materials that pose an imminent threat to all units. Likewise, Bigley and Roberts (2001) noted that loose and tight coupling is an issue in firefighting operations when different units attack different sides of a building. Breaking a window or opening a door at the back can suddenly disturb the smoke balance, triggering a flashover scenario for units entering the front of the building. As interdependencies can change rapidly in response operations, it's crucial for crisis managers to stay aware of the interplay between loose and tight coupling.

In sum, the literature on control shows that in crisis situations, commanders often retain flexibility by giving the initiative back to frontline commanders based on the principle of commanders' intent. This enables units on scene to adapt and operate within the broader operational mandate through self-synchronization. Organizing control in this way works when the operation remains loosely coupled. However, the risk is that operations tend to become tightly coupled in unexpected moments, resulting in unintended consequences for the actions of other units. The challenge of control is thus to retain flexibility while avoiding the creation of intended and unintended effects on the operations of other units involved in responding to the crisis.

The 4Cs in Action: Operational Challenges during the Turkish Airlines Crash

In the following sections, we will explore how the 4Cs of crisis management play a role in the response operation to the Turkish Airlines crash. We will use the public investigation reports that appeared in the aftermath of the crash as an illustration of the main challenges in response operations (Inspectorate of Justice and Safety, 2009; Dutch Safety Board, 2010). Our analysis indicates that cognition, communication, coordination, and control each have a distinct role to play in the response operation, but also directly and indirectly influence each other.

Locating the crash site. The first challenge in the report of the DSB (2010) identified that the first fire engines responding from both Schiphol Airport and the regional fire stations had trouble locating the crash site. Crash tenders drove down the runway and did not see the aircraft, because it crashed behind a dike that obscured the view from the runway. Accidentally, around the same time, an ambulance passing by on the A9 highway from the adjacent safety region 'Noord-Holland-Noord' spotted the aircraft. The driver passed the information to his Emergency Response Center (ERC) in Alkmaar. However, the location of the crash site was not communicated to the ERC in Haarlem, which was responsible for the dispatch to the crash site. In the ERC in Haarlem, several calls came in from citizens who had seen the crash site, but this information was not shared with the dispatchers in the ERC working in the same room, in the first chaotic moments of the response operation (often symbolically characterized as the 'fog of war'). Consequently, as the first official call came from the Schiphol tower that had lost the aircraft on the radar, the ERC dispatchers (incorrectly) activated the VOS6 procedure meant for a plane crash on the Schiphol Airport grounds. However, the actual crash occurred in a ploughed field just outside the Schiphol Airport perimeter. The consequence was that all incoming units were directed to UGS A (a designated staging area at Schiphol), as the VOS6 procedure prescribes, instead of directly to the crash site.

The logic behind the VOS procedure is that emergency services cannot freely drive on the airport grounds, but must be marshaled by airport police to avoid collision with aircrafts and other airport traffic. The activation of the VOS6 procedure thus let first responders believe that they were responding to a crash on the airport grounds. When they could not locate the crash site on the airport grounds, a new search had to be initiated in the surrounding areas. Valuable time was lost due to this confusion. The DSB concluded that '*the consequence of activating a VOS6 was that the regional fire department reached the crash site only after approximately half an hour*' (DSB, 2010, p. 6).

In the first moments of the response operations, we see that responders are challenged by a combination of communication and coordination issues. Variable disjunction of information occurred when the location of the crash site was not shared immediately between two different ERCs in the cities of Alkmaar and Haarlem, who developed their own perspective on the incident. The disjunction of information prompted the ERC in Haarlem to activate the VOS6 protocol, as they were under the assumption that the plane crash occurred on the Schiphol Airport grounds.

The trouble with locating the crash site and the discussion around activating the correct (and ultimately incorrect) procedures illustrates that crisis managers have to make quick decisions, often based on incomplete information. These decisions, in the first moments of the response operation, are often hard to revise once they have been made. Like the actual use of the VOS6 procedure shows, contingencies in the response operation often turn out to be more complex than anticipated in the original procedures. As a consequence, once responders arrive at the disaster scene, predetermined plans need to be adapted to the dynamically unfolding situation at hand.

We thus have to question the effectiveness of coordinating based on predefined plans and procedures in fast-paced environments. Still, the activation of the VOS6 procedure also had a positive side to it. When we interviewed the field commander several months after the response operation, he explained that for him and other units, it was a blessing that VOS6 procedure had been activated. Once the crash site was located, it meant that the Schiphol military police units were positioned at strategic points on the airport to guide the emergency units from the UGS to the crash site. This allowed a faster guidance of units and resources, once the crash site was located.

Counting the number of victims. The second challenge described in the public investigation reports was that common understandings between different organizational actors were compromised and disrupted at several moments. A problematic understanding of the number of victims who were transported to different hospitals occurred during the response operation (IoJS, 2009, p. 13).

> At a certain point no-one knows who is doing what. That the victims are transported to hospitals rather quickly, is because of the professionals in the field who just transported the patients to a hospital, despite of a missing command structure.
>
> *(IoJS, 2009, p. 97)*

Tactical and strategic command units had trouble getting validated information from the field. Improvised action at the crash site by medics triggered new information flows and obstructed existing information flows in the network of collaborating actors. The following example shows clearly how this occurred.

At the moment the first ambulance arrived at the crash site 18 minutes after the crash at 10:44 AM, its crew started a triage of the amount and the severity of wounded victims. The incident report describes that this is immediately problematic, as several victims have already left the crash site by themselves and were transported to a temporary shelter, a nearby barn, with help from bystanders, fire department, and police units (IoJS, 2009). Sometime later, two trauma doctors arrived at the temporary shelter, observed the situation, and decided to intervene. They believed it was necessary to perform a second triage. The trauma doctors assessed that 19 victims were incorrectly identified as slightly wounded (Triage Category 3); 17 were seriously injured (Triage Category 2), and 2 of them were severely injured (Triage Category 1). In addition, the doctors judged that all of these victims needed to be transported to the hospital to check for a 'high energetic trauma', due to the severity of the crash speed of 180 km/h (IoJS, 2009, p. 91). As a result, the 19 victims were transported to the hospital immediately; the remaining passengers were transported at a later stage.

The information about the second triage and the new triage status of the victims never reached the other crisis management teams (IoJS, 2009, p. 66). Due to the different locations where the triage took place, different numbers of victims with different triage statuses spread throughout the continuously evolving and expanding response network. For a long time, it was unclear to the public authorities how many wounded there were and what their status was. In the end, it took *four* days to validate the incomplete lists gathered from various on-site medical teams with lists in the 13 involved hospitals (IoJS, 2009, pp. 93–94). The final count showed that 57 victims were transported in ambulances from the crash site, 42 victims were transported from the temporal wounded facility, and 25 victims were transported with own means of transportation. These numbers illustrated the diffuse situation the crisis teams had to deal with.

Triage is a medical decision-making process meant for prioritizing transport of injured to the hospital, and for assessing the medical capacity required for the transport (Koenig & Schultz, 1994). Yet, the previous situation shows that triage information is also used for interpreting the number and the severity of wounded by other (non-medical) response organizations. It is a well-known concern in response operations that crisis managers with different backgrounds, specialized operational expertise, and different professional languages need to coordinate across their jurisdictional and organizational boundaries (Comfort & Kapucu, 2006). This offers a multilayered coordination challenge, as the gathering of victim information requires the crossing of jurisdictional boundaries, which includes the regulation of authority, legitimization, and the application of expertise. This was especially the case for communicating information about the number and severity of wounded. Providing the correct number of victims is an important aspect for different response organizations in their (public) crisis communication. When multiple response organizations use and interpret triage information, misunderstandings about the status and number of victims will likely reverberate throughout the entire response network, causing extensive challenges. Moreover, the expert assessment of passengers needing to be checked for a high energetic trauma in a hospital posed a formidable logistical task for the medical agencies.

In the aftermath of the Turkish Airlines crash, the responders faced a combination of challenges. A key element underlying the problematic administration of victim numbers is cognition. The trauma doctors made sense of the consequences the impact of the crash could have on the trauma of the patients. This enabled them to make a future projection in their situational awareness. The 'expert' on-scene reassessment for another triage by the trauma doctors also directly fed into the variable disjunction of information. Processes of cognition and communication became intertwined in the course of events, as professionals in different locations developed a diverging understanding of the triage process. By undertaking the reassessment, trauma doctors also directly intervened in ongoing coordination processes. The second triage conflicted with the ongoing administration of triage classifications, and thus influenced the validity of the ongoing triage numbers between the involved command centers. The issue of triage can also be viewed from the challenge of control in terms of tight and loose coupling. Normally medical aid on the disaster site is loosely coupled, as medical teams take care of individual patients and perform multiple rounds of triage updates. The reason is that the condition of patients can change over time because of treatment. In this case, reassessing the triage status of all passengers created a tightly coupled system, which caused extensive control and coordination problems with other actors in the response system.

The triage process in the aftermath of the Turkish Airlines crash showed that the interdependence between cognition, communication, coordination, and control develops too fast to engage in extensive and continuous consultation. Crisis managers need to work in an environment that is unknown, difficult to oversee, and that is characterized by unexpected and continuous change. This dynamic environment, in combination with various information system-mediated communication, makes it very difficult to develop and sustain common understanding (Gephart, 2004). Moreover, action and expertise are often distributed and need to be employed immediately, to prevent the situation from escalating or deteriorating.

Command Centers are Deprived of Information. The third challenge described in the public investigation reports was the information management between the different crisis management teams, operational in the GRIP3 emergency state. Several agencies and teams were active quite rapidly, but were deprived of information for several hours (IoJS, 2009, p. 66). This led to coordination problems between the medical organizations in the now rapidly expanding response network. Providing care for 86 wounded persons overwhelmed the local medical response capacity, but fortunately the VOS6 protocol didn't only designate staging areas; it also activated the procedures to call 3 Mobile Medical Trauma teams and 64 ambulances to the crash site (IoJS, 2009). Furthermore, it notified dispatchers that between 7 and 13 hospitals had to be warned to create trauma room capacity. Emergency response centers throughout the Netherlands received the call and rerouted their ambulances to the crash site.

While the initial dispatch of 64 ambulances was fast, the quick capacity buildup created additional problems. In the heat of the moment, dispatchers only warned six hospitals and failed to call in the three mobile medical trauma teams in first instance (DSB, 2010). As the focus was on building ambulance response capacity, limited attention was paid to the information needs of other partners in the medical response network. This led to several problems in the periphery of the network. As no calls came in, several hospitals anticipated on a large amount of wounded at own initiative, kept trauma rooms at bay, and called in additional surgical capacity. This forced several hospitals to cancel their planned surgeries to keep trauma care available, but they were not notified when the number of severely wounded was far less than expected (IoJS, 2009).

It is a well-known phenomenon in acute medical care that organizing a coherent triage, transportation, and registration during mass casualty situations leads to coordination issues (Tierney, 1985; Koenig & Schultz, 1994). Monitoring the status and location of casualties requires consistent communication between a wide spectrum of medical actors: the medical officer, casualty transport coordinator, mobile field hospital commander, ambulances crews, emergency response centers, national ambulance dispatch center, and hospitals. To make matters more complicated, police and municipalities share responsibility for casualty registration and communicating information to victims' relatives.

An important coordination challenge of networked coordination is that as new organizations are included in the network, information sharing becomes increasingly complex, as information flows through network from various positions at different times. This occurs because response organizations have operational field units at different levels, different functional command structures, and separate back-offices for information and resource management (Comfort & Kapucu, 2006). Therefore, a rapidly evolving network triggers an information flow that is in flux.

The common solution for structuring communication and enabling fast decision-making is to increase control by employing a centralized command and control structure, in which communication lines and authority are formalized. Command and control structures are known for their hierarchical decision capacities and clear role structures, and are a powerful instrument for accomplishing tasks characterized by repetition and uniformity (Quarantelli & Dynes, 1977). Its underlying premise is that when the organizations involved in the response operation match the existing command structure, centralized coordination forms a quick and effective solution. Yet, such a system is difficult to maintain in a dynamic environment in which a large number of organizations become involved and membership fluctuates over time. In these situations, command and control structures insufficiently account for the decentralization and flexibility that are required during the response operation.

Similarly, the coordination process in the aftermath of the Turkish Airlines crash shows that the dynamics occurring around medical logistics cannot be completely understood in

Table 2.1 The 4Cs in Action during the Turkish Airlines Crash Response Operation

	Locating the crash site	*Counting number of victims*	*Deprived of information*
Cognition	VOS6 procedure activated for crash on airport grounds, while actual crash site was still unknown	Trauma doctors found it necessary to perform a second triage on-scene because of high-energetic trauma	Teams at tactical and strategic level were unable to make sense of the situation in the first hours
Communication	112 calls with correct location reached response center in adjacent region and were not communicated	Information about second triage never reached other crisis management teams	Hospitals and trauma teams were initially not warned and received little updates
Coordination	VOS6 procedure directed units to incorrect staging area	Second triage collided with coordination of ongoing transportation	Ambulances took patients to a range of hospitals, while others kept trauma capacity available
Control	Response center in control was too busy to receive other information	Many different actors responsible for triage and registration	Actors responsible for coordination received little information and had limited overview

terms of command and control. The problems response organizations are confronted with outgrow the span of control of the existing command and control structure, as organizational and jurisdictional boundaries need to be crossed. This calls for a coordination structure that is able to account for the distributed nature of this problem. Due to its enhanced capacity for adaptation to fluctuations in the environment, networked collaboration is found to be more effective to deal with the distributed nature of information and decisional challenges under pressure (Moynihan, 2008; Moynihan, 2009). Therefore, centralized command structures become gradually extended with or transformed into interorganizational networks to provide a structure through which distributed crisis response activities can be coordinated (Topper & Carley, 1999; Moynihan, 2008) (Table 2.1).

Key Dilemmas Across the 4Cs: Toward a Research Agenda

The case of the Turkish Airlines crash illustrates that adapting to the contingencies of the crisis creates tensions between cognition, communication, coordination, and control. Crisis management organizations excel in mounting a rapid operation according to plan, but as the events on the incident scene often turn out to be more complex and unpredictable, plans need to be adapted. The role of the 4Cs in the Turkish Airlines crash teaches us that it is crucial to adapt, but it also suggests that when people confront turbulent and hazardous situations they seek structures to create stability.

This tension is well known in the literature on resilience that offers some important insights on the challenge of adapting in turbulent and volatile settings. Resilience is often defined as '*the capacity to cope with unanticipated dangers after they have become manifest, learning to bounce back*' (Wildavsky, 1988, p. 77). Some have argued that bouncing back is not enough, and that true resilience also means being able to come away from the event with a greater capacity to prevent and contain future errors (Weick et al., 1999). In any case, what is central in the research on resilience is that managing by anticipation – that is to predict and prevent potential dangers before damage is done – turns out to be an ineffective strategy when uncertainty and volatility increase (De Bruijne et al., 2010). In the organizational and management literature, an important work on resilience is the functioning of high-reliability organizations (Weick & Sutcliffe, 2001). Findings from this literature indicate that organizations develop the capacity for high-reliable performance when they are able to combine anticipation with adaptation (LaPorte & Consolini, 1991).

In crisis management, the dilemma of anticipation and adaptation is prominent when crisis managers are forced to adapt, while they are also inclined to hold on to existing structures. Crisis managers are trained to deal with this dilemma by adapting elements of incident command structures (Bigley & Roberts, 2001). In order to facilitate a fast response, many of the organizing processes on the incident scene have been prestructured through incident command structures (Boersma et al., 2014). In practice, crisis managers are specifically trained to elaborate these structures, and switch between different roles in the command structures (Bigley & Roberts, 2001). Such adaptation strategies are known in organization and management studies as 'bricolage'. Bricolage is a way to respond to surprises by experimenting with alternative courses of action by rearranging existing structures (Bechky & Okhuysen, 2011). In terms of resilience, bricolage relies on a combination of anticipation and adaptation, as the elements of the structures have been created in advance. The issue with bricolage is that in order to do so, actors require shared social cognitive resources to foster the collectively held knowledge about how a task should be performed (Duymedjian & Rüling, 2010). However, in response operations where professionals from different response organizations need to come together at unexpected moments, these shared social cognitive resources do not always exist (Comfort & Kapucu, 2006; Uhr et al., 2008).

The tension between anticipation and adaptation in crisis management provides the foundation for a future research agenda concerning the 4Cs. Based on our analysis of the role of the 4Cs in the response operation to the Turkish Airlines crash, we highlight three research themes: *ad-hoc teaming, command tactics,* and *information management.*

First, the tension between anticipation and adaptation highlights the role of ad-hoc teaming. As a crisis intensifies the nature of the on-scene, collaboration tends to become more ad-hoc and distributed (Majchrzak et al., 2007). Crises like the Norway Breivik terror attack (Rimstad & Sollid, 2015) and the attacks in Paris (Hirsch et al., 2015) have shown that response operations unfold in unexpected ways and take place at multiple sites. The key challenge for crisis management research is to investigate how ad-hoc teams in the frontline react to an unexpected event, how they adapt, and how they can be managed. Research on adaptation has predominantly explored the structural means of adaptation, such as structure elaborating and role switching (Bigley & Roberts, 2001). Future research may address the dynamics that takes place outside formal response structures, as ad-hoc adaptation is likely to emerge when the crisis takes an unexpected turn, or requires a simultaneous response in different locations. The processes of cognition, communication, coordination, and control are likely to play a foundational role in fostering adaptation and improvisation. This will feed into, and requires more knowledge, about challenges of keeping situational awareness, interpreting in what way people adapt from standard operating procedures, and how to retain control over a response that is characterized by improvisation.

Second, as ad-hoc teaming and adaptation become increasingly important, the command tactics also have to be updated. It is difficult to account for the unexpected and multi-sited dynamics of crisis situations with traditional hierarchal command and control tactics. The consequence of ad-hoc teaming in crisis situations is that decision-making is pushed down to the frontline (Gephart, 1993). When multiple teams engage in different aspects of the response operation, it creates separate pockets of control, which results in the variable disjunction of information (Wolbers et al., 2017). Coordination based on anticipation gets increasingly difficult as different teams adapt in an unpredictable manner. Instead, crisis managers will need to adapt their command tactics toward more open-ended tactics like commander's intent. The key challenge for future crisis management research is to explore how response teams are commanded in a distributed setting, so that they are able to synchronize their actions and information sharing at different hierarchical levels and at different times. It might very well be the case that this requires crisis managers to adopt a more diverse set of command tactics in different phases of a response operation. Adapting the command tactics will affect the processes of cognition, communication, coordination, and control. Giving more freedom to the frontline operations means that it becomes more difficult to interpret what is going on, assess when to or not to communicate, understand what kind of new interdependencies arise, and keep track of when units reinterpret their commander's intent.

Third, when the nature of teaming and command tactics changes, this must be supported by a more flexible and agile information management process. To date, the common response in developing information management technology entails centralizing information streams in a shared platform so that different actors and organizations can develop a common operational picture (COP) (Comfort, 2004). The underlying premise of a COP is that when all units can access relevant information, they are able to self-synchronize. The COP research has a predominant technical focus, as most attention is given to how information can be collected, sorted, and represented. However, studies into information management have pointed out important caveats like information overload (Bharosa et al., 2010), insufficient evaluation/validation of the information (Rake & Nja, 2009), insufficient attention to sharing data with others (Dearstyne, 2007), scarce attention to the role of sensemaking (Wolbers & Boersma, 2013), and limited collaboration awareness (Treurniet et al., 2012). These issues show that the information management process is far more extensive than only collecting and sorting information. Future research may address what role information management plays in fostering cognition, communication, coordination, and control so that it supports a more flexible crisis management process. Key issues are how to retain situational awareness using a common operational picture as the response is underway, how to translate meanings and interests between different actors, and how to develop swift trust for sharing information between actors that are not familiar with each other. Overall, information sharing should trigger a process where actors develop a better idea of what is going on, while they challenge each other's action and assumptions to be able to question dominant beliefs and frames of the situation. How this process unfolds and can best be supported provides an interesting avenue for future research into crisis management.

Conclusion

In this chapter we have sought to answer the research question: *what is the role of cognition, communication, coordination, and control in crisis management?* Our discussion of the literature indicates that through the process of *cognition*, crisis managers strive to recognize the degree of emerging risk. Subsequently, they face the challenge of *communicating* the state of affairs to other stakeholders, and jointly advance a *coordinated* response. Throughout this process, crisis managers need to retain *control* to keep all actions focused on a shared goal. Our analysis of the Turkish Airlines crash response operation shows that these four crisis management processes are highly interrelated. Organizing an effective response entails awareness in all these four processes. As the nature of the on-scene collaboration in crisis is volatile and distributed, the future challenge is to study the 4Cs of crisis management in relation to ad-hoc teaming, command tactics, and information management.

References

Alberts D. S., & Hayes R. E. (2003). Power to the edge: Command and control in the information age. Office of the Assistant Secretary of Defense Washington DC Command and Control Research Program (CCRP), Washington DC.

Bechky, B. A., & Okhuysen G. A. (2011). Expecting the unexpected? How SWAT officers and film crews handle surprises. *Academy of Management Journal*, 54(2), 239–261.

Bharosa, N., Lee, J., & Janssen, M. (2010). Challenges and obstacles in sharing and coordinating information during multi-agency disaster response: Propositions from field exercises. *Information Systems Frontiers*, 12(1), 49–65.

Bigley, G. A., & Roberts. K. H. (2001). The incident command system: High-reliability organizing for complex and volatile task environments, *The Academy of Management Journal*, 44(6), 1281–1299.

Boersma, F. K., Comfort L. K., Groenendaal J., & Wolbers J. (2014). Incident Command Systems: A dynamic tension among goals and rules. *Journal of Contingencies and Crisis Management*, 22(1), 1–4.

Chen, R., Sharman, R., Rao, H. R., & Upadhyaya, S. J. (2008). Coordination in emergency response management. *Communications of the ACM*, 51(5), 66–73.

Cohen-Hatton, S. R., Butler, P. C., & Honey, R. C. (2015). An investigation of operational decision making in situ: Incident command in the UK Fire and rescue service. *Human Factors*, 57(5), 793–804.

Comfort, L. K., Ko, K., & Zagorecki, A. (2004). Coordination in rapidly evolving disaster response systems: The role of information. *American Behavioral Scientist*, 48(3), 295–313.

Comfort, L. K. (2007). Crisis management in hindsight: Cognition, communication, coordination, and control. *Public Administration Review*, 67(s1), 189–197.

Comfort, L. K., & Kapucu N. (2006). Inter-organizational coordination in extreme events: The world trade center attacks, September 11, 2001. *Natural Hazards*, 39(2), 309–327.

Cornelissen, J. P., Mantere, S., & Vaara, E. (2014). The contraction of meaning: The combined effect of communication, emotions, and materiality on sensemaking in the Stockwell shooting. *Journal of Management Studies*, 51(5), 699–736.

Cowper, T. J. (2000). The myth of the "military model" of leadership in law enforcement. *Police Quarterly*, 3(3), 228–246.

De Bruijne, M., Boin, A., & van Eeten, M. (2010). Resilience: Exploring the concept and its meanings. *Designing Resilience: Preparing for Extreme Events*, 13–32.

Dearstyne, B. (2007). The FDNY on 9/11: Information and decision making in crisis. *Government Information Quarterly*, 24(1), 29–46.

Dutch Safety Board. (2010). *Hulpverlening na vliegtuigongeval Turkish Airlines, Haarlemmermeer. 25 Februari 2009*, Den Haag.

Duymedjian, R., & Rüling, C. C. (2010). Towards a foundation of bricolage in organization and management theory. *Organization Studies*, 31(2), 133–151.

Endsley, M. R. (1995). Toward a theory of situation awareness in dynamic systems. *Human Factors: The Journal of the Human Factors and Ergonomics Society*, 37(1), 32–64.

Faraj, S., & Xiao Y. (2006). Coordination in fast-response organizations. *Management Science*, 52(8), 1155–1169.

Gephart, R. P. (1993). The textual approach: Risk and blame in disaster sensemaking. *Academy of Management Journal*, 36(6), 1465–1514.

Gephart, R. P. (2004). Sensemaking and new media at work. *American Behavioral Scientist*, 48(4), 479–495.

Hirsch, M., Carli, P., Nizard, R., Riou, B., Baroudjian, B., Baubet, T., … & Fontaine, J. P. (2015). The medical response to multisite terrorist attacks in Paris. *The Lancet*, 386(10012), 2535–2538.

Inspectorate of Security and Justice. (2009). *Poldercrash 25 Februari 2009*. Een onderzoek door de Inspectie Openbare Orde en Veiligheid in samenwerking met de Inspectie voor de Gezondheidszorg. IOOV, Den Haag.

Kapucu, N. (2006). Interagency communication networks during emergencies: Boundary spanners in multiagency coordination. *The American Review of Public Administration*, 36(2), 207–225.

Keithly, D. M., & Ferris, S. P. (1999). Auftragstaktik, or directive control, in joint and combined operations. *Parameters*, 29(3), 118.

Kellogg, K. C., Orlikowski W. J., & Yates J. (2006). Life in the trading zone: Structuring coordination across boundaries in postbureaucratic organizations. *Organization Science*, 17(1), 22–44.

Klein, G. A. (1993). *A Recognition-Primed Decision (RPD) Model of Rapid Decision Making* (pp. 138–147). New York: Ablex Publishing Corporation.

Klein, G. A., Calderwood, R., & Clinton-Cirocco, A. (1986). Rapid decision making on the fire ground. In: *Proceedings of the Human Factors Society Annual Meeting* (Vol. 30, No. 6, pp. 576–580). Los Angeles, CA: SAGE Publications.

Klein, K. J., Ziegert., J. C., Knight, A. P., & Xiao Y. (2006). Dynamic delegation: Shared, hierarchical, and deindividualized leadership in extreme action teams. *Administrative Science Quarterly*, 51(4), 590–621.

Koenig, K. L., & Schultz C. H. (1994). Disaster medicine: Advances in local catastrophic disaster response. *Academic Emergency Medicine*, 1(2), 133–136.

Lagadec, P. (2007). Crisis management in the twenty-first century: "unthinkable" events in "inconceivable" contexts. In: *Handbook of Disaster Research* (pp. 489–507). New York: Springer.

Landgren, J., & Nulden, U. (2007). A study of emergency response work: Patterns of mobile phone interaction. In: *Proceedings of the SIGCHI conference on Human factors in computing systems* (pp. 1323–1332). ACM.

LaPorte, T. R., & Consolini, P. M. (1991). Working in practice but not in theory: Theoretical challenges of "high-reliability organizations". *Journal of Public Administration Research and Theory*, 1(1), 19–48.

Maitlis, S., & Christianson, M. (2014). Sensemaking in organizations: Taking stock and moving forward. *Academy of Management Annals*, 8(1), 57–125.

Majchrzak, A., Jarvenpaa S. L., & Hollingshead A. B. (2007). Coordinating expertise among emergent groups responding to disasters. *Organization Science*, 18(1), 147–161.

Manoj, B. S., & Baker, A. H. (2007). Communication challenges in emergency response. *Communications of the ACM*, 50(3), 51–53.

Marincioni, F. (2007). Information technologies and the sharing of disaster knowledge: The critical role of professional culture. *Disasters*, 31(4), 459–476.

Moynihan, D. P. (2008). Combining structural forms in the search for policy tools: Incident Command Systems in US crisis management. *Governance*, 21(2), 205–229.

Moynihan, D. P. (2009). The network governance of crisis response: Case studies of Incident Command Systems. *Journal of Public Administration Research and Theory*, 19(4), 895–915.

Moynihan, D. P. (2012). A theory of culture-switching: Leadership and red-tape during hurricane Katrina, *Public Administration*, 90(4), 851–868.

Morris, J. C., Morris, E. D., & Jones, D. M. (2007). Reaching for the philosopher's stone: Contingent coordination and the military's response to hurricane Katrina. *Public Administration Review*, 67(s1), 94–106.

Netten, N., & van Someren, M. (2011). Improving communication in crisis management by evaluating the relevance of messages. *Journal of Contingencies and Crisis Management*, 19(2), 75–85.

NRC-Next. (2009). 'No disaster after the disaster'. NRC-Next, February 27th, 2009, p. 1.

Okhuysen, G. A., & Bechky B. A. (2009). Coordination in organizations: An integrative perspective. *The Academy of Management Annals*, 3(1), 463–502.

Pearson, C. M., & Clair, J. A. (1998). Reframing crisis management. *Academy of Management Review*, 23(1), 59–76.

Perrow, C. (1999). *Normal Accidents: Living with High Risk Technologies*. 2nd Edition. Princeton University Press.

Quarantelli, E. L. (1997). Ten criteria for evaluating the management of community disasters. *Disasters*, 21(1), 39–56.

Quarantelli, E. L., & Dynes, R. R. (1977). Response to social crisis and disaster. *Annual Review of Sociology*, 3(1), 23–49.

Rake, E. L., & Njå, O. (2009). Perceptions and performances of experienced incident commanders. *Journal of Risk Research*, 12(5), 665–685.

Reddy, M. C., Paul, S. A., Abraham, J., McNeese, M., DeFlitch, C., & Yen, J. (2009). Challenges to effective crisis management: Using information and communication technologies to coordinate emergency medical services and emergency department teams. *International Journal of Medical Informatics*, 78(4), 259–269.

Rico, R., Sánchez-Manzanares M., Gil F., & Gibson C. (2008). Team implicit coordination processes: A team knowledge–based approach. *Academy of Management Review*, 33(1), 163–184.

Rimstad, R., & Sollid, S. J. (2015). A retrospective observational study of medical incident command and decision-making in the 2011 Oslo bombing. *International Journal of Emergency Medicine*, 8(1), 4.

Roux-Dufort, C. (2016). Delving into the roots of crises The genealogy of surprise. *The Handbook of International Crisis Communication Research*, 43, 24.

Sandberg, J., & Tsoukas, H. (2015). Making sense of the sensemaking perspective: Its constituents, limitations, and opportunities for further development. *Journal of Organizational Behavior*, 36(S1).

Schakel, J. K., van Fenema, P. C., & Faraj, S. (2016). Shots fired! Switching between practices in police work. *Organization Science*, 27(2), 391–410.

Schutz, A. (1973). On multiple realities. In: *Collected Papers I: The Problem of Social Reality* (pp. 201–259). The Hague, the Netherlands: Martinus Nijhoff.

Shamir, E. (2010). The long and winding road: The US Army managerial approach to command and the adoption of Mission Command (Auftragstaktik). *The Journal of Strategic Studies*, 33(5), 645–672.

Shattuck, L. G. (1995). *Communication of intent in distributed supervisory control systems* (Doctoral dissertation, The Ohio State University).

Snook, S. A. (2000). *Friendly Fire: The Accidental Shootdown of US Black Hawks over Northern Iraq*. Princeton University press.

Sommer, A., & Pearson, C. M. (2007). Antecedents of creative decision making in organizational crisis: A team-based simulation. *Technological Forecasting and Social Change*, 74(8), 1234–1251.

Tierney, K. J. (1985). Emergency medical preparedness and response in disasters: The need for inter-organizational coordination. *Public Administration Review*, 45(S1) 77–84.

Topper, C. M., & Carley K. M. (1999). A structural perspective on the emergence of network organizations. *Journal of Mathematical Sociology*, 24(1), 67–96.

Treurniet, W., van Buul-Besseling, K., & Wolbers, J. (2012). *Collaboration Awareness – A Necessity in Crisis Response Coordination*. Vancouver, Canada: Simon Fraser University.

Tsai, J. S. & Chi, C.S. (2012). Cultural influence on the implementation of incident command system for emergency management of natural disasters. *Journal of Homeland Security and Emergency Management*, 9(1), 1–22.

Turner, B. A. (1976). The organizational and interorganizational development of disasters. *Administrative Science Quarterly*, 378–397.

Uhr, C., Johansson, H., & Fredholm, L. (2008). Analysing emergency response systems. *Journal of Contingencies and Crisis Management*, 16(2), 80–90.

Van Creveld, M. L. (1989). *Technology in War*. New York: The Free Press.

Van De Ven, A. H., Delbecq A. L., & Koenig R. (1976). Determinants of coordination modes within organizations. *American Sociological Review*, 41(2), 322–338.

Vaughan, D. (1999). The role of the organization in the production of techno-scientific knowledge. *Social Studies of Science*, 29(6), 913–943.

Williams, T. A., Gruber, D. A., Sutcliffe, K. M., Shepherd, D. A., & Zhao, E. Y. (2017). Organizational response to adversity: Fusing crisis management and resilience research streams. *Academy of Management Annals*, 11(2), 733–769.

Weick, K. (1979). *The Social Psychology of Organisations*. Reading, MA: Addison-Westly.

Weick, K. E. (1993). The collapse of sensemaking in organizations: The Mann Gulch disaster. *Administrative Science Quarterly*, 628–652.

Weick, K. E. (1995). *Sensemaking in Organizations* (Vol. 3). Sage Publishing.

Weick, K. E. (1998). Foresights of failure: An appreciation of Barry Turner. *Journal of Contingencies and Crisis Management*, 6(2), 72–75.

Weick, K. E., & Roberts, K. H. (1993). Collective mind in organizations: Heedful interrelating on flight decks. *Administrative Science Quarterly*, 357–381.

Weick, K. E., Sutcliffe, K. M., & Obstfeld, D. (1999). Organizing for high reliability: Processes of collective mindfulness. In: S. Sutton and B. M. Staw (eds.), *Research in Organizational Behavior, Volume 1* (pp. 81–123). Stanford, CA: Jai Press.

Weick, K., & Sutcliffe, K. (2001). Managing the unexpected: Assuring high performance in an age of uncertainty. *San Francisco: Wiley*, 1(3), 5.

Wildavsky, A. B. (1988). *Searching for Safety* (Vol. 10). Transaction Publishers.

Wolbers, J., & Boersma K. (2013). The common operational picture as collective sensemaking, *Journal of Contingencies and Crisis Management*, 21(4), 186–199.

Wolbers, J., Boersma, K., & Groenewegen, P. (2017). Introducing a fragmentation perspective on coordination in crisis Management. *Organization Studies*.

3

POST-DISASTER RECOVERY
Pathways for Fostering Disaster Risk Reduction

Loïc Le Dé and Sushma Shrestha

Introduction

Disasters, whether they are linked to quick or slow onset hazards, affect local communities in many ways, generating human, physical, economic, social and emotional impacts. Disasters may displace some populations, damage or destroy houses, affect the means by which people generate income, impact infrastructure and make public services non-operational. Recovery, therefore, implies the rebuilding of infrastructure and re-establishment of telecommunication systems and other public services needed for a society to function (Amaratunga & Haigh, 2011). Recovery is also about revitalizing people's livelihoods that have been disrupted (Khan et al., 2015), and the local and/or national economy. Disaster-affected people must also recover psychosocially in order to overcome any emotional shock or trauma arising from the event (Diaz, Srinivasa Murthy & Lakshminarayana, 2006). Lastly, recovery is about reducing risk and preventing other disasters from occurring (Christoplos, 2006; Wisner, Gaillard & Kelman, 2012).

The recovery after disaster has captured much attention among scholars and practitioners regarding many issues including people-based resources and mechanisms, equitability and effectiveness of recovery programs, power relationship in the decision-making process, policies implementation and more recently the application of sustainable development principles (Bolin & Stanford, 1998; Olson, 2000; Nakagawa & Shaw, 2004; Ingram et al., 2006; Lizarralde, Johnson & Davidson, 2009). The recovery of those affected by disasters is complex and still not very well understood (Smith & Wenger, 2007). Furthermore, the challenges linked to the post-disaster recovery have increased because of the high number of stakeholders at play in highly mediatized events.

Since the 1970s, international institutions and non-governmental organizations (NGOs) have increased support for the so-called developing countries with recovery efforts following disasters. For example, from the 1950s to the 1990s, external assistance covering post-disaster reconstruction costs more than quadrupled (Freeman, 2004). The involvement of more aid agencies has meant the greater availability of financial resources, thus potentially creating the conditions for effective and sustainable recovery (Christoplos, 2006). At the same time, it meant that the challenges associated with the recovery process were amplified. Therefore, the coordination of the recovery efforts, delivery of aid that matches local needs, accountability toward disaster-affected communities and participation of local people within such process became more complex.

Until the mid-1990s, international aid directed toward the post-disaster recovery was largely about returning to normalcy as quickly as possible. However, this approach started to appear problematic since it implied returning to the situation of vulnerability that led to the disaster, reproducing the conditions for another disaster to happen (Wisner et al., 2012). Thus, the recovery process has progressively been associated with Disaster Risk Reduction (DRR). The concept of 'Building back better' became popular within the international aid community. It emphasized the need to rebuild with an approach that reduces disaster risks and generates sustainable development (Kennedy et al., 2008).

To date, there are very few examples where post-disaster recovery subsequently contributed to DRR and generated sustainable development (e.g., Alexander, et al., 2007; Lizarralde, Johnson & Davidson, 2009; Davis, 2011). Generally, short-term responses to address immediate needs of those affected – shelter, food, water and sanitation – prevail over longer-term actions that address development matters and DRR. The research question explored in the chapter is, 'how can disaster recovery be accomplished in ways that also allow for DRR and the future pursuit of sustainable development goals?' Emphasis is placed on the interaction between what we term *outsiders*, being the aid agencies involved in developing recovery programs, and *insiders*, in other words those affected by disasters and developing strategies to recover. The next section reviews the concept of disaster recovery and emphasizes why an integrative approach that involves insiders' and outsiders' views and efforts is essential to effective disaster recovery and DRR. Section 3 identifies the difficulties and challenges for implementing such an approach. Finally, Section 4 advances ways to overcome such challenges so DRR can be included within the recovery process and lead to sustainable development outcomes.

Disaster, Recovery and Risk Reduction

Defining Post-disaster Recovery

Post-disaster recovery refers to the period or process in the aftermath of a disaster when the affected communities work to recover from the losses and damages they have experienced (see, for example, Kates & Pijawka, 1977; Davis, 1978; Cuny, 1983; Oliver-Smith, 1986; Ingram et al., 2006; Amaratunga & Haigh, 2011). It is recognized that people recover in many different ways depending on what aspects of their lives are affected. Recovery is contextual and dependent on the scale and impacts of the disaster, the investment in recovery and the capacity and motivation of those impacted. Recovery measures commonly include the reconstruction of housing and other built necessities, the invigoration of people's livelihoods and the local economy as well as psychological and physical support (Cuny, 1983; Oliver-Smith, 1986; Ingram et al., 2006; Smith & Wenger, 2007; Lizarralde, Johnson & Davidson, 2009; Amaratunga & Haigh, 2011; Duyne & Leemann, 2012).

In the literature, disaster recovery is generally perceived as a situation after a disaster with little links to the conditions prior to the disaster. Preexisting conditions of the disaster-affected communities equally matter and often remain the underlying factor to shape communities' recovery. It is often assumed that disasters are a departure from 'normal' social functioning and that recovery means a return to 'normal' (Wisner et al., 2003: 10). Such a perspective has been questioned (IFRCRCS, 2001; Wisner et al., 2003; Clinton, 2006). The validity of viewing disasters as a departure from normal social functioning is contradicting with the idea inherent in the concept of vulnerability. The concept of vulnerability is used to demonstrate that in much of the world, daily life is often difficult to distinguish from disaster (O'Keefe, Westgate & Wisner, 1976; Susman, O'Keefe & Wisner, 1983; Wisner, 2003), and to argue that disasters occur because people are vulnerable prior to a hazardous event. On this basis, if recovery in the aftermath of a disaster aims only to reinstate the pre-disaster state, the affected population remains at least as vulnerable as before, making it possible for a hazard to turn into another disaster (IFRCRCS, 2001; Wisner et al., 2003). Thus, recovery is increasingly understood not as the process of returning to preexisting status quo, but as moving forward, which involves addressing and reducing the vulnerabilities that led to the initial disaster.

At the same time, the literature (e.g., Bolin & Patricia, 1978; Quarantelli, 1978; Susman, O'Keefe & Wisner, 1983; Blaikie et al., 1994; Nigg, 1995) has also indicated communities' preexisting conditions as important in determining how recovery proceeds after disaster. Such understanding has further reinforced recent academic research, which clearly illustrates that a disaster is not a unique, isolated event, and neither is recovery (Shrestha, 2016). Rather, both disaster and recovery are deeply embedded in the social system in which they occur, especially in relation to social structure and fabric of the society. The recovery process reflects the day-to-day struggle of the affected people and communities with respect to both their pre-disaster situation and their post-emergency conditions.

Recovery as Opportunity for DRR

It is now widely recognized that in the aftermath of disasters, an opportunity is created, potentially permitting recovery efforts that reduce the risk of future disasters (Cuny, 1983; Anderson & Woodrow, 1989; Christoplos, 2006). This opportunity is linked to economic, institutional, technical and social factors. First, while there is typically limited funding available for DRR pre-disaster, funding commitments are generally very high post-disaster. Donors, government agencies and international NGOs (INGOs) tend to mobilize huge financial resources for reconstruction and recovery. Such massive flow of financial resources, if managed appropriately, can make post-disaster recovery an opportunity for DRR and sustainable development (Shaw, 2014). Second, poorly built and vulnerable infrastructure have been destroyed, thus the recovery provides an opportunity to build them back better and safer (Lyons, Schilderman & Boano, 2010). Third, disasters expose mistakes of past development strategies and reveal institutional failures or weaknesses such as corruption that contributed to create or increase disaster risk. As a result, governments display greater political will to act, often visibly, and reduce the risk of disaster (Christoplos, 2006).

The recovery also provides an opportunity to draw upon the resources from local communities, in other words insiders. In the aftermath of disaster, there is a high awareness and engagement of people on risks associated with natural hazards, permitting both outsiders and insiders to reflect upon the root causes that led to the disaster (ADPC, 2015). Indeed, the recovery process is seen as an opportunity for change and transformation where local people can have a key role to play. For example, after Hurricane Mitch, reconstruction and recovery plans used catch phrases such as "transforming El Salvador to reduce its vulnerabilities" and "the government invites you to transform Nicaragua together" (Bradshaw, 2002: 871). The recovery potentially enables outsiders to include DRR planning post-disaster and allow local people to participate, including the poorest and the marginalized.

During and after disaster, local people are not passive or helpless nor are they massively traumatized over a long period, but are rather willing to recover as fast as possible

(Quarantelli, 2008). They are capable of much more than what is typically expected by outside agencies. Indeed, local people often display coping and recovery mechanisms to overcome disasters. Such mechanisms are based on their capacities, which refer to the resources and assets that they mobilize during and after such events. These capacities include local and traditional knowledge, social organizations and solidarity networks and skills and technologies (Gaillard, 2010). For example, social capital was a critical driver of fast and effective recovery post-Kobe and Gujarat earthquakes (Nakagawa & Shaw, 2004). Likewise, different researchers emphasized the key role played by cooperation systems, kinship and reciprocity in recovering from disasters (Campbell, 2006; Aldrich, 2012; Le Dé, Gaillard, Friesen & Smith, 2015). Others indicated the importance of traditional knowledge and skills to rebuild back housing affected by cyclones (Paulson, 1993; Mercer et al., 2007).

Integrating DRR measures and fostering sustainable development imply an integrative process where the resources from outside stakeholders (e.g., financial, institutional, technical) are effectively mobilized and amalgamated with that of local people (e.g., local knowledge, livelihoods mechanisms, perceptions) (Gaillard & Mercer, 2013). External aid is indispensable in reducing vulnerability and tackling the root causes that led to the disaster. At the same time, effective recovery with DRR only happens when local people actively participate in the decision-making process and when programming draws on their capacities (Oliver-Smith, 1991). However, despite the existing window of opportunity, there are only a handful of case studies in which the recovery significantly contributed to DRR. There are different challenges linked with outsiders' understanding of local communities' recovery, governance system and scale of the decision-making process as well as difficulties in reaching those most vulnerable so inequalities are not reproduced or increased. These challenges are critically analyzed in the next section.

Challenges for Fostering DRR in the Recovery Process

Governance and Issues of Scale

Cultural, ethnic, religious and socioeconomic contexts vary among communities or regions impacted by disasters. Likewise, local communities (i.e., suburbs, villages, tribes, neighborhoods) vary from place to place, so their capacities, perceptions, challenges faced and mechanisms developed to recover from disasters also vary. Decentralizing the decision-making process for fostering DRR in the recovery is therefore essential (Wisner et al., 2012). This implies the need to involve disaster-affected people and those at risk in the decision-making process and integrate their views and priorities on recovery and DRR (Shaw, 2014; Daly & Brassard, 2011). However, in post-disaster situations, the decision-making process is generally more centralized than in non-disaster time (Blaikie et al., 1994; Moatty, Gaillard & Vinet, 2017). Moreover, recovery necessitates rapid solutions, while DRR is a lengthy process that requires dialogue between outsiders and insiders so that consensus can be reached on the measures and actions to undertake (Christoplos, 2006). It is therefore very difficult to include stakeholders at different scales, both from the bottom-up (i.e., disaster-affected people) and the top-down (e.g., central government, INGOs, international organizations). This is particularly challenging in large-scale events since media attention is very high and places pressure on the central government and aid agencies to provide responses very quickly. During large-scale events, there is also an important number of stakeholders arriving on site to fulfill their aid delivery role (Zanotti, 2010; Barber, 2015). For example, in the aftermath of the 2004 tsunami, there were more than 463 aid agencies carrying out about

2,000 projects in the sole Aceh province in Indonesia, making a coordinated and decentralized recovery process difficult (Masyrafah & McKeon, 2008).

Over the past ten years, the United Nations (UN) cluster system has increasingly been used for disaster reconstruction and recovery. The UN cluster system involves the formation of clusters or committees defined in function of sectorial activities (e.g., shelter, water sanitation and hygiene, livelihoods). This governance system aims to enable dialogue between different aid actors in order to foster more coordinated efforts for relief and reconstruction, avoid the duplication of aid delivered and optimize the resources allocated to recovery. The UN clusters encompass experts, donors, decision-makers and representatives from civil society. Despite the goal of including stakeholders from different scales, the UN cluster approach rarely involves those affected and small local actors in the decision-making process (Boon, 2012; Humphries, 2013). For example, after the 2010 earthquake in Haiti, local NGOs were excluded from the facilities where cluster meetings were held. Cluster meetings were conducted in languages spoken only by foreigners, and the viewpoints of local organizations were systematically neglected (O'Connor, 2011; Benton Heath, 2014). Benton Heath (2014) further acknowledged that the gender-based violence sub-cluster refused to allow Haitian grassroots women's groups to participate in the planning and implementation of activities designed to address sexual violence experienced in displacement camps. Similarly, the limited involvement of local people and small-scale actors was reported after the 2007 earthquake in Pakistan (Street & Parihar, 2007) and more recently in the Philippines (Abaya, 2017). Focusing on typhoon Haiyan in the Philippines, Abaya (2017) shows that even though the UN cluster system had merged with the national governance system, small and local actors were still excluded from the decision-making process post-typhoon Haiyan. Eventually, this centralized governance system places a great emphasis on outsiders' viewpoints about disaster recovery and their operational role within it. This constitutes a barrier to foster DRR and sustainable development in the recovery.

Questioning the Operational Understanding of Disaster and Disaster Recovery

The operational definitions and frameworks of disaster recovery have largely failed in tapping the 'comprehensiveness' of this process and disproportionally emphasized a few aspects of disaster recovery. The recovery models (e.g., Kates & Pijawka, 1977; Cuny, 1983) that have shaped the current understanding of the recovery process explain the process as a number of sequential periods, each characterized by particular, dominant activities. Standard classification that has emerged is an *emergency phase*, a *transitional phase* (or rehabilitation phase) and a *reconstruction phase*. The emergency phase is characterized by the actions necessary to save lives, while the transitional phase includes people's return to work, and the permanent repair of infrastructure and damaged buildings and those other actions necessary to help the population rebuild its way of life as quickly as possible. The final reconstruction phase is generally characterized by building new houses, repairing of roads and other community facilities, and re-establishing the economy.

Breaking down recovery into phases is generally helpful to guide aid agencies in designing, funding, implementing and evaluating their respective programs. Indeed, such partitioning of well-defined boundaries largely reflects aid agencies' understanding of recovery. This suggests linear and sequential recovery, which many development agencies have adopted. For example, the UNDP emphasizes "early recovery", while others differentiate "relief", "rehabilitation", "reconstruction" and "recovery and development". However, while the operational definitions and classifications of the recovery process have provided clear and simplified models of recovery, many fundamental aspects of the actual form of community recovery are missed and pose challenges to effective recovery and fostering DRR.

First, the understanding of the recovery process depicted in these models is operationalized within a context where external aid agencies are key components, with little consideration of the knowledge and experience of those affected by disasters. This has huge implications on how responses and recovery programs are designed. Predominantly shaped by outsiders' views, disasters are dealt with as special "events", different from the day-to-day conditions of peoples' everyday life (UNISDR, 2015). Response, recovery and risk reduction within these operational frameworks continue to be practiced principally as disaster management and as a set of instrumental and administrative mechanisms to protect against "tangible external threats". However, such an approach is misleading because viewing disaster solely as an event, and relief and recovery as mechanisms to manage that event, deflects attention from the need to address the vulnerabilities resulting from the social processes which underpin, create and foster disaster risk. This current operational understanding provides no links to preexisting socioeconomic and political systems. This has resulted in a disproportionate focus on external interventions to meet short-term needs (Wisner et al., 2012).

Second, the simplified sequential phases identified in the recovery models are not necessarily in tune with the reality experienced by those trying to recover (Smith & Wenger, 2007). Recovery is often patchy, uncertain and is shaped by different elements. This includes the nature of disaster and its impact in recovery. For example, the disaster recovery process associated with recurrent disasters is frequently interrupted, often on a regular basis, by newly emergent disasters, and therefore takes the form of a complex and multidirectional process, completely different from what has been operationalized in the standard recovery models (Shrestha, 2016). Similarly, other elements such as power relationship within society, past experiences of disasters, the nature of recovery programs implemented, people's capacity to access adequate resources as well as class, gender and age all add up to make the process complex and nonlinear. Thus, the current conceptualization of recovery is oversimplifying and does not acknowledge that recovery is not homogenous. Inequalities may also be prolonged not only between the rich and the poor but also within poor communities (Bradshaw, 2002). Eventually, recovery often reproduces vulnerabilities, failing to foster, or even "recover" development (Anderson & Woodrow, 1989).

Third, the linear models do not take into consideration the pre-disaster conditions and the impacts these have post-disaster. For example, in the longer term, communities that are extremely poor prior to the disaster respond differently than do comparatively richer communities. According to Shrestha (2016), the former prioritizes day-to-day survival over recovery, while the latter prioritizes recovery and attempts addressing future risks. The integration of pre- and post-disaster phases is elaborated by Turner (1976) in the five stages he documented. In the first three stages, Turner explains the different stages of the development of disaster, and thus highlights the strong connection of disaster event—"the onset" to the pre-disaster conditions—and illustrates "the onset" as a consequence of the accumulation of events and process prior to the disaster. Further, the final stage is described as attempts of adjustments made to integrate to the new normal such as merging to the social system. The recent academic research by Shrestha (2016) expands this understanding. It demonstrates the strong linkage between disaster, recovery and the social system, and concludes that the normative system and power structure of the affected communities in existence prior the disaster, including their socioeconomic conditions, carry the possibilities for their recovery or failure to recover. Recovery therefore implies a wider social process that is largely shaped by both pre- and post-disaster conditions.

Lastly, the focus of current operational understanding on reconstruction and recovery in the aftermath of the disaster is still limited to the built environment including the repair, reconstruction and rehabilitation of infrastructure, public services and housing (Ingram et al., 2006; Lizarralde, Johnson & Davidson, 2009; Jha et al., 2010; Practical Action & IFRC, 2010; Amaratunga & Haigh, 2011). While these aspects are essential for effective recovery, little attention is directed toward the fundamental socioeconomic and political components that often led to a disaster, thus failing to address the underlying causes of disaster. Thus, the Building Back Better approach aims to reduce the risk of future disaster faced by local communities. However, the use of this approach remains largely limited to building protection against hazards rather than increasing people's ability to overcome disasters.

These different elements show the dominance of outsiders' perceptions on the operational understanding of disaster and disaster recovery. This is clearly reflected in the global and national policies, governance systems and practices that focus on disaster recovery. However, such an approach, as discussed here, is not only contradicting the long evolved learnings and conceptual understanding of disaster recovery but has also encouraged misguided recovery actions on the ground, thus implying poor utilization of investments, resources and therefore often increased disaster risk on people.

Recovery of Vulnerability and Risk?

In the aftermath of disasters, the poor and marginalized citizens generally cannot afford to wait for the potential benefits of any longer-term government-sponsored development. They are often obliged to rebuild to a level just as vulnerable as before disaster (Susman, O'Keefe & Wisner, 1983; IFRCRCS, 2001; Gaillard & Cadag, 2009; Davis, 2011). In some cases, the recovery might even increase vulnerabilities, inequalities and risks. The case of community disaster recovery in the aftermath of recurrent small-scale disasters in Nepal studied by Shrestha (2016) clearly illustrates this point. In this study, communities were located in remote, hilly Nepal where recurrent disasters are part of a long-term process. Scarcity of agricultural land and lack of alternative economic opportunities are core reasons why people are forced to adopt unsustainable land use practices that result in intensive hill erosion, and this process has been going on since decades. Population growth, a shrinking resource base and poverty have long been identified as the key reasons behind increased soil degradation. The steep, eroded hills, when subject to heavy and prolonged monsoon rains, become destabilized. Given the unequal power relations within communities and between communities and external authorities, relationships rooted in traditional norms and systems, a majority of residents in small rural communities are particularly vulnerable to natural hazards of all kinds. The phenomenon of disaster occurrence and knowledge of the local context are crucial factors in understanding the causes of these disasters, and thus in shaping the appropriate responses to landslides.

However, in the aftermath of multiple small-scale disasters, external interventions did not recognize and consider the driving forces behind risk and disaster. Efforts for landslide response included gabion walls, check dams and other engineering techniques to stop their advance, but the underlying factors of daily life that promote vulnerability and risk were largely ignored. As a result, instead of contributing to recovery, the policies implemented after a disaster commonly worsened the already harsh living conditions of local residents. With no appropriate external support to address the preexisting vulnerability, the pressures on land resources increased, promoted increased unsustainable land use and, in turn, continued land degradation and increased disaster risk. The recurrence of landslides became almost inevitable followed by greater impact and loss, forcing the affected population toward a greater level of poverty and misery. Moreover, with the inappropriate focus of the interventions, the poorest and the disadvantaged groups had to completely rely on the skewed power structure preexisting in these communities for their survival, thus eventually forcing them to greater sufferings, both physically and socially. Affected communities remain somewhat deterministic of their environment and official policies – or gaps in these policies – and how they are implemented. Meanwhile, national resources that could be used to support the recovery process are often absorbed for inappropriate and inadequate interventions that make no positive contribution to recovery.

Another example is the Erasma area of Orissa in India. A year after the cyclone of 1999, the region had not recovered in any way. Indeed, the population was even more vulnerable than before despite a huge influx of humanitarian aid. The IFRCRCS (2001: 14) described the situation: "uprooted trees littered the landscape. Everywhere people were rebuilding, in many cases literally reconstructing the risk. While villagers were aware that at least community buildings should be cyclone-proof, there simply weren't the resources to achieve this goal". This is not an isolated case study (e.g., Susman, O'Keefe & Wisner, 1983; Gaillard & Cadag, 2009; Davis, 2011). For example, the Payatas trash slide in the Philippines studied by Gaillard and Cadag (2009) shows how the inability to recover in the aftermath of a disaster may result in a worsening of the living conditions of the poor and the marginalized. Before the disaster, those people were already living in deprived conditions in hazard-prone areas, on the largest dumpsite in the country and with limited economic resources or livelihoods alternatives. Gaillard and Cadag (2009) labeled this example "from marginalization to further marginalization".

Rahmato (1991) explains well that a return to the pre-disaster situation and/or reverting to a worse position than before is failed recovery: "It's in the years of recovery that the seeds of famine are actually sown" (Rahmato, 1991, pp. 13–18). By this, Rahmato (1991) suggests that the failure of an affected population to respond appropriately to a disaster may be the starting point for further hardships. Blaikie et al. (1994) explain such failed recovery using the ratchet effect, a phenomenon well established in the theoretical and empirical literature of development studies (Chambers, Longhurst & Pacey, 1981). In a disaster situation, the ratchet effect occurs as part of the process of marginalization, which links the increasing vulnerability of disaster-affected people with decreasing access to resources. Less or no access to those resources necessary to recover from disaster results in further marginalization and a higher degree of deprivation. In effect, hardships, if not addressed, can create and increase the vulnerability of those affected and may even expose them to greater risks (Shrestha, 2016). Addressing these issues is challenging yet indispensable to both effective recovery and avoiding the reproduction or worsening of disaster risk.

Pathways for Recovery that Foster DRR

Addressing Pre- and Post-disaster Vulnerability

The literature has long established links between vulnerability, disaster occurrence and severity of its impacts, and people's ability to recover and bounce forward. As discussed, pre-disaster conditions play a strong role in shaping people's vulnerability to natural hazards, their impacts and recovery. These include socioeconomic aspects, gender relations, legal rights and other sociopolitical arrangements (O'Keefe, Westgate & Wisner, 1976; Susman, O'Keefe & Wisner, 1983; Blaikie et al., 1994). These same conditions have been shown to be vital for shaping the abilities of local people to respond to and recover from disaster (Shrestha & Gaillard, 2013). Despite significant external efforts to support disaster recovery, there has been limited success in either addressing or reducing disaster risk. Approaches to reduce vulnerability and the notion of building back better are less evident in practice (IFRCRCS, 2001; Cadag & Gaillard, 2009; Shrestha, 2016).

Recovery implies reducing vulnerabilities, thus addressing the drivers of disaster risk and eventually helping communities to recover in meaningful terms. It is widely recognized that recovery post-disaster depends largely on the conditions existing pre-disaster (Blaikie et al., 1994). Indeed, the difficulties and constraints pre-disaster tend to continue post-disaster. Understanding the local context, including economic, social, cultural and political aspects of the affected area is therefore essential to quickly implement recovery programs. This also enables recovery workers to anticipate both challenges and opportunities to provide solutions that are adapted to the disaster-affected area (Bolin & Stanford, 1998). This approach helps reduce the time needed to identify and deal with economic constraints, political conflicts and challenges as well as the sociocultural elements that shape a disaster-affected community (Moatty, Gaillard & Vinet, 2017).

Focusing on the 1991 Mt Pinatubo eruption in the Philippines, Gaillard (2008) shows how recovery programs need to appraise pre-disaster conditions, or else post-disaster interventions might increase vulnerability and risk. Studying Hurricane Mitch in Nicaragua, Christoplos et al. (2010) document different livelihood programs developed post-disaster in order to reduce vulnerability and foster development. Yet, to be successful, such recovery programs need to carefully assess vulnerability pre- and post-disaster, otherwise they will not benefit the poorest who have been affected by the event (Christoplos et al., 2010). Different researchers and practitioners emphasized that recovery that fosters DRR happens when recovery programs are embedded within development initiatives existing pre-disaster (Oliver-Smith, 1991; Anderson & Woodrow, 1989). In the same vein, Kelman and Mather (2008) argue for a sustainable livelihoods approach and emphasize the need to embed DRR measures within the life conditions of local people. However, too often, disasters are managed as events disconnected from the conditions and activities existing pre-disaster, thus leading to short-term responses that do not tackle the root causes of disasters.

Decentralizing the Decision-Making Process

Pathways for integrating DRR in the recovery are not necessarily "elusive" (Christoplos, 2006) or impossible to achieve as demonstrated in different cases (e.g., Alexander, 2004; Lyons, 2009). For example, Hill and Gaillard (2013) show that after the 1931 earthquake in New Zealand, the recovery led to the reduction of disaster risk at both local and national levels. Hill and Gaillard (2013) emphasized the benefits of a decentralized and integrative decision-making process, highlighting that the extensive and meaningful participation of local people led to effective DRR in the recovery. This was also possible because of a good understanding of pre-disaster vulnerability, constraints and opportunities for effective recovery. As a result, recovery programs provided a balance of change, critical to foster DRR, and continuity to ensure that the links between the community and its place were maintained (Hill & Gaillard, 2013). In the same vein, post-2009 tsunami in Samoa, some of the villages highly impacted decided to move back inland away from the tsunami-prone area, while rebuilding on the beach the touristic accommodations on which their livelihoods depend. This decision came from the local community and involved risk assessment and dialogue with outsiders, including scientists and the National Disaster Management Office

(Daly et al., 2010). This option contributed to reduce the risk of future disasters, while en-suring to achieve sustainable development goals through the recovery of tourism activities. Tourist accommodations were rebuilt to better withstand hazards and preparedness activities conducted to deal with hazards such as tsunamis or cyclones.

Local communities are demonstrably knowledgeable about disasters and disaster recovery as these events form a major part of their day-to-day experience. The affected populations who directly experience disasters are the key actors in post-disaster recovery. Their perspec-tives are based on their own knowledge, which is an enormous resource gained through experience and innovation, tested and refined by multiple personal trials (Chambers, 1995; 2006). Integrating people's viewpoints and knowledge in the reconstruction and recovery leads to risk-reduction measures that are more robust and fit the local context (Oliver-Smith, 1991). Failure to involve them in the decision-making process can mean that local people recover only partly or that disaster risk is increased. For example, in Sri Lanka after the 2004 tsunami, a decision was made by outsiders to relocate affected people far away from the coastlines in order to reduce the risk of future disaster. However, this decision process did not involve those local residents affected nor did it consider the fact that the livelihoods of locals depended on resources located on the coast. As a result, newly built houses inland remained largely un-inhabited, people failed to recover quickly and local residents were ex-posed to new hazards in the relocated area (Ingram et al., 2006). Thus, it is important to note that local people's perspectives are valuable and should occupy a central role in the recovery because no one is more interested than disaster-affected people themselves in the need to re-duce the risk of another disaster. And the participation of local people in the recovery process does not preclude the key contribution of outsiders. Fostering DRR requires involving local people together with a large array of stakeholders external to local communities (Gaillard & Mercer, 2013; Le Dé, 2017).

Building on Local People's Capacities and Resources

Recovery provides an opportunity to build on local peoples' capacities and resources. Such an approach promotes self-help and empowers local people with their own recovery (Schilderman & Lyons, 2011; Campbell, 2015). It is generally a cost-effective approach since local people's knowledge, skills and expertise are already at hand. Building on local resources and capacities also helps to avoid the presence of large, foreign workforce coming from out-side the impacted area. Such massive inflow of external workers often has negative effects at the local level such as the emergence of high inflation post-disaster (Wisner & Walker, 2006). In addition, involving locals increases the chances of fast and effective recovery in the sense that it matches local people needs, fits their cultural practices and addresses DRR and long-term development. Studying the recovery of people from Yungay in Peru, Oliver-Smith (1986) found that sustainable recovery objectives could only be achieved when the recovery programs included local communities' capacities and matched with their priorities. Such an approach enables one to address inequality issues and adopt risk-reduction measures within the recovery process (Oliver-Smith, 1986). In turn, external assistance that does not draw on local peoples' resources may result in increased dependency on outside aid, lead to unsustain-able recovery solutions and fail in generating sustainable development (Blaikie et al., 1994; Bolin & Stanford, 1998; Wisner et al., 2012; Le Dé et al., 2018).

Community-based disaster recovery draws upon an approach that emphasizes the partic-ipation of those affected in both the evaluation of their recovery needs and in ways of sustain-ing them. Academics and practitioners have indicated the relevance of a community-based approach for including DRR planning within the recovery process (Bolin & Stanford, 1998; Daly et al., 2010). Different community-based disaster recovery programs have been effective with the recovery process. For example, academics and practitioners emphasized that involving local people in housing reconstruction through participatory and stakeholder programming (e.g., owner-driven reconstruction program) can be very beneficial to the recovery. It may generate both tangible and intangible outcomes such as an increase of self-esteem and psychosocial recovery and strengthening of social relationship and trust in outside/institutional agencies (Barakat, 2003; Barenstein, 2006). In the same vein, cash for work aims at involving locals in the cleanup and reconstruction tasks post-disaster while building on the local capacities such as knowledge and skills. Such programming contributed post-2004 tsunami to good recovery by enabling the revitalization of households' livelihoods and helping those impacted to achieve longer-term economic recovery while reducing feelings of trauma and stress post-disaster (Doocy, Gabriel, Collins, Robinson & Stevenson, 2006).

Nonetheless, community-based disaster recovery is not without difficulties. For example, cash for work and owner-driven reconstruction programs requires taking into account different parameters in order to produce a successful process that generates sustainable outcomes (Nakagawa & Shaw, 2004; Doocy et al., 2006; Davidson et al., 2007). There are difficulties associated with monitoring and controlling the quality of the rebuilding taking place post-disaster. For example, most of the houses rebuilt post-2004 tsunami in Banda Aceh, using an owner-driven reconstruction program approach, were more vulnerable to earthquakes than they were before this event (Vinet et al., 2011). Similarly, the Post Disaster Needs Assessment (PDNA) is a critical tool to inform outsiders on the needs for recovery and DRR, and initiatives have involved local people in the use of such a tool. While insiders' participation in the needs assessment provides many advantages (e.g., timeframe and relevance of information, cost-effective, empowering process), it also requires that local communities feel confident with the PDNA and thus are trained before disaster. If this is not the case, the information might not be adequate and may delay the recovery process (Moatty, Gaillard & Vinet, 2017). In addition, international agencies need to be aware that there are mechanisms in place for local people to carry out PDNA. This was emphasized post-2015 Cyclone Pam in Vanuatu, coming from both a lack of knowledge of the local context from outside agencies and weak leadership at national level (Le Dé et al., 2018). Indeed, without strong leadership at national and local community levels, adequate training pre-disaster and a good understanding from outside agencies of the local context, community-based disaster recovery can be quite challenging or even unsuccessful in fostering DRR. It requires an integrated approach that includes both initiatives from local people and action from aid agencies.

Concluding Remarks

This chapter explored how disaster recovery can be achieved in ways that foster DRR and sustainable development. Different authors have long pointed out the window of opportunity existing in the aftermath of disasters (Cuny, 1983; Anderson & Woodrow, 1989; Christoplos, 2006; Lyons, Schilderman & Boano, 2010). Opportunity is linked with important financial resources mobilized post-disaster, greater political will, past development and exposure of planning mistakes as well as greater awareness from the local people and government agencies about disaster risk. This window of opportunity is often "elusive", and goals of DRR and sustainable development are rarely achieved in practice (Christoplos, 2006).

After reviewing some of the challenges associated with fostering DRR (see Section 3), we suggest pathways to overcome them.

The chapter highlighted the need to redefine our understanding of recovery. Recovery should be understood not as the process of returning a community to its preexisting status quo, but as a process of moving forward that involves addressing and reducing the vulnerabilities that led to the initial disaster. Similarly, recovery is rarely manifested in the linear and episodic life cycles that are commonly depicted in the existing scholarly models (e.g., Kates & Pijawka, 1977; Cuny, 1983). Both disaster and recovery are closely embedded in the social system in which they occur. Recovery is therefore an ongoing and recursive process shaped by vulnerabilities and capacities present within such system. Recovery interventions designed to protect against a tangible external threat do not generate sustainable solutions. Rather, they may create the conditions for another disaster. Fostering risk reduction in the recovery process should therefore encourage the adoption of an approach that not only encompasses disaster management, but combines actions that directly target, address and reduce vulnerabilities that have been incubated through preexisting social, economic and political processes and systems.

Fostering DRR in the recovery requires that the resources from outside agencies are integrated together with local communities' resources (Lyons, 2009; Gaillard & Mercer, 2013). Support from the outside is essential to reduce vulnerability and tackle the root causes of disaster. At the same time, reducing disaster risk can only occur if recovery programs build on local people's capacities and involve them in the decision-making process (Oliver-Smith, 1991; Daly & Brassard, 2011). This implies the need for outsiders to understand pre-disaster conditions at the local level, including the constraints and opportunities to apply recovery programs (Oliver-Smith, 1991; Lyons, 2009). Dialogue and consensus building are therefore essential to reduce risk post-disaster. The dangers of highly centralized disaster recovery processes have been discussed and include the fact that such an approach might provide measures and actions that do not match local needs, do not address root causes of disaster and overall lead to unsustainable or failed recovery.

The points developed in this chapter have different implications for research, policy and practice. First, there is a need for aid agencies to revisit their operational understanding of disaster and recovery. This requires agencies to understand disasters, both their occurrence and recovery, as a part of a preexisting social, economic and political system in which they occur. Understanding developed in this way will help design recovery interventions that will actually help move beyond the conventional short-term disaster management approaches and contribute to reducing disaster risk. Second, fostering the participation of local communities in the recovery process is essential. More efforts are needed to give more voice to local people in addressing DRR and sustainable development. Focus should be placed on tools and mechanisms for the assessments post-disaster, monitoring of aid effectiveness and recovery of disaster-affected communities. Lastly, there is a need for more accountability of governments and aid agencies toward affected people (Twigg, 1999). Currently, there are no standards or guidelines that disaster response and recovery agencies could or should commit to in order to effectively foster DRR in the recovery process (Wisner et al., 2011; Gaillard & Mercer, 2013). However, some standards do exist for humanitarian intervention (i.e. HAP, 2010; The Sphere Project, 2011). Thus, as for the humanitarian sector, standards or guidelines for integrating DRR within the recovery process could be developed. Commitment to those standards might be monitored by all stakeholders involved in the recovery, including local communities. This approach could greatly contribute to foster DRR in the reconstruction and recovery process.

References

Abaya, M. (2017). Improving coordination between disaster relief agencies: The cluster approach in the Philippines. Master dissertation of Emergency Management, Auckland University of Technology, New Zealand.

Aldrich, D. P. (2012). *Building Resilience: Social Capital in Post-disaster Recovery*. Chicago, IL: University of Chicago Press, p. 232.

Alexander, D. (2004). Planning for disaster risk reduction. In *Proceedings of the 2004 International Conference and Student Competition on Post-disaster Reconstruction*. Université de Montréal, Montréal. [Cited 11 July 2012.] Available from URL: www.grif.umontreal.ca/pages/papers2004/Paper%20-%20Alexander%20D.pdf.

Alexander, D., Davidson, C. H., Fox, A., Johnson, C., & Lizarralde, G. (2007). *Post-disaster Reconstruction: Meeting Stakeholder Interests*. Florence: Firenze University Press.

Amaratunga, D., & Haigh, R. (Eds.). (2011). *Post-disaster Reconstruction of the Built Environment Rebuilding for Resilience*. Oxford: Wiley- Blackwell

Anderson, M. B., & Woodrow, P. (1989). *Rising from the Ashes: Development Strategies in Times of Disasters*. Boulder, CO and San Francisco, CA: Westview Press/Unesco, p. 338.

Asian Disaster Preparedness Centre (ADPC) (2015). Disaster Recovery Toolkit, Tsunami Global Lessons Learned Project. www.adpc.net/tgllp/drt.

Barakat, S. (2003). Housing Reconstruction after Conflict and Disaster. Oversee Development Institute HPN Network Paper No. 43, London.

Barber, R. (2015). One size doesn't fit all. Tailoring the international response to the national need following Vanuatu's cyclone Pam. A contribution to the Pacific regional consultation for the world humanitarian summit. Save the Children Australia.

Barenstein, J. D. (2006). *Housing Reconstruction in Post-earthquake Gujarat: A Comparative Analysis*. Network Paper 54, Humanitarian Practice Network, London.

Benton Heath, J. (2014). Managing the Republic of NGOs: Accountability and legitimation problems facing the UN Cluster System. *Vanderbilt Journal of Transnational Law*, 47: 239, 294.

Blaikie, P., Cannon, T., Davis, I., & Wisner, B. (1994). *At Risk: Natural Hazards, People's Vulnerability, and Disasters*. London and New York: Routledge.

Bolin, R., & Patricia, T. (1978). Modes of family recovery following disaster: A Cross- National Study. In E. L. Quarantelli (Ed.), *Disasters: Theory and Research*. Beverly Hills, CA: SAGE Publications.

Bolin, R., & Stanford, L. (1998). The Northridge earthquake: Community-based approaches to unmet recovery needs. *Disasters*, 22(1): 21–38.

Boon, L. (2012). The cluster approach: Working towards best practices in humanitarian response. University of Denver.

Bradshaw, S. (2002). Exploring the gender dimensions of reconstruction processes post-Hurricane Mitch. *Journal of International Development*, 14(6): 871–879.

Gaillard, J. C., & Cadag, J. R. D. (2009). From marginality to further marginalization: Experiences from the victims of the July 2000 Payatas Trashslide in the Philippines. *JAMBA: Journal of Disaster Risk Studies*, 2: 197–215.

Campbell, J. R. (2006). *Traditional Disaster Reduction in Pacific Island Communities*. GNS Science.

Campbell, J. R. (2015). Development, global change and traditional food security in Pacific Island countries. *Regional Environmental Change*, 15(7): 1313–1324.

Chambers, R. (1995). Poverty and livelihoods: Whose reality counts? *Environment and Urbanization*, 7(1): 173–204.

Chambers, R. (2006). Participatory mapping and Geographic Information Systems: Whose map? Who is empowered and who is disempowered? Who gains and who loses? *The Electronic Journal on Information Systems in Developing Countries*, 25(2): 1–11.

Chambers, R., Longhurst, R., & Pacey A. (Eds.). (1981). *Seasonal Dimensions to Rural Poverty*. London: Frances Pinter.

Christoplos, I. (2006). The elusive 'window of opportunity' for risk reduction. Provention Consortium Forum 2006, 2–3 February 2006, Bangkok, Thailand.

Christoplos, I., Rodríguez, T., Schipper, E. L. F., Narvaez, E. A., Bayres Mejia, K. M., Buitrago, R., Gómez, L. and Pérez, F. J. (2010). Learning from recovery after Hurricane Mitch. *Disasters*, 34(2): 202–219.

Clinton, W. J. (2006). *Lessons Learnt from Tsunami Recovery: Key Propositions for Building Back Better*. New York: Office of the UN Secretary-General's Special Envoy for Tsunami Recovery.

Cuny, F. C. (1983). *Disaster and development*. New York: Oxford University Press.

Daly, P., & Brassard, C. (2011). Aid accountability and participatory approaches in post-disaster housing reconstruction. *Asian Journal of Social Sciences*, 39(1): 508–533.

Daly, M., Poutasi, N., Nelson, F., & Kohlhase, J. (2010). Reducing the climate vulnerability of coastal communities in Samoa. *Journal of International Development*, 22(1): 265–281.

Davidson, C. H., Johnson, C., Lizarralde, G., Dikmen, N., & Sliwinski, A. (2007). Truths and myths about community participation in post-disaster housing projects. *Habitat International*, 31(1): 100–115.

Davis, I. (1978). *Shelter after Disaster*. Oxford: Oxford Polytechnic.

Davis, I. (2011). What have we learned from 40 years' experience of Disaster Shelter? *Environmental Hazards*, 10(1): 193–212.

Diaz, J. O. P., Srinivasa Murthy, R., & Lakshminarayana, R. (Eds.). (2006). Advances in Psychological and Social Support after Disasters. American Red Cross, India Delegation.

Doocy, S., Gabriel M., Collins, S., Robinson, C., & Stevenson, P. (2006). Implementing cash for work programmes in post-tsunami Aceh: Experiences and lessons learned. *Disasters*, 30(3): 277–296.

Duyne, J. E., & Leemann, E. (Eds.). (2012). *Post-disaster Reconstruction and Change: Communities' Perspectives*. CRC Press.

Freeman, P. K. (2004). Allocation of post-disaster reconstruction financing to housing. *Building Research and Information*, 32(5): 427–437.

Gaillard, J. C. (2008). Alternative paradigms of volcanic risk perception: The case of Mt. Pinatubo in the Philippines. *Journal of Volcanology and Geothermal Research*, 172(1): 315–328.

Gaillard, J. C. (2010). Vulnerability, capacity and resilience: Perspectives for climate and development policy. *Journal of International Development*, 22(2): 218–232.

Gaillard, J. C., & Cadag, J. R. D. (2009). From marginality to further marginalization: Experiences from the victims of the July 2000 Payatas trashslide in the Philippines. *Journal of Disaster Risk Studies*, 2: 197–215.

Gaillard, J. C., & Mercer, J. (2013). From knowledge to action Bridging gaps in disaster risk reduction. *Progress in Human Geography*, 37(1): 93–114.

Hill, M., & Gaillard, J. C. (2013). Integrating disaster risk reduction into post-disaster reconstruction: A long-term perspective of the 1931 earthquake in Napier, New Zealand. *New Zealand Geographer*, 69(1): 108–119.

Humanitarian Accountability Partnership (HAP). (2010). *The 2010 HAP Standard in Accountability and Quality Management*. Chatelaine, Switzerland: HAP International.

Humphries, V. (2013). Improving humanitarian coordination: Common challenges and lessons learned from the cluster approach. *The Journal of Humanitarian Assistance*. Retrieved from http://sites.tufts.edu/jha/archives/1976.

Ingram, J. C., Franco, G., Rio, C. R. D., & Khazai, B. (2006). Post-disaster recovery dilemmas: Challenges in balancing short-term and long-term needs for vulnerability reduction *Environmental Science and Policy*, 9(1): 607–613.

International Federation of Red Cross and Red Crescent Societies (IFRCRCS) (2001). World Disasters Report: Focus on recovery. Geneva, Switzerland: International Federation of Red Cross and Red Crescent Societies. Retrieved from www.ifrc.org/Global/Publications/disasters/WDR/21400_WDR2001.pdf.

Jha, A. K., Duyne, J. B., Phelps, P., Pittet, D., & Sena, S. (2010). *Safer Homes, Stronger Communities: A Handbook for Reconstructing after Natural Disasters*. Washington, DC: The World Bank.

Kates, R. W., & Pijawka, D. (1977). From Rubble to Monument: The Pace of Reconstruction. In J. E. Haas, R. W. kates and M. J. Bowden (Eds.), *Reconstruction Following Disaster* (pp. 1–20). Cambridge, MA and London: The MIT Press.

Kelman, I., & Mather, T. A. (2008). Living with volcanoes: The sustainable livelihoods approach for volcano-related opportunities. *Journal of Volcanology and Geothermal Research*, 172(1): 189–198.

Kennedy, J., Ashmore, J., Babister, E., & Kelman, I. (2008). The meaning of « Build Back Better »: evidence from post-tsunami Aceh and Sri Lanka. *Journal of Contingency and Crisis Management*, 16(1): 24–36.

Khan, K. S., Shanmugaratnam, N., & Nyborg, I. L. P. (2015). Recovering from disasters: A study of livelihoods in post-quake villages in northern Pakistan. *Disasters*, 39(2): 339–361.

Le Dé L. (2017). Connecting knowledge and policy for disaster risk reduction including climate change adaptation. In I. Kelman, J. Mercer and J. C. Gaillard (Eds.), *Routledge Handbook of Disaster Risk Reduction Including Climate Change Adaptation* (pp. 274–285). London and New York: Routledge.

Le Dé, L., Gaillard, J. C., Friesen, W., & Smith, F. M. (2015). Remittances in the face of disasters: A case study of rural Samoa. *Environment, Development and Sustainability*, 17(3): 653–672.

Le Dé L. Rey T., Leone F., & David G. (2018). Sustainable livelihood and effectiveness of disaster responses: TC Pam in Vanuatu as case study. *Natural Hazards.* https://doi.org/10.1007/s11069-018-3174-6.

Lizarralde, G., Johnson, C., & Davidson, C. (2009). *Rebuilding after Disasters: From Emergency to Sustainability.* Oxford: Taylor and Francis.

Lyons, M. (2009). Building back better: The large-scale impact of small-scale approaches to reconstruction. *World Development*, 37(1): 385–398.

Lyons, M., Schilderman, T., & Boano, C. (2010). *Building Back Better: Delivering People-Centred Housing Reconstruction at Scale*, London: Practical Action Publishing, p. 388.

Masyrafah, H., & McKeon, J. M. J. A. (2008). Post-tsunami aid effectiveness in Aceh. Proliferation and coordination in reconstruction. Wolfensohn center for development. Working paper 6.

Mercer, J., Dominey-Howes, D., Kelman, I., & Lloyd, K. (2007). The potential for combining indigenous and western knowledge in reducing vulnerability to environmental hazards in small island developing states. *Environmental Hazards*, 7(4): 245–256.

Moatty, A., Gaillard, J. C., & Vinet F. (2017). From disaster to development: Challenges and opportunities of the post-disaster recovery. *Annales de Geographie*, 714(1): 169–194.

Nakagawa, Y., & Shaw, R. (2004). Social capital: A missing link to disaster recovery. *International Journal of Mass Emergencies and Disasters*, 22(1): 5–34.

Nigg, J. M. (1995). *Disaster recovery as a social process.* Newark: University of Delaware.

O'Connor, M. (2011). Does International Aid Keep Haiti Poor? Slate. Retrieved March 10, 2017 from www.slate.com/articles/news_and_politics/dispatches/features/2011/does_international_aid_keep_haiti_poor/the_un_cluster_system_is_as_bad_as_it_sounds.html.

O'Keefe, P., Westgate, K., & Wisner, B. (1976). Taking the naturalness out of natural disasters. *Nature*, 260(1): 566–567.

Oliver-Smith, A. (1986). *The Martyred City: Death and Rebirth in the Andes.* Albuquerque: University of Mexico Press.

Oliver-Smith, A. (1991). Successes and failures in post-disaster resettlement. *Disasters*, 15(1): 12–23.

Olson, R. S. (2000). Toward a politics of disaster losses, values, agendas, and blame. *International Journal of Mass Emergencies and Disasters*, 18(1): 265–287.

Paulson, D. D. (1993). Hurricane hazard in Western Samoa. *Geographical Review*, 83(1): 43–53.

Practical Action & IFRC. (2010). *Building Back Better: Delivering People-Centred Housing Reconstruction at Scale* (M. Lyons, T. Schilderman & C. Boano Eds.). Practical Action Publishing Ltd.

Quarantelli, E. L. (Eds.). (1978). *Disasters: Theory and Research.* London and Beverly Hills, CA: SAGE Publications Inc.

Quarantelli, E. L. (2008). Conventional beliefs and counterintuitive realities. *Social Research*, 75(3): 873–904.

Rahmato, D. (1991). *Famine and Survival Strategies: A Case Study from Northeast Ethiopia.* Sweden: Swedish International Development Authority (SIDA).

Schilderman, T., & Lyons, M. (2011). Resilient dwellings or resilient people? Towards people centred reconstruction. *Environmental Hazards*, 10(1): 218–231.

Shaw, R. (Eds.). (2014). *Disaster Recovery. Used or Misused Development Opportunity.* Japan: Springer Japan, p. 429.

Shrestha, S., & Gaillard, J. C. (2013). Small-Scale Disasters and the Recovery Process. Paper presented at the I-Rec Conference 2013: Sustainable Post-disaster Reconstruction: From Recovery to Risk Reduction, Ascona, Switzerland. Retrieved from www.grif.umontreal.ca/i-Rec2013/43-54_Shresta.pdf.

Shrestha, S. (2016). Exploring Recovery from Small-Scale Disasters: Examples from Remote Nepal. Doctoral thesis, The University of Auckland, Auckland, New Zealand.

Smith, G. P., & Wenger, D. (2007). Sustainable disaster recovery: Operationalizing an existing agenda. In H. Rodríguez, E. L. Quarantelli and R. R. Dynes (Eds.), *Handbook of Disaster Research* (pp. 234–257). New York: Springer.

Street, A., & Parihar G. (2007). The UN cluster approach in the Pakistan response: An NGO perspective. Humanitarian Exchange. *The Humanitarian Practice network*, 37, 32–34. London.

Susman, P., O'Keefe, P., & Wisner, B. (1983). Global disasters, a radical interpretation. In K. Hewitt (Dir.), *Interpretation of calamities*, The Risks and Hazards Series 1 (pp. 263–283). Boston, MA: Allen and Unwin Inc., pp. 263–283.

The Sphere Project (2011). Humanitarian charter and minimum standards in humanitarian response. Available at: www.sphereproject.org.

Turner, B. A. (1976). Organizational and interorganizational development of disasters. *Administrative Science Quarterly*, 21 (3): 378–397.

Twigg, J. (1999). The age of accountability? Future community involvement in disaster reduction. *The Australian Journal of Emergency Management*, 14: 51–58.

United Nations International Strategy for Disaster Reduction (UNISDR) (2015). *Global Assessment Report on Disaster Risk Reduction 2015*. UNISDR.

Vinet, F., Gaillard, J. C., Denain, J. C., Clave, E., Leone, F., Giyarsih, S., & Bachri, S. (2011). Enjeux et modalités spatiales de la reconstruction post-tsunami à Banda Aceh. In F. Lavigne et R. Paris (Dir.), *Tsunarisque : le tsunami du 26 décembre 2004 à Aceh, Indonésie* (pp. 233–270). Paris: Publications de la Sorbonne, Paris.

Wisner, B. (1993). Disaster vulnerability: Scale, power and daily life. *Geo Journal*, 30(2): 127–140.

Wisner, B. (2003). Assessment of capability and vulnerability. In G. Bankoff, G. Frerks and D. Hilhorst (Eds.), *Mapping Vulnerability: Disasters, Development, and People* (pp. 183–193). London: Earthscan.

Wisner, B., Blaikie, P., Cannon, T., & Davis, I. (2003). *At Risk: Natural Hazards, People's Vulnerability and Disasters* (2nd ed.). New York: Routledge.

Wisner, B., Gaillard, J. C, & Kelman, I. (Eds.). (2012). *Handbook of Hazards and Disaster Risk Reduction*. London: Routledge.

Wisner, B., Kent, G., Carmalt, J., Cook, B., Gaillard, J. C., & Lavell, A. (2011). Political will for disaster reduction: What incentives build it, and why is it so hard to achieve? A Contribution to the Review of the draft UNISDR Global Assessment Report 2011. Geneva: UNISDR.

Wisner, B., & Walker, P. (2006). Getting tsunami recovery and early warning right. *Open House International*, 31(1): 54–61.

Zanotti, L. (2010). Cacophonies of aid, failed state building and NGOs in Haiti: Setting the stage for disaster, envisioning the future. *Third World Quarterly*, 31(5): 755–771.

4

CRISIS COMMUNICATION
The Best Evidence from Research

W. Timothy Coombs

A crisis can be viewed as the manifestation of risk resulting in the potential for harm to befall stakeholders and/or the organization. A crisis can harm or kill stakeholders and always inflict at least some reputation damage on an organization (Barton, 2001). Quick actions taken by crisis managers can prevent or limit the harm a crisis can inflict. Those harms can be bodily, property-related, financial, or reputational. It is the potential harm posed by a crisis that makes it a concern for both managers and stakeholders. The investment in crisis management is designed to mitigate and to limit the harm a crisis can produce.

This chapter highlights the critical role crisis communication plays in crisis management. Drawing upon the most reliable empirical studies, the chapter documents the various ways crisis communication can have a positive effect on crisis outcomes. However, these positive outcomes are only achieved when crisis communication is properly executed. The main focus of this chapter involves synthesizing and articulating what research indicates is the proper way to engage in crisis communication. The chapter begins by defining and refining key terms, and then moves to a review of the empirically based crisis communication research.

Clarification of Key Concepts

Crisis communication can be defined as the strategic use of words and actions to manage information and meaning during the crisis process (Coombs, 2010). This is a broad view of crisis communication that will be refined in order to articulate the evidence-based crisis communication knowledge that can benefit managers. The refinement process begins by defining how I am using the terms crisis and crisis process. These two terms are critical contextual factors for understanding crisis communication.

There are many definitions of crises that range from the general to the specific. The variability of crisis definitions results in confusion when people compare or integrate research using very different conceptualizations of crisis. Therefore, it is critical in any discussion of crisis communication to specify how crisis is being defined. For this chapter, crisis is defined as the perceived violation of stakeholder expectations that can result in harm to the organization and/or its stakeholders. The focus is on what can be called organizational crises rather than disaster or emergencies. Organizational crises are managed primarily by the organization, while disasters are the purview of governmental agencies.

Crises are driven by violations of stakeholder expectations, meaning an organization does something stakeholders do not think it should have done. Expectation-violation examples include industrial facilities catching fire, products making customers ill, chemical releases endangering nearby communities, and trains derailing. Crises have a strong perceptual element. Many crises are event-driven, such as a plane crash, but others are driven by perceptions of the stakeholders. For instance, stakeholders might perceive a product as problematic, while managers think it is fine, or many stakeholders might view sourcing as irresponsible, while managers believe the sourcing is appropriate. The perceptual element of crises reflects the process view of crisis championed by many writers (e.g., Roux-Dufort, 2007).

Let us return to the process nature of crisis. A crisis is not one thing or just an event. Experts have long recognized that crises have phases that reflect a process. Crisis communication is linked to the crisis process because different crisis phases produce different communicative demands for crisis managers (Coombs, 2015). This chapter is guided by a two-step process of crisis known as the regenerative model of crisis communication. Roux-Dufort (2007) has rightly argued that crises are not always linear. The regenerative model of crisis reflects complex process rather than linearity. We can think of crises as having two phases, pre-crisis and post-crisis. What separates the two can be clearly defined or quite vague. It is clearly defined when there is an identifiable event such as an explosion at a facility. It is rather vague when management must reach the realization that a situation is a crisis. Examples of such realizations include a product possibly posing harm to customers or workers possibly being treated in irresponsible ways. We can label the event or management's realization of a crisis as the trigger event, which is the point where the organization moves from pre-crisis to post-crisis phase.

There are times when significant shifts occur in how the crisis is viewed. These shifts cause people to see the crisis in a different light. An example of a shift would be the findings of an investigation that reveal a crisis was a result of management negligence and not accidental. The shift is a new trigger event. After the shift occurs, all the previous time becomes pre-crisis and a new post-crisis phase is defined. In other words, what was once the post-crisis phase becomes redefined as pre-crisis. Figure 4.1 illustrates the process nature of the regenerative crisis model (Coombs, 2017). The point is a crisis can be fluid, and the communicative demands can change as the crisis morphs. Crisis managers must be prepared to revise their communicative efforts when a shift in the crisis occurs.

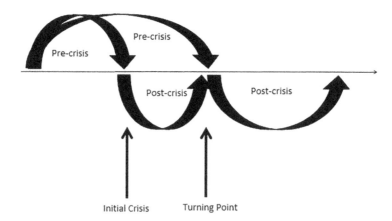

Figure 4.1   Regenerative Crisis Model (Coombs, 2017)

Crisis Communication Definition Revisited

With the contextual factors in place, we can elaborate on the initial definition of crisis communication as the strategic use of words and actions to manage information and meaning during a crisis. Strategic communication is designed to achieve specific objectives. Crisis communication seeks to protect stakeholders and organizations from crises. Objectives related to crisis communication can include protecting stakeholder safety, restricting reputational damage, and limiting the negative effects on purchase intentions and share prices (Coombs, 2015). Crisis communication is not only what management says but what management does. Actions communicate symbolically to stakeholders. The CEO visiting the scene communicates that the organization takes the crisis seriously; offering compensation shows the organization is taking victim concerns seriously.

Crisis communication has two general elements: managing information and managing meaning. Managing information is about collecting and disseminating crisis information. This can include internal and external information management. Internal information management involves crisis team's efforts to collect and to process information to aid in decision-making. External information management includes warning stakeholders about a crisis danger. Managing meaning is about influencing how people perceive the crisis and/or the organization in crisis. Crisis communication often is used to shape perceptions of the crisis by influencing how much crisis responsibility is attributed to the organization and shaping perceptions of the organization in crisis by providing positive information about the organization (Coombs, 1995, 2007).

Crisis Response Strategies

The aforementioned definition of crisis communication is very broad, and the demands of this book require further refinement. The book, in part, seeks to highlight research that provides solid evidence and rationales that can inform the actions of crisis managers. The bulk of crisis communication research has been on public efforts to manage information and public communication designed to manage meaning. The focus on the public aspects of crisis communication allows us to leverage research focused on the three primary categories of crisis response strategies derived from the works of Sturges (1994): instructing information, adjusting information, and reputation management.

Instructing information encompasses information designed to help people protect themselves physically from a crisis. Examples of instructing information include recall information about a product harm situation or warnings to evacuate because of a hazardous chemical release (Holladay, 2009). Instructing information is primarily managing information. Adjusting information corresponds to messages designed to help people cope psychologically with a crisis. Examples of adjusting information include expressions of sympathy, actions taken to prevent a repeat of the crisis, counseling for trauma, and the basic information about the crisis event. Adjusting information is a mix of managing information and meaning. Both instructing and adjusting information reflect a concern for the victim and should be the first strategies employed by crisis managers (Sturges, 1994).

Reputation management strategies are attempts to mitigate or to repair the reputational damage a crisis inflicts on an organization. The various reputation management strategies can be placed into four groups: denial, diminish, rebuild, and bolster (Coombs, 2015). Denial and diminish strategies seek to manage meaning by trying to influence how people perceive the crisis. Denial argues the organization has no responsibility for the crisis. Either there really is no crisis or some other actor is to blame for the crisis. If the organization has no perceived crisis responsibility, it should suffer little to no harm from the crisis (Coombs, 2007). The diminish strategy attempts to reduce the perceived responsibility for the crisis. Managers can argue they lacked control over events or that accidents just happen. If people accept the diminish strategy, attributions of crisis responsibility are reduced.

Rebuild and bolster strategies seek to influence perceptions of the crisis by enhancing how people perceived the organization in crisis. Rebuild approaches take positive actions intended to address victim concerns such as an apology or compensation. By helping victims, organizations can improve how people view the organizations. Bolstering seeks to associate positive actions or messages with the organization. Managers might praise those who helped during the crisis or remind people of the past or current good works by the organization. Bolstering adds positive information to the negatives generated by the crisis in an attempt to offset some of those negatives (Coombs, 2007).

Situational crisis communication theory (SCCT) places the three primary reputation management strategies on a continuum from defensive to accommodative. Defensive strategies prioritize protecting the organization, while accommodative strategies emphasize helping the crisis victims. Denial is defensive, rebuild is accommodative, and diminish is in between the two. Bolstering tends to be defensive when the emphasis is on past actions of the organization, but somewhat accommodative when it praises stakeholders. Bolstering is only somewhat accommodative because praising stakeholders does not address their concerns directly. Returning to the first two crisis response categories, strategies aligned with both instructing information and adjusting information are accommodative because the focus is on addressing victim needs. With the key terms defined, we have parameters to guide the analysis of research findings related to crisis communication.

Crisis Communication Research Findings

A number of disciplines have examined crisis communication with the bulk of the research appearing in corporate communication, public relations, and marketing disciplines. This section reviews the crisis communication research to find the best evidence for the various effects crisis communication can have during a crisis. The research findings have been clustered into four groups: (1) the effects of crisis response strategies, (2) the timing of crisis responses, (3) monitoring media and other stakeholder reactions to crisis communication, and (4) spokespersons.

Effects of Crisis Response Strategies

SCCT is a dominant theory in crisis communication related to the effectiveness of crisis response strategies (Avery, Lariscy, Kim & Hocke, 2010). SCCT research utilizes experimental methods to test causal relationships involving crisis response strategies. SCCT posits that as attributions of crisis responsibility increase, managers need to use more accommodative strategies to be effective at protecting reputational and other organizational assets. Accommodative responses focus on victim needs as opposed to more defensive strategies that privilege organizational needs. Moreover, reputation management is attempted only after the managers provide instructing and adjusting information (Coombs, 2007). There is a long-established relationship between attributions of crisis responsibility and organizational damage from a crisis originating in the marketing literature (Mowen, 1980; Stockmyer, 1996). SCCT uses crisis responsibility as a basis for the selection of crisis response strategies.

The crisis type is the primary determinant of how people will perceive crisis responsibility. There are three crisis types or frames for organizational crises in SCCT: victim, accidental, and intentional. Victim crises produce very minimal attributions of crisis responsibility because the organization is considered a victim of the crisis as well. Victim crises include product tampering and workplace violence. Accidental crises produce minimal attributions of crisis responsibility because the organization has little control over events leading to a crisis. Accidents and product harm crises precipitated by technical/mechanical failures represent the accidental crises. Intentional crises produce strong attributions of crisis responsibility because managers knowingly place stakeholders at risk and/or knowingly violate laws (Coombs, 2007). Managers can have a rough gauge of crisis responsibility by identifying the crisis type—how the crisis is being framed in the media.

Prior reputation and history of past crises have been found to intensify attributions for crisis responsibility. A negative prior reputation and other crises serve to increase the crisis responsibility stakeholders assign to a crisis. However, positive and neutral prior reputations both have been found to have ameliorating effects on crisis responsibility, providing evidence against a strict halo effect for prior reputations (Coombs, 2004; Coombs & Holladay, 2006). SCCT suggests a two-step process for assessing crisis responsibility. The first step is to determine the crisis type, while the second step is to account for intensifiers such as prior reputation and crisis history (Coombs, 2007).

SCCT recommends using instructing and adjusting information any time a crisis has the potential to harm others. Instructing and adjusting strategies, as per Sturges (1994), should be considered as separate from any reputation repair strategies such as the rebuild strategies. When crises generate strong attributions of crisis responsibility, managers should add one or more of the rebuild crisis responses to maximize the benefits from crisis communication. Bolstering can be used with any crisis response but should be used only as a secondary response to complement the primary crisis response strategies (Coombs, 2015). The research generally supports the advice on using instructing and adjusting information, as well as various actions from the rebuild strategy (Ma & Zhan, 2016).

SCCT uses reputation as the primary outcome variable for crisis communication. The idea is to understand how various crisis response strategies can be used to protect the very valuable reputation asset (Coombs & Holladay, 2006). However, SCCT research has also examined the effects of crisis communication on affect, purchase intention, and negative word-of-mouth. Crisis response strategies can be used to reduce the anger generated by a crisis, to protect purchase intention, and to reduce negative word-of-mouth (e.g., Coombs & Holladay, 2005, 2007).

Despite its usefulness, it is important to move beyond just SCCT in order to examine the general effects found when using various crisis response strategies. In doing so, we should consider how crisis response strategies are used in real crises and the effects created by those strategies. The general discussion of crisis response strategies will be organized using the three crisis response categories: (1) instructing information, (2) adjusting information, and (3) reputation management.

The research on instructing information represents a much smaller collection of works than that involving the other two crisis response categories. Instructing information has been linked with technical translation strategies (Chung & Lee, 2016) or the ways organizations deliver complex information to stakeholders (Stephens & Malone, 2009). More precisely, the direct presentation of information without contextual form of technical translation fits with the idea of instructing information. An examination of crisis response strategies in the chemical industry found very limited use of instructing information (Holladay, 2009).

There is some research on compliance with instructing information such as following recalls with limited data for making conclusions. Freberg (2012) found that people were more likely to comply with food recall requests when the organization was the source rather than individuals on social media. What we do know is that compliance with recall messages, especially in the food industry, is very low (Hallman, Cuite & Hooker, 2009). More research is required to find ways to increase compliance with instructing information that provides recommendations about safety.

One very interesting study compared the technical translation strategies (both instructing and adjusting information in this instance) to reputation management strategies using online reactions of people to the messages. The data found people were much more accepting of the technical translation strategies than the reputation management strategies. The crisis in the study was a product harm crisis involving salmonella—a food safety crisis. The results support the value of instructing, and adjusting information being the initial response in a crisis (Chung & Lee, 2016).

Adjusting information also has been linked with the technical translation strategies of elucidating, engaging the transformative, and providing the quasi-scientific (Stephens & Malone, 2009). The elucidating technical translation strategy helps people to understand why a product is now safe. The transformative technical translation strategy is used to provide details about the new and safer product. The quasi-scientific technical translation strategy helps people to understand the process used to make a product safer (Chung & Lee, 2016). The three technical translation strategies constitute various ways of explaining the corrective actions the organization is taking to prevent a repeat of the crisis. Seo, Miao, Almanza, and Behnke (2018) found that food companies regularly used the three technical translation strategies when responding to food safety crises.

Sympathy is the most widely studied aspect of adjusting information. The research on sympathy is closely connected to studies of apology, hence it blends with the research on reputation management strategies. Researchers are interested in any differences in the effects of sympathy and apology on how people react to crises. The sympathy/apology comparison is important because apologies carry with them a legal liability. Apologies involve the organization accepting responsibility for the crisis, while sympathy does not. Both are victim-centered; hence, the two strategies could produce similar effects. Studies generally find similar effects for sympathy and apology. Compensation is included in the studies because it is a rebuild strategy like apology, but does not directly take responsibility for the crisis.

The general findings from experimental studies is that sympathy and apology produce similar effects on perceptions of reputation and feelings of anger. Compensation is similar to apology and sympathy, but in some cases it has not been as effective as the other two (Coombs & Holladay, 2008; Kiambi & Shafer, 2016). Chen and Reber (2017) found no difference between apology and compensation for reputation, negative word-of-mouth intention, and negative online crisis-reaction in a study using an airline crash as the crisis. Only one study found a significant difference between sympathy and apology. It should be noted that this study used a crisis with nine deaths that were preventable, creating a crisis with very high attributions of crisis responsibility (DiStaso, Vafeiadis & Amoral, 2015). SCCT recommends that managers should add apology to the expression of sympathy for a crisis with high attributions of responsibility. The work by DiStaso et al. (2015) supports this recommendation because sympathy alone was much less effective at protecting the reputation than an apology.

SCCT argues that bolstering is a secondary strategy because it makes little sense as the only response to a crisis. Park's (2017) experiment found that bolstering alone was no more effective at protecting reputations and increasing supportive behavioral intentions than no response. Interestingly, bolstering is among the most frequently used crisis response strategies (Kim, Avery & Lariscy, 2009). This finding is logical because bolstering can be used in combination with any crisis response strategy as it is consistent with all the strategies (Coombs, 2007). Nonetheless, there is limited evidence indicating bolstering strategies are generally beneficial to organizations. This appears to be one of the points where theory and practice are not consistent with one another. Interestingly, an important variant of bolstering has emerged in management research, corporate social responsibility (CSR), and there is some supportive evidence for its effects.

CSR refers to pro-social efforts of organizations such as fair treatment of workers, ethical sourcing, and community philanthropy. Studies using an event-based methodology in management have found that CSR is a common response after a crisis, as organizations often respond by publicly communicating about their CSR activities. This is a form of bolstering because it highlights the good works of the organization and offers positive information designed to offset the negative information created by the crisis. Noack, Miller, and Smith (2017) studied responses of food companies to product recalls (product harm crises). It should be noted they only coded for CSR messages and no other crisis response strategies. Their data found that CSR was a common response and was associated with improving the valuation of a firm after a product recall. The one limitation they found was for firms with prior strong reputations, which benefited less than firms with weaker prior reputations. Moreover, a delayed CSR response was more effective for prior strong reputation firms than an immediate response. Again, we do not know what other crisis response strategies were used by these firms, so we do not know if the CSR/bolstering was the only strategy being used. However, the event studies data do suggest bolstering using CSR messages can help to mitigate stock valuation losses from a crisis.

Stock valuation is a key outcome in the marketing and management research that examines crisis response strategies. Research studies find that product recalls, boycotts, and management misconduct crises can all have adverse effects on stock prices (Marcus & Goodman, 1991; Long & Rao, 1995; King, 2011). By far, product recall is the most intensely researched area for crisis effects on stock prices. Part of that research includes how crisis response strategies affect post-crisis stock prices. Recall crisis response research focuses on remedies, and "a remedy is the corrective or compensation measure the companies provide for the defective products" (Liu, Liu & Lou, 2016, p. 79). The belief is that remedies demonstrate responsible behavior by the company. Remedies would include corrective actions (the recall itself is corrective action) and compensation. Apology also is an option during product recalls as well (Marcus & Goodman, 1991).

The recall crisis communication research places response options on two different but conceptually similar continuums: (1) proactive or passive, and (2) defensive or accommodative. Proactive recall response takes action before there are public reports of complaints or incidents, while passive strategies react to complaints or government calls for action (Zhao, Li & Flynn, 2013). The proactive recall strategy is similar to stealing-thunder research which emphasizes the organization being the source of the crisis information (Claeys & Cauberghe, 2012). Siomkos and Kurzbard (1994) identified four crisis response strategies for product recalls: denial, involuntary recall, voluntary recall, and super-effort. Denial is when managers claim there is no problem with the product, while involuntary recall is when the government forces management to take action. A voluntary recall is when management recalls the product without government intervention. The super-effort response is when the actions of management correspond to "demonstrating concern with consumer welfare"

(Siomkos & Kurzbard, 1994, p. 32). A super-effort involves communicating early and often with consumers as well as making the recall process as easy as possible. Denial and involuntary recalls are passive, while voluntary recalls and super-efforts are proactive.

The defensive and accommodative recall strategies reflect management's degree of accepting responsibility for the crisis. Accommodative strategies are associated with managers recognizing the problem and accepting responsibility for it, while defensive strategies are associated with managers focusing on organizational concerns and seeking to avoid responsibility (Marcus & Goodman, 1991). Defensive and accommodative form the more comprehensive framework and can absorb the proactive and passive continuum. Essentially, passive strategies are defensive, while proactive strategies are accommodative. Hence, it is accurate to place all response options along the defensive and accommodative continuum. Table 4.1 places the various strategies discussed thus far with the defensive and accommodative continuum.

At first glance, the findings on recall crisis communication appear inconsistent. There seems to be advantages to both accommodative and defensive crisis response strategies. A closer examination reveals it is the focal stakeholder that is making the difference. Accommodative recall messages create positive reaction from consumers because the strategy demonstrates concern for consumers (Chen, Ganesan & Liu, 2009; Zhao et al., 2013). Similarly, Siomkos and Kurzbard (1994) found their super-effort crisis response strategies were the most effective in their experimental studies when the respondents most closely resembled consumers. Accommodative crisis response strategies signal the organization is willing to take responsibility for the crisis, which means the organization will incur financial costs as well. The accommodative crisis response strategies highlight the liability and financial loss from a recall and has a negative effect on immediate stock valuation (Chen et al., 2009). Moreover, Marcus and Goodman (1991) found product recall crises frequently used a defensive response in order to limit the negative financial effects of the crisis.

The key lesson is that an accommodative crisis response strategy is effective for consumers, while a defensive crisis response strategy is effective for investors. That perspective changes when we take a longer view of the crisis. Both reputational and stock valuation data show a similar pattern during crises with accommodative crisis response strategies. The proactive accommodative crisis response strategy initially creates greater damage to reputation and stock valuation, but both recover much more than when a defensive and reaction response is used (Moran & Gregory, 2014; Raithel, 2014). The data would suggest that accommodative crisis response strategies are a wise long-term investment for organizations in crisis.

Table 4.1 Summary of Crisis Response Strategies

	Defensive ⟵―――――――――――⟶ *Accommodative*			
Coombs (2007)	Denial	Diminish	Bolstering	Rebuild Adjusting information Instructing information
Marcus and Goodman (1991)	Defensive			Accommodative
Siomkos and Kurzbard (1994)	Denial	Involuntary recall	Voluntary recall	Super-efforts
Zhao et al. (2013)		Reactive		Proactive

Timing of Crisis Communication

Timing involves when an organization speaks about the crisis. The focus is on whether or not the organization is the first to speak about the crisis. When an organization is the first to speak, managers are engaging in stealing thunder. Multiple research studies have found that a crisis inflicts less damage on an organization when managers in the organization are the first to disclose the existence of a crisis (Arpan & Pompper, 2003). Stealing thunder is a concept from law that finds if defense is the first to discuss a weakness in its own case, the weakness has less of a negative effect on the jury. Claeys (2017) and her associates have done an outstanding job of mapping the effects of stealing thunder and proving the robustness of the effect (Claeys & Cauberghe, 2012; Clays, Cauberghe & Keysen, 2013; Clayes, Cauberghe & Pandelaere, 2016). For instance, the stealing-thunder research found that benefits from post-crisis response strategies depend upon whether or not managers had stolen thunder. When managers steal thunder, the selection of post-crisis response strategies matters less. However, when managers do not steal thunder, the selection of post-crisis response strategies matters more (Claeys & Cauberghe, 2012).

Lee (2016) studied the effects of brand attachment (an individual difference) on stealing thunder. The research found that the stealing-thunder effect intensifies as brand attachment becomes stronger. It would seem that effects of stealing thunder are even stronger among those who have positive associations with the organization in crisis. Furthermore, research has yielded insights into why managers avoid stealing thunder instead of embracing the concept. Claeys and Opgenhaffen (2016) interviewed senior communication managers about stealing thunder. Three reasons emerged for why managers often do not steal thunder. First, some managers feel it is best to wait before taking action. There is a fear of acting too soon because the organization might be able to settle the matter internally and avoid any public disclosure of the situation. Second, stealing thunder is viewed as situationally based and not an absolute. Managers look for the right conditions for stealing thunder. The right conditions tend to be when the crisis involves external concerns and greater extent of harm. Third, the legal and managerial implications are weighed against the value of stealing thunder. There could be important legal or managerial concerns that prevent the use of stealing thunder (Claeys & Opgenhaffen, 2016).

While there are consistent findings related to efficacy, stealing thunder does have limitations such as prior reputation. Organizations with negative reputations prior to a crisis find lesser benefit than do organizations with more favorable reputations (Beldad, Hegner & van Laar, 2017). This is consistent with the earlier discussion of crisis responsibility and its effect on organizations.

Monitoring Media and Other Stakeholder Reactions

Modern crisis communication naturally integrates digital channels into a crisis response. However, we are still learning the best way to make use of these new channels and the data these channels offer to crisis managers. Crisis managers have always had a need to monitor how stakeholders are reacting to their crisis communication efforts. Early designs for crisis communication centers included televisions to monitor media coverage as a source of data for crisis communication effectiveness (Barton, 2001). News reports help to indicate how well or how poorly an organization's crisis response message is being adopted. For instance, Holladay (2009) found that in chemical accidents, a small percentage of news stories were using the chemical firms as sources, limiting the ability of these firms to tell their side of the crisis story.

As digital channels emerged, computer monitors were added to the mix, and researchers began to explore the utility of these new data for crisis managers. Two monitoring uses have emerged: (1) reactions to the crisis and (2) reactions to the crisis communication. Choi and Lin (2009) were among the first to use digital channels to assess how people were reacting to a crisis. They studied Mattel's product recall over lead paint in toys for emotional reactions in online bulletin boards. By coding for various emotions, the researchers found the online bulletin boards provided a rich source of information on emotions created by the crisis (Choi & Lin, 2009).

Coombs and Holladay (2012, 2014) are among those who have done work to explicate the use of digital media reactions to assess crisis communication efforts. Amazon.com had a crisis unfold online when it had to remove unlicensed George Orwell books from people's Kindle reading devices. The initial crisis response was an email that had a rather technical explanation of the situation that confused many Kindle owners. The Kindle Community discussion board had a number of very negative posts regarding the initial message. The CEO, Jeff Bezos, then posted an apology to the Kindle Community discussion board. The responses were coded to determine if people seemed to accept the apology and the effect the crisis and response had on stated purchase intentions. Over 200 responses were content-analyzed. The results showed the vast majority of people accepted the apology and that those indicating purchase intentions in their messages were favorable toward Amazon.com. The responses would suggest the crisis response was effective. However, the messages were not a representative sample of Kindle users, meaning the results must be interpreted with caution.

Another concern with digital channels (often just called social media) is that the channels are fragmented and not monolithic. The rhetoric arena is a multi-vocal approach to crisis communication. The perspective holds that multiple voices appear during a crisis in what is called the rhetorical arena. Each of these voices can affect the outcome of the crisis management efforts (Frandsen & Johansen, 2017). Due to the fragmented nature of digital channels, it is likely that sub-arenas emerge. A sub-arena represents a specific digital channel that creates a limited space where a message is heard. In other words, there may be little crossover in the audiences for various digital channels discussing crisis. Hence, each channel might present a different view of how people are reacting to the crisis communication effort. To directly examine sub-arenas, the Lance Armstrong resignation from the board of Livestrong has been studied. The resignation occurred when Armstrong seemed to admit guilt for doping by dropping his appeal. Two sub-arenas were examined: the Livestrong blog and a Huffington Post story about the situation coupled with the story's related blog. The Livestrong blog is a supportive environment because most blog readers like the blog (Kent, 2008). The Huffington Post is one of the most popular online news sources, and those posting comments for one of its articles will not necessarily be supporters of Lance Armstrong and Livestrong. The blog posts were analyzed for positive and negative valence. The Livestrong blog was much more supportive of Lance Armstrong than the Huffington Post comments (95%–25% positive comments) and slightly more supportive of Livestrong (97%–87% positive). The data show that aggregating social media data can hide important insights. Different sub-arenas may hold different reactions to the crisis communication, and this information can be useful to crisis managers (Coombs & Holladay, 2014).

These initial studies were based on small data sets both in terms of news media coverage and digital media posts. Van der Meer (2016b) and his research partners have pioneered the use of semantic-network analysis to examine large data sets in order to determine frames as a means of assessing the outcomes of crisis communication efforts. Framing can be defined in the following terms: "to select some aspects of a perceived reality and make them more salient in the communicating context, in such a way as to promote a particular problem definition, causal interpretation, moral evaluation and/or treatment recommendation for the item described" (Entman, 1993, p. 52). Framing seeks to shape how people interpret events by highlighting specific aspects of a situation or event and hiding others. Moreover, framing analysis can be used to understand how various stakeholders are interpreting the crisis event which provides one measure of the effectiveness of crisis communication (Gerken, Van der Land & van der Meer, 2016).

Crisis frame alignment is a means of assessing how well the organization's frame for the crisis aligns with news media and stakeholder frames (van der Meer, Verhoeven, Beentjes & Vliegenthart, 2014). The organization's crisis frame is determined by analyzing the crisis response messages created by management. The news media and stakeholder frames are determined by analyzing news stories and social media posts about the crisis. In this type of analysis, frames are the key words being used to discuss the crisis and do not reflect the earlier discussion of crisis types as crisis frames. The news media and social media posts can generate large amounts of data to code. Semantic-network analysis can be conducted using automated content analysis to analyze the texts for the co-occurrence of words or what is known as implicit frames. For instance, when examining an explosion at a chemical facility, the initial frame emphasized the words "residents," "safety region," and drinking water" reflecting a frame emphasizing safety and the potential dangers for residents from the explosion (van der Meer et al., 2014). The various frames or patterns of words are then compared to see if there is convergence or divergence in words being used to frame the crises. Again, the analysis is examining words and not specifically any particular crisis type. (See van der Meer (2016a, 2016b) for more detailed explanation of the analysis process.)

This type of frame analysis has found a pattern of words where frames are divergent, then begin to converge after the initial coverage, and then diverge again after the media coverage begins to fade (e.g., van der Meer & Verhoeven, 2013; van der Meer et al., 2014). The researchers who studied the aforementioned explosion found a pattern of divergence-convergence-divergence in the news media (newspapers) and public (social media) frames for four different crises. The initial crisis time frame had divergence, for example, the news media frame was about safety, while the public frame was about terrorism. In the second phase, when the media coverage was extensive, the news media and public frames began to converge around an information frame that focused on the investigation. The third phase, after the extensive media coverage ended, found the public and news media frames diverging once more. Correlational analysis of the words was used to demonstrate the divergence and convergence of the frames (van der Meer et al., 2014). Convergence of the frames is used as evidence of successful crisis communication (Gerken et al., 2016). For example, a Dutch company used a denial strategy in response to a crisis. At first, stakeholders were skeptical and the frames were divergent. But, over time, the stakeholders accepted the denial frame as the two frames began to align (van der Meer, 2014). The computer-based content analysis for framing can be used to analyze large data sets in order to determine if stakeholders and the news media are agreeing or disagreeing with the organization's crisis frame providing an important piece of information for managers seeking to assess the effectiveness of their crisis communication efforts.

Spokesperson Issues

A long-time element in crisis communication research and practice has been the spokesperson (Barton, 2001). The spokesperson is the individual (or perhaps a group of individuals) that answers media questions about the crisis either at a news conference or during an interview. There is a growing trend of companies placing crisis response videos (usually apologies from the CEO) online. Tesco, Maple Foods, JetBlue, and Dominos have posted such videos. This trend requires the spokesperson role be expanded to include the individual appearing in a videotape presenting the organization's crisis response. The expansion is rather simple because the key delivery skills remain the same across the two domains. The only difference is the spokesperson in the video does not answer questions.

Researchers have been trying to determine who should be the spokesperson and what qualities the spokesperson should have to maximize the benefits of crisis communication. Arpan (2002) examined spokesperson ethnicity because of the multinational nature of many crises. She found that it was best to match the ethnicity of the spokesperson and the target audience when the audience is likely to have a strong ethnic identity. Similarly, Crijn, Claeys, Cauberghe, and Hudders (2017) found gender similarity enhances empathy which can enhance a reputation, but only during a preventable crisis. Overall, ethnicity and gender of the spokesperson can have some influence on the effectiveness of crisis communication. Also, the data support the idea that organizations frequently need to have more than one spokesperson in order to match various audiences.

Gorn, Jiang, and Johar (2008) explored the baby-faced effect for a spokesperson. Their research was inspired by the effects of baby-faced endorsers in advertising (e.g., Guido & Peluso, 2009). The baby-face effect relates to people liking and trusting people with baby-faces more than those with mature-faces. The data showed that baby-facedness did increase judgments of innocence and created more favorable evaluations of the spokesperson and the organization. Essentially, innocence increased perceived credibility, and perceived credibility improved attitudes toward the organization. However, the effect was not found when the crisis was severe. Moreover, the cause of the crisis affected whether a baby-faced or mature-faced spokesperson was more effective. The baby-faced spokesperson was more effective when the source of the crisis was due to potential dishonesty, while a mature-faced spokesperson was preferable when the crisis was caused by a lack of vigilance (Gorn et al., 2008). Additional research should be conducted to verify the reported effects of a baby-faced or matured-face spokesperson.

Research has begun to move beyond the appearance of the spokesperson to the quality of the spokesperson's voice. Claeys and Cauberghe (2014) examined the nonverbal expression of power as manifest in voice pitch. A lower-pitched voice is considered more powerful. Their initial findings indicated a lower-pitched voice was perceived as more competent than a higher-pitched voice. The study probed further to examine if there were differences in the utility of voice between an immediate crisis response (immediately after the trigger event) and, later, post-crisis responses. The results indicate that a powerful voice (lower-pitched) is preferable immediately after a crisis because it increases perceptions of confidence which, in turn, enhanced the organizational reputation. During the post-crisis response, a powerless voice (higher-pitched) is preferable because it increases perceptions of sincerity which, in turn, enhanced the organizational reputation (Claeys & Cauberghe, 2014). Spokespersons should vary their pitch between the immediate and the post-crisis communication responses to maximize the value that pitch can add to the crisis communication messages. The researchers are currently conducting additional studies to build additional support and refine our understanding of the pitch effects for spokespersons.

DeWaele, Claeys, and Cauberghe (2015) examined the interplay between voice pitch and speech rate, during an apology crisis response. Two combinations of the cues produced the most desired effects. First, reputation was stronger when the lower-pitched voice was paired with the slow speech rate compared to lower-pitched voice and fast speech rate. Second, reputation was stronger when the higher-pitched voice was paired with the higher speech rate compared to higher-pitched voice and a slow speech rate. Unlike the Claeys & Cauberghe (2014) study, this experiment examined responses at only one point in time and not immediate and post-crisis. Nonetheless, the pairing of the pitch and speech rate seems to play a role in creating the right vocal attractiveness and the desired positive effect on reputation (DeWaele et al., 2015). We do know that low pitch and slow rate seem to fit best with an immediate crisis, while high pitch and fast rate seem to fit best in post-crisis communication.

Conclusion

There continues to be a significant portion of the crisis communication research that is case-study-based, making it more speculation than evidence-based. This chapter has drawn heavily upon the experimental studies in crisis communication in order to articulate the emerging and expanding evidence-based knowledge that is being generated. Table 4.2 provides a summary of the key lessons this research offers crisis communicators. The extant research has validated the importance of both instructing and adjusting information for an initial crisis response. Moreover, the sympathy in adjusting information is typically as effective as accommodative strategies such as apology and compensation. Apology seems to enhance a response when a crisis has strong crisis responsibility. Moreover, accommodative crisis responses produce long-term benefits. Generally, organizations fare better on important outcomes when managers steal thunder. News stories and social media posts can be content-analyzed in various ways to determine how people are reacting to crises and crisis responses. Finally, we found some insights into the verbal cues utilized by spokespersons. Crisis communication is a dynamic field, and research will continue to improve our understanding of the practice.

Table 4.2 Summary of Crisis Communication Advice

Effectiveness of Crisis Response Strategies
    When there are victims or potential victims, use adjusting and instructing information which should include expression of sympathy and corrective action
    Rebuild strategies *can* help to reduce the damage to organizational assets
    Bolstering *can* provide limited protection for organizational assets
Timing of Crisis Response Strategies
    Stealing thunder does protect organizational assets during a crisis
    Stealing thunder is unlikely to be used if managers feel the crisis can be contained internally
Monitoring Crisis Reactions
    Monitoring traditional and social media can provide insights into how people are defining the crisis and reacting to crisis response strategies
Spokesperson
    A baby-faced spokesperson works best when the crisis involves dishonesty and is not severe
    A mature-faced spokesperson works best when the crisis is a result of lack of vigilance
    The immediate response benefits from spokesperson with a lower-pitched voice
    Post-crisis responses benefit from a spokesperson with a higher-pitched voice
    A lower-pitched voice works best with a slower speech rate for a spokesperson
    A higher-pitched voice works best with a higher speech rate for a spokesperson

References

Arpan, L. M. (2002). When in Rome? The effects of spokesperson ethnicity on audience evaluation of crisis communication. *The Journal of Business Communication (1973), 39*(3), 314–339.

Arpan, L. M., & Pompper, D. (2003). Stormy weather: Testing "stealing thunder" as a crisis communication strategy to improve communication flow between organizations and journalists. *Public Relations Review, 29*(3), 291–308.

Avery, E. J., Lariscy, R. W., Kim, S., & Hocke, T. (2010). A quantitative review of crisis communication research in public relations from 1991 to 2009. *Public Relations Review, 36*(2), 190–192.

Barton, L. (2001). *Crisis in organizations II* (2nd ed.). Cincinnati, OH: College Divisions South-Western.

Beldad, A. D., Hegner, S. M., & van Laar, E. (2017). Proactive crisis communication when precrisis reputation is rotten? The moderating roles of precrisis reputation and crisis type in the relationship between communication timing and trust and purchase intention. In M. Stieler (Ed.), *Creating marketing magic and innovative future marketing trends* (pp. 679–684). Cham, Switzerland: Springer.

Chen, Y., Ganesan, S., & Liu, Y. (2009). Does a firm's product-recall strategy affect its financial value? An examination of strategic alternatives during product-harm crises. *Journal of Marketing, 73*(6), 214–226. doi:10.1509/jmkg.73.6.214

Chen, Z. F., & Reber, B. H. (2017). Examining public responses to social media crisis communication strategies in the Unites States and China. In L. Austin & Y. Jin (Eds.), *Social media and crisis communication* (pp. 114–126). New York: Routledge.

Choi, Y., & Lin, Y. H. (2009). Individual difference in crisis response perception: How do legal experts and lay people perceive apology and compassion responses? *Public Relations Review, 35*(4), 452–454.

Chung, S., & Lee, S. (2016). Crisis communication strategy on social media and the public's cognitive and affective responses: A case of foster farms salmonella outbreak. *Communication Research Reports, 33*(4), 341–348.

Claeys, A. S. (2017). Better safe than sorry: Why organizations in crisis should never hesitate to steal thunder. *Business Horizons, 60*(3), 305–311.

Claeys, A. S., & Cauberghe, V. (2012). Crisis response and crisis timing strategies, two sides of the same coin. *Public Relations Review, 38*(1), 83–88.

Claeys, A. S., & Cauberghe, V. (2014). Keeping control: The importance of nonverbal expressions of power by organizational spokespersons in times of crisis. *Journal of Communication, 64*(6), 1160–1180.

Claeys, A. S., Cauberghe, V., & Leysen, J. (2013). Implications of stealing thunder for the impact of expressing emotions in organizational crisis communication. *Journal of Applied Communication Research, 41*(3), 293–308.

Claeys, A. S., Cauberghe, V., & Pandelaere, M. (2016). Is old news no news? The impact of self-disclosure by organizations in crisis. *Journal of Business Research, 69*(10), 3963–3970.

Claeys, A. S., & Opgenhaffen, M. (2016). Why practitioners do (not) apply crisis communication theory in practice. *Journal of Public Relations Research, 28*(5–6), 232–247.

Coombs, W. T. (1995). Choosing the right words: The development of guidelines for the selection of the "appropriate" crisis response strategies. *Management Communication Quarterly, 8,* 447–476.

Coombs, W. T. (2004). Impact of past crises on current crisis communications: Insights from situational crisis communication theory. *Journal of Business Communication, 41,* 265–289.

Coombs, W. T. (2007). Attribution theory as a guide for post-crisis communication research. *Public Relations Review, 33,* 135–139.

Coombs, W. T. (2010). Crisis communication: A developing field. In R. L. Heath (Ed.), *Handbook of public relations* (2nd ed.) (pp. 477–488). Thousand Oaks, CA: Sage.

Coombs, W. T. (2015). *Ongoing crisis communication: Planning, managing, and responding* (4th ed.). Thousand Oaks, CA: Sage.

Coombs, W. T. (2017). Digital naturals and the rise of paracrises: The shape of modern crisis communication. In S. Duhé (Ed.), *New media and public relations* (3rd ed.) (pp. 281–290). New York: Peter Lang.

Coombs, W. T., & Holladay, S. J. (2005). Exploratory study of stakeholder emotions: Affect and crisis. In N. M. Ashkanasy, W. J. Zerbe, & C. E. J. Hartel (Eds.), *Research on emotion in organizations: Volume 1: The effect of affect in organizational settings* (pp. 271–288). New York: Elsevier.

Coombs, W. T., & Holladay, S. J. (2006). Halo or reputational capital: Reputation and crisis management. *Journal of Communication Management, 10,* 123–137.

Coombs, W. T., & Holladay, S. J. (2007). The negative communication dynamic: Exploring the impact of stakeholder affect on behavioral intentions. *Journal of Communication management, 11*(4), 300–312.

Coombs, W. T., & Holladay, S. J. (2008). Comparing apology to equivalent crisis response strategies: Clarifying apology's role and value in crisis communication. *Public Relations Review, 34*(3), 252–257.

Coombs, W. T., & Holladay, S. J. (2012). Amazon.com's Orwellian nightmare: Exploring apology in an online environment. *Journal of Communication Management, 16*(3), 280–295.

Coombs, W. T., & Holladay, S. J. (2014). How publics react to crisis communication efforts: Comparing crisis response reactions across sub-arenas. *Journal of Communication Management, 18*(1), 40–57.

De Waele, A., Claeys, A. S., & Cauberghe, V. (2015). The organizational voice: The importance of voice pitch and speech rate in organizational crisis communication. *Communication Research*. doi:10.1177/0093650217692911

DiStaso, M. W., Vafeiadis, M., & Amaral, C. (2015). Managing a health crisis on facebook: How the response strategies of apology, sympathy, and information influence public relations. *Public Relations Review, 41*(2), 222–231.

Entman, R. M. (1993). Framing: Toward clarification of a fractured paradigm. *Journal of communication, 43*(4), 51–58.

Frandsen, F., & Johansen, W. (2017). *Organizational crisis communication: A multivocal approach*. London: Sage.

Freberg, K. (2012). Intention to comply with crisis messages communicated via social media. *Public Relations Review, 38*(3), 416–421.

Gerken, F., Van der Land, S. F., & van der Meer, T. G. (2016). Crisis in the air: An investigation of AirAsia's crisis-response effectiveness based on frame alignment. *Public Relations Review, 42*(5), 879–892.

Gorn, G. J., Jiang, Y., & Johar, G. V. (2008). Babyfaces, trait inferences, and company evaluations in a public relations crisis. *Journal of Consumer Research, 35*(1), 36–49.

Guido, G., & Peluso, A.M. (2009). When are baby-faced endorsers appropriate? Testing effects on credibility and purchase intention. *Journal of Current Issues & Research in Advertising, 31* (2), 67–74.

Hallman, W. K., Cuite, C. L., & Hooker, N. H. (2009). Consumer responses to food recalls: 2008 national survey report. Retrieved from http://foodpolicy.rutgers.edu/docs/news/rr-0109-018.pdf.

Holladay, S. J. (2009). Crisis communication strategies in the media coverage of chemical accidents. *Journal of Public Relations Research, 21*, 208–215.

Kent, M. L. (2008). Critical analysis of blogging in public relations. *Public Relations Review, 34*, 32–40.

Kiambi, D. M., & Shafer, A. (2016). Corporate crisis communication: Examining the interplay of reputation and crisis response strategies. *Mass Communication and Society, 19*(2), 127–148.

Kim, S., Avery, E. J., & Lariscy, R. W. (2009). Are crisis communicators practicing what we preach?: An evaluation of crisis response strategy analyzed in public relations research from 1991 to 2009. *Public Relations Review, 35*(4), 446–448.

King, B. G. (2011). The tactical disruptiveness of social movements: Sources of market and mediated disruption in corporate boycotts. *Social Problems, 58*(4), 491–517.

Lee, S. Y. (2016). Weathering the crisis: Effects of stealing thunder in crisis communication. *Public Relations Review, 42*(2), 336–344.

Liu, A. X., Liu, Y., & Lou, T. (2016). What drives a firm's choice of product recall remedy? The impact remedy cost, product hazard, and the CEO. *Journal of Marketing, 80*(3), 79–95. doi:10.1509/jm.14.0382

Long, D. M., & Rao, S. (1995). The wealth effects of unethical business behavior. *Journal of Economics and Finance, 19*(2), 65–73.

Ma, L., & Zhan, M. (2016). Effects of attributed responsibility and response strategies on organizational reputation: A meta-analysis of situational crisis communication theory research. *Journal of Public Relations Research, 28*(2), 102–119.

Marcus, A. A., & Goodman, R. S. (1991). Victims and shareholders: The dilemmas of presenting corporate policy during a crisis. *Academy of Management Journal, 34*, 281–305.

Moran, R., & Gregory, J. R. (2014). Post crisis: Engage—or fly low? *Brunswick Review, 8*, 52–54.

Mowen, J. C. (1980). Further information on consumer perceptions of product recalls. *Advances in Consumer Research, 8*, 519–523.

Noack, D., Miller, D. R., & Smith, D. (2017). Let me make it up to you: Understanding the mitigative ability of corporate social responsibility following product recalls. *Journal of Business Ethics*. doi:10.1007/s10551-017-3639-7.

Park, H. (2017). Exploring effective crisis response strategies. *Public Relations Review, 43*(1), 190–192.

Raithel, S. (2014). Negative celebrity endorser publicity and stock returns: How critical are immediate form reaction? Annual Meeting of the International Crisis and Risk Communication Conference, Orlando, FL.

Roux-Dufort, C. (2007). A passion for imperfections: Revisiting crisis management. In C. M. Pearson, C. Roux-Dufort, & J. A. Clair (Eds.), *International handbook of organizational crisis management* (pp. 221–252). Thousand Oaks, CA: Sage.

Seo, S., Miao, L., Almanza, B., & Behnke, C. (2018). How have restaurant firms responded to food safety crises? Evidence from media coverage. *Journal of Foodservice Business Research, 21*(1), 83-105.

Siomkos, G. J., & Kurzbard, G. (1994). The hidden crisis in product harm crisis management. *European Journal of Marketing, 28*(2), 30–41.

Stephens, K. K., & Malone, P. C. (2009). If the organizations won't give us information…: The use of multiple new media for crisis technical translation and dialogue. *Journal of Public Relations Research, 21*(2), 229–239.

Stockmyer, J. (1996). Brands in crisis: Consumer help for deserving victims. *Advances in Consumer Research, 23*, 429–435.

Sturges, D. L. (1994). Communicating through crisis: A strategy for organizational survival. *Management Communication Quarterly, 7*, 297–316.

van der Meer, T. G. (2014). Organizational crisis-denial strategy: The effect of denial on public framing. *Public Relations Review, 40*(3), 537–539.

van der Meer, T. G. (2016a). Automated content analysis and crisis communication research. *Public Relations Review, 42*(5), 952–961.

van der Meer, T. G. (2016b). *Communication in times of crisis: The interplay between the organization, news media, and the public.* Amsterdam: Amsterdam School of Communication Research.

van der Meer, T. G., & Verhoeven, P. (2013). Public framing organizational crisis situations: Social media versus news media. *Public Relations Review, 39*(3), 229–231.

van der Meer, T. G., Verhoeven, P., Beentjes, H., & Vliegenthart, R. (2014). When frames align: The interplay between PR, news media, and the public in times of crisis. *Public Relations Review, 40*(5), 751–761.

Zhao, X., Li, Y., & Flynn, B. B. (2013). The financial impact of product recall announcements in China. *International Journal of Production Economics, 142*(1), 115–123. doi:10.1016/j.ijpe.2012.10.018

5

COLLECTIVE FIT FOR EMERGENCY RESPONSE TEAMS

April D. Schantz and Juanita M. Woods

Few issues in psychology have been as pervasive as the one concerning the interaction between an individual and his or her environment (Schneider, 2001). Importantly, the implications of this interaction are quite pronounced in emergency and community services. For instance, a peace officer may have a temperament better suited to financial crimes than to traffic control and therefore function better in a unit focused on such crimes. Some emergency responders may prefer trauma calls, while others prefer medical calls; some firefighters may choose to work in locations where wildland fires are common, while others are better suited to structural fire scenarios. The common trend in these cases is that success in each situation depends in part on the harmony between the individuals and environmental factors present in their jobs. This idea of harmony is known as person-environment fit, defined as the congruence, match, compatibility, or similarity between the person and his or her environment (Kristof-Brown and Guay, 2011).

Compatibility with the characteristics of one's direct task environment is not, however, the whole picture. Because an emergency responder often works in a team, he or she must also demonstrate compatibility with the other members of the work team. When a firefighter on an engine crew "clicks" with others, he or she is more likely to demonstrate better performance on emergency calls. Compatibility between the individual and his or her work team is known as person-group fit. Person-group fit, which represents one part of overall person-environment fit, is focused on the compatibility between an individual and the values, personalities, and abilities represented in his or her workgroup or team (Seong and Kristof-Brown, 2012). Emergency response teams must function in situations that erratically alternate between routine and non-routine events, in unpredictable, time-pressured, and sometimes hazardous conditions. In these situations, performance effectiveness is essential but potentially hindered by a lack of compatibility between team members.

Based on these realities, we extend the individually focused concept of person-environment fit by developing the concept of collective fit as a team characteristic that arises from the shared perceptions of team members' relatedness (Kozlowski and Ilgen, 2006; Kristof-Brown, Seong, Degeest, Park, and Hong, 2014). Specifically, we suggest that collective fit is the result of dynamic interactions among team members' shared experiences over time. Additionally, as teams are embedded in organizations and influenced by their overall fit to the task and organizational environments (DeRue and Hollenbeck, 2007; Klein and

Kozlowski, 2000), our integrated model considers the effects of individual, organizational, and task characteristics on this team-level perception of fit. Implications for team effectiveness also are emphasized.

The propositions presented in this chapter are unique and offer several contributions to current research on person-environment fit and team effectiveness. As such, they offer unique and important insights into research on best practices in emergency management. First, previous researchers investigating person-environment fit typically have focused on the individual, rather than the team, when examining fit. Person-environment fit research has demonstrated significant relationships with individual job attitudes (such as satisfaction or organizational commitment), turnover and absenteeism, performance, and counterproductive work behaviors (Kristof-Brown and Guay, 2011). Still, there is a need to further investigate how the relationship between fit and outcomes actualizes in teams (Kozlowski and Bell, 2013). Second, research investigating team properties has also neglected the unique needs inherent in emergency response teams. Individuals in emergency response teams serve as the safety net for the public, often functioning in dangerous or hazardous conditions, while also dealing with dynamic team processes and organizational constraints.

To address these gaps, we present a novel application of person-environment fit in emergency response contexts. First, we discuss the importance of fit in emergency response teams, followed by an overview of research related to person-environment fit. Second, we develop the concept of collective fit as a team-level property and explore individual, environmental, and contextual influences on collective fit in emergency response teams. Finally, we conclude with implications for emergency responders and those concerned with their well-being and effectiveness at work. Our model highlights opportunities for leaders to realize the benefits of fit in emergency response teams, with potential applications related to organizational policies, teams, and interagency human-resource management standards.

The Importance of Fit in Emergency Response Teams

In a general sense, teams are groups of individuals who work interdependently toward shared goals, work within organizational boundaries, and are perceived by others as a single unit (Kozlowski and Bell, 2013). Emergency response teams are one type of team where individuals work together in risky and unpredictable situations to achieve mutual and clear goals. Specifically, emergency response teams are hierarchically structured teams with clearly defined team roles (Archer, 1999) that face high pressure to perform without failure (Colquitt, LePine, Zapata, and Wild, 2011; Jehn and Techakesari, 2014). Sometimes these teams consist of members who have essentially the same training and job tasks and work in unison, such as those typically staffing an ambulance. Other times, emergency response teams include individuals who, regardless of any similarity of training, are responsible for a specific team task, such as a group of firefighters working on one Truck/Ladder unit. In both situations, there exists a need for individuals to trust that other team members are completing their tasks because each member has only enough time to focus on his or her duties. For teams to function well, both mutual respect and interdependence must exist between team members (Cohen and Bailey, 1997; Kozlowski and Bell, 2013). An inability for a team to meet these requirements results in second-guessing and lack of trust, which can lead to errors and costly failure (Weick, 1993). Errors by emergency response teams can be very costly in both financial (Shackford, Hollingsworth-Fridlund, McArdle, and Eastman, 1987) and human terms (Davis and Mosesso, 1998).

Because of the need for high performance in uncertain and risky contexts, emergency response team members must be able to work seamlessly together to minimize loss of property and life in crisis situations. Crisis situations, as high-risk and unpredictable events, require both a high level of competence and confidence from each responder, clear understanding of roles, and a high level of team member integration (Subramaniam, Ali, and Mohd Shamsudin, 2010). In other words, all members of the team must "fit" with the other members of the team like gears in a watch, both supplementing and complementing the skills, values, and personalities of their teammates. To support the need for high performance, we present a framework built on person-environment fit. Within this framework, we explore the underlying processes within emergency response teams that contribute to team effectiveness outcomes.

Person-Environment Fit

The notion of individuals responding in different ways to various environmental influences is universally accepted, beginning with Lewin (1951), who posited human behavior arises as a function of the person and environment. Person-environment fit suggests that human behavior can only be understood by investigating joint effects between the characteristics of an individual and his or her environment, and not the environment or the individual in isolation (Harrison, 1978; Lewin, 1951; Muchinsky and Monahan, 1987). From this theoretical perspective, researchers have elaborated the concept of person-environment fit to examine various forms of fit in the workplace (Kristof-Brown and Guay, 2011). Examples include fit between individuals and their chosen vocations, their organizations, their coworkers, their supervisors, and their assigned jobs. Person-environment fit broadly captures the notion of compatibility between a person and relevant environmental characteristics, as indicated by three core dimensions: supplementary fit, complementary demands-abilities fit, and complementary needs-supplies fit, which we briefly address in the following section.

Dimensions of Person-Environment Fit

The evaluation of fit in the workplace is based on two psychological processes: similarity-attraction and needs fulfillment (Kristof-Brown and Guay, 2011; Muchinsky and Monahan, 1987). *Supplementary fit* occurs through the similarity-attraction mechanism, which suggests that a person fits into some environmental context because he or she possesses characteristics similar to other individuals in that context (Muchinsky and Monahan, 1987). The mechanism of similarity-attraction suggests that individuals are attracted to people and organizations with whom they perceive an affinity or similarity (Schneider, 1987). People who work as emergency responders are attracted to the job initially because they are interested in the work or want to emulate some others already in the field; research confirms this "birds of a feather" behavior by demonstrating the shared characteristics of individuals within emergency services (Klee and Renner, 2013). Similarity-attraction also explains why so many members of para-military organizations and former military personnel seek each other out ("Operation Dispatch" 2012; Worrall and Zhao, 2003). This perception of similarity through supplementary fit has been found to facilitate a smoother working environment (Cable and DeRue, 2002) and increase organizational commitment (Kristof-Brown, Zimmerman, and Johnson, 2005).

Complementary fit relies on the drive for needs fulfillment from both the perspective of the organization and of the individual. A fundamental principle of needs fulfillment suggests that individuals engage in work-related behaviors and take on job-related tasks to increase their self-esteem (Lawler, 1973). Complementary fit emphasizes compatibility such that "characteristics of an individual serves to 'make whole' or complement the characteristics of an environment" (Muchinsky and Monahan, 1987, p. 271) and vice versa. From the organizational perspective, the degree to which an individual's knowledge, skills, and abilities fulfill environmental or organizational demands refers to *demands-abilities fit* (French, Caplan, and Harrison, 1982). From the person's perspective, *needs-supplies fit* refers to work environment characteristics that fulfill a person's needs, desires, motives, or goals (Caplan, 1987; French et al., 1982). Therefore, complementary fit can refer to either an individual's knowledge, skills, or abilities meeting environmental job demands as in demands-abilities fit, or to an environment that meets the individual's need for growth, recognition, or achievement as in needs-supplies fit. We observe demands-ability fit in emergency response organizations that require individuals to pass a physical test (such as the Candidate Physical Abilities Test for firefighters) before they can be hired (Ryan and Ployhart, 2000). An example of needs-supplies fit includes situations where individuals seek to increase the security of their communities by joining law enforcement agencies. In considering demands-abilities and needs-supplies at the same time, the ability to meet the demands of a challenging task (e.g. successfully retrieving victims from a house fire) may also meet one's needs of meaningfulness or recognition (e.g. saving lives).

Perceived fit is manifested by both supplementary and complementary fit peculiar to the work environment context (Harrison, 1978; Seong and Kristof-Brown, 2012) and can occur via several mechanisms. For instance, a job environment can provide resources desired by an individual, or that individual can provide abilities required by the job environment. Additionally, both the individual and the organization can share characteristics. It is also important to note that any combination of these scenarios can occur to provide an overall level of perceived fit (Harrison, 1978).

Outcomes of Person-Environment Fit

Outcomes of person-environment fit include job satisfaction, organization commitment, turnover, psychological and physical well-being, and better job performance (Cable and DeRue, 2002; Edwards and Harrison, 1993; Kristof-Brown, Zimmerman, et al., 2005). Research has shown the supplementary and complementary dimensions of person-environment fit are highly related to each other but contribute uniquely to outcomes (Cable and DeRue, 2002). Person-environment fit has also demonstrated consistent effects across the different forms of person-environment fit in workplaces (e.g. between an individual and his or her organization, vocation, group, or job; Kristof-Brown, Zimmerman, et al., 2005). Finally, person-environment fit demonstrates an influence on outcomes after controlling for the effects of other positive workplace factors (such as organizational support or altruistic behaviors; Cable and DeRue, 2002).

Despite the large body of research on person-environment fit, there is limited research that examines outcomes for emergency services. The few examples include Carless' (2005) study that found moderately strong relationships between person-job and person-organization fit for entry-level police officers and their commitment to and intent to remain in the force, and Ingram's (2013) study that examined the impact of sergeant-officer supplementary fit on officer's perception of role ambiguity. Schantz' (2018) investigation examined the role of needs-supplies fit on strain and well-being outcomes for emergency services personnel. Findings suggested that fit between an emergency responder's preference for and presence of corresponding job attributes (such as feedback, task significance, and skill variety) were influential in burnout and compassion satisfaction outcomes (Schantz, 2018). At an organizational level, Sinclair, Doyle, Johnston, and Paton (2013) used a person-environment fit framework to guide their examination of demands-abilities fit in the context of training for emergency operations center activations in Canada, New Zealand, and the United States. Overall, however, research considering fit in the field of emergency response personnel is limited.

As a theory applied to all forms of fit in the workplace, person-environment fit crosses different levels of analysis, as researchers investigate fit between an individual and his or her job, between an individual and his or her team, or between an individual and his or her organization. Cross-level relationships suggest multilevel phenomena are at play, and at the intermediate level between the individual members of the organization and the organization itself, the team represents an optimum point for investigation of multilevel phenomena (Kozlowski, Chao, Grand, Braun, and Kuljanin, 2013). Because research identifies stronger relationships when examining relationships at the same level of analysis (individual characteristics and individual outcomes, or organizational characteristics and organizational outcomes), we need to consider a team-level construct that captures the team's collective perception of team fit to identify effects at the team level (Klein and Kozlowski, 2000; Kristof-Brown, Zimmerman et al., 2005). In other words, person-environment fit fundamentally focuses on an individual characteristic with individual-level consequences, but collective fit, as we propose here, describes a team-level characteristic that demonstrates team-level consequences. Our conceptualization of collective fit thus refers to a team-level characteristic that is consistent with the form and nature of person-environment fit.

Collective Fit

To lay a foundation for developing our model of collective fit, we now step aside to discuss the structure and nature of multilevel models in organizational research. Multilevel models must specify functional relationships among constructs at the various levels of analysis, indicate the nature of the higher-level construct, and identify how the construct should be measured (Chan, 1998; Klein and Kozlowski, 2000). Because of this, special attention to both the form of fit (such as person-job, person-group, and person-organization) and the measurement of fit at different levels is essential.

In general, the level of analysis investigated is a function of the structure of the organization studied, as typically found in businesses, schools, and military. For example, individual firefighters are grouped within specific work groups and assigned to a particular station that is part of a larger district, county, and region within the state. This distinction is especially salient to the study of person-environment fit as the construct itself is cross-level because it describes relationships between individuals and some aspect of their work environment (such as job, team, or organization). Outcomes relevant to the total work experience (e.g. tenure or intent to quit) are more likely influenced across levels and through multiple forms of fit (Kristof-Brown, Zimmerman, et al., 2005).

Thus, our model of collective fit builds on processes occurring at multiple levels that contribute to team outcomes. The two fundamental processes of interest to our model are 1) top-down contextual forces arising from the organization and task environment and 2) bottom-up forces arising from interactions within the team (Kozlowski et al., 2013) and individual perceptions of fit with the group. *Top-down forces* include the effects of organizational policies and procedures, organizational structure, or individual reward systems on the team (Schneider, 1987). For example, organizational cultures differ based on the unique

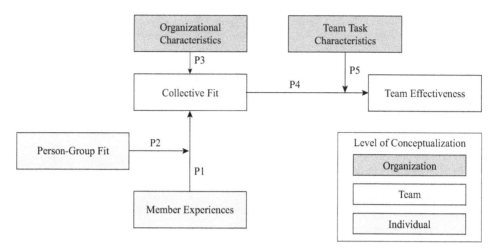

Figure 5.1 Multilevel Model of Collective Fit

characteristics, behaviors, and shared values of the organizational members. The organizational culture would represent a top-down force that influences norms of teamwork within a team. In emergency service and response organizations, a command-and-control culture would be one example that influenced how leadership at the station or equipment level might be enacted. *Bottom-up forces* include the effects on the team from interactions between individuals within the team (Schneider, 1987). For instance, when firefighters work a consistent shift, over time, the repeated interactions with the other emergency responders who work the same shift may introduce similarities in behaviors or attitudes among all members of that shift (such as food and exercise choices or attitudes about the community). We demonstrate the complexity of both top-down and bottom-up forces on team functioning in our multilevel model of collective fit (Figure 5.1).

To explain our model and distinguish between person-group fit and collective fit, we first examine the theoretical foundation that supports collective fit as an emergent state in teams. Second, we explore the bottom-up processes that influence the emergence of collective fit. Third, we investigate the top-down organizational characteristics that affect the development of collective fit in teams. Finally, we examine outcomes of collective fit and how task characteristics may moderate the relationship between collective fit and team effectiveness outcomes.

The Emergence of Collective Fit

Researchers focused on groups and teams leverage several theoretically important factors in order to shed light on the types of issues that we are studying in this chapter. These factors include the level of analysis, the role of time, process mechanisms, and contextual constraints and influences (Kozlowski et al., 2013). The first three of these describe the dynamic interactions that occur in teams that give rise to team processes and shared team characteristics. Specifically, emergent processes and characteristics of the team develop into *emergent states* over time and are influenced by individual, team, and organizational characteristics and behaviors (see Figure 5.2; Kozlowski et al., 2013). Contextual constraints and characteristics that influence group outcomes are discussed later in the chapter. For now, we discuss three key influencers of the emergence of collective fit.

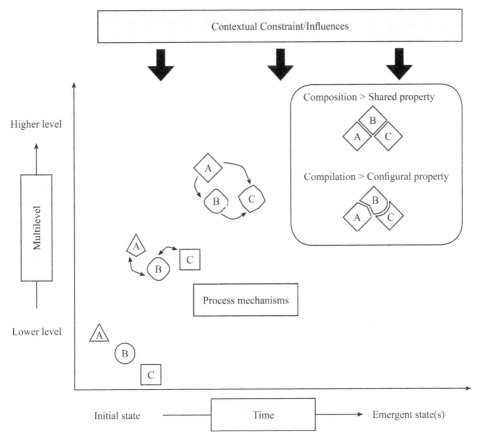

Figure 5.2 Key Influencers of Emergent States (Kozlowski et al., 2013)

Emergent team phenomena may be *multilevel* if they encompass at least two different levels of analysis, with one level indicating where the process originates and the second level indicating where the outcomes manifest. For example, an emergent state that starts at the team level could manifest as a new organizational structure at the department, district, or regional level. Additionally, contextual effects from the organization or region in which the team operates may affect the development of team characteristics and phenomena. For instance, teams may develop an overall emotional state, or group affective tone, influenced by both individual-level team member characteristics and organizational-level norms that regulate appropriate emotional expression (Woods, 2016). In this example, group affective tone is a team-level characteristic that influences team effectiveness above and beyond the effect of individual emotions on team outcomes.

Emergent states are *temporal* in that recurrent patterns of interactions at a lower level contribute to more-or-less stable higher-level phenomena (Kozlowski and Klein, 2000). The time required for emergence may be very brief or very long, depending on the phenomenon of interest and other contextual effects. For example, specialized teams that form to address a specific mission or crisis response with clearly defined individual roles may require minimal time for the emergence of team cohesion. In contrast, product development teams may need longer periods of time to develop distinct team-level characteristics because of the learning processes required to understand how team member's expertise can support long-term project objectives. In other words, specific circumstances at all levels (i.e. individual, group, department, and organization) influence the timing of emergence.

Emergent states also can be the result of team processes that are driven by characteristics of team members (Kozlowski and Klein, 2000), and identified through the composition or compilation of individual attributes into a team-level phenomenon (see Figure 5.2). The compositional approach suggests that team processes drive the convergence of similar individual characteristics to form a team-level property that is essentially the same (in nature) as the underlying components. This process mechanism leads to a *shared team property* (i.e. structure). Compositional, or shared, properties are measured by adding together or averaging individual team member characteristics (e.g. "I like to socialize with my team") to generate a value for a team-level characteristic. It can also be measured by asking team members to evaluate a team-level characteristic (for instance, "our team likes to socialize together"; Chan, 1998; Klein and Kozlowski, 2000).

Combining different individual properties into a team-level property of similar function (Kozlowski and Klein, 2000) is the compilational, or configural, approach to forming team phenomena. For example, a wide range of different individual emergency response experiences would emerge as a new shared team-level experience property. One team member might have extensive experience in commercial fire response, while another has experience in dealing with hazardous materials, while yet another comes from a forest fire response background. Thus, we may describe the team as having a broad, versus narrow, experience background, which provides a broader range of knowledge and experience for the team to draw on in a specific emergency response. Team experience background becomes a *configural team property*, which is a team characteristic that emerges due to variability, rather than similarity, within a group (Klein and Kozlowski, 2000; Seong, Kristof-Brown, Park, Hong, and Shin, 2015). Unlike shared properties, configural team properties are indicated by the diversity or spread of team member attributes (measured by range or variability).

The Role of Shared Experiences on the Emergence of Collective Fit

As with many other team phenomena, collective fit emerges over time through the repeated interactions of team members, ultimately resulting in a team-level characteristic of fit that contains both shared and configural properties (Kristof-Brown et al., 2014). Collective fit develops as team members spend time together – working through tasks, facing challenges, establishing group norms, and reflecting on past performance. While an individual team member may feel he or she fits well with the team, collective fit shifts the focus of perceptions of group fit to the team. Specifically, even if individual team members feel confident in their abilities to perform their job function, this does not imply that team members collectively believe their team is up to the demands of the team's job.

Similar to the multidimensionality of person-group fit, collective fit is also multidimensional. Supplementary fit has its analog in shared team properties, while complementary fit is analogous to configural team properties. Shared and configural team properties contribute to a shared sense of compatibility within the team and confidence in the match between the team and the team's organizational and task environment (DeRue and Hollenbeck, 2007; Kristof-Brown et al., 2014). Shared properties represent the overall composition of the team regarding experiences, values, or characteristics held in common by all team members (Klein and Kozlowski, 2000; Seong et al., 2015). Team members can share personality characteristics; for instance, emergency response teams tend to be composed of individuals who are more excitement-seeking than the norm (Salters-Pedneault, Ruef and Orr, 2010). Also, standardized training and educational requirements exist that all team members must go through, such as a fire academy or passing the state EMT licensing exam. Thus, all members of an emergency response team share a common educational background; even if they did not participate in training at the same time. Common job experiences over which everyone can bond may also be shared. For instance, members of the team have experienced, at different times, responding to a barking dog call or assisting with a drug overdose victim. On the other hand, configural properties emerge from individual team member characteristics that are diverse, yet functionally similar. For example, one team member has experience with high-rise fires and another team member may have extensive experience in residential fires, but the experiences of both members contribute to the team's ability to address crisis situations confidently as knowledge is shared (Seong et al., 2015). Through repeated interactions with other members of the team, these common and unique experiences are recognized by the team as a whole, and add to the team's repertoire of experience. Therefore, a group's repertoire of experience is not only a collection of events that the team experiences together, but is also a collection of separate individual experiences. In other words, each member's distinct experiences contribute to team experience, measured as the range of experiences held by the team (Kozlowski and Klein, 2000).

Consistent with this discussion, both shared and configural properties in the context of collective fit contribute to a team-level perception of fit within the team and between the team and its task and organizational environment. Shared properties develop from the team's assessment of how well the team fits together in terms of personality, shared values, and experiences (a measure of supplementary fit), whereas configural properties develop as the team experiences outcomes enhanced by their different experiences and skills (a measure of complementary fit). Our conceptualization of collective fit further expands the construct of collective fit as a team-level emergent state, indicated by its shared and configural team properties, and separate from aggregated person-group fit perceptions.

In summary, building on earlier models of team-level collective fit (Kristof-Brown et al., 2014), we suggest that collective fit emerges over time through shared and divergent experiences within the team, which is consistent with the nature of emergence. The nature of collective fit as a higher-order construct represented by the team's shared and configural properties is in line with the conceptualization of person-environment fit, discussed earlier (Kozlowski et al., 2013; Seong and Kristof-Brown, 2012). Therefore, collective fit originates with individual team member level characteristics and experiences, but becomes apparent as a team-level phenomenon. Collective fit occurs when the team integrates over time shared and unique team member experiences and characteristics.

Proposition 1: Collective fit represents an emergent state that manifests at the team level through processes of shared and individual experiences over time.

The Role of Person-Group Fit on the Emergence of Collective Fit

In addition to being influenced by shared and divergent member experiences, the development of collective fit in a team may also be influenced by each individual team member's perception of his or her fit with the group. Person-group fit refers to interpersonal compatibility between employees and their work groups (Kristof-Brown et al., 2014), and describes how an individual's characteristics interact with those of other team members (known as interpersonal compatibility) to predict individual-level outcomes (Kristof-Brown, Zimmerman, et al., 2005). An example of this may occur with a new firefighter, as he or she may feel that he or she does not fit with the more experienced members of their team. A recent meta-analysis indicated significant relationships between person-group fit and several workplace outcomes, such as increased job satisfaction, coworker satisfaction, supervisor satisfaction, contextual performance, and reduced intention to quit (Kristof-Brown, Zimmerman, et al., 2005). Subsequent person-group research has found relationships between goals congruence (i.e. supplementary fit; Kristof-Brown and Stevens, 2001) and perceptions of fit among team members (i.e. complementary fit; Kristof-Brown, Barrick, and Stevens, 2005) with team satisfaction, work satisfaction, and team performance.

As mentioned previously, shared and distinctive member experiences contribute to the emergence of a team-level collective fit. Individual perceptions of fit with the group may influence how strong these effects are. Having shared and distinctive experiences may be only part of the story. Overall levels of person-group fit perceptions may be just as or more important than shared experiences (Seong and Kristof-Brown, 2012). When team members feel they fit with the team, they are more likely to discuss their experiences and to learn from the experiences of other team members. Referring back to the new firefighter, he or she may be more likely to learn from the experiences of more-seasoned veterans if he or she feels he or she is a good fit with the group in other ways. Given that person-group fit is an individual-level perception, we propose that the emergence of collective fit, arising from shared and individual experience, is facilitated by the level of homogeneity of perceptions of person-group fit held by members of the team.

Proposition 2: Homogeneity of person-group fit strengthens the effects of shared and individual member experiences on the emergence of collective fit.

The Influence of the Organizational Environment on the Emergence of Collective Fit

To continue building our multilevel model of collective fit, we now turn to the embeddedness of teams in organizational environments that set constraints on team functioning (Kozlowski and Ilgen, 2006). Technology, structure, reward systems, organizational culture, and leadership represent various aspects of the organizational environment that influence team processes (DeRue and Hollenbeck, 2007; Kozlowski and Ilgen, 2006). For example, the fit of technology to the tasks performed by a team has demonstrated both positive and negative relationships with team performance (Fuller and Dennis, 2008). Fuller and Dennis (2008) demonstrated that, poor fit between task and technology initially reduced team effectiveness; however, after a few days, team performance improved as the team adapted to the technology. This can be seen when a new piece of equipment is introduced to a station; it takes time to figure out how the equipment will work with the station's existing skillsets.

Organizational structure also constrains team effectiveness; for example, divisionally structured teams with broadly based roles may perform better than functionally structured teams with narrowly defined roles when the task requires adaptive or creative problem solving (Hollenbeck et al., 2002). Another organizational characteristic, reward systems, influences team effectiveness. Team-based reward systems appear to be more effective in teams that have interdependent work styles and task environments (Beersma, Hollenbeck, Humphrey, Moon, Conlon, and Ilgen 2003). When emergency response teams are rewarded as a team on successful calls, this may motivate members of the team to engage in fewer freelancing behaviors. Organizational culture, as the collection of assumptions held by an organization or group (Schein, 1990), is another environmental characteristic that has demonstrated positive relationships with organizational and individual outcomes (Barney, 1986), as well as with team outcomes (King, 2002). For instance, when organizational members perceived that their values align with the values of their organization, they demonstrated higher levels of satisfaction and commitment (Ostroff, Shin, and Kinicki, 2005). These relationships held true when the individuals perceived a fit between their preferences and organizational culture (O'Reilly III, Chatman, and Caldwell, 1991).

Finally, leadership demonstrates a role in outcomes of person-organization fit such that group-focused transformational leadership behaviors contribute to group effectiveness when group members perceive a congruence in values with the organization (Hoffman, Bynum, Piccolo, and Sutton, 2011). Research has demonstrated the contextual effect of leadership in work teams, such that negative and positive outcomes result depending on whether leader behaviors were directed toward individual team members differentially or toward the workgroup as a whole (Jiang, Gu, and Wang, 2014). Even leaders' moods have been found to influence team effectiveness in relationships between the mood of the leader and the moods of team members as well as overall team performance (Volmer, 2012).

In summary, the organization influences the team in various ways: technology can help or hinder team performance, structure can strengthen or weaken team effectiveness, reward systems can support or hinder team-focused behaviors, organizational culture can enhance or undermine a focus on the team, and leadership can foster or hinder team outcomes. These examples demonstrate that a given set of organizational practices that fit in one type of task, context, or team may not necessarily fit with a different task, context, or team (DeRue and Hollenbeck, 2007).

The influence of the organizational context on the emergence of collective fit relies on the same underlying mechanism as person-environment fit at the individual level. As stated earlier, perceived fit at the individual level might be present in a job environment that provides resources wanted by the person, a person who provides abilities required by the job environment, a situation where the person and organization share fundamental characteristics, or any combination of these. Collective fit, built on individual team member's perceptions of their fit with the team, is a compilation of all the team member's perception of fit plus a team-level perception of fit. The team perception of fit also arises in a work environment that provides resources wanted by the team, a team ability to meet demands required by the environment, a situation where the team and the environment share fundamental characteristics, or a combination of these. When teams are embedded in organizations that demonstrate an appreciation for effective teamwork through appropriate reward systems and structure, teams may feel more confident in their ability to supply the necessary skills and experience to support the needs of the organization. Additionally, leaders who create a culture of excellence in teamwork may give rise to teams that feel an overall positive fit with the demands of the organization. Thus, realizing that the organizational environment influences the development of collective fit, we suggest the following proposition.

Proposition 3: The organizational environment influences the emergence of collective fit.

Outcomes of Collective Fit

Team effectiveness is a global concept that relates to outcomes of teamwork composed of multiple factors. Organizations and researchers evaluate team effectiveness by objective and subjective indicators of individual outcomes, group outcomes, and organizational outcomes (Cohen and Bailey, 1997; Mathieu, Maynard, Rapp, and Gilson, 2008). For instance, emergency response organizations may measure station effectiveness by the number of calls responded to with successful outcomes or the number of near-miss incidents reported.

Near-miss incidents may arise from unsuccessful team coordination or team member behaviors that jeopardize the outcomes of emergency calls.

Team effectiveness outcomes are influenced by team coordination and interpersonal processes that convert task, individual, group, and organizational characteristics into team effectiveness outcomes (Mathieu et al., 2008). Important for our purposes, collective fit is likely to drive useful team coordination and interpersonal processes. Such fit is likely to create commitment to the productivity and safety of teammates, as well as commitment to the overall success of the team. Although sparse, prior research related to collective fit suggests that such fit is a team-level characteristic that contributes to team effectiveness through psychosocial team processes (Kristof-Brown et al., 2014).

Proposition 4: Collective fit demonstrates positive relationships with objective and subjective measures of team effectiveness.

The Role of the Team Task Environment on the Outcomes of Collective Fit

We have discussed how members of a team and the organization influence the development of collective fit, and propose that collective fit has a positive relationship with team effectiveness outcomes. However, what about the role of the team task environment? In all types of teams, the nature of the team task environment influences team processes and outcomes (Salas, Stagl, Burke, and Goodwin, 2007). As such, potential role ambiguity, time constraints, and the unknown aspects of the team's task characterize the nature of the team task environment and determines the primary focus of team member activities (DeRue and Hollenbeck, 2007).

The team task environment becomes even more important for emergency response teams that function in uncertain and potentially hazardous conditions. In addition to the environmental factors such as the specific culture or climate of the agency in which they work, there are concerns about situations in which emergency response personnel place themselves. These situational demands (Kozlowski and Ilgen, 2006) may add to or detract from a team's performance. Further, highly interdependent tasks may inhibit team performance if there is ambiguity in roles and responsibilities among members of the team (Campion, Medsker, and Higgs, 1993). This role and responsibility ambiguity may also negatively influence multiteam situations with shared roles. Because task ambiguity causes stress and dysfunction, it can interfere with the generally positive effects of collective fit on team effectiveness. For instance, multiple emergency management services (EMS) teams arriving at a multi-incident crisis scene may waste time, resources, and potentially cost human lives if there are no protocols to define which teams are responsible for different areas of the incident.

Time constraints may also play a role in reducing the normally positive effects of collective fit on team performance. Emergency response situations require quick action on the part of emergency responders. This need for quick action may cause some team members to jump in, especially when lives are at stake. The act of improvising a response without feedback from team members is known as freelancing and may be dangerous to the team (Bigley and Roberts, 2001). If not successful, freelancing as a result of time constraints negatively affects the team by subverting the role of the team to the actions of the individual (Bigley and Roberts, 2001).

Unknown aspects of the team's task also have the potential to moderate the link between collective fit and effectiveness. For example, although decked with appropriate gear and equipped with extensive training to minimize physical risk, there are still task characteristics that are out of the control of emergency response teams by the nature of their work. Even in a well-contained house fire, there could be hidden structural damage or the presence of explosive materials such as bullets. Even with plenty of police backup, there could be another suspect somewhere in the immediate area. Due to these unknowns and the potentially dangerous environments, it becomes even more important for responders to be able to trust their team and feel as though the team is a cohesive unit. Thus, uncertainty and ambiguity likely influence the linkage between collective fit and team outcomes.

Based on this reasoning, we suggest the following proposition to capture the role of task characteristics.

Proposition 5: Task characteristics moderate the relationship between collective fit and team effectiveness outcomes.

Concluding Remarks

While individual contributions to team functioning will always be essential and primary, team-level collective fit provides an essential contribution to team effectiveness. In our multilevel model of collective fit, "we wish both to understand the whole and keep an eye on the parts" (Kozlowski and Klein, 2000, p. 54).

In this chapter, we have examined person-group fit and the emergence of collective fit as a team-level latent construct manifested in shared and configural team properties. As a reflection of team member characteristics, collective fit offers a way to measure team members' perceptions of team fit and the team's fit with its environment. We suggest that collective fit is an emergent team-level state that develops over time and through shared experiences among team members. Collective fit also contributes uniquely to the effectiveness of teams, over and above the influence of combined team member person-group fit (Kristof-Brown et al., 2014). Emergency response teams working together through tasks, challenges, and events represent the shared and divergent experiences of the team, and these shared events are suggested as the primary processes in which collective fit emerges (Kozlowski et al., 2013). Individual member's perception of person-group fit and contextual effects from organizational environments also influence the emergence of collective fit. Additionally, task characteristics may moderate the relationship between collective fit and team outcomes.

Our overriding purpose was to propose a multilevel model of collective fit, including contributing individual-level factors, the influence of external organizational and team task factors, and the potential for contributing to team effectiveness. Recent empirical findings have brought team-level collective fit to the forefront of team dynamics research. Essentially, this team-level construct has been found to be related to both team- and individual-level outcomes over and above relationships found by examining team member's characteristics individually (Kristof-Brown et al., 2014). Using collective fit as our focal construct, our multilevel model proposes factors affecting the emergence of, moderators to, and outcomes of collective fit for teams, with a focus on emergency response teams. Our model adds to previous ideas related to the origins of collective fit, and to ideas related to how collective fit influences team effectiveness.

To build our model, we identified the emergency response team as a unique type of team. Effective teamwork within emergency response teams has high-stakes consequences focused on preventing human pain and suffering, and in the protection of private property as well as human lives, making the benefits of good team fit even more important. Although some translation may be necessary, our work provides a model that emergency management leaders and administrators can use to strengthen the development of collective fit in emergency response teams. For example, emergency management leaders may focus on team building within emergency response teams to foster a sense of shared identity and perception of team fit with the team's environment. Emergency management leaders may also act as guardians, protecting the team from organizational factors that could negatively impact the emergence of collective fit and its outcomes. Emergency management administrators responsible for decisions about selection processes, training, and resource allocation may utilize our model to support their decisions.

In summary, this chapter and our model provide a foundation for exploring team effectiveness outcomes associated with the dynamic and synergistic combination of team collective fit and team member group fit. Additionally, the ability to examine both individual and collective contributions simultaneously enables identification of individual, team, task, and organizational factors as well as their relative importance for team outcomes. The ability to identify those factors that contribute to overall team effectiveness will make for stronger emergency response teams and more consistent success in emergency and crisis responses.

Acknowledgement

Authors would like to extend an acknowledgment to colleague Anastasia Miller, for her helpful comments and feedback during early development of this chapter.

References

Archer, David. 1999. "Exploring "Bullying" Culture in the Para-military Organisation." *International Journal of Manpower* 20 (1/2): 94–105. doi:10.1108/01437729910268687.

Barney, Jay B. 1986. "Organizational Culture: Can It Be a Source of Sustained Competitive Advantage?" *Academy of Management Review* 11 (3): 656–665. doi:10.5465/AMR.1986.4306261.

Beersma, Bianca, John R. Hollenbeck, Stephen E. Humphrey, Henry Moon, Donald E. Conlon, and Daniel R. Ilgen. 2003. "Cooperation, Competition, and Team Performance: Toward a Contingency Approach." *Academy of Management Journal* 46 (5): 572–590. www.jstor.org/stable/30040650.

Bigley, Gregory A., and Karlene H. Roberts. 2001. "The Incident Command System: High-Reliability Organizing for Complex and Volatile Task Environments." *Academy of Management Journal* 44 (6): 1281–1299. doi: 10.2307/3069401.

Cable, Daniel M., and D. Scott DeRue. 2002. "The Convergent and Discriminant Validity of Subjective Fit Perceptions." *Journal of Applied Psychology* 87 (5): 875–884. doi:10.1037/0021–9010.87.5.875.

Caplan, Robert D. 1987. "Person-Environment Fit Theory and Organizations: Commensurate Dimensions, Time Perspectives, and Mechanisms." *Journal of Vocational Behavior* 31 (3): 248–267. doi:10.1016/0001–8791(87)90042-X.

Campion, Michael A., Gina J. Medsker, and A. Catherine Higgs. 1993. "Relations between Work Group Characteristics and Effectiveness: Implications for Designing Effective Work Groups." *Personnel Psychology* 46 (4; winter): 823–847. doi:10.1111/j.1744–6570.1993.tb01571.x.

Carless, Sally A. 2005. "The Influence of Fit Perceptions, Equal Opportunity Policies, and Social Support Network on Pre-entry Police Officer Career Commitment and Intentions to Remain." *Journal of Criminal Justice* 33 (4): 341–352. doi:10.1016/j.jcrimjus.2005.04.004.

Chan, David. 1998. "Functional Relations among Constructs in the Same Content Domain at Different Levels of Analysis: A Typology of Composition Models." *Journal of Applied Psychology* 83 (2): 234–246. doi:10.1037/0021–9010.83.2.234.

Cohen, Susan G., and Diane E. Bailey. 1997. "What Makes Teams Work : Group Effectiveness Research from the Shop Floor to the Executive Suite." *Journal of Management* 23 (3): 239–290. doi:10.1177/014920639702300303.

Colquitt, Jason A., Jeffery A. LePine, Cindy P. Zapata, and R. Eric Wild. 2011. "Trust in Typical and High-Reliability Contexts: Building and Reacting to Trust among Firefighters." *Academy of Management Journal* 54 (5): 999–1015. doi:10.5465/amj.2006.0241.

Davis, Eric. A., and Vincent N. Mosesso. 1998. "Performance of Police First Responders in Utilizing Automated External Defibrillation on Victims of Sudden Cardiac Arrest." *Prehospital Emergency Care* 2 (2): 101–107. doi:10.1080/10903129808958851.

DeRue, D. Scott, and John R. Hollenbeck. 2007. "The Search for Internal and External Fit in Teams." In *Perspectives on Organizational Fit*, edited by Cheryl Ostroff and Timothy A. Judge, 259–285. New York: Lawrence Erlbaum Associates. doi:10.4324/9780203810026.

Edwards, Jeffrey R., and R. Van Harrison. 1993. "Job Demands and Worker Health: Three-Dimensional Reexamination of the Relationship between Person-Environment Fit and Strain." *Journal of Applied Psychology* 78 (4): 628–648. doi:10.1037/0021–9010.78.4.628.

French, John R. P., Robert D. Caplan, and R. Van Harrison. 1982. *The Mechanisms of Job Stress and Strain*. Chichester, UK: Wiley.

Fuller, Robert M., and Alan R. Dennis. 2008. "Does Fit Matter? The Impact of Task-Technology Fit and Appropriation on Team Performance in Repeated Tasks." *Information Systems Research* 20 (1): 2–17. http://pubsonline.informs.org/doi/abs/10.1287/isre.1070.0167.

Harrison, R. Van. 1978. "Person-Environment Fit and Job Stress." In *Stress at Work*, edited by Cary L. Cooper and R. Payne, 23–55. New York: John Wiley & Sons.

Hoffman, Brian J., Bethany H. Bynum, Ronald F. Piccolo, and Ashley W. Sutton. 2011. "Person-Organization Value Congruence: How Transformational Leaders Influence Work Group Effectiveness." *Academy of Management Journal* 54 (4): 779–796. http://amj.aom.org/content/54/4/779.abstract.

Hollenbeck, John R., Henry Moon, Aleksander P. J. Ellis, Bradley J. West, Daniel R. Ilgen, Lori Sheppard, Christopher O. L. H Porter, and John A. Wagner III. 2002. "Structural Contingency Theory and Individual Differences: Examination of External and Internal Person-Team Fit." *Journal of Applied Psychology* 87 (3): 599–606. doi:10.1037/0021–9010.87.3.599.

Ingram, Jason R. 2013. "Supervisor-Officer Fit and Role Ambiguity Attitudinal Relationship." *Policing: An International Journal of Police Strategies & Management* 36 (2): 375–398. doi:10.1108/13639511311329750.

Jehn, Karen A., and Pirathat Techakesari. 2014. "High Reliability Teams: New Directions for Disaster Management and Conflict." *International Journal of Conflict Management* 25 (4): 407–430. doi:10.1108/IJCMA-02–2014–0019.

Jiang, Wan, Qinxuan Gu, and Greg G. Wang. 2014. "To Guide or to Divide: The Dual-Side Effects of Transformational Leadership on Team Innovation." *Journal of Business and Psychology* 30 (4): 677–691. https://link.springer.com/article/10.1007/s10869-014-9395-0.

King, Granville. 2002. "Crisis Management & Team Effectiveness: A Closer Examination." *Journal of Business Ethics* 41 (3): 235–249. https://link.springer.com/article/10.1023/A:1021200514323.

Klee, Stephanie, and Karl-Heinz Renner. 2013. "In Search of the 'Rescue Personality'. A Questionnaire Study with Emergency Medical Services Personnel." *Personality and Individual Differences* 54 (5): 669–672. doi:10.1016/j.paid.2012.11.006.

Klein, Katherine J., and Steve W. J. Kozlowski. 2000. "From Micro to Meso: Critical Steps in Conceptualizing and Conducting Multilevel Research." *Organizational Research Methods* 3 (3): 211–236. doi:10.1177/109442810033001.

Kozlowski, Steve W. J., and Bradford S. Bell. 2013. "Work Groups and Teams in Organizations." In *Handbook of Psychology, Volume 12, Industrial and Organizational Psychology, 2nd Edition*, edited by Irving B. Weiner, Neal W. Schmitt, and Scott Highhouse, 412–469. Hoboken, NJ: John Wiley & Sons, Inc. www.wiley.com/WileyCDA/WileyTitle/productCd-0470768878.html.

Kozlowski, Steve W. J., Georgia T. Chao, James A. Grand, Michael T. Braun, and Goran Kuljanin. 2013. "Advancing Multilevel Research Design: Capturing the Dynamics of Emergence." *Organizational Research Methods* 16 (4): 581–615. http://orm.sagepub.com/content/16/4/581.abstract.

Kozlowski, Steve. W. J., and Daniel R. Ilgen. 2006. "Enhancing the Effectiveness of Work Groups and Teams." *Psychological Science in the Public Interest* 7 (3): 77–124. doi:10.1111/j.1529-1006.2006.00030.x.

Kozlowski, Steve W. J., and Katherine J. Klein. 2000. "A Multilevel Approach to Theory and Research in Organizations: Contextual, Temporal, and Emergent Processes." In *Multilevel Theory, Research, and Methods in Organizations: Foundations, Extensions, and New Directions*, edited by Katherine J. Klein and Steve W. J. Kozlowski, 3–90. San Francisco, CA: Jossey-Bass, Inc.

Kristof-Brown, Amy, Murray R. Barrick, and Cynthia Kay Stevens. 2005. "When Opposites Attract: A Multi-Sample Demonstration of Complementary Person-Team Fit on Extraversion." *Journal of Personality* 73 (4): 935–957. doi:10.1111/j.1467–6494.2005.00334.x.

Kristof-Brown, Amy, and Russell P. Guay. 2011. "Person–environment Fit." In *APA Handbook of Industrial and Organizational Psychology, Vol 3: Maintaining, Expanding, and Contracting the Organization.*, edited by Sheldon Zedeck, 3–50. Washington, DC: American Psychological Association. doi:10.1037/12171-001.

Kristof-Brown, Amy L., Jee Young Seong, David S. Degeest, Won-Woo Park, and Doo-Seung Hong. 2014. "Collective Fit Perceptions: A Multilevel Investigation of Person-Group Fit with Individual-Level and Team-Level Outcomes." *Journal of Organizational Behavior* 35 (7): 969–989. doi:10.1002/job.1942.

Kristof-Brown, Amy L., and Cynthia Kay Stevens. 2001. "Goal Congruence in Project Teams: Does the Fit between Members' Personal Mastery and Performance Goals Matter?" *Journal of Applied Psychology* 86 (6): 1083–1095. doi:10.1037/0021–9010.86.6.1083.

Kristof-Brown, Amy L., Ryan D. Zimmerman, and Erin C. Johnson. 2005. "Consequences of Individuals' Fit at Work: A Meta-Analysis of Person-Job, Person-Organization, Person-Group, and Person-Supervisor Fit." *Personnel Psychology* 58 (2): 281–342. doi:10.1111/j.1744–6570.2005.00672.x.

Lawler, Edward E. 1973. *Motivation in Work Organizations.* Monterey, CA: Brooks/Cole Pub. Co.

Lewin, Kurt. 1951. *Field Theory in Social Science.* New York: Harper & Row.

Mathieu, John, M. Travis Maynard, Tammy Rapp, and Lucy Gilson. 2008. "Team Effectiveness 1997–2007: A Review of Recent Advancements and a Glimpse into the Future." *Journal of Management* 34 (3): 410–476. doi:10.1177/0149206308316061.

Muchinsky, Paul M., and Carlyn J. Monahan. 1987. "What Is Person-Environment Congruence? Supplementary versus Complementary Models of Fit." *Journal of Vocational Behavior* 31 (3): 268–277. doi:10.1016/0001–8791(87)90043-1.

"Operation Dispatch." Operation Dispatch. 2012. Accessed July 18, 2017. www.myfloridacfo.com/division/sfm/OperationDispatch.htm.

O'Reilly III, Charles A., Jennifer Chatman, and David F. Caldwell. 1991. "People and Organizational Culture: A Profile Comparison Approach to Assessing Person-Organization Fit." *Academy of Management Journal* 34 (3): 487–516.

Ostroff, Cheri, Yuhyung Shin, and Angelo J. Kinicki. 2005. "Multiple Perspectives of Congruence: Relationships between Value Congruence and Employee Attitudes." *Journal of Organizational Behavior* 26 (6): 591–623.

Ryan, Ann Marie, and Robert E. Ployhart. 2000. "Applicants' Perceptions of Selection Procedures and Decisions: A Critical Review and Agenda for the Future." *Journal of Management* 26 (3): 565–606. doi:10.1177/014920630002600308.

Salas, Eduardo, Kevin C. Stagl, C. Shawn Burke, and Gerald F. Goodwin. 2007. "Fostering Team Effectiveness in Organizations: Toward an Integrative Theoretical Framework." In *Modeling Complex Systems*, edited by B. Shuart, W. Spaulding and J. Poland. Nebraska Symposium on Motivation, 185–243. Lincoln: University of Nebraska Press.

Salters-Pedneault, Kristalyn, Anna M. Ruef, and Scott P. Orr. 2010. "Personality and Psychophysiological Profiles of Police Officer and Firefighter Recruits." *Personality and Individual Differences* 49 (3): 210–215. doi:10.1016/j.paid.2010.03.037.

Schantz, April D. 2018. "Impact of Person-Environment Fit upon Strain and Well-Being for Emergency Responders." PhD diss., Florida International University.

Schein, Edgar. H. 1990. "Organizational Culture." *American Psychologist* 45 (2): 109–119. doi:10.1037/0003–066X.45.2.109.

Schneider, Benjamin. 1987. "The People Make the Place." *Personnel Psychology* 40 (3): 437–453. doi:10.1111/j.1744–6570.1987.tb00609.x.

Schneider, Benjamin. 2001. "Fits about Fit." *Applied Psychology-An International Review* 50 (1): 141–152. doi:10.1111/1464–0597.00051.

Seong, Jee Young, Amy L. Kristof-Brown, Won-Woo Park, Doo-Seung Hong, and Yuhyung Shin. 2015. "Person-Group Fit." *Journal of Management* 41 (4): 1184–1213. doi:10.1177/0149206312453738.

Seong, Jee Young, and Amy L. Kristof-Brown. 2012. "Testing Multidimensional Models of Person-group Fit." *Journal of Managerial Psychology* 27 (6): 536–556. doi:10.1108/02683941211252419.

Shackford, Steven R., Peggy Hollingsworth-Fridlund, Maureen Mcardle, and A. B. Eastman. 1987. "Assuring Quality in a Trauma System-the Medical Audit Committee: Composition, Cost, and Results." *Journal of Trauma and Acute Care Surgery* 27 (8): 866–875. www.ncbi.nlm.nih.gov/pubmed/3612863.

Sinclair, Helen, Emma E. H. Doyle, David M. Johnston, and Douglas Paton. 2013. "The Use of Emergency Operations Centres in Local Government Emergency Management Government Emergency Management." *International Journal of Emergency Management* 9 (3): 205–228. doi:10.1504/IJEM.2013.058542.

Subramaniam, Chandrakantan, Hassan Ali, and Faridahwati Mohd Shamsudin. 2010. "Understanding the Antecedents of Emergency Response: A Proposed Framework." *Disaster Prevention and Management: An International Journal* 19 (5): 571–581. doi:10.1108/09653561011091904.

Volmer, Judith. 2012, "Catching Leaders' Mood: Contagion Effects in Teams." *Administrative Sciences* 2 (3): 203–220. doi:10.3390/admsci2030203.

Weick, Karl E. 1993. "The Collapse of Sensemaking in Organizations: The Mann Gulch Disaster." *Administrative Science Quarterly* 38 (4): 628–652.

Woods, Juanita M. 2016. "The Role of Group Affective Tone in Shaping Outcomes of Team-Focused Leadership." Ph.D. dissertation, Florida Atlantic University, Boca Raton, FL.

Worrall, John L., and Jihong Zhao. 2003. "The Role of the COPS Office in Community Policing." *Policing: An International Journal of Police Strategies & Management* 26 (1): 64–87. doi:10.1108/13639510310460305.

PART III

Theoretical Viewpoints and Methods

6

RISK, CRISIS AND ORGANIZATIONAL FAILURE

Toward a Post-rationalist View

Thomas D. Beamish

Introduction

Underneath an isolated oil field on California's windswept central coast sits the second largest petroleum spill in the U.S. history. At more than 20 (or more) million gallons, the Guadalupe Dunes spill was recognized in 1990 after 38 years of spillage; it was a known yet unacknowledged problem for much of that time. Unlike the massive oil spills that ensconce it on a list of the U.S.'s largest—the Deepwater Horizon platform blowout and the Exxon Valdez tanker spill—the Guadalupe Dunes spill is little known because it was neither acute nor dramatic (Beamish 2002a: 3). Dubbed the "Silent Spill" in local press accounts, the ongoing spillage was familiar to the oil field workers where it originated, to regulators who frequented the Dunes, and locals who visited the adjacent ocean beach, even though it went unadmitted as an "oil spill." Until the late 1980s, the common petroleum sheens that formed on the nearby Santa Maria River and the Pacific Ocean raised little concern (Beamish 2002b). An oil field worker's call would set the state's regulatory apparatus in motion. Yet, response to the spill would soon become an interorganizational headache for 18 federal, state, and local regulators; a $300 million-dollar problem for Unocal Corporation (the spiller); and a sore spot for community members who no longer trusted any of the involved organizations—government or industry—to protect them from harm (Beamish 2001). The Guadalupe Dunes spill represented a clear case of organizational failure on a grand scale.

The Guadalupe spill, like other well-known cases of organizational failure, provides the pretext for asking and answering important questions of organizational administrators and personnel about how they address "organizational risk" (Turner 1978; Gephart 1984; Calhoun and Hiller 1988; Lee and Ermann 1999; Perrow 1999). These questions include "how do administrators perceive contexts and circumstances that involve the risk of organizational mistake, misconduct, accident, and crisis (hereafter *organizational failure*)?" How does the risk of organizational failure influence administrative and general personnel decision-making? What is more, how does an organization's configuration—its formal structure(s)—influence the risk of failure? How do informal social processes and organizational culture figure in the risk of organizational failure? And, finally, how are the risks of organizational failure typically managed by administrators and mainline members? These questions are central to the tasks of risk and crisis management practitioners and influence how managers will handle emergency scenarios. Answers to such questions are needed so managers can proactively plan and self-consciously respond in ways that avert organizational failures.

Given these terms will be used frequently, I define *risk* here as a situation in which something of value (human well-being, property, or morals or beliefs) is threatened and their future status is uncertain (Jaeger et al. 2001; Beamish 2015: 8–9). Harm, both what is important and why it matters, reflects who is doing the assessing and therefore what is deemed to be "at stake." *Organizational risk*, or what is "organizationally at stake," can reflect many different concerns, from the loss of money, time, or other scarce resources, to loss of legitimacy and damaged reputation—particularly when persons are injured or killed—to total system(s) breakdown and organizational failure. Organizational risk can also reflect the breach of moral or ethical standards rather than simply a material loss, such as when a failure is deemed to have negatively impacted something of sacred value (Douglas 2002).

Characteristically, in answering questions regarding organizational risk(s), analysts and managers have assumed formal organizations to be "rational constructs" whose failures reflect management error, missing or misbegotten rules, or even misconduct (Vaughan 1998). The most common explanation for organizational failure is that of "operator error"—an explanation in which the organizational system is spared critique because blame is placed on the individual practitioner (Perrow 1999: 174). If operator error is not found to be the cause of failure, then it is often assumed to be the result of formal-rational and deliberate aspects of the organizational system itself, such as poorly devised rules and policies. Therefore, risk and crisis management practitioners seeking to avoid organizational failure or those who must investigate its unfortunate occurrence often focus on the formal chain of command and allocation of responsibility, formal decision-making processes, formal training and staff incentives, and formal processes and resource allocation(s) (Kaplan and Mikes 2012). Of course, either operator error or organizational malfunction or both can be the cause of organizational failure(s). There is no denying this.

Research that has relaxed the rationalist assumptions associated with the classical managerialism of Taylorism and Weberianism as well as contingency theory and organizational economics, however, has made significant strides in understanding organizational failure. This scholarship has shown how putatively "rational organizational systems" can produce and reflect unforeseen and unintended outcomes (Merton 1940, 1957; Selznick 1957; Meyer and Rowan 1977). Some of these studies have sought to further understand how seemingly "normal" elements of organizational systems (i.e., rationally conceived and configured) can interact in unpredictable ways to produce accidents (Perrow 1999). In these studies, scholars have found that specific organizational characteristics pre-structure, embed, and predict future accidents (i.e., failures), the sources of which are systemic and structural rather than limited to individual operator errors or faulty components.

Still other studies have sought to better understand how "normative" and informal organizational processes can encourage "good people" to do "dirty work" (see Hughes 1962 for original reference; Vaughan 1983; Beamish 2000). In the normative approach, it is in social and cultural processes, native to all formal and informal social organization, that the seeds for failure are sown. By shaping group perceptions in systematic ways, this research has found that processes of institution-making and cultural reproduction can normalize risk, leaving it hidden from operators and therefore heightening the chance of organizational failure (Turner 1978; Janis 1983).

Indeed, early 20th-century organizational research showed that in any given organization's "manifest system" of formal bureaucratic rules, hierarchies, and responsibilities, members always create a parallel set of informally generated normative institutions that can complement, contradict, and even be decoupled from formal organizational directives (Selznick 1949). Therefore, to understand how the risks associated with organizational failure occur, are perceived, and how decisions regarding them are made, one must address not only organizations as putatively rational constructs, but also how the *normal* and *normative* aspects of organization can lead in predictably unpredictable directions.

Thus, this essay provides a "post-rational view" of organizational failure. I focus on the interactive role that normal organizational structures and normative social and cultural processes play in the generation of organizational risks that hold the potential to promote failure. The view I emphasize has found that organizational failure(s) frequently reflect the very normal aspects of formal organization that classical theorists like Weber (1978) differentiated from other types of social groups and associations and that make formal organizations the most powerful instruments for goal achievement known to human kind. The research I emphasize suggests that normative social processes can unintentionally make formal organizations very risky too.

The rest of this essay is structured into four parts. I begin with attention to the role and relation that organizational outcomes have with internal processes of institution building, native to all forms of social organization. Next, I address research on disaster and industrial crises that emerged in the post-World War II era and the legacy it had on the study of organizational failure. Then I develop a view that emerged in dialogue with this prior scholarship, while breaking with it, called "Normal Accidents Theory" (NAT). The NAT approach was soon joined by research that developed the role that "normative social processes" can play in both generating and hiding risks that can lead to organizational failure. Ironically, perhaps, I briefly touch on a rival argument, "High Reliability Theory" (HRT), that contends a "culture of reliability" can avert organizational failure. I close with attention to what risk and crisis management practitioners can learn from a post-rational view.

Institutions, Organizations, and Risk

During the 1950s, sociologists were developing ideas regarding the "organic qualities" expressed within bureaucratic organizations (Merton 1940; Parsons 1951; Gouldner 1954; Selznick 1957). These organic qualities were thought to reflect the social "functions" that different manifest and latent aspects of the social organization served in supporting the integrity of the greater organizational whole. According to functionalist theory, the development of latent social institutions functioned to address issues of group adaptation, goal achievement, integration, and maintenance, issues that Selznick (1949) highlighted in his research on "institutionalization processes" in organization.

"Institutionalization processes" are native to all human groups and their interactions. According to Selznick, they are also a means by which formal organizations gain their unique "character." Upon joining an organization, members who bring with them their beliefs and values quickly generate commitments to one another that then infuse an organization's formal structures with latent meanings and character from which emerges an organization's distinctive "identity" (Selznick 1949: 40). Thus, while the formally planned and "rational" aspects of organization do make them tools for achieving specific goals, once infused with latent institutions, an organization gains a life of its own.

Institutionalizing processes therefore involve and reflect organizational members, within formal contexts, informally creating shared expectations for conduct that promote more reliable interaction. Yet, if mutual understanding and predictability are one side of such "institutionalization processes," then "social inertia" (Becker 1995), "groupthink" (Janis 1983), and "normalized deviance" (Vaughan 1996) can be another side of it. As members conventionalize norms, shared understanding, and means of coordination, change or "newness" can challenge their continued high-fidelity interactions (Freeman et al. 1983; Biggart and Beamish 2003). Given the influence exerted by such informal social processes within and between organizations, it is therefore important to consider concepts and ideas identified and developed by Selznick (1996) and later by neo-institutionalists that are important to understanding organizational failure (Meyer and Rowan 1977; Suchman and Edelman 1996; Scott 2008). Doing so will help clarify the role that latent aspects of formal organization can play in failures.

The Institutionalization Process in Formal Organizations

Philip Selznick (1949), in his landmark study *TVA and the Grass Roots*, was the first to show how social institutions emerged from the interactions and shared experiences of those who populated organizational contexts. Selznick defined the institutionalization process as "the emergence of orderly, stable, socially integrating patterns out of unstable, loosely organized, or narrowly technical activities" (Broom and Selznick 1955: 238). Selznick viewed emergent institutions to be as important to formal organizations as the formal and structural aspects. He argued that the very "emergence of organization" is best considered a mutually constitutive process that involves both (1) the manifest, formal, and structural aspects and (2) the latent, tacit, and informal social and institutional aspects of organizations. Institutions emerge because those who co-inhabit formal organizational systems endeavor to "humanize" them as they go, so that they are locally understandable and therefore made actionable.

Like many of his contemporaries, Selznick (1949: 10) considered formal organizations to be "tools" that differed from other sorts of human association. Yet, unlike his contemporaries, Selznick also found that the tool-like aspects of organizations could be shaped, altered, and even challenged by the emergent institutions generated by organizational members. He found this to be the case through his landmark investigation of the Tennessee Valley Authority (TVA). Founded in 1933, the TVA was a U.S. government-sponsored depression era project meant to alleviate poverty through social and economic development. In this research, Selznick asked a relatively straightforward organizational question: *how effective of a "tool" was the TVA at achieving its stated mission*? The TVA's mission was to generate jobs, promote local education, improve farming techniques, bring electricity to the region, and ultimately promote prosperity in a historically impoverished region.

Selznick found that in seeking to fulfill the TVA's mission, managers incorporated local elites into their plans, but in doing so they began to take on elite views. That is, the administrators were "co-opted." Selznick coined the term co-optation to capture the latent tendency for organizational members to adopt the views and ideas of those with whom they frequently interact. Through his observations of institutionalization and the resultant cooptation at the TVA, he showed how it had veered from its official mission. Instead, it enriched regional elites and did little to address regionally endemic poverty. In a word, the TVA's formal mission had become *decoupled* from its practical accomplishment. As such, co-optation promoted the TVA's failure insofar as it diverted the organization away from its initial, formal mandate.

The ideas that emerged from Selznick's research showed that organizations are much more than the rational tools of classical management theory that Frederick Taylor (2006) articulated in his principles of scientific management, or even in the theory of rational bureaucracy developed by Weber (1978). Selznick emphasized that, although heavily influenced by rationally conceived structures and administrator decisions, these actions and their outcomes are not simply a reflection of "mechanically" rational considerations. Rather, in Selznick's analysis, the TVA's mission-drift reflected administrators vigorously pursuing the TVA's mission through participatory management and community outreach that ended in their co-optation. The universal human practice of meaning-making and developing commitments carries with it the organizational risk of decoupling when formal organizational policies and goals no longer align with the way they are fulfilled (Boxenbaum and Jonsson 2008).

Research on Disasters, Accidents, and Failures

At about the same time Selznick was developing his ideas regarding institutions in organization, emerging studies of disasters and industrial accidents were also uncovering insights into how organizations perform under stress. Following World War II, the study of disasters gained a good deal of federal support as disaster research provided a means of exploring societal reaction(s) to large-scale disruptions to draw inferences regarding how society might respond to a nuclear attack. The raft of studies that followed focused on post-impact analysis since the problem was what would happen after a disaster struck, not before it. As defined in Fritz's iconic characterization,

> Disasters are events concentrated in time and space, in which society... undergoes severe danger and incurs such losses to its members and physical appurtenances that social structure is disrupted and the fulfillment of all or some of the society's essential functions of the society is prevented.
>
> *(1961: 655)*

A post-impact emphasis is implicit in this definition.

Given that researchers like Fritz sought to understand unforeseen and unforeseeable disaster events, post-impact analysis made good sense. Hence, a variety of models were developed, most sharing a socio-historical approach in which the general stages of collective response were documented and verified (Quarentelli and Dynes 1977). Disaster research of this sort therefore sought to elucidate the communication strategies used, how untrue myths and rumors spread, and the myriad forms that collective behavior takes in the aftermath of disaster. The study of natural disasters such as earthquakes, tornadoes, floods, and fires lent themselves to these research objectives.

The examination of natural disasters was soon joined by a growing interest and scholarship on the social and technological causes and consequences of disasters and accidents. The prior agenda associated with the study of "natural disaster," however, strongly influenced this early research on social and technological disasters, insofar as it involved a continued focus on post-impact conditions and response rather than on possible explanations for such accidents and technological failures. The post-impact emphasis therefore failed to clarify either how one might detect impending crises or what the signs of organizational failure might be.

Indeed, organizational disasters constitute a subtype within the broader category of "socio-technical disasters," but they were noticeably absent from these early treatments (Turner 1978). Until the 1980s, very few studies examined the role business corporations or government agencies played in fomenting conditions that might lead to disaster (Torry et al. 1979; Gephart 1984). Until this time, the precursors to organizational failure received little attention because the presumption was that the causes of organizationally inspired mishap, like the causes of natural disasters and nuclear attack, reflected "exogenous forces" such as foreign powers, chance, or technological failure. The continued influence of the post-impact model can still be observed in organizational manuals, protocols, regulatory statutes, and legislation that guide many risk and crisis management practitioners and remedial action(s) today.

As I will share in what follows, both formal organizational structures and latent social processes native to organizations have been found to play important, if paradoxical, roles in both fomenting organizational failure and providing potential remedies. These qualities were largely if not entirely missed when the emphasis remained post-disaster.

The Antecedents to Industrial Disasters

In the 1980s, Barry Turner (1978) was perhaps the first to identify the importance of pre-cipitating conditions in what he termed "socio-technical disasters" (1978: 86). According to Turner, in his ground-breaking book *Man-Made Disasters* (MMD), industrial disasters are rarely "bolts from the blue." Rather, the so-called accident scenarios often reveal important preconditions such as early signs of decline that are misinterpreted, signals of impending failure that are ignored, or indications of breakdown that are not communicated to a wider audience of operators, leaving the conditions to grow worse and increasing the odds of disaster (Turner 1978: 86). Indeed, terming them "accidents" is a misnomer since they are rarely a reflection of coincidence. Turner claimed that "information deficit" and "communication failure" were almost always culprits in industrial disasters.

Therefore, to understand industrial disasters, Turner stressed that they must be investigated both for their antecedent conditions and socio-technical outcomes since they typically reflect the organizational intertwining of social and technical processes. Specifically, Turner's MMD model focused on the life cycle of industrial disasters that originated in normative elements such as accepted standards of safety and standard operating procedures (SOP), often considered unthreatening by those who performed them. Indeed, Turner found that in the industrial disasters he studied, operator recognition of risk was often prevented or undermined by tacit assumptions that emerged as plant staff became familiar with SOP.

This further reflects the mismatch of SOP and the pragmatic work routines that emerge overtime in industrial and other organizational contexts. SOP are formal-structural means of guiding operator conduct that typically assume and imply that work process reflects a stepwise approach to task completion. Yet, research has exposed that operators, as they become familiar with their duties, typically rely on pragmatic understandings of those work processes, not stepwise SOP (Baccus 1986). These can take shape as ad hoc and informal recipes for action (Bensman and Gerver 1963; Gephart 1997) and can even become quasi-formalized as rules-of-thumb or "social heuristics" (Beamish and Biggart 2011). In Turner's original research, normative processes associated with SOP both produced and concealed from operators the conditions that preceded (and predicted) the accident and that if recognized might have stopped it.

Turner's focus on the interaction of structure, culture, and technical aspects/technological assets was born out of his redefinition of industrial disaster; a definition that contrasts with Fritz's (1961) iconic definition of disaster as a post-impact phenomenon (shared earlier). Turner defined disaster as "a significant disruption of the existing cultural beliefs and norms about hazards, and for dealing with them and their impacts" (1978: 381). For Turner, similar to observations made by Selznick, industrial disasters typically reflect a mismatch between formal-technical and latent-cultural systems.

In identifying disasters as involving patterns, Turner further distinguishes industrial "accidents" from industrial "disasters." Turner was emphatic on the point that industrial disasters were not coincidental occurrences, but were the outcome of incompatibility between formal-technical-organizational and informal-social-cultural assumptions and "real" conditions. Turner's basic argument, then, is that the events that culminate in industrial disasters are typically overlooked, ignored, and misinterpreted by organizational operators; they reflect "false assumptions, poor communication, cultural lag, and misplaced optimism" (Turner, 1976: 395). Turner's (1976) "man-made disaster" model of organizational disasters thus pivots on the distinction between operator misperceptions and the objective world outside their subjective perceptions. Turner's solution is therefore to gain "truer" information about the "real" disaster potential in an organization in order to prevent them. Rational steps must be taken to overcome what he saw as a "subjectivity" problem.

The weakness of Turner's theory is therefore that it rests on a presumption of a singular objective reality that can be accessed, conditioned, even controlled via further rational planning and closer alignment with "true reality." As will become clear, more organizational rationality (and rationalization) can itself be risky.

Normal Organizational Structures and Organizational Failure

Soon after the publication of Turner's research, Charles Perrow argued something very different in *Normal Accidents* ([1984] 1999): even highly rational and rationally devised organizational systems will "normally" fail. This concern emerged from Perrow's participation on a congressional panel tasked with investigating the nuclear meltdown at the Three Mile Island Nuclear Generating Station in Dauphin County, Pennsylvania. Perrow developed a structural explanation for what had until then been largely viewed as a technical failure involving operator error. Focusing on organizational characteristics, Perrow demonstrated that the source of this organizational failure was systemic rather than component-based or founded in operator mistake. He specifically highlighted the role that the system characteristics of "interactive complexity" (parts of a system that exhibit the potential for unpredictable synergy) and "tight component coupling" (parts of a system that exhibit small margins of error) play in organizational failure. Both interactive complexity and tight coupling are normal organizational conditions that characterize many of today's high-risk technological infrastructures (Perrow 1999: 327).

Importantly, while technical systems like these are inherently complicated, their interactive complexity and tight coupling also reflect the efficiency preferences of the engineers and technical managers who design and administer them. That is, technocrats have historically preferred "efficient systems" that produce enhanced outputs from reduced or equivalent inputs and therefore waste less energy, time, and/or resources. Tight coupling and interactive complexity typically fulfill and reflect this preference for highly efficient systems; technical systems are therefore frequently designed with this in mind. It is also important to specify what Perrow meant by "normal" to avoid confusion. The term "Normal" in relation to accidents as used in NAT refers to common properties and structures inherent in an organization's technological system that create unexpected interactions among systems components. Normal does not mean good or desired in this context.

Why does Perrow argue that these organizational qualities inexorably lead to normal accidents? On the one hand, interactively complex systems hold the potential for random interactions among component(s) that are outside the standard linear production sequences designed by engineers, and that are characteristic of most industrial processes. The assembly line is a classic example of a "linear" production system. In a scenario involving a factory assembly line, breakdown will be relatively obvious to operators: the functions downstream of a failure will be left waiting, while the functions and products upstream of it will quickly pile up, leading operators to shut the system down. By contrast, in the nonlinear subsystem of a nuclear facility, some parts hold multiple functions. If such a multi-function component fails, technically unrelated problems can arise simultaneously, making recognition that something has gone wrong slow to manifest as the complexity of the system makes the production processes opaque (Perrow 1999: 72–73).

The other dimension of normal accidents theory is tight coupling. The more tightly coupled an organizational system, the higher the degree of time-dependence among systems components. Based in this tightness, such a system holds far less "slack" and therefore a smaller margin for error. A smaller margin for error makes system breakdown both more likely and quicker to occur.

To combat system breakdowns like these, engineers, designers, and administrators tend to favor system redundancy. Yet, redundancies tend to increase the complexity of the overall system reducing its ability to absorb a malfunction, which raises the risk of normal accident. Examples of organizational systems that reflect high complexity and tight coupling include nuclear power facilities, chemical/petroleum refineries, ocean-going cargo ships, biotechnology, airline flight, and modern energy grids.

As for solutions to normal accidents, Perrow suggests two ways to reduce the threat posed by such high-risk systems. These include design considerations and abandoning systems that involve high catastrophic potential and low societal benefit. Organizational factors that influence design considerations include management goals and reward structures that typically stress power, speed, and efficiency over ease of operation, maintenance, and safety (Perrow 1983: 521–522). Perrow also suggests that an engineering design preference for "efficient systems" reflects an engineering rubric that prefers increasingly complex and tightly coupled systems that ought to be conscientiously relaxed since the potential for "normal accidents" increases with them (Perrow 1999: 72–73). Perrow also provides a societal risk-to-benefit classification system for technical systems. Perrow argues that in organizational systems where the risk of catastrophic failure outweighs the benefit to society, they should simply be abandoned. Nuclear power and nuclear weapons fall into this category (Perrow, 1999: 14; 304–24).

The distinction between NAT and prior theories of accidents rests in the assertion that the risks posed by such systems are inherent to them given the normal structural configurations such systems deploy. In effect, they reflect the rational origination of organizational failure. This argument stands in marked contrast to what had been typically asserted previous to this research: attributing organizational failure to operator self-interest, operator errors, or simple component failure. It is thus from highly rationalized structures that organizational irrationalities emerge—mishaps, accidents, and the heightened potential for disaster.

An Intersectional Account of Industrial Accidents

Influenced by the works of both Turner and Perrow, Paul Shrivastava developed his own account of the precursors to organizational failure using the Union Carbide pesticide plant disaster in Bhopal, India, as a case. The Union Carbide disaster involved the accidental release of deadly methyl isocyanate (MIC) gas into neighborhoods adjacent to the plant, immediately killing 300 (or more) persons and injuring some 200,000. Recent estimates by the Indian government put the total number directly killed by the release at 15,000, with those exposed to the toxic gases at 600,000, making it the worst chemical spill in history (Taylor 2014). Shrivastava found Union Carbide's deadly MIC release to reflect both logistical contradictions at the plant and feedback loops that increased the severity of these contradictions and that precipitated a catastrophic organizational failure (Shrivastava et al. 1988; Shrivastava 1992, 1994).

Shrivastava labels his approach an "intersectional account of industrial disaster" insofar as the vast chemical release reflected the intersection of technical/technological aspects of the plant and production processes characteristic of industrial organizations. Accordingly, on the one hand, organizational contradictions reflect conflicting forces within an industrial organization that create tensions by generating incompatible demands on it. Incompatibility promotes organizational failure because operators are less likely to notice or acknowledge such breakdowns, since they reflect SOPs (even if they are in contradiction). On the other hand, vicious circles involve sequenced and repetitive activities that, over time, work to intensify the contradictions and dangerous feedback loops. In short, vicious circles amplify organizational contradictions, pushing them toward failure and industrial disaster (Shrivastava 1994: 241).

At Union Carbide's plant, organizational contradictions included incompatible goals like striving to reduce the costs of production, maintaining an aggressive production schedule, and ensuring overall plant efficiency while also maintaining a safe facility for workers and the surrounding city. Commitment to plant "efficiency" lay behind the decision to store highly toxic MIC in a single 40-ton underground tank. The single storage tank was chosen by the plant's management because it could store more MIC for a lower cost and because it was also an easier means of storage. However, single tank storage was also a less "flexible" and robust form of storage and therefore less safe than individual 40 gallon barrels. Barrel storage would have allowed more control, more effective monitoring, and therefore a safer workplace and local environment. If an individual (or even multiple) barrels of MIC had been breached, it would have been far less destructive.

The contradiction between "productivity/efficiency" and "flexibility/safety" at the plant reflected managerial decisions that emphasized efficiency (i.e., cost savings), productivity (i.e., profits), and costs (i.e., overhead) over control, pliancy, and safety. In the end, management's commitment to productivity/efficiency blinded them to issues of system pliancy and plant safety, both setting the stage for the MIC release as well as an inability to effectively respond to the tank-breach and stop it.

Putting Normal Accidents Theory to the Test

A criticism of NAT research has been its selection of cases on the dependent variable—that is, organizational failures—from which to draw conclusions. The focus on failure, critics suggest, does not provide a clear picture of high-performing organizations that have yet to fail, or those that very rarely fail, and when they do, they react in a manner that avoids disaster (La Porte and Consolini 1991). Researchers have developed an alternative to NAT, called "High Reliability Theory" (HRT), that has focused on organizations that manage highly complex and hazardous technologies in some of the world's most hostile environments while compiling a record of very few mistakes and very little misconduct.

Scott Sagan in *Search for Safety* (1993) sought to address these competing theses regarding organizational performance through a comparative study of NAT and HRT. Sagan compares them using the U.S. nuclear weapons program as a historical case. As discussed earlier, NAT contends organizational accidents are inherent to complex, tightly coupled organizational systems. HRT, by contrast, suggests that organizational elements like design, culture, and managerial decision-making can provide a counter-weight to these organizational risks.

Sagan tested the causal mechanisms located in both theoretical models, using the record of accidents and near misses in the U.S. nuclear weapons program over four decades. These included whether higher levels of technological complexity and component and personnel redundancy increased or decreased an organizational system's reliability and whether those charged with managing America's nuclear arsenal had learned from their mistakes and near misses over time. He also assessed whether strong socialization and a "culture of reliability" in the military units that are charged with securing the U.S. nuclear arsenal moderate failure and promote reliable performance.

Sagan's conclusion was that the causal mechanisms HRT theorists described as mitigating or even halting "normal accidents" did not stop near misses and accidents from occurring in the U.S. nuclear weapons program. Sagan argued that NAT better explained the many near-miss accidents than HRT explained their reliable avoidance. Sagan, however, notes that this does not mean that HRT is invalid or that its advice for risk and crisis management practitioners should be ignored. His was a theoretical test and therefore should not be taken as an outright dismissal of HRT.

Through case studies, NAT theorists have exposed the risk-paradox of formal organization. As a civilization, we have tasked formal organizations with securing society from risk, but in seeking to do so these same organizations must also manage the world's most hazardous technical and technological systems. As a consequence, formal organizations tasked with securing society from risk simultaneously expose it to risk. According to NAT, then, managers not only confront the risk(s) that formal organizations were created to secure, but they must also confront the risk(s) they pose via their potential to fail. Something NAT reminds us is a "normal" aspect of their operation. This state of affairs also suggests that formal organizations fulfill a third and significant role in the contemporary: they routinely define and accept risk on behalf of the public.

Trustee Organizations, Normal Accidents, and Acceptable Risk

Research regarding how organizations plan for and manage risk has also exposed the contemporary role formal organizations play in assessing, accepting, or rejecting risks on behalf of society. In this regard, many complex formal organizations in industry, government, and civil society act as societal "trustees" (Beamish 2000: 7, 2015: 9). This is another dimension of NAT. Not only should accidents be considered normal under specific organizational conditions, but when accidents do occur, the organizations charged with responding to them can also "fail" for predictable reasons, putting the organizations involved and the general public at risk.

For example, in *Acceptable Risk*, Lee Clarke (1989) investigated the polychlorinated biphenyl (PCB) contamination of a federal office building in Binghamton, New York. PCBs are known to cause cancer in animals and are probable human carcinogens too. The ambiguous risk posed by PCBs along with a lack of coherent rules for response to such a chemical contaminant left government health and safety organizations without clear responsibilities, effective means of coordination, or specific response protocols. The lack of a clear set of guidelines led to poor organizational decision-making, exacerbating the PCB release by unnecessarily exposing many more persons and property to continued and greater levels of contamination. Clarke therefore exposed the "inter-organizational chaos" that reigned because regulators had no scientifically established "safe" level of PCB exposure to draw on, no consensus on monitoring of PCB contamination, and no tested method to either clean up or neutralize PCBs.

What is more, because the contamination context of risk identification, risk monitoring, and risk mitigation required interorganizational attention, it also necessitated high levels of interorganizational coordination. Yet, no charter existed to guide interactions. Clarke's research therefore also highlights how interorganizational decisions concerning what were novel risks and ambiguous circumstances led authorities to apply already "known solutions"— for example, using unspecialized janitorial services to clean up the PCB-contaminated office building—to an "unknown problem"—PCB contamination—that increased rather than decreased the risk of harm. Clarke finds that the agencies responsible for the cleanup of the site therefore engaged in an assortment of ineffective behaviors. In the end, the interorganizational response to the PCB contaminants worsened the outcome and increased the risks.

In this instance, the very "normal" structural qualities and responsibilities of contemporary trustee organizations involved in managing hazardous technologies (or in responding to hazardous scenarios), while reflecting high levels of rational planning, inevitably generate "irrationalities" too that reflect unpredictable interactions, systemic contradictions, feedback loops, and intraorganizational chaos to name but four covered in the above. Yet, formal structures are only one aspect of any given organizational system. Risks, research suggests, can also emerge from the informal and cultural dimensions of formal organization as well.

Normative Organizational Processes and Organizational Failure(s)

Research has also shown how organizational failure can reflect the tacit assumptions, culturally shaped perceptions, and the faulty interpretations forged within rationally planned organizational processes. In what follows, I develop some of the key pieces of scholarship that address both the social psychological and cultural-institutional basis for organizational failure.

Bounded Rationality and Groupthink

Social psychologist Herbert Simon (1957) was an early pioneer in seeking to understand how organizations shape members' perceptions and decision-making. Simon's view has had a profound impact on the understanding of normative thinking in organizations. Importantly, Simon's view contrasted with conventional assumptions about organizational members and their decision-making habits and capacities. He specifically problematized conventional assumptions regarding the comprehensively "rational individual," wherein individual decision-makers are presumed to solve problems by *comprehensively searching* for and identifying all the possible options for solving a problem, *assessing* the total cost-to-benefit of each option via comparison, and, finally, *selecting* the option that promises to yield the greatest benefit.

By contrast, Simon found comprehensive rationality uncharacteristic of individual human decision-makers both inside and outside formal organizations. Simon coined the term "satisficing" to capture how individual rationality is always constrained by limited information, limited cognitive capacities, and limited aspirations among other restrictions on choice(s). Simon also held that the simplifying assumptions individuals relied on in their thinking and decision-making limited their potential to be comprehensively rational. He called this limited cognitive state "bounded rationality." Simon believed that if formal organizations were effectively managed they could promote collective rationality that surpassed that of their individual operators. This could be accomplished by systematically focusing operator attention by task and responsibility and therefore bounding their rationality to create supra-rational organizations that can better achieve their preferred ends.

The bounded rationality concept soon became widely applied in domains well outside of Simon's originally targeted administrative units within formal organizations. Simon's subsequent research with James March (1958) and March's own work (1978, 1994) sought to further situate bounded rationality in administrative systems to better reveal how it shaped organizational outcomes including mistakes and misconduct. This research helped to open organizational scholarship to the influence that structures and institutions have in in shaping individual perceptions and organizational outcomes including failures.

Another early social psychological account of the normative shaping that organizational contexts have on individual and group perceptions was that of Irving Janis. Janis (1983) developed the idea of "groupthink" to explain catastrophic policy failures. The groupthink concept was Janis's explanation for how exceptionally talented, high-level administrative decision-making groups could significantly miscalculate in their planning and execution, leading to disastrous policy failures. Janis (1972) in *Victims of Groupthink* used the Kennedy administration's 1961 Bay of Pigs Invasion as an exemplar. Janis's analysis of the Bay of Pigs debacle focused on the impact normative group dynamics can have on the psychology and the judgments of highly rational experts in organizational contexts. Janis exposed conditions native to administrative groups that can influence collective perceptions, decisions, and therefore outcomes. Janis's theory purported that cohesive groups were especially susceptible to "groupthink." Groupthink occurs when a group makes faulty decisions because group pressures lead to a deterioration of "mental efficiency, reality testing, and moral judgment" (Janis 1983: 9). Groups engaged in groupthink tend to prematurely converge on solutions as individual decision-makers succumb to group conformity. Both bounded rationality and groupthink are indispensable tools for organization scholars and should be for risk and crisis management practitioners as each seeks to better understand and avoid organizational failure(s).

Organizational Culture and Normalizing Risks

Research on the role culture plays in structuring operator rationality also has a long-standing place in the study of organizational failure, as Gephart's research on "cultural rationalities" and organizational crisis attests (Gephart 1984, 1993, 1997). Gephart defines organizational culture as "constituted by its members' activities, which produce for them the sense that a shared framework of meaning exists for interpreting the world. Culture is the sense of intersubjective meanings that members develop and use. Culture is thus a process" (Gephart 1993: 1469). Gephart sought to understand how organizationally inspired environmental disasters are differently understood by organizational stakeholders such as administrators in government and industry as well as their public critics. Gephart's definition of culture in organizational contexts as an inter-subjective process fits well with a number of other scholarly efforts to understand the role culture plays in organizational failure (Vaughan 1999; Beamish 2000; Snook 2000; Unseem 2016).

In groundbreaking research, Diane Vaughan (1996) explored the role cultural-institutions played in interpretations of risk in a complex and technologically intensive endeavor—the manufacture and launch of the Space Shuttle Challenger. Her investigation of NASA's Space Shuttle Challenger accident focused on what led up to the fateful decision to launch in adverse weather conditions. Vaughan's research resulted in a theory of risky decision-making that might best be termed a "*normative* accidents theory." Vaughan's treatment corresponds with NAT insofar as she to seeks to expose the "normal" aspects of organization that unintentionally lead to organizational failure. Yet her treatment focuses on cultural processes rather than formal structures of complexity and coupling.

On January 28, 1986, seventy-three seconds after liftoff, the Challenger Space Shuttle 51-L exploded mid-flight, killing its crew of seven, as millions of Americans watched the live broadcast. In addition to the loss of life and national trauma, $55 million dollars was lost and the space shuttle program at NASA was thrown into doubt—a condition from which it never completely recovered. The failure arose out of the engineering and NASA work-group culture, competing objectives and mandates at NASA, and overlapping hierarchies that prevailed at NASA and its subcontractor Morton Thiokol. The Challenger accident demonstrated the role that culture and flawed decision-making can play in organizational failures.

The Challenger Launch was the culmination of years of work and millions spent, yet a three-way teleconference call the night before launch stands in as a proxy for the dysfunctional decision-making that Vaughan sought to understand and which she used to explain the faulty decision to launch. The call involved Morton Thiokol engineers who sought to persuade NASA and Morton Thiokol managers to abort the launch based on their concerns about cold AM temperatures and the resiliency of O-rings designed to seal the joints (i.e., segments) of the Challenger's solid rocket boosters. Combustible gases had leaked, charring and even eroding the O-rings in prior cold weather launches; the engineers Arnie Thompson and Roger Boisjoly worried that a failure to seal during launch due to cold-temperature hardening could threaten the mission's safety (Vaughan 1996: 286). Responding to the plea of their engineers to abort, Morton Thiokol's lead managers conferred, and in an oft-quoted sequence, Senior Vice President Jerry Mason asked Vice President Robert Lund to "take off his engineering hat, and put on his management hat" to make his final decision. Lund rejected the no-launch recommendation of the project engineers and sided with the other managers who wanted to proceed with the launch (Vaughan 1996: 316).

To understand what led to this fateful decision—a managerial override of sound engineering reasoning—Vaughan emphasized the intersecting role cultural domains, professional cosmologies, and production pressures had on what aeronautics engineers judged to be acceptable risk. Put in the language developed in her analysis, Vaughan exposed the role that *"production culture"* centered in NASA's work groups and its commercial subcontractors, the *"culture of production"* reflected in NASA's competitive environment, political pressure, and perpetual resource scarcity, and the *"structural secrecy"* that prevailed within NASA and between NASA and its contractors interactively played in sowing the seeds for the eventual Challenger accident. She found that these internal cultural elements at NASA and its subcontractors, along with political pressures exerted from outside NASA that stressed the need for a successful launch, conjoined to encourage miscalculation regarding a known risk(s): the temperature tolerance of a rubber O-ring seal on the shuttle's solid rocket boosters. It was therefore the nexus of a "production culture," a "culture of production," and the "structural secrecy" that prevailed within NASA and between NASA and its contractors that sowed the seeds for organizational failure and therefore the catastrophic Challenger accident.

Normative Organizational Accommodation and Crescive Risks

Tom Beamish (2002a) further developed an understanding of the normative tendencies in organizations through his study of an enormous oil spill on the Central California Coast that evaded official recognition for four decades. The Guadalupe Spill involved 20 million spilled gallons of a refined petroleum similar to diesel or kerosene called "diluent" that was used to thin the thick peanut butter like crude-oil native to Central California. Diluent was injected into well-heads, making the thick crude oil easier to pipe to storage tanks and refining facilities on site. The spill reflected nearly four decades of routine small-, medium-, and, by the late 1980s, relatively large oil leaks and spills at an oil field and an adjacent beach in Central California's Guadalupe Dunes.

Beamish found the spill's slow and cumulative origination and the interorganizational response it gained—slow, halting, and once acknowledged actively denied and mismanaged—were evocative of both organizational behavior and the kind of risk it represented. Beamish termed this kind of risk a "crescive trouble" (Beamish 2002a: 4, 2002b: 151–152). Crescive literally means in the growing stages and comes from the Latin root *crescere* meaning to grow. Crescive captures phenomena that gradually accumulate, becoming well-established over time. Beamish found that crescive troubles vex organizational systems for intersecting perceptual, technical, and strategic reasons. Initially, because crescive troubles emit low or muted signals of danger, they tend to be overlooked and even actively accommodated by organizational personnel who must routinely interact or monitor them such as those in industry, regulators, and even nearby community members. Once discovered, the long-term gestation of such crescive problems makes organizational cover-up, and therefore misconduct, much more likely.

The history of the spill's discovery exposed how and why crescive troubles confound organizational systems. Unocal Corporation, who operated the field, state regulators, and local community members who frequented the beach and dunes had all experienced the sight and smell of petroleum so often it was an "expected" part of work at the field or a visit to the beach. Overtime, as the spilled petroleum accumulated, signs of an alarming "spill" mounted. By the late 1980s and early 1990s, some of those who frequented the oil field began to acknowledge that something wasn't right.

Yet organizational response was initially muted, halting, and confused for two primary reasons, one *normative*, the other *strategic* (Beamish 2000). On the one hand, because the emergent spill risk had occurred and been accommodated for decades, what might be alarming to an outsider was unsurprising (i.e., *normative*) to insiders at the field who regularly worked with oil and saw signs of oil spillage but did not attribute urgency to them. On the other hand, once the spill was deemed an obvious organizational issue, detection, responsibility, and report became a *strategic issues* as well. Identifying a spill-problem that had been visible but ignored for three decades generated concern about sanction, both from sources internal to the oil-field and from those external to it. Internally, organizational careers could be ruined and field jobs lost if a large spill were discovered while one worked or managed there. Careers in organizations typically don't advance when they are associated with large financial losses or shameful media debacles, like those associated with industrial disasters. Externally, reporting the event would trigger state investigation, fines, and ultimately blaming rituals—which, in the end, occurred. Therefore, "self-reporting" the spill—as the law and ethics requires (US EPA 1990; King and Lennox 2000; Beamish 2002)—was also resisted by both field workers and managers for strategic reasons (i.e., self-interest).

Finally, much like the interorganizational chaos Clarke (1989) documented, the slow and muddled response by a disorganized interorganizational array of federal, state, and local regulators also shows how the Silent Spill defied formal definitions and organizational protocols. The lack of "fit" between the crescive trouble they collectively confronted and the policies and mandates they sought to fulfill led to interorganizational difficulties and then a response that was more befitting of an "acute oil spill disaster" than one tailored for a badly contaminated and environmentally fragile dunes ecosystem (Little et al. 1997).

The research shared in this section has shown how the "normal structural" and "normative-cultural" aspects characteristic of contemporary organizational systems can lead to organizational failure. What is more, the tendency of organizational actors to fail to notice or take action can also reflect strategic behavior on the part of organizational personnel, whose failure to act can reflect personal ambitions, intraorganizational hierarchy, interorganizational relations, and the overarching policy context within which they operate. In such cases, it isn't simply "mistake" but also misconduct.

Normative Organizational Processes and Highly Reliable Performance

Having developed the role that normal and normative aspects of organization play in organizational failure, one might rightly ask if these conditions simply reflect the "darkside" of organization (c.f., Vaughan 1999). The answer is no. Indeed, as touched on above, Hight Reliability Theory (HRT) provides a strong counterpoint to NAT insofar as it rejects the basic premise that the structural characteristics and normative processes in organizations will ultimately undermine even the most determined efforts at avoiding failure.

HRT highlights cases of successful risk management not failure. Specifically, HRT has focused on organizations that have successfully managed highly complex and hazardous technologies in some of the world's most hostile environments while compiling "highly reliable" performance records—very few, if any recorded failures. Cases HRT scholars have investigated include both governmental and commercial enterprises that oversee chemical plants, air traffic control systems, firefighting squads, energy grids, emergency hospitals, nuclear power facilities, and nuclear waste management (Weick 1993; Bierly and Spender 1995; Porte and Consolini 1998; Boin and Schulman 2008; Wheeler et al. 2013). They have also followed U.S. military units charged with managing modern weapons systems, including case studies of the U.S. aircraft carriers and nuclear submarines (Bierly and Spender 1995).

HRT researchers argue that while organizations like these are routinely challenged by structural and institutional qualities that NAT highlight, they rarely, if ever, fail (Roberts et al. 2001). When mistakes are made, they are minimized in frequency and severity by robust response and high levels of organizational resilience (Sutcliffe 2011).

From their research, HRT has identified a set of characteristics that promote organizational robustness and resilience and therefore highly reliable organizational performance. These include (1) safety as a priority for organizational elites, (2) decentralized decision-making, (3) high levels of personnel and technological redundancy, (4) effective trial and error learning from previous failures and mistakes, and (5) developed "culture of reliability" that reflects intense training and socialization. This last, a culture of reliability, emerges with the prior four elements and promotes operators who can anticipate organizational failure and act to stem it before it occurs (Weick and Roberts 1993).

Given what has been emphasized in the forgoing chapter, HRT's claim that a "culture of reliability" can vastly improve organizational performance presents a point of convergence with NAT, albeit with diametrically opposed outcomes in mind. For example, Rochlin et al. (1998) investigated flight operations on a U.S. aircraft carrier where flight controllers were highly reliable because the organizational culture prioritized a "mistake free operation." A culture of reliability, according to Weick and Roberts (1993), involves what they term "collective mind." Collective mind is the degree to which organizational members contribute in a manner that converges, supplements, and assists the imagined requirements that flow from the organization on whose behalf they act (paraphrased, see Weick and Roberts, 1993: 365). Reliable performance and collective mind further promote the "heedful interrelating" between organizational personnel and organizational technologies. Culturally induced heedfulness promotes consistently thoughtful member performance without the rigidity and even carelessness frequently associated with SOP's and largely reactive bureaucratic rules (Weick and Roberts 1993).

According to Weick and Roberts, then, such heedful interrelating can address and even correct for the unexpected interactions that occur in complex and tightly coupled organizations that are hard to see, hard to believe (i.e., assumed), and that NAT contends can quickly cascade into crisis. Weick and Roberts further identify three important capacities that heedful interrelating provide: heedfulness provides continuity across time, heedfulness provides continuity across activity, and heedfulness provides pragmatic comprehension from experienced personnel who can then convey it to inexperienced personnel (Weick and Roberts 1993: 365–368). Heedful interrelating enhances coordination because it involves personnel spanning the typical divisions that formally structure organizational activity. This includes bureaucratic and purely technical functions that are reflected in an organization's divisions, projects, or missions, and hierarchies of authority (i.e., squadrons, maintenance teams, and ships command on board an aircraft carrier) (Rochlin et al. 1998). In short, a culture of reliability promotes (and reflects) heedful interrelating and collective mind, which heightens organizational reliability by reducing errors and improving response to error and accident, and with the reduction and improved response lowers the chance of organizational failure.

While Weick has championed the role organizational culture can play in helping to foment highly reliable performance, he has also conceded that such a cultural prescription can have a darker side. In order to avoid failure and maintain highly reliable performance, Wieck suggests organizational personnel must remain ever-vigilant, not becoming inured by SOP or disregard changing conditions (Weick 1987). This is of course why normalized deviance in crescive scenarios is so organizationally dangerous: operators don't typically recognize they have become habituated and complacent until it's too late. Though they admit the organizational risks, in the main HRT theorists' adhere to a view best summed in a Roberts quote: "Reliance on risky technologies is a fact of life. Our position is that since this is a given we must do all we can to increase reliability in such technologies" (Bourrier 2005: 97).

Conclusion

The introduction opened with the story of a crescive petroleum spill disaster that vexed the organization that caused it and the interorganizational systems responsible for interdicting and cleaning it up. From this case of organization failure, I forwarded a handful of basic questions regarding how the risks of organizational failure are perceived, addressed, structured, and influenced by informal social processes. To answer these questions, I focused on the interactive role that *normative social processes* and *normal organizational structures* play in the generation of and response to organizational failure. Indeed, the views and treatments I developed showed that organizational failure frequently reflects the very rational aspects of formal organization that have been used to define them as humanity's preeminent tool. In this essay, then, I suggest that the "irrationality of rationality," as observed in the organizational cases and treatments I conveyed, provides the basis for what might be best termed a "post-rational view" of organizational failure(s).

I began with attention to the relation that organizational failure has with normative aspects of organization, like the institutionalization process identified by Selznick (1949) in his classic work regarding the TVA. Selznick exposed how organizations often engage in unintended and even unacknowledged behavior that can become detached from official goals and can therefore put an organization at risk of failure.

I then took up research on disaster and industrial accident that emerged in the post-World War II context and the legacy this had on the study of organizational failure for organizational scholars, regulators, and managers. This was evident in the early focus on post-impact analysis wherein industrial accidents were approached as chance events, acts of god, or technical failure(s). Barry Turner was one of the first to study the antecedents of industrial accidents, rejecting the accident nomenclature for one focused on the a priori conditions that lay the basis for what he termed "industrial disasters."

Having established the connection between normal structures and normative processes and the antecedents to organizational disaster, I subsequently developed research that has explicitly focused on the "normal" bases for organizational failure. This line of research, known loosely as NAT, has sought to explain how normal operations, in rationally planned organizational systems, can systematically produce risks that result in organizational failure(s). Perrow (1999) was the first to identify system-wide structural conditions that promoted nonlinear interactions from which emerge "normal accidents." Shrivastava also developed a general model of industrial disaster, in which he argues risk and crisis management practitioners must be cognizant of the intersection of technologies and organizational processes, where contradictions and feedback loops can precipitate organizational failure and catastrophe. Risk and crisis management practitioners should also critically assess organizational commitments to efficiency and productivity, since NAT forewarns us that these can be overemphasized in design and processes changes, increasing the odds of failure.

A related strand of research emerged soon after NAT that stressed the "normative social processes" associated with organizational failure. As highlighted in research by Vaughan (1996) on the Space Shuttle Challenger disaster, the institutions organizational members generate provide them with cultural scripts and schema that enable them to coordinate behavior and fill gaps inherent to formal structures. Yet this can also lead down the path of "normalized deviance" that carries the risk of organizational failure. Risk and crisis management practitioners should be aware that deploying unaffiliated administrators or outside experts to judge conduct and/or organizational processes, where those judgments are free of constraint, is one means of catching groupthink and normalized deviance before it results in failure(s).

In addition to "normal structures" and "normative processes," I also showed that certain types of problems profoundly vex organizational systems for intersecting cultural and structural reasons. On this, as detailed in Clarke's (1989) research regarding the PCB contamination of a government building, because protocols to address PCB contamination had yet to be defined, uncertainty reigned among the interorganizational mélange of regulators charged with securing the contaminated site. Their decisions, reflective of an "inter- organizational garbage can," increased the number of persons and property exposed to PCBs and therefore increased rather than moderated the risks it posed.

Beamish (2002b) also studied an ambiguous problem with no clear solution: a petroleum spill that was long-term, incremental, and cumulative, and that would become one of the nation's largest on record. Crescive troubles initially emit muted signals of risk that tend to be overlooked and even actively accommodated by organizational personnel who must regularly interact with them (Beamish 2002a: 4). Once exposed, the long-term gestation of such problems also makes strategic cover-up, and therefore misconduct, much more likely since those who might report them are usually implicated given the timespan in which crescive problem gestated. As a consequence, crescive troubles present an especially pernicious kind of organizational problem.

Finally, I close the chapter with brief attention to HRT. HRT researchers have argued that if properly harnessed, normative socialization processes in organizations can lead to "culture of reliability" in ways that can stave off organizational failure. These strategies, pursued by organizations that work with some of the world's most dangerous technologies in some of the most unforgiving environments, have been shown by HRT researchers to improve organizational performance and push organizations that manage hazardous technologies toward higher reliability and lower risk operation.

In closing, then, I have sought to expose the "normal" organizational structures and "normative" organizational processes involved in the organizational risk of failure. I have outlined a number of lessons that risk and emergency managers ought to find useful. One can characterize the treatments I have highlighted as "post-rational" insofar as those I have highlighted approach and understand the risk of organizational mistake, misconduct, accident, and crisis as outcomes associated with rationally planned organizations reliant on routine structures and processes. Much as Weber sought to understand how in the process of rationalizing a social order, irrationality could result (i.e., the irrationality of rationality), the research I have featured on organizational failure(s) has sought to better understand how putatively rational organizational systems can pursue reasoned lines of action that end in organizational failure.

Approaching organizational behavior from such a post-rationalist position should sensitize risk and crisis management practitioners to the range of threats common to organizations—risks that have been found linked with many types and forms of organizational failure. Indeed, the design preference of engineers and risk managers for ever more "efficient organizations" is a case in point: if pursued without reflection, this can inexorably lead to normal accidents. What is more, building organizational systems without acknowledging that the humans who populate them will fill out such formal systems with latent cultural understandings and relationship is to miss half or more of what one must manage in these contexts. In short, in approaching organization(s) itself as a double-edged sword, rather than panacea, risk and crisis management practitioners will be better able to anticipate and plan for organizational failure(s).

References

Arthur D. 1997. Little is association with Fugro West, Headley Associates, Marine Research Specialists, and Science Application Corp. "Guadalupe Oil Field Remediation and Abandonment Project."

Baccus, M. D. 1986. "Multi-piece Truck Wheel Accident and Their Regulations." In *Ethnomethodological Studies of Work*, edited by H. Garfinkel, pp. 21–58. London and New York: Routledge.

Beamish, Thomas D. 2000. "Accumulating Trouble: Formal organization, a Culture-of-Silence, and a Secret Spill." *Social Problems* 47(4):473–498.

Beamish, Thomas D. 2001. "Environmental Threat and Institutional Betrayal: Lay Public Perceptions of Risk in the San Luis Obispo County Oil Spill." *Organization and Environment* 14(1):5–33.

Beamish, Thomas D. 2002a. *Silent Spill the Organization of an Industrial Crisis*. Cambridge, MA: MIT Press.

Beamish, Thomas D. 2002b. "Waiting for Crisis: Regulatory Inaction and Ineptitude and the Case of the Guadalupe Dunes Oil Spill." *Social Problems* 49(2) (May):150–177.

Beamish, Thomas D. 2015. *Community at Risk: Biodefense and the Collective Search for Security*. Palo Alto, CA: Stanford University Press.

Beamish, Thomas D. and Nicole Woolsey Biggart. 2011. "The Role of Social Heuristics in Project Centered Production Networks: Insights from the Commercial Construction Industry." *Engineering Project Organization Journal* 1(4):57–70.

Becker, Howard. 1995. "The Power of Inertia." *Qualitative Sociology* 18:301–309.

Bensman, Joseph and Israel Gerver. 1963. "Crime and Punishment in the Factory: The Function of Deviancy in Maintaining the Social System." *American Sociological Review* 28(4):588–598.

Bierly, Paul E. and J. C. Spender. 1995. "Culture and High Reliability Organizations: The Case of the Nuclear Submarine." *Journal of Management* 21(4):639–656.

Biggart, Nicole Woolsey and Thomas Beamish. 2003. "The Economic Sociology of Conventions: Habit, Custom, Practice and Routine in Market Order." *Annual Review of Sociology* 29:443–464.

Boin, Arjen and Paul Schulman. 2008. "Assessing NASA's Safety Culture: The Limits and Possibilities of High-Reliability Theory." *Public Administration Review* 68(6):1050–1062.

Bourrier, Mathilde. 2005. "An Interview with Karlene Roberts." *European Management Journal* 23(1):93–97.

Boxenbaum, Eva and Stefan Jonsson. 2008. "Isomorphism, Diffusion and Decoupling." In *The Sage Handbook of Organizational Institutionalism*, edited by R. Greenwood, C. Oliver, R. Suddaby, and K. Sahlin, pp. 79–98. Thousand Oaks, CA: Sage.

Broom, Leonard, and Philip Selznick. 1955 *Sociology: A Text with Adapted Readings.* New York: Row, Peterson.

Calhoun, Craig and Henryk Hiller. 1988. "Coping with Insidious Injuries: The Case of Johns-Manville Corporation and Asbestos Exposure." *Social Problems* 35(2):162–181.

Clarke, Lee Ben. 1989. *Acceptable Risk? Making Decisions in a Toxic Environment.* Berkeley: University of California Press.

Douglas, Mary. 2002. *Purity and Danger: An Analysis of the Concepts of Pollution Taboo.* 2nd ed. London, New York: Routledge.

US EPA. 1990. Oil Pollution Act of 1990. Retrieved March 26, 2017 (www.epa.gov/laws-regulations/summary-oil-pollution-act).

Freeman, John, Glenn R. Carroll, and Michael T. Hannan. 1983. "The Liability of Newness: Age Dependence in Organizational Death Rates." *American Sociological Review* 48(5):692–710.

Fritz, C. E., ed. 1961. *Disaster.* New York: Harcourt Brace & World Press.

Gephart, Robert P. 1984. "Making Sense of Organizationally Based Environmental Disasters." *Journal of Management* 10(2):205–225.

Gephart, Robert P. 1993. "The Textual Approach: Risk and Blame in Disaster Sensemaking." *The Academy of Management Journal* 36(6):1465–1514.

Gephart, Robert P. 1997. "Hazardous Measures: An Interpretive Textual Analysis of Quantitative Sensemaking during Crises." *Journal of Organizational Behavior* 18:583–622.

Gouldner, Alvin Ward. 1954. *Patterns of Industrial Bureaucracy.* Glencoe, IL: Free Press.

Hughes, Everett C. 1962. "Good People and Dirty Work." *Social Problems* 10(1):3–11.

Jaeger, Carlo C., Ortwin Renn, Eugene A. Rosa, and Thomas Webler. 2001. *Risk, Uncertainty, and Rational Action.* London; Sterling, VA: Earthscan.

Janis, Irving L. 1983. *Groupthink: Psychological Studies of Policy Decisions and Fiascoes.* 2nd ed. Boston, MA: Houghton Mifflin.

Janis, Irving Lester. 1972. *Victims of Groupthink: A Psychological Study of Foreign-Policy Decisions and Fiascoes.* Boston, MA: Houghton Mifflin Company.

Kaplan, Robert S. and Anette Mikes. 2012. "Managing Risks: A New Framework." *Harvard Business Review* 90(6):49–60.

King, Andrew and Michael Lennox. 2000. "Industry Self-Regulation Without Sanctions: The Chemical Industry's Responsible Care Program." *Academy of Management Journal* 43(4):698–716.

La Porte, Todd R. and Paula M. Consolini. 1991. "Working in Practice but Not in Theory: Theoretical Challenges of 'high-Reliability Organizations.'" *Journal of Public Administration Research and Theory* 1(1):19–48.

Lee, Matthew T. and M. David Ermann. 1999. "Pinto 'Madness' as a Flawed Landmark Narrative: An Organizational and Network Analysis." *Social Problems* 46(1):30–47.

March, James G. 1994. *A Primer on Decision Making: How Decisions Happen.* New York: The Free Press.

March, James G. 1978. "Bounded Rationality, Ambiguity, and the Engineering of Choice." *Bell Journal of Economics* 9(2):587–608.

March, James G. and Herbert Simon. 1958. *Organizations.* New York: John Wily and Sons, Inc.

Merton, Robert K. 1936. "The Unanticipated Consequences of Purposive Social Action." *American Sociological Review* 1(6):894–904.

Merton, Robert K. 1940. "Bureaucratic Structure and Personality." *Social Forces* 18:560–568.

Merton, Robert K. 1957. *Social Theory and Social Structure.* New York: Free Press.

Meyer, John and Brian Rowan. 1977. "Institutionalized Organizations: Formal Structure as Myth and Ceremony." *American Journal of Sociology* 83:340–363.

Parsons, Talcott. 1951. *The Social System.* Glencoe, IL: Free Press.

Perrow, Charles. 1983. "The Organizational Context of Human Factors Engineering." *Administrative Science Quarterly* 28(4):521–541.

Perrow, Charles. 1999 [1984]. *Normal Accidents: Living with High Risk Technologies.* 2nd ed. Princeton, NJ: Princeton University Press.

Porte, Todd La and Paula Consolini. 1998. "Theoretical and Operational Challenges of 'high-Reliability Organizations': Air-Traffic Control and Aircraft Carriers." *International Journal of Public Administration* 21(6–8):847–852.

Quarentelli, Enrico Luis and Russell Dynes. 1977. "Responding to Social Crises and Disaster." *Annual Review of Sociology* 3(1):23–49.

Roberts, Karlene H., Denise M. Rousseau, and Todd R. La Porte. 1994. "The Culture of High Reliability: Quantitative and Qualitative Assessment Aboard Nuclear-Powered Aircraft Carriers." *The Journal of High Technology Management Research* 5(1):141–161.

Roberts, Karlene, Bea Robert, and Dean L. Bartles. 2001. "Must Accidents Happen? Lessons from High-Reliability Organizations." *Academy Management Executive* 15(3):70–79.

Rochlin, Gene, Todd R. La Porte, and Karlene H. Roberts. 1998. "The Self-Designing High-Reliability Organization: Aircraft Carrier Flight Operations at Sea." *Naval War College Review* 51(3):97–113.

Sagan, Scott D. 1993. *The Limits of Safety: Organizations, Accidents, and Nuclear Weapons*. Princeton, NJ: Princeton University Press.

Scott, W. Richard. 2008. *Institutions and Organizations: Ideas and Interests*. Los Angeles, CA: Sage Publications.

Selznick, Philip. 1949. *TVA and the Grass Roots: A Study in the Sociology of Formal Organization*. Berkeley: University of California Press.

Selznick, Philip. 1957. *Leadership in Administration: A Sociological Interpretation*. New York: Harper and Row.

Selznick, Philip. 1996. "Institutionalism 'Old' and 'New.'" *Administration Science Quarterly* 41(2):270–277.

Shrivastava, Paul. 1992. *Bhopal: Anatomy of a Crisis*. 2nd ed. London: P. Chapman Pub.

Shrivastava, Paul. 1994. "Technological and Organizational Roots of Industrial Crises: Lessons from Exxon Valdez and Bhopal." *Technological Forecasting and Social Change* 45(3):237–253.

Shrivastava, Paul, Ian I. Mitroff, Danny Miller, and Anil Miclani. 1988. "Understanding Industrial Crises." *Journal of Management Studies* 25(4):285–303.

Simon, Herbert A. 1957. *Models of Man: Social and Rational; Mathematical Essays on Rational Human Behavior in Society Setting*. New York: Wiley.

Snook, Scott A. 2000. *Friendly Fire: The Accidental Shootdown of U.S. Black Hawks Over Northern Iraq*. Princeton, NJ: Princeton University Press.

Suchman, M. C. and L. B. Edelman. 1996. "The New Institutionalism in Organizational Analysis - Powell, W. DiMaggio, P J." *Law and Social Inquiry-Journal of the American Bar Foundation* 21(4):903–941.

Sutcliffe, Kathleen M. 2011. "High Reliability Organizations (HROs)." *Best Practice & Research Clinical Anesthesiology* 25(2):133–144.

Taylor, Alan. 2014. "Bhopal: The World's Worst Industrial Disaster, 30 Years Later." *The Atlantic*. Retrieved August 24, 2017 (www.theatlantic.com/photo/2014/12/bhopal-the-worlds-worst-industrial-disaster-30-years-later/100864/).

Taylor, Frederick Winslow. 2006. *The Principles of Scientific Management*. New York: Cosimo Classics.

Torry, William I., William A. Anderson, Donald Bain, Harry J. Otway, Randall Baker, Frances D'Souza, Philip O'Keefe, Jorge P. Osterling, B. A. Turner, David Turton, and Michael Watts. 1979. "Anthropological Studies in Hazardous Environments: Past Trends and New Horizons." *Current Anthropology* 20(3):517–540.

Turner, Barry A. 1976. "The Organizational and Inter-Organizational Development of Disasters." *Administrative Science Quarterly* 21(3):378–397.

Turner, Barry A. 1978. *Man-Made Disasters*. London: Wykeham Science Press.

Unseem, Jerry. 2016. "What Was Volkswagen Thinking?" *The Atlantic* (January/February). Downloaded from www.theatlantic.com/magazine/archive/2016/01/what-was-volkswagen-thinking/419127/ on August 7, 2018.

Vaughan, Diane. 1983. *Controlling Unlawful Organizational Behavior: Social Structure and Corporate Misconduct*. Chicago, IL: University of Chicago Press.

Vaughan, Diane. 1996. *The Challenger Launch Decision: Risky Technology, Culture, and Deviance at NASA*. Chicago, IL: University of Chicago Press.

Vaughan, Diane. 1998. "Rational Choice, Situated Action, and the Social Control of Organizations." *Law & Society Review* 32(1):23–61.

Vaughan, Diane. 1999. "The Dark Side of Organizations: Mistake, Misconduct, and Disaster." *Annual Review of Sociology* 25:271–305.

Weber, Max. 1978. *Economy and Society: An Outline of Interpretive Sociology.* Berkeley: University of California Press.

Weick, Karl E. 1987. "Organizational Culture as a Source of High Reliability." *California Management Review* 29(2):112–127.

Weick, Karl E. 1993. "The Collapse of Sensemaking in Organizations: The Mann Gulch Disaster." *Administrative Science Quarterly* 38(4):628–652.

Weick, Karl E. and Karlene H. Roberts. 1993. "Collective Mind in Organizations: Heedful Interrelating on Flight Decks." *Administrative Science Quarterly* 38(3):357–381.

Wheeler, Derek S., Gary Geis, Elizabeth H. Mack, Tom LeMaster, and Mary D. Patterson. 2013. "High-Reliability Emergency Response Teams in the Hospital: Improving Quality and Safety Using In Situ Simulation Training." *BMJ Quality and Safety* 22:507–514.

7

RISK SENSEMAKING

Robert P. Gephart, Jr. and Max Ganzin

Risk sensemaking, a common feature of everyday life, is the verbal, intersubjective process of noticing, interpreting and explaining actions and events to assess their potential to become risks and dangers that produce extensive harm. It is the primary agentive process (Emirbayer & Mische, 1998) through which intentional choices and actions are made to influence risk, crisis and emergency management, and an important focus in social research (Lupton, 1999; Gephart, Van Maanen, & Oberlechner, 2010, p. 141).

Risk, defined as the probability of an event multiplied by the magnitude of loss or gain that results (Lupton, 1999), is essential for economic gain, and the dominant logic of capitalist wealth production assumes that risk and wealth are compatible (Beck, 1992, p. 154). But risk has a more sinister character in late modernity (Beck, 1992): it is a source of threats that can damage an organization, its stakeholders, products and reputation (Barton, 1992, p. 2). And the logic of late capitalism has shifted from one of wealth production to a logic of risk society that assumes the *in*compatibility of distributions of wealth and risk, and the *competition* of their 'logics' (Beck, 1992, p. 154). The logic of risk society is reducing and remediating the accumulated damage from prior wealth production.

Given the importance of risk sensemaking in contemporary society and in crises, the primary objective of this chapter is to describe, explain and compare two important approaches to risk sensemaking: (1) ethnomethodology (Garfinkel, 1967), a micro-sociological approach considered "the science of sensemaking" (Heap, 1976), and (2) Weick's (1995, 2001) social psychological approach. Both approaches share common ideas but also differ (Weick, 1995, p. 11). Weick views sensemaking as a subjective, cognitive process triggered by cognitive dissonance (1995). Weick's interest in sensemaking was inspired by conversations with Harold Garfinkel, the originator of ethnomethodology, whose famous jury decision-making study uncovered the retrospective nature of sensemaking critical to Weick's perspective (Weick, 1995, p. 10). Weick's approach to sensemaking has been widely cited in the management and organization studies area. Ethnomethodology offers important means to advance sensemaking research but is not as well known. It is thus important to explain and compare the approaches so that scholars interested in risk sensemaking may better understand and use the two perspectives more effectively in research and practice. To do so, we provide examples of crisis research done using each approach, highlight the topics explored, address advantages of each approach and provide guidance for future research on risk sensemaking.

The Ethnomethodological Approach to Sensemaking

Ethnomethodology, a micro-sociological approach, provides a "descriptive science of sensemaking" (Heap, 1976, p. 107) to understand how common sense knowledge is produced and used in everyday practical reasoning (Garfinkel, 1967; Leiter, 1980, pp. 3–4). The term "ethnomethodology" (Garfinkel, 1974) refers to the everyday sensemaking methods (interpretive practices) social actors use to construct social reality and sustain a sense that the world has a factual character they can share with one another even if they disagree (Leiter, 1980). The sense of shared agreement is signaled when the sensemaking practice of "let it pass" is operating. This sense of shared reality is fragile and perishes when the interaction ends or sensemaking is disrupted.

Ethnomethodology conceives sensemaking as an agentive, intersubjective process undertaken through verbal communication in situated interaction that creates a sense of shared meaning among members (Garfinkel, 1967; Leiter, 1980). Sensemaking can be studied directly by observing the talk, textual work and discourse of members of society (Gephart, 1993, p. 1470). The socially constructed world produced by sensemaking is a real world that must be continuously reproduced: there is no time out from sensemaking (Leiter, 1980, p. 173).

Breaching expectancies and sensemaking practices. Ethnomethodology's conception of sensemaking practices builds on Schutz's (1973a, 1973b) formulation of background expectancies (Garfinkel, 1967, p. 37): elemental interpretive processes that inform all efforts at creating meaning or sensibility (Freeman, 1980, p. 139). Garfinkel (1967) designed experiments to breach expectancies in ways that make trouble and render the interpretive practices visible to permit Garfinkel to explore how they work (1967, p. 37). Disruptions of the sensemaking practices produced senselessness, bewilderment, anxiety, indignation and disorganized interaction. These outcomes confirm the practices are essential for normal interaction. For example, Garfinkel (1967) asked 49 undergraduate sociology students to spend 15–60 minutes imagining, and then act as boarders in their home: to behave in a circumspect, polite fashion, use formal address, avoid being personal, and speak only when spoken to (Garfinkel, 1967, p. 47). Only 40 students actually acted as boarders. Their "family members were stupefied" (p. 47) and demanded explanations, asking them if they were sick. Reactions included "astonishment, bewilderment, shock, anxiety, embarrassment, and anger" (p. 47). A mother shrieked angrily at her daughter for being disrespectful and a father berated his daughter for "acting like a spoiled child" (p. 48). When students explained their behavior was an experiment, their families "were not amused" (p. 48) because the disruption of expectancies produced anger, confusion and interpersonal conflict.

Sensemaking practices are explicit and tacit assumptions and actions that create and sustain a sense of shared meaning during face-to-face interaction and restore social order after breaches. Four general practices identified by Garfinkel (1967) are, first, the *reciprocity of perspectives* that assumes that "participants in conversation understand one another and can experience the same perspective on the world" even if they disagree (Gephart, 1993, p. 1472). This practice is enacted by acknowledging another's talk was heard ("uh huh"). In the boarder study, breaches of expectations prevented family members from understanding students's (qua boarders') perspectives so they did not confirm this reciprocity. Second, members construct and expect others to construct *normal forms* of phenomena: recognizable words and behaviors others can comprehend. The boarder role required abnormal forms of talk (politeness) that deviated from the informal behavior expected and demanded explanations of deviant behavior. Third, vague and incomplete features of conversation are sustained as normal forms by using *the etcetera sensemaking practice* with two aspects: an assumption that features of phenomena that are unclear will be filled in or interpreted by the hearer (etcetera assumption) or clarified later (retrospective-prospective interpretation assumption). Family members waited when the student's talk was unclear, and then employed a sensemaking practice term called 'the etcetera clause' to elicit missing information that was not provided. This was done by using questions (e.g. are you ill?) to understand the unusual behavior.

Finally, members use *descriptive vocabularies as indexical expressions* by assuming non-sensible terms, and utterances will be interpreted later using contextual knowledge to give meaning to expressions. Family members used knowledge of the household context to comprehend the student talk as abnormal but failed to uncover contextual information that made the behavior sensible, and hence they became angry. The boarder example shows how sensemaking practices are used to create organizations (the family) and selves (student, boarder) as sensemaking resources. Risk was created in the boarder experiment when simple breaches of expected role behavior disrupted interactions and caused unease, anger, confusion and interpersonal conflict.

Risk sensemaking: the ethnomethodological view. Risk sensemaking involves noticing, interpreting and explaining phenomena that humans encounter as risks and dangers by offering accounts and verbal explanations of events (Gephart, 1992, p. 118; Weick, 1997, p. 271). Ethnomethodological studies of risk sensemaking address intersubjective properties of sensemaking in talk and texts related to risks, harms and dangers. Ethnomethodologists prefer to study risk sensemaking done in real settings where risks and crises are discussed and assume the disruption of ongoing sensemaking is a cue signaling the emergence of crisis.

Risk sensemaking is the fundamental agentive process involved in risk and crisis management. Agency is the human ability to undertake intentional actions based on reasons that can be explained to others (Mayr, 2011). It is the dialogical process that social actors use to engage in temporally constructed and structured environments using "habit, imagination and judgment… to transform structures in response to problems" (Emirbayer & Mische, 1998, p. 970). The three temporally constructed dimensions of agency are future, present and past addressed respectively by projection, iteration and practical evaluation.

Agency emphasizes projectivity (future-oriented sensemaking) used by social actors to imagine possible future trajectories of action where structures are reconfigured in relation to the future (Emirbayer & Mische, 1998). Projectivity draws on past experiences and reactivates habits and routines to identify present actions to manage the future. Projectivity connects to past and present because actors relate to all three temporal dimensions at any moment. Ethnomethodology thereby rescues projectivity "from its subjectivist ghetto" (1998, p. 991) to respecify it as an intersubjective phenomenon accomplished in social interaction.

Projectivity mobilizes past knowledge, habits and routines in present settings to predict the future and to plan strategies to prevent, manage or remediate risks, crises and disasters associated with them. Risk sensemaking also involves retrospective sensemaking done in present settings (e.g. a public hearing into a disaster) to locate past causes of crises. In general, risk sensemaking reviews past trajectories of agentive action and imaginatively anticipates present and future trajectories of action to address future crises or to allocate responsibility for past crises.

Risk sensemaking addresses how organizations and selves are constructed as interpretive schemes, and how these schemes are used prospectively and retrospectively to identify causes and outcomes of risks and crises in specific contexts. Three themes are used to construct organizations (Gephart, 1993, pp. 1470–1471; Bittner, 1965). First, organization is constructed as a model of functional integrity specifying organizational needs that must be met for the organization to function and survive. Actions that threaten to need fulfillment are constructed as risks, dangers and harms. Second, organizations are constructed as a model of compliance where rules and policies describe appropriate behaviors that produce safety and inappropriate behaviors that create risks. Third, organizations are constructed as informal models of style that specify acceptable behavior. Actions that are inconsistent with models of style can be interpreted as disruptive and threatening.

The process of constructing selves for persons provides reasons and motives for action in relation to risky events. Four themes composing selves have been observed (Gephart, 1979, 533–537). The professional self is constructed by stating features of a person's career, training and professional activities. The social psychological self is constituted by a person's styles and habits as well as their general traits and motivations. The financial self is constructed in terms of wealth, occupation, professional experience and financial status of a person and their economic features, status and needs. Finally, the physiological self is constructed in terms of a person's physical capabilities, physical features and health.

Risk sensemaking at a public hearing. Public hearings are a primary societal venue for retrospective sensemaking concerning the causes and consequences of disaster and the actions of those involved (Gephart, 1993, p. 1474; 1997). Hearings occur post-disaster to facilitate cultural adjustment (Turner, 1976; Gephart, 2008). The ethnomethodological approach to risk sensemaking is illustrated by a study of sensemaking at a National Energy Board of Canada (NEB) public inquiry into a fatal accident on a pipeline system in Canada (Gephart, 1992, 1993) held in March 1985. The accident occurred during efforts by a pipeline maintenance crew to repair a leak of natural gas liquids (NGLs) from the pipeline. Five pipeline workers were seriously burned during the repair effort, and two workers subsequently died. The participants in the hearing included the NEB, the pipeline firm and legal counsel for the widow of the pipeline foreman (Gephart, 1993, p. 1476).

Ethnography and documentary analysis were used to explore sensemaking that emerged during the public inquiry into the accident (Gephart, 1992, 1993). The goal was to understand "how are sensemaking practices used in the interpretation of disasters" (Gephart, 1993, p. 1475)"? Data included field notes on hearing activities, official proceedings of testimony at the hearing, and the NEB's official report. These data provide descriptions of risk sensemaking about the accident undertaken during the hearing (Gephart, 2008) and were analyzed using computer-aided interpretive text analysis (Gephart, 1993, 1997; Kelle, 1995) to develop textual exhibits and textual tables. Textual exhibits containing detailed passages of data tell the stories of the Assistant District Manager (ADM), pipeline maintenance worker, DM (District Manager), and Board. The stories were analyzed using expansion analysis to explicate the background information participants used to understand and highlight the theoretical processes operating in the discourse (Gephart, 1993, pp. 1484–1485). Textual tables present sentences from testimony and documents that include all occurrences of key word uses by witnesses. Key words reflect the central issues uncovered at the hearing using ethnographic observations. The textual analysis of data explained how participants interpreted the hearing discourse, uncovered workers' tacit background knowledge, and described discursive processes in sensemaking. The storied accounts of the four different actors underwent comparative analysis.

Stories of risk sensemaking. The Assistant District Manager's Story. Company policies state: "On a major NGL leak the best course of action may be to ignite it. Once ignited, the danger of a growing and drifting explosive cloud is eliminated" (Gephart, 1993, p. 1488). The ADM as on-site authority during the accident noted: "it was a major break...I stated we seriously needed to consider the option of flaring" (p. 1488). "He [the District Manager] felt strongly that we shouldn't flare it offand [should] approach the repair by setting an upstream stopple and he followed that comment with however if we were unless we were 100 percent sure that all was safe" (p. 1488).

The pipeline worker' story. The worker described flaring as a team decision involving the DM, ADM and pipeline foreman: "If three agree to it… it is usually done" and "I would have assumed that their decision would have been strong enough to flare". "John approached me and he expressed his danger. He thought we should get out of here, and I was kind of in a state of I agree with you" (Gephart, 1993, p. 1490). A media account notes, "A man who outran the flames from a pipeline flash fire recalled… hearing his co-workers cry out as each was caught by the rolling inferno". This testimony "left the widow of his former foreman in tears" (p. 1490).

The District Manager's story. During the DM's direct testimony, the company's legal counsel asks, "Why you did not want to flare at night?" The DM replied that he thought the situation was under control and "I think we just took it for granted it would be a stopple job [a normal repair] before the fire". After aggressive questioning, the DM replied "I personally didn't want to flare. There is no hiding that". He was concerned flaring the leak would ignite the 18,000 barrels of highly flammable NGLs in the 14.4 km pipeline segment and impact two pipelines just meters away (Field notes summarized from Gephart, 1993, p. 1492).

The Board's final report states: "The district manager did not relay to the director of operations the recommendations of the Assistant District Manager and foreman to flare escaping gas prior to installing a stopple" (in Gephart, 1993, p. 1494).

Interpreting stories of risk. The stories show that public inquiries are important sites for sensemaking about organizational risks and dangers. Inquiries address risk sensemaking situated in the present (the hearing site) and retrospectively account for the original crisis event. Key words that described risk, danger, responsibility, safety, hazards and fears were normal form terms that played important roles in the accounts of all parties. Flaring (voluntarily igniting) the vapor cloud was a key concern as a hazardous last resort for controlling a dangerous fire. The key concepts members used made the hearing sensible as a response to a tragic event and allocated responsibility for safe practices to decisions of managers. Attributions of blame were important in framing the inquiry and allocating responsibility, but blaming was beyond the scope of the inquiry.

Further, all parties used sensemaking practices to sustain and control discourse and to create and negotiate meanings for the organization and its actions. The Board and the ADM thereby developed the sense they shared the view that the situation was out of control and flaring the leak would have been the safest action. In contrast, the DM viewed the situation idiosyncratically: the fire was under control and flaring would be dangerous.

Sensemaking practices were used by stakeholders to construct divergent schemes of organizations and individuals to interpret risks and dangers. The workers, foreman, ADM and the Board constructed the organization as a hierarchy where the DM, ADM and pipeline foreman had authority to give orders to workers. The Board and ADM sought to use their authority to prevent harm to the pipeline crew and the public. In contrast, the DM portrayed his authority as ambiguous and de-centralized. He was criticized for using incorrect organizational schemes that caused the accident and sought to avoid monetary loss from incinerating an expensive product and danger from starting an uncontrollable control fire.

Responsibility for crises was thereby created by constructing organizational schemes that allocate responsibility to specific positions, and then using these schemes to interpret behavior as laudable or problematic. Critical interpretations are imposed on events when the schemas used by on-site organizational agents diverge from or contradict the prior organizational schemes constructed and used by legitimate institutional agents.

Finally, the study shows sensemaking is largely a social not psychological process. A social perspective is needed to address how different interpretations and divergent views among groups are addressed through collective action, to account for cultural categories used in sensemaking and to understand how social actors in accidents are demonized or valorized. The social perspective can provide knowledge of how features of settings influence sensemaking, offer knowledge of how sensemaking practices are used and disrupted, create understanding of institutional contexts where risks and dangers emerge in discourse, address the history of groups involved in the sensemaking and uncover the background knowledge members use to do sensemaking.

Safety logics. Risk sensemaking research has also explored the role of safety logics in accidents. Baccus (1986, pp. 22–27) reviewed regulatory actions and investigations and observed truck tire servicing to understand how competing versions of safety – top down hierarchical logics of regulators and workers' in-situ logics of safe practice – were used to produce safety in multi-piece truck wheel accidents. A multi-piece truck wheel is "a rim base over which a truck tire is mounted and a wheel center which is bolted onto the axle of the vehicle" (Baccus, 1986, p. 20). Because of the design, locking failure is common: between 1969 and 1974, a total of 500 explosive separations caused over 90 deaths and 300 injuries (p. 27), although a safer single piece rim was available.

The Occupational Health and Safety Administration (OSHA) created a safety regulation using a top-down, hierarchical control logic (Baccus, 1986, p. 32) to address wheel separations. Hierarchical logic provides regulations that, if followed, would prevent accidents. For example, OSHA uses regulatory logic and requires safety cage utilization to contain wheels that could separate during repair (Baccus, 1986, p. 44).

Baccus also found the existence of in-situ local safety logics that create ad hoc safeguarding activities (p. 43) that are outcomes of interacting with the wheels but not part of OSHA standards (Baccus, 1986, p. 42). For example, the goal of "seating" the ring to prevent explosive separations (Baccus, 1986, p. 46) requires interaction with the rim without a safety cage during inflation while maintaining contact with the ring parts by "using a hammer on the ring" (p. 47) and poking and tapping the ring to ensure proper seating. Yet the official wall chart repair guide states: "NEVER [red caps] hit tire or rim with a hammer" (p. 47).

Thus, competing versions of safety emerge. Formal safety logic involves top-down application of standards that are deductively effective, and official safety logic ignores local practice (Baccus, 1986, p. 48). Strategies such as the "safety cage" are remedial measures that do not address how accidents are created but instead ensure that anything that occurs is ignored if accidents do not occur. In contrast, situated logics of practice and personal safeguarding logics create safe practice for workers. Accidents can be understood using situated logics of practice that formal accident theory cannot address. As a consequence, regulation is not straightforward (Baccus, 1986, p. 50) and does not ensure safe work. Rather, one needs to understand the structures of local practice and the situated logics of effective and safe procedures that are unexamined and untouched by formal safety theory to unravel how accidents are produced and to alter the processes that produce them.

Extending social studies of risk and crisis. Four areas related to risk sensemaking illustrate emerging extensions: temporalities, institutional rhetoric, riskwork and riskification.

Temporalities and risk. Studies of risk sensemaking that address the past, present and future temporal aspects of sensemaking are rare (Wiebe, 2010), and the "present" dimension of time has largely been viewed retrospectively (Weick, 1995, 2001). Yet, temporalities are important for risk sensemaking (Gephart, Topal, & Zhang, 2010) because sensemaking is often undertaken to anticipate the future, deal with current problems and learn from the past. The agentivity perspective central to sensemaking (Emirbayer & Mische, 1998) encourages a concern with temporalities and emphasizes projection as the primary dimension of sensemaking. Projection can create regulations to ensure future safety and is critical for risk management.

A study of future-oriented sensemaking addressed an energy board hearing to assess an application by an oil and gas firm to drill and operate two sour gas (H_2S) wells on land owned by a local resident (Gephart, Topal, & Zhang, 2010). The key risk was a potential leak of the gas that is fatal at concentrations above 400 ppm. The public hearing was a suitable site to explore how risk temporalities operate in projective sensemaking (Gephart, Topal, & Zhang, 2010, pp. 286–287). Data included the official hearing transcript and the final report by the hearing board. The documents were analyzed with computer-supported qualitative data analysis to code and interpret data (Gephart, 1993, 1997).

Sensemaking practices helped participants construct and project hypothetical entities into the future by constructing an unfolding future trajectory that was retrospectively located in the past. For example, testimony by a company official noted that "it is expected that the new wells that are proposed will produce sweet gas...however the prospect of sour gas produced from the... well, which also targets the slightly sour Nordegg formation, is clearly recognized at this time" (Gephart, Topal, & Zhang, 2010, p. 304). Embedding entities in past and present enhanced peoples' expectations that projected entities will become real, and histories for entities were described as linear sequences of events moving from past to future. Thus, standard institutional steps from the past became next steps projected into the future. Finally, professionals involved in these projections were constructed as "experts" legitimately qualified to project the future.

Past schemes were constructed in the present, and then shaped into future projections of hypothetical entities using selective reconstruction, creative elaboration of prior entities and inventing new entities. The vagueness of past meanings made future projections more open to innovation. As well, expertise was created in hearings by describing the qualifications of persons and degrees from the past. For example, a company official noted "I'm a graduate with distinction from the University of Regina... and use the title of professional engineer" (Gephart et al., p. 303). Extensive and important links to the past made future projections more certain and sensible than projections without connections to the past or present.

Institutions were legitimated and sustained by future-oriented sensemaking that established how the projected risks of future projects could be safely managed or prevented. Projection was done using discourse grounded in past routines, and in structures used in the present to create plans and images of the future. Experts are authorities that are institutionally sanctioned to do future-oriented sensemaking and project hypothetical entities. Their projections are hard to challenge by non-experts, and experts with similar background seldom challenge other experts' projections.

Institutional rhetoric. Institutional rhetoric (Lynch & Bogen, 1996; Clarke, 1999, 2006) examines how social institutions persuade others to accept interpretations (Gephart, Topal, & Zhang, 2010, p. 283), regulate communication in public inquiries (Lynch & Bogen, 1996; Gephart, 2007) and create plans and planning (Clarke, 1999). Plans are the means used by organizations to know the future (Clarke, 1999, p. 40). Functional plans require meaningful data to estimate probabilities. If probabilities cannot be assigned, plans are "fantasy documents" – imaginative fictions that may or may not anticipate future crises (Clarke, 1999, pp. 16–19). Institutional rhetoric is relevant to risk sensemaking that often addresses phenomena that are not probabilistic but that are used to develop institutional plans. Thus, risk sensemaking is often negotiated in institutional settings, and is the agentive organizational core for decision-making about past, present and future actions that select risks for management attention.

Emerging extensions. Riskwork (Power, 2016) refers to discursive practices used to ascertain and address risk. Risk workers are institutional agents embedded in the "dominant paradigm" of risk management. They routinely address established risks, emerging risks and eliminating risks in their ongoing jobs (Hardy & Maguire, 2016, p. 144). The conceptualization of riskwork is used to develop foundations for a bottom-up approach to understanding risk sensemaking done by risk professionals. The approach is credited in part to ethnomethodology (Power, 2016, p. 5) and its continuing influence on Weickian sensemaking. Riskwork is similar to risk sensemaking from an ethnomethodological point of view. For Power (2016), this "broad micro-sociological point of view...defines the space of the chapters [in Power's book] and their common focus on the work of managing risk" (p. 8). However, Power's conception of riskwork emphasizes risk as a form of work in common, everyday work of institutional agents rather than riskwork undertaken during disasters and crisis: "the turn to work [in risk studies] requires a provisional bracketing of the disaster bias...in order to bring to the surface the assumptions that sustain the practices of risk management" (p. 9). Riskwork thus addresses ethnomethodological concerns but reframes them in terms of formal institutional constraints. There is great potential for future riskwork research to advance social approaches to risk and crisis sensemaking.

Riskification theory. "Riskification" is a post-structural constructivist approach to understanding organizational risk discourse based on a Foucaultian perspective (Hardy & Maguire, 2016). Constructivism is an interpretive perspective that differs from social constructionism (Berger & Luckmann, 1966) through its greater emphasis on subjective interpretations and its treatment of discourses as integrated, reified and objective products of prior communication that exist outside of particular actors. Discourses impose identities and thereby constrain or preempt agentive action. In contrast, ethnomethodology conceives discourse as a process of agentive action accomplished through communication involving talk and texts. Discourse is a process that must be accomplished in an ongoing manner, and the factual nature of discourses must be created and sustained through sensemaking not assumed a priori.

The constructivist approach to understanding riskwork offers a perspective that conceives of sensemaking as a process with limited agency relative to the highly agentive approach of ethnomethodology. Thus, comparative analyses of crises using different approaches can advance sensemaking research by exploring the boundaries of agency in accidents and crises. We turn now to a discussion of Weickian sensemaking.

The Weickian Approach to Sensemaking

Sensemaking (Weick, 1995, p. 14) is the invention process done through human senses that precedes interpretation and constructs that which becomes sensible. In sensemaking, people generate and interpret the social world (Weick, 1995, p. 13; Weick, Sutcliffe, & Obstfeld, 2005, p. 409) by "comprehending, understanding, explaining...and predicting" events (Starbuck & Milliken, 1988, p. 10). Weick conceptualizes crises, but not risk. Crises are "low probability, high-consequence events that threaten the most fundamental goals of an organization... defy interpretations and impose severe demands on sensemaking" (Weick, 2001, p. 224). Crisis sensemaking is an episodic process triggered by exogenous events that interrupt plans or cognitive structures underway, and it ends when a disruption ends.

Weick distinguishes interpretation from sensemaking (Weick, 1995, p. 6). Sensemaking assumes authoring and action are interwoven (Weick, 1995, p. 13), highlights the interpretation of traces (p. 13) and addresses puzzles quickly. Interpretation is both a process and a product; it is more detached and engaged than sensemaking, and it discovers something "there" (1995, p. 14). If interpretations fail, other interpretations are used with little impact on peoples' sense of self. Loss of interpretation is a nuisance, not a crisis (p. 14).

Sensemaking is an outcome of peoples' attempts to manage equivocality in social life (Weick, 2001, p. 9). "What sensemaking is not is a metaphor" – it is literally "making something sensible" (Weick, 1995, p. 16); hence, sensemaking creates social reality. Sensemaking has more impact than interpretation and failures of sensemaking question the nature of the world (p. 14).

Organizing as natural selection. Weick (1979, p. 133) offers a recipe for sensemaking. "How can I know what I think until I see what I say?" anticipates Weick's model of "organizing as natural selection" (1979, p. 130) where communication precedes cognition and means that action creates material for sensemaking rather than the reverse. Sensemaking begins when ecological change causes enactment, selection, retention (Weick, 1979, pp. 132–137) and remembering (Weick, 2001). Ecological change triggers sensemaking (Weick, 2001, p. 97) if important objects unexpectedly appear and/or are absent when expected (Weick, 2001, p. 97 following Mandler, 1997, p. 74). Sensemaking processes reciprocally influence each other to reveal "the circularity involved in most sensemaking" (p. 135).

People produce the raw material that is made sensible through enactment (Weick, 1979, p. 133). This involves the selective, retrospective refinement and interpretation of retrospective cues, connecting cues with plausible stories and highlighting credible aspects of accounts to enact an environment. Enactment is "more influential" for "sensemaking" than the environment (Weick, 2001, p. 177) because actions that create the environment also produce self-fulfilling prophecies that constrain actions (p. 176). Selection is similar to enactment (Weick, 2001, p. 237).

Retention (Weick, 2001, p. 305) stores enacted meanings that are consistent with prior interpretations retained in organizational memories. Retention is similar to believing. It is guided by plausibility based on successful past sensemaking. Remembering recalls and uses retained information. It can mislead when it relies on preconceptions, knowledge that is incomplete or distorted by recall, or fails to consider the unknowns that are unexplained (Weick, 2001, p. 358). Complex remembering that directs attention to salient cues may miss other cues and overdetermine action.

Organizational crisis sensemaking. All crises have an enacted quality (Weick, 2001, p. 228): initial crisis responses determine the trajectory of a crisis. This is illustrated in the Bhopal disaster (Weick, 2001, pp. 228–233) where the plant became susceptible to crisis due to management's beliefs that led to policies at the Bhopal Plant in India that signaled the plant was unimportant to Union Carbide. The signals led to cost-cutting that enacted further deteriorations in working conditions causing a methyl isocyanate leak that killed over 3,000 people (Shrivastava, 1987).

The enactment perspective suggests crisis events are more controllable than previously thought (Weick, 2001, p. 234) despite a necessary tradeoff between dangerous actions that create better understanding and safe but ineffective actions that produce confusion (p. 274). Effective crisis management needs to lower the intensity of crises, increase skills to expand perception, appreciate how small actions produce large consequences, improve awareness of commitments that bias diagnoses and reduce tight coupling and interactive complexity in the system (p. 235).

The collapse of sensemaking at Mann Gulch. A lightning storm ignited a small fire in Mann Gulch on August 4, 1949. Firefighters expected to control the fire by the next morning when they parachuted into the area on August 5 at 4 p.m.; however, they found dangerous conditions: a temperature of 97°F, strong winds and a high fire danger rating. While hiking to the fire, Dodge, the foreman, saw the fire cross the gulch 200 yards ahead and race toward them. He headed up a 76% ridge toward the top with the men behind, chased by 30-foot high flames. Dodge suddenly lit a fire, ordered the crew to drop their tools and told them to lie down in the burned area. The 13 mainly young men ignored him, raced for the ridge and were burned to death. Two men stuck together and made it over the ridge, and they survived as did Dodge the leader. It took 450 firefighters over 5 days to gain control of the fire (summary of Weick, 2001, pp. 100–102).

Weick's (2001) detailed and nuanced analysis of the disaster explores how "minimal organization" makes organizational members subject to "cosmology events" (p. 104) and thereby

> susceptible to sudden losses of meaning (p. 105) when surprises or incomprehensible events occur. In cosmology events, people's understanding of the world is breached, they feel the universe is no longer a rational, orderly world, and they experience "collapse of sensemaking and structure".
>
> *(p. 105)*

Weick's analysis of the disaster argues that the loss of intersubjectivity among members of the group who perished was the key to the disastrous outcome because it created existential confusion leading to complex interaction among systems factors.

Seven properties of sensemaking and the Mann Gulch disaster. The following illustrative analysis was created to show how Weick's seven properties of sensemaking can be used as a "rough guideline for inquiry" (Weick, 1995, pp. 17–18) to understand the Mann Gulch data. First, sensemaking is grounded in identity construction and constructs the selves of the sensemaker.

Second, sensemaking is retrospectively done by reviewing past experience to understand a present or future situation. Sensemaking collapsed at Mann Gulch because the men used past experience to incorrectly anticipate a controllable fire (retrospective sensemaking).

Third, sensemaking enacts sensible environments. Conditions were rapidly changing on the ground as the fire rapidly advanced toward them and leadership was blurred. The ability to comprehend context was disrupted, and there was no ongoing sensemaking (difficulty enacting a sensible environment).

Fourth, sensemaking is social and creates shared meanings and coordinates action (p. 42). At Mann Gulch, the organization began to dissipate as individual behavior emerged and leadership became unclear. The lack of role specificity impeded development of clear identities for crew members: they did not know their role or roles of others, and hence they didn't know how to act and interact (loss of social).

Fifth, arousal is activated if ongoing sensemaking is interrupted. The intensity of the fire and situation on the ground, the fire's rapid growth, the loss of organization and the leaders's behavior disrupted sensemaking and caused men to panic.

Sixth, sensemaking addresses extracted cues (p. 50): familiar phenomena that can "seed" (p. 50) development of a larger sense of what is happening. The cues extracted from the leader's behavior such as reversing direction and starting a fire were surprising and hard to interpret (lack of clear cues).

Finally, sensemaking is driven by plausibility not accuracy. It is concerned with filters and embellishments that influence sensemaking. Sensemaking seeks to provide coherent, reasonable, credible and socially acceptable accounts (p. 61). And the most plausible action based on past experience was to run to escape the fire (plausibility of escape by running versus lighting another fire).

Weick's recommendations for preventing the collapse of sensemaking encourage development of capabilities that enhance organizational resilience. He recommends more extensive use of intra-group verbal and non-verbal communication to coordinate complex systems that are susceptible to catastrophes (Weick, 2001, p. 115), creating structure with both an inverse and a direct relationship between meaning and structure (p. 117), recognizing the limitations of non-disclosive intimacy (p. 118) and developing emotional ties in groups to keep panic under control (p. 118).

Making sense of an airline disaster. The Tenerife air disaster in 1977 caused 583 deaths when a KLM Flight departing from Los Rodeos Airport collided with a Pan Am Flight taxiing on the runway. Weick's analysis (2001) addresses the processes that amplify the effects of small events to produce disasters (p. 125) and demonstrates how processes in tightly coupled systems produce more errors and reduce the means to detect them.

On March 27, 1977, a KLM flight bound from Amsterdam to the Canary Islands, and a Pan Am Flight bound from New York to the Canary Islands, were diverted to Los Rodeos Airport at Tenerife after their original destination – Las Palmas Airport – was bombed. Los Rodeos Airport is a small airport with limited facilities or parking for aircraft, and the Pan Am flight had to park behind the KLM flight. The KLM flight taxied onto the active runway at 4.56 p.m. prior to takeoff and was told by control to turn and hold at the end of the runway. The Pan Am pilot was ordered to taxi down the active runway behind the KLM flight. The KLM flight reached the end of the runway, turned and the captain pushed the thrusters to move forward. The co-pilot said "Wait a minute we do not have ATC clearance", and the pilot responded "No I know go ahead and ask". After the request, the co-pilot quickly said, "We are uh taking off" or "We are at takeoff". The Pan Am flight, engulfed in fog, was not visible to the KLM crew or the control tower. The pilot stated he would report when he was off the runway and the KLM engineer asked the KLM pilot "Is he not clear then, that Pan Am?" and the pilot replied "yes". And 13 seconds later, the collision with the Pan Am flight occurred killing 583 people [Summarized from Weick, 2001, pp. 126–140].

Weick (2001) analyzes the voice recording of cockpit conversations to explore environmental demands and stress, individual and group capacities, the breakdown of group behavior into individualism, the role of speech exchange (communication) systems and the need to manage interactive complexity.

The airport environment was stressful due to the bombing at the Las Palmas Airport; other factors were fear that Los Rodeos Airport could also be bombed, limited space to park or maneuver aircraft, flight crew fatigue and fog obscuring the runway. These factors could impair the crew's performance and create small discrepancies that cause the greatest stress. Further, the Dutch law limited the allowable monthly flying time for pilots, permitted no flexibility to extend duty time, used a system that made it was impossible for pilots to calculate remaining flight hours, and violations could trigger fines, imprisonment and loss of one's pilot license. The incident occurred near the end of the month when KLM pilots were close to their flying time limits and needed to depart within 2 hours to avoid exceeding their flying time limits. The Pan Am crew also faced stress because their flight was blocked from leaving for 2.5 hours by the KLM flight.

The setting was unusual. The KLM flight captain was a member of the top management team, head of KLM flight training for 10 years and had not flown regular routes for 12 weeks. Training captains follow a flight script and the training captain – not the control tower – gives permission for takeoff. Simulated flights are common in training and simulated takeoff occurs without any permission given. The captain had given the young co-pilot (the First Officer), who was new to his job, his qualification recently. The co-pilot's comments were ambiguous attempts to influence the takeoff decision and indicated the co-pilot was surprised and was trying to alert others to the takeoff.

A problem with lack of communication meant the existence of organization became problematic as the crew acted like individuals not as a team. A well-functioning team can transform a complex task into simpler tasks that are less susceptible to disruptive effects of arousal. And incoherent and misunderstood communications disrupted interpretations and routines and created confusion. Further, hierarchical communication systems can produce false hypotheses when accuracy is needed under certain conditions – all of which were present at the time (Weick, 2001, p. 137). Subordinates often distort messages to please a superior and reduce role overload, which may account for the co-pilot's limited talk and action.

Finally, the interactive complexity at Los Rodeos Airport increased during the day (Weick, 2001, p. 138). There was no place to park aircraft and aircraft maneuvers were restricted (e.g. 148° turns) or impossible due to the 75-foot wide runway. The initial loosely coupled linear airline system became a more tightly coupled non-linear system later as more aircraft arrived, making it difficult for the airline crews and the controllers to create and maintain a sensible environment.

These stressors thus produced regression to first learned responses including the pilot's adoption of flight training officer behavior during takeoff without ATC clearance, and the co-pilot's passive, deferential behavior toward the pilot that reflected a trainee role not a co-pilot role. Weick (2001, p. 131) attributes some of these stress-based effects to "autonomic activity" – a physical reaction following an interruption that creates arousal, limits information processing capacity and reduces sensed cues available for interpretation.

The flight crews almost coped. The KLM pilot saw the Pan Am flight during departure and tried to climb over it, but the KLM flight struck the Pan Am flight with its wheels and crashed.

Extending Weickian sensemaking. Organizational scholars have extended Weick's crisis sensemaking research (Weick, 1988, 1993, 2001) to different contexts, for example, during unfolding crises as well as in the aftermath when the crises have ended (Maitlis & Christianson, 2014). And crisis sensemaking concepts have been used to map new domains of risk, for example, ecological sensemaking and environmental risk (Whiteman & Cooper, 2011) and ethics (Thiel et al., 2012).

Recent studies have addressed sensemaking during unfolding crises including mining disasters (Wicks, 2002), climbing disasters (Kayes, 2004), building collapses (Christianson et al., 2009) and disasters in entertainment events (Vendelo & Rerup, 2009). Insights from this research address the normalization of deviance that emerges when people take deviant behaviors for granted, ignore cues of possible risks and hinder sensemaking in ways that lead to disasters. Dunbar and Garud (2009) report normalization of the protective foam shed from the Columbia space shuttle caused the loss of the vehicle and crew. Similarly, Wicks (2002) found that miners became accustomed to conceiving of dangerous conditions as normal, and this normalization led to the Westray mine disaster. Further Kayes (2004) reported that overly optimistic statements by mountaineers prevented them from noticing a serious problem that ultimately led to the deaths of eight climbers. This shows that overly optimistic outlooks can be detrimental to crisis management.

Post hoc investigations of public inquiries into crises included an inquiry into children's deaths and injuries at a UK hospital (Brown, 2000), an inquiry into an industrial accident that destroyed an offshore oil platform (Brown, 2004), an inquiry into the collapse of Barings Bank (Brown, 2005) and an inquiry into the deaths of people caused by a heat wave in France (Boudes & Laroche, 2009). These studies provide insights into how post-crisis sensemaking restores trust and legitimizes institutions. Instead of blaming and assigning responsibility, public inquiry accounts can be rhetorical and use overly optimistic statements to create an account of the crisis that ultimately legitimates the institution under investigation (Maitlis & Sonenshein, 2010).

Researchers have also mapped new territories of contemporary risks. The concepts of ecological sensemaking developed by Whiteman (Whiteman & Cooper, 2011; Whiteman, 2012) and planetary risk (Whiteman & Williams, Chapter 13) refer to "the process used to make sense of material landscapes and ecological processes" (Whiteman & Cooper, 2011, p. 889). Ecological sensemaking can help people notice and make sense of material cues in the environment that impede prevention and management of crises caused by the natural environment and action on climate change (Whiteman, 2012). The predisposition to ecological sensemaking is very important in organizations operating in specific contexts such as wilderness and forests (Weick, 1993; Whiteman & Cooper, 2011), sub-arctic ecosystems (Whiteman & Cooper, 2011) and aquatic environments. A predisposition to planetary risk management is essential for planetary survival (Whiteman & Williams, Chapter 13; Gephart, 1984).

Another emerging issue is developing sensemaking models for ethical decision-making (Thiel et al., 2012; Bagdasarov et al., 2016) to address the increasing complexity of the environment in contemporary organizations and the challenging ethical risks faced in environmental decision-making. Sensemaking is inevitable in complex high-risk situations with difficult ethical dilemmas. Recent research has developed several intentional strategies for sensemaking that mitigate risks in ethical decision-making (Thiel et al., 2012, p. 55).

Finally, sensemaking research on established risk topics is growing. Maitlis and Sonenshein (2010) argue shared meaning and emotion are important for risk sensemaking. While positive emotions including hope and relief are found in risk sensemaking, Maitlis and Sonensheim argue that negative emotions, such as anxiety, fear, panic and desperation are prevalent in crisis situations and can significantly impede sensemaking. Cornelissen, Mantere and Vaara (2014) also show how emotions and materiality in sensemaking under pressure operated in the context of the Stockwell shooting that caused the killing of an innocent person during a police anti-terrorism operation. Finally, Winch and Maytorena (2009) studied sensemaking in the context of risky decision-making and found levels of education and training improved sensemaking, whereas experience impeded sensemaking due to a check box mentality.

Comparing Weickian and Ethnomethodological Sensemaking Perspectives

Weickian sensemaking is theoretically eclectic and methodologically diverse. Sensemaking is a real, retrospective, episodic, subjective, cognitive process triggered by environmental disruptions that dissipates when disruptions end. Risk sensemaking is conceptualized in terms of crises. In contrast, ethnomethodology is grounded in interpretive social science and linguistics. Sensemaking is an ongoing intersubjective process altered by breaches of expectancies that trigger repair efforts to restore a sense of order. If the restoration works, the crisis will be averted. If it fails, the group may lack a sense of shared meaning and a crisis may occur. Risk sensemaking in ethnomethodology involves moments of intersubjective sensemaking directed to phenomena constructed as past, present or future risks, harms and dangers as conceived by members. Sensemaking always orients to all three temporal modes.

Table 7.1 Comparison of Weickian and Ethnomethodological Approaches to Risk Sensemaking

Dimension	Weickian sensemaking	Ethnomethodology
Theoretical foundations	Pragmatism, ethnomethodology, social psychology, cognitive dissonance, organization theory	Social phenomenology, symbolic interactionism, interpretive sociology, linguistics
Sensemaking	• The invention process using human senses that precedes interpretation and constructs that which becomes sensible • Episodic • Sensemaking is a metaphor • Sensemaking is making sense	• The verbal, intersubjective process of interpreting actions and events • Continuous • Sensemaking is an ongoing process of noticing, interpreting and acting that occurs in social interaction
Risk sensemaking	• Risk not explicitly conceptualized • Crises involve interruptions of plans or cognitive structures that are underway	Intersubjective communication that seeks to interpret and account for risks, hazards and crises
Intersubjectivity	3 levels: Intersubjective, generic subjective, extrasubjective	The sense that people can understand the point of view of others in a conversation and see the world from this point of view
The organization	• A collection of people trying to make sense of what is happening to them • open systems and interpretive systems that do more than individuals can	A linguistic device and resource constructed through sensemaking and descriptive accounts done in face-to-face settings and in texts
Levels of analysis	• Psychological level: individual and group perception and cognition • Individual in group or unit context	• Micro-sociological level: face-to-face communication in real settings • Micro-level communication among people
Temporalities	Sensemaking is primarily retrospective in focus but can be forward-oriented and is done in a present	Sensemaking is oriented to the future, founded on the past and done in the present
Data	• Secondary data: detailed narratives of crisis events assembled from government reports, expert analyses and non-fiction literature • Key focus = how cues become visible as crises, how adaptation prevents adaptability, exogenous influences on situated crises	• Primary data: transcripts of face–to-face communication in specific settings. Secondary textual data including investigative report data and transcripts of hearings • Key focus = detection, interpretation and repair of disruptions in sensemaking during pre-crisis, crisis and post-crisis phases
Data analysis	Experiments, documentary analysis, grounded theorizing, essays writing	Conversational analysis, ethnography, grounded theorizing, expansion analysis

(Continued)

Dimension	Weickian sensemaking	Ethnomethodology
General applications	• Analysis of broad features of sensemaking observed in interaction or textual accounts + imputed cognitions depicted in secondary sources • Explore cognitive and spoken manifestations of sensemaking	• Fine-grained, precise and detailed description and analysis of conversations and interactions in real settings to uncover sources of disruptions, routines and breaches, and communicative practices for restoring meaning • Explore the deepest levels of sensemaking and culture
Risk, crisis and emergency management applications	• Uncover and identify triggers of the collapse of sensemaking • Explore how adaptations can prevent adaptability • Understand how organizations unravel and how to make organizations resilient • Retrospective analysis of crises and disasters • General focus and broad theoretical commitments allow far ranging analyses of large-scale disasters	• Understand how sensemaking practices are used to interpret and manage risks and crises • Uncover sources of communicative disruptions • Explore how order is restored after disruptions • Multi-temporal analysis of risks, crises and disasters • Focus on situated communication to precisely describe and analyze sensemaking in specific risk and crisis settings

Organization is created with language in Weickian theory that also often reifies the organization as an entity outside of human agency and applies generic theoretical concepts to understand organizations as, for example, open systems theory. Ethnomethodology de-reifies the organization using a radically process-oriented perspective that assumes organization exists only in and through the communicative practices that renders it visible. The organization is a linguistic device constructed through conversation and becomes a reified entity through sensemaking. Weickian sensemaking presupposes a stable order of things as a prelude to sensemaking. Ethnomethodology investigates this stable order as the ongoing practical accomplishment made possible in and through sensemaking.

Data and analyses in Weickian sensemaking research involve experiments, documentary analysis and writing empirically based essays. A variety of data and sources are used to study organizational sensemaking, including secondary evidence from media or literature. In the approach, triggers of risk are discerned, disruptive adaptations are identified, retrospective interpretations of crisis are provided and general (generic) concepts are used to interpret phenomena given the broad theoretical and epistemological commitments of Weick's perspective. Data and data analyses in ethnomethodology tend to utilize primary or secondary data that describe face-to-face interaction in specific settings including institutions and textual accounts of organizational action. The general goal is to create fine-grained descriptions and precisely detailed qualitative analyses that provide insights into how sensemaking practices create a sense of social order and how this sense of order is disrupted and restored in interaction.

This comparison shows Weickian sensemaking and ethnomethodological sensemaking are similar: they both draw inspiration and foundational concepts from philosophical traditions associated with interpretive sociology. They differ because the Weickian perspective orients more to positivist literatures of organization theory and cognitive psychology and conceives sensemaking as a cognitive process. In contrast, ethnomethodology orients more to interpretive sociology, anthropology and linguistics, and conceives sensemaking as a micro-social process. The respective conceptions of organization and risk/crisis reflect the more realist view of Weick and the process-oriented interpretive view of ethnomethodology. Weickian sensemaking also emphasizes retrospect, whereas ethnomethodology addresses all three temporal dimensions.

Methodologically, the two approaches differ in terms of how data are collected and used. Weickian research uses traditional qualitative and quantitative designs and methods to create large-grained analyses of phenomena that extend the sensemaking perspective outward to address a wide range of topics using diverse theoretical views. Sensemaking as a cognitive process is not an observable process but is inferred and can be studied with causal mapping (Weick, 2001). In contrast, ethnomethodology applies linguistically oriented analytical approaches directly to traces of sensemaking: transcripts of situated talk, descriptions of settings and texts. Broadly expressed, Weickian sensemaking research is theory-driven, uses a diverse set of positivist and interpretive ideas and methods and selectively applies theory and concepts to examples of data. In contrast, ethnomethodological research is data-driven, selects concepts and theory based on what emerges in data, uses abductive methods and is exhaustive in analysis of an entire corpus of data.

Discussion and Conclusion

Ethnomethodology addresses certain aspects of sensemaking more readily than Weickian sensemaking and other extensions, and these are areas where the social approach to sensemaking has the greatest potential to advance sensemaking research in general. We conclude by discussing the contributions that could emerge from addressing these issues.

Ethnomethodology uncovers and addresses divergent views of the world and multiple realities where risks and crises are addressed and interpreted. The chapter shows how different people and groups can have radically different cosmologies and conceptions of risks, danger and crises. Weickian sensemaking assumes sensemaking is problematic when it diverges from reality and thus seeks to reconcile divergent views both against one another and against a singular objective reality. This privileges the dominant view as the true view and reflects positivist ontology. For ethnomethodology, divergent views create multiple realities that are intersubjectively shared by collectivities. The analyst is not an arbiter of truth, but a descriptor of differing rationalities whose task is to describe the interpretive processes that produce different "realities" and allow one conception of the world to dominate others (Gephart, 1984). Ethnomethodology can thus help advance sensemaking theory and research by providing tools to examine and analyze situations where multiple realities exist and truth is elusive to understand the conversational processes that constitute negotiated agreement on realities, and the interactional consequences of the competing or differing realities.

Second, Weickian research is broad-brush research that uses general background knowledge and generic concepts to tell interesting stories about uncommon phenomena using secondary accounts of events or large-grained descriptions that provide limited, selective details of interaction. These descriptions could be complemented by more fine-grained descriptions such as those composed by ethnomethodology to provide more detailed, precise and accurate records of interaction for analysis.

Third, Weickian sensemaking research emphasized retrospective sensemaking and views the present through the past. In contrast, ethnomethodology and extensions address all three temporalities and focuses on projectivity – the future-oriented work of sensemaking.

Weickian approaches and sensemaking research in general can benefit by incorporating all temporal dimensions in analysis and can be guided in by the ethnomethodological approach to temporalities and agency.

Fourth, ethnomethodology's concern with accuracy contrasts with Weick's plausibility criterion. The plausibility criterion means that filters and embellishments that influence sensemaking may not be understood because they are not adequately described. Accurate descriptions of sensemaking as action are needed to uncover such filters. A focus on accuracy and precision in description and analysis using ethnomethodology could also bring sensemaking research closer to conventional scientific practice and thus advance the field. Further, a focus on plausibility in members' accounts rather than accuracy can help both perspectives grasp situated logics and reasoning that differ from scientific and other rational methods.

Fifth, Weick uses deductive logic to apply generic concepts to data, and abduction to depict concepts of social actors in their own terms. The deductive and abductive moments are therefore not tightly connected in Weickian research when general concepts such as open systems theory are applied to abductively created descriptions in a top-down manner. Risk sensemaking research, and particularly Weickian research, can be advanced by using the fully developed abductive process advocated by Schutz (1973) to create abductively consistent scientific concepts (Gephart, 2018).

Finally, Weickian sensemaking explores local practices in descriptive data on human behavior, but it becomes distant from local knowledge and concepts of members by imposing top-down logics and "reality" on situated logics and subjectively rendered decision outcomes. Ethnomethodology addresses situated logics of practice and local safeguarding logics of members and contrasts these with top-down hierarchical knowledge rather than reality. These situated logics and local practices are examined but not deeply probed in Weickian and other studies where realities are known from the outside, not the inside. The situated logics that Weickian sensemaking uncovers can be explored more fully by attending to the social level using ethnomethodological practices. Working together, these sensemaking approaches can unpack the elusive processes that produce accidents and find ways for enabling humans to intervene in crises and prevent them.

References

Baccus, M. D. (1986). Multi-piece truck wheel accidents and their regulation, pp. 20–59. In H. Garfinkel (Ed.) *Ethnomethodological studies of work*. London and New York: Routledge and Kegan Paul.

Bagdasarov, Z., Johnson, J. F., MacDougall, A. E., Steele, L. M., Connelly, S., & Mumford, M. D. (2016). Mental models and ethical decision making: The mediating role of sensemaking. *Journal of Business Ethics, 138*(1), 133–144.

Beck, U. (1992). *Risk society: Towards a new modernity*. London: Sage Publications, Ltd.

Berger, P., & Luckmann, T. (1966). Society as a human product, pp. 51–61. In *The social construction of reality: A treatise in the sociology of knowledge*.

Bittner, E. (1965). The concept of organization. *Social research, 32*, 239–255.

Brown, A. D. (2000). Making sense of inquiry sensemaking. *Journal of Management Studies, 37*, 45–75.

Brown, A. D. (2004). Authoritative sensemaking in a public inquiry report. *Organization Studies, 25*(1), 95–112.

Brown, A. D. (2005). Making sense of the collapse of Barings Bank. *Human Relations, 58*, 1579–1604.

Boudes, T., & Laroche, H. (2009). Taking off the heat: Narrative sensemaking in post-crisis inquiry reports. *Organization Studies, 30*(4), 377–396.

Christianson, M. K., Farkas, M. T., Sutcliffe, K. M., & Weick, K. E. (2009). Learning through rare events: Significant interruptions at the Baltimore and Ohio Railroad Museum. *Organization Science, 20*, 846–860.

Clarke, L. (1999). *Mission probable: Using fantasy documents to tame disaster.* Chicago, IL: University of Chicago Press.

Clarke, L. (2006). *Worst cases: Terror and catastrophe in the popular imagination.* Chicago, IL: University of Chicago Press.

Cornelissen, J. P., Mantere, S., & Vaara, E. (2014). The contraction of meaning: The combined effect of communication, emotions, and materiality on sensemaking in the Stockwell shooting. *Journal of Management Studies, 51*(5), 699–736.

Dunbar, R. L. M., & Garud, R. (2009). Distributed knowledge and indeterminate meaning: The case of the Columbia shuttle flight. *Organization Studies, 30,* 397–421.

Emirbayer, M., & Mische, A. (1998). What is agency? *American Journal of Sociology, 104*(4), 962–1023.

Freeman, G. H. (1980). Fitting two-parameter discrete distributions to many data sets with one common parameter. *Applied Statistics, 29,* 259–267.

Garfinkel, H. (1967). *Studies in ethnomethodology.* Englewood Cliffs, N.J.: Prentice Hall.

Garfinkel, (1974). The origins of the term 'Ethnomethodology', pp. 15–18. In R. Turner (Ed.), *Ethnomethodology.* Harmondsworth, England: Penguin Books.

Gephart, R. P. (1979).*Making Sense of Succession.* Unpublished PhD dissertation, University of British Columbia, Vancouver.

Gephart, R.P. (1984). Making sense of organizationally based environmental disasters. *Journal of Management,* 10, 205–225.

Gephart, R. P. (1992). Sensemaking, communicative distortion and the logic of public inquiry legitimation. *Industrial and Environmental Crisis Quarterly, 6,* 115–135.

Gephart, R. P. (1993). The textual approach: risk and blame in disaster sensemaking. *Academy of Management Journal, 36*(6), 1465–1514.

Gephart, R. P. (1997). Hazardous measures: an interpretive textual analysis of quantitative sensemaking during crises. *Journal of Organizational Behaviour,* 18: 583–622.

Gephart, R. P. (2007). Hearing discourse, pp. 239–260. In M. Zachry & C. Thralls (Eds.) *The cultural turn: Perspectives on communication practices in workplaces and the professions.* Amityville, NY: Baywood Press.

Gephart, R. P. (2008). Crisis sensemaking and the public inquiry, pp. 123–160. In C. Pearson, C. Roux-Dufort, & J. Clair (Eds.), *International handbook of organizational crisis management.* Thousand Oaks, CA.: Sage Publications.

Gephart, R. (2018). Qualitative research as interpretive science, pp. 33–68. In C. Castells, A. Cunliffe, & G. Grandy, (Eds.), *The Sage handbook of qualitative business and management research methods: History and traditions.* London: Sage Publications.

Gephart, R., Topal, C. & Zhang, Z. (2010). Future oriented sensemaking: Temporalities and institutional legitimation, pp. 275–311. In T. Hernes & S. Maitlis (Eds.), *Process, sensemaking & organizing.* New York: Oxford University Press.

Hardy, C. & Maguire, S. (2016). "Organizing risk: discourse, power and "riskification". *Academy of Management Journal, 41*(1), 80–108.

Heap, J. (1976). "What are sense making practices?" *Sociological Inquiry, 46,* 107–115.

Kayes, D. C. (2004). The 1996 mount everest climbing disaster: The breakdown of learning in teams. *Human Relations, 57,* 1263–1284.

Kelle, U. (1995). *Computer-aided qualitative data analysis: Theory, methods and practice.* London: Sage Publications.

Leiter, K. (1980). *A primer in ethnomethodology.* New York: Oxford University Press.

Lupton, D. (1999). *Risk.* New York: Rutledge.

Lynch, M., & Bogen, D. (1996). The spectacle of history: Speech, text, and mat the iran-contra hearings. Durham, NC: Duke University Press.

Maitlis, S., & Christianson, M. (2014). Sensemaking in organizations: Taking stock and moving forward. *The Academy of Management Annals, 8*(1), 57–125.

Maitlis, S., & Sonenshein, S. (2010). Sensemaking in crisis and change: Inspiration and insights from Weick (1988). *Journal of Management Studies, 47*(3), 551–580.

Mandler, G. (1997). *Human nature explored.* Oxford University Press.

Mayr, E. (2011). *Understanding human agency.* Oxford University Press.

Power, M. (2016). Introduction, pp. 1–25. In M. Power (Ed.), *Riskwork: Essays on the organizational life of risk management.* New York: Oxford University Press.

Schutz, A. (1973a). Common-sense and scientific interpretation of human action, pp. 1–47. In M. Natanson (Ed.), *Alfred Schutz Collected Papers I: The problem of social reality*. The Hague: Martinus Nijhoff.

Schutz, A. (1973b). Concept and theory formation in the social sciences, pp. 48–66. In M. Natanson (Ed.), *Alfred Schutz Collected Papers I: The problem of social reality*. The Hague: Martinus Nijhoff.

Starbuck, W. H., & Milliken, F. J. (1988). Challenger: Fine-tuning the odds until something breaks. *Journal of Management Studies, 25*(4), 319–340.

Thiel, C. E., Bagdasarov, Z., Harkrider, L., Johnson, J. F., & Mumford, M. D. (2012). Leader ethical decision-making in organizations: Strategies for sensemaking. *Journal of Business Ethics, 107*(1), 49–64.

Vendelo, M. T., & Rerup, C. (2009). Weak cues and attentional triangulation: The Pearl Jam concert accident at Roskilde Festival. Paper presented at the Academy of Management Annual Meeting, Chicago, IL.

Weick, K. E. (1988). Enacted sensemaking in crisis situations. *Journal of management studies, 25*(4), 305–317.

Weick, K. E. (1993). The collapse of sensemaking in organizations: The Mann Gulch disaster. *Administrative Science Quarterly, 38*, 628–652.

Weick, K. (1995). *Sensemaking in organizations*. Thousand Oaks, CA.: Sage Publications.

Weick, K. (2001). *Making sense of the organization*. Oxford, UK: Blackwell Publishers.

Weick, K. E., Sutcliffe, K. M., & Obstfeld, D. (2005). Organizing and the process of sensemaking. *Organization Science, 16*(4), 409–421.

Whiteman, G. (2012). Ecological sensemaking and climate change. *RSM Discovery-Management Knowledge, 9*(1), 8–10.

Whiteman, G., & Cooper, W. H. (2011). Ecological sensemaking. *Academy of Management Journal, 54*(5), 889–911.

Wicks, D. (2002). Institutionalized mindsets of invulnerability: differentiated institutional fields and the antecedents of organizational crisis. *Organization Studies, 22*, 659–692.

Winch, G. M., & Maytorena, E. (2009). Making good sense: Assessing the quality of risky decision-making. *Organization Studies, 30*(2–3), 181–203.

8

ISSUES AND TRENDS IN RESEARCH METHODS

How We Learn Affects What We Learn about Crises, Risks, and Emergency Responses

Rob Austin McKee, Connor Lubojacky, and C. Chet Miller

Introduction

Organizations and the individuals inside them must manage both chronic and acute risks. In addition, they often must confront specific crises that have developed, and facilitate or provide emergency responses. Indeed, in an increasingly complex and interdependent world, effective approaches to risk, crisis, and emergency management have become exceptionally important. In response, these aspects of modern life have become focal points for academic research.

A substantial number of studies have appeared over the past ten years, not only in response to the evolving risk-crisis context but also in response to an oft-cited call for additional research (Pearson, Roux-Dufort, & Clair, 2007). Indeed, the number of published studies has more than quintupled in the past decade. This rapid expansion has been needed and has produced some interesting and important findings, yet the expansion also suggests it is time to pause and reflect on our collective work. Have we been making the best choices and engaging the best practices in our methodologies as the field's scale has dramatically increased? From a very general perspective, assessing methodological choices and practices is important for at least two reasons, as discussed in the following paragraph.

First, the overall usefulness of knowledge and prescriptions generated by individual studies largely depends on the appropriateness and rigor of the research methods used (Pfeffer, 1993; P. R. Sackett & Larson, 1990). Thus, the accumulation, breadth, and depth of knowledge across a discipline are contingent on the research designs found in individual studies (Allen, Eby, O'Brien, & Lentz, 2008). In addition, as a discipline grows, matures, and becomes whole, research questions addressed by the discipline necessarily become more complex, and research methods should therefore concomitantly evolve in terms of robustness and sophistication (Asare, Yang, & Brashear Alejandro, 2012). This evolution, however, is not always seen. Particular research practices often become institutionalized within a discipline and thus become resistant to change even when they can be shown to be less effective and efficient than other methods (McKee & Miller, 2015). Thus, research methods that were appropriate earlier in a discipline's history may continue to be heavily used despite becoming obsolete as the discipline has advanced (Cumming et al., 2007; Dacin, Goodstein, & Scott, 2002; Fidler & Cumming, 2007; Labovitz, 1972).

Second, research choices and practices within a discipline affect perceptions of the discipline's legitimacy (Wagenmakers, Lee, Lodewyckx, & Iverson, 2008), which affects recognition by external stakeholders and the ability of a field to disseminate knowledge beyond its boundaries (Buelens, Van De Woestyne, Mestdagh, & Bouckenooghe, 2008). Assessing a discipline's current research practices provides diagnoses of strengths and weaknesses, and ultimately generates ideas for advancing the field (Casper, Eby, Bordeaux, Lockwood, & Lambert, 2007; Scandura & Williams, 2000).

Related to the aforementioned motivation for evaluating methodological choices and tactics, questions currently abound regarding the validity and veracity of research findings across fields, including medicine, psychology, and the field focused upon in this book. Sadly, some critics have gone so far as to say that, for a variety of reasons, most published research findings are false (Cumming et al., 2007; Fidler, Cumming, Burgman, & Thomason, 2004; Goodman & Greenland, 2007; Ioannidis, 2005; Moonesinghe, Khoury, & Janssens, 2007). Indeed, a number of recent investigations of the replicability of key research results have been troubling (Bettis, Ethiraj, Gambardella, Helfat, & Mitchell, 2016; Open Science Collaboration, 2015).

Interestingly, observable problems in research reports may mask more consequential but otherwise less observable problems in the underlying research. For instance, failure by a research team to provide crucial information about basic study design, such as the time horizons for retrospective studies, can be observed, but the underlying causes of the omissions cannot be (accidental omission of key information vs. an editorial decision to trim the reporting in order to shorten the paper vs. purposeful blurring by the researchers of what was actually done). As another example, a very high proportion of supported hypotheses in a published quantitative study can be observed, but the drivers of such outcomes cannot be (well-done research vs. lucky research vs. unscrupulous research in the form of post hoc hypothesizing, selective use of participants/variables, or playing any number of statistical games that affect p-values) (Cumming, 2013; Simmons, Nelson, & Simonsohn, 2011). Inferences, however, can be made at the field level if a very high proportion of hypotheses are supported across existing quantitative studies. Given the complex contexts being examined in organizational research, and given the desire for novel theoretical ideas at most journals, the probability of a very high proportion of supported hypotheses is not high if unbiased scientific processes have been dominant (see, for example, Cardinal, Kreutzer, & Miller, 2017).

The goals of this chapter are to (1) investigate the current state of research methodology and reporting in the crisis, risk, and emergency management literatures; (2) identify practices shaping the field; and (3) provide recommendations for moving forward based on rigorous evaluations of the methods and practices that we identify. To accomplish our goals, we consider a set of 139 studies that appeared in published articles from 2006 to 2016. Thus, we provide a targeted review that aligns with the recent expansion of the field.

Quantitative vs. Qualitative Orientations as a Starting Point

Perhaps the most fundamental distinction that can be made in the research community relates to quantitative vs. qualitative work (see, for example, Miles, Huberman, & Saldaña, 2014). For the first of these, systematic measures such as scales or counts are used to assign numbers to all variables of interest across all units of analysis (organizations, teams, and so on). These numbers are then used either descriptively or inferentially to understand the subject matter better. Quantitative research frequently is positioned as deductive in its origins, but it need not be. Regardless, it is often designed to directly and immediately contribute to a cumulative knowledge base that can be used in evidence-based management (e.g., Avery, Graham, & Park, 2016; Kaplan, LaPort, & Waller, 2013; Pramanik, Ekman, Hassel, & Tehler, 2015).

For the qualitative approach, systematic measures give way to more flexible assessment approaches, and numbers typically give way to words or images (which ultimately might be coded and perhaps quantified in some way). Qualitative data can be particularly useful for studying processes and states for which very limited understanding exists a priori. Such data tend to be richly grounded in specific empirical contexts and provide deep, contextualized insights into how people think and act. Qualitative research frequently is positioned as inductive, but it need not be. Regardless, it is often designed to produce guidance for downstream quantitative studies (e.g., Bergeron & Cooren, 2012; Patvardhan, Gioia, & Hamilton, 2015; Sabatino, 2016).

In our examination of research related to risk, crisis, and emergency management, we separately examine quantitative and qualitative studies in recognition of the non-trivial differences in epistemology. Despite the separate examinations, we focus our attention on a set of common concerns across the two streams, including preferences for theory-driven or phenomenon-driven underpinnings, the use of archival vs. more proximate data sources, emphases on real-time vs. retrospective vs. prospective data, and the surfacing of victims's voices rather than only those of elites. Each of these methodological issues previously has been identified as important and influential, as discussed later. For the quantitative stream, we also assess the percent of hypotheses supported (as an indirect indicator of possible bias), as well as sample sizes and types of data. For the qualitative stream, we assess the apparent ontology, and for those studies on the more "objective reality" side of the coin, we assess the use of inter-coder reliability estimates and triangulation.

Methods

Literature Search and Inclusion Criteria

We initially identified candidate articles through an automated search of the *Web of Science* database, using the search terms "risk" and "crisis" while specifying "topic" as the search target. Next, we directly examined titles and abstracts of articles to identify those that fit the research stream of interest. In this step, articles focused on the potential for crises involving organizations, actual organizational crises, and/or organizational responses to emergencies were sought. In addition, the following definition from Pearson and Clair (1998) served to orient us to the proper domain (although focused on crises, the definition proved to be useful as general frame): "An organizational crisis is a low-probability, high-impact event that threatens the viability of the organization and is characterized by ambiguity of cause, effect, and means of resolution, as well as by a belief that decisions must be made swiftly" (p. 60). Three-hundred and nineteen articles entered our preliminary database through the preceding process. Finally, we applied a number of specific criteria to create our final database, including whether a particular article was (1) a primary empirical study as opposed to a meta-analysis, theory piece, or scale-development paper; (2) grounded in social/organizational science as opposed to engineering practice or financial economics (in keeping with the foci of this book); (3) published between January 2006 and December 2016; (4) published in a peer-reviewed journal; and (5) published in English. One-hundred and thirty-five journal articles remained after the application of these criteria (see Appendix A). The articles had been published in 60 journals (see Appendix B), but only two journals contributed more than ten articles each (*Journal of Contingencies and Crisis Management* and *Journal of Business Research*).

Coding Process

As mentioned earlier, we assessed the studies in our database using several dimensions (e.g., theory-driven vs. phenomenon-driven). Some of these dimensions apply to (nearly) every field of social science, while others are (nearly) idiosyncratic to the crisis, emergency, and risk management literatures. We discuss the dimensions and their importance in the next section.

Two of the authors coded 15% of the articles. Agreement ranged from 68% to 100% across the coded dimensions, with the average being 83%. Disagreements were resolved through discussion, and the coding protocols were refined. One of the authors then coded the remaining articles.

Findings

Surprisingly, we found that only 46% of the studies in our database were quantitative in orientation, while 49% were qualitative, with approximately 5% exhibiting both approaches. These relative emphases have remained constant over time, with one exception – studies incorporating both approaches rather than one or the other have increased from non-existent during the first half of our time period to a non-trivial presence in the second half (7%). This trend is welcome given that the strengths of one approach can compensate for the weaknesses of the other. Within the same overall project, quantitative research can be very useful for solidifying knowledge when positioned as a counterpoint or follow-up to ideas and propositions developed in qualitative work.

Despite the usefulness of dual-approach research, the almost equal devotion to quantitative and qualitative approaches at the field level is somewhat worrisome given the age of the risk, crisis, and emergency management field. As a field of inquiry matures, it is not unreasonable to expect a greater proportion of work to embody the quantitative tradition. Normal science based at least somewhat on shared paradigms should begin to emerge as a field matures (see, for example, Kuhn, 1962). Although some might fear the creation of conceptual and empirical straightjackets through this process, effective contributions to evidence-based management historically have been tied to quantitative work (Pfeffer, 2015; Pfeffer & Sutton, 2006; Rousseau, 2006; Rynes, Rousseau, & Barends, 2014). Rich insights from qualitative work are always critically important, but consolidating and cumulating knowledge in more quantitative ways tends to be helpful for a field that has aspirations for relevance and impact in the world of practice (Cardinal et al., 2017). As is widely known, medicine was transformed from a mysterious and problem-plagued field to a respected evidence-based field through a shift to careful, quantitatively focused studies (Greenhalgh, Howick, & Maskrey, 2014; Rosenberg & Donald, 1995; D. L. Sackett, Rosenberg, Gray, Haynes, & Richardson, 1996; Smith & Rennie, 2014).

Theory-Driven vs. Phenomenon-Driven Research

Some research is predominately theory-driven while other research is predominately phenomenon-driven (see, for example, Cotteleer & Wan, 2016; Hambrick, 2007; Schwarz & Stensaker, 2014; Van de Ven et al., 2015). For the first of these, attention in the initial phases of a project is generally focused on new deductions from existing theory, older ideas from existing theory, and/or contradictions across two or more theoretical traditions. For the second, initial attention is directed toward events, incidents, and/or empirical puzzles in the world around us. Repeated use of the term "theory" vs. repeated use of the term "phenomenon" can be seen in the research literature as individuals emphasize one or the other.

Both types of research can be positive. On the one hand, theory-driven work helps to organize lines of inquiry in a field, and it can generate a certain level of continuity over time as researchers seek to develop existing lines of inquiry (Van de Ven, 1989). Moreover, theories are often necessary for taming very complex aspects of organizational life. To put this idea another way, theories can facilitate effective inquiry because they distinguish figure from ground. As the old quip suggests, "there is nothing so practical as a good theory" (Lewin, 1951, p. 169). Phenomenon-driven research, however, also has its place. Such research connects the field directly and richly to events and incidents that matter, and it provides an epistemological avenue to important empirical discoveries (Bamberger & Ang, 2016; Van de Ven et al., 2015). In addition, such research tends to be problem-focused, where the studied problems resonate with practitioners. Recent commentaries have suggested that fields prosper when embracing problem-focused research (Drnevich, Mahoney, & Schendel, 2016; Van de Ven, 2016). Interestingly, more Nobel Prize winners have been phenomenon-driven than theory-driven (Haig, 2005).

Overall, both approaches to research are useful and important. Thus, balance in a given field is probably a positive standard. Too much theory-driven work can crowd out rich, new empirical discoveries, as theories can act as straightjackets that limit the scope and openness of research (Hambrick, 2007; Lynch, Alba, Krishna, Morwitz, & Gürhan-Canli, 2012; Schwarz & Stensaker, 2014). Too much phenomenon-driven research can crowd out the consolidation of gains and accumulation of findings related to particular questions, although such research perhaps should be emphasized in younger fields.

For quantitative research in the field of crisis, risk, and emergency management, we found a worrisome imbalance, with more than 90% of studies being theory-driven while only 2% have been phenomenon-driven. Eight percent have exhibited a blend of the two approaches (see Figure 8.1). In the past five years, these numbers have worsened, with 93% of studies exhibiting a theory-driven approach. For qualitative research, we found greater balance, but phenomenon-driven work has still lagged in this area – only 25% of studies have reflected a phenomenon-driven approach, with another 16% of studies exhibiting a blended approach. Across recent years, however, there has been a trend toward more phenomenon-oriented research in the qualitative world, shifting from 19% in the early portion of our time period (4 of 21 studies) to 28% in the latter portion (13 of 47 studies).

Overall, more quantitative research perhaps should be phenomenon-driven, with a discovery orientation (Bamberger & Ang, 2016). This suggestion, however, should not be taken too far because qualitative research is currently producing some phenomenon-based inputs for downstream quantitative studies. That is positive and productive, yet qualitative research seems to make up too much of the overall portfolio, as suggested earlier.

Archival Data vs. Key Informants

Selecting appropriate data sources is a crucial consideration for researchers. Benefits and costs must be weighed before choosing to emphasize archival data sources (e.g., databases and extant reports) or non-archival data sources (e.g., key-informant interviews and broad-based surveys) (Edmondson & Mcmanus, 2007; Podsakoff & Organ, 1986; Venkatraman & Ramanujam, 1986). Importantly, there is often little or only modest correlation between a variable assessed through an archival source and the same variable assessed through a non-archival source (Boyd, Dess, & Rasheed, 1993; e.g., Tan & Peng, 2003).

Archival data provide researchers with several advantages and disadvantages. On the positive side, these data are convenient and available to all researchers (though often at a cost), which facilitates replication and comparison across studies (Boyd et al., 1993). Also, relative to non-archival sources, archival data generally are seen as less prone to various biases (Huber & Power, 1985), though, of course, even archival data are reported by *someone* who is fallible (Gupta, Shaw, & Delery, 2000). Finally, archival data sometimes are extensive in terms of number of organizations covered and number of years represented, which sets the stage for higher levels of statistical power as well as longitudinal analyses (Payne, Finch, & Tremble, 2003). On the negative side, data available through archival sources may not correspond closely to theoretical constructs of interests, leading to less-than-ideal fit between data and the conceptual space of a given construct (Boyd et al., 1993). As one corollary, the same data may represent different constructs across studies, and the same constructs may be represented by different data. Such inconsistency can impede validity in the interpretations of findings and the comparability of various studies, which in turn can lead to problems in cumulative theory building and knowledge generation (Boyd et al., 1993).

Non-archival data sources also have both positive and negative aspects. Surveys, which often involve key informants but sometimes involve a broader base, are a cornerstone of quantitative research (Forza, 2002; Pinsonneault & Kraemer, 1993). They are quite useful for reaching large numbers of people who have information unavailable through archival means. Surveys, however, do pose a range of problems such as non-response bias and fatigue driven by "over-surveying" (Rogelberg & Stanton, 2007). Interviews typically involve key informants and are useful for generating in-depth data regarding feelings, opinions, and behaviors about which only a few well-placed organizational members may be knowledge-able or willing to discuss (Glick, Huber, Miller, Doty, & Sutcliffe, 1990; Gupta et al., 2000; Kumar, Stern, & Anderson, 1993). Despite the benefits of using key informants, there are notable limitations. The accuracy of key informants has been called into questioned in some instances (March & Sutton, 1997), as informants can be affected by biases resulting from divergent organizational roles and impression management (Phillips, 1981; Seidler, 1974).

Based on the review of the advantages and disadvantages for the field's two fundamental data sources, projects that include both an archival study and a non-archival study would seem to be quite valuable. If such a project produced similar findings across the two approaches, both of which are far from perfect, then relatively strong confidence would be

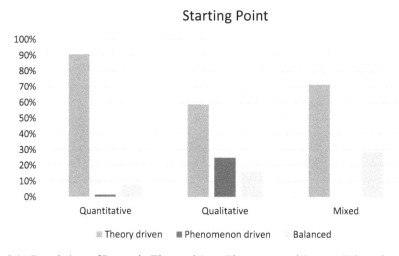

Figure 8.1 Foundations of Research: Theory-driven, Phenomenon-driven, or Balanced

generated in the findings. In essence, within-study replication would have been offered using different methods, and that is a very useful outcome (see, for example, Bettis et al., 2016; Miller & Bamberger, 2016). Alternatively, a project that blends the two approaches in one study also would have value (e.g., independent variables assessed through key informants while intermediate and outcome variables are assessed through archival means). Unfortunately, our critical review did not reveal a single project that followed the first of these two strategies, and it did not reveal a single quantitative project that followed the second.

Overall, we found that 44% of quantitative studies relied exclusively on archival sources while 56% relied exclusively on non-archival sources. For qualitative work, the profile was 44% and 43%, with the remaining 13% of qualitative studies having both types of data represented (see Figure 8.2). There were no major differences between the early and later time periods for either quantitative or qualitative research. Overall, there seems to be too much reliance on a single type of data, although some studies can only be based on one type or the other given the research questions being addressed.

Retrospective vs. Real-time vs. Prospective Data

Retrospective reports require eyewitnesses, senior officials, and other key informants to provide non-contemporaneous recollections of events, actions, feelings, and so on. Such reports are commonly used in research, and in courtroom proceedings, legislative debates, and other investigatory venues. They, however, present a number of potential problems, including lapses of memory, over-simplifications, post hoc rationalizations, and erroneous post hoc attributions (Golden, 1992; Huber & Power, 1985; Wolfe & Jackson, 1987). These problems can and do result in flawed research findings and conclusions (Huber & Power, 1985). While the careful use of retrospective reports can be valuable (Miller, Cardinal, & Glick, 1997), a field's overreliance on them would be a cause for concern.

In our work, we found that 26% of the quantitative studies were retrospective, defined in terms of new data being collected for a focal event (e.g., natural disaster, public relations fiasco) that occurred more than 30 days prior. Sixty-eight percent were real-time (data collection within 30 days of the event), and 6% were prospective (dealing with planning for the

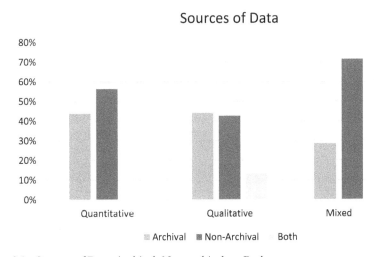

Figure 8.2 Sources of Data: Archival, Non-archival, or Both

Temporal Window

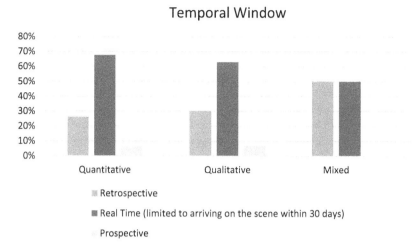

Figure 8.3 Temporal Window: Retrospective, Real-time, or Prospective

future). For qualitative research, we saw a similar pattern: 30% retrospective, 63% real-time, and 7% prospective (see Figure 8.3). The overall pattern suggests a reasonably healthy state, as over-reliance on potentially problematic retrospective reports has not occurred.

Three issues, however, do exist. First, retrospective studies have become more prevalent over time, particularly in quantitative research. Second, a number of these studies exceed the two-year time horizon often depicted as the limit for effectively looking backward in time (e.g., Miller et al., 1997). In the set of quantitative studies with a retrospective approach, 18% exhibit this issue. In the set of qualitative studies, 26% have long backward time horizons. Third, a number of the retrospective studies have unclear time horizons, which makes evaluations and interpretations of the underlying research difficult. Thirty-two percent of retrospective quantitative studies and 57% of retrospective qualitative studies fall into the unclear category. This lack of clarity should be avoided going forward.

We should note that we are primarily concerned with research that requires participants to put themselves back in time more than 24 months in order to recall subjective experiences, including feelings and opinions. We are slightly less concerned with research that asks participants to recall more concrete phenomena. Our contention is that at the individual researcher level, extended-horizon retrospective research is appropriate as long as sufficient justification exists to warrant new data-collection on dated event(s), and assuming underlying measures (scales, interview questions) are exceptionally high in quality and focused on facts rather than opinions, emotions, and other subjective phenomena (Miller et al., 1997). At the collective field level, however, a high incidence of older focal events would be undesirable, because of threats to the reliability of data and thus the conclusions garnered from research. Moreover, as mentioned, lack of clarity about the backward time horizon must be avoided. Without clear knowledge in this area, readers are denied a crucial contextual element regarding the research methodology.

Voices of Victims vs. Elites

For a well-rounded field, it is imperative that voices of victims be heard. If only the voices of elites are captured (e.g., senior government officials, senior managers from firms that helped to handle the problem, and senior company officials from firms that actually experienced the problems), then our field could be flavored by self-interested portrayals of events and incidents. Indeed, the voices of elites could subdue the voices of victims ('t Hart, Heyse, & Boin, 2001). Elites are more identifiable, even if less accessible, and their words might be seen as more important because of greater perceived legitimacy and stronger underlying information advantages (Lalonde, 2012). Also, there might be some impetus on the part of elites to stifle the voices of victims under the presumption that the victims' voices could instigate increased public and media scrutiny of the elites, thereby spurring elites to expend resources and take remedial actions they otherwise may have been able to avoid (Boin & 't Hart, 2004; 't Hart et al., 2001). Thus, when common citizens are victims, they may have to work together to make their voices heard (Lalonde, 2012). At the other extreme, if only the voices of victims and potential victims are captured, then our field could be pervaded by overly narrow perspectives and too much raw emotion.

For quantitative research, we found that 34% of the studies in our database presented the direct voices of victims, with 40% doing so in the most recent five years (up from 21% in the earlier time period). For qualitative research, we found that 31% of the studies presented the direct voices of victims (see Figure 8.4), with 32% doing so in the most recent five years (up from 29% in the earlier time period). Greater attention to victim's voices would be positive, but the trends over time are in the right direction.

Additional Aspects of Quantitative Research

Publication bias is a major problem for quantitative research in a host of fields (Bettis, 2012; Miller & Bamberger, 2016). Indeed, a crisis of faith related to this issue has swept across the academic landscape (Bettis et al., 2016; Ioannidis, 2005; Open Science Collaboration, 2015). In essence, publication bias corresponds to published evidence not being representative of all existing evidence (Cardinal et al., 2017). It is created by author choices regarding what to submit to journals, and editor/reviewer choices concerning what to publish (Schmidt & Oh, 2016). In both of these cases, choices typically hinge on statistical support for novel hypotheses (Barley, 2015; Bettis, 2012; Cardinal et al., 2017; Davis, 2015; Miller & Bamberger, 2016;

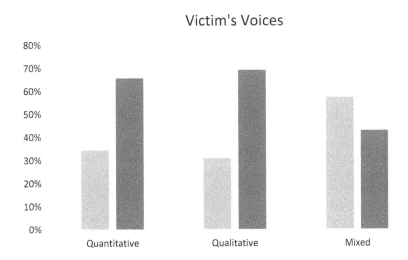

Figure 8.4 Victims' Voices Directly Represented: Yes or No

Starbuck, 2016; Tsui, 2013). Related to this, HARKing can be an issue. HARKing (**H**ypothesizing **A**fter the **R**esults are **K**nown) has been defined as "presenting a post hoc hypothesis in the introduction of a research report as if it were an a priori hypothesis" (Kerr, 1998). Authors might HARK in order to ensure empirical "support" for novel "hypotheses."

To assess publication bias, we examined the percentage of hypotheses supported in quantitative research (Cardinal et al., 2017). Overall, 79% of the hypotheses proffered by studies in our data set were fully (~73.5%) or partially supported (~5.6%), without any discernable trend toward higher or lower rates over time. This relatively high proportion of supported hypotheses is problematic for the field because it likely indicates some degree of publication bias, and perhaps HARKing (Fanelli, 2010; Mazzola & Deuling, 2013). With non-significant findings hiding in file drawers, it is difficult to assess actual effect sizes for various independent variables (Rosenthal, 1979). Some effect sizes that appear to be substantial actually could be negligible across all credible studies that have been conducted, only a fraction of which appear in the published literature.

We also examined sample sizes and exact sources of data used (archival databases, archival reports, archival photos, surveys, interviews, direct field observations, field experiments, lab experiments, vignettes, and eye tracking). Across our database of studies, the average sample size was 2,477, which is quite substantial and a driver of strong statistical power. This number, however, is inflated by archival studies and semantic network analyses (for which the average sample sizes were 6,000 and 12,000 observations, respectively). Removing those data sources yielded an average sample size of 248, which is still reasonable. Regarding sources of data, the plurality of studies was based on surveys (44%), with archival databases (25%) and archival reports (14%) being the next most common data types. Surveys, archival databases, archival reports, and/or interviews appeared in 96% of the studies. All other data types were somewhat limited, appearing in approximately 15% of the studies. Overall, this pattern reveals substantial breadth in data types, which seems useful for rich examinations of varied research questions in a dynamic field.

Additional Aspects of Qualitative Research

Qualitative research comes in many flavors. One basic distinction relates to objective ideology (non-interpretive) vs. subjective ideology (interpretive). Both of these ideologies are very valuable, but the former might provide some advantage in legitimacy outside of the field, with senior managers, policy makers, and members of the media. Based on our examination of ontological language used in the articles, 91% of the qualitative studies in our database do, in fact, exhibit an objective, non-interpretive ideology. While this percentage might be somewhat inflated by an undercount of interpretive work (interpretive researchers may have been forced to alter their language in order to be successful in the review processes at some journals), it does seem to indicate a strong emphasis on more objective ideologies.

We examined triangulation in the non-interpretive studies. Triangulation can be defined broadly to include aspects of measurement, data collection, and research strategy (Scandura & Williams, 2000), but we limit our examination to straightforward consistency checks on information that has been received. In essence, our focus lies with reliability and robustness of the data, which in turn affect researchers' abilities to yield strong conclusions of value to the field as well as to practitioners (see, for example, Jick, 1979; McGrath, 1981; Scandura & Williams, 2000). Unfortunately, only one study in our database demonstrated substantial efforts to assure consumers of the research that data triangulation had occurred (i.e., specifics of multiple triangulation efforts were provided in the article). In only another 12% of the studies, triangulation was briefly mentioned (no specifics or actual outcomes provided). For most of the non-interpretive qualitative studies (87%), there was no mention of triangulation. This lack of triangulation limits the field's ability to justify and support findings (i.e., data, knowledge) derived from a particular research method (Flick, 2004). It also limits our ability to detect trends in triangulation methods.

An Assessment of Our Current Dilemmas

Contributors to the risk, crisis, and emergency management field have produced a number of strong or reasonably strong studies, for example Haddon et al. (2015). These authors created a dual-approach study (both qualitative and quantitative) with a retrospective time horizon of less than two years and strong triangulation. Interestingly, they report that important effects related to leader communication during crisis would not have been apparent with only a quantitative study. Rizzuto and Maloney (2008) provide another example. They blended phenomenon-driven and theory-driven foundations, and incorporated a limited retrospective time horizon and some triangulation. Through their efforts, these authors generated important insights related to the protection of animals during and after natural disasters, with Hurricane Katrina as the empirical backdrop.

Although a number of positive examples can be identified, there are several challenges in the research literature, as our analysis has indicated. These include (1) a portfolio of quantitative and qualitative research that seems to lean more than it should to the qualitative side, (2) a portfolio of phenomenon-driven and theory-driven research that is too heavy on the theory-driven side, (3) use of both archival and non-archival data in too few projects, (4) lack of clarity in reporting retrospective time horizons in too many papers, (5) support for all or the vast majority of hypotheses in too many published papers, and (6) triangulation efforts that do not seem strong enough in too many cases (for a summary of the findings that we have been discussing, see Table 8.1).

Regarding our findings, qualitative methods and theory-driven approaches seem to represent institutionalized practices. Qualitative methods, often necessary in a nascent field, arguably should yield to a higher proportion of quantitative methods as a field matures (Edmondson & Mcmanus, 2007). This shift, however, does not seem to have occurred yet in risk, crisis, and emergency management research. Much more disquieting is the nearly three to one ratio of theory-driven to phenomenon-driven studies (almost ten to one in quantitative research). Crises, risks, and emergencies seem to be particularly fruitful areas for discovery-oriented, phenomena-based research, but such research is quite limited. It is to this key challenge that we now turn our full attention.

The overemphasis on theory-driven work seems to be part of a strong institutionalized pattern reinforced by the training of new researchers in their doctoral programs and by journal editors and reviewers who seem to prize theory-driven work relative to phenomenon-driven work. Within the context of doctoral training programs, the relative prominence of theory versus application has experienced ebbs and flows, but recent analyses indicate an increasingly heavy emphasis on theory (Wren, Buckley, & Michaelsen, 1994; Wren, Halbesleben, & Buckley, 2007). Regarding the overall management and organizations field, Roy Suddaby has described the evolving situation in the following way: "a growing tendency amongst management scholars to be increasingly fetishistic about theory, often at the expense of phenomena" (Birkinshaw, Healey, Suddaby, & Weber, 2014, p. 42). Julian Birkinshaw, another noted organizational scholar, has cogently argued that most management and organization research should be phenomenon-driven, emerging from heretofore unexamined

Table 8.1 Core Findings Related to Research Methods

| | | Number (%) | | | | | | | | | | |
| | | Starting point | | | Sources of data | | | Time horizon | | | Direct voices of victims | |
		Theory-driven	Phenomenon-driven	Balanced	Archival	Non-archival	Both	Retrospective	Real time	Prospective	Yes	No
Quantitative	2006–2011	16 (84)	1 (5)	2 (11)	8 (42)	11 (58)	0 (0)	3 (17)	13 (72)	2 (11)	4 (21)	15 (79)
	2012–2016	42 (93)	0 (0)	3 (7)	20 (44)	25 (56)	0 (0)	14 (30)	31 (66)	2 (4)	18 (40)	27 (60)
	2006–2016	58 (91)	1 (2)	5 (8)	28 (44)	36 (56)	0 (0)	17 (26)	44 (68)	4 (6)	22 (34)	42 (66)
Qualitative	2006–2011	14 (67)	4 (19)	3 (14)	10 (48)	6 (29)	5 (24)	6 (27)	14 (64)	2 (9)	6 (29)	15 (71)
	2012–2016	26 (55)	13 (28)	8 (17)	20 (43)	23 (49)	4 (9)	16 (31)	32 (63)	3 (6)	15 (32)	32 (68)
	2006–2016	40 (59)	17 (25)	11 (16)	30 (44)	29 (43)	9 (13)	22 (30)	46 (63)	5 (7)	21 (31)	47 (69)
Mixed	2006–2011	0 (0)	0 (0)	0 (0)	0 (0)	0 (0)	0 (0)	0 (0)	0 (0)	0 (0)	0 (0)	0 (0)
	2012–2016	5 (71)	0 (0)	2 (29)	2 (29)	5 (71)	0 (0)	4 (50)	4 (50)	0 (0)	4 (57)	3 (43)
	2006–2016	5 (71)	0 (0)	2 (29)	2 (29)	5 (71)	0 (0)	4 (50)	4 (50)	0 (0)	4 (57)	3 (43)

contemporary phenomena that require explanations, or from experimentation that reveals novel phenomena, or from a mismatch between theory and observable practice (Birkinshaw et al., 2014). The consequences of unchecked veneration of theory include new knowledge being grounded in existing research papers rather than actual experience and observation in the world, and new knowledge being created only incrementally based on increasingly narrow research questions (Birkinshaw et al., 2014).

The inertia of institutionalized practices can be difficult to overcome. Though researchers often study the institutionalization of organizational practices, they rarely reflect on the institutionalization of their own practices with regard to research design and methodology (McKee & Miller, 2015). Such practices are upheld by mutually reinforcing cognitive, normative, and regulative pillars (Scott, 2008a, 2008b). These pillars encompass how individuals, as members of collectives, habitually think, feel, and act as a result of socio-cultural forces, as well as the regulative power held by organizational gatekeepers (McKee & Miller, 2015). Thus, researchers tend to engage in certain types of research (e.g., theory-driven) relative to other types (e.g., phenomenon-driven) because they are more accustomed to and conversant in those methods, because their colleagues also do so, and because reviewers and editors have rewarded their prior institutionalized behavior with acceptances and publications. Using atypical research designs or methods is risky. First, researchers must learn them, which is effortful and time-consuming and entails a gamble involving the opportunity costs of forgoing more familiar types of projects. Researchers also risk exclusion by colleagues for violating socio-cultural norms, as well as rejection by journal editors and reviewers for not adhering to dominant practices.

Fortunately, increasing attention is being given to the relative importance of and concurrent lack of phenomenon-driven research (Mathieu, 2016; Schwarz & Stensaker, 2016). Fields as diverse as change management, economics, sociology, and consumer psychology recently have heard rallying cries for more phenomenon-driven work (Schwarz & Stensaker, 2014). At the Academy of Management, a new journal devoted to discovery-oriented research has been developed (*Academy of Management Discoveries*). In addition, theory constraints were relaxed at the Academy of Management's standard-bearing empirical journal (*Academy of Management Journal*) for a 2016–2017 special issue on grand challenges (see George, Howard-Grenville, Joshi, & Tihanyi, 2016). The crisis, risk, and emergency management literatures can benefit from this momentum.

The field can begin to build a stronger relationship with phenomenon-driven research by first recognizing and returning to the foundations of the field, rooted in real managerial and organizational issues (Schwarz & Stensaker, 2014). Indeed, crises, risks, and emergencies are inherently phenomenon-focused, as crises and emergencies, in particular, are defined by distinguishable focal events. As a further impetus, the field should recognize that contemporary problems may be different from those faced in the past (Schwarz & Stensaker, 2014). Studying contemporary phenomena may challenge, refine, expand, or even make obsolete existing knowledge or theory (von Krogh, Rossi-Lamastra, & Haefliger, 2012).

Although the heavy reliance on theory-driven research is concerning for the field overall, the use of that approach by any one member of the field represents a defensible choice. The same can be said about the use of only qualitative data and the use of only one type of data source. On the other hand, repeatedly offering statistical support for all or the vast majority of hypotheses against a backdrop of novelty and complexity creates some uncomfortable questions (Bettis, 2012; Bettis et al., 2016; Bosco, Aguinis, Field, Pierce, & Dalton, 2016; Byington & Felps, 2017; Cardinal et al., 2017; Miller & Bamberger, 2016). Failures to fully describe retrospective time horizons creates less serious but still noteworthy questions, as do failures to implement or describe triangulation fully.

In some cases, there might be a lowering of professional standards in response to publication pressures. Most worrisome, there might be HARKing, p-hacking, and intentional hiding of important non-significant results as a response to the field's obsession with novel hypotheses and statistical support for those hypotheses (Barley, 2015; Bettis, 2012; Cardinal et al., 2017; Davis, 2015; Miller & Bamberger, 2016; Starbuck, 2016; Tsui, 2013). To the extent that such problems exist, individual researchers probably should not be blamed, as the issues are systemic. Editors and other leaders of the field must take responsibility for the dysfunctional culture and reward system. In this spirit, several editors from the broad management and organizations area have recently highlighted the value of publishing null findings as well as the value of replication studies – these, in point of fact, are crucial elements of a truly evidence-based field (e.g., Bettis et al., 2016; Miller & Bamberger, 2016).

Less worrisome, there might be purposeful hiding of information related to time horizons and triangulation in order to publish research that otherwise would not quite satisfy legitimate standards in the review process. Going forward, editors and editorial board members should not allow papers to be published without clear descriptions of all key methodological attributes and choices.

Conclusion

It is important to review the state of research in all fields periodically, but it is particularly important to do so in rapidly growing fields such as crisis, risk, and emergency management. Thus, our work has an element of timeliness. And while many of our findings suggest strong research in the field, several findings suggest weaknesses for which deliberate action is warranted. For example, editors, editorial board members, and individual researchers probably should take a fresh look at the somewhat low proportion of quantitative work. This type of work is useful for supporting evidence-based management, which makes its current underrepresentation worrisome in a field that has aspirations for strong relevance. The underutilization of phenomenon-driven underpinnings also merits attention. Increasing the use of such underpinnings would likely help the field stay current on dynamics in the world around it, and would be consistent with trends in a number of other fields. Furthermore, additional investigations into the causes of apparent publication bias are clearly warranted, as are additional investigations into the drivers of limited triangulation in non-interpretive qualitative research. Overall, research in the field of crisis, risk, and emergency management seems poised for a bright future, but this is not assured without attention to weaker aspects of our empirical research.

References

Allen, T. D., Eby, L. T., O'Brien, K. E., & Lentz, E. (2008). The state of mentoring research: A qualitative review of current research methods and future research implications. *Journal of Vocational Behavior, 73*(3), 343–357. https://doi.org/10.1016/j.jvb.2007.08.004

Asare, A. K., Yang, J., & Brashear Alejandro, T. G. (2012). The state of research methods in personal selling and sales management literature. *Journal of Personal Selling & Sales Management, 32*(4), 473–489. https://doi.org/10.2753/PSS0885-3134320405

Avery, E. J., Graham, M., & Park, S. (2016). Planning makes (Closer to) perfect: Exploring United States? Local government officials? Evaluations of crisis management. *Journal of Contingencies and Crisis Management, 24*(2), 73–81. https://doi.org/10.1111/1468-5973.12109

Bamberger, P., & Ang, S. (2016). The quantitative discovery: What is it and how to get it published. *Academy of Management Discoveries, 2*(1), 1–6. https://doi.org/10.5465/amd.2015.0060

Barley, S. R. (2015). 60th anniversary essay. *Administrative Science Quarterly, 61*(1), 1–8. https://doi.org/10.1177/0001839215624886

Bergeron, C. D., & Cooren, F. (2012). The collective framing of crisis management: A ventriloqual analysis of emergency operations centres: The collective framing of crisis management. *Journal of Contingencies and Crisis Management, 20*(3), 120–137. https://doi.org/10.1111/j.1468-5973.2012.00671.x

Bettis, R. A. (2012). The search for asterisks: Compromised statistical tests and flawed theories. *Strategic Management Journal, 33*(1), 108–113. https://doi.org/10.1002/smj.975

Bettis, R. A., Ethiraj, S., Gambardella, A., Helfat, C., & Mitchell, W. (2016). Creating repeatable cumulative knowledge in strategic management: A call for a broad and deep conversation among authors, referees, and editors. *Strategic Management Journal, 37*(2), 257–261. https://doi.org/10.1002/smj.2477

Birkinshaw, J., Healey, M. P., Suddaby, R., & Weber, K. (2014). Debating the future of management research: Debating the future of management research. *Journal of Management Studies, 51*(1), 38–55. https://doi.org/10.1111/joms.12061

Boin, A., & 't Hart, P. (2004). Coping with crisis complexity: Trends, challenges and pathways. In R. Fisch & D. Beck (Eds.), *Komplexitätsmanagement* (pp. 233–248). Wiesbaden: VS Verlag für Sozialwissenschaften. https://doi.org/10.1007/978-3-322-89803-6_15

Bosco, F. A., Aguinis, H., Field, J. G., Pierce, C. A., & Dalton, D. R. (2016). HARKing's threat to organizational research: Evidence from primary and meta-analytic sources. *Personnel Psychology, 69*(3), 709–750. https://doi.org/10.1111/peps.12111

Boyd, B. K., Dess, G. G., & Rasheed, A. M. A. (1993). Divergence between Archival and perceptual measures of the environment: Causes and consequences. *The Academy of Management Review, 18*(2), 204–226. https://doi.org/10.2307/258758

Buelens, M., Van De Woestyne, M., Mestdagh, S., & Bouckenooghe, D. (2008). Methodological issues in negotiation research: A state-of-the-art-review. *Group Decision and Negotiation, 17*(4), 321–345. https://doi.org/10.1007/s10726-007-9097-3

Byington, E. K., & Felps, W. (2017). Solutions to the credibility crisis in management science. *Academy of Management Learning & Education, 16*(1), 142–162. https://doi.org/10.5465/amle.2015.0035

Cardinal, L., Kreutzer, M., & Miller, C. (2017). An aspirational view of organizational control research: Re-invigorating empirical work to better meet the challenges of 21st century organizations. *Academy of Management Annals.* https://doi.org/10.5465/annals.2014.0086

Casper, W. J., Eby, L. T., Bordeaux, C., Lockwood, A., & Lambert, D. (2007). A review of research methods in IO/OB work-family research. *Journal of Applied Psychology, 92*(1), 28–43. https://doi.org/10.1037/0021-9010.92.1.28

Cotteleer, M. J., & Wan, X. (2016). Does the starting point matter? The literature-driven and the phenomenon-driven approaches of using corporate archival data in academic research. *Journal of Business Logistics, 37*(1), 26–33. https://doi.org/10.1111/jbl.12114

Cumming, G. (2013). The new statistics. *Psychological Science, 25*(1), 7–29. https://doi.org/10.1177/0956797613504966

Cumming, G., Fidler, F., Leonard, M., Kalinowski, P., Christiansen, A., Kleinig, A., … Wilson, S. (2007). Statistical reform in psychology: Is anything changing? *Psychological Science, 18*(3), 230–232.

Dacin, M. T., Goodstein, J., & Scott, W. R. (2002). Institutional theory and institutional change: Introduction to the special research forum. *Academy of Management Journal, 45*(1), 45–56.

Davis, G. F. (2015). Editorial essay. *Administrative Science Quarterly, 60*(2), 179–188. https://doi.org/10.1177/0001839215585725

Drnevich, P. L., Mahoney, J. T., & Schendel, D. E. (2016). The logic of discovery in strategic management research: Taking stock and looking ahead. In *Academy of Management Proceedings* (Vol. 2016, p. 12615). Academy of Management.

Edmondson, A. C., & Mcmanus, S. E. (2007). Methodological fit in management field research. *Academy of Management Review, 32*(4), 1155–1179. https://doi.org/10.5465/AMR.2007.26586086

Fanelli, D. (2010). Do pressures to publish increase scientists' Bias? An empirical support from US States Data. *PLoS ONE, 5*(4), e10271. https://doi.org/10.1371/journal.pone.0010271

Fanelli, D. (2012). Negative results are disappearing from most disciplines and countries. *Scientometrics, 90*(3), 891–904. https://doi.org/10.1007/s11192-011-0494-7

Fidler, F., & Cumming, G. (2007). Lessons learned from statistical reform efforts in other disciplines. *Psychology in the Schools, 44*(5), 441–449.

Fidler, F., Cumming, G., Burgman, M. A., & Thomason, N. (2004). Statistical reform in medicine, psychology and ecology. *The Journal of Socio-Economics, 33*(5), 615–630.

Flick, U. (2004). Triangulation in qualitative research. In U. Flick, E. von Kardoff, & I. Steinke (Eds.), *A companion to qualitative research* (pp. 178–183). London; Thousand Oaks, CA: Sage.

Forza, C. (2002). Survey research in operations management: A process-based perspective. *International Journal of Operations & Production Management, 22*(2), 152–194. https://doi.org/10.1108/01443570210414310

George, G., Howard-Grenville, J., Joshi, A., & Tihanyi, L. (2016). Understanding and tackling societal grand challenges through management research. *Academy of Management Journal, 59*(6), 1880–1895. https://doi.org/10.5465/amj.2016.4007

Glick, W. H., Huber, G. P., Miller, C. C., Doty, D. H., & Sutcliffe, K. M. (1990). Studying changes in organizational design and effectiveness: Retrospective event histories and periodic assessments. *Organization Science, 1*(3), 293–312. https://doi.org/10.1287/orsc.1.3.293

Golden, B. R. (1992). Research notes. The past is the past—or is it? The use of retrospective accounts as indicators of past strategy. *Academy of Management Journal, 35*(4), 848–860. https://doi.org/10.2307/256318

Goodman, S., & Greenland, S. (2007). Why most published research findings are false: Problems in the analysis. *PLoS Medicine, 4*(4), e168. https://doi.org/10.1371/journal.pmed.0040168

Greenhalgh, T., Howick, J., & Maskrey, N. (2014). Evidence based medicine: A movement in crisis? *BMJ, 348*(jun13 4), g3725–g3725. https://doi.org/10.1136/bmj.g3725

Gupta, N., Shaw, J. D., & Delery, J. E. (2000). Correlates of response outcomes among organizational key informants. *Organizational Research Methods, 3*(4), 323–347. https://doi.org/10.1177/109442810034002

Haig, B. D. (2005). An abductive theory of scientific method. *Psychological Methods, 10*(4), 371–388. https://doi.org/10.1037/1082-989X.10.4.371

Hambrick, D. C. (2007). The field of management's devotion to theory: Too much of a good thing? *Academy of Management Journal, 50*(6), 1346–1352. https://doi.org/10.5465/AMJ.2007.28166119

Huber, G. P., & Power, D. J. (1985). Retrospective reports of strategic-level managers: Guidelines for increasing their accuracy. *Strategic Management Journal, 6*(2), 171–180. https://doi.org/10.1002/smj.4250060206

Ioannidis, J. P. A. (2005). Why most published research findings are false. *PLoS Medicine, 2*(8), e124. https://doi.org/10.1371/journal.pmed.0020124

Jick, T. D. (1979). Mixing qualitative and quantitative methods: Triangulation in action. *Administrative Science Quarterly, 24*(4), 602–611. https://doi.org/10.2307/2392366

Kaplan, S., LaPort, K., & Waller, M. J. (2013). The role of positive affectivity in team effectiveness during crises. *Journal of Organizational Behavior, 34*(4), 473–491. https://doi.org/10.1002/job.1817

Kerr, N. L. (1998). HARKing: Hypothesizing after the results are known. *Personality and Social Psychology Review, 2*(3), 196–217. https://doi.org/10.1207/s15327957pspr0203_4

Kuhn, T. S. (1962). *The structure of scientific revolutions* (1st ed.). Chicago, IL: University of Chicago Press.

Kumar, N., Stern, L. W., & Anderson, J. C. (1993). Conducting interorganizational research using key informants. *The Academy of Management Journal, 36*(6), 1633–1651. https://doi.org/10.2307/256824

Labovitz, S. (1972). Statistical usage in sociology sacred cows and ritual. *Sociological Methods & Research, 1*(1), 13–37.

Lalonde, C. (2012). A diagnostic method for the study of disaster management: A review of fundamentals and practices. In J. Tiefenbacher (Ed.), *Approaches to managing disaster – Assessing hazards, emergencies and disaster impacts.* InTech.

Lewin, K. (1951). *Field theory in social science: Selected theoretical papers.* New York: Harper & Row.

Lynch, J. G., Alba, J. W., Krishna, A., Morwitz, V. G., & Gürhan-Canli, Z. (2012). Knowledge creation in consumer research: Multiple routes, multiple criteria. *Journal of Consumer Psychology, 22*(4), 473–485. https://doi.org/10.1016/j.jcps.2012.06.004

March, J. G., & Sutton, R. I. (1997). Crossroads—organizational performance as a dependent variable. *Organization Science, 8*(6), 698–706. https://doi.org/10.1287/orsc.8.6.698

Mathieu, J. E. (2016). The problem with [in] management theory. *Journal of Organizational Behavior, 37*(8), 1132–1141. https://doi.org/10.1002/job.2114

Mazzola, J. J., & Deuling, J. K. (2013). Forgetting what we learned as graduate students: HARKing and selective outcome reporting in I–O journal articles. *Industrial and Organizational Psychology, 6*(03), 279–284. https://doi.org/10.1111/iops.12049

McGrath, J. E. (1981). Dilemmatics: The study of research choices and dilemmas. *American Behavioral Scientist, 25*(2), 179–210.

McKee, R. A., & Miller, C. C. (2015). Institutionalizing bayesianism within the organizational sciences: A practical guide featuring comments from eminent scholars. *Journal of Management, 41*(2), 471–490. https://doi.org/10.1177/0149206314546750

Miles, M. B., Huberman, A. M., & Saldaña, J. (2014). *Qualitative data analysis: A methods sourcebook* (Third edition). Thousand Oaks, CA: SAGE Publications, Inc.

Miller, C. C., & Bamberger, P. (2016). Exploring emergent and poorly understood phenomena in the strangest of places: The footprint of discovery in replications, meta-analyses, and null findings. *Academy of Management Discoveries, 2*(4), 313–319. https://doi.org/10.5465/amd.2016.0115

Miller, C. C., Cardinal, L. B., & Glick, W. H. (1997). Retrospective reports in organizational research: A reexamination of recent evidence. *Academy of Management Journal, 40*(1), 189–204. https://doi.org/10.2307/257026

Moonesinghe, R., Khoury, M. J., & Janssens, A. C. J. W. (2007). Most published research findings are false—but a little replication goes a long way. *PLoS Medicine, 4*(2), e28. https://doi.org/10.1371/journal.pmed.0040028

Open Science Collaboration. (2015). Estimating the reproducibility of psychological science. *Science, 349*(6251), aac4716-aac4716. https://doi.org/10.1126/science.aac4716

Patvardhan, S. D., Gioia, D. A., & Hamilton, A. L. (2015). Weathering a meta-level identity crisis: Forging a coherent collective identity for an emerging field. *Academy of Management Journal, 58*(2), 405–435. https://doi.org/10.5465/amj.2012.1049

Payne, S. C., Finch, J. F., & Tremble, T. R. (2003). Validating surrogate measures of psychological constructs: The application of construct equivalence to archival data. *Organizational Research Methods, 6*(3), 363–382. https://doi.org/10.1177/1094428103254455

Pearson, C. M., & Clair, J. A. (1998). Reframing crisis management. *Academy of management review, 23*(1), 59–76. https://dx.doi.org/10.2307/259099

Pearson, C. M., Roux-Dufort, C., & Clair, J. (Eds.). (2007). *International handbook of organizational crisis management*. Los Angeles, CA: Sage Publications.

Pfeffer, J. (1993). Barriers to the advance of organizational science: Paradigm development as a dependent variable. *Academy of Management Review, 18*(4), 599–620.

Pfeffer, J. (2015). *Leadership BS: fixing workplaces and careers one truth at a time* (First edition). New York, NY: Harper Business, an imprint of HarperCollins Publishers.

Pfeffer, J., & Sutton, R. I. (2006). *Hard facts, dangerous half-truths, and total nonsense: Profiting from evidence-based management*. Boston, MA: Harvard Business School Press.

Phillips, L. W. (1981). Assessing measurement error in key informant reports: A methodological note on organizational analysis in marketing. *Journal of Marketing Research, 18*(4), 395. https://doi.org/10.2307/3151333

Pinsonneault, A., & Kraemer, K. (1993). Survey research methodology in management information systems: An assessment. *Journal of Management Information Systems, 10*(2), 75–105. https://doi.org/10.1080/07421222.1993.11518001

Podsakoff, P. M., & Organ, D. W. (1986). Self-reports in organizational research: problems and prospects. *Journal of Management, 12*(4), 531–544. https://doi.org/10.1177/014920638601200408

Pramanik, R., Ekman, O., Hassel, H., & Tehler, H. (2015). Organizational adaptation in multi-stakeholder crisis response: An experimental study: Organizational adaptation in multi-stakeholder crisis response: An experimental study. *Journal of Contingencies and Crisis Management, 23*(4), 234–245. https://doi.org/10.1111/1468-5973.12094

Rizzuto, T. E., & Maloney, L. K. (2008). Organizing chaos: Crisis management in the wake of Hurricane Katrina. *Professional Psychology: Research and Practice, 39*(1), 77. https://dx.doi.org/10.1037/0735-7028.39.1.77

Rogelberg, S. G., & Stanton, J. M. (2007). Introduction. *Organizational Research Methods, 10*(2), 195–209. https://doi.org/10.1177/1094428106294693

Rosenberg, W., & Donald, A. (1995). Evidence based medicine: An approach to clinical problem-solving. *BMJ, 310*(6987), 1122–1126. https://doi.org/10.1136/bmj.310.6987.1122

Rosenthal, R. (1979). The file drawer problem and tolerance for null results. *Psychological Bulletin, 86*(3), 638.

Rousseau, D. M. (2006). Is there Such a thing as "Evidence-Based Management"? *Academy of Management Review, 31*(2), 256–269. https://doi.org/10.5465/AMR.2006.20208679

Rynes, S. L., Rousseau, D. M., & Barends, E. (2014). From the guest editors: Change the World: Teach evidence-based practice! *Academy of Management Learning & Education, 13*(3), 305–321. https://doi.org/10.5465/amle.2014.0203

Sabatino, M. (2016). Economic crisis and resilience: Resilient capacity and competitiveness of the enterprises. *Journal of Business Research, 69*(5), 1924–1927. https://doi.org/10.1016/j.jbusres.2015.10.081

Sackett, D. L., Rosenberg, W. M. C., Gray, J. A. M., Haynes, R. B., & Richardson, W. S. (1996). Evidence based medicine: What it is and what it isn't. *BMJ, 312*(7023), 71–72. https://doi.org/10.1136/bmj.312.7023.71

Sackett, P. R., & Larson, J. R. (1990). Research strategies and tactics in industrial and organizational psychology. In M. D. Dunnette & L. M. Hough (Eds.), *Handbook of industrial and organizational psychology* (Vol. 1, pp. 419–489). Palo Alto, CA: Consulting Psychologists Press.

Scandura, T. A., & Williams, E. A. (2000). Research methodology in management: Current practices, trends, and implications for future research. *The Academy of Management Journal, 43*(6), 1248–1264. https://doi.org/10.2307/1556348

Schmidt, F. L., & Oh, I.-S. (2016). The crisis of confidence in research findings in psychology: Is lack of replication the real problem? Or is it something else? *Archives of Scientific Psychology, 4*(1), 32–37. https://doi.org/10.1037/arc0000029

Schwarz, G. M., & Stensaker, I. G. (2014). Time to take off the theoretical straightjacket and (Re-)introduce phenomenon-driven research. *The Journal of Applied Behavioral Science, 50*(4), 478–501. https://doi.org/10.1177/0021886314549919

Schwarz, G. M., & Stensaker, I. G. (2016). Showcasing phenomenon-driven research on organizational change. *Journal of Change Management, 16*(4), 245–264. https://doi.org/10.1080/14697017.2016.1230931

Scott, W. R. (2008a). Approaching adulthood: The maturing of institutional theory. *Theory and Society, 37*(5), 427–442.

Scott, W. R. (2008b). *Institutions and organizations: Ideas and interests* (3rd ed.). Thousand Oaks, CA: Sage.

Seidler, J. (1974). On using informants: A technique for collecting quantitative data and controlling measurement error in organization analysis. *American Sociological Review, 39*(6), 816–831. https://doi.org/10.2307/2094155

Simmons, J. P., Nelson, L. D., & Simonsohn, U. (2011). False-positive psychology. *Psychological Science, 22*(11), 1359–1366. https://doi.org/10.1177/0956797611417632

Smith, R., & Rennie, D. (2014). Evidence-based medicine—An oral history. *JAMA, 311*(4), 365. https://doi.org/10.1001/jama.2013.286182

Starbuck, W. H. (2016). 60th anniversary essay. *Administrative Science Quarterly, 61*(2), 165–183. https://doi.org/10.1177/0001839216629644

't Hart, P., Heyse, L., & Boin, A. (2001). New trends in crisis management practice and crisis management research: Setting the agenda. *Journal of Contingencies and Crisis Management, 9*(4), 181–188. https://doi.org/10.1111/1468-5973.00168

Tan, J., & Peng, M. W. (2003). Organizational slack and firm performance during economic transitions: Two studies from an emerging economy. *Strategic Management Journal, 24*(13), 1249–1263. https://doi.org/10.1002/smj.351

Tsui, A. S. (2013). Making research engaged: Implications for HRD scholarship. *Human Resource Development Quarterly, 24*(2), 137–143. https://doi.org/10.1002/hrdq.21161

Van de Ven, A. H. (1989). Nothing is quite so practical as a good theory. *Academy of Management Review, 14*(4), 486–489.

Van de Ven, A. H. (2016). Grounding the research phenomenon. *Journal of Change Management, 16*(4), 265–270. https://doi.org/10.1080/14697017.2016.1230336

Van de Ven, A. H., Ang, S., Arino, A., Bamberger, P., LeBaron, C., Miller, C., & Milliken, F. (2015). Welcome to the Academy of Management Discoveries (AMD). *Academy of Management Discoveries, 1*(1), 1–4. https://doi.org/10.5465/amd.2014.0143

Venkatraman, N., & Ramanujam, V. (1986). Measurement of business performance in strategy research: A comparison of approaches. *Academy of Management Review, 11*(4), 801–814.

von Krogh, G., Rossi-Lamastra, C., & Haefliger, S. (2012). Phenomenon-based research in management and organisation science: When is it rigorous and does it matter? *Long Range Planning, 45*(4), 277–298. https://doi.org/10.1016/j.lrp.2012.05.001

Wagenmakers, E.-J., Lee, M., Lodewyckx, T., & Iverson, G. J. (2008). Bayesian versus frequentist inference. In H. Hoijtink, I. Klugkist, & P. A. Boelen (Eds.), *Bayesian evaluation of informative hypotheses* (pp. 181–207). New York: Springer.

Wolfe, J., & Jackson, C. (1987). Creating models of the strategic decision making process via participant recall: A free simulation examination. *Journal of Management, 13*(1), 123–134. https://doi.org/10.1177/014920638701300110

Wren, D. A., Buckley, M. R., & Michaelsen, L. K. (1994). The theory/applications balance in management pedagogy: Where do we stand? *Journal of Management, 20*(1), 141–157.

Wren, D. A., Halbesleben, J. R. B., & Buckley, M. R. (2007). The theory-application balance in management pedagogy: A longitudinal update. *Academy of Management Learning & Education, 6*(4), 484–492.

9

RESEARCHING RISK, EMERGENCY AND CRISIS

Taking Stock of Research Methods on Extreme Contexts and Moving Forward

Markus Hällgren and Linda Rouleau

Introduction

Within the broader field of management and organization studies, risk, emergency and crisis research has attracted an increasing interest among scholars over the past decades. Reviews show that research has been published in a variety of outlets and that the literature is based on different theoretical and methodological approaches (Buchanan & Denyer, 2013). As a result, there have been repeated calls for integration (Bundy et al., 2017; James et al., 2011; Williams et al., 2017). In a recent literature review based on 138 papers from top-tier journals published between 1980 and 2015, we suggest that the notion of extreme contexts would be useful for reducing the fragmentation characterizing risk, emergency and crisis research (Hällgren, Rouleau, & de Rond, 2018). Put differently, the idea of extreme contexts brings together resemblances across different areas of research; therefore, it can be used to identify common denominators. The aim of this chapter is to examine the methodological trends and opportunities in the empirical papers we reviewed, in order to identify some patterns and trajectories.

To accomplish this, we draw on Cunliffe (2011) and examine the methodological sections of the papers within the dataset. According to Cunliffe, a research design generally contains four types of interrelated elements. First, researchers elaborate their research strategies and explain why they have chosen qualitative, quantitative or mixed research designs. In this subsection, they introduce the characteristics of their case study or dataset. Second, researchers usually discuss the level of analysis: individual, team, organizational or society-wide. Third, they describe the data collection techniques they used and the processes by which they gathered them (e.g., interviews, questionnaires, public reports or observations). Fourth, researchers portray the multiple steps in which they analyzed the data (e.g., grounded theory, regression analysis or content analysis). A careful examination of these elements allowed us to discover trends within the literature that have hitherto been somewhat obscured.

We identify three periods characterized by different research design patterns: *emergence* (1980–1994), *expansion* (1995–2004) and *consolidation* (2005–2015). In the emergence period, research was focused on illustrative examples and spectacular events and provides context-specific explanations. In the expansion period, there was a tendency to draw on public hearings and expand explanations to organizations and industry or society at large. Finally, in the consolidation period, the methods used were more driven toward generalization to non-extreme contexts, and we saw an emerging set of innovative and fresh insights used by researchers for designing their research on extreme contexts.

This chapter is organized into four parts. After defining what we mean by extreme contexts, we explain how the dataset was built and analyzed. Then, the findings are described according to each period. Finally, we discuss the methodological evolution of research on extreme contexts and provide some reflections for future directions.

Extreme Contexts

The notion of extreme contexts is not new, and there is a plethora of related ones in use in management and organization theory literature, including "extreme environments," "high reliability organizations," "adverse events," "crises," "risks," "emergencies" and "disasters." (For a full review of the definition of these related terms, see Hällgren, Rouleau, & de Rond, 2018). While we are highly appreciative of the insights provided by such a diversity of terms, common features within the literatures have been left unexplored (Bundy et al., 2017; Williams et al., 2017). Such features include but are not limited to distinguishing between crises in non-extreme contexts vs extreme contexts, financial risks vs physical risks, and resilient operations in regular organizations vs organizations that have no margin to fail. Thus, referring to extreme contexts is useful for describing the resemblances across the literature.

According to Hannah et al. (2009: 898), extreme events "(1) have the potential to cause massive physical, psychological, or material consequences that occur in physical or psychosocial proximity to organization members, (2) the consequences of which are thought unbearable by those organization members, and (3) are such that they may exceed the organization's capacity to prevent those extreme events from actually taking place." According to these authors, extreme contexts are

> where one or more extreme events are occurring or are likely to occur that may exceed the organization's capacity to prevent and resulting in an extensive and intolerable magnitude of physical, psychological, or material consequences to – or in close physical or psycho-social proximity to organization members.
>
> *(Hannah et al., 2009: 898)*

Consequently, a financial crisis at a business school would be excluded, while a madman's shooting at the same business school would not. The aftermath of the latter would have more in common with, for example, the compassion displayed after a natural disaster than behaviors after a financial crisis.

Our literature on extreme contexts is based on the previous distinction between extreme "events" and "contexts" (Hällgren, Rouleau, & de Rond, 2018). However, we further operationalize the definition to explore the context's specificities. We distinguish contexts that are prepared to handle events from those that are not, and events that have happened from those that have not. This leaves us with three types of extreme contexts: *risky contexts* (R), which are continuously exposed to potentially extreme events and are prepared accordingly (e.g., high-reliability organizations, Nascar racing and even mountaineering); *emergency contexts* (E), where extreme events have occurred but where the members are trained to handle them (e.g., firefighters and police officers); and *disruptive contexts* (D), where extreme events have befallen unprepared people and organizations (e.g., the Holocaust or natural disasters).

Adopting this context-specific approach allowed us to group together diverse literatures according to context rather than their disciplinary approaches (e.g., high-reliability organizations, crises and emergencies). While the purpose of this review was to look for research patterns *within* the RED category, this chapter aims to describe methodological patterns and trajectories *across* the dataset.

Researching Extreme Contexts

Though we can find an extensive variety of empirical research on risk, emergency or crisis, the methodological challenges researchers face when trying to capture the essence of extreme contexts have not been sufficiently addressed. Buchanan and Denyer (2013: 2006) posit that studies on crisis, disasters and other extreme events

> have been required to adopt designs and methods considered unconventional in other areas, and to use data from sources normally considered unreliable and biased. This is a field where a qualitative-processual paradigm is dominant, and theory-building is often based on idiosyncratic cases and small-n studies.

Therefore, they identify four main challenges that such research faces: the problem of relying on retrospective research designs, the difficulty of accessing sensitive data, the question of generalizing explanations based on an extreme event and the difficulty of addressing context-specific ethical concerns. To shed further light on how research on extreme contexts has developed methodologically, we proceed in three steps.

First, we draw on the dataset built in a previous paper on research on extreme contexts (Hällgren, Rouleau, & de Rond, 2018). The paper is based on a selective review of nine top-tier European and North American management and organization journals: *Academy of Management Journal, Academy of Management Review, Administrative Science Quarterly, Organization Science, Strategic Management Journal, Journal of Management, Journal of Management Studies, Human Relations* and *Organization Studies.* These journals pride themselves on publishing papers with strong theoretical contributions relying on methodological rigor. The selected articles (138) should thus represent most of the significant contributions to the area, but there is always the possibility that we have ignored important contributions (for more details about the constitution of the dataset, see the methodological section in Hällgren, Rouleau & de Rond, 2018). Next, we eliminated 18 papers that were not based on empirical research.

Three papers excluded from our dataset specifically deal with methodological challenges. George and Clegg (1997) relate the difficulties young and junior researchers might experience when trying to get access to participants in a context where the safety of researchers and participants is a major constraint. This constraint impedes the ability to properly evaluate the costs and duration of the fieldwork. When getting access to informants, researchers themselves are subjectively embedded in a set of socio-political and emotional dynamics. Having been posted in Jerusalem to study the Israeli-Palestinian conflict, Prasad (2014) reflects on each day spent interacting with gatekeepers and native people on a strategic border. Drawing on conversations, memos, voices recordings and diaries, the paper shows the discursive impact of such a ritual on the researchers and their interpretations of the data collected. Even analyzing primary as well as secondary data from an extreme context is difficult, since they both convey confusing, complex and sensitive interactions between actors' interpretations, organizational and institutional norms and structures. In a pedagogical note, Weick (2007) recounts how he gradually became familiar with and involved in the analysis process of the

Table 9.1 Three Periods of Extreme Context Research

	Emergence (1980–1994) (21 papers)	Expansion (1995–2004) (29 papers)	Consolidation (2005–2015) (70 papers)
Research strategies	Case-based studies and illustrative examples Brief descriptions of the events and organizations where they may happen Comparative, multiple and single-case studies based on spectacular events	Case studies and databases Increased detail of descriptions of events and organizations in where they do or may happen Single-case and multiple comparative case studies related to already known extreme events	Case studies, databases and surveys Detailed descriptions of contexts Embedded, multiple and single-case studies, multimodality and distributed activities, less focused on extreme events
Levels of analysis	Intraorganizational Technical or cultural contingency factors, coordination, and sensemaking	Individual and intraorganizational Sensemaking, learning, leadership, politics, and stakeholder-oriented	Individual and intraorganizational Sensemaking, learning, and stakeholder-oriented
Data collections	Final reports and books, interviews and surveys	Final reports and inquiry documentation, interviews, simulations and surveys	Interviews and observations, documentation (reports or transcripts), databases and surveys. Some experimental methods (movies, actor network theory or auto-biographic)
Data analyses	Data analyses generally not that explicit, except for just a few (e.g., Gephart, 1984)	Data analyses inspired mainly by variations of grounded theory and content analysis.	Data analyses inspired mainly by variations of grounded theory. Various statistical methods (regressions analysis and others also used)
Examples	(Weick, 1990) (Roberts, 1990) (Weick & Roberts, 1993) (Gephart, 1984, 1993) (Shrivastava et al., 1988) (Starbuck & Milliken, 1988)	(Carroll, 1998) (Brown, 2000, 2003) (Hoffman & Ocasio, 2001) (Bigley & Roberts, 2001) (Rudolph & Repenning, 2002) (Haunschild & Sullivan, 2002) (Edmondson, 2003)	(Majchrzak et al., 2007) (Quinn & Worline, 2008) (Thornborrow & Brown, 2009) (Madsen & Desai, 2010) (Bechky & Okhuysen, 2011) (Whiteman & Cooper, 2011) (Cornelissen et al., 2014)

Mann Gulch disaster. He proposes a set of lessons for generating richness when analyzing data from extreme contexts – a boon for any qualitative researcher.

Second, we draw on Cunliffe (2011), for whom research designs consist of an interrelated set of elements that form the methodological assemblage around which a study is articulated. Accordingly, we operationalized the methodological research sequence in four parts: (1) Researchers elaborate their *research strategies* and indicate the research positioning or the choices and justifications they adopted to answer their research questions. In this subsection, they introduce the characteristics of their case studies or datasets, depending on whether they chose qualitative, quantitative or mixed research designs. (2) They often refer, explicitly or not, to the *level of analysis*. Extreme events can be examined from many levels of analysis, for example, individual or "intra" or "extra"-organizationally. (3) Researchers explain how they accessed data and which *data collection* techniques they used to gather them (e.g., interviews, questionnaires, public reports or observations). (4) They portray the multiple steps they went through during the data analysis phase and explain why they chose one technique or another (e.g., grounded theory, regression analysis or content analysis). The coherence between these elements is key for assessing the robustness of the methodological sections.

Finally, we built a matrix in which we looked at the four elements presented previously (research strategies, level of analysis, data collection and data analysis) for each paper in our dataset. The data enabled us to clearly identify three periods characterized by different patterns, namely *emergence* (1980–1994), *expansion* (1995–2004) and *consolidation* (2005–2015). The following section describes these periods and will be followed by a discussion about the methodological challenges and opportunities in research on extreme contexts and suggests future avenues (see Table 9.1 for a summary).

The Emergence Period (1980–1994)

Historically, studies on extreme contexts have been interested in industrial accidents and safety (Gherardi et al., 1998; Turner, 1978). In the early 1980s, however, there occurred a shift from a more technically oriented perspective toward the exploration of what makes certain organization less prone to failure. Following the same trend, research during this first period generally relied on a qualitative research design. Explicit arguments for the choice of a particular design were largely missing, due to the dominance of the literature on high-reliability organizations, which argues that case studies can be used for illustrative purposes and that organizations operating in extreme contexts are interesting for developing fail-proof organizations (Roberts, 1990; Shrivastava et al., 1988; Weick, 1990; Weick & Roberts, 1993).

Devoted to an increased understanding of human and organizational behavior, the level of analysis in the early period tended to be intraorganizational. For example, researchers explored how safety and resilience were built into how organizations operated by paying unproportioned attention to potential safety threats in all aspects of the organization, ranging from structure to culture (e.g., Gephart, 1984, 1993; Roberts, 1990; Shrivastava et al., 1988; Weick, 1993; Weick & Roberts, 1993). Analytically, most papers do not offer explicit analytical frameworks, perhaps as an effect of the dominance of illustrative examples that unfold over time. On the one hand, exceptions include, but are not limited to, Cooper and Mitchell (1990), who use bivariate and multivariate descriptive analysis in their investigation of how nurses deal with being close to death (see also Argote, 1982; George et al., 1993). On the other hand, those with less elaborate analytical frameworks are among the papers with the most impact. For example, Weick and Roberts (1993) is the most cited paper (1,323 citations in *Web of Science*), but there is less of an explicit discussion about the analysis. Still, the impact of heedful interrelating and its use within management and organization studies is undisputed.

As a result of their reliance on illustrative examples and cases and their interest for high-reliability organizations, the papers of this period relied on data containing mainly transcripts, final reports, essays and interviews/observations with people involved in extreme events or organizations operating in extreme contexts. For example, Weick (1990) used transcripts of conversations between pilots and air traffic control to explore why a plane was allowed to take off on the same runway as another plane was landing. Relying on the transcripts, he explains how multiple small behaviors and changes in activities influenced how the system operated and the cognitive abilities among the actors to identify the accident waiting to happen (see also Anderson, 1983). Similarly, explorations relied on interviews (mixed with observations in some cases) of high-reliability organizations. For example, Weick and Roberts (1993) explored life onboard an aircraft carrier and used three out of four illustrative examples there from to explain how heedful interrelating is constructed (see also Argote, 1982; Lanzara, 1983). Others in turn used final reports to investigate how extreme events come about. For example, Vaughan (1990) explored the Challenger disaster with multiple sources of data, such as the final report of the accident, interviews and other documentation to develop a multi-level explanation (see also Starbuck & Milliken, 1988). Another trend of the emergence period is the use of essays, often relying on books. Karl Weick illustrates the skillful use of such an approach in his investigation of the Mann Gulch disaster. In the investigation, he used Norman Maclean's (2010) *Young Men and Fire* to explore why experienced elite firefighters attempted to outrun a roaring fire while still carrying their heavy equipment (see also Dietrich, 1981; Nelkin, 1988; Shrivastava et al., 1988).

The data analysis sections of papers published during the emergence period generally contain few details about how researchers constructed their explanations. Moreover, these explanations generally consist of factors or dimensions explaining the phenomena under review. For example, Shrivastava et al. (1988: 288) propose a model of industrial crisis by developing their "key defining characteristics" based on three illustrative examples (Bhopal, Tylenol poisoning and Challenger). The textual analysis proposed by Gephart (1993: 1465) constitutes a notable exception, however. The documents gathered via an ethnographic research process were analyzed "via an integrated combination of methods: theoretical sampling, computer-facilitated qualitative data analysis, and expansion analysis."

In sum, while there are exceptions, case-based research designs are common to the emergence period. Several of the cases we relied on are high-profile illustrative events, predominantly analyzed on an intraorganizational level. The use of narrative data and interview explorations from the emergence period have sensitized us to the causes of and reactions to rather spectacular events and to how people react to sustained experienced exposure to extreme contexts. With respect to risk, crisis and emergency, we see common denominators across the literature, rather than theoretical boundaries.

The Expansion Period (1995–2004)

The popularity of extreme context research published in top-tier journals, though still rare in this decade, has increased if we compare it to the last 15 years. Overall, we observe a diminishment of the popularity of high-reliability organization studies to the benefit of crisis and disaster research during this decade (e.g., Rudolph & Repenning, 2002). It is important to mention that a more critical vision of the nature and phenomenon of extreme contexts developed during this decade (Brown, 2000, 2002; Douglas & Mars, 2003).

Qualitative research designs utilizing single and sometimes multiple and comparative case studies are still dominant, but the reasons provided by researchers for their choices deserve stronger justification. While spectacular cases from the previous period are still central in these works (e.g., Bhopal, Mount Everest), they are less used in order to illustrate arguments than before. While the context description remains the largest part of research designs, we can nevertheless see a stronger preoccupation from researchers to propose coherent research strategies. For example, Bowman and Kunreuther (1988) and Kunreuther and

Bowman (1997) sketch an interpretive research design in order to investigate the influence of the Bhopal accident on decision-making 10 years after the event. They thus present how they articulated their methodological procedures for gathering the data by constantly paying attention to not introduce bias in the different stages of the research. Nevertheless, there are still many papers that propose a general account of an extreme event (e.g., Reed et al., 1997). Besides the trend of relying on spectacular events, other types of events such as the Westray mining disaster (Hynes & Prasad, 1997) are introduced.

Following the influence of Weick and Gephart from the previous period, interpretation and sensemaking became important aspects. The focus shifted to the exploration of dynamics before or during an extreme event, or after through public hearings. Building on Gephart's (1993) work, Brown (2000, 2003) developed the notion of "inquiry sensemaking." The approach invited researchers to examine the impact of extreme research at the field level. Nevertheless, studies produced between 1995 and 2004 are situated mainly on the intraorganizational level, as they seek to explain what happens to organizations and teams exposed to extreme events. For example, Edmondson (2003) investigated how leaders in a healthcare context promote speaking up among their staff. She finds that the managers help the teams learn through their communication style and the reduction of power and status differences (see also Feldman, 2004). While not dominant, others are applying a more individual level of analysis, which was largely absent in the emergence period. Such research includes Fraher (2004), whose autobiographic study of the wake of 9/11 explains why American pilots are in favor of carrying guns. While the level of analysis is individual, parts of the explanation are provided by American culture (see Mintzberg, 2001; Morris & Moore, 2000). In either case, most of the explanations are still focused on the event per se.

Largely consistent with a reliance on single and multiple cases, but in contrast to a previous focus on illustrative examples, books and reports, data collection techniques were dominated by interviews and observations during the expansion period. These interviews and observations became increasingly elaborate, however, as the research increased the level of sophistication. By sophistication, we allude to the fact that the number of interviews and observations was discussed and increased. For example, Bigley and Roberts (2001) conducted their study into fire departments in three phases: Phase 1: unobtrusive observation, informal interviews and internal documents; Phase 2: 15 semi-structured interviews with managers and frontline informants; Phase 3: 15 semi-structured interviews with firefighters. This observation could in part be an indication of a rising maturity within the theoretical genre on one hand, and the requirements associated with the journals in question on the other. Notably, the reliance on books and secondary material was decreasing (but see Weick, 1996; Kayes, 2004; Stein, 2004), and when secondary material was used, it was repurposed. The repurposing included, for example, Weick (1996), who relied on his now famous paper on the Mann Gulch firefighters (Weick, 1993) to extend the implications to scientific work, or extend the case to other cases (Feldman, 2004).

Data analysis presentations were more explicit than during the previous period. Articles more thoroughly discussed the choices made and how the data were analyzed. Proximal variations of themes identifying methods, such as grounded theory, were frequent. For example, Edmondson (2003) used a mixed method where themes were identified within her qualitative research and then used to analyze quantitative data (see also Bigley & Roberts 2001). Some exceptions could, however, be noted where material based on either databases, surveys or simulations or qualitative material was quantitatively analyzed through regression analysis or other methods (see, e.g., Waller, 1999; Hofmann and Stetzer, 1998). We could also find a derivative of a discursive content analysis applied to an inquiry report, which was typical of this period (Brown, 2000, 2002). Despite the advancement in the way data analyses were generally performed between 1995 and 2004, the development of types and the description of critical factors remained the prominent forms of explanations and contributions (Reed, Leamk, & Hesser, 1997; Nelkin, 1988).

Overall, this period was still characterized by qualitative research designs, dominated by qualitative single or multiple case studies. In contrast to the previous period, data collections relied less on illustrative examples and more on interviews and databases. We also observed a refinement in terms of data analysis.

The Consolidation Period (2005–2015)

The last decade is characterized by a significant increase in the interest of research on extreme contexts, as 70 papers have been published in top-tier journals during this period. This is partly explained by three special issues on "Organizations and the management of risk" (Scheytt et al., 2006), "Organizations and risk in the late modernity" (Gephart et al., 2009) and "Experiencing the improbable" (Lampel et al., 2009). Nevertheless, the methodological trends observed from the beginning of the 1980s are still relevant in this period even though it is marked by innovation, fresh insights and maturity.

During the past decade, interest in qualitative research design based on single or comparative case studies has been proportionally increasing compared to previous periods. More than 50 papers out of 70 are based on events widely published in the news media during the past decade. In contrast to past periods, the empirical settings and the sorts of extreme events are different. For example, we observed an interest in "disruptive" extreme contexts, such as natural disasters (Majchrzak et al., 2007; Shepherd & Williams, 2014), terrorist attacks (Cornelissen et al., 2014; Quinn & Worline, 2008) and humanitarian and societal crises (Lamberg & Pajunen, 2010; Muller & Kräussl, 2011). In contrast to the emergence period, we observed a tendency to compare extreme with conventional contexts instead of trying to distinguish them and insist on the specificities of extreme contexts. For example, Bechky and Okhuysen (2011) examined a police crew and a film production team. They justify their research strategies by emphasizing their similarities. Such a research design allowed them to explore how their findings can legitimately contribute to the advancement of knowledge in their case of organizational bricolage under time pressure.

During the previous periods, researchers mainly investigated the factors and processes explaining why an accident, a crisis or a disaster happened or not. Now we observe a displacement toward the consequences of experiencing extreme events. Put differently, the qualitative research design trend observed until now is bolstered by a stronger interest in learning (Desai, 2015; Haunschild et al., 2015; Vashdi et al., 2012) and resilience (Busby, 2006; Carroll et al., 2006; Leveson et al., 2009). On these aspects, the level of analysis becomes central, as learning takes on the eternal question of whether or not individuals and organizations learn from extreme events (see Starbuck, 2009). In this respect, Madsen (2009) proposes a model of individual, organizational and field learning from disasters and minor events. Of course, this multilevel positioning remains an exception, as most research was conducted on an individual or intraorganizational level during the last period (continuing from the expansion period). It should be noted that the individual level of analysis produced original findings on compassion (Powley, 2009), dirty work among police officers (Dick, 2005) or how people see their jobs as including a level of "necessary evils" (Margolis & Molinsky, 2008). Additionally, researchers are becoming more sophisticated, as they organize their data by extracting episodes from interviews (Barton & Sutcliffe, 2009) or by targeting a set of critical events (Quinn & Worline, 2008). Finally, we observed a tendency in which more multi-modality dimensions are taken into account, including materiality, sensemaking and diverse types of organizational behaviors (e.g. Cornelissen et al., 2014; Hawkins, 2015; Shattuck & Williams, 2006).

Regarding the data collection process, our observations are consistent with the previous trend, as documentations and interviews (mainly from inquiry reports) are prevalent. However, datasets are increasingly extensive and mature (Margolis & Molinsky, 2008; Thornborrow & Brown, 2009; Valentine & Edmondson, 2015). For example, we have seen detailed documentation with multiple stages of analysis (Colville et al., 2013; Cornelissen et al., 2014), more interviews (Lindberg & Rantatalo, 2014) and longer periods of observation (Bechky & Okhuysen, 2011; Candrian, 2014). Numerically, but not proportionately, the number of studies using extensive databases (Baum & Dahlin, 2007; Vashdi et al., 2013) and surveys (Bacharach & Bamberger, 2007; Nembhard & Tucker, 2011) is increasing. Quantitative design research is also drawing on more expansive databases than before (Baum & Dahlin, 2007; Desai, 2011, 2015). Finally, a few studies have used a mixed methods approach (database and documentation), while we have also observed more playful and experimental approaches to data collection. For example, Godfrey et al. (2012) analyzed the movie "Jarhead" to investigate the relationship between masculinity, the body and the military body. Whiteman and Cooper (2011) drew on auto-ethnographic insights gained from sub-Arctic Canada to make a comparative analysis with the well-known Mann Gulch disaster (see also, e.g., Valentine & Edmondson, 2015).

The most important change observed since 2005 relates to data analyses, which have become more rigorous and extended. In general, data analyses are more concerned with modeling and/or testing hypotheses and propositions, including those adopting qualitative methods. For example, Desai (2011) tested how an entire industry reacts when threatened by adverse events, or the relation between safety and profitability, where Madsen (2013) found that airlines performing above their aspirations tended to pay less attention to safety. Moreover, variations of grounded approaches in qualitative design research are becoming more robust. Researchers do not only mention the analysis in a paragraph or two, relating to reading, coding and returning to the literature until theory saturation, but they are "breaking the case into events" (Quinn & Worline, 2008) or describing a set of analytical steps that clearly explain how they proceeded. For example, Whiteman and Cooper (2011) propose seven analytical steps: (1) ethnography, (2) writing narrative accounts, (3) initial coding, (4) identifying emergent themes with reflexivity, (5) analyzing other contexts, (6) further integration of theory and refinement of coding, and (7) validity checks. Increasingly, researchers also include their data structures and provide complementary data in appendices (e.g., Shepherd and Williams, 2014). By being more rigorous, researchers have been able to open the black box of micro-processes and practices inherent to extreme contexts. For example, Busby (2006: 1375) explains how "processes of systemic reform co-exist with a set of phenomenon that tend to undermine them." Haunschild et al. (2015) highlight the oscillation process of learning in which organizations such as NASA have learning and forgetting periods. All these analytical improvements contribute to reinforcing theory and contributions based on unique cases.

In sum, the consolidation period is characterized by a significant increase in the sophistication of the methodological choices. The research design is still dominated by qualitative research, relying on single and multiple cases, but several of the articles also use quantitative methods for data collection and/or analysis. It should be noted that there is less a reliance on the same events, and more attention to how unspecified events transform within and between organizations. The data collection and analysis techniques used are becoming more rigorous and sophisticated.

Discussion

The goal of this chapter was to review the methods sections of 120 empirical contributions on extreme contexts published in top-tier journals between 1980 and 2015. The growing popularity of extreme context research (70 of the 120 articles were published in the past 10 years) has contributed to accentuating the fragmentation of this literature (Bundy et al., 2017; Hällgren, Rouleau, & de Rond, 2018; James et al., 2011; Williams et al., 2017). While we agree with this claim, our review of these papers' Methods sections (research strategy, level of analysis, data collection and analysis) demonstrates that they are rather homogenous. Based on our main observations, we will now discuss four suggestions for the future: (1) introducing mixed research designs, (2) redirecting the focus to spectacular events, (3) looking for innovative data collection techniques and (4) increasing rigor in data analyses.

Introducing Mixed Research Designs

The distribution and ratio of research strategies (qualitative case or quantitative dataset) appears to be fairly consistent across the three periods. This homogeneity has served to establish the research area, and has made important contributions to a better understanding of how people and organizations react to adverse events, for example, how people and organizations react compassionately (Shepherd & Williams, 2014) or courageously (Quinn & Worline, 2008), or how safety is temporally achieved even in highly complex and uncertain situations (Weick & Roberts, 1993). That said, innovative research strategies for exploring sensitive data – however significant for the advancement of the field (Buchanan & Denyer, 2013) – remain rare. Of course, there are notable exceptions over time (e.g., from our sample: Barton & Sutcliffe, 2009, Bechky & Okhuysen, 2011; Cooren et al., 2008; Gephart, 1993; Quinn & Worline,2008; Whiteman & Cooper, 2011). Moreover, the development of quantitative and mixed methods is limited, and we have just started to scratch the surface of modeling and testing assumptions on a broader scale.

While researchers with an interest in extreme contexts should continue to promote case-based research, innovative and sophisticated designs are still possible. For example, they can draw on fiction (e.g., film or novels) or adopt real-time or prospective research designs (Buchanan & Denyer, 2013). The latter are difficult to carry out during extreme events, but more realistic in the so-called risky contexts that are prepared to handle extreme events that might occur in the future (Hällgren, Rouleau, & de Rond, 2018). Of course, the volume of information and their access render retrospective designs more convenient despite the problems associated with them (e.g., memory loss and interpretation bias). Nevertheless, we see a potential in more mixed-method research, which would be as helpful for qualitative as for quantitative research.

Redirecting the Focus to Spectacular Events

There is a tendency to focus on spectacular events. Some researchers have chosen events that few have done any research on, but they are spectacular nonetheless (e.g., the Alpha Piper disaster (Brown, 2003), the collision of two trains (Busby, 2006) and the Westray coal mining disaster (Hynes & Prasad, 1997)). Others revisit the same events, including the Mann Gulch disaster (Weick, 1993; Whiteman & Cooper, 2011), the Challenger disaster (Starbuck & Milliken, 1988; Vaughan, 1990), the 1996 Everest disaster (Elmes & Frame, 2008; Kayes, 2004), the Bhopal disaster (Bowman & Kunreuther, 1988; Weick, 2010), the shooting of Charles Menendez (Colville et al., 2013; Cornelissen et al., 2014) and the Holocaust (Dietrich, 1981; Marti & Fernandez, 2013). Considering the empirical and theoretical impact of these events, it is understandable that researchers would revisit them. On the one hand, organizing is about events (Weick, 1979: 1) and thus important for advancing theory. On the other hand, by choosing the same spectacular events, the literature risks romanticizing and exaggerating the differences between extreme contexts and non-extreme contexts. Moreover, it is not only significant events that are responsible for how things turn out. There are also dynamic non-events (Weick, 2011), and even in extreme contexts, most activities are rather trivial (Hällgren, Rouleau, & de Rond, 2018). To further the potential of research on extreme contexts, researchers could consider their units of analysis by using, for example, temporal bracketing (Langley, 1999) or critical incidents analysis (Quinn & Worline, 2008) or redirecting attention to individual activities instead of being centered on the events (Barton & Sutcliffe, 2009). By decentering the research from the event-sequence narrative, researchers would potentially access under-examined levels of analysis and provide multi-level explanations.

Looking for Innovative Data Collection Techniques

Researchers have made remarkable efforts to draw on innovative ways of collecting and analyzing data in extreme contexts. These include action research (Vashdi et al., 2013), video-ethnography (Cooren et al., 2008), film (Godfrey et al., 2012) and self-report methods (Bacharach & Bamberger, 2007; Margolis & Molinsky, 2008). Still, some innovative methods have become mainstream (e.g., public inquiries or public hearing reports (Brown, 2003; Cornelissen et al., 2014; Gephart, 1993)). In addition, research is dominated by more conventional ways of collecting data (e.g., interviews (Argote, 1982; Catino & Patriotta, 2013; Roth et al., 2006), simulations (Carroll et al., 2006; Waller, 1999), surveys (Colquitt et al., 2011; Katz-Navon et al., 2005; Klein et al., 1995) and, to a limited extent, observations (Waring & Currie, 2009; Woolley, 2011)).

To study extreme events in situ requires a certain amount of luck and methodological innovation, particularly given that extreme contexts are potentially dangerous to the researcher (Buchanan & Denyer, 2013). To ensure that the previous directions outlined in this research agenda are undertaken, future research should explore the "everyday" life of contexts in which extreme events are likely to occur, or have occurred. For example, "passing organizational ethnography" (Cooren et al., 2008) might be a relevant way of better understanding the processes and practices at play in risk, emergency and crisis research, and visual research methods could offer greater opportunities for capturing both their discursive and material aspects. A future possibility lies in the use of social media (e.g., blogs, Facebook and Twitter). Social media offer potential real-time data, and in-house production of audio and video constitutes new possibilities for collecting data in extreme contexts. Thus, the emotional labor and access problems of extreme contexts may be reduced (see Prasad, 2014; George & Clegg, 1997).

Finally, efforts should continue to be made to compare empirical insights from conventional contexts with insights in extreme contexts and vice versa (e.g., Garud et al., 2011; Haunschild et al., 2015). Such research can better address the similarities and differences between conventional and extreme contexts and allow researchers to better investigate how organizing is embedded in larger organizational and institutional structures.

Increasing Rigor in Data Analyses

Most studies in our dataset relied on case studies and variations inspired by grounded theory/theme-building analysis. Unlike us, some have concerns about generalizing from such data, and we see that, for instance, adopting processual and practice approaches can help make the data analysis more systematic while building relational and contextual explanations. Such approaches can also provide opportunity for "naturalistic generalization" or "analytical refinement" (Buchanan & Denyer, 2013: 218). That said, balance is often useful. Therefore, an increased use of narrative comparison (Whiteman & Cooper, 2011) and statistical methods such as regression analysis (Desai, 2011) could be valuable. In terms of quantitative design, Morgeson et al. (2015) call for hierarchical linear modeling in order to track down the interdependence of multiple events.

In recent papers, however, data analyses have expanded in variety and rigor by providing coherent and systematic explanations. Regardless of the type of analysis, there is still a need for researchers interested in extreme contexts to continue to be more rigorous and sophisticated. By its nature, research on extreme contexts is based on counterintuitive and unconventional data. We should therefore also cherish these characteristics and use the analyses in innovative ways to generate richness (Weick, 2007) and to advance what we know about extreme contexts in general, and management and organization theory in particular.

Conclusion

In this chapter, we have reviewed 120 articles on extreme contexts published in top-tier journals, identifying patterns related to three main research periods. We suggest that extreme contexts would be useful for increasing the integration of a rather theoretically fragmented and methodologically homogenous literature. We find that the methodological challenges to which research on extreme contexts is exposed relate to this homogeneity. There is a tendency to examine the same spectacular events, with identical or similar designs and strategies based on conventional data and increasingly rigorous data analysis processes. While the literature may carry the key to addressing today's major challenges, there is a need for a greater spectrum of methods and multi-level investigations that take the everyday activities of organizations operating in extreme contexts seriously. The turning point that occurred 10 years ago is very encouraging for the future of this body of research, at least for publishing in top-tier journals.

References

Anderson, P. A. (1983). Decision making by objection and the Cuban missile crisis. *Administrative Science Quarterly, 28*(2), 201–222.

Argote, L. (1982). Input uncertainty and organizational coordination in hospital emergency units. *Administrative Science Quarterly, 27*(3), 420–434.

Bacharach, S. B., & Bamberger, P. A. (2007). 9/11 and New York City firefighters' post hoc unit support and control climates: A context theory of the consequences of involvement in traumatic work-related events. *Academy of Management Journal, 50*(4), 849–868.

Barton, M. A., & Sutcliffe, K. M. (2009). Overcoming dysfunctional momentum: Organizational safety as a social achievement. *Human Relations, 62*(9), 1327–1356.

Baum, J., & Dahlin, K. (2007). Aspiration Performance and Railroads' patterns of learning from train wrecks and crashes. *Organization Science, 18*(3), 368–385.

Bechky, B. A., & Okhuysen, G. A. (2011). Expecting the Unexpected? How Swat Officers and film crews handle surprises. *The Academy of Management Journal (AMJ), 54*(2), 239–261.

Bigley, G., A., & Roberts, K. H. (2001). The incident command system: High reliability organizing for complex and volatile task environments. *Academy of Management Journal, 44*(6), 1281–1299.

Bowman, E., & Kunreuther, H. (1988). Post-Bhopal behaviour at a chemical company. *Journal of Management Studies, 25*(4), 387–400.

Brown, A. D. (2000). Making sense of inquiry sensemaking. *Journal of Management Studies, 37*(1), 45–75.

Brown, A. D. (2003). Authoritative sensemaking in a public inquiry report. *Organization Studies, 25*(1), 95–112.

Buchanan, D. A., & Denyer, D. (2013). Researching tomorrow's crisis: Methodological innovations and wider implications. *International Journal of Management Reviews, 15*(2), 205–224.

Bundy, J., Pfarrer, M. D., Short, C. E., & Coombs, W. T. (2017). Crises and crisis management. *Journal of management, 43*(6), 1661–1692.

Busby, J. S. (2006). Failure to mobilize in reliability-seeking organizations: Two cases from the UK railway. *Journal of Management Studies, 43*(6), 1375–1393.

Candrian, C. (2014). Taming death and the consequences of discourse. *Human Relations, 67*(1), 53–69.

Carroll, J. S. (1998). Organizational learning activities in high-hazard industries: The logics underlying self-analysis. *Journal of Management Studies, 35*(6), 699–717.

Carroll, T. N., Gormley, T. J., Bilardo, V. J., Burton, R. M., & Woodman, K. L. (2006). Designing a new organization at NASA: An organization design process using simulation. *Organization Science, 17*(2), 202–214.

Catino, M., & Patriotta, G. (2013). Learning from errors: Cognition, emotions and safety culture in the Italian air force. *Organization Studies, 34*(4), 437–467.

Colquitt, J. A., LePine, J. A., Zapata, C. P., & Wild, R. E. (2011). Trust in typical and high-reliability contexts: Building and reacting to trust among firefighters. *Academy of Management Journal, 54*(5), 999–1015.

Colville, I., Pye, A., & Carter, M. (2013). Organizing to counter terrorism: Sensemaking amidst dynamic complexity. *Human Relations, 66*(9), 1201–1223.

Cooper, C. L., & Mitchell, S. (1990). Nursing the critically Ill and dying. *Human Relations, 43*(4), 297–311.

Cooren, F., Brummans, B. H. J. M., & Charrieras, D. (2008). The coproduction of organizational presence: A study of Medecins Sans Frontieres in action. *Human Relations, 61*(10), 1339–1370.

Cornelissen, J. P., Mantere, S., & Vaara, E. (2014). The contraction of meaning: The combined effect of communication, emotions, and materiality on sensemaking in the stockwell shooting. *Journal of Management Studies, 51*(5), 699–736.

Cunliffe, A. L. (2011). Crafting qualitative research: Morgan and Smircich 30 years on. *Organizational Research Methods, 14*(4), 647–673.

Desai, V. M. (2011). Mass media and massive failures: Determining organizational efforts to defend field legitimacy following crises. *Academy of Management Journal, 54*(2), 263–278.

Desai, V. (2015). Learning through the distribution of failures within an organization: Evidence from heart bypass surgery performance. *Academy of Management Journal, 58*(4), 1032–1050.

Dick, P. (2005). Dirty work designations: How police officers account for their use of coercive force. *Human Relations, 58*(11), 1363–1390.

Dietrich, D. J. (1981). Holocau-st as public policy: The third reich. *Human Relations, 34*(6), 445–462.

Edmondson, A. C. (2003). Speaking up in the operating room: How team leaders promote learning in interdisciplinary action teams. *Journal of Management Studies, 40*(6), 1419–1452.

Elmes, M., & Frame, B. (2008). Into hot air: A critical perspective on Everest. *Human Relations, 61*(2), 213–241.

Feldman, S. P. (2004). The culture of objectivity: Quantification, uncertainty, and the evaluation of risk at NASA. *Human Relations, 57*(6), 691–718.

Fraher, A. L. (2004). 'Flying the Friendly Skies:' Why US Commercial Airline Pilots Want to Carry Guns. *Human Relations, 57*(5), 573–595.

Garud, R., Dunbar, R. L., & Bartel, C. A. (2011). Dealing with unusual experiences: A narrative perspective on organizational learning. *Organization Science, 22*(3), 587–601.

George, R., & Clegg, S. R. (1997). An inside story: Tales from the field—Doing organizational research in a state of insecurity. *Organization Studies, 18*(6), 1015–1023.

George, J. M., Reed, T. F., Ballard, K. A., Colin, J., & Fielding, J. (1993). Contact with AIDS patients as a source of work-related distress: Effects of organizational and social support. *Academy of Management Journal, 36*(1), 157–171.

Gephart, R. P. (1984). Making sense of organizationally based environmental disasters. *Journal of management, 10*(2), 205–225.

Gephart, R. P. (1993). The textual approach: Risk and blame in disaster sensemaking. *Academy of Management Journal, 36*(6), 1465–1514.

Gephart, R. P., Van Maanen, J., & Oberlechner, T. (2009). Organizations and risk in late modernity. *Organization Studies, 30*(2–3), 141–155.

Gherardi, S., Nicolini, D., & Odella, F. (1998). What do you mean by safety? Conflicting perspectives on accident causation and safety management in a construction firm. *Journal of Contingencies and Crisis Management, 6*(4), 202–213.

Godfrey, R., Lilley, S., & Brewis, J. (2012). Biceps, bitches and borgs: Reading Jarhead's representation of the construction of the (masculine) military body. *Organization Studies, 33*(4), 541–562.

Hällgren, M., Rouleau, L., & De Rond, M. (2018). A matter of life or death: How extreme context research matters for management and organization studies. *Academy of Management Annals, 12*(1), 111–153.

Hannah, S. T., Uhl-Bien, M., Avolio, B. J., & Cavarretta, F. L. (2009). A framework for examining leadership in extreme contexts. *The Leadership Quarterly, 20*(6), 897–919.

Haunschild, P. R., Polidoro Jr, F., & Chandler, D. (2015). Organizational oscillation between learning and forgetting: The dual role of serious errors. *Organization Science, 26*(6), 1682–1701.

Haunschild, P. R., & Sullivan, B. N. (2002). Learning from complexity: Effects of prior accidents and incidents on airlines' learning. *Administrative Science Quarterly, 47*(4), 609–643.

Hawkins, B. (2015). Ship-shape: Materializing leadership in the British Royal Navy. *Human Relations, 68*(6), 951–971.

Hoffman, A. J., & Ocasio, W. (2001). Not all events are attended equally: Toward a middle-range theory of industry attention to external events. *Organization Science, 12*(4), 414–434.

Hofmann, D. A., & Stetzer, A. (1998). The role of safety climate and communication in accident interpretation: Implications for learning from negative events. *Academy of Management Journal, 41*(6), 644–657.

Hynes, T., & Prasad, P. (1997). Patterns of 'Mock Bureaucracy' in mining disasters: An analysis of the Westray coal mine explosion. *Journal of Management Studies, 34*(4), 601–623.

James, E. H., Wooten, L. P., & Dushek, K. (2011). Crisis management: Informing a new leadership research agenda. *The Academy of Management Annals, 5*(1), 455–493.

Katz-Navon, T., Naveh, E., & Stern, Z. (2005). Safety climate in health care organizations: A multidimensional approach. *Academy of Management Journal, 48*(6), 1075–1089.

Kayes, C., D. (2004). The 1996 Mount Everest climbing disaster: The breakdown of learning in teams. *Human Relations, 57*(10), 1263–1284.

Klein, R. L., Bigley, G. A., & Roberts, K. H. (1995). Organizational culture in high reliability organizations: An extension. *Human Relations, 48*(7), 771–793.

Kunreuther, H., & Bowman, E. H. (1997). A dynamic model of organizational decision making: Chemco revisited six years after Bhopal. *Organization Science, 8*(4), 404–413.

Lamberg, J.-A., & Pajunen, K. (2010). Agency, institutional change, and continuity: The case of the Finnish Civil War. *Journal of Management Studies, 47*(5), 814–836.

Lampel, J., Shamsie, J., & Shapira, Z. (2009). Experiencing the improbable: Rare events and organizational learning. *Organization Science, 20*(5), 835–845.

Langley, A. (1999). Strategies for theorizing from process data. *Academy of Management Review, 24*(4), 691–710.

Lanzara, G. F. (1983). Ephemeral organizations in extreme environments: Emergence, strategy, extinction. *Journal of Management Studies, 20*(1), 71–95.

Leveson, N., Dulac, N., Marais, K., & Carroll, J. (2009). Moving beyond normal accidents and high reliability organizations: A systems approach to safety in complex systems. *Organization Studies, 30*(2–3), 227–249.

Lindberg, O., & Rantatalo, O. (2014). Competence in professional practice: A practice theory analysis of police and doctors. *Human Relations, 68*(4), 561–582.

Maclean, N. (2010). *Young men and fire*: University of Chicago Press.

Madsen, P. M. (2009). These lives will not be lost in Vain: Organizational learning from disaster in US Coal mining. *Organization Science, 20*(5), 861–875.

Madsen, P. M. (2013). Perils and profits: A reexamination of the link between profitability and safety in U.S. Aviation. *Journal of management, 39*(3), 763–791.

Madsen, P. M., & Desai, V. (2010). Failing to learn? The effects of failure and success on organizational learning in the global orbital launch vehicle industry. *Academy of Management Journal, 53*(3), 451–476.

Majchrzak, A., Jarvenpaa, S. L., & Hollingshead, A. B. (2007). Coordinating expertise among emergent groups responding to disasters. *Organization Science, 18*(1), 147–161.

Margolis, J. D., & Molinsky, A. (2008). Navigating the bind of necessary evils: Psychological engagement and the production of interpersonally sensitive behavior. *Academy of Management Journal, 51*(5), 847–872.

Marti, I., & Fernandez, P. (2013). The institutional work of oppression and resistance: Learning from the Holocaust. *Organization Studies, 34*(8), 1195–1223.

Mintzberg, H. (2001). Managing exceptionally. *Organization Science, 12*(6), 759–771.

Morgeson, F. P., Mitchell, T. R., & Liu, D. (2015). Event system theory: An event-oriented approach to the organizational sciences. *Academy of Management Review, 40*(4), 515–537.

Morris, M. W., & Moore, P. C. (2000). The lessons we (don't) learn: Counterfactual thinking and organizational accountability after a close call. *Administrative Science Quarterly, 45*(4), 737–765.

Muller, A., & Kräussl, R. (2011). Doing good deeds in times of need: A strategic perspective on corporate disaster donations. *Strategic Management Journal, 32*(9), 911–929.

Nelkin, D. (1988). Risk reporting and the management of industrial crises. *Journal of Management Studies, 25*(4), 341–351.

Nembhard, I. M., & Tucker, A. L. (2011). Deliberate learning to improve performance in dynamic service settings: Evidence from hospital intensive care units. *Organization Science, 22*(4), 907–922.

Powley, E. H. (2009). Reclaiming resilience and safety: Resilience activation in the critical period of crisis. *Human Relations, 62*(9), 1289–1326.

Prasad, A. (2014). You can't go home again: And other psychoanalytic lessons from crossing a neo-colonial border. *Human Relations, 67*(2), 233–257.

Quinn, R. W., & Worline, M. C. (2008). Enabling courageous collective action: Conversations from United Airlines flight 93. *Organization Science, 19*(4), 497–516.

Reed, R., Lemak, D. J., & Hesser, W. A. (1997). Cleaning up after the Cold War: Management and social issues. *Academy of Management Review, 22*(3), 614–642.

Roberts, K., H. (1990). Some characteristics of one type of high reliability organization. *Organization Science, 1*(2), 160–176.

Roth, E. M., Multer, J., & Raslear, T. (2006). Shared situation awareness as a contributor to high reliability performance in railroad operations. *Organization Studies, 27*(7), 967–987.

Rudolph, J. W., & Repenning, N. P. (2002). Disaster dynamics: Understanding the role of quantity in organizational collapse. *Administrative Science Quarterly, 47*(1), 1–30.

Scheytt, T., Soin, K., Sahlin-Andersson, K., & Power, M. (2006). Introduction: Organizations, risk and regulation. *Journal of Management Studies, 43*(6), 1331–1337.

Shattuck, L. G., & Williams, N. L. (2006). Extending naturalistic decision making to complex organizations: A dynamic model of situated cognition. *Organization Studies, 27*(7), 989–1009.

Shepherd, D. A., & Williams, T. A. (2014). Local venturing as compassion organizing in the aftermath of a natural disaster: The role of localness and community in reducing suffering. *Journal of Management Studies, 51*(6), 952–994.

Shrivastava, P., Mitroff, I. I., Miller, D., & Miclani, A. (1988). Understanding industrial crises. *Journal of Management Studies, 25*(4), 285–303.

Starbuck, W. H. (2009). Perspective-cognitive reactions to rare events: Perceptions, uncertainty, and learning. *Organization Science, 20*(5), 925–937.

Starbuck, W. H., & Milliken, F. J. (1988). Challenger: Fine-tuning the odds until something breaks. *Journal of Management Studies, 25*(4), 319–340.

Stein, M. (2004). The critical period of disasters: Insights from sense-making and psychoanalytic theory. *Human Relations, 57*(10), 1243–1261.

Thornborrow, T., & Brown, A. D. (2009). 'Being Regimented': Aspiration, discipline and identity work in the British Parachute Regiment. *Organization Studies, 30*(4), 355–376.

Turner, B., A. (1978). *Man-made disasters.* London, UK: Wykeham Press.

Valentine, M. A., & Edmondson, A. C. (2015). Team scaffolds: How mesolevel structures enable role-based coordination in temporary groups. *Organization Science, 26*(2), 405–422.

Vashdi, D. R., Bamberger, P. A., & Erez, M. (2012). Can surgical teams ever learn? The role of coordination, complexity, and transitivity in action team learning. *Academy of Management Journal, 56*(4), 945–971.

Vashdi, D. R., Bamberger, P. A., & Erez, M. (2013). Can surgical teams ever learn? The role of coordination, complexity, and transitivity in action team learning. *Academy of Management Journal, 56*(4), 945–971.

Vaughan, D. (1990). Autonomy, interdependence, and social control: NASA and the space shuttle challenger. *Administrative Science Quarterly, 35*(2), 225–257.

Waller, M. J. (1999). The timing of adaptive group responses to nonroutine events. *Academy of Management Journal, 42*(2), 127–137.

Waring, J., & Currie, G. (2009). Managing expert knowledge: Organizational challenges and managerial futures for the UK medical profession. *Organization Studies, 30*(7), 755–778.

Weick, K. E. (1979). *The social psychology of organizing* (2nd ed.). New York: McGraw-Hill.

Weick, K. E. (1990). The vulnerable system: An analysis of the Tenerife air disaster. *Journal of management, 16*(3), 571–593.

Weick, K. E. (1993). The collapse of sensemaking in organizations: The mann gulch disaster. *Administrative Science Quarterly, 38*(4), 628–652.

Weick, K. E. (1996). Drop your tools: An allegory for organizational studies. *Administrative Science Quarterly, 41*(2), 301–313.

Weick, K. E. (2007). The generative properties of richness. *Academy of Management Journal, 50*(1), 14–19.

Weick, K. E. (2010). Reflections on enacted sensemaking in the Bhopal disaster. *Journal of Management Studies, 47*(3), 537–550.

Weick, K. E. (2011). Organizing for transient reliability: The production of dynamic non-events. *Journal of Contingencies and Crisis Management, 19*(1), 21–27.

Weick, K. E., & Roberts, K. H. (1993). Collective mind in organizations: Heedful interrelating on flight decks. *Administrative Science Quarterly, 38*(3), 357–381.

Whiteman, G., & Cooper, W. H. (2011). Ecological sensemaking. *Academy of Management Journal, 54*(5), 889–911.

Williams, T., Gruber, D., Sutcliffe, K., Shepherd, D., & Zhao, E. Y. (2017). Organizational response to adversity: Fusing crisis management and resilience research streams. *Academy of Management Annals, 11*(2), 733–769.

Woolley, A. W. (2011). Playing offense vs. defense: The effects of team strategic orientation on team process in competitive environments. *Organization Science, 22*(6), 1384–1398.

10

LOCAL TRANSLATIONS OF OPERATIONAL RISK[1]

Barbara Czarniawska

Regulations, even those that concern numerical procedures, are texts. As a rule, texts say more and less than that their authors wish; translations (linguistic or not) can change the text beyond recognition (for better and for worse), and institutional sediments are much more resistant to change than the eager change agents wish. In the global world, ideas travel around the planet, but are then translated locally. The result may be that the same idea differs every place it lands, that different ideas may lead to similar practices, and that the final combination of global ideas and local practices is almost inevitably difficult to foresee, but fascinating to study.

In what follows, I address the concept of operational risk management as launched by Basel II Accord, and the way it has been translated in two countries – Sweden and Poland – both relatively untouched by the financial crisis of 2008–2012. The analysis is preceded by a short introduction to the theory of translation – the framework used in this text.[2]

The Notion of Translation Applied to Financial Regulations

In order to denote the transfer of ideas and practices from one context to another, scholars have traditionally spoken of *diffusion*, following Rogers (1962), who borrowed this concept from Gabriel Tarde (1890/1903). But to most people, "diffusion" suggests a movement subject to the laws of physics, quite contrary to Tarde's intentions; he proposed that molecules move like ideas, not the other way around. Yet Tarde was forgotten, and the physicalist understanding of the term gained the upper hand, followed by a further train of physical metaphors, such as "saturation" or "resistance". Latour (1986), inspired by the philosophy of Michel Serres, proposed its replacement with the word *translation*, calling attention to the richness of meanings associated with this term, only some of which are evoked in everyday speech.[3] Translation, he said, is a *transportation* combined with a *transformation*. Drawing from the same source, Callon (1980) suggested that "[t]translation involves creating convergences and homologies by relating things that were previously different" (p. 211).

It is important to stress that the meaning of "translation" in this context surpasses the linguistic interpretation. It means "displacement, drift, invention, mediation, creation of a new link that did not exist before and modifies in part the two agents" (Latour, 1993, p. 6), the two agents being those who translate and that which is translated. It is this richness of meaning, evoking associations with both movement and transformation, embracing both linguistic and material objects, that makes translation a key concept for understanding organizational change (Czarniawska & Sevón, 1996). It comprises what exists and what is created: the relationships between humans and ideas, ideas and objects, and humans and objects.[4]

How can the notion of translation be useful in understanding globalization processes? Globalization is often depicted as a process that contributes to the compression of the world, a variation on the well-known definition by Robertson (1992, p. 8). But, as Sahlins (2001) has pointed out "[e]ven as the world becomes more integrated globally, it continues to differentiate locally – the second in some measure stimulated by the first" (p. 170). Thus, Robertson suggested that a more useful term could be *glocalization* or "telescoping *global* and *local* to make a blend" (Robertson, 1995, pp. 28–29).

Precisely because of its polysemic character, the concept of translation helps us to understand how this blend is achieved and how various types of connections are constructed around the globe. Translation thus understood means transformation, and transference not only of utterances, but of anything. The concept thus redefined is meant to attract attention to the fact that anything – an idea, a practice – moved from one place to another cannot reappear unchanged. To set something in a new place is to construct it anew. Thus, translation immediately evokes symbolic associations; yet, scholars of translation emphasize that at the same time translation is inevitably material, because only a thing can be moved from one place to another and from one time to another. Ideas must materialize; symbols must be inscribed. A practice cannot travel; it must be simplified and abstracted into an idea, and thereby converted into words and images. A similar translation is required in the opposite direction: no abstract model, no best practice description, and no manual can guarantee that actions inspired by it will be identical.

The result of translation is always a change – a change in what was translated, and a change in the translator. The change may create improvement or deterioration, enrichment or impoverishment. Even copying machines do not produce copies identical to the original. Changes can be due to a faulty imitation, to a conscious adaptation to local circumstances, to the hidden hand of the past (sediments in new institutional theory), but also because institutions are inscribed in machines (Joerges & Czarniawska, 1998), and machines – especially computers – play a central role in glocalization processes.

The travel of the idea of "operational risk" is one of many that could well illustrate such a process (Power, 2007), even if this text focuses on only a small part of this travel; in fact, it can be seen as an addendum to Power's story of its earlier peregrinations. It also shows, as every translator knows, that even when the translation remains limited to a linguistic practice, translation is a destabilizing operation. It destabilizes the text under translation, which is taken from its original cultural context and fit onto another, even if the context is in itself cross-cultural, as in the case of global accords. Furthermore, the language into which the translation is made is destabilized, if ever so little, with every translation made – thus the need for the stabilizing role of dictionaries. One could claim that the text of the Basel II Accord was such a stabilizing dictionary (Power [2007], called it a "boundary object"). Yet a dictionary, no matter how perfect, does not guarantee the perfection of translation. It remains local, especially when words are being translated into practices.

Operational Risk: A Swedish Translation

When I began to question my Swedish colleagues about the connections between risk management and accounting, I was directed to a doctoral dissertation describing the history of public sector accounting in Sweden from the times of Gustaf Vasa to the present (Sandin, 1991). I consulted the work in question somewhat warily (in my early study of municipal reforms, I was told that they were initiated by the Vikings, which I believed for a while), and indeed, I found nothing on the topic. But at least two pieces of information captured my interest: the origin of Swedish accounting and the increased competence of accountants. Since the end of the 19th century, especially since the establishment of the Institute of Chartered Accountants in England and Wales, Swedish accounting and auditing were modeled after England's (Sandin, 1991, p. 43). During the same period of time there was a wave of frauds, falsifications, and embezzlements. The solution was seen to be an increase in the competence of accountants and auditors (the Swedish Audit Society was founded in 1899) and a strong emphasis on impartial and competent auditing. Two central auditing organizations were created at the beginning of the next century, one for private companies and the other for public administration organizations. The notion of "risk" was not mentioned. The elimination of frauds and misappropriation was to be achieved by a stronger control: a retrospective rather than a prospective monitoring of economic activity.

A popular accounting textbook (four editions between 1983 and 1997) mentions "risk" on one page and defines it as a decision situation between complete certainty and complete uncertainty of its consequences. A situation is risky, then, when one knows the possible consequences of a given decision and their respective probabilities (Göran Andersson, 1997, p. 38). Later in the text, two paragraphs were dedicated to "risk analysis" (pp. 195–196). Things have changed since 1983, however, in Sweden as elsewhere. A 1995 doctoral dissertation dedicated to risk and efficiency in interbank payment systems (Martin Andersson, 1995) contained a simulation of system risk in payments. Operational risk was seen as consisting of administrative risk and risk of fraud, and was commented upon in two half pages. But it was clear that risk management was becoming a central issue in financial institutions. An explosion of the concept transformed this local, US finance (or military) invention into a global trait (Power, 2004).

As commonly claimed, the problematic liquidation of a German bank in 1974 required that the G10 nations form the Basel Committee on Banking Supervision, which reached its first accord in 1988: the so-called Basel I. Much attention was paid there to the notion of *credit risk*, soon to be complemented by *market risk*, and then, in Basel II (2004), by *operational risk*. It has been argued that such events as 9/11 and rogue trading at Société Générale, Barings, Allied Irish Banks (AIB), and National Australia Bank convinced the committee that risk management extends beyond market and credit risk.

Indeed, when the translation of ideas into actions is well advanced, the actors involved feel a need to mythologize by dramatizing origins. It may well be that, in the reconstruction of the past, an event is chosen or invented because it is rhetorically convenient – a logical starting point for a story. Alternatively, the incidental and disruptive character of the initial events is stressed in order to demonstrate an incredible touch of luck in the timely arrival of the idea. Both types of memories serve the same purpose: to tie, meaningfully, the arrival of an idea to present problems experienced by people in organizations or attributed to the organizations. There is often an attempt to portray the process as functional; this idea was spotted and adopted because it served well in resolving a specific difficulty or in creating a new opportunity in situations of stagnation. Although the label "operational risk" has existed since the beginning of the 1990s, Power (2007) has noted that the banking community tends to relate it to the collapse of Barings Bank in 1995.

The Basel Committee defined operational risk in 2001, so that Gunnar Wahlström was able to interview Swedish bank managers that year (Wahlström, 2006, 2009a) and again in 2005 (Wahlström, 2009b). As the title of one of his articles suggests ("Risk in practice", 2009a), he was interested in risk management in banking. There are no Swedish textbooks dedicated to risk management and accounting, and textbooks dedicated to risk management tend to treat it in general terms (e.g. Hamilton, 1985/1996). Perhaps because Swedish students – and bankers – read English, there is no need for linguistic translations of texts dedicated to such issues. There is only one reference to a Swedish text in Wahlström's three articles, although he quotes many Swedish and Nordic authors. In both his studies (2001 and 2005), he interviewed representatives of four Swedish banks that differ in size and in degree of centralization. In both cases, positive as well as negative aspects of the idea of measuring operational risk were raised.

The positive opinions formulated in 2001 emphasized several aspects noted by the interviewees when the Basel Committee published its definition of operational risk[5]: "the risk of direct and indirect loss resulting from inadequate or failed internal processes, people and systems or from external events" (Wahlström, 2006, p. 498). The measurement of operational risk provides management with better grounds for decision-making, at the same time leading to a more positive image of the bank (low operational risk indicates higher competence, and permits a lower level of regulatory capital). Operational risk measurement was also seen as a valuable complement to credit and market risk measurements, touching such potentially threatening areas as fraud and embezzlement, which often create crisis, but were not previously covered by risk measurements.[6] Additionally, the procedure was seen as enhancing the banks' relationships with other industries by improving clients' understanding of the bank's situation and by providing clients with a model of a successful procedure that includes operational risk – a procedure that they may consider imitating in their own risk management.

The critique of the notion of operational risk began with the opinion that Basel II's definition was vague and abstract, thus making its proper measurement deeply problematic. The second criticism was more psychological, placing in doubt employees' willingness to expose their failings.[7]

All in all, Wahlström (2006) concluded that the interviewed managers were strongly in favor of the innovation, and he attempted to explain this somewhat surprising (in the face of criticism) enthusiasm:

> The Basel Committee's communication in the accord and its supporting documents is highly persuasive. The claims for the new accord are put forward in a technical way without discussion of potential advantages and disadvantages, and thus it lulls the reader into a false sense of security, believing that the new accord is appropriate, valuable and represents knowledge that can prevent future financial crises. (…) In addition, the accord's approach to measuring risk by rigorous statistical models such as VaR is deeply rooted in the society and is manifested in a conviction that it is possible and appropriate to measure risk.
>
> *(Wahlström, 2006, p. 512)*

Wahlström is symmetric in his approach to the field studies, in that he does not issue a priori judgments. But in communicating the results, he is clearly referring to the critical and sociological school of accounting studies.

In addition to collecting the interviewees' opinions about Basel II, Wahlström also asked them what they perceived as being the greatest risks in their work (Wahlström, 2009a). By his own admission, the answers puzzled him. He expected them to talk about "risk measurement, as described in leading [read 'mainstream', BC] scientific journals and in textbooks (...) Instead, the interviewees talked much more about risks that they could not measure" (Wahlström, 2009a, p. 291). Indeed, senior bank managers agreed that the greatest risk areas are those that defy quantified measurement, and pointed out that their most challenging task is to solve unanticipated problems. This second statement corresponds well to other studies of risk, in that it highlights the importance of "well-practiced improvisation" (Czarniawska, 2009). Although Wahlström's study was conducted in 2001, the article was written during the financial crisis of 2007–2010, and he therefore concluded that risk measurement could create a false sense of safety, whereas a financial crisis can drastically change perceptions of what is the greatest threat. In this he agreed with Broadbent et al. (2008), who suggested that risk measurement could silence other risk assessments.

After the Basel II Accord was accepted, Wahlström returned to the four banks and conducted a new series of interviews. As before, opinions were divided into positive and negative, and as before, there was general support for Basel II. The positive opinions stressed the concordance of suggestions in the accord and actual banking practices (which may partly explain the tendency among Swedish organizations to implement the EU's and other international regulations well in advance; see Jacobsson, 1993). The interviewees were also pleased by the fact that the accord permitted the banks to use their own measurement models, whereas the requirement for a measurement (not an assessment) of risks imposed a desirable uniformity on the banks. The criticisms revealed large gaps among the groups, however: managers with operational functions (usually older), and staff specialists in risk management (usually younger, with higher levels of education). The staff people, not surprisingly, thought all was well with operational risk measurement, whereas the operational people took a relatively critical view of the younger group, claiming a fissure in "our risk organization, with its PhDs and statisticians on the one side, and the managers who run the bank on the other". As one operational manager said, sarcastically, risk management "forms its own tradition in the theoretical world and at the universities. And soon there will be just three people in each bank who really understand the rules and can explain them" (Wahlström, 2009b, p. 61). Managers involved in running the operations noted that implementation of Basel II was costly (indeed, there are many IT companies that started to specialize in appropriate systems and software), but, more importantly, given the abstractness of Basel II, its relationship to reality is doubtful. Additionally, they saw Basel II as supporting a tendency toward centralization, which the more decentralized banks saw as a threat. As always, when ideas are translated into practices, they involve people and objects, identities, and computers.

The critics were well aware of the need for local translations. They pointed out that the accord itself was vague, but was considerably clarified when the Swedish Financial Supervisory Authority introduced its interpretation, based on a dialogue with the banks. As one CFO said, however,

> We are afraid that the Swedish Supervisory Authority will interpret the regulation more strictly than the supervisory authorities in other countries. So we are afraid that there may be competitive disadvantages for Swedish banks with non-Swedish banks, including those with branches here in Sweden.
>
> *(Wahlström, 2009b, p. 63)*

So now I inspect another local translation – this time in Poland.

Operational Risk: A Polish Translation

For historical background, it is not necessary to return to the time of Gustaf Vasa or even to the time of Sigismund Vasa, a joint king of Poland and Sweden. The relevant history of Polish accounting starts in 1989, but until 1995, the transformed economy faced so many tasks and challenges that accounting served only as a basis for tax calculations and national statistics. The Bill of 1995 changed this situation, by emphasizing the role of financial accounting and requiring the creation of jobs responsible for external reporting, while separating tax law and law regulating financial statements. The modernization of accounting principles in 2002 further widened the gap, as did the introduction of the International Accounting Standards of 2005. Coping with these often-contradictory demands resulted in almost complete neglect of management accounting. It was not until the 2007 tax reform that the idea of an integrated accountancy model came to the fore, together with the promise of new IT systems and software, grouped under the name of Business Intelligence (Kucharski & Kucharska, 2010).

The novelty of management accounting and the necessity of linguistic translations of such international standards and accords as Basel II may explain the massive number of textbook chapters and popular articles, all but absent in Sweden, explaining the relationships between risk management and accounting. Indeed, the textbook edited by Edward Nowak (2010) was entitled "Accounting and company risk management".[6] The starting definition of risk is the same as in Göran Andersson's work (1983/1997), but in contrast, all 302 pages of Nowak's edited volume are dedicated to the topic. Operational risk is separated from financial risk, and a great many aspects of risk management are explained and illustrated by fictive cases. No research results are quoted. References are dominated by those in Polish, with UK and US positions in second and third place, with UK references outnumbering US references in most chapters.

An all-encompassing textbook, "Risk management", edited by Krzysztof Jajuga (2009), begins with a theoretical introduction to the concept of risk; moves toward risk measurements; and then discusses separately market risk, credit risk, and, in the part dedicated to risk management in banks, operational risk. The chapter dedicated to operational risk begins with the Basel Committee definition quoted previously and includes a list of new phenomena in banking that caused the committee's concern. It also contains a reference to an article in *Gazeta Bankowa* (a practitioners' newspaper), quoting in turn a study undertaken by the Risk Management Association (most likely in the USA) that revealed the percentage of the four components of operational risk: 64% procedures, 25% people, 2% systems, and 7% external events (Gospodarowicz, 2009, p. 270). The chapter proceeds by listing various typologies of operational risk (including the Basel II typology; see Endnote 2), and states that its measurement is extremely difficult. Another statement, which was meant seriously, I assume, maintains that the measurement of operational risk is 80% art and 20% science, given that "the losses that determine the level of operational risk are under a strong influence of human behaviors, which are difficult to foresee and often unrepeatable" (Gospodarowicz, 2009, p. 273). Measurement methods can be qualitative (scenario analysis, Delphi method) or quantitative, the latter dividable into top-down and bottom-up (English in original). Another division differentiates between internal and external methods, and yet another between basic and advanced, the latter to be used only after permission of the supervisory authority has been granted. The chapter continues by presenting four methods of growing complexity (the most advanced is Loss Distribution Approach), and concludes that banks will certainly take several criteria into account when determining the method to be used. The last paragraph mentions a growing supply of IT systems specializing in the measurement of operational risk, as exemplified by Canadian Algorithmics (their product is called AlgoSuite) and Viennese BOC Information Technologies Consulting (system called ADONIS). Here, references contain even German positions.

"Management accounting: Strategic and operational approach", edited by Irena Sobańska (2010), extends the topic in another direction, toward management accounting in general. The chapter on risk deals with many types of risk and concentrates primarily on mathematical algorithms, permitting the calculation of probabilities in decision-making under uncertainty and imperfect information. The chapter contains many mathematical examples (using, e.g., Bayesian analysis) and ends with a student assignment requiring calculation.

The second edition of "Operational Risk in Management Sciences"[8] (edited by Staniec & Zawiła-Niedźwiecki, 2015) connects operational risk to the new managerial fashion, Business Continuity Management. Again, their work is a textbook, even if one chapter contains a case study of a project that, instead of conducting risk analysis, conducted SWOT analysis, which turned out to be unsatisfactory.

Still looking for research results, I consulted the three most-quoted articles from *Bank i Kredyt*, a peer-reviewed journal published by the National Bank of Poland. The first (Lewandowski, 2001) was published the year the Basel Committee began presenting its suggestions. It quotes a 1997 survey undertaken by the British Banking Association and Coopers & Lybrand, according to which more than 69% of surveyed persons (bankers?) stated that operational risk is as important or even more important than market and credit risks. The author suggested that the supervising authority should open a dialogue with the banks in order to achieve a local interpretation of the coming accord, and listed three of the four methods mentioned earlier (Loss Distribution Approach was not included).

The same author wrote another article in 2004, when the Basel Committee was ending its consultations. It begins with a definition of operational risk, and contains a presentation of ten principles of "Developing an Appropriate Risk Management Environment" contained in *Sound Practices for the Management and Supervision of Operational Risk* (Basel Committee on Banking Supervision, 2003). The article ends with an expression of the hope that these principles will guide Polish banks in the years ahead (Lewandowski, 2004). "Sound practices" have been rendered in Polish as "Best Practices".

After the 2007 tax reform and the Banking Supervision Committee (since then incorporated into Financial Supervision Committee) presented its interpretation of Basel II (I was unable to establish if it happened in a dialogue with the banks, as it had in Sweden), Bancarewicz (2007) wrote an article that she began by quoting an assessment of risk (25%–30% operational risk, 65%–70% credit risk, and 10% market risk). The original article by Lenczewski, Martin, and Niedziółka (2005) refers only to "research results", however, without specifying who conducted this research or where. Bancarewicz (2007) quoted the same percentages of causes as Gospodarowicz (2009) did in his chapter, but increased their visibility by presenting them graphically. The main part of the article, to quote its English abstract, "shows relevant difficulties and challenges that a bank may come across while collecting loss data and modeling operational risk" (Bancarewicz, 2007, p. 96). The analysis is purely speculative; in two places unspecified "other European banks" are mentioned.

Lenczewski, Martin, and Niedziółka's (2005) article presents some research results, but primarily speculations and assessment, as their study was done immediately after Basel II and before the interpretation by Banking Supervision Committee. They predicted some of the same problems as Wahlström did, albeit some in the opposite direction. Different local translations may cause problems for international banks in Poland, not the other way around (although it is not spelled out that Polish interpretations are likely more tolerant).

The classification of events included in operational risk may be a problem: the same events can be classified as market and operational risk, they can be wrongly monitored, and their consequences may be difficult to ascribe to an appropriate category. And, as in Sweden, many speculations concern the impact of operational risk on the required level of regulatory capital; but, unlike in Sweden, the expectation was that the measuring of operational risk would raise rather than lower this level.

I have finally located in "Risk in accounting" – an ambitious co-authored work edited by Anna Karmańska (2008) – a small study that can be compared to Wahlström's. The entire book has nine authors, runs for 535 pages, and can probably be characterized as a handbook. It has no assignments and cases like other textbooks typically do. The 17 chapters are primarily encyclopedic, although each begins with a motto borrowed from a philosopher, a novelist, or even Yogi Berra, and some contain hypothetical examples. There are 234 pages of lists, organized with the help of Arabic numbers, Roman numbers, capitals, low caps, bullets, and dashes; 141 pages contain tables, many with lists. Only 24 pages contain equations, and as many have graphs or figures.

The survey of interest to me was presented on the last four pages of the text, with questions addressed to four top-level managers, who were well acquainted with both financial accounting and management accounting procedures. They were shown a risk report form, constructed according to suggestions from the authors of the volume, in which risk was separated into several categories, relating primarily to market and credit risk. The first question to these four managers was whether or not such a report was needed for financial analysis. The general answer was "yes", with the specification that if the report were to be correct, it had to remain internal information, and it would be of more use to large- and middle-sized companies than to small companies. The second question concerned the suggested structure of the report, which achieved disparate responses. Two of the managers liked it, one was uncertain, and the fourth thought that open questions invited politically correct answers, although the same person admitted that closed questions could be difficult to formulate. The question concerning possible arenas of use raised some anxiety about the report becoming obligatory, but three persons saw it as a useful source of managerial information. Asked if some parts of the report should be better developed, the respondents protested, which can probably be explained by their answer to the next question, in which they estimated the preparation as time- and effort-consuming, at least the first time around. In their opinion, such a report should be prepared by their finance department. When asked if they had competent personnel who could accomplish the task, only the manager from a large company answered positively, yet added immediately that someone that competent should be occupied with more creative tasks. The other three managers answered negatively, as they considered their companies too small to include such personnel, the lack of which would require a preparation time of between two months and two years. In addition, three of the mangers were convinced that if the report had an external function, it would be no doubt manipulated.

The editor ended the volume by emphasizing the complexity of risk reporting and suggesting that a great many empirical studies were needed in the future. The fact that the sample used for the survey has been so limited is easier to understand in the light of the fact that Cap Gemini failed to conduct "Basel II Survey" among Polish banks in 2004. The response rate was so low that it was impossible to draw any conclusions from their study. The reporter who wrote the article reporting this failure asked several top managers for reasons (Gamdzyk, 2004). Those from other industries suggested that banks did not have and still do not collect appropriate data, and that bank managers were afraid of spending money on uncertain investments. Indeed, the bank representatives suspected IT companies of trying to make quick money on new systems and software, and indicated that the Polish banks are still relatively poor compared to other European equivalents. Thus, they were unwilling to spend money on fulfilling requirements that were still far from being well specified in 2004.

They were better specified in the new recommendation of the Polish Financial Supervision Authority from 2013, which includes the following paragraph:

> Operational risk, due to its complex nature, can have a significant impact on the business and situation of banks, especially as its source, besides the environment and external events, is the banking organization itself. According to available studies, operational risk is the second most important type of risk in banks after credit risk. Moreover, analyses of spectacular losses in the financial system in the world indicate that, despite their exposure to credit or market risk, their actual source was operational risk.

The recommendation does not contain any references to those studies, and nothing in its 59 pages suggests that the Polish banks were consulted.

Translations Compared

The picture of the introduction of Basel II in Sweden confirms many similar observations made on various previous occasions. In describing how Sweden followed EU rules even before joining the Community,

> Swedish administration had often imported management ideas. Lübeck ran the City of Stockholm as an enterprise. German Conrad von Pyhy saw to it that Gustaf Vasa had the most modern accounting system of the time at his disposal, so that taxes could be properly collected. We allowed the most dedicated capitalists we knew, the Dutch, to build and start Gothenburg. The Swedish state and municipal administration often drew inspiration from the outside. These ideas were then modified in encounter with local traditions.
>
> *(Jacobsson, 1993, p. 113; my translation, BC)*

Indeed, studies from various times and of various areas show a similar picture: the Swedish public administration is always *au courant* with the newest fashions in what was previously called administration, and is now called management. As a "negotiated economy" (Hernes, 1978), it was and is in constant dialogue with the private sector. For many years, it was a global "fashion leader", proudly presenting "the Swedish model" of a welfare state to visitors; later, it admitted its demise (Czarniawska, 1996) and started sending envoys to New Zealand, the Mecca of New Public Management. Swedish city management is alert to all city fashions: fast trams, smart cities, and the Ferris wheel. But, as Jacobsson pointed out, new ideas are transformed in encounters with local customs, in a pragmatic way – not least because the voices of practitioners are seriously considered. It is therefore justifiable to apply this frame of reference to the reaction of the Swedish banks to Basel II. They were eager to implement it, being satisfied with the fact that the required procedures corresponded to their own. The Swedish Financial Supervision Authority interpreted the abstract requirements in a dialogue with the banks. The main split is between the older and the younger generations, corresponding to the split between operational and staff duties shown in Wahlström's (2009b) research. The older, operational managers are skeptical, especially about the cost of new IT systems and the correspondence between abstract models and measurements derived from them; the younger, staff people are enthusiastic.

No such gap can be found in Poland, for two reasons. Because of the dramatic change of the political regime and the consequent changes in running the economy, there are no "old, experienced bankers". Furthermore, one may suspect a common positive perception of abstract models and numeric calculations across generations, due to an anti-pragmatic attitude, which I called "merciless idealism" in my city study (Czarniawska, 2002, p. 119). One of its elements is "trust in numbers" (Porter [1995]; but also "trust in models"; Power [2007, p. 120]), albeit with a local twist. Numbers were commonly manipulated during the socialist regime, but faith in "correct numbers" remains – the correct numbers guaranteed by a non-ideological science.

Rottenburg (1994) described a similar attitude in managers from East Germany at the time of unification – an attitude that he called "socialist monism": "that definitions of reality are either ideological constructs and, therefore, false, or they correspond to reality and are, therefore, valid" (p. 89). The pragmatist conviction that words and numbers can be compared only with other words and other numbers (Rorty, 1980) did not gain any ground; the correspondence theory of truth rules unquestioned. This attitude is not limited to Poland, of course; indeed, Power (2007) spoke of "calculative idealists" (p. 120). In Poland, their dominance seems to be absolute.

Another observation concerns the fact that although both Sweden and Poland largely follow the UK example in accounting for risk management, the Polish imitation stops at dialogue with practitioners, common in the UK (see, e.g., NAO, 2004). There are no traces of any official dialogue between law enforcers and practitioners in Poland, but neither are there studies of practice, apart from the limited survey and the case of failed survey mentioned above. There are, of course, serious differences between the case studies commissioned by the UK National Audit Office (NAO) and those conducted by Wahlström, but these are expected differences – differences between official investigations and scholarly research. Furthermore, even in Sweden, the media are often necessary mediators among researchers, politicians, and officials. But the contacts and mediations do happen, and researchers are often asked to join or lead official investigations.

Was it always like that? Mostly. Between 1972 and 1980, I served as a methodological consultant and researcher in a research program "Managing enterprises – participants in the consumer goods market" (Beksiak, 1978), in which an extensive field study of actual management practices was conducted, probably for the first time, and under a strong methodological influence of our Swedish colleagues. Field studies in Poland have not vanished, for Polish and foreign researchers are conducting organizational ethnographies (see, e.g., Kostera, 2011). But such studies, being unquantifiable, are seen as being of no use in an official context. Textbooks and journal articles offer a linguistic translation and an explication of official documents, now and then quoting survey results from other countries (for a recent example, see Ramotowski, 2017). "Calculative pragmatists" (Power, 2007, p. 121) seems to be an empty category, or at least a not-yet-located group.[9]

The label is a good fit with the older operation managers interviewed by Wahlström. Indeed, Sweden has a long pragmatist tradition revealed in multiple field studies and studies of practices, and in this aspect, does not have to imitate UK. A critical and sociological take on accounting, however, is clearly a UK influence. In contrast, I am not sure if Polish accounting scholars are at all aware that accounting can be a social science. (Neither *Accounting, Organizations and Society* nor *Critical Perspectives on Accounting* were to be found in Warsaw University Library.) As I see it, "socialist monism" has been replaced in the official discourse by "capitalist monism"; the "top-to-bottom" approach in centrally steered initiatives remains, as does the role of the researchers as translators of top leaders' intentions to the wider public.

However, this analysis must not be read as a eulogy for the Swedish way of translating global trends and a critique of the Polish ways of doing so. Some aspects of the Swedish translation are no doubt positive – the dialogue of authorities with practitioners and the problematizing attitude of researchers. Some aspects of the Polish translation are easy to understand in the light of the past and present economic situation. Yet both countries set to translate global directives without, it seems, ever asking a question whether they make sense in their locality or not.

Operational Risk Is Not Alone

The case of varied translations of operational risk into the practices of different countries ought not to be seen as special or exceptional. On the contrary, the idea was to illustrate the travel of various rules and regulations across the globe, always characterized by two elements. The first is the seeming belief of the regulators that, if all goes well, the regulation will be introduced in the same way everywhere. This old belief was at the base of the popular version of diffusion theory: Ideas (innovations, regulations) should diffuse smoothly and without change. Tensions, frictions, and changes disturb the proper process of diffusion and must be combatted with all possible strength. The second is the actual course of the spreading, which always encounters various obstacles and is an object of more or less thorough translations. What these texts suggest, in line with the translation theory presented at the outset, is the necessity of change of attitude. Instead of assuming that changes and deviations are problems to be avoided (an attitude that famous economist Albert O. Hirschman called "fracasomania" [1991]), it is possible to think that frictions and tensions animate discussions and lead to a serious consideration of rules and regulations. The practical results would be that, in each country, the actors involved (ministries, banks, unions, companies) will together analyze a new global or international regulation, and decide what variant would best fit their problems and their needs.

Notes

1 An earlier version of this chapter has been published in *Contemporary Economics*, 2012 (2): 26–39. Since then, a Basel III Accord has been reached, adding liquidity risk to previous types of risk. It is to be introduced (voluntarily) between 2013 and 2019. The general attitude toward risk measurements hasn't changed, though.
2 I would like to express sincere thanks to Maciej Ramus and Gunnar Wahlström for their helpful comments.
3 A brief but instructive introduction to Serres' work can be found in Steven D. Brown (2002).
4 It differs from the interpretation of Keith Robson, to whom translation is "the process through which often pre-existing accounting techniques, and their associated roles, are articulated discoursively" (Robson, 1991, p. 550).
5 The categories of operational risk listed by Basel II:
Internal Fraud – misappropriation of assets, tax evasion, intentional mismarking of positions, bribery.
External Fraud – theft of information, hacking damage, third-party theft, and forgery.
Employment Practices and Workplace Safety – discrimination, workers' compensation, employee health and safety.
Clients, Products, and Business Practice – market manipulation, antitrust, improper trade, product defects, fiduciary breaches, account churning
Damage to Physical Assets – natural disasters, terrorism, vandalism.
Business Disruption and Systems Failures – utility disruptions, software failures, hardware failures
Execution, Delivery, and Process Management – data entry errors, accounting errors, failed mandatory reporting, negligent loss of client assets.

6 The managers' optimism concerning the role of operational risk measurement as protection against financial crisis was proven ungrounded by the latest events. I would predict that asked the same question today, the managers would still divide into two groups. Those who were positive would claim that more and better measurement of operational risk is needed and those who were negative would claim that their fears were founded.

7 By now, the employees are probably well trained in the popular use of a management technology called SWOT, which is supposed to disclose the strengths and weaknesses of an organization. The standard weakness thus revealed is a lack of resources, thereby turning a self-evaluation into a tactical move toward top management.

8 The title of the previous edition was "Managing Operational Risk" (*Zarządzanie ryzykiem operacyjnym*, 2008); the previous title likely suggested reports from practice.

9 Calculative pragmatists "…are more sceptical about the role of numbers in managing operational risk (...) They typically regard them as attention-directive devices with no intrinsic claims to represent reality (...) They are more pluralistic about operational risk management, partly because they think capital should not be the sole foundation of risk management practice" (Power, 2007, p. 121).

References

Andersson, Göran (1983/1997). *Kalkyler som beslutsunderlag* [Calculations as the basis for decisions]. Lund: Studentlitteratur.

Andersson, Martin (1995). *Kontroll av bankernas betalningssystem* [Controlling banks' payment systems]. Stockholm: Nerenius & Santérus Förlag.

Bancarewicz, Grażyna (2007). AMA—selected issues in the areas of operational risk data and operational risk modeling. *Bank i Kredyt*, August–September, 96–105.

Beksiak, Janusz (Ed.) (1978). *Zarządzanie przedsiębiorstwami – uczestnikami rynku dóbr konsumpcyjnych* [Corporate governance – market participants, consumer goods]. Warszawa: PWN.

Broadbent, Jane, Gill, Jas, & Laughlin, Richard (2008). Identifying and controlling risk: The problem of uncertainty in the private finance initiative in the UK's national health service. *Critical Perspectives on Accounting*, 19(1), 40–78.

Brown, Steven D. (2002). Michel Serres. Science, translation and the logic of parasite. *Theory, Culture & Society*, 19(3), 1–27.

Callon, Michael (1980). Struggles to define what is problematic and what is not: The socio-logic of translation. In Karin Knorr Cetina, Roger Krohn, & Richard Whitley (Eds.). *The social process of scientific investigation: Sociology of the sciences*, Vol. IV (pp. 191–217). Dordrecht: D. Reidel.

Czarniawska, Barbara (1996). Changing times and accounts: Tales from an organization field. In Roland Munro, & Jan Mouritsen (Eds.). *Accountability. Power, ethos and the technologies of managing* (pp. 308–328). London: Thomson Business Press.

Czarniawska, Barbara (2002). *A tale of three cities, or glocalization of city management*. Oxford: Oxford University Press.

Czarniawska, Barbara (2009). Conclusions: Plans or well- practiced improvisations? In Barbara Czarniawska (Ed.). *Organizing in the face of risk and threat* (pp. 166–196). Cheltenham: Edward Elgar.

Czarniawska, Barbara, & Sevón, Guje (1996). Introduction. In Barbara Czarniawska, & Guje Sevón (Eds.). *Translating organizational change* (pp. 1–12). Berlin: de Gruyter.

Gamdzyk, Przemysław (2004). Daleko do Bazylei [Far from Basel]. *ComputerWorld*, 30 August. Retrieved from www.computerworld.pl/artykuly/43665/ Daleko.do.Bazylei.html (2011–10–16).

Gospodarowicz, Andrzej (2009). Ryzyko operacyjne w banku [Operational risk in banks]. In Krzysztof Jajuga (Ed.). *Zarządzanie ryzykiem* [Risk management] (pp. 269–284). Warszawa: PWN.

Hamilton, Gustav (1985/1996). *Risk management 2000*. Lund: Studentlitteratur.

Hernes, Gudmund (1978). *Forhandlingsøkonomi og blandingsadministrasjon* [Negotiated economy and mixed administration]. Bergen: Universitetetsforlag.

Hirschman, Albert O. (1991). *The rhetoric of reaction. Perversity, futility, jeopardy*. Cambridge, MA: Belknap Harvard.

Jacobsson, Bengt (1993). Europeisering av förvaltningen [Europeanization of public administration] *Statsvetenskaplig Tidskrift*, 96(2), 113–137.

Joerges, Bernward, & Czarniawska, Barbara (1998). The question of technology, or how organizations inscribe the world. *Organization Studies*, 19(3), 363–385.

Karmańska, Anna (Ed.) (2008) *Ryzyko w rachunkowości* [The risk in accounting]. Warszawa: Difin.

Komisja Nadzoru Finansowego (Financial Supervision Authority) (2013). *Rekomendacja M dotycząca zarządzania ryzykiem operacyjnym w bankach*. Warszawa: KNF.

Kostera, Monika (Ed.) (2011). *Etnografia organizacji: Badania polskich firm i instytucji* [Ethnography of organization: Research of Polish companies and institutions]. Sopot: GWP.

Kucharski, Adam, & Kucharska, Natalia (2010). Czy wdrożenie zintegrowanego modelu rachunkowości może ograniczyć ryzyko podatkowe? [Is the implementation of integrated accounting model can reduce the tax risk?] 1 September. Retrieved from www.parkiet.com/artykul/964087.html (2011–10–16).

Latour, Bruno (1986). The powers of association. In John Law (Ed.). *Power, action and belief* (pp. 261–277). London: Routledge and Kegan Paul.

Latour, Bruno (1993). *We have never been modern*. Cambridge, MA: Harvard University Press.

Lenczewski, Martins Carlos, & Niedziółka, Paweł (2005). Kwantyfikacja ryzyka operacyjnego w banku oraz jego wpływ na wymóg kapitałowy [Quantification of operational risk in the bank and its impact on capital requirement]. *Bank i Kredyt*, May, 28–41.

Lewandowski, Dariusz (2001). Ryzyko operacyjne w działalności banków – nowe wyzwania, pilna konieczność zarządzania [Operational risk in banks – new challenges, the urgent need to manage]. *Bank i Kredyt*, May, 29–35.

Lewandowski, Dariusz (2004). Ryzyko operacyjne w bankach – zarządzanie i audyt w świetle wymagań Bazylejskiego Komitetu ds. Nadzoru Bankowego [Operational risk in banks management and audit in light of the requirements of the Basel Committee on Banking Supervision]. *Bank i Kredyt*, April, 48–55.

NAO (2004) Managing risks to improve public services. Case studies. Report by the Comptroller and Auditor General. HC 1078-II Session 2003–2004: 22 October. London: The Stationery Office.

Nowak, Edward (2010). *Rachunkowość w zarządzaniu ryzykiem w przedsiębiorstwie* [Accounting for risk management in the enterprise]. Warsaw: Polskie Wydawnictwo Ekonomiczne S.A.

Power, Michael (2004). *The risk management of everything*. London: Demos.

Power, Michael (2007). *Organized uncertainty. Designing a world of risk management*. Oxford: Oxford University Press.

Ramotowski, Jacek (2017). Bazylea IV utknęła w martwym punkcie [Basel IV got stuck]. *Obserwator Finansowy*, 22 February.

Robertson, Roland (1992). *Globalization. Social theory and global culture*. London: Sage.

Robertson, Roland (1995). Glocalization: Time-space and homogeneity-heterogeneity. In Mike Featherstone, & Scott Lash (Eds.). *Global* modernities (pp. 25–44). London: Sage.

Robson, Keith (1991). On the arenas of accounting change: The process of translation. *Accounting, Organizations and Society*, 16(5/6), 547–570.

Rogers, Everett (1962). *Diffusion of innovation*. New York: Free Press.

Rorty, Richard (1980). *Philosophy as the mirror of nature*. Oxford: Basil Blackwell.

Rottenburg, Richard (1994). From socialist realism to postmodern ambiguity. *Industrial & Environmental Crisis Quarterly*, 8(1), 71–91.

Sahlins, Marshall (2001). "Sentimental pessimism" and ethnographic experience or, why culture is not a disappearing "object". In Lorraine Daston (Ed.). *Biographies of scientific objects* (pp. 178–202). Chicago, IL: University of Chicago Press.

Sandin, Alf (1991). *Statlig redovisning i förändring. Från Gustaf Vasa till nutid* [Governmental accounting in transition. From Gustavus Vasa to the present]. Gothenburg: Gothenburg School of Economics and Commercial Law.

Sobańska, Irena (Ed.) (2010). *Rachunkowość zarządcza. Podejście operacyjne i strategiczne* [Management accounting. Operational and strategic approach]. Warszawa: Wydawnictwo C.H. Beck.

Staniec, Iwona, & Zawiła-Niedźwiecki, Janusz (Eds.) *Ryzyko operacyjne w naukach o zarządzaniu* [Operational risk in management sciences]. Warszawa: Wydawnictwo C.H. Beck.

Tarde, Gabriel (1890/1903). *The laws of imitation*. New York: Henry Holt.

Wahlström, Gunnar (2006). Worrying but accepting new measurements: the case of Swedish bankers and operational risk. *Critical Perspectives on Accounting*, 17, 493–522.

Wahlström, Gunnar (2009a). Risk in practice – senior bank managers at work. *International Journal of Critical Accounting*, 1(3), 287–305.

Wahlström, Gunnar (2009b). Risk management versus operational action: Basel II in a Swedish context. *Management Accounting Research*, 20, 53–68.

PART IV

Types of Crises

11

THE CO-EVOLUTION OF REPUTATION MANAGEMENT, GOVERNANCE CAPACITY, LEGITIMACY AND ACCOUNTABILITY IN CRISIS MANAGEMENT

Tom Christensen, Per Lægreid, and Lise H. Rykkja

Introduction

Dealing with crises is a main responsibility of government authorities. Crises strike at the core of democratic governance and challenge not only capacity but also legitimacy and accountability. They are a test of whether an organization can meet citizens' expectations. Crisis management studies often focus on *governance capacity*, investigating how the government can effectively prepare for, handle and learn from different crises. One way to do this is to study how governments structure their organizations responsible for crisis and how they use their overall capacity and resources (Christensen, Lægreid, & Rykkja, 2016).

Governance capacity hinges on a set of important *accountability* relationships. A crucial question is to whom account is to be rendered and what one is accountable for. When there are many accountability forums, the problem of "many eyes" may arise (Day & Klein, 1987). This question normally concerns the formal accountability of the government to parliament, the accountability of the administrative leadership, the accountability of professional groups and how accountability is handled with respect to laws and rights. In most cases, there are multiple accountability relations (Bovens, 2007).

Our argument is that a well-functioning crisis management system needs both governance capacity and governance legitimacy (Lægreid & Rykkja 2018). While governance capacity relates to more formal accountability relations, *governance legitimacy* can involve what is called horizontal or societal accountability, meaning that the political and administrative leaderships try to justify or win support for their actions from the population and the media without having any formal obligation to do so (Schillemans, 2011). Thus, governance legitimacy is partly based on citizens' trust in government (Easton, 1965). One can distinguish between input legitimacy, judged in terms of responsiveness to citizens, throughput legitimacy, judged in terms of the quality of governance processes, and output legitimacy, judged in terms of effectiveness of policy outcomes (Sharpf, 1999; Schmidt, 2012). In this perspective, governance legitimacy has a dynamic relationship to governance capacity. High governance capacity may enhance governance legitimacy, and a high level of governance legitimacy may help achieve more governance capacity.

Furthermore, governance legitimacy is quite often connected to the emergence of *reputation management*, that is, when public bodies try to influence how external stakeholders or constituencies perceive the government's actions. In contrast to stable, routine situations, crises represent unsettled and transitional situations, which make accountability relations more ambiguous, complex and uncertain (Christensen & Lægreid, 2017). The uncertainty and complexity vis-à-vis stakeholders, problems and solutions that characterize crisis make reputation management more challenging.

Thus, the quality of crisis management depends on both government capacity and government legitimacy and can therefore be coupled to two more distinct lines of enquiry: accountability and reputation management. In this chapter, we will explore how this coupling could be analyzed, with our goal being to provide new insights concerning the quality of governmental institutions' crisis management. We claim that there is a merit in looking for mutually affecting processes and co-evolution between governance capacity, governance legitimacy, accountability and reputation management. Subsequently, we will try to answer the following question:

• What is the relationship between governance capacity, accountability, governance legitimacy and reputation management in crisis management? To what extent do these elements co-evolve?

We begin the chapter by presenting some of the basic concepts, such as crisis and crisis management, governance capacity, governance legitimacy, accountability and reputation management. We then present our theoretical perspectives – an instrumental and an institutional one. Third, we analyze the dynamic relationship between our central concepts before concluding the chapter with a summarizing discussion

Basic concepts: Crises, Crisis Management, Governance Capacity, Governance Legitimacy, Accountability and Reputation Management

A *crisis* may be defined as "a situation in which there is a perceived threat to the core values or life-sustaining functions of a social system that requires urgent remedial action in uncertain circumstances" (Rosenthal, Charles, & 't Hart, 1989: 10). Crises are often a threat to an organization's reputation, and affect how stakeholders interact with the organization (Coombs, 2007). One way to characterize crises is in terms of their *cause(s)*, whether they are intentional or non-intentional (Smith, 2006). Another way is to look at crisis management *phases*. One can distinguish between prevention, preparation, mitigation and aftermath (Boin et al., 2005). A third dimension is to consider the *degree of uncertainty* and the *uniqueness* of a crisis (Gundel, 2005), and a fourth one concerns the *degree of transboundary features* (Ansell, Boin, & Keller, 2010). A fifth dimension is how a crisis is *perceived* by different actors. This includes a subjective element which ties in with legitimacy (Christensen, Lægreid & Rykkja, 2016). Handling a crisis may involve balancing different considerations, for instance a need for increased prevention against a need for a stronger response, or a strategy emphasizing more resilience (Wildavsky, 2003). When a crisis is characterized by uncertainty, ambiguity and unpredictability, decisions are often made in complex, disorganized and dynamic circumstances. Furthermore, transboundary crises transcend the borders of ministerial areas and administrative levels which may create serious coordination problems (Kettl, 2003).

Public organizations have to deal with crises. *Crisis management* can therefore be defined as the processes by which a public organization systematically deals with a crisis. It may include preventive aspects, operative aspects and learning and/or change aspects. This involves processes of identification, assessment, understanding and coping. Crisis management also has a technical and instrumental aspect, as well as a broader institutional-cultural aspect, which embraces how to understand conflicts, power, trust and legitimacy. Both the technical and the institutional-cultural features affect the way the political and administrative leadership faces and handles crises.

Governments have to allocate resources to different purposes and policies, of which handling crises is just one of many. *Governance capacity* in crisis management thus includes formal structural and procedural features and how they work in practice (Christensen, Lægreid, & Rykkja, 2016). Overlapping domains among public organizations are often necessary in crisis management, because they function as back-up systems (Landau, 1969). However, overlap may also lead to conflicts and turf wars, making it difficult to develop "positive" coordination and coherence. "Underlap" and "negative coordination", where the actors avoid interfering in each other's programs and policies, is more common (Scharpf, 1994; Lodge & Wegrich, 2014) and often seen in administrative systems with strong line ministries, departmentalization and silo arrangements. Moving from negative to positive coordination by building integrated and coherent programs, arrangements and services is often a major challenge (Bouckaert, Peters, & Verhoest, 2010).

One can distinguish between four types of governance capacity (Lodge & Wegrich, 2014): coordination, analytical, regulation and delivery. *Coordination capacity* is about bringing together disparate organizations to engage in joint action, which means that capacity or resources "find each other" via positive coordination. Normally, coordination challenges are at the forefront in crisis (Boin & Bynander, 2014). *Analytical capacity* is about analyzing information and giving advice as well as assessing risk and vulnerability. *Regulation capacity* is about control, surveillance, oversight and auditing, which may have preventive effects. *Delivery capacity* is about the handling of the crisis in practice.

Any government is dependent on the participation and trust of citizens for handling crises. *Governance legitimacy* accordingly focuses on the relationship between government authorities and citizens or between government authorities and the media (Christensen, Lægreid, & Rykkja, 2016). It concerns citizens' perceptions of whether the authorities' crisis management is desirable and appropriate – that is, whether they match generally held norms, values and beliefs (Suchman, 1995; Jann, 2016). Governance legitimacy may deal with the degree of cultural support for the action the public leadership takes during a crisis (Selznick, 1957; Meyer & Scott, 1983). However, such perceptions may also reflect institutional myths, "social constructions of reality" and "taken-for-grantedness" (Meyer & Rowan, 1977). Legitimacy affects how people understand government but also how they act toward government authorities in crises. Easton (1965) makes a useful distinction between *diffuse* and *specific* support, which means that people may either generally trust government institutions and their actors or trust specific institutions and actors. If citizens generally trust institutions, they will potentially regard crisis management efforts positively and be willing to participate, giving the system some resources to fall back on (Cyert & March, 1963).

Legitimacy is difficult to define, but related concepts like trust, confidence, satisfaction and reputation have been used as proxies (Christensen, Lægreid & Rykkja, 2016). According to Scharpf (1999), there are three types of government legitimacy: *input legitimacy, throughput legitimacy* and *output legitimacy* (see also Schmidt, 2013). Input legitimacy focuses on citizens' assessment and acceptance of government. In crises, this relates to support, participation, representativeness and responsiveness. Throughput legitimacy focuses on processes within the administrative apparatus and peoples' perceptions of these. It concerns organization, resources and competence, but also fairness, impartiality and openness. Output legitimacy deals with perceptions of policies, means and measures related to crisis management.

One central aspect of legitimacy is making actors in the government accountable. Bovens (2007: 447) defines *accountability* as "the relationship between an actor and a forum, in which the actor has an obligation to explain and justify his or her conduct, the forum can pose questions and pass judgment, and the actor may face consequences". Therefore, the basic factors in accountability relations are information, debate and consequences. In contrast to responsibility, which is more about entrusting someone with a task, accountability is generally retrospective, that is, an organization or person is held to account or has to answer for something that has already happened. In a crisis, accountability relations are often ambiguous (Christensen, Lægreid & Rykkja, 2016). Public organizations face the *problem of many eyes* or who the subordinate actors are supposed to *account to* and which criteria should be used to judge them. This is quite difficult in a complex and hybrid public apparatus. Public organizations also face the problem of *many hands*, meaning whether it is individuals or organizations, political or administrative executives, street-level bureaucrats or managers who should account to superior forums for their actions (Thompson, 1980). Consequently, actors may be held to account by a number of different forums, and there are different ways of categorizing who is accountable to whom (Romzek & Dubnick, 1987; Bovens, 2007; Willems & Van Dooren, 2011).

There are also several different types of accountability. *Political accountability* is a key feature in the chain of delegation implied by the "the primacy of politics" (Pollitt & Hupe, 2011). The cabinet is accountable to the parliament and the civil service is accountable to the political executive. Here, the accountability relationship is mainly seen as a vertical one in which the hierarchy gives the forum formal power over the actor.

Administrative accountability is based on a person's position in a political-administrative hierarchy where an administrative superior may call a subordinate to account for his or her performance of delegated duties. Traditional administrative accountability is chiefly concerned with compliance with process features like rules and procedures. *Managerial accountability* is connected to performance management, output and outcomes, and makes those with delegated authority answerable for carrying out tasks according to agreed performance criteria (Day & Klein, 1987; Askim, Christensen, & Lægreid, 2015).

Professional accountability focuses on the importance of professional peers or peer review. Professions in public organizations are constrained by codes of conduct – a system marked by deference to expertise (Mulgan, 2000) and a reliance on the technical knowledge of experts (Romzek & Dubnick, 1987). *Judicial accountability* deals with the rule of law and actors' formal rights.

Bovens, Schillemans & Hart (2008) add another dimension by distinguishing between mandatory *vertical accountability* of the types explained earlier, and voluntary *horizontal accountability or societal/social accountability*. In the second instance, the actor may feel pressure from the environment to justify or defend his or her actions, particularly when governance legitimacy and reputation management are at stake.

The accountability debate has traditionally revolved around principal-agent issues and "agency drift", but it has to a lesser degree addressed the problem of "forum drift" (Schillemans & Busuioc, 2014). In crisis or unsettled situations, some ambiguity or uncertainty often surrounds who the agents and the principals are. Therefore, there is a need to go beyond the principal-agent model. Our suggestion would be to supplement it with a combined structural-instrumental and cultural-institutional approach (Olsen, 2015; Christensen & Lægreid, 2017).

Reputation and *reputation management* are treated in studies of branding, mission statements, image-building and self-presentation (Carpenter, 2010; Wæraas, Byrkjeflot, & Angell, 2011;

Carpenter & Krause, 2012; Maor, 2010). These use theory from anthropology (Goffman, 1959), political science (Edelman, 1964) and organization theory (Meyer & Rowan, 1977; Brunsson, 1989; Czarniawska & Sevon, 1996).

Reputation is often both complex and hybrid. How well an organization meets stakeholder expectations based on its past behavior (Wartick, 1992) derives a reputation. *Organizational reputation* may be defined as "a set of beliefs about an organization's capacities, intentions, history, and mission that are embedded in a network of multiple audiences" (Carpenter, 2010: 33). This means that in their reputation management, political and administrative executives systematically use symbols that appeal to diverse actors in their environment in order to build a reputation (Wæraas & Maor, 2015: 4). Reputation management focuses on the core mission and tasks of an organization, which reflect its historical path, on its main resources and competences and on its outputs and outcomes. It both facilitates and guides members of the organization but also helps external constituencies to understand its activities (Morphew & Harley, 2006: 457). Whether leaders manage the reputation of their organization successfully depends not only on the agency's ability to present itself, but also on the perceptions of the "networks of multiple audiences", including the balance between the perceptions of internal and external actors. Their "presentation of self in everyday life" (Goffman, 1959) is particularly challenging if the gap is large between the mainly symbolic "front-stage" and "back-stage" where the "real" action takes place.

One of the main goals of reputation management is to strike a balance between being "excessively vague or unrealistically aspirational or both" (Morphew & Harley, 2006: 457). An organization's reputation can be managed in different ways. One way is to develop a rather narrow, integrated and specific profile (van Riel & Fombrun, 2007). The advantage is that both the members of the organization and the external stakeholders know what the organization stands for, which may enlist support. The disadvantage is that this does not sufficiently communicate the complexity and different interests of the organization (Wæraas & Solbakk, 2009: 459). This may create conflicts if members of an organization are required to actively represent it. The other option is to have a rather broad identity profile, encompassing a range of internal and external stakeholders. The advantage of using such broad symbols is that they have a "bridging" function (Røvik, 2002) and can communicate different and flexible messages to different audiences in what has been labeled "polyphony" (Christensen & Lægreid, 2005). The disadvantage of this is that trying to please everybody may result in a profile that is overly ambiguous and a general set of symbols that do not say anything to anyone.

Reputation management is also linked to accountability (Busuioc & Lodge, 2016). Accountability is to a great extent about managing and cultivating an organization's reputation vis-à-vis different stakeholders and audiences and addressing issues of "path-dependency" and appropriateness, fairness and reliability (Jann, 2017). Accountability is related to justifying the organization's existence and to preserving its identity, building alliances and enhancing political support and survival (Busuioc & Lodge, 2016). In this sense, reputation comes close to legitimacy (Suchman, 1995). One difference, though, is that reputation can be managed, and hence manipulated, while legitimacy cannot. Thus, legitimacy is a broader concept than reputation (Jann, 2017).

Analytical Framework: Combining a Structural/Instrumental and an Institutional Perspective

In order to understand the relationship and potential co-evolution between governance capacity, governance legitimacy, accountability and reputation management during crises, we advocate applying a combined structural/instrumental and an institutional approach

(Christensen et al., 2016). This implies that there is a need to study *organizational structures* for governance capacity but also *cultural* and *symbolic features* linked to governance legitimacy, accountability and reputation.

An instrumental organizational perspective focuses on the formal structures of public organizations (Christensen et al., 2007). Formal organization is seen as an instrument for achieving goals, and it channels and influences the models of thought and the decision-making behavior of civil servants (Simon, 1957; Egeberg, 2012). It is based on a "logic of consequence", where "bounded" rational actors can predict the consequences of their choices and find the appropriate means (Simon, 1957; March & Olsen, 1989). It is assumed that leaders will score high on rational calculation and political control (Dahl & Lindblom, 1953), meaning that they have relatively clear intentions and goals, choose structures that correspond with these goals, have insight into the potential effects and have the power to control decision-making processes and implement their decisions. The assumption is that there is a tight coupling between formal policy, daily practice and intended outcome. We use the perspective to focus on the relationship between governance capacity on the one hand, and governance legitimacy and reputation management on the other. This means that formal organization and capacities may both influence and be influenced by legitimacy and reputation, in a co-evolutionary way.

A cultural perspective emphasizes informal norms, values and practices that have developed over time through a process of institutionalization. Central organizational features result from mutual adaptation to internal pressure, reflecting what internal actors have brought into the organization and how they interact with it, and to external pressure. Together, these create the organization's unique cultural identity (Selznick, 1957). A crucial argument concerns *path-dependency*, meaning that contexts, norms and values surrounding the establishment of a public organization – its "roots", in other words – will strongly influence the "route" or path it takes later (Krasner, 1988). Also related to core organization, competence, goals and services is the "logic of appropriateness" (March, 1994). The assumption is that every institution over time develops such a logic. When actors face a crisis, they try to match the situation with their own institutional identity and with various decision-making rules. We use the perspective primarily to discuss the relationship and potential co-evolution between accountability on the one hand, and legitimacy and reputation on the other.

A version of this perspective assumes that major crises can produce a "punctuated equilibrium" implying a shock effect that can alter institutionalized beliefs and routines and open the way for more radical change (Baumgartner & Jones, 1993). Streeck and Thelen (2005) stress the more general argument that institutional changes may differ depending on whether they are incremental or abrupt, and on whether the result is continuity or discontinuity. In some crisis situations, there might also be "punctuated backsliding" due to a combination of external and internal forces (Kettl, 2007).

A symbolic or myth perspective addresses the institutional environment, consisting of myths and symbols, and standards or scripts that are taken for granted about how to develop and organize an institution (Meyer & Rowan, 1977). According to DiMaggio and Powell (1983), nonmaterial myths and symbols spread fast between nations and organizations, either making organizations similar or isomorphic or else being translated and edited as they travel around (Røvik, 2002; Wedlin & Sahlin, 2017). One of the reasons for adapting to or importing such myths and symbols about an organization's reputation is that they may enhance the legitimacy of a public organization. Balancing talk and action gives the leadership more flexibility and makes it look modern and rational (Brunsson, 1989). A loose coupling between "front stage" talk, representing "window-dressing" and image building, and "backstage" action makes this possible and desirable. Public leaders cannot deliver on all talk and promises because of lack of motivation, resources or knowledge (Goffman, 1959). In the end, there may be a loose coupling between formal policy and daily practice, but also between daily practice and intended outcome (Bromley & Powell, 2012). Accordingly, we use the perspective primarily to look at the relationship between legitimacy and reputation, on the one hand, and capacity and accountability, on the other.

The Relationship between Governance Capacity and Governance Legitimacy

The links between governance capacity and governance legitimacy in crisis situations have received little attention (Christensen, Lægreid, & Rykkja, 2016). However, the relationship between governance capacity and governance legitimacy might be a two-way street. First, seen from an instrumental perspective, strong governance capacity is a major precondition for scoring high on governance legitimacy, and hence developments in governance capacity may affect legitimacy. If a government is able to prevent a crisis, or handle it well, citizens will probably trust and support it. However, a government may have problems with showing the efficacy of capacity when the government's prevention or handling of a crisis is not very visible, for example when there are major issues of secrecy involved (Christensen & Lodge, 2018). The same may happen when the effects are disputed. It may also depend on the viewpoint of stakeholders or citizens, some of whom will have more knowledge of governance capacity than others, or if the effects of the capacity are diverse.

The extent to which the various types of governance capacity translate into governance legitimacy depends on how visible they are for the citizens. Coordination and delivery capacity may have a rather high public profile during crises, and the legitimacy may be rather low when these "capacities don't find each other" and handling is flawed. Analytical capacity, on the other hand, is normally rather hidden but is nonetheless critical for dispelling the impression that the responsible organizations do not have the relevant competence. Finally, regulation capacity is also rather invisible to most people. It usually becomes relevant in the aftermath of crises, especially when learning processes assume legitimacy.

Conversely, governance legitimacy might affect governance capacity. When people's trust in government is high, ensuring the various kinds of governance capacity required for crisis management is easier. It gives the government a greater degree of freedom in coordinating, analyzing, regulating and delivering. A high level of diffuse support gives the government more leeway for preventing and handling crises (cf. Easton, 1965). In these situations, the flawed handling of one particular crisis will not normally have long-term consequences. If legitimacy is based on more specific support, however, this limits governance capacity.

Our argument is that the match or mismatch between governance capacity and citizens' expectations will affect perceptions of the quality of crisis management (Schneider, 2011; Christensen, Lægreid, & Rykkja, 2016). Not only what the government does, but also how it is assessed by citizens, matters. The more legitimacy the government has, the better it can perform its tasks (Rothstein, 1998). When there is a gap between capacity and expectations, crisis management runs into trouble. This gap can be closed either by strengthening capacity or by reducing expectations, or a combination of the two.

The Relationship between Accountability and Governance Legitimacy

The connection between accountability and legitimacy is blurred and contested, often due to a lack of conceptual clarification and operationalization (Jann, 2017). Furthermore, it is often seen as a phenomenon with reciprocal effects. First, scoring high on most accountability types may enhance governance legitimacy, but how visible the different types of accountability are for the general public and media varies, which may foster more use of symbols. The media tend to focus on political accountability, so this may be a critical factor influencing governance legitimacy. If government is perceived as weak, this may have a negative impact on legitimacy. Another aspect of political accountability is also important, namely, the relationship between the political and administrative leadership. Normally the administrative apparatus will have little reason to make its own government or ministry look bad vis-à-vis the parliament, but internal tensions may affect legitimacy in a negative way. Administrative, managerial, professional and judicial accountability will normally have a rather loose connection with legitimacy, but may become more exposed in a crisis. The ambiguity of accountability is especially clear when things go wrong (Gregory, 1998). Managerial accountability might be biased toward hierarchy and punishment and thus might tend to undermine trust and legitimacy (Behn, 2001).

One of the major features of horizontal or societal accountability is that it aims to improve governance legitimacy, which often includes both cultural and symbolic elements. The other types of accountability also play into this relationship. The fact that this type of accountability is not mandatory gives it more flexibility. This means that the government can more systematically target certain stakeholders with specific messages to increase its legitimacy. One problem with this is that it is often difficult to predict how actors in the environment will react to the government's justification for structural and policy changes. This type of accountability exposes governmental actors and may increase insecurity in public decision-making processes. Overall, it is not easy to discover to what extent and how accountability impacts on legitimacy (Jann, 2017).

Second, scoring high on legitimacy will generally enhance the score on most accountability types and relationships in crisis management. If the government enjoys overall strong trust and diffuse support, political accountability will probably be easier to fulfill, because the information given by the government to parliament, or by administrative leaders to the political executive, will be judged in a generally positive way because of strong societal support. Furthermore, administrative and managerial accountability will go more smoothly and with less public exposure. Professional accountability will be easier to handle, because professional autonomy and competence are seen in a more positive light. The same goes for judicial accountability, that is, there will be fewer questions about due process, the rule of law and users'/citizens' rights. And there will be fewer reasons to try to further societal accountability toward the media and the general public.

The Relationship between Governance Capacity and Reputation Management

Different types of governance capacity may have diverse effects on reputation management. Lack of coordination or delivery capacity, both instrumental features, may severely limit what kind of symbols that can be used, or it may have negative effects on those that are used. Analytical capacity normally remains under the radar when it comes to reputation management, but professional reputation may be spotlighted if competence is disputed. Regulation capacity has been rather loosely connected to reputation management, but this has changed in the last decade. One example of this is the increasing tendency to establish public oversight and audit units with communications expertise, which may combine instrumental and symbolic features. These units have a tendency to pursue the control of public and private organizations more aggressively, which leads to more pressure on reputation management.

Reputation management, meaning that the right use of myths and symbols will portray the prevention and handling of a crisis as a success, may facilitate governance capacity. Balancing talk and action may be difficult for public leaders, however, and often there is a tendency to oversell success. This may be enhanced by the so-called superstitious learning (March & Olsen, 1975), where the probability of success is exaggerated, while lack of knowledge or changing conditions are under-communicated. This again may give rise to counter-myths and problems of reputation management. Leaders face the challenge of supporting capacity with the right reputation symbols, but at the same time being careful not to undermine that capacity when conditions change and the gap between talk and action increases.

The literature on the relationship between governance capacity and organizational reputation has mainly been preoccupied with traditional hierarchies (Carpenter, 2001; Roberts, 2006; Maor, 2010), but it is also relevant for the organization of networks, including those involved in crisis management. Network actors may be driven by a desire to protect their reputation by avoiding blame. A study of blame avoidance and reputation in the crisis response network after Hurricane Katarina reveals that network members tend to be concerned about their extra-network organizational reputation, which might enhance blame avoidance strategies when failure occurs (Moynihan, 2012). Such behavior might also undermine intra-network relationships. It is therefore important to understand how crisis communication can be used to protect reputation during a crisis (Coombs, 2007).

Second, successful reputation management potentially enhances governance capacity and leeway in crisis management. Agencies tend to strive for autonomy, and some agencies achieve it through a favorable reputation. Organizations with a positive reputation among social groups are better able to create and maintain autonomy (Carpenter, 2001). However, reputation is also an unstable source of autonomy (Roberts, 2006). In a politicized bureaucracy, the reputation of groups critical to fulfilling its public mission can be a potent but also fragile source of autonomy.

Not only social groups but also professions might play a role in building and maintaining a reputation. If an organization has a positive image, it will gain acceptance for a wider range of actions, and subpar performance will have fewer negative consequences. Therefore, combining talk and symbols on the one hand, and action on the other, overall generates more capacity than relying on action alone would (Brunsson, 1989). Nevertheless, there are potential problems with reputation management that may affect governance capacity (Wæraas & Maor, 2015). Government organizations may have limited discretion in branding their own organization. They may have problems choosing a consistent image, they may struggle with symbols if they are strongly regulative or if they have unpopular "unsolvable" tasks, or else they may try to be too unique and oversell their performance and competence. These aspects may all limit governance capacity in crisis management.

The Relationship between Accountability and Reputation Management

Different types of reputation symbols may be influenced by the diverse accountability types in a variety of ways. Political and societal accountability are interesting, and it is therefore not surprising that the number of employees with communication tasks in the government has increased. Political accountability has two dynamic relationships – between government and parliament and between the political and administrative leaderships. A majority government may find it easier to portray itself as strong vis-à-vis parliament, while a minority government may have more problems with what Wæraas and Byrkjeflot (2012: 193–200) label the "consistency problem", especially when there is a coalition government. There is a consistency problem when the government seeks to communicate what it stands for collectively while single parties push their favorite issues. This is compounded by the "politics problem", meaning that political and administrative leaders may disagree on how to pursue reputation management, either because of disagreement about the profile to be furthered, because of general conflicts in their relationship or because the government will manage its reputation differently in dealing with the parliament than in dealing with its own administrative apparatus.

Scoring high on societal accountability gives government actors more flexibility, including in reputation management, but there might also be a "consistency problem", suggesting that it may be difficult to put across a consistent message (Wæraas & Byrkjeflot, 2012). Especially if the public organization is heterogeneous and different messages are presented to different stakeholders, there is a potential problem of conflict. The "charisma problem" deals with the fact that government organizations often have to deal with complex and not easily solved problems. It is easier to sell programs and policies that have positive and less complicated connotations. The "uniqueness problem" deals with trying to create an image that may cause internal problems, especially in heterogeneous public organizations. Finally, the "excellence problem" is about the backlashes and critique that an organization may receive if it tries to oversell its own performance and competence.

The general message is that successful reputation management makes accountability relationships instrumentally easier to handle. Another message is that there is a need for different types of symbols and myths for different types of accountability. Collective symbols are often connected with political accountability. Administrative leaders try to cater to collective purposes when they are accountable. The symbols used are internally directed when talking about administrative and managerial accountability. In the case of crisis management, this would mean focusing on whether adequate plans have been made and executed in the correct manner, or it may relate to specific performance indicators in crisis management. The symbols related to professional accountability are more divided between internal and external purposes. Judicial accountability also has the same divided profile: internally the symbols are about due process, while the external symbols concern rule of law and peoples' rights. Symbols connected with societal accountability are often diverse and external, for example when a public organization tries to convince the public as well as specific stakeholders that it has handled a crisis well.

Discussion and Conclusion

The main argument is this chapter is related to the dynamic coevolution of governance capacity, legitimacy, accountability and reputation in crisis management. We have shown the mutual influence between these crucial elements of crisis management, where governance capacity and accountability both influence and are influenced by governance legitimacy and reputation management. Thus, we are facing coevolution and mutual affected processes.

The relationship between governance capacity and governance legitimacy is under-researched. Following Suchman (1995), we believe there is a need to examine how governments handle legitimacy in crises using both an instrumental and an institutional approach. During and after a crisis, a main challenge is to maintain and restore trust in the capacity of government to deal with such situations. Without citizens' trust in government bodies, there is no legitimacy, and the implementation of societal security policies is likely to fail. In order to ensure this legitimacy, governance capacity needs to be in place. However, governance capacity is not only a question of policy design and efficient implementation by crisis management bodies, but also about citizens' perceptions of the governance apparatus (Rothstein, 1998). The complexity, ambiguity and uncertainty of crises pinpoint accountability issues that go beyond traditional instrumental principal-agent relations (Olsen, 2017). Accountability in such situations might be an issue of political communication, and reputation management is often important because the system is exposed and lack of cultural compatibility may hamper changes (Carpenter, 2010; Carpenter & Krause, 2012; Christensen & Lægreid, 2015). From a myth perspective, reputation is about understanding the role of ideas and evolving belief in organizations (DiMaggio & Powell, 1983). Reputation is then about how ideas shape agencies.

In this chapter, we have argued that more governance capacity, especially in the form of "better structures" or technical solutions, will not necessarily lead to better crisis management. Governance capacity may thus enhance or weaken governance legitimacy, accountability and reputation. Likewise, governance legitimacy, accountability and reputation may strengthen or constrain government capacity. Thus, we have to ask how trust in crisis management institutions as well as their reputation affects crisis management capacity. Not only what crisis management bodies do, but also citizens' expectations regarding what they should do, matter for governance legitimacy, accountability and reputation (Lodge & Wegrich, 2014).

Handling the relationships between governance capacity, legitimacy, accountability and reputation management in unsettled and turbulent crises is a key challenge. These are frequently mutually affecting processes, resulting in ambiguities and hybrid and complex relationships. We argue that there is a need to go beyond vertical principal-agent approaches and rethink these relationships in a way that resonates with the new reality of modern governance systems in turbulent times (Lægreid, 2014; Ansell, Trondal, & Øgård, 2017). Simply reinstalling hierarchical principal-agent-based relationships is problematic in the current more complex state. Especially in unexpected, unruly and unsettled situations, we face mutually dynamic relationships between governance capacity, legitimacy and accountability and reputation management. The crisis management apparatus is characterized by diversity and interdependencies, and there are tensions for which there is no optimal, simple or general solution (Bossong & Hegemann, 2015; Christensen et al., 2016). Mixtures and layering rather than substitution of one arrangement by another is a main trend, which tends to enhance ambiguity, and the relationship between accountability and legitimacy is rather scattered (Jann & Lægreid, 2015). In such circumstances, there is a need for pragmatism (Ansell, 2011) and to analyze how multiple and hybrid relationships interact and change over time. To understand such relationships we need to combine structural/instrumental, cultural/institutional and myth approaches.

The use of symbols and myths is common in the construction of governance capacity and central forms of accountability in crisis management. These are frequently invoked to enhance governance legitimacy and societal horizontal accountability. The development of governance legitimacy may be influenced by dynamics between cultural and symbolic processes. Or else pressure from the environment may be modified by a combination of cultural norms and symbols, as seen in situations when crisis-induced pressure to merge military and civilian crisis management organizations produces few results (Christensen, Lægreid, & Rykkja, 2015). The symbolic or myth perspective is also central in reputation management. We see it when attempts are made to present crisis management organizations as modern, rational and catering to the concerns of different stakeholders.

When we face turbulent, unpredictable crisis situations it is rather unrealistic to assume clear and simple relationships between governance capacity, legitimacy, accountability and reputation management. Restoring simple one-way relationships is probably not the way forward. We have to accept the increasing complexity of such situations and perhaps consider each situation separately. A main lesson is to start with an analysis of how public organizations actually work in practice in such circumstances, rather than engaging in unrealistic and wishful thinking about how they ought to work. This approach might be less heroic, but hopefully more realistic. The real challenge is to move toward a more responsible crisis management that incorporates governance capacity, accountability, reputation, responsiveness to citizens' demands and governance legitimacy, so that it can act decisively for the public good (Kettl, 2009).

In working toward this goal, crisis management faces important methodological issues. The research field is dominated by case studies. We know fairly little about how stakeholders react to crises or to the crisis response strategies used. Experimental methods might be a way forward (Coombs, 2007). On the empirical side, there is a need to study in more detail the relationship between governance capacity, legitimacy, accountability and reputation in different types of crises and in different countries. On the theoretical side, the administrative system is characterized by mixed order and compound relations, implying difficult dilemmas and trade-offs. We need to take into account that public administration consists of a diverse repertoire of coexisting, overlapping, partly competing and mutually affecting relationships, especially in crisis situations (Olsen, 2010). Institutional syncretism might be a way for crisis management to change, in between instrumental design and path dependencies characterized by recombination, refashioning and repurposing of existing crisis management organizations in an adaptive way (Ansell, Trondal, & Øgård, 2017). In this perspective, achieving resilience after crises is less a question of engineering resilience by reducing complexity and bringing the system back to a pre-crisis equilibrium, and more a question of establishing complex and dynamic resilience by absorbing hybridity and complexity.

A possible way to handle and manage unruly and wicked crises might be to adopt a probing strategy whereby feedback obtained via small investigations can form a strategy of response (Ansell, 2017). It is often difficult to anticipate and predict a crisis, and it might call for difficult trade-offs and produce unintended consequences. In such situations, it might be better to allow small-scale experimentation, adaptability and resilience. Unpacking this mixed order and understanding the dynamic relationships between governance capacity, governance legitimacy, accountability and reputation management seems a promising way forward in public administration research on crisis management as well as on reputation management.

References

Aberbach, J. D., & Christensen, T. (2007). The Challenges of Modernizing Tax Administration Putting Customers First in Coercive Public Organizations. *Public Policy and Administration*, 22(2): 155–182.

Ansell, C. (2011). *Pragmatic Democracy*. Oxford: Oxford University Press.

Ansell, C., Boin, A., & Keller, A. (2010). Managing Transboundary Crises: Identifying Building Blocks of an Effective Response System. *Journal of Contingencies and Crisis Management*, 18(4): 205–217.

Ansell, C., Trondal, J., & Øgård, M. (2017). *Governance in Turbulent Times*. Oxford: Oxford University Press.

Ansell, C. (2017). Turbulence, Adaptation and Change. In Ansell, C., Trondal, J., & Øgård, M. (Eds.). *Governance in Turbulent Times*. Oxford: Oxford University Press.

Askim, J., Christensen, T., & Lægreid, P. (2015). Accountability and Performance Management: The Norwegian Hospital, Welfare and Immigration Administrations. *International Journal of Public Administration*, 38: 971–982.

Behn, R. (2001). *Rethinking Democratic Accountability*. Washington, DC: Brookings Institution Press.

Boin, A., & Bynander, F. (2014). Explaining Success and Failure in Crisis Coordination. *Geografiska Annaler*, Series A, 97(1): 123–135.

Boin, A., Stern, E., 't Hart, P., & Sundelius, B. (2005). *The Politics of Crisis Management: Public Leadership under Pressure*. Cambridge: Cambridge University Press.

Bossong, R., & Hegemann, H. (Eds.). (2015). *European Civil Security Governance*. London: Palgrave.

Bouckaert, G., Peters, B. G., & Verhoest, K. (2010). *The Coordination of Public Sector Organization*. Basingstoke: Palgrave Macmillan.

Bovens, M. (2007). Analyzing and Assessing Public Accountability: A Conceptual Framework. *European Law Journal*, 13(4): 837–868.

Bovens, M., Schillemans, T., & Hart, P. T. (2008). Does public accountability work? An assessment tool. *Public Administration, 86*(1): 225–242.

Bromley, P., & Powell, W. W. (2012). From Smoke and Mirrors to Walking the Talk: Decoupling in the Contemporary World. *The Academy of Management Annals*, 6(1): 483–530.

Brunsson, N. (1989). *The Organization of Hypocrisy. Talk, Decisions and Actions in Organizations*. Chichester: Wiley.

Busuioc, E. M., & Lodge, M. (2016). The Reputational Basis of Public Accountability. *Governance*, 29(2): 247–263.

Carpenter, D. P. (2001). *Forging Bureaucratic Autonomy*. Princeton, NJ: Princeton University Press.

Carpenter, D. P. (2010). *Reputation and Power. Organizational Image and Pharmaceutical Regulation at FDA*. Princeton, NJ: Princeton University Press.

Carpenter, D. P., & Krause, G. A. (2012). Reputation and Public Administration. *Public Administration Review*, 12(1): 26–32.

Christensen, T., & Lægreid, P. (2005). Trust in Government: The Relative Importance of Service Satisfaction, Political Factors, and Demography. *Public Performance & Management Review*, 28(4): 487–511.

Christensen. T., & Lægreid, P. (2015). Reputation Management in Times of Crisis—How the Police Handled the Norwegian Terrorist Attack in 2011. In Major, M., & Wæraas, A. (Eds.). *Organizational Reputation in the Public Sector*. London: Routledge.

Christensen, T., & Lægreid, P. (2017). Accountability Relations in Unsettled Situations: Administrative Reform and Crises. In Christensen, T., & Lægreid, P. (Eds.). *The Routledge Handbook to Accountability and Welfare States Reforms in Europe*. London: Routledge.

Christensen, T., Lægreid, P., & Rykkja, L. H. (2016). Organizing for Crisis Management: Building Governance Capacity and Legitimacy. *Public Administration Review*, 76(6): 887–897.

Christensen, T., & Lodge, M. (2018). Reputation Management in Societal Security: A Comparative Study. *American Review of Public Administration*, 48(2): 119–132.

Christensen, T., Danielsen, O. A., Lægreid, P., & Rykkja, L. H. (2016). Comparing Coordination Structure for Crisis Management in Six Countries. *Public Administration*, 94(2): 316–332.

Christensen, T., Lægreid, P., Roness, P. G., & Røvik, K. A. (2007). *Organization Theory and the Public Sector. Instrument, Culture and Myth*. London and New York: Routledge.

Coombs, W. T. (2007). Protecting Organization Reputations During a Crisis: The Development and Application of Situational Crisis. *Communication Theory*, 10(3): 163–176.

Czarniawska, B., & Sevón, G. (Eds). 1996. *Translating Organizational Change*. Berlin: De Gruyter.

Day, P., & Klein, R. (1987). *Accountability. Five Public Services*. London: Tavistock Publishers.

DiMaggio, P. J., & Powell, W. W. (1983). The Iron Cage Revisited: Institutional Isomorphism and Collective Rationality in Organizational Fields. *American Sociological Review*, 48(2): 147–160.

Easton, D. (1965). *A Systems Analysis of Political Life*. New York: Wiley.

Edelman, M. (1964). *The Symbolic Uses of Politics*. Urbana: University of Illinois Press.

Egeberg, M. (2012). How Bureaucratic Structure Matters: An Organizational Perspective. In Peters, B. G., & Pierre, J. (Eds.). *The Sage Handbook of Public Administration*, 2nd Ed. London: Sage.

Goffman, E. (1959). *The Presentation of Self in Everyday Life*. New York: Anchor Books.

Gregory, R. (1998). Political Responsibility for Bureaucratic Incompetence: Tragedy at Cave Creek. *Public Administration*, 76: 519–538.

Gundel, S. (2005): Towards a New Typology of Crises. *Journal of Contingencies and Crisis Management*, 13(3): 106–151.

Jann, W. (2016). Accountability, Performance and Legitimacy. In Christensen, T., & Lægreid, P. (Eds.). *The Routledge Handbook on Accountability and Welfare State Reforms in Europe*. London: Routledge.

Jann, W., & Lægreid, P. (2015). Reforming the Welfare State: Accountability, Management, and Performance. *International Journal of Public Administration*, 38(13): 941–946.

Kettl, D. F. (2003). Contingent Coordination: Practical and Theoretical Puzzles for Homeland Security. *American Review of Public Administration,* 33(3): 253–277.

Kettl, D. F. (2007). *System under Stress. Homeland Security and American Politics.* Washington, DC: CQ Press.

Kettl, D. F. (2009). *The Next Government of the United States: Why Our Institutions Fail Us and How to Fix Them.* New York: W.W. Norton.

Krasner, S. (1988). Sovereignty: An Institutional Perspective. *Comparative Political Studies*, 21: 66–94.

Lodge, M., & Wegrich, K. (2014). *The Problem Solving Capacity of the Modern State.* Oxford: Oxford University Press.

Lægreid, P. (2014). Accountability and New Public Management. In Bovens, M., Goodin, E., & Schillemans, T. (Eds.). *The Oxford Handbook of Public Accountability.* Oxford: Oxford University Press.

Lægreid, P., & Rykkja, L. H. (Eds.). (2018). *Societal Security and Crisis Managment. Governance Capacity and Legitimacy.* London: Routledge.

Maor, M. (2010). Organizational Reputation and Jurisdictional Claims: The Case of the U.S. Food and Drug Administration. *Governance*, 23(1): 133–159.

March, J. G. (1994). *A Primer in Decision Making.* New York: Free Press.

March, J. G., & Olsen, J. P. (1975). The Uncertainty of the Past: Organizational Learning Under Ambiguity. *European Journal of Political Research*, 3(2): 147–171.

March, J. G., & Olsen, J. P. (1989). *Rediscovering Institutions: The Organizational Basis of Politics.* New York: The Free Press.

Meyer, J. W., & Rowan, B. (1977). Institutionalized Organizations: Formal Structure as Myth and Ceremony. *American Journal of Sociology*, 83(September): 340–363.

Meyer, J. W. & Scott, W.R. (1983). Centralization and the Legitimacy Problems of Local Government. In Meyer, J. W. & Scott, W.R (Eds.). *Organizational Environments: Ritual and Rationality.* Beverly Hills, CA: Sage Publications, 199–215.

Moynihan, D. P. (2012). Extra-Network Organizational Reputation and Blame Avoidance in Networks: The Hurricane Katarina Example. *Governance*, 25(4): 567–588.

Morphew, C. C., & Harley, M. (2006). Mission Statements: A Thematic Analysis of Rhetoric across Institution Types. *Journal of Higher Education,* 77(3): 456–471.

Mulgan, R. (2000). Accountability: An Ever-expanding Concept? *Public Administration*, 78(3): 555–573.

Pollitt, C., & Hupe, P. (2011). Talking about Government. The Role of Magic Concepts. *Public Management Review*, 13(5): 641–658.

Olsen, J. P. (2010). *Governance through Institution Building.* Oxford: Oxford University Press.

Olsen, J. P. (2015). Democratic order, autonomy, and accountability. *Governance*, 28(4): 425–440.

Olsen, J. P. (2017). *Democratic Accountability, Political Order, and Change.* Oxford: Oxford University Press.

Roberts, P. (2006). FEMA and the Prospects of Reputation-Based Autonomy. *Studies in American Political Development*, 20(1): 57–87.

Romzek, B., & Dubnick, M. (1987). Accountability in the Public Sector: Lessons from the Challenger Tragedy. *Public Administration Review*, 47: 227–238.

Rothstein, B. (1998). *Just Institutions Matter: The Moral and Political Logic of the Universal Welfare State.* Cambridge: Cambridge University Press.

Røvik, K. A. (2002). The Secrets of the Winners: Management Ideas That Flow. In Sahlin-Andersson, K., & Engwall, L. (Eds.). *The Expansion of Management Knowledge – Carriers, Flows and Sources*, Stanford, CA: Stanford University Press

Scharpf, F. W. (1994). Games Real Actors Could Play: Positive and Negative Coordination in Embedded Negotiations. *Journal of Theoretical Politics*, 6(1): 27–53.

Scharpf, F. W. (1999). *Governing in Europe: Effective and Democratic?* Oxford: Oxford University Press.

Schillemans, T. (2011). Does Horizontal Accountability Work? Evaluation Potential Remedies for the Accountability Deficits of Agencies. *Administration and Society*, 43(4): 387–416.

Schillemans, T., & Busuioc, M. (2014). Predicting Public Sector Accountability. From Agency Drift to Forum Drift. *Journal of Public Administration Research and Theory*, 25: 191–215.

Schmidt, V. A. (2012). Democracy and Legitimacy in the European Union Revisited. Input, Output and 'Throughput'. *Political Studies*, 61(1): 2–22.

Schneider, S. K. (2011). *Dealing with Disaster. Public Management in Crisis Situations*, 2nd Ed. Armonk: E. Sharp.

Selznick, P. (1957). *Leadership in Administration*. New York: Harper & Row.

Simon, H. A. (1957). *Administrative Behaviour*. New York: Macmillan.

Streeck, W., & Thelen, K. (Eds). (2005). *Beyond Continuity: Institutional Change in Advanced Political Economies*. Oxford: Oxford University Press.

Suchman, M. C. (1995). Managing Legitimacy. Strategic and Institutional Approaches. *Academy of Management Review*, 20(3): 571–610.

Thompson, D. F. (1980). Moral Responsibility of Public Officials: The Problem of Many Hands. *American Political Science Review*, 74(4): 905–916.

Van Riel, C. B. M., & Fombrun, C. (2007). *Essentials of Corporate Communications*. London: Routledge.

Wedlin, L., & Sahlin, K. (2017). The Imitation and Translation of Management Ideas. In Greenwood, R., Oliver, C., Lawrence, T., & Meyer, R. (Eds). *The SAGE Handbook of Organizational Institutionalism*, 2nd Ed. London: Sage Publications, 102–127.

Willems, T., & Van Dooren, W. (2011). Lost in Diffusion? How Collaborative Arrangements Lead to an Accountability Paradox. *International Review of Administrative Sciences*, 77(3): 505–530.

Wæraas, A., & Byrkjeflot, H. (2012). Public Sector Organizations and Reputation Management: Five Problems. *International Public Management Journal*, 15(2): 186–206.

Wæraas, A., Byrkjeflot, H., & Angell, S. I. (Eds). (2011). *Substans og framtreden. Omdømme-håndtering i offentlig sektor* (Substance and appearance. Reputation management in the public sector). Oslo: Universitetsforlaget.

Wæraas, A., & Maor, M. (Eds.). (2015). *Organizational Reputation in the Public Sector*. London: Routledge.

Wæraas, A., & Solbakk, M. N. (2009). Defining the Essence of University: Lessons from Higher Education Branding. *Higher Education*, 57(4): 449–462.

12

RELATIVE RISK CONSTRUCTION THROUGH A RISK BOUNDARY AND SET OF RISK RITUALS

The Mining Context in the Soma Disaster

Cagri Topal, Cagatay Topal, and Fatma Umut Beşpınar

Introduction

This study looks into the question of how or through what mechanisms social, political, and economic contexts shape social actors' risk meanings regarding an organizational activity. Organizational risk research shows the contextual effect on the construction of risk meanings (Gamson & Modigliani, 1989; Gephart & Pitter, 1993; Jasanoff, 1988; Nelkin, 1988; Perrow, 1984). Yet, except for social-cultural rationalities emerging and embedded within particular contexts (Beamish, 2001; Gephart, Steier, & Lawrence, 1990; Kamoche & Maguire, 2011; Lane & Quack, 1999), no explicit mechanism, which carries the contextual effect into the actors' risk construction, is clearly identified by the research. This study explores some other contextual mechanisms, which enable or constrain the development of specific risk meanings. In addition, it shows the relative character of risk construction when the context refers to the existence of other risk sources different from the focal organizational activity.

In order to explore those mechanisms and relative risk construction, the study applies the anthropologist Mary Douglas's (1966, 1992) concepts of boundary, which refers to a social-economic context and related categorization of social objects and practices as acceptable or unacceptable, and ritual, which refers to a social activity against boundary breaches, to the worst industrial disaster case in the Turkish history, which claimed the lives of 301 miners and hurt many others. The case is about a coal mine in Soma, a district within the western part of Turkey and near the Aegean Sea. For many miners in Soma, as well as outside observers, something was expected, and concerns regarding the risk in the Soma mines had been repeatedly raised. In fact, many deadly accidents occurred before the disaster. Still, the disaster with such a huge magnitude was shocking and led to a general questioning of the mining context in Soma. This study is one of those emerging out of this general critical questioning among the researchers and citizens. It develops an analysis of the production process in the mine and related employment dynamics within Soma and its environment, which are very much revealing of the complex interlinkages between risk meanings and contextual currents at the micro and macro levels.

The analysis of the case shows that the existing employment context of mining production works as a risk boundary for the miners to make sense of the risk in the mine, and this boundary is sustained by the miners' work and non-work practices and relationships work-ing as risk rituals. There are three contextual mechanisms, which are not rituals but have a ritualistic character in that they give a reproductive form to practices and relationships and thus turn those elements into rituals that maintain the current employment context. The mechanisms include a relative risk rationality arising from the high degree of unemploy-ment and low possibility of alternative employment, controls over the individual agency of the miners due to lack of an effective labor union and lack of job and safety training, and relational networks of the miners composed of the family (and its consumption needs) and employer (and its production pressures). Hence, the miners evaluate the risk within the employment context of mining production, a boundary referring mainly to the distinction between the norm of being employed in the mine and risk of being unemployed or employed in a minimum-wage job, which is considered not different from being unemployed. Within this risk boundary, the risk in the mine is constructed or made meaningful by the miners as relatively acceptable because of the alternative risk of unemployment. The three contextual mechanisms facilitate this relative construction process by confining the miners' daily prac-tices and relationships to this boundary and transforming them into risk rituals.

Therefore, the study demonstrates that in the risk construction process, social actors ex-perience the context as a boundary through the contextual mechanisms of a specific risk rationality, controls over individual agency, and relational networks. Working as a risk boundary, the context realizes its effect over the actors' understanding of risk with the help of those mechanisms, which turn social practices and relationships into risk rituals. Also, the contextual boundary indicates an alternative risk not directly generated by the focal organizational activity. Such a boundary gives a comparative and thus relative character to risk construction. The alternative risk becomes a major factor to make the focal activity meaningful, as risky or safe.

Organizational Research on Risk Context and Rationality

There are two groups of organizational studies that examine the effect of social, political, and economic contexts on risk construction. The first group directly demonstrates the ef-fect of different contexts with no or little attention to specific mechanisms through which the effect is realized (Gamson & Modigliani, 1989; Gephart & Pitter, 1993; Jasanoff, 1988; Nelkin, 1988; Perrow, 1984). The second group highlights certain social-cultural rationali-ties as a contextual mechanism to give some form to risk meanings (Beamish, 2001; Gephart et al., 1990; Kamoche & Maguire, 2011; Lane & Quack, 1999).

Context and Risk Construction

Social, political, and economic contexts are institutional settings characterized by a particular distribution of power and associated formal or informal norms and practices, which guide and limit the way the actors give meaning to organizational activities as risky or safe (Shrivastava, 1995; Stein, 2011). They are one of the bases of social-cultural rationalities, which also shape risk construction (Shrivastava, 1995; Stein, 2011). The contexts provide a legitimation ground for dominant risk rationalities and the power of social classes benefiting from those rationalities (Gephart & Pitter, 1993; Perrow, 1984).

In many organizational studies, the context of risk construction is an issue not richly discussed, or in some cases even surfaced in any explicit way. In the study looking into the Mann Gulch forest fire (Weick, 1993), for example, the context appears to be a kind of social disorder where organizational structures and teams no longer make sense. Most members of the firefighter team in the Mann Gulch construct the orders of the leader as invalid and risky, disregard them, and are not able to escape the fire in the field. Similarly, a governmental inquiry into the attacks of a nurse on the patients in a UK hospital refers to the institutional context of the national health system and how it makes the nurse and her actions seem normal and safe (Brown, 2000). The nurse is seen to be exploiting this institutional setting by meeting its formal requirements and successfully concealing her real self and attacks behind it. NASA's political context shaped by schedule pressures and cost concerns is another example (Dunbar & Garud, 2009). This context facilitates the decision of the Columbia's launch, which is constructed as safe despite the existence of serious problems in the shuttle and the following disaster. The different constructions of terrorism risk in the aviation and travel industries also refer to the effect of the context shaped by recent events and experiences (Sullivan-Taylor & Wilson, 2009). The managers in the aviation industry are highly concerned about the terrorism threat and develop measures proactively, whereas in the travel industry, the terrorist threat is not a big concern and the response is only reactive.

There are also organizational studies explicitly exploring the relationship between social, political, and economic contexts and risk construction. A number of studies, for example, argue that the capitalist institutional context facilitates the construction of complex organizational systems as safe, although such systems are highly unpredictable (Gephart & Pitter, 1993; Perrow, 1984, 2006). The context, which helps define such systems as generally safe, is actually shaped by the economic and political power of business and government elites who keep high-risk systems in operation in their pursuit of profit and tax revenues. In this context, risks are legitimized with the service of technical and legal experts and discourses as they seem to be professionally handled (Perrow, 1984; Zyglidopoulos & Fleming, 2011).

Public inquiries and hearings constitute another, more specific, context, in which risks created by organizational activities are constructed as legitimate (Brown, 2000, 2003; Gephart, 1992, 2007; Gephart & Pitter, 1993; Habermas, 1975; Topal, 2009). The inquiries and hearings restrict the discussion of those activities through institutional procedures (Gephart, 1992). In most cases, they are dominated by legal and technical discourses not easily accessible by the general public (Topal, 2009; Tsoukas, 1999). Also, they direct the public's attention away from systemic problems toward human errors (Brown, 2003; Elliot & Smith, 2007) and provide normalizing interpretations embedded in formal reports (Brown, 2000, 2003; Gephart, 2007).

The restricted, expert-based construction of risks is partly overcome in the context of the mass media (Gamson & Modigliani, 1989; Nelkin, 1988; Stallings, 1990). The media facilitate a more participative construction through a relatively open discussion. They partially reflect the perspectives of laypeople. The media provide critical schemes of interpretation for the public to make sense of industrial activities (Gamson & Modigliani, 1989; Stallings, 1990). Yet, the media are also selective in reporting and covering risks (Nelkin, 1988; Stallings, 1990). The media allow access for and empower particular groups of experts, politicians, and laypeople, which can affect public discussions and policy decisions regarding risks.

The legal context also shapes the construction of risk meanings (Jasanoff, 1988). For example, in the context of US public law, which is composed of government regulations and standards for licensing and monitoring risky organizational activities, risks are evaluated in terms of aggregate impacts at the population level. Risks are thus constructed with a focus on collective interests. The engagement of risk producers in risk management and compensation is limited. In contrast, the private law, which develops through disputes and litigations among private individuals or groups resolved through the courts in line with past precedents, subjects risks to an individualized evaluation in terms of impacts on individuals. Risks are thus constructed without regard to collective benefits. Risk producers are required to satisfactorily manage risks and fully compensate individual victims for any impacts.

Contextual Rationality and Risk Construction

Social actors' construction of risk is also shaped by social-cultural rationalities embedded within social, economic, and political contexts. Social-cultural rationalities are formal or informal knowledge sets such as technical or legal knowledge and local experiences (Beamish, 2001, 2002; Gephart et al., 1990; Kamoche & Maguire, 2011). The actors generally adopt a specific rationality as a meaning framework to interpret whether an organizational activity is a risk source or not.

Several studies implicitly show the effect of social-cultural rationalities in developing risk meanings. For example, the study analyzing the Bhopal disaster with 3,000 casualties due to a fatal gas leak in chemical factory points to the cost-cutting rationality of the factory owners (Weick, 1988). Accordingly, the safety procedures are routinely ignored to reduce the cost and the operations are constructed as not risky until the disaster. The cost-cutting logic is also observed in another factory in which the managers force the workers to comply with new behavioral measures by putting almost all the burden of safety on the workers (Rasmussen, 2010). The workers are considered as a source of risk as well as cost when they question the new measures. Another example is the use of quantitative sensemaking practices by both the government board and the operator company in a public inquiry to understand a well blowout (Gephart, 1997). Through a quantitative logic, the board and company interpret the blowout as an unusual case of risk, which otherwise is considered measurable and controllable.

In addition to these studies, some organizational studies directly analyze the link between social-cultural rationalities and risk meanings. It is demonstrated, for example, that the community members' risk meanings for the Guadalupe oil spill in California is embedded within a local rationality (Beamish, 2001, 2002). This rationality is shaped by the members' experiences with business and government authorities, which cover up similar cases of pollution. The rationality leads to mistrust on the part of the members who develop a chronic sense of contamination risk. Likewise, in order to assess risks, the tunnelers in a UK coal mine rely on their local pit sense, which they acquire within daily practices and preserve as an experience set to guide the work (Kamoche & Maguire, 2011). The tunnelers resist the new bureaucratic procedures embedded in formal safety rules but not in line with their pit sense. The procedures are unrelated to their local setting and thus considered abstract.

In a public inquiry into a fatal pipeline accident, the meanings of the inquiry participants regarding the accident are shaped by particular risk rationalities (Gephart et al., 1990). Among the three main participant groups, the government board follows a hierarchical rationality based on formal industry rules. The accident constitutes a risk of legitimacy for the government as it indicates a breach of the rules. In contrast, the pipeline company has a market rationality with a focus on wealth production. It is concerned about regulatory interventions to force costly operational changes and decreased profits. Finally, the workers and their families interpret the accident with a sectarian rationality. They focus on safety and highlight such risks as failures of equipment, exposures to toxic gas, and physical injuries. Hierarchical and market rationalities are also observed in a cross-cultural analysis of the German and British banks (Lane & Quack, 1999). The German banks assess the risk of financing small- and medium-sized firms through a hierarchical logic. They work closely with the government hierarchy to carry out banking policies and develop strong ties with public and private institutions to collect risk information. In the British banking industry, on the contrary, the involvement of the government is limited. The risk is mainly on the banks, which search for more profits through more credits and reflect the risk onto the creditor firms with risk premiums and collaterals.

Summary: Relative Neglect of Contextual Mechanisms of Risk Construction

Organizational studies on risk construction basically demonstrate that social, political, and economic contexts shape social actors' risk meanings. Social-cultural rationalities, which are generally an outcome of complex contextual factors, emerge as a mechanism that conveys the effect of the context onto the actors' meanings. Except for social-cultural rationalities, organizational research does not specifically look into different contextual mechanisms of risk construction. In the literature, the question of how the context is related to the development of risk meanings regarding organizational activities is not sufficiently explored. To address this situation, this study utilizes the ideas of Mary Douglas (1966, 1973, 1992) on risk construction.

Group Context, Boundary, and Ritual

One of the most comprehensive risk analyses, which emphasizes the effect of the context and has influenced organizational risk studies (Gephart, 1993; Gephart et al., 1990; Gephart, Van Maanen, & Oberlechner, 2009; Lane & Quack, 1999), is from the anthropologist Mary Douglas. Douglas (1966, 1973, 1992) focuses on the roots and results of cultural-contextual classifications with a structural analysis of everyday phenomena representing those classifications. The pertinent studies in the organizational field generally utilize the group-grid model (Gephart et al., 1990; Lane & Quack, 1999) developed by Douglas (1973) and Douglas and Wildavsky (1982) to categorize the empirical findings in different cases. Though generally neglected by organizational researchers, Douglas's concepts of boundary and ritual are also strong analytical tools to understand the relationship between the context and risk construction process.

Boundary and Risk Construction

A boundary refers to a social-economic context and the associated classification of social objects, events, relationships, and practices as acceptable or unacceptable for a particular cultural group (Douglas, 1966, 1973; Douglas & Wildavsky, 1982). It indicates the existence of a distinct group with certain contextual norms and thus differentiates the group from other groups. Douglas (1966) looks into everyday phenomena to understand the boundaries of a group. She is mainly interested in the meaning of dirt (see especially "Purity and Danger", 1966). What the members of a group consider as dirty or clean gives clues about the norms and boundaries of the group. To the extent that those norms are reflected in the members' ongoing, everyday practices and relationships, the meaning of dirt implies and derives from the reality of the group including social, cultural, and economic classifications and related boundaries. The boundaries in turn both encourage and force the practices and relationships to remain within the group norms. Hence, the same meaning of dirt, together with the norms, is reproduced within and through those daily practices and relationships of the group members. In other words, the group and dirt are always intertwined, the dirt having no meaning without a group. The group declares its boundaries through and becomes the ultimate reference for the meaning of dirt. It makes known acceptable or unacceptable roles to occupy, practices to perform, and ways to relate to other members and groups with its specific definition of dirt and related boundaries between the dirty and clean.

The concept of risk refers to potential dirt and is closely linked to the concept of boundary (Douglas & Wildavsky, 1982). Like dirt, risk is rooted and results in a particular boundary. The group members evaluate certain sets of events, activities, and objects as risky and others as non-risky based on their group's adopted or imposed realities and norms. The boundary can take both material and symbolic forms between the two sets. Risky and non-risky locations are marked for the members. For example, coal mining is considered relatively dirty and more risky in residential areas while being seen as relatively clean and less risky in industrial areas. Coal mines are generally physically distant from residential areas, and ordinary citizens are not allowed to enter mining sites surrounded by fences or walls. This refers to a normative as well as material risk boundary between industrial and residential areas in modern cities. Therefore, the group communicates and demands attention for its risk meanings with the help of a particular boundary and restricts access to risky areas (Douglas, 1992; Douglas & Wildavsky, 1982). In general, the members' individual experiences related to risk, for example accidents or disasters in coal mines, form a common pattern within the group. This pattern reinforces the group-specific risk meanings and helps construct them as a social norm. It is actually the basis of the norm (coal mining is risky and thus not acceptable in a residential area) and associated risk boundary (residential and industrial areas are separated by fences, walls, long distances, and access rules). Risk meanings appear to be factually developed as well as normatively sustained. In fact, the members' norms and their practices and relationships shaped by patterned experiences are transformed into one another in the construction process of a common risk meaning and boundary, which the members eventually take for granted.

Ritual and Risk Construction

Risk boundaries are concretized by rituals. Rituals are symbolic and material activities developed and performed against boundary breaches. They reproduce the contextual distinction between what is dirty (or risky) and clean (or not risky) (Douglas, 1966). Boundary breaches are actually a threat to group norms, and associated practices and relationships as well as meanings. Rituals are the group's risk measures to prevent or correct boundary breaches and resulting breaks in common meanings. They show and reconfirm the proper location of risky activities and objects, referring to and defending the boundary and norm behind, which set them apart from other, non-risky activities and objects. They push risky activities and objects, which cross over the boundary and break the norm, back to their legitimate location. Hence, rituals reestablish the group order every time they are performed.

Therefore, rituals are essential to preserve the consistency of risk meanings across different individual settings and situations (Douglas, 1975). For example, the operation of a coal mine very close to a residential area might be prevented by the order of a court, a process of risk ritual, which reconfirms the residential area as not a place to run an industrial operation. Conversely, the court might decide that the operation is non-risky and acceptable if accompanied by certain safety measures, also rituals of risk management, which symbolically reproduce the boundary between the residential and industrial areas while protecting the residents to a certain extent. In both cases, the rituals support the meaning of residential areas as a safe place to live and of coal mines as a source of manageable risks from which to profit. Risk management measures are there to prevent any boundary breach such as a mining accident in the first place. But if an accident occurs, they are also available to address the situation and restore the order as quickly as possible. Thus, risk rituals both symbolically and materially reestablish risk boundary and meaning in an ongoing manner. When risk boundary represents deep-rooted group norms, practices, and relationships, risk rituals are especially emphasized. For example, in a residential area where there has never been an industrial operation, the residents are likely to consider a new coal mine as a significant source of risks including possible landslides, environmental pollution, and heavy traffic. The mining company might be required to develop and routinely utilize numerous risk measures, materially reestablishing the boundary between the residential life and industrial operation. Alternatively, the mining company might issue daily statements about the nature of possible problems and use of risk measures to assure the residents of safety, symbolically reestablishing the boundary. Together with the existing risk boundary, the existing risk meaning is reconfirmed by both rituals of risk measures and statements: it is still a residential area safe for living, and the industrial operation is already and continues to be isolated.

The continuity of risk rituals is important so as not to allow a transitional state to emerge. A transitional state emerges when the boundary between the risk and non-risk is unclear for a long period of time (Douglas, 1966). It is a serious threat to the group order because it indicates the possibility of an alternative order, which can destabilize the existing practices and relationships. As the coexistence of the existing and alternative orders persists, new risk norms and meanings embedded within the alternative are accepted by more and more group members. A new risk boundary begins to emerge while the unity of the group erodes. The long-term existence of a risky industrial operation near a residential area, for example, might normalize risk for some residents while others might keep struggling to replace the operation. The residents might be divided, some accepting the operation as an employment opportunity and others rejecting it as a pollution source. New employment relationships or safety practices might emerge, gradually replacing the existing ones. New norms might arise from the debate around employment and pollution. The new boundary is likely to include the risky operation within the safe zone.

In order to avoid a transitional state and an eventual loss of group coherence, rituals in most cases are not a special occasional event at the group level but an ordinary daily activity, which repeatedly refers to the existing order and leaves little space for alternatives to appear at the individual level. Simple speech acts, communications, or discourses, which routinely emphasize certain boundary issues, are an example (Douglas, 1975). The group members' daily communications are generally framed or restricted by those issues. Restricted speech acts mark the ongoing role of those issues in shaping the members' practices and relationships, discursively reconfirming this role. For example, when unemployment is a boundary issue for coal miners to evaluate or compare with the risk in the mine, it is likely to observe repeated references to unemployment risk in daily discourses. The miners reproduce the boundary between employment and unemployment in those discourses while experiencing it in their practices and relationships in the mine or outside. Their everyday discourses or conversations thus turn out to be a risk ritual, which keeps emphasizing this risk boundary and unemployment risk.

Summary: Ritualistic Contextual Mechanisms of Risk Boundary and Risk Construction

The concept of boundary implies that risk meanings are related to a set of contextual norms and practices for a particular cultural group. Risk refers to a possible breach of the group's normative-practical boundary. For example, accidents in a coal mine are a risk because they indicate a breach of safety norms and practices. Similarly, unemployment is a risk as it indicates a breach of the norm and practice of being employed and getting paid. Group members respond to risk with rituals such as taking safety precautions and following workplace rules to ensure the sustainability of the group's risk boundary and reestablish related meanings of risk. The normative-practical boundary between risk and non-risk is thus reproduced through risk rituals. Rituals repair boundary breaches and associated breaks in risk meanings in an ongoing manner and protect the unity of the group. Hence, together with risk boundary, they have an important role in risk construction. This study conceptualizes a mining employment context, both as a risk boundary and as a source of risk rituals, and analyzes related contextual mechanisms as the link between the boundary and rituals. It thus applies these two concepts to address the organizational literature's relative neglect of the role of contextual mechanisms in risk construction.

Methodology

According to the report of TEPAV (The Economic Policies Research Foundation of Turkey) (2014), Turkey was the second worst after China in death ratio per million ton of coal production between 2007 and 2012. Yet, the death ratio in China has decreased by 75% since 2012, while production has increased almost 100% per year. Hence, Turkey has become the worst in death ratio in recent years. The case we examined is the deadliest industrial disaster in Turkey. The disaster happened in Soma on May 13, 2014, leaving 301 dead and 90 injured. The deaths were due to the fire started by an explosion because of oxidation inside the main gallery and the consequent large amount of carbon monoxide permeating into other galleries (TBB, 2014). The coal mine in question was originally built in 1990 and operated by the state (Turkish Coal Enterprises) for about 15 years. In 2006, the state transferred the operational right to a private firm (Park Technique Company). This firm left the mine in 2009, reporting that it was not economically viable to safely operate due to the highly flammable nature of coal in the mine (TMMOB, 2014). In 2009, the current firm (Soma Coal Enterprises) was granted the license, and it operated until the disaster. During this entire period, the state retained the ownership of the mine as well as the right to monitor the operation (TBB, 2014).

The Soma Disaster Report by the TMMOB (Union of Chambers of Turkish Engineers and Architects) mentioned that a disaster was already expected by the miners. The report confirmed that the coal seams in the mine were flammable by themselves and the temperature in the mine was extraordinarily high for some time before the disaster. The report argued that the event took place due to the oxidation of coal at a distance of approximately 1,350 meters from the main gate. The oxidation was transformed into open flame, which set on fire the transportation line, electricity cables, wooden support columns, and plastic fresh-air pipes. In addition, the power in the mine was cut due to the fire, and the backup ventilators would not work. The resultant thermodynamic disequilibrium made way for the dissemination of intensive carbon monoxide (TMMOB, 2014, p. 24). The technique of black tumbling used to extract the coal in the mine, which is in fact forbidden in the Western countries, was considered as another factor for the event to turn into a disaster. The black tumbling on that day left flammable coal after the extraction. This already oxidized coal became a sufficient ground for the flame and prevented proper ventilation during the event (KDK, 2014, p. 72).

The event was realized and responded to around 15:00. After the management noticed the seriousness of the situation, the miners from the neighboring mines were called for help.

At around 17:00, many miners were able to come out of the mine. Meanwhile, it was already announced that it was an emergency situation and the urgent transfer of the national rescue teams started (TMMOB, 2014, p. 25). In a common report prepared by the TMMOB and the TTB (The Turkish Medical Association) in 2016, it was stated that the initial rescue attempts were quite disorganized. Crisis management was poor, and there was no control on the entrance into or the exit from the area. The involvement of unauthorized and unqualified people, though with good intentions, created new problems. Due to disorganization and mismanagement, the expert rescue teams coming from other mining towns of Turkey could not enter the mine until 15 hours after the event. The report indicated that there was an obvious lack of an explicit rescue plan (TMMOB and TTB, 2016, p. 28).

During our research, we used a qualitative design as our focus was the risk meanings of social actors (Denzin & Lincoln, 2000; Gephart, 2004). As the worst industrial disaster in Turkey, the case was a very rich source of risk meanings, especially those of the miners (Stake, 2000). To understand those meanings, we conducted, and used as the main source of data, in-depth interviews with the miners and representatives of non-governmental organizations amounting to 19 hours in total. Interviews were completed within June 2015 in Soma, Kınık, and Akhisar districts. Some of the miners interviewed were employed at the site of the disaster, and others in the neighboring mines. Several of the miners lost their jobs after the disaster, and several others were transferred to other mines. To better understand the context, we also referred to various reports and documents prepared by the special commission of the Grand National Assembly of Turkey, the Union of Chambers of Turkish Engineers and Architects (TMMOB), the Union of Turkish Bar Associations (TBB), expert authorities charged by the courts, the research centers and the concerned scholars. In the interviews, we asked our respondents the meaning of mining and mining risks. The disaster being the background, we asked them about the conditions of mining before and after. We also asked the effects of the disaster on their lives.

The data gathered through the interviews were analyzed through an iterative, collaborative process (Gephart, 1997; Silverman, 2006). We all read through the interview data, often referring to the supplementary reports and documents, to clarify specific as well as general contextual issues regarding the case and mining industry (Gephart, 1997). After this general reading and familiarization, we then discussed emerging contextual issues, which were generally beyond the control of, but emphasized by, individual miners in the interviews. After moving back and forth within the data and resulting discussions, we noted that the miners regularly referred to the problem of unemployment. Unemployment seemed to be the most visible aspect of the context. We also established that unemployment was often given meaning together with the conditions of employment and needs of family. Unemployment was compared to mining and other jobs. Between unemployment and employment was the precarious position of family. Therefore, using problem of unemployment, employment conditions, and family needs as sensitizing concepts (Gephart, 1993; Glaser & Strauss, 1967), we returned back to the data and identified the textual segments where these issues were discussed in detail. Reviewing the textual segments, we recognized six common themes in the discourse of different interviewees. The themes included intensity of unemployment, low number of non-mining jobs, lack of an effective labor organization, lack of employee training, production pressure of the mining firms over the miners, and living needs of the miners' families. Next, as researchers, we exchanged ideas about what these themes would indicate in general and whether there could be higher order categories in which to group them. This collective and collaborative elaboration resulted in three general categories (Silverman, 2006), which we argue shaped the risk construction process and thus meanings of the miners. The categories were relative risk rationality embedded within unemployment intensity and within lack of alternative jobs, controls over individual miners due to the lack of an effective labor union and due to the lack of job and especially safety training, and miners' relational networks focused on their family's consumption needs and on the firm's production demands. Lastly, we utilized the concepts of boundary and ritual (Douglas, 1966, 1973) to theoretically interpret our empirical findings. We tried to theoretically ground the findings by relating the miners' risk meanings and contextual mechanisms of meanings to those theoretical concepts (Gephart and Pitter, 1995).

Results

The miners make sense of risk with respect to the employment context of mining production. In this context, the norm for the male workforce is to be employed by a mining firm, and thus the main contextual risk is to be unemployed with no wages or out of the mining sector with very low wages. This context operates as a risk boundary, categorizing mining employment as acceptable, and unemployment or other employment as unacceptable. It is supported by three contextual mechanisms. These mechanisms are ritualistic because they give a form of risk ritual to the miners' practices, relationships, and discourses, which in turn result in the reproduction of the employment context. Hence, the mechanisms facilitate this reproduction by establishing the link between the general context and daily activity.

The first ritualistic mechanism we observe is relative risk rationality. This is rooted in the relative risk of unemployment together with lack of alternative jobs. The second mechanism is control over individual agency due to the limited power of the miners, who do not have access to the institutional support of a labor union or to the capacity-building potential of job training. Finally, relational networks indicate that the miners are caught between the consumption demands of family and the production pressures of the mining firm.

Relative Risk Rationality

Unemployment intensity. For the last two decades, there has been a process of economic restructuration in the agricultural sector. Both the proportion of agricultural fields and the number of registered workers in the sector have decreased. Turkey has long become a net importer of agricultural products. The debts of farmers have considerably increased. This process has triggered unemployment, the transfer of fields to commercial banks, and migration of agricultural population to urban areas. Parallel to this process, the primary agricultural product in Soma, tobacco, has lost its economic value due to the end of government subsidies for the small farmers. The process has created a massive low-skilled labor pool to be employed in the service and mining sectors, which are the only alternatives left. Thanks to the very large reserves of coal in the area, Soma is also a major destination for migrant workers, especially from other mining regions. The continuous migration exacerbates the problem of unemployment in Soma. Added to this is the fact that the mine where the disaster took place is now closed. The mine was one of the largest in the region, sustaining many jobs directly in mining and indirectly in other sectors. Under the conditions of this high unemployment, the mining job is invaluable:

> Why do they continue [to work]? How many people are unemployed in Turkey? The question is simple. How many unemployed? When you speak up, they show you the people at the gate. I'll tell you something. When your child comes and says to you, 'father, give me a [Turkish] Lira', would you like to die or give the money?
>
> *(Interview)*

The engineers in the mine also mention that there is no other option for work. Yet, the mining work is not secure. There are some hidden rules not to be fired. One of those rules, also mentioned in the court minutes on the disaster, is forced participation in the meetings of the governing party. An engineer explains this issue:

> There is a rule of fear. There is fear in each worker from the past. There is a political pressure. Workers are forced to participate in the meetings of the ruling party. If a worker does not participate, he is considered absent at work, too.
>
> *(Interview)*

Lack of alternatives. People are pushed to work in the mines. Mining becomes the most advantageous alternative among others for survival. For the low-skilled ex-farmers, for example, the service and mining sectors seem to be the only alternatives. Compared to the service jobs, which are likely to be unregistered and very low-paid, the mining sector offers a registered job with early retirement and income above the legal minimum wage. The mining job becomes the only way for a relatively decent living. Mining gradually equals to employment and appears as the only option for living:

> This is the only work opportunity for people here. This is the only reason; it is a remedy for unemployment here. There is no other purpose in the mining work. It is completely about fear of unemployment.
>
> *(Interview)*

The fear of unemployment and lack of alternative employment dominate the miners' experiences and discourses. For adequate living conditions, the employment context of Soma offers only two options according to those discourses:

> If you are not a government employee, you are a miner. That is, there is no other work here.
>
> *(Interview)*

Following Douglas (1966, 1973, 1992) and Douglas and Wildavsky (1982), we argue that the mining employment operates as a norm in Soma. Unemployment together with employment in another low-wage sector is seen as the biggest risk and the opposite of the norm of employment. The mining employment becomes a common code of a moral order. As such, it is reemphasized as the only acceptable and available contextual fact in all the discourses among the workers and families. In all the occasions, gatherings, and breaks, it is reaffirmed that there is no other option but to descend into the mine. There are actually two choices: either to work in a mine or to starve. The employment context, which sets the mining employment apart from all other options, then appears as an essential boundary for the miners to make sense of the risk in mining. This risk boundary indicates the existence of a relative risk rationality, which makes the miners continuously compare the risks of mining and of unemployment. As the components of the boundary, the intensity of unemployment and lack of alternative employment lead to the development of such a rationality that puts these two different risks in the same context (Beamish, 2001; Lane & Quack, 1999; Perrow, 1984; Shrivastava, 1995; Stein, 2011). Hence, this relative rationality works as a mechanism to sustain the current context of employment. The mining risk is made meaningful in relation to the risk of unemployment in this context. Relative risk rationality dominates the miners' repeated discourses of or conversations on risk, which actually reflect their daily experiences and relationships with the employer and other miners, turning those into risk rituals to reproduce the contextual boundary and strongly define the mining employment and unemployment, respectively, as the norm and the ultimate risk. Unemployment intensity combined with almost no alternative opportunity makes this relative rationality so strong, as a ritualistic mechanism, that the repeated comparisons in daily conversations include the concepts of death, accident, starvation, and unemployment. In turn, the rationality helps sustain the context of mining employment by shaping the miners' meanings of risk through comparative employment evaluations and transforming their daily discourses of risk into reproductive speech acts, and make the context an omnipotent risk boundary. Accordingly, the miners' discourses or conversations act as a risk ritual and mark unemployment as the ultimate risk or boundary breach despite the existence of fatal risks in the mine. The discourse indicates that such a breach is to be fully repaired with other mining employment and, in fact, most unemployed miners look for another mining job. Hence, the miners' speech acts reproduce the context of mining employment as a risk boundary, to which both unemployment and mining risks refer.

Control over Individual Agency

Lack of an effective labor union. The proportion of workers organized in trade unions in Turkey is about 11.5%. This proportion increases to 18% in the mining sector (DİSK report, 2016). This is still very much behind the worldwide averages. Turkey comes last in unionization within the OECD countries (Hürriyet, 2014). The most important reason for this, which we observe also in the case, is the belief of workers that labor unions do not represent them or protect their rights (Öke & Kurt, 2013). Although the miners in the case are the members of a union, many of them do not trust the union. They think the union is under the strong influence of the employer and managers. The union is even considered to be a representative of the employer. One miner states that the union collects monthly payments from the workers but defends the employer's interests. Despite this, the miners do not speak up and ask for their own rights. The same miner mentions that the miners are suppressed and afraid of getting fired. Another miner points out that the directors of the union are paid by the employer.

Another issue is that most miners are not aware of their own rights and the real function of a union to defend those rights. Hence, they do not attempt to work for a positive change in the union. It seems usual when the union does not lead to any positive outcome in their lives:

> The miners do not even know what a trade union is and what its purpose is. As a matter of fact, until now, the union has not worked for the interests of the miners.
>
> *(Interview)*

Lack of safety and job training. According to the occupational chambers in Turkey, in the last decade, the number of work accidents, especially in the mining and construction sectors, has considerably increased (Evrensel, 2015). One critical factor for this increase, also mentioned by our interviewees, is lack of occupational safety and job training. The miners also point out lack of safety equipment. When the equipment is available, the miners are not provided with sufficient knowledge of its use and/or are not always permitted to use it. One miner explains:

> We have masks for the last five years. This is thanks to the work safety law. However, we have not been trained. I do not know how to use a mask. Besides, you are not allowed

to open the mask. You may be penalized for opening it. And, most of the masks do not function at all. They are outdated and low quality. They do not help you survive.

(Interview)

The employer thinks that safety measures slow down the production and thus does not properly implement them. There is no real safety in the mine. A miner, for example, mentions there is no underground emergency gathering area. He adds that in an accident, it is difficult to reach the onsite clinic due to the distance. The safety problem is heightened because the government does not properly monitor the mining site. Besides, the occupational safety expert does not carry out his inspection duty effectively because he is paid by the employer. Given these consistently unsafe practices, lack of job training seems usual. An engineer who worked in the mine before the disaster considers it as the biggest problem. He relates the high number of deaths in the disaster to this problem and mentions that the miners get fast and poor training for a day only. The training must continue at least for a week. This is rarely the case. The miners are generally required to sign a document after a day of training as if they got the whole training. Without proper training, the miners easily act in improper ways and become more vulnerable to accidents. Some miners, for example, want the job done fast, being unaware of the risk of death.

In this whole picture, the miners have little control over their employment context. A miner states that "workers are the last to speak for security issues" (interview). The existing safety measures and training programs are "for saving the day or the shift" (interview). The most important thing is to get the job done. Hence, the miners work under intense pressure to increase their productivity regardless of improper and unsafe employment conditions. Relative lack of training complements those conditions because proper training would rather empower the miners to individually or collectively challenge the same conditions. The miners' agency is further restrained by the union, the so-called collective organization of workers, which actually serves the individual interests of the employer, union directors, and uncle-chiefs in this context (uncle-chief, Dayıbaşı in Turkish, is a local term used by the miners to define the chiefs in the mine who informally recruit and then formally supervise the miners and whose informal power in many cases dominates the miners' other formal relations). The union increases the pressure on the miners. Deprived of an effective collective force, the miners are forced to deal with their problems individually. Yet, without proper training, they are not equipped to effectively formulate and communicate specific safety problems and thus exercise their individual agency. This strengthens the agency of the employer over and against that of the miners. Hence, the overall outcome of lack of an effective labor union and lack of safety and job training is general control over the agency of the miners, a ritualistic mechanism to reproduce the existing employment context as a risk boundary. Through this control, which deprives the miners of the power to change the existing context and redefine the boundary, the miners' daily relationships with the employer, uncle-chiefs, union directors, and other miners are contained and tamed. The relationships thus turn out to be risk rituals themselves as they continuously reestablish the imbalance of power between the miners and the employer. As a result, unemployment continues to be the ultimate risk for the miners, and the risks related to the relative absence of a labor union and of job training, which include unsafe conditions and low wages, are blurred by this ultimate risk. Within their unequal relationships working as risk rituals, the miners repeatedly experience the union as ineffective and training as ignored. The miners, who lack protection by the union and capacity by training, try to avoid the risk of unemployment through those submissive relationships. As individuals without any meaningful agency of change against the power of the employer, they are inevitably involved in the reproduction of the employment context characterized by the ongoing risk of unemployment.

Relational Networks

Family and consumption needs. The employment context of Soma is perhaps best analyzed in terms of the miners' relational networks. There are two sets of relations including those with the family household and within the workplace. The needs of family are more vital than any other consideration. The survival for the miners means the survival of the family. The most significant risk for the miner is an inability to maintain the unity of the family. Working in the mining industry in this sense appears as the best way since it makes the miner more or less able to support the family. One miner is clear on the risk:

> If you want to live here, you need to work in the mining sector. I have five children, how can I survive with 800 Turkish Liras; with the wage of a sales person. I pay rent for my house.
>
> *(Interview)*

They are aware of and yet try to endure the poor conditions of the mine for their families. They cannot risk the life of the family. One miner asserts that "the miners all know that they are oppressed and exploited" (interview). He adds that they are afraid of being fired because they have to pay the family debts and school expenses for their children.

"Cause of living" is a key phrase to understand the miners' sense of risk. This is a classical phrase in Turkish to demonstrate how respectful it is to work for the family. "Cause of living" not only identifies the current situation of the miners but also is a legitimate source to endure the same situation. Because it is ultimately about the family, it is uttered with an inherent legitimacy:

> There is pressure by the employer and union; people cannot even move. For, this is a cause of living. The workers say that they have children, they pay rent and credit debts. No one dares to resist.
>
> *(Interview)*

This is not to say that all the miners fear the employer. One miner says that this is the fear of living, which is very similar to cause of living. Both indicate the fact that the miners work mostly for a simple but essential reason, their family's basic consumption needs including daily bread, credit debts, school expenses, and rent payments. For the miners, the family and the mine are so much intertwined that the work and non-work are barely distinguishable in terms of risks. The miners make sense of the risks from within their family relationships, which routinely emphasize the survival of the family.

Employer and production pressures. The mine is hardly a place where people work without any sense of fear. The miners desire to work in safety. One miner thinks that a mine with proper security measures will be successful anyways. But, this is not the case for most mines in Soma. The biggest concern for the employer is not safety, but production. This is generally formulated by the miners as production pressure:

> Production will not stop. Those coal bands continuously operate. The transfer lasts for 24 hours. The bands stop only during the Feasts of the Ramadan and the Sacrifice. There is a lasting production pressure.
>
> *(Interview)*

It seems that while the family is the most important value for the miners, it is the coal production that is valued the most by the employer. The consumption pressure that the miners feel within the family relationships at home is parallel to the production pressure they feel within their relationships at work. An engineer argues that it is mainly an administrative pressure supported by a bonus system. The engineer says that "more coal means more money for the miners" (interview). However, the bonus system hardly pays anything to the miners. Due to the very tough conditions in the mine, most miners cannot complete the full-month work-day, which is the criterion to qualify for the bonus. But the same bonus system works very well for the uncle-chiefs, who usually occupy the position of foreman. The uncle-chiefs thus increase the pressure on the miners even though no miner under their supervision will be qualified for the bonus. The uncle-chiefs' authority is not simply formal, though. The uncle-chiefs are generally senior miners. They are well known to other miners and attributed a kind of traditional authority. In fact, most miners are hired through informal ways, generally based on local relationships or townsman ties, by a particular uncle-chief, who then becomes their formal supervisor. The chiefs' formal authority combined with informal power greatly intensifies the production pressure. This system of uncle-chiefs is maybe the most essential part of coal production. The engineer highlights the power of as well as the need for the uncle-chiefs:

> Why then dayıbaşı (uncle-chief) system is needed? Why does the firm not recruit by advertisement? To manage low-skilled workers with little or no education. When I yell at a miner, he may disregard me (as an engineer). When an uncle-chief yells at a miner, the miner worships him like a god.
>
> *(Interview)*

According to the engineer, the existence of this system is closely connected to the insufficient degree of professionalization in the mine. He argues that some uncle-chiefs are individually paid 50–60 thousand Turkish Liras (TL) a month (as opposed to 1.5–2 thousand TL for the miners) depending on the volume of coal production. This amounts to 600 thousand TL in a year, which is enough to train 1,000 workers. Yet, training, as discussed in the previous section, would empower the workers to question the existing employment context. Thus, the uncle-chief system is a necessary element of the current context to operationally substitute for training, render production pressure continuous, and harshly suppress any challenge from the miners.

Therefore, the relational networks composed of work and non-work fields are the third mechanism to support the employment context in Soma, which promotes the mining job. The miners are caught within both the family network shaped by basic consumption needs and work network formed by production pressures. These networks as a whole constitute a means to carry the effect of the context of mining employment as a risk boundary into the miners' specific relationships. The family relationships become risk rituals, which directly point to the necessity of being employed in a mine. The workplace relationships similarly function as risk rituals, which indirectly upholds the norm of mining employment as the miners continue to work despite the very difficult, often inhumane conditions. As the two networks are complementary, one in the consumption and the other one in the production side, there seems to be no escape for the miners from the effect of the employment context, which is experienced over and over within any relationship. The relationships with the uncle-chiefs are especially important, embodying the interdependence between family needs and employer demands. With their informal ties to the miners and families and with their formal workplace positions over the miners, the uncle-chiefs actually bridge the family and work networks. They have the power to keep the miners employed or unemployed, potentially changing the miners' status within both networks. Hence, they literally show how work and non-work are contextually interwoven to form a specific risk boundary, which seems to be irrational, yet operational. Moreover, through their informal and formal relationships with the miners, they are a key participant in risk rituals that reproduce the boundary. Supported by tightly coupled domestic and workplace networks and associated relationships of ritual, the risk boundary thus shapes the miners' meanings of mining risk to revolve around the norm of employment and risk of unemployment. The miners' repeated conversations on survival concerns and ongoing references to fear of subsistence reflect this effect of the boundary and norm of employment and, as discursive risk rituals, accompany their relational risk rituals at home and at work to reaffirm the boundary. The appendix provides additional representative examples of the miners' statements regarding relational networks and the other two contextual mechanisms.

Conclusion

This paper offers an analysis of how contextual dynamics influence the risk meanings of the coal miners after the deadliest industrial disaster of Turkey in the mining town of Soma. In our analysis, we employ Mary Douglas's (1966, 1992) concepts of boundary and ritual. While boundary refers to a social-economic context and the related distinction between acceptable and unacceptable norms and practices, ritual is a reaffirmation of this context as a boundary. This paper analyzes the employment context of mining production in Soma as such a boundary. It then identifies three ritualistic contextual mechanisms: (1) relative risk rationality embedded within unemployment intensity and lack of employment alternatives, (2) control over individual agency due to lack of effective labor union and lack of safety and job training, and (3) relational networks shaped by family needs and production pressures. The employment context, which overemphasizes the norm of being employed in the mine (and not in other sectors) and risk of being unemployed (or employed in other sectors), functions as a risk boundary through the contextual mechanisms of relative risk rationality, controls over individual agency, and relational networks, which convey the effect of the context into the daily relationships and discourses of the miners and turn them into risk rituals reproductive of the same context as a boundary and of a specific risk meaning associated with this boundary.

Therefore, the risk construction of the miners takes place within a specific employment context working as a risk boundary. This boundary differentiates between employment defined as having a job in the mine and unemployment defined as having a job in other sectors with the minimum wage level or no job at all. The main risk then is to be outside what this boundary defines as the norm and contextually unemployed. The risk in the mine seems to be different and independent from this risk of unemployment. Yet, the miners experience and give meaning to the mining risk within a particular context of employment, normalizing it as a secondary risk. The practical and moral burden of unemployment leads to this relative construction of risk in the mine. The three contextual mechanisms, which are themselves not rituals but ritualistic, facilitate and provide a ground for the relative construction of risk. It is a ground of risk rituals including ongoing, daily relationships, practices, and discourses, through which the miners reemphasize, reestablish, and reproduce a relative risk meaning embedded within the employment context of mining production, a dominant risk boundary, in Soma. The ritualistic mechanisms thus constitute a link between this boundary and related rituals or the context and practice.

The relationship between the risk in the mine and risk of unemployment shows that the miners do not give meaning to the mining risk in isolation. This is a relative construction and refers to a social-economic context. Unemployment (and sustainable employment) is a common problem in Soma and a major component of the context. The context seems to maintain mining employment vis-à-vis unemployment as a social norm, which is reflected in the miners' risk evaluations and meanings. Within this particular context of employment, the risk in the mine is acceptable as compared to the risk of unemployment. Meanwhile, risk management, which is actually another risk ritual used to clarify and confirm the norms of the current context, loses its material quality in spite of the existence of the risk with a catastrophic potential (already realized in the case) and turns out to be a symbolic activity, which simply reminds the miners of the risk boundary between the mining employment and unemployment. Lack of an effective labor union and safety/job training, both of which can be used as risk management tools, indicates this symbolic role of risk management in this context. Risk management does not focus on the risk in the mine. Rather, as a ritual, it tries to protect the current boundary that makes the same risk acceptable to the miners and their families. In this sense, the union is a symbolic entity in terms of safety, materially focusing on the protection of the existing status quo and associated interest groups including the mining firms and union leaders. This function of the union is not questioned by the miners who are afraid of unemployment and thus whose relationships with the union can hardly be termed as other than a ritual. Hence, the union is not forced to develop a representative capacity for the miners. On the contrary, it becomes one of the symbols of the status quo while symbolically representing the miners.

This paper argues that risk and related meanings cannot be properly analyzed outside the local social-economic context of the organizations producing those risks. In fact, what the miners do in the case is a local risk assessment. The miners go beyond the legal-technical assessments of business and government institutions oriented toward individual operations, and make sense of the risk in terms of local life practices and possibilities including mining employment, other minimum-wage employment, and unemployment. Similarly, risk management tools reflect the social-economic context as their boundary. They are effective to the extent permitted by this context, and they sometimes include simple symbolic responses to safety problems as in the case of Soma. In Soma and similar contexts, it is unlikely that risk management will be materially meaningful without considering local social-economic conditions and developing corresponding policies, for example, by creating other acceptable employment opportunities. This means that risk management is not simply a legal-technical issue that individual firms can solve. Successful risk management is a political activity that considers and, if necessary, transforms local conditions. Hence, the local experiences of those who are routinely exposed to risk should be the key input in risk evaluations and risk management formulations. Otherwise, risk disappears within the boundary and rituals of the social-economic context even though it will possibly be realized as a disaster sooner or later.

References

Beamish, T. D. (2001). Environmental hazard and institutional betrayal: Lay-public perceptions of risk in San Luis Obispo county oil spill. *Organization and Environment*, 14(1), 5–33.

Beamish, T. D. (2002). *Silent spill: The organization of an industrial crisis*. Cambridge, MA: The MIT Press.

Brown, A. D. (2000). Making sense of inquiry sensemaking. *Journal of Management Studies*, 37(1), 45–75.

Brown, A. D. (2003). Authoritative sensemaking in a public inquiry report. *Organization Studies*, 25(1), 95–112.

Denzin, N. K., & Lincoln, Y. S. (2000). Introduction: The discipline and practice of qualitative research. In N. K. Denzin & Y. S. Lincoln (Eds.), *Handbook of qualitative research* (pp. 1–32). London: Sage.

DİSK-Türkiye Devrimci İşçi Sendikaları Konfederasyonu Araştırma Enstitüsü (The Research Institute of the Confederation of Progressive Trade Unions of Turkey) (2016). *İşsizlik ve İstihdam Raporu, Kasım 2016*. İstanbul.

Douglas, M. (1966). *Purity and danger: An analysis of the concepts of pollution and taboo*. New York: Praeger.

Douglas, M. (1973). *Natural symbols: Explorations in cosmology*. New York: Pantheon Books.

Douglas, M. (1975). *Implicit meanings: Essays in anthropology*. London: Routledge and Paul.

Douglas, M. (1992). *Risk and blame: Essays in cultural theory*. London: Routledge.

Douglas, M., & Wildavsky, A. (1982). *Risk and culture*. Berkeley: University of California Press.

Dunbar, R. L. M., & Garud, R. (2009). Distributed knowledge and indeterminate meaning: The case of the Columbia Shuttle Flight. *Organization Studies*, 30(4), 397–421.

Elliot, D., & Smith, D. (2007). Cultural readjustment after crisis: Regulation and learning from crisis within UK soccer industry. *Journal of Management Studies*, 43(2), 289–317.

Evrensel. (2015, January 26). Sendika istatistiklerine göre iş kazası sayısı yüzde 291 arttı.

Gamson, W. A., & Modigliani, A. (1989). Media discourse and public opinion on nuclear power: A constructionist approach. *American Journal of Sociology*, 95(1), 1–37.

Gephart, R. P. (1992). Sensemaking, communicative distortion, and the logic of public inquiry legitimation. *Industrial and Environmental Crisis Quarterly*, 6(2), 115–135.

Gephart, R. P. (1993). The textual approach: Risk and blame in disaster sensemaking. *Academy of Management Journal*, 38(6), 1465–1514.

Gephart, R. P. (1997). Hazardous measures: An interpretive textual analysis of quantitative sensemaking during crises. *Journal of Organizational Behavior*, 18, 583–622.

Gephart, R. P. (2004). From the editors: Qualitative research and the Academy of Management Journal. *Academy of Management Journal*, 47(4), 454–462.

Gephart, R. P. (2007). Crisis sensemaking in the public inquiry. In C. M. Pearson, C. Roux-Dufort, & J. A. Clair (Eds.), *International handbook of organizational crisis management* (pp. 123–160). Thousand Oaks, CA: Sage.

Gephart, R. P., & Pitter, R. (1993). Organization basis of industrial accidents in Canada. *Journal of Management Inquiry*, 2(3), 238–252.

Gephart, R. P., & Pitter, R. (1995). Textual analysis in technology research: An investigation of the management of technology risk. *Technology Studies*, 2(2), 325–356.

Gephart, R. P., Steier, L., & Lawrence, T. B. (1990). Cultural rationalities in crisis sensemaking: A study of a public inquiry into a major industrial accident. *Industrial Crisis Quarterly*, 4(1), 27–48.

Gephart, R. P., Van Maanen, J., & Oberlechner, T. (2009). Organizations and risk in late modernity. *Organization Studies*, 30(2–3), 141–155.

Glaser, B. G., & Strauss, A. L. (1967). *The discovery of grounded theory: Strategies for qualitative research*. Chicago, IL: Aldine Publishing Company.

Habermas, J. (1975). *Legitimation crisis*. Boston: Beacon Press.

Hürriyet. (2014, October 28). Türkiye en kötü sendilaşma oranı ile OECD sonuncusu.

Jasanoff, S. (1988). Judicial gatekeeping in the management of hazardous technologies. *Journal of Management Studies*, 25(4), 353–371.

Kamoche, K., & Maguire, K. (2011). Pit sense: Appropriation of practice-based knowledge in a UK coalmine. *Human Relations*, 64(5), 725–744.

KDK-Kamu Denetçiliği Kurumu (Ombudsman) (The Public Inspection Institution) (2014). Kömür Madenciliğinde İş Sağlığı ve Güvenliği Özel Raporu.

Lane, C., & Quack, S. (1999). The social dimensions of risk: Bank financing of SMEs in Britain and Germany. *Organization Studies*, 20(6), 987–1010.

Nelkin, D. (1988). Risk reporting and the management of industrial crisis. *Journal of Management Studies*. 25(4), 341–351.

Öke, M. K., & Kurt, S. (2003). Yeni süreç ve sendikaların temsil sorunu. In A. H. Köse, F. Şenses, & E. Yeldan (Eds.), *İktisat Üzerine Yazılar I: Küresel Düzen, Birikim, Devlet ve Sınıflar* (pp. 191–218). İstanbul: İletişim.

Perrow, C. (1984). *Normal accidents: Living with high-risk technologies*. New York: Basic Books.

Perrow, C. (2006). Culture, structure, and risk. In I. K. Richter, S. Berking, & R. Muller-Schmid (Eds.), *Risk society and the culture of precaution* (pp. 47–58). New York: Palgrave MacMillan.

Rasmussen, J. (2010). Enabling selves to conduct themselves safely: Safety committee discourse as governmentality in practice. *Human Relations*, 64(3), 459–478.

Shrivastava, P. (1995). Ecocentric management for a risk society. *Academy of Management Review*, 20(1), 118–137.

Silverman, D. (2006). *Interpreting qualitative data: Methods for analysing talk, text, and interaction.* London: Sage.

Stake, R. E. (2000). Qualitative case studies. In N. K. Denzin & Y. S. Lincoln (Eds.), *Handbook of qualitative research* (pp. 443–466). London: Sage.

Stallings, R. A. (1990). Media discourse and the social construction of risk. *Social Problems*, 37(1), 80–95.

Stein, M. (2011). A culture of mania: A psychoanalytic view of the incubation of the 2008 credit crisis. *Organization*, 18(2), 173–186.

Sullivan-Taylor, B., & Wilson, D. C. (2009). Managing the threat of terrorism in British travel and leisure organizations. *Organization Studies*, 30(2–3), 251–276.

TBB-Türkiye Barolar Birliği (The Union of Turkish Bar Associations) (2014). *Soma Maden Faciası raporu.* Ankara.

TMMOB-Türk Mühendis ve Mimar Odaları Birliği (The Union of Chambers of Turkish Engineers and Architects) (2014). Soma Maden Kazası Raporu. Ankara.

TMMOB-Türk Mühendis ve Mimar Odaları Birliği (The Union of Chambers of Turkish Engineers and Architects) & Türk Tabipler Birliği (The Turkish Medical Association) (2016). Soma Maden Faciası İnceleme Raporu. Ankara.

Tepav-Türkiye Ekonomi Politikaları Araştırma Vakfı (The Economic Policies Research Foundation of Turkey) (2014). Kömür madeni işletmelerinde verimlilik ve iş güvenliği. Ankara.

Topal, Ç. (2009). The construction of general public interest: Risk, legitimacy, and power in a public hearing. *Organization Studies*, 30(2–3), 277–300.

Tsoukas, H. (1999). David and goliath in the risk society: Making sense of the conflict between shell and Greenpeace in the North Sea. *Organization*, 6(3), 499–528.

Weick, K. E. (1988). Enacted sensemaking in crisis situations. *Journal of Management Studies*, 25(4), 305–317.

Weick, K. E. (1993). The collapse of sensemaking in organizations: The Mann Gulch disaster. *Administrative Science Quarterly*, 38(4), 628–652.

Zyglidopoulos, S., & Fleming, P. (2011). Corporate accountability and the politics of visibility in late modernity. *Organization*, 18(5), 691–706.

APPENDIX

Illustrative Statements on Contextual Mechanisms

Relative risk rationality	Unemployment intensity	"There is a political pressure (over the miners) to vote for the ruling the party. As a result, the workers have the opinion that if the ruling party is gone, they will be unemployed and cannot find a job."
		"The members of the ruling party visit the mines and talk to the miners. The managers of the firm tell (as a threat) that if the ruling party will not win the elections again, the firm will be shut down."
		"Those who find a job in the mine keep their mouth shut as they fear to be fired."
		"The only reason is that the mine solves the problem of unemployment."
		"Even though 300 miners are killed here, new miners come from Zonguldak and Ordu (mining cities in the north of Turkey) and there are already so many unemployed in Soma."
	Lack of alternatives	"If there was any other opportunity for employment, I am sure they will not prefer mining."
		"Mining in Soma means the source of life. If you want to live here, you will go down the mine; you do not have any chance and any other alternative."
		"Under the current economic structure, there is nothing but coal as a source of income."
		"They do not make money from agriculture. The people living here have nothing other than mining."
		"He and his wife work, both earning the minimum wage (in other jobs). In the mine, I myself make the same amount of money that both make together."
Control over individual agency	Lack of an effective labor union	"Trade-unionist is the man of the company not of the state (public authority)."
		"When you say the Union, you actually refer to three bases: the state, the firm, and the union. These three work together to prevent workers from getting organized."
		"What can you expect from a union whose director or representative stands and shouts at the production line 'Give me more coal'?"
		"What did the union do when the firm fabricated evidence of absence or disobedience to punish the miners?"
		"The union could have kept those miners from entering the mine. It had the authority not to let them in. What did it do? It acted with the employer."

(Continued)

211

	Lack of safety and job training	"This huge number of deaths is due to lack of training. They are not trained enough. They are given a three-day initial training. In Soma Coal Enterprises, this is one day only." "It is due to lack of inspection. If the workers had training and if the success of this training was inspected, it would be very different." "After a day of training, they go down into the mine. They continue to work in the mine on the next two days as well. On the fourth day, they take an exam for formality only." "There is nothing in the name of training. There is no training, exercise, or something like that. A one-day training is for show only. They give you a file to sign that you read and understand the file. Then, you go down and mine." "Can you give training to a miner leaving his night shift? Can a job training take 15–20 minutes?"
Relational networks	Family and consumption needs	"We do a heavy work. They give 1500 TL. How can I live with it? I give 400 TL for rent. There are two children at school. That is, we live under difficult conditions." "The worker says 'I can't lose my bread; I have a child. I live in a rented apartment and I have a credit debt. Who will pay it?'" "There are 100 thousand people living in Soma and 13–15 thousand of them are miners. Considering the families of these miners, we have 45 thousand people living on the wages from the mines." "The miners should do something for the future. If not for themselves, they should do for their children." "They fear that they might be fired. They have debts and children attending the school."
	Employer and production pressures	"There is an administrative pressure. There is always an enormous pressure over the workers for the coal extraction." "It is production pressure. If I stop the production line due to a problem production decreases. There is competition between the shifts for example. We ask those leaving their shift about how much coal they extracted and we are required to extract more." "They died one by one. We knew most of the reasons of why they died. Excessive production, excessive production." "Each uncle-chief has 100–200 miners and earns 50 TL per miner. In addition, as the coal production increases, the uncle-chief gets his share from the increase, earning on the labor of the miners. The hiring and firing of the miners is completely at his discretion." "As long as there is production pressure, there is no way to keep that danger away."

13

SYSTEMIC PLANETARY RISKS
Implications for Organization Studies

Gail Whiteman and Amanda Williams

Environmental risks to humans are not new – history is replete with examples of societies that collapsed alongside ecosystem change (Diamond, 2005). We know that numerous societies have suffered because of environmental pollution from organizational operations (King & Lenox, 2000; Maguire & Hardy, 2009, Maguire & Hardy, 2013) and from industrial accidents (Gephart, 1984: Tsoukas, 1999).

However, the scale of environmental risks has changed over the course of the 20th century from locale-specific threats to those arising at a planetary level (Rockström et al., 2009a, 2009b; Whiteman, Walker, & Perego, 2013). Natural scientists now estimate that four of the nine essential planetary processes needed to sustain life have exceeded safe thresholds and now represent significant risks to humanity (Rockström et al., 2009a, 2009b; Steffen et al., 2015a). In particular, climate change and land-system change are well past safe thresholds and have entered the zone of increasing risk where the rate of biodiversity loss and phosphorus and nitrogen release pose high levels of planetary risk. In such a world, organizational "processes of risk calculation used in modern society fail to work in risk society because risks are no longer localized and are long term in nature" (Gephart, Van Maanen, & Oberlechner, 2009, p. 145).

Natural scientists further argue that there are solid data to suggest that organizational and economic activities over time have been the driving force behind the planetary shift away from the stable Holocene period into what has been called the Anthropocene (Steffen et al., 2015b) – what Nobel Prize winner Paul Crutzen and colleagues describe as period of time commencing with the industrial revolution where human impact on the environment became the paramount force of change (Steffen, Crutzen, & McNeill, 2007). The central role of organizations within these shifts seems likely.

However, the complex role of organizations as collective contributors to and recipients of systemic risks at the planetary level remains underexplored (Winn, Kirchgeorg, Griffiths, Linnenluecke, & Gunther, 2011). While the organizational risk management literature is vast, organizational studies of risk seldom integrate environmental threats into conceptual frameworks (cf. Bundy, Pfarrer, Short, & Coombs, 2017). In addition, the handful of studies on environmental risk within the corporate sustainability literature are firm-specific and focus more on supply chain or operational risks from specific natural events – in terms of extreme weather (e.g. Linnenluecke & Griffiths, 2013)– or risks to the natural world through organizational accidents such as Exxon Valdez (Shrivastava, 1994) or Deepwater Horizon

(Bozeman, 2011). Integration of planetary risks to, and from, collections of organizational actors over time is lacking.

The aim of this chapter is to address these gaps. We ask the question, 'How can researchers of organization theory collaborate with managers of organizations to better conceptualize systemic ecosystems risks and develop strategies to insure these are addressed?' Building upon advances in Earth System Science, we present a framework for analyzing systemic planetary risks and consider the role of collections of organizational actors. Our chapter is organized as follows: we first set the broader context by reviewing the literature on environmental risk at the planetary scale and on global business discussions on risk. We then review the organizational literature on environmental risks, and identify the gaps in the organizational literature evident from the issue addressed in systemic research on environmental risk at the planetary scale. To help address these gaps in our understanding of organizations and risk, we present a framework that encapsulates a systemic view of social-ecological risk and organizations. We close with a discussion of future research needs.

The Landscape of Planetary Risk

To support more effective risk management at the global level, earth system science indicates that there are nine key global ecosystem processes that collectively interact to create a 'safe operating space for humanity' (Rockström et al., 2009a; Whiteman et al., 2013). These processes include climate change, biochemical flows of phosphorus and nitrogen, freshwater use, land-system change, biosphere integrity (biodiversity); ocean acidification, stratospheric ozone depletion, atmospheric aerosol loading (air pollution); and novel entities (chemical pollution) (Figure 13.1).

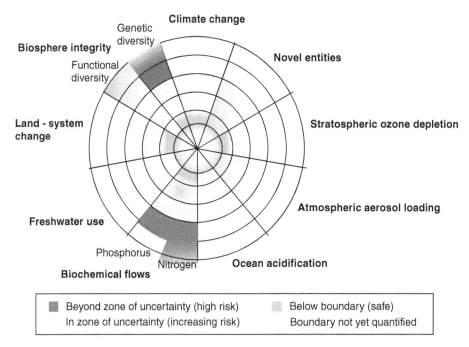

Figure 13.1 Planetary Boundaries and Safe Thresholds

Source: Steffen et al. Planetary Boundaries: Guiding Human Development on a Changing Planet, *Science*, 16 January 2015a. (Credit: F. Pharand-Deschênes /Globaïa).

The nine boundaries are dynamically interconnected, so risks in one area will trigger increasing risks in others. An analysis of systemic risk factors at the planetary level, which captures both spatial and temporal dimensions, is thus important. For some parts of the world, including the Arctic and drought-ridden parts of Africa, the United States and Australia, climate change impacts are happening already (2018) (droughts, floods, fire, etc.; cf. IPCC, 2015) alongside degradation of land, water, and air pollution (see Le De and Shrestha, 2018, this volume). In other parts of the world, planetary risks are the most serious under future scenarios – thus, risks may be mitigated to some extent if deep de-carbonization occurs in the near-term. While the highest risks of climate change or ocean acidification have not yet materialized into catastrophic tipping points, the window of opportunity to address the increasing (and significant) risks of climate change is closing fast (Figueres et al., 2017). Thus, planetary risk management requires that the world deal urgently with the emissions crisis in the near-term, in order to provide us with a safer space to tackle other entrenched ecosystem problems.

Scholars have identified the period since World War II as the "Great Acceleration," whereby industrial processes dramatically accelerated their impact on the structure and functioning of key ecosystem resources including rapidly increasing levels of carbon dioxide, nitrous oxide, methane, stratospheric ozone loss, surface temperature, ocean acidification, tropical forest loss, and terrestrial biosphere degradation (Steffen et al., 2015b). While causality has yet to be conclusively proven, given the complexity of these effects, it is highly plausible that cumulative and collective organizational action is correlated with or related to systemic degradation of the planet's key ecosystem processes. Furthermore, these human-led impacts have, over time, introduced a new landscape of planetary risk that poses complex and uncertain threats for humanity and for the organizations that collectively make up the world as we know it (see Rockström et al., 2009a, 2009b; Steffen et al., 2015a; Whiteman et al., 2013). Natural science data thus support the social science argument (Beck, 1992; Beck & Holzer, 2007) on risk societies: that "the success of the wealth-generating industrial society has produced a situation in which the risks and problematic by-products of wealth generation have become the new basic organizing principle and a key concern for society (Lupton 1999b, p. 59)" (in Gephart et al., 2009, p. 145). We argue that this is an area ripe for conceptual and empirical development for organization studies.

Organizational Literature on Risk and the Natural Environment

The literature on risks and the natural environment has shown that organizations can reduce vulnerability to risks by preparing for potential disturbances and by developing coordination techniques within organizations and with other stakeholders (Williams, Gruber, Sutcliffe, Shepherd, & Zhao, 2017). Two main streams of research explain how managers prevent crises through effective risk management. The internal perspective focuses on organizational preparedness and how managers build capabilities to manage unexpected events (Bundy et al., 2017). For example, research on high-reliability organizations demonstrates that effectively correcting errors and remaining flexible can prevent crisis (Weick & Sutcliffe, 2001). The external perspective suggests that relationships with stakeholders influence managerial capacity to manage risks (Bundy et al., 2017). Relationships with stakeholders can provide the knowledge and resources necessary to facilitate recovery after a crisis (Williams & Shepherd, 2016; Le De & Shrestha, Chapter 3).

A review of the management literature suggests: (1) the natural environment is notably absent from leading organizational risk frameworks (see, e.g. Figure 1 in Bundy et al., 2017,

Table 13.1 Overview of Organizational Risk Literature Concerning the Natural Environment

Risk type	Studies focused on threats <u>from</u> the natural environment <u>to</u> organizations	Studies focused on organizational threats <u>to</u> the natural environment	Systemic studies examining the feedback loops across organizations and between socio-ecological systems
Discrete events	- Mann Gulch (Weick, 1993) - Victoria Bushfires (Linnenluecke & Griffiths, 2013) - Climate risks (Beerkhout et al., 2006; Beermann, 2011) - Droughts and floods (Gasbarro, Rizzi, & Frey 2016) - Pollution (Dobler, Lajili, & Zéghal 2014) - Hurricanes (Delp, Podolsky, & Aguilar 2009)	- Bhopal (Shrivastava, 1992) - Oil spills (Pauchant & Mitroff, 1992) - Fukushima - Other toxic releases - High risk technologies (Gephart, 2004)	- Firm contribution to climate change and climate impacts on the firm (Weinhofer & Busch, 2012)
Processes over time	- Supply chain risks (Hofmann, Busse, Bode, & Henke 2014) - Chemical industry supply chain risk (Kleindorfer & Saad, 2005) - Mann Gulch (Whiteman & Cooper 2011) - Social and environmental practices (Ortiz-de-Mandojana & Bansal, 2016) - Climate change (Hahn, Reimsbach, & Schiemann 2015; Pinkse & Gasbarro, 2016)	- Climate risks (Kolk & Pinkse, 2005) - Sustainable energy (Kondoh, 2009) - Eco-certification (Melo & Wolf, 2005)	- Toledo water supply and Lake Erie phosphorus bloom (Whiteman & Kennedy, 2016)

p. 1665) due to the implicit assumption of a stable natural environment, or one that faces linear change, (2) risk studies from the corporate sustainability literature are either focused on episodic threats from natural environment (e.g., through extreme weather) or are focused on organizationally produced risks to the natural environment through industrial accidents, and (3) there are limited studies that examine systemic feedback loops between organizations and dynamic ecosystem processes facing threats (see Table 13.1). In Table 13.1, we provide an overview of the literature along two dimensions. First, we examine if environmental risks are considered at a discrete point in time or a risk that unfolds as a process over time and space. Then we consider the directionality of the threat.

On the positive side, organizational researchers recognize that numerous companies, including the insurance sector, have begun to seriously consider the threat of climate change over the last ten years, but have failed to integrate climate change risk into corporate governance structures (Thistlethwaite, 2012; Thistlethwaite & Wood, 2087). Despite a relatively late recognition of the need for corporate sustainability research to focus on climate change (Goodall, 2008), there is now a good understanding of drivers of carbon reporting and lobbying, clear knowledge of institutional drivers of carbon accounting regimes, evidence of financial risks for a firm from climate change (Hahn et al., 2015), and a growing understanding of the physical risks from climate change such as those from extreme weather (Linnenluecke & Griffiths, 2013; Weinhofer & Busch, 2013). There is also continuing research focus on managing the risks from natural disasters or extreme weather events – fires, floods, drought – both in terms of supply chain risk and response (Linnenluecke & Griffiths, 2013) and philanthropic disaster response (Muller & Whiteman, 2009). In addition, the organizational adaptation literature has focused on building organizational resilience in the face of changing climate conditions (Linnenluecke & Griffiths, 2010; Williams, T. A. et al., 2017). Collectively, these studies provide new insights into risk management, noting that organizations can build resilience and adaptive capacity by creating network responses and sensemaking capabilities and encouraging flexibility (Linnenluecke & Griffiths, 2013).

Research also shows that risk perception is an important factor in determining a firm's selective attention to climate change risks; however, firms tend to focus on short-term risks that are of immediate concern for business decisions (Pinkse & Gasbarro, 2016). A temporal bias thus prevents firms from considering risks that will materialize in the distant future (Pinkse & Gasbarro, 2016). Managers tend to overlook risks when the temporal and spatial attributes, or scale of the processes related to the risk being observed, are not aligned with their cognition (Bansal, Kim, & Wood, 2017). Corporations that operate in more dynamic and competitive environments are more likely to implement adaptation strategies in the face of climate risks (Berkhout, Hertin, & Gann 2006). Companies that perceive long-term organizational survival is threatened by climate change are more likely to invest in risky environmental technologies to enhance organizational resilience (Kolk & Pinkse, 2008). Climate change may jeopardize long-term organizational survival. Nuclear power reduces carbon dioxide emissions but increases the nuclear threats such as exposure to radioactivity creating a risk tradeoff (Kondoh, 2009). In addition, if nuclear waste storage zones are in geographic areas which may be affected by rising sea levels or extreme weather, then new risks may arise.

To date, there is little crossover between the corporate sustainability literature and the organizational literature on risk and crisis management, which implicitly assume a stable natural environment (cf. Gephart et al., 2009; Bundy et al., 2017). Overall, most studies are firm- and industry-focused, and few, if any, attempt to analyze cumulative, interrelated systemic risks at global, regional, and local levels over time (Whiteman et al., 2013). Integrative frameworks of organizational crisis and risk implicitly assume a stable (and therefore invisible) natural environment, which is not identified as an explicit variable or dynamic context shaping risk (Bundy et al., 2017). Firms' individual and collective actions also contribute significantly to global warming and other planetary boundaries, and co-create the threats that increase risks to their operations and financial stability. In the next section, we propose an integrative framework (Figure 13.3) to help organizational scholars examine feedback loops across organizations and between social-ecological systems.

A Framework for Analyzing Systemic Planetary Risks

The outstanding question for organizational scholars is how can we contribute to the conversation about systemic planetary risks? The answer, from our perspective, is threefold:

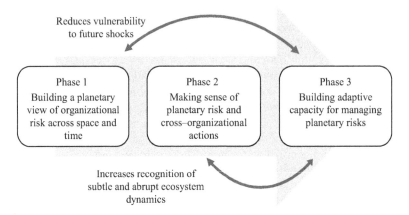

Figure 13.2 A Framework for Analyzing Systemic Planetary Risks

we can incorporate planetary risk into our view of organizational risk; second, we can help organizations make sense of planetary risks; and third, we can identify how managers can build more adaptive capacity through systemic risk management programs across scale, and across organizational actors. To do so, we offer a framework (summarized in Figure 13.2) which consists of three iterative phases (1) building a planetary view of organizational risk across temporal and spatial scales, (2) making sense of organizational actions in the context of planetary risks, and (3) building adaptive capacity to mitigate planetary risks.

Phase 1: Building a Planetary View of Organizational Risk across Temporal and Spatial Scales

Risks from climate change, lack of fresh water, land use pressures, air pollution (aerosol loading), ocean acidification, and chemical pollution (or more broadly, the release of hazardous entities) pose significant material risks to companies and societies – and critically can be tied back to economic activity across companies and organizations over temporal and spatial scales (Steffen et al., 2015a; Clift et al., 2017). Planetary risks are systemic in nature and need to be examined at local, regional, and global levels (Steffen et al., 2015a; Whiteman et al., 2013).

We therefore suggest that risk management decisions today need to be influenced by an understanding of these ecosystem risks which are interconnected at global, regional, and local scales overtime. Figure 13.3 depicts safe and unsafe risk pathways in relation to planetary boundaries, shows trends in global, regional, and local risks over time, and provides the background for the discussion that follows.

Companies should take a long-term perspective to evaluate which risks could materialize at different time scales, and assess both the materiality of those risks to firm operations, and unintended externalities that arise from organizational actions which may amplify planetary risks. Integrating the planetary boundaries framework to risk management ensures that a more systemic approach is adopted which incorporates cross-organizational, cumulative organizational actions. This also reflects the growing systemic perspective of global economic actors, such as the World Economic Forum which argues that "[a] key characteristic of global risks is their potential systemic nature – they have the potential to affect an entire system, as opposed to individual parts and components" (WEF, 2014).

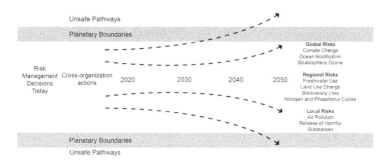

Figure 13.3   Cross-organizational View of Long-term Planetary Risks over Time and Space

The planetary boundaries framework (Figure 13.1) outlines the nine key ecosystem processes which collectively delineate the safe space for humanity. By incorporating this framework into our discipline, a key implication is to explicitly consider how organizational actions contribute (or detract) from pathways which may (or may not) lead to a safe space for humanity (Rockström et al., 2009a, 2009b, 2013; Whiteman et.al., 2013; Steffen et al., 2015a). Safe pathways are those that mitigate planetary risks. Unsafe pathways are those that (intentionally or unintentionally) amplify planetary risks.

A systemic perspective requires a cross-organizational collective view of planetary risks over both time and space. Issues of scale are important when managers identify risks (Bansal et al., 2017). We discuss these in more detail in the following section.

Temporal Scales

Temporal scale is "the patterned variations in processes over time" (Bansal et al., 2017, p. 12). Long-term organizational survival depends on managers capacity to manage intertemporal tradeoffs (Bansal & DesJardine, 2014). Inability to manage short-term and long-term risks exposes the firm to risks across scales (Bansal & DesJardine, 2014). Figure 13.3 adopts a ten-year time interval (up to 2050) given that global societal and economic risks have been defined as "an occurrence that causes significant negative impact for several countries and industries over a time frame of up to 10 years" (WEF, 2014). In Figure 13.3, we have suggested time intervals including 2020, 2030, 2040, and 2050. Most of these intervals have coincided with existing globally agreed-upon frameworks and scientific targets. The year 2020 has been proposed as the turning point for bending the global emissions curve in order to achieve the climate targets set by the Paris Agreement (Figueres et al., 2017). In addition, the UN Sustainable Development Goals (SDGs), agreed upon by 193 member states of the UN, set the global development agenda until 2030. The 17 SDGs and 169 targets set broad social and environmental goals. If seriously implemented by governments, regulations and investment flows are expected to align with the SDGs. To account for future risks and opportunities, managers should map their current operations against the SDGs and align their strategy with the SDGs. The SDG Compass, a guide for business action on the SDGs, provides advice for companies to understand the impacts of the SDGs (GRI, UNGC, & WBCSD, 2015). The guide suggests identifying high-impact areas and then evaluating the risks and opportunities that the prioritized areas present. The guide also identifies specific open-access tools and indicators for each SDG that can be useful during the process. By 2050, climate scientists agree that net zero emissions should be reached (Rockström et al., 2017).

Our framework explicitly identifies these four intervals given the need for firm behavior to collectively be aligned with global agreements and scientific thresholds to mitigate long-term social-ecological risks. Managers can, in collaboration with scientists, further identify and refine time intervals such that they are most pertinent and relevant for firm-specific operations. Nevertheless, the collective systemic targets and time frames remain relevant for each firm as it operates within the collective behaviors of multiple firms and societies. In order to effectively and robustly evaluate future risks to and from the natural environment, managers should also account for cross-scale feedbacks over time. For example, infrastructure decisions made by countries, cities, and companies cannot be assessed without a systemic appreciation of risks from the natural environment. There are some encouraging signs that this approach is being applied in cities like London, which are evaluating green infrastructure decisions on transport, water, and energy to both accommodate a growing population and make the city more resilient to the effects of climate change. In general, our framework suggests that organizational decisions made today will positively and negatively impact social-ecological systems over time and across different geographic scales. If the feedback from these decisions is not accounted for today, organizations will be left vulnerable to unexpected future shocks.

Spatial Scales

Achieving sustainability requires addressing interactions across spatial scales (Starik & Rands, 1995). Spatial scale is "the geographical area in which the dominant process(es) of interest manifest" (Bansal et al. 2017, p. 12). In Figure 13.3, we have identified a number of organizational risks that materialize at global, regional, and local spatial scales related to the planetary boundaries processes. In order to do so, we build upon prior transdisciplinary work that considers the spatial implications of planetary risks to organizational behavior (Whiteman et al., 2013).

Using a spatial application of the planetary boundaries concept to organizations in the natural environment, Whiteman et al. (2013, p. 324) show that "corporate sustainability is anchored within an analysis of how the company (and industry at a higher scale) affects all nine boundary processes within specific bounded geographies – at the local, regional, continental, and planetary level." One empirical example of this type of approach is an organizational analysis of cumulative cross-scale risks from phosphorus overload in Lake Erie (Whiteman & Kennedy, 2016). This study used the Lake Erie water system as the focal unit of analysis rather than starting with specific organizational actors (e.g., farmers or agricultural companies). A spatial and temporal analysis necessitates a broader investigation of the biophysical processes surrounding Lake Erie as well as the collective and cumulative actions of multiple actors shaping the agricultural sector (e.g., regulators, seed manufacturers, farmers, fertilizer manufacturers, retailers, transportation), as well as those from shipping, recreation, retail, and water management.

Figure 13.3 provides examples of risks that may arise at different spatial scales including global, regional, and local (summarized on the right side of Figure 13.3). Thus, cross-organizational actions must simultaneously consider spatial and temporal scales across social, ecological, economic, and organizational subsystems. A processual view collapses the notion that "crisis" can be avoided, but rather it is part of a complex process unfolding with risks to be limited or contained (Whiteman & Kennedy, 2016, Williams, T. A. et al., 2017).

Phase 2: Making Sense of Planetary Risk and Organizational Actions

Organizational studies indicate that knowledge and information about risks is important for framing and deciding upon courses of action (Sullivan-Taylor & Wilson, 2009).

When information is scarce, the level of risk and exposure to the risk increases (Sullivan-Taylor & Wilson, 2009).

Encouragingly, "real-world" discussions of global risk have begun to make sense of planetary risks. For example, each year, the World Economic Forum (WEF) issues an influential report on Global Risk. Based upon feedback from 750 global experts, WEF identifies the top risks facing world leaders, including the private sector (WEF, 2017). For much of its history, the WEF Global Risk Report has short-listed risks from civil unrest, war, market turbulence, and supply chain disruption. But in recent years, the global risk landscape changed, and WEF's reports (e.g., 2017) recognize the natural environment and extreme weather as the source of the top risk to humankind – the threat of climate change was ranked as the #1 risk facing the world because of both the growing likelihood of this occurring and the increasing scope of the potential impacts. "Research indicates that unbridled anthropogenic climate change would be most likely to play out in a disruptive and irreparable way" (Schellnhuber, Rahmstorf, & Winkelmann, 2016, p. 650). WEF actively supports work on other planetary risks like water, and has convened numerous workshops on the implications of planetary boundaries for various sectors, nations, and within various types of organizations (Rockström, personal communication).

Economic discussions of planetary risks are also a topic within the corporate boardroom. Unilever, for instance, has explicitly considered planetary boundaries risks to and from their value chain (Clift et al., 2017). Planetary boundary processes such as climate change, fresh water use, and nitrogen and phosphorus flows pose significant risks to food security at local and regional scales.

At the same time, such discussions remain more well developed on single-topic issues such as ozone depletion or the climate change front. For instance, Mark Carney, Governor of the Bank of England and Chair of the G-20 Financial Stability Board, argues that climate change poses physical, liability, and transition risks to markets and firms (Carney, 2016, pp. 2–4). More work is required to integrate the systemic nature of planetary risk into these arenas and to more effectively make sense of complex feedbacks across different spatial and temporal scales. Weinhofer and Busch (2012) suggest, for instance, that future research should examine a two-dimensional risk perspective on climate change including both an "inside-out" perspective which acknowledges the firm's contributions to climate change and an "outside-in" perspective which acknowledges the impact of climate risks on the firm. However, they do not discuss the interaction of inter-related risks over time.

We also know that risk sensemaking is critical to understanding the threat of high-risk technologies to the natural environment (Gephart, 2004). In general, organizational sensemaking contributes to effective crisis and risk management by helping organizational actors identify and develop a shared understanding and set of responses to emerging risks (cf. Williams, T. A. et al., 2017). But research on ecological sensemaking further suggests that ecological crises occur when individuals – and by extension, organizations – are disembedded from the natural environment (Whiteman & Cooper, 2000). "To the unseasoned, the dynamics of nature may appear as undifferentiated flux, but to the more experienced, this ecological flux contains important raw data that can signal danger" (Whiteman & Cooper, 2011, p. 891). Ecological sensemaking is "the process by which actors identify and make sense of complex ecological systems that unfold over space and time" (p. 890). Proponents of ecological sensemaking "explicitly recognize that the natural environment consists of material and physical elements" (p. 889) and the ability to make sense of subtle and abrupt ecosystemic dynamics across time and space can enhance organizational resilience at both the individual and collective levels: "if local actors are not routinely engaging in ecological sensemaking, and/or this expertise is not effectively transferred 'across scale,' hidden vulnerability can escalate into crisis" (p. 908).

Here we argue that cross-organizational sensemaking of planetary risks can be facilitated by combining local data on ecosystem change, and by using science-based boundary objects to formulate a collective strategy to address pressing global environmental issues. Framing of global systemic risks may also be an avenue for organizational scholars to pursue. Bundy et al. (2017, p. 11), for instance, show that "leaders who frame crises as threats react more emotionally and are more limited in their efforts, while leaders who frame crises as opportunities are more open-minded and flexible."

Phase 3: Building Adaptive Capacity for Managing Planetary Risks

We explained how organizational risks in our complex planetary system can be understood, and we now suggest how managers could collectively build adaptive capacity to cope with long-term systemic risks.

When levels of uncertainty are high and information is scarce, management techniques which emphasize prediction and planning are insufficient (Sullivan-Taylor & Wilson, 2009). In order to cope with systemic long-term risks arising from transgressed planetary boundaries, managers can build long-term adaptive capacity to systemic ecosystem risks. A key implication of Figure 13.3 is for organization scholars to consider the interrelated risks of other social-ecological systems, such as biodiversity, nitrogen/phosphorus use, and ozone depletion on organizational adaptation strategies (Whiteman et al., 2013), over time (Bansal & DesJardine, 2014). An example of this approach to organizational studies of risk is found in Whiteman and Kennedy (2016) in their systemic analysis of the phosphorus threat facing the city of Toledo, Ohio.

The adaptive capacity of organizations within nested social-ecological systems is one of the key mechanisms to managing planetary risks. Adaptability is "the capacity of actors in a system to influence resilience" (Folke et al., 2010, p. 3), in order to "avoid crossing into an undesirable system regime, or to succeed in crossing into a desirable one" (Walker & Salt, 2006, p. 163). To respond effectively to systemic shocks arising from increasing volatility of the planetary system, organizations can build flexible and adaptive systems. Self-organizing systems tend to be highly adaptive. Heightened sensemaking of ecological risks may initiate organizational adaptation strategies to build the required resilience (Clément & Rivera, 2016). For instance, studies have shown that considering how to manage risks posed by climate change, mitigation can improve long-term resilience capabilities (Beermann, 2011). Yet adaptive capacity to climate change cannot be developed in isolation from other planetary boundaries. For example, land degradation, another planetary boundary, is affected by climate change. Further, a forest fire contributes to climate change by releasing carbon stored in the trees that are burned and leaves fewer trees for carbon storage in remaining woodlands. Such risks are intrinsically intertwined, and adaptive capacity is a cross-organizational and systemic phenomenon.

After an understanding of the planetary system is developed, managers may build adaptive or transformative capacity to cope with long-term risks. For example, managers of high-reliability organizations (HROs), or organizations in high-risks industries which rarely fail, build adaptive capacity for organizational resilience (Weick & Sutcliffe, 2001).

Research also suggests that the resilience of ecosystem services is enhanced when governance systems encourage learning and experimentation, foster an understanding of complex systems, promote participation, and implement polycentric governance (Biggs et al., 2012).

Managers can thus encourage diversity and redundancy as well as manage feedbacks and connectivity to enhance the resilience of ecosystem services (Biggs et al., 2012; Winn & Pogutz, 2013). More resilience is not necessarily better. Often systems that are too resilient become rigid and unable to undertake necessary change until it is too late (Walker, Holling, Carpenter, & Kinzig, 2004). When adaptation limits are reached, transformative change may be necessary (Walker et al., 2004; Clément & Rivera, 2016), which may, in turn, require the reduction in resilience within the old system. Resilience of existing structures and behaviors must be reduced in order to introduce new variables into the system to allow for transformative change (Walker & Salt, 2004). (Ecological) transformability is "the capacity to create a fundamentally new system when ecological, economic or social structures make the existing system untenable" (Walker et al., 2004). Organizations, including companies, have important roles to play within the transformation of market systems through eco-innovation and novelty (Loorbach, van Bakel, Whiteman, & Rotmans, 2010; Kennedy, Whiteman, & van den Ende, 2017).

Given the spatial scale of global risks (see Figure 13.3), we suggest organizations need to build adaptive or transformative capacity collectively. For example, research on recovery operations after New Zealand earthquakes finds that organizations embedded in strong networks are able to better organize after a disaster (Stevenson et al., 2014). If connectedness is low in networks of organizations, vulnerabilities to global risks may increase. Some network structures could be more vulnerable when a node is removed compared to others (van der Vegt, Essens, Wahlström, & George, 2015). Research on resilience in organizational networks would be particularly relevant for supply chains, where organizational connectedness is high. More knowledge is needed to understand cross-organizational resilience, adaptation, and transformation as responses to long-term global systemic risks.

Organizational scholars should also examine how cross-organizational governance structures influence responses to global systemic risks. Governance and compensation structure may influence the probability of a crisis (Bundy et al., 2017). Companies that wish to avert possible climate change risks may rely on changes in compensatory benefits (Kolk & Pinkse, 2005). Although research has yet to explore the impact of tying compensation structures to global risks or to assess the subsequent impacts on organizational resilience, the structure of corporate boards may need to be revised to include a role for chief climate officers or a planetary risk committee.

Conclusion

We proposed in this chapter that organizational studies of risk can benefit from the wealth of natural science insights on systemic ecosystem risks at the planetary scale. Hoskisson, Chirico, Zyung, and Gambeta (2017, p. 156) posit that the dominant organizational theories such as agency theory or the behavioral theory of the firm that are used to understand managerial risk-taking tend to focus on solely risks that are economic or financial in nature. The authors argue that the boundary conditions of risk theories should therefore be reconsidered. Alternative theories are needed to redefine risk-taking and consider risks beyond firm-level financial risks (Hoskisson et al., 2017). This chapter has contributed to the advancement of the literature on organizational risk by a long-term, systemic perspective on planetary risks that recognizes the embeddedness of organizations in the natural environment.

Further, given the ongoing escalation of planetary risks related to key ecosystem processes, we proposed a three-phase framework for analyzing systemic planetary risks (Figure 13.2) that can contribute to reduction of these risks by establishing ways for organizations to build a planetary view of organizational risk across temporal and spatial scales, make sense of organizational actions in the context of planetary risks, and build adaptive capacity to mitigate planetary risks.

Critically, our framework highlights the importance of making managerial decisions as soon as possible to take into consideration safe pathways within the boundaries of the planet (Steffen et al., 2015a). To manage the long-term systemic risks of organizations, we suggest principles of adaptive capacity and resilience can prepare managers for unanticipated risks from the natural environment and enhance managers collectively ability to respond to long-term planetary risks driven by feedback loops across local, regional, and global scales. One example is Action 2020, the collective strategy of the World Business Council for Sustainable Development, which utilized the planetary boundaries framework to develop science-based targets for collective business action in an effort to mitigate systemic risks from the natural environment.

We have also suggested several areas of research including sensemaking, organizational networks, and governance in the discussion that organizational scholars can undertake to contribute to a better understanding of planetary risks.

We also note that our framework has limitations. In particular, we pay little attention to social risks in our framework (Leach, Raworth, & Rockström, 2013). However, we recognize that planetary environmental risks are deeply intertwined with pressing societal issues, and the interaction between these systems needs greater exploration in terms of cross-organizational behaviors. In addition, future empirical research is needed to explore barriers and enablers to our collective framework, including a deeper analysis of the role of entrenched vested interests and power relations. Future research on bounded rationality in managerial risk perceptions across scales is required, especially given that prior research indicates that firms tend to focus on short-term risks when making business decisions (Pinkse & Gasbarro, 2016).

We thus encourage organizational scholars to research long-term systemic risks that have yet to receive scholarly attention. For example, the WEF's *The Global Risks Report 2017* found that social instability, migration, and water crises are the most critical societal risks for businesses in 2017 (WEF, 2017). Amongst the top environmental risks are biodiversity loss and ecosystem collapse. However, our review of the literature shows that these risks have received little attention. We urge organizational scholars to devote more attention to these pressing global risks.

Finally, we argue that a cross-organizational and transdisciplinary approach is necessary – organization scholars cannot effectively address planetary risks to and from organizations without collaborating with our natural science colleagues. We thus reiterate the long-standing call in sustainability research for greater transdisciplinary integration and closer collaboration between social scientists and natural scientists to help to fill these gaps. While it may be true that past societies have been surprised by catastrophic environmental risks, we argue that a transdisciplinary approach to organizational risk can help us learn from the mistakes of the past and collectively contribute to a safe space for humanity. There is no time to lose.

References

Bansal, P., Kim, A., & Wood, M. (2017). Hidden in Plain Sight: The Importance of Scale on Organizational Attention to Issues. *Academy of Management Review*, 43(2), 217–241.

Bansal, P., & DesJardine, M. (2014). Business Sustainability: It's about Time. *Strategic Organization*, 12(1), 70–78.

Beck, U. (1992). *Risk Society: Towards a New Modernity.* Thousand Oaks, CA: Sage.

Beck, U., & Holzer, B. (2007). Organizations in World Risk Society. In C. Pearson, C. Roux-Dufort, & A. J. Clair (Eds.), *International Handbook of Organizational Crisis Management* (pp. 3–24). Thousand Oaks, CA: Sage.

Beermann, M. (2011). Linking Corporate Climate Adaptation Strategies with Resilience Thinking. *Journal of Cleaner Production,* 19(8), 836–842.

Berkhout, F., Hertin, J., & Gann, D. M. (2006). Learning to Adapt: Organisational Adaptation to Climate Change Impacts. *Climatic Change,* 78(1), 135–156.

Biggs, R., Schlüter, M., Biggs, D., Bohensky, E. L., BurnSilver, S., Cundill, G., et al. (2012). Toward Principles for Enhancing the Resilience of Ecosystem Services. *Annual Review of Environment and Resources,* 37(1), 421–448.

Bozeman, B. (2011). The 2010 BP Gulf of Mexico Oil Spill: Implications for Theory of Organizational Disaster. *Technology in Society,* 33, 244–252.

Bundy, J., Pfarrer, M. D., Short, C. E., & Coombs, W. T. (2017). Crises and Crisis Management: Integration, Interpretation, and Research Development. *Journal of Management,* 43(6), 1661–1692.

Carney, M. (2016). Resolving the Climate Paradox. Speech Given at the Arthur Burns Memorial Lecture (Berlin). Retrieved from www.fsb.org/wp-content/uploads/Resolving-the-climate-paradox.pdf.

Clément, V., & Rivera, J. (2016). From Adaptation to Transformation An Extended Research Agenda for Organizational Resilience to Adversity in the Natural Environment. *Organization & Environment,* 30(4), 346–365.

Clift, R., Sim, S., King, H., Chenoweth, J., Christie, I., Clavreul, J., et al. (2017). The Challenges of Applying Planetary Boundaries as a Basis for Strategic Decision-Making in Companies with Global Supply Chains. *Sustainability,* 9(279), 1–23.

Delp, L., Podolsky, L., & Aguilar, T. (2009). Risk Amid Recovery: Occupational Health and Safety of Latino Day Laborers in the Aftermath of the Gulf Coast Hurricanes. *Organization & Environment,* 22(4), 479–490.

Diamond, J. (2005). *Collapse: How Societies Choose to Fail or Succeed.* New York: Viking Press.

Dobler, M., Lajili, K., & Zéghal, D. (2014). Environmental Performance, Environmental Risk and Risk Management. *Business Strategy and the Environment,* 23(1), 1–17.

Folke, C., Carpenter, S. R., Walker, B., Scheffer, M., Chapin, T., Rockström., J., et al. (2010). Resilience Thinking: Integrating Resilience, Adaptability and Transformability. *Ecology and Society,* 15, 20.

Figueres, C., Schellnhuber, H. J., Whiteman, G., Rockström, J., Hobley, A., & Rahmstorf, S. (2017). Three Years to Safeguard Our Climate. *Nature,* 546, 593–595.

Gasbarro, F., Rizzi, F., & Frey, M. (2016). Adaptation Measures of Energy and Utility Companies to Cope with Water Scarcity Induced by Climate Change. *Business Strategy and the Environment,* 25(1), 54–72.

Gephart, R. P. (1984). Making Sense of Organizationally Based Environmental Disasters. *Journal of Management,* 10, 205–225.

Gephart, R. P. (2004). Normal Risk: Technology, Sense Making, and Environmental Disasters. *Organization & Environment,* 17(1), 20–26.

Gephart, R. P., Van Maanen, J., & Oberlechner, T. (2009). Organizations and Risk in Late Modernity. *Organization Studies,* 30, 141–155.

Goodall, A. H. (2008). Why Have the Leading Journals in Management (And Other Social Sciences) Failed to Respond to Climate Change? *Journal of Management Inquiry,* 17, 408–420.

GRI, UNGC, & WBCSD. (2015). SDG Compass the Guide for Business Action on the SDGs. Retrieved from www.sdgcompass.org.

Hahn, R., Reimsbach, D., & Schiemann, F. (2015). Organizations, Climate Change, and Transparency: Reviewing the Literature on Carbon Disclosure. *Organization & Environment,* 28(1), 80–102.

Hofmann, H., Busse, C., Bode, C., & Henke, M. (2014). Sustainability-Related Supply Chain Risks: Conceptualization and Management. Business Strategy and the Environment, 23(3), 160–172.

Hoskisson, R. E., Chirico, F., Zyung, J., & Gambeta, E. (2017). Managerial Risk Taking: A Multitheoretical Review and Future Research Agenda. *Journal of Management,* 43(1), 137–169.

IPCC. (2015). *The AR5 Synthesis Report.* Geneva: IPCC.

Kennedy, S., Whiteman, G., & van den Ende, J. (2017). Radical Innovation for Sustainability: The Power of Strategy and Open Innovation. *Long Range Planning,* 50(6), 712–725.

King, A. A., & Lenox, M. (2000). Industry Self-Regulation Without Sanctions: The Chemical Industry's Responsible Care Program. *Academy of Management Journal*, 43, 698–716.

Kleindorfer, P. R., & Saad, G. H. (2005). Managing Disruption Risks in Supply Chains. *Production and Operations Management*, 14(1), 53–68.

Kolk, A., & Pinkse, J. (2005). Business Responses to Climate Change: Identifying Emergent Strategies. *California Management Review*, 47(3), 6–20.

Kolk, A., & Pinkse, J. (2008). A Perspective on Multinational Enterprises and Climate Change: Learning from "An Inconvenient Truth"? *Journal of International Business Studies*, 39(8), 1359–1378.

Kondoh, K. (2009). The Challenge of Climate Change and Energy Policies for Building a Sustainable Society in Japan. *Organization & Environment*, 22(1), 52–74.

Leach, Melissa, Raworth, Kate & Rockström, Johan. (2013). Between Social and Planetary Boundaries: Navigating Pathways in the Safe and Just Space for Humanity. In *World Social Science Report 2013: Changing Global Environments*. Paris: OECD Publishing, UNESCO Publishing.

Linnenluecke, M. K., & Griffiths, A. (2013). The 2009 Victorian Bushfires: A Multilevel Perspective on Organizational Risk and Resilience. *Organization & Environment*, 26, 386–411.

Loorbach, D., van Bakel, J., Whiteman, G., & Rotmans, J. (2010). Business Strategies for Transitions towards Sustainable Systems. *Business Strategy and the Environment*, 19, 133–146.

Maguire, S., & Hardy, C. (2009). Discourse and Deinstitutionalization: the Decline of DDT. *Academy of Management Journal*, 52, 148–178.

Maguire, S., & Hardy, C. (2013). Organizing Processes and the Construction of Risk: A Discursive Approach. *Academy of Management Journal*, 56, 231–255.

Melo, C. J., & Wolf, S. A. (2005). Empirical Assessment of Eco-Certification: The Case of Ecuadorian Bananas. *Organization & Environment*, 18, 287.

Muller, A., & Whiteman, G. (2009). Exploring the Geography of Corporate Philanthropic Disaster Response: A Study of Fortune Global 500 Firms. *Journal of Business Ethics*, 84, 589–603.

Ortiz-de-Mandojana & Bansal, P. (2016). The Long-term Benefits of Organizational Resilience through Sustainable Business Practices. *Strategic Management Journal*, 37, 1615–1631.

Pauchant, T. C., & Mitroff, I. I. (1992). *Transforming the Crisis-Prone Organization: Preventing Individual, Organizational, and Environmental Tragedies*. San Francisco, CA: Jossey-Bass.

Pinkse, J., & Gasbarro, F. (2016). Managing Physical Impacts of Climate Change: An Attentional Perspective on Corporate Adaptation. *Business & Society*. Downloaded from http://journals.sage pub.com/doi/10.1177/0007650316648688. August 18, 2018.

Rockström, J., Gaffney, O., Rogelj, J., Meinshausen, M., Nakicenovic, N., & Schellnhuber, H. J. (2017). A Roadmap for Rapid Decarbonization. *Science*, 355, 1269–1271.

Rockström, J., Steffen, W., Noone, K., Persson, Å., Chapin, F. S. III, Lambin, E. F., et al. (2009a). A Safe Operating Space for Humanity. *Nature*, 461, 472–475.

Rockström, J., Steffen, W., Noone, K., Persson, Å., Chapin, F. S. III, Lambin, E. F., et al. (2009b). Planetary Boundaries: Exploring the Safe Operating Space for Humanity. *Ecology and Society*, 14(2), 32.

Schellnhuber, H. J., Rahmstorf, S., & Winkelmann, R. (2016). Why the Right Climate Target Was Agreed Upon in Paris. *Nature Climate Change*, 6, 649–653.

Shrivastava, P., (1992). *Bhopal: Anatomy of a Crisis*. London: P. Chapman Pub.

Shrivastava, P. (1994). Technological and Organizational Roots of Industrial Crises: Lessons from Exxon Valdez and Bhopal. *Technological Forecasting and Social Change*, 45, 237–253.

Starik, M., & Rands, G. (1995). Weaving an Integrated Web: Multilevel and Multisystem Perspectives of Ecologically Sustainable Organizations. *Academy of Management Review*, 20(4), 908–935.

Steffen, W., Crutzen, P. J., & McNeill, J. R. (2007). The Anthropocene—Are Humans Now Overwhelming the Great Forces of Nature. *Ambio*, 36, 614–621.

Steffen, W., Richardson, K., Rockström, J., Cornell, S.E., Fetzer, I. et al. (2015a). Planetary Boundaries: Guiding Human Development on a Changing Planet. *Science*, 347(6223), 649–653.

Steffen, W., Broadgate, W., Deutsch, L., Gaffney, O., & Ludwig, C. (2015b). The Trajectory of the Anthropocene: The Great Acceleration. *The Anthropocene Review*, 2(1), 81–98.

Stevenson, J. R., Chang-Richards, Y., Conradson, D., Wilkinson, S., Vargo, J., et al. (2014). Organizational Networks and Recovery Following the Canterbury Earthquakes. *Earthquake Spectra*, 30(1), 555–575.

Sullivan-Taylor, B., & Wilson, D. C. (2009). Managing the Threat of Terrorism in British Travel and Leisure Organizations. *Organization Studies*, 30(2/3), 251–276.

Thistlethwaite, J. (2012). The ClimateWise Principles: Self-Regulating Climate Change Risks in the Insurance Sector. *Business & Society*, 51(1), 121–147.

Thistlethwaite, J., & Wood, M. (2018). Insurance and Climate Change Risk Management: Rescaling to Look Beyond the Horizon. *British Journal of Management*, 29, 279–298.

Tsoukas, H. (1999). David and Goliath in the Risk Society: Making Sense of the Conflict between Shell and Greenpeace in the North Sea. *Organization*, 6(3), 499–528.

Walker, B., Holling, C. S., Carpenter, S. S. R., Kinzig, A. (2004). Resilience, Adaptability and Transformability in Social–Ecological Systems. *Ecology & Society*, 9, 5.

Walker, B., & Salt, D. (2006). *Resilience Thinking: Sustaining Ecosystems and People in a Changing World*. Washington, DC: Island Press.

WEF. (2014). Global Risks 2014: Understanding Systemic Risks in a Changing Global Environment. Retrieved from http://reports.weforum.org/global-risks-2014/part-1-global-risks-2014-understanding-systemic-risks-in-a-changing-global-environment/?doing_wp_cron=1515420545.865283966064453125000.

WEF. (2017). Global Risks Report 2017. Retrieved from http://reports.weforum.org/global-risks-2017/global-risks-of-highest-concern-for-doing-business-2017/.

Weick, K. E., & Sutcliffe, K. (2001). *Managing the Unexpected—Assuring High Performance in the Age of Complexity*. San Francisco, CA: Jossey-Bass.

Weinhofer, G., & Busch, T. (2013). Corporate Strategies for Managing Climate Risks. *Business Strategy and the Environment*, 22(2), 121–144.

Whiteman, G., & Cooper, W. (2000). Ecological Embeddedness. *Academy of Management Journal*, 43(6), 1265–1282.

Whiteman, G., & Cooper, W. H. (2011). Ecological Sensemaking. *Academy of Management Journal*, 54(5), 889–911.

Whiteman, G., & Kennedy, S. (2016). Sustainability as Process. In A. Langley & H. Tsoukas. (Eds.), *Sage Handbook of Process Organization Studies* (pp. 417–431). Los Angeles, CA: SAGE Publications.

Whiteman G., Walker, B., & Perego, P. (2013). Planetary Boundaries: Foundations for corporate sustainability. *Journal of Management Studies*, 50, 307–336.

Williams, A., Kennedy, S., Philipp, F., & Whiteman, G. (2017). Systems Thinking: A Review of Sustainability Management Research. *Journal of Cleaner Production*, 148(1), 866–881.

Williams, T. A., Gruber, D. A., Sutcliffe, K. M., Shepherd, D. A., & Zhao, E. Y. (2017). Organizational Response to Adversity: Fusing Crisis Management and Resilience Research Streams. *Academy of Management Annals*, 11(2), 1–70.

Williams, T. A., & Shepherd, D. (2016). Building Resilience or Providing Sustenance: Different Paths of Emergent Ventures in the Aftermath of the Haiti Earthquake. *Academy of Management Journal*, 59(5), 2069–2102.

Winn, M. I., Kirchgeorg, M., Griffiths, A., Linnenluecke, M. K., & Günther, E. (2011). Impacts from Climate Change on Organizations: A Conceptual Foundation. *Business Strategy & the Environment*, 20, 157–173.

Winn, M. I., & Pogutz, S. (2013). Business, Ecosystems, and Biodiversity: New Horizons for Management Research. *Organization & Environment*, 26(2), 203–229.

Van der Vegt, G. S., Essens, P., Wahlström, M., & George, G. (2015). Managing Risk and Resilience. *Academy of Management Journal*, 58, 971–980.

14

EVENT RISKS AND CRISES

Barriers to Learning

Christian Huber and Tobias Scheytt

Introduction

We were writing the last pieces of this chapter when we heard the shocking reports about the Las Vegas shooting, an event crisis in 2017, where over 50 people were killed and 500 injured while participating in an outdoor music festival that took place near to Las Vegas Boulevard. This example of event crises and many others, including the bombings at the Boston Marathon 2013 (New York Times, April 16, 2013), the Manchester concert hall terrorism attack in 2017, the shooting at the Bataclan concert hall in Paris in 2015, or the attack at the Christmas market in Berlin in 2016, exemplify in the most dreadful manner that public events can be impacted by numerous high-profile risks. Public events are manifold and diverse and so are the risks and crises associated with them. These events are a specific form of planned "social occasion" (cf. Merriam-Webster Dictionary) and, when used in the context of event management, refer to formally organized mass gatherings. To differentiate our understanding from other uses of the word event, we use the phrase *public events* (Public Event Law and Legal Definition, 2017). Our motivation is that public events that involve large masses of people constitute specific challenges to organizing due to the inherent risks they pose and their potential for producing crises. This claim is demonstrated by many studies of public events including cultural and arts festivals, concerts, sports events including the Olympic Games, and other mass participation events. It is the chief aim of this chapter to address and integrate aspects of the various bodies of literature in a multitude of disciplines that address public events and provide learning and insights into the management of event risks and crises.

Our focus lies on both, the risks and the crises involved in holding public events. This double focus is motivated by the fact that most studies of public events address events where risks emerged and finally ended in disaster (Soomaroo & Murray, 2012). In order to differentiate the factors by which risks and crises are caused, we refer to Shrivastava's (1992) seminal work on the Bhopal disaster. In his view, a crisis differs from an accident in that it is not adequately dealt with for a prolonged time. For crisis management, this distinction is crucial. It is near-impossible to avoid all accidents, owing to the technical complexity of public events. Hence, dealing with accidents in a meaningful manner forms a central challenge to organizing and managing public events. Confining our discussion to crises, however, would limit our attention to those public events where accidents have not been adequately dealt with. Moreover, those who are organizing and managing public events face additional challenges *before* the actual event takes place. Dealing with such challenges may be best grasped, understood quite broadly, under the term risk management. We therefore take both risks and crises as our starting point and understand risk management as the bundle of practices enacted to deal with event risks and crises. We assume here that risks that exist prior to events can engender crises.

This endeavor is truly interdisciplinary as the volume of research shows. Soomaroo & Murray (2012) have identified 156 academic texts for the period between 1971 and 2011, although only 21 of these texts were published in peer-reviewed journals. This points toward the importance of "grey" or unpublished literature in the scholarly field of crisis management. And practitioner-oriented publication outlets have suggested that the number of accidents and crises at public events is much larger. This is further substantiated by the website by Still (2017), a renowned expert on crowd safety, and the impressive web application developed by Asgary (2017) that collects fact files on worldwide crowd disasters. In addition, the analyses of sources, antecedents, and consequences of public event risks and crises touch upon insights from several academic fields including research in social psychology studying crowd behavior and decision-making related to large numbers of people (Zeitz, Tan, Grief, Couns, & Zeitz, 2012) as well as theories of risk management (Flyvbjerg, Bruzelius, & Rothengatter, 2003), sensemaking (Gephart Jr., 1993), and normal accident theory (Perrow, 1999). The heterogeneity of these approaches motivates our attempt to organize our discussion around a specific type of event rather than around disciplinary fields or trajectories.

While it is conventional wisdom that a myriad of risks and potentialities for crises are part of organizing public events, current research on risk management does not fully address events as a specific topic, nor does it understand "event risks" or "event studies" in economics that address how events impact the value of firms. A possible reason for the absence of such a sub-discipline may be the multifaceted nature of public events. Additionally, public events touch upon many important, yet usually separated, themes in organization theory, like space, time, accountability, crowd control, management control, and rules and regulations. Therefore, in this chapter, we suggest understanding public events as a fruitful site for exploring the unique features of event risks and to reflect on how they vary from other types of risks and crises. Such an approach can yield important insights into public event risks and crises that are significant for scholars and practitioners alike, who are working in the risk, crisis, and emergency management domain.

We thus provide an overview of some of the most pertinent themes of studying risks and crises of public events in order to make two principle contributions. First, we ask "What are the role of human, organizational and technological factors in public event risks and crises?" To do so, we explain Shrivastava's (1992) HOT (human, organizational, technological) framework and use this to identify a common core of issues of importance to studies focusing on public event crises. We suggest that the temporal-spatial constraints on activities at public events pose special challenges, a finding supported by research on temporary organizations. By reviewing and synthesizing these past studies, we identify key features of managing public events successfully. Second, we focus on the unintended side effects that frequently emerge from event risks and crises, in particular, the failure to learn from experience in depth during or after event risks and crises. We ask "What are the key internal and external barriers to learning that occur because of the temporary nature of event organizations?" To answer this question, we apply the HOT framework to examples of event crises to develop a general set of the most prominent barriers to organizational learning from past public event crises. The chapter also contributes to practitioner as well as theoretical discourses on risk and crisis management by providing insights developed by synthesizing the diverse and distributed insights from the field into suggestions that can contribute to public safety. A key concern is to demonstrate and explain how and why it is so difficult to learn from event risks and crises.

Key Features of Public Event Crises

Different studies from diverse fields have discussed public events, but there has been little systematic dialogue. To facilitate the start of such a dialogue, we draw on the established HOT-framework as proposed by Shrivastava (1992, pp. 40–47). HOT stands for the human, organizational, and technological factors that lead to accidents. The framework's aim is to show "how antecedent conditions for [an] accident developed and how a complex set of interacting failures lead to [a] disaster" (p. 40). *Human factors* concern the role of individuals or groups of individuals (machine operators, managers, etc.) in socio-technical systems. Problems accruing from human factors include inadequate staffing or training, insufficient information, or mundane human errors. *Organizational factors* comprise strategic issues that produce an environment in which operating policies potentially affect the safety of operations. Strategic issues include the ascribed importance of a specific location for an organization, or larger structural determinants such as top-management (dis)continuity. *Technological factors* relate to the degree by which individual components are coupled to each other, and the (non)linearity of interactions between individual components (Perrow, 1984; Shrivastava, 1992, p. 45). The antecedents for technical systems, subsystems, and components include design, equipment, supplies, and operating procedures (Shrivastava, 1992, p. 46). Table 14.1 presents examples for what is specific about public event risks and crises.

Table 14.1 HOT-factors of Public Event Risks and Crises

Human factors	Organizational factors	Technological factors
• Large crowds may follow crowd dynamics as sociopsychologically defined. • Events are accessible to a large and heterogeneous public. • Crowds may show emotional excitement. • Errors of judgment can occur due to misconception of large numbers of people.	• Events are usually organized in and by project and temporary organizations. • Project and event organizations are usually organized embedded in networks of organizations with lateral relations. • Planning before and planning after the event can become decoupled. • Events can be usually subject to a range of regulations from diverse regulatory agencies. • Organizational learning is limited due to the uniqueness of events that do not recur.	• Events commonly unfold under the condition of limited time. • Events are held in a context where there is limited physical space. • Information and communication technology is critical to managing emerging risks and crises, and communication failures can be hazardous. • Effective crown surveillance technology is critical; failure of this technology can be hazardous.

The *human factors* found in almost all accounts of crises associated with large public gatherings relate, in one way or another, to the large number of participants. Some events turn into accidents and crises because of crowd dynamics. Injuries and deaths resulting from stampedes or crushing are examples here: the disasters at the LoveParade, a stampede at a festival due to limited physical space and regulatory confusion (Dempsey, 2010), or at the Roskilde Festival, a stampede at a rock festival caused by errors of judgment and crowd dynamics (New York Times, 2000). Such accidents and crises might be obscure from an individual participant's perspective. Eyewitnesses' accounts regularly highlight that the disaster took place, although the overall spatial conditions were unproblematic. Many individuals do not take notice of the tragic events until they notice emergency forces rushing into the area. Psychological research on crowd behavior has stressed the influence of emotions, especially when people become engaged in a public event (Zeitz et al., 2012) and when they assume a collective identity (Hopkins & Reicher, 2016). Studies from social and cognitive psychology have also shown that people have systematic problems with estimating large numbers (Gigerenzer & Gaissmaier, 2010; Tversky & Kahneman, 1971). Such wrong estimations, among planners and / or participants, can lead to errors of judgment, making the planning and operational management especially difficult when large numbers of people are involved.

Organizational factors defining public event risks and crises relate to the organizational forms associated with public events. Usually, a network of organizations is involved in dealing with the risks of public events. For example, a rock festival is the product of an event organizer, bands and their management, caterers, private securities, local police forces, the municipality which governs the physical space of the festival, and so forth. In many cases, there is a stable organizational structure. For a sports game, the stadium and the home team are stable across many public events. These stable organizations are confronted with non- or semi-routine tasks, such as when local police forces have to provide security for a large political demonstration. Moreover, the network of organizations is complemented by a temporary organization (e.g. the organization responsible for running the Olympic Games in a city) or a stable organization in a temporarily unusual setting (e.g. the visiting team at a football game). Networks of organizations are difficult to regulate, and so large public events face a mix of regulations, ranging from local fire prevention rules to crowd control regulations to road safety regulations. Regulatory oversight and defining accountability can be tricky in such settings.

Technological factors are the third defining set of features specific to event risks and crises. Communication (speakers, social media) and surveillance (cameras) technologies play a crucial role in controlling crowds. What stands out about the technological factors of public events, however, are their temporal and spatial limitations. Technology, understood as design and architecture, materializes the spatial limitations of a festival venue, a football stadium, or an event center. Technologies also define the temporal limitations of public events. IT and communication technologies are widespread in event planning and preparation (Lundin & Söderholm, 1995). The functioning of such technologies is, however, even more crucial during the short life of an event, because organizers need multiple time-keeping technologies such as clocks, schedules or timers, and structures that allow immediate coordination. Spatial technologies are also tightly connected in public events – gates, scaffolding, seating, and fencing are put together, but only for short periods of time. Think of a football stadium in which the technical infrastructure, paths to the concession stands, and parking lots are only used for a few hours each year. The likelihood that this building turns into a risky site, or potential crisis zone, is highest during these brief periods.

The analysis of these human, organizational, and technological factors is the key feature for managing public event risks and crises. They have multiple consequences for the organizers, attendants, and other stakeholders. One organizational factor, however, can have more consequences compared to others, as it can have great influence on the mindfulness necessary in situation of event crises: organizational learning and possible barriers to learning.

Barriers to Learning

Scholars have suggested that the failure to learn from disasters or crises is one of the main reasons why crises continue to happen (Turner, 1978/1997). The literature on event risks and crises may be dispersed, but it repeatedly identifies some barriers to learning as crucial impediments for future success of public events. Table 14.2 offers a summary of the most important barriers to learning in which we have distinguished between barriers which are intraorganizational and those which are in the organization's environment.

In principal, these barriers are a result of the characteristics of public events discussed in the previous sections – human and organizational complexities as well as temporal/spatial limitations. However, not all aspects of public events pose direct barriers to learning. Some barriers directly affect the organizations which manage the public event, while other barriers stem from the organization's environment. Our final point, namely, that there is a gulf between ex-ante and ex-post perspectives on event risks and crises, is brought about by the fact that different stakeholders have different perspectives. For example, legal authorities have a different view on the same event before (ex-ante) the actual event (e.g. in the form of municipalities granting permissions) and after (ex-post) the event (potentially in the form of a district attorney in case of an accident). We will discuss this point separately at the end of this section and start with a description of the intra- and extra-organizational barriers to learning.

Intraorganizational Barriers to Learning

Different bodies of literature suggest that organizations preparing and managing public events face three principal barriers to learning, each of which leads to the continued occurrence of public event crises and catastrophes. There are barriers stemming from the temporal challenges of organizing public events, barriers originating from networked forms of organizing, and barriers resulting from bad planning or errors of judgment.

Table 14.2 Barriers to Learning. Adapted for Event Risks Based on Turner (1978/1997), Pidgeon and O'Leary (2000), and Smith and Elliott (2007)

Intraorganizational barriers	*Barriers in the organizations' environment*
• Complexity of planning events. • Time pressure. • Networked character of event organizations can challenge communication and make dissemination of the knowledge that was learned difficult. • Fewer routines exist in temporary organizations. • Misjudgments/misconceptions can occur.	• External agents will likely blame event organizers if something goes wrong. • A culture of fear can emerge, with organizational members manifesting defensiveness against learning so that prior mistakes are not known and thus they can avoid potential consequences. • Regulatory confusion due to regulatory complexity may result in ambiguity about who could learn and how they could learn.
• A gulf or distance can emerge between ex-ante and ex-post perspectives on event risks and crises.	

The semi-regularity with which public events often occur can easily lead to them being treated as idiosyncratic and singular. While some public events such as a regular season base-ball game may be less susceptible to such an assumption, other types of public events, like an annual music festival which changes locations, may be more prone to over-emphasizing id-iosyncrasy. The assumption that no event is like the other – a widespread assumption among practitioners of event management – effectively keeps event organizations from learning from past experiences. This argument is echoed by Roux-Dufort (2007) who argues that crises may be rare events, but should be studied in the (situational and temporal) context in which they evolve. In many cases, this is not very idiosyncratic. Crisis management should therefore not be limited to the management of exceptions, but instead should be incorpo-rated into more routine forms of dealing with risk and uncertainty.

Planning errors are frequently cited as causes for disasters during public events. Clarke (1999) has persuasively argued that plans for any situation when uncertainty is high are merely fantasy documents. They mirror wishes and assumptions, rather than provide tools for realistically coordinating action. Public event management may be especially prone to engaging in unrealistic or useless planning, not only because they face high uncertainty, such as regarding crowd behavior. Rather, the tight timeframe often shifts the practical lens from planning to improvisation. To be sure, improvisation is not only a problem, but also a widely accepted, and in some situations a necessary practice in event organizations. How-ever, knowledge about how to improvise well is usually embodied in individuals and can be easily lost in cases of high staff turnover.

Public events are often organized by temporary or project organizations (Flyvbjerg et al., 2003). Such organizations have a networked character (Easterby-Smith, Lyles, & Tsang, 2008; Getz, Andersson, & Larson, 2006), composing of different sub-organizations which have their own cultures and structures for organizing. A festival, for instance, in addition to the event management organization, may include a private security firm, a caterer, performers who each have their own crew and others. Learning in network organizations faces several obstacles (Larsson, Bengtsson, Henriksson, & Sparks, 1998), the key one of which is the difficulties with building routines. That is to say, the aforementioned temporal challenges are also a source for problems with learning from routines. Routines have enjoyed much attention from or-ganizational scholars following the seminal publication of Feldman & Pentland (2003). Some accounts have explored how routines work in dealing with risks (e.g. Danner-Schröder & Gei-ger, 2016). Others have explored how routines in networks may emerge (Feldman, Pentland, D'Adderio, & Lazaric, 2016, p. 8). The problem with network organizations, in short, is that building routines is difficult. Important communication processes take place between organi-zations, rather than in one organization, which makes fostering shared organizational memory in such networks a challenge. The absence of routines, because it hampers learning, can lead organizations and the individuals therein to repeat mistakes (Levinthal & Rerup, 2006).

The human factors in event risks and crises that we identified in Table 14.1 relate primarily to errors in human judgment when people appear in large numbers. Such errors repeatedly concern misconceptions regarding the behavior of masses. Literature has also stressed that large numbers are often misjudged in planning processes. Even when past information is available, such errors of judgment may inhibit organizers from learning valuable lessons. For example, a major aspect of cost estimations is their persistent tendency of being too low. This is caused partially by human and technical limitations of estimating costs in big projects (Flyvbjerg et al., 2003). Local micro politics and developments in the larger political economy impact financial resources and play a role here, both of which are especially important for large events given the length of time usually spent for planning and coordinating (Horne & Manzenreiter, 2004).

Barriers to Learning in the Organization's Environment

An organization's environment is the second source for barriers to learning. Various stakeholders, such as local authorities, interest groups, businesses, or regulators can impact how experiences from public events are retained (or not). Barriers resulting from the constellation of the organization's environment fall into two broad categories: (i) a strong cultural inclination to attribute or find causes that focus on blame and fear, and (ii) regulatory confusion.

Event organizations face substantial demands from the public and political stakeholders. Sometimes, an intense political debate is associated with determining accountability and responsibility. Actors often seek to pass the buck in what is often referred to as the "blame game" (Hood, 2002). Apart from the search for a guilty party, the blame game is said to cause an overall defensive stance. Power (2007) has outlined how the exponential growth in resources devoted to risk management in organizations is linked to deeper changes in organizational practices. Public and private organizations develop routines which may not always be appropriate for engaging with the challenges of future uncertainties, but rather shift attention to maintaining a publicly acceptable image of the organization's risk management (Power, 2009). Hence, while accountability and transparency may be useful concepts in general, too much focus on them may hamper effective risk management. Moreover, too much focus on the past, and concentrating on the historically identified risks, can keep organizations from effectively looking at the future.

Regulation by public authorities is in high demand, yet difficult, owing to the human, organizational, and technological factors marking public events. Good regulation should, in theory, foster learning by bringing stability to situations perceived as instable within project organizations. Additionally, good regulation should help to avoid incorrect or superstitious learning. However, unclear regulation may have the opposite effect. Regulatory heterogeneity is often cited as having negative effects on organizational learning. Regulatory regimes across the world also differ with respect to the types of risk which they target. New risk categories keep entering public debate, as the growing concern for reputational risks illustrates (Power, Scheytt, Soin, & Sahlin, 2009). Reputational risks have not only been identified as important for regular events such as the Olympic Games or the Super Bowl, but also provide a nexus of professional concerns, ranging from fields of expertise in marketing, branding, accounting, and communication (Coaffee & Rogers, 2008; Jennings, 2012; Power et al., 2009).

The Gulf between Ex-ante and Ex-post Perspectives

In our review of the different strands of literature dealing with public event risks and crises, we noticed a strange divide between ex-ante (before the event) and ex-post (after the event) perspectives. Practitioners and academic experts alike experience a gulf between ex-post and ex-ante analyses of event risks. This divide may also hinder learning from diverse cases. Ex-ante perspectives are often focused on questions of financial and security risks, while ex-post perspectives are often limited to issues of preventing or recovering from disasters, and are mainly concerned with questions of accountability. Again, the underlying problem of such a divide is that it complicates learning *between* events. For instance, the ex-post focus on disasters ignores the potential learning from successfully managed event risks. Such a feed-forward of experience and key learning could be usefully incorporated in ex-ante risk and crisis management.

What also strengthens the ex-ante-ex-post divide is that ex-ante perspectives usually ignore learning from near misses (Weick & Sutcliffe, 2007). Accordingly, accounts of events which have ended in disaster have received substantially more scrutiny from academics and the public alike. In some cases, as for the Hillsborough soccer disaster (see description later), the ex-post analysis took almost 25 years. To put it even stronger: ex-ante concepts for managing risks of public events rarely look for best practices, nor do they pay attention to events that faced a potential for disaster, but managed to navigate risks successfully. Drawing on the example of the European Capital of Culture 2010 (Essen for the Ruhr Area), Crepaz, Huber, and Scheytt (2016) show how successful events, even if they were originally estimated as bearing high risk, ended with only some media coverage and eventually economic winding-up of the event organization, but did not result in learning for event risk management.

Examples of Event Risks and Crises

We will now illustrate our reflections on event risks and crises with two examples from sports events, both well known for their (potential) ending in crisis and, in one case, a tragic outcome. In the first example, the 2012 Olympic Games, we focus on risks, whereas the second example, a 1989 soccer game in Sheffield, England (named the Hillsborough disaster for the stadium where it occurred), will deal with a crisis. We chose these two examples because they are well documented in the literature and emphasize different aspects of our notional framework, including the identified barriers to learning. We draw on secondary sources for our empirical examples. Since the principal arguments of this chapter are about the state of the literature, we will also illustrate how such arguments map onto the framework outlined earlier. Table 14.3 summarizes our key illustrations from each case.

Table 14.3 Comparison of the Empirical Examples

Categories \ Cases	2012 Olympic Games	Hillsborough disaster
Type of public event	A mega-event comprising multiple smaller events	A semi-regular soccer cup match
Risks/crises	Despite multiple risks ranging from transportation to terrorism, no major crisis occurred	96 dead and many more injured in a stampede led to a decade-long struggle with the consequences
Human factors	Complex decision-making, difficult planning, largely unproblematic human behavior	Crowd panic, mismanagement, and cover-up by the local police forces
Organizational factors	A mix of stable organizations (IOC, London Police Force) and project-organizations specifically established for the Games (e.g. local organizing committee)	A stable local organization (Sheffield United Football Club) interacts with local authorities and a visiting organization (Liverpool Football Club)
Technological factors	Large infrastructure investments, combined with the use of many preexisting facilities (e.g. tube network)	Overcrowding due to unclear access policies; fences against which victims were crushed
Barriers for learning	Temporal challenges, network organization	Culture of fear, focus on blame

Example 1: Olympic Risks – Diversity of Risks and the Rise of Risk Management Before Mega-Events

The Olympics in the modern era have not only an unparalleled standing in the world of sports, but have also received much attention from practitioners as well as organization and management scholars. In 2012, the Olympics held in London saw a host of over 10,000 athletes from over 200 countries; it cost more than 15 billion USD (including infrastructure investments), and more than 7 million tickets were sold (IOC, 2017). Even under normal circumstances, an event of such a magnitude bears many risks. In addition, the 1970s to 1990s have politicized the Olympics that had until then enjoyed a rather positive reputation with the public. Disputes between the USA and the Soviet Union had led to partial boycotts of the 1980 Games in Moscow and the 1984 Games in Los Angeles. Palestinians taking hostages and killing athletes at the 1972 Munich Games had equally robbed the Olympics of their innocence. The bombing during the 1996 Games in Atlanta by a Christian religious extremist was the most recent reveal of the risks implicated in such a mega-event. Less spectacular, but with a lasting effect, the question of financial risk associated with the Olympics has become central in public discussion, as the examples of the Montreal in 1976, and Rio in 2016, illustrate. In the following, we describe a specific combination of human factors (complex planning), organizational factors (networked organizations with intricate structure and varying stability), and technological factors (production of infrastructure), which led to barriers for learning (idiosyncrasies of regular events).

In the case of the Olympic Games, HOT-factors (Shrivastava, 1992) and barriers for learning are both dependent on the temporal structure of the events (long preparation, similar events for the past century) and the Games' character as an event of events (a mega-event comprising many individual events, each with their own potential for crisis). The Olympic Games, both in summer and winter, have not only exponentially increased in terms of cost and revenue, but they also have become ever more explicitly framed in terms of risk management. An especially well-documented case is the 2012 Summer Games in London. The sensitivity for risks and security is traditionally high in the United Kingdom, and this mindset had been cemented by a coincidence which appeared on July 7, 2005 – the announcement that London had won the bidding for the 2012 Games and the terrorist attacks on the London tube occurred on the same day. Jennings (2012) has argued that "[r]isk is now an organizing principle at all levels of Olympic governance – and in most organizational functions – from finance to security to construction to contingency planning".

Olympic Games illustrate the temporal nature of event risks very well. Timing is crucial, yet peaks occur at different time periods for different risks. The long bidding phases are accompanied by the risk of wasting resources on an unsuccessful bid. For the host city winning the bid, the risks shift to inaccurate estimations in the bidding document – which is the norm due to the many uncertainties involved in such a mega-project (Jennings, 2012). Increases in scope and costs are risks which peak years before the actual Games, especially during the phase when the technical infrastructure is planned. Workplace accidents are most likely during the building phases. During the actual Games, the risk of terrorist attacks and mass panic is highest. But even during the Games, not all periods of time are equally risky. For example, the organization committee of the 2006 Turin Games identified those timeslots in which large masses of people are transported to and from venues as the most vulnerable ones. In addition to event-specific risks, other risks such as theft and other petty crimes usually peak during the Games (for a detailed discussion, see Jennings, 2012, p. 58ff).

Jennings (2012) also illustrates the difficulties in assessing the risk associated with the rise in costs and over-estimation of benefits. The infamous cost explosion of the 1976 Montréal Games (by more than 1,000%) has given the Olympics a troublesome financial reputation. Since then, however, the losses that organizing cities and states suffered have increased immensely.

Underlying the highly publicized debates are difficulties in calculating the costs and benefits. While cost-benefit analyses are carried out regularly, getting the numbers right is difficult. Cost calculations suffer from extremely high levels of aggregation and problems of defining which costs need to be directly attributed to the Games themselves, and which are general infrastructure investments. Equally, benefits are difficult to discern, as direct effects (e.g. ticket revenues), indirect effects on the local economy, and induced effects (proportion of income re-spent within the economy) are muddy ex-ante categories (Jennings, 2012, p. 105f). Ex-post analyses of costs and benefits are also far from being uncontestable, as macro-economic factors that cannot be attributed to the Games directly influence the result.

The Olympic Games illustrate some of the barriers for learning we outlined earlier. While the organization is hardly unexpected and the event at its core is similar across time, the local setting, budget, magnitude, and network of organizations involved vary considerably. Financial risks, for instance, were already known to be of crucial importance to the success of Games since the problems at the Montréal Games. Yet, this knowledge alone did not prevent the London Games from making their own plans and generating their own planning assumptions. Bad planning and misjudgment could be prevented, but not specifically through learning processes.

In sum, we suggest three main points to take away from the example of the Olympic Games in London 2012. First, public events can be idiosyncratic and special, even if they occur semi-regularly and are prepared well in advance. Second, the Games are organized by a vast network of organizations and multiple stakeholders. In character, the Olympic Games are an event which combines multiple public events, each of them prone to risks and crises on their own. These can aggregate and add to those risks associated with the mega-event. Third, we see that there can be risks without crises. While risk became a logic of organizing (Power et al., 2009), crises did not emerge on a large scale. Future Games could learn from what went well in London.

Example 2: Hillsborough – the Long Struggle for Justice

Our second example concentrates on a soccer match that ended in a mass panic and catastrophe. After the initial confusion about the number of away fans attending an English soccer cup game and a resulting confusion among security staff about how many people can be granted access, 96 people were crushed and killed on an overcrowded stand, while many more were injured. The Hillsborough disaster is named after the soccer stadium of Sheffield, which hosted the FA Cup semi-final game between Liverpool FC and Nottingham Forrest on April 15, 1989. This event crisis is an archetypical example of the risk of overcrowding. It is particularly interesting because it complements the first example in that it was a distinct crisis at a much more regular type of event. It also illustrates different barriers to learning.

The disaster of Hillsborough is not only tragic in its scope but also in its long and difficult history of reconstructing what happened. Despite the event happening in 1989, an inquiry into its causes was only concluded after an independent panel presented a report in 2012, and a jury case in 2016. The following presents an excerpt from the executive summary of the report (Hillsborough Independent Panel, 2012):

On 15 April 1989 over 50,000 men, women and children travelled by train, coach and car to Hillsborough Stadium, home of Sheffield Wednesday Football Club, to watch an FA Cup [a competition between English soccer teams; the authors] Semi-Final between Liverpool and Nottingham Forest. It was a sunny, warm, spring day and one of the high points of the English football season.

Hillsborough was a neutral venue, like so many stadia of its time a mix of seated areas and modified standing terraces. As the match started, amid the roar of the crowd it became apparent that in the central area of the Leppings Lane terrace, already visibly overcrowded before the kick-off, Liverpool fans were in considerable distress.

In fact, the small area in which the crush occurred comprised two pens. Fans had entered down a tunnel under the West Stand into the central pens 3 and 4. Each pen was segregated by lateral fences and a high, overhanging fence between the terrace and the perimeter track around the pitch. There was a small locked gate at the front of each pen.

The crush became unbearable and fans collapsed underfoot. To the front of pen 3 a safety barrier broke, creating a pile of people struggling for breath. Despite CCTV cameras transmitting images of distress in the crowd to the Ground Control Room and to the Police Control Box, and the presence of officers on duty on the perimeter track, it was a while before the seriousness of what was happening was realized and rescue attempts were made.

As the match was stopped and fans were pulled from the terrace through the narrow gates onto the pitch, the enormity of the tragedy became evident. Fans tore down advertising hoardings and used them to carry the dead and dying the full length of the pitch to the stadium gymnasium.

Ninety-six women, men, and children died because of the crush, while hundreds more were injured and thousands traumatized. In the immediate aftermath, there was a rush to judgment concerning the cause of the disaster and culpability. In a climate of allegation and counter-allegation, the government appointed Lord Justice Taylor to lead a judicial inquiry.

What makes Hillsborough an especially interesting case is how the narrative surrounding the incident has been reconstructed over time by different actors. It took decades after the event to fully recall what happened and attribute accountability accordingly. The story is an exemplar for how the idea of justice is tied to competing narratives of past events and sensemaking of (failing) technologies (see also Gephart, 2007). For example, most of the struggles of the victims' families have been concerned with correcting the story. But the long struggle for justice has faced two principle obstacles: (i) a systematic cover-up by the police, and (ii) misrepresentations of the event presented in the media, especially by a popular London-based tabloid. Both the police and the media cultivated the myth that Liverpool FC supporters had themselves caused the crush and committed atrocities to victims' bodies. As later reports gradually exposed, the police systematically promoted the false narrative to divert blame from their insufficient handling of the situation on site (Scraton, 1999, 2004; Teff, 1992). Some media, however, continued to disseminate the police version of events despite numerous divergent eyewitnesses' accounts, leading to boycotts. Formal condemnation of the narrative by the then Prime Minister David Cameron, and apologies by the media, were only made nearly 25 years after the tragedy (Hillsborough Independent Panel, 2012).

Together with the Heysel stadium disaster, during which 39 soccer supporters died just four years earlier (Young, 1986), the Hillsborough disaster has led to numerous changes in public safety policies at soccer stadiums. For example, one direct consequence is that the standing view areas were replaced by areas with seating, which is still the norm in the United Kingdom and at European club and national games (Sports Grounds Safety Authority, 2017).

As in the first example, human factors (crowd movement, police decision-making on site), organizational factors (insufficient policing policies), and technological factors (fences, pens, stadium architecture) combined during the emergence of the disaster. But in the Hillsborough case, the temporality of the event was much more predictable. While the same football stadium had already hosted thousands of games, it was not prepared for this specific constellation of fans, crowd movement, and policing errors. Some learning did occur prior to the disaster as the introduction of seating at English football games after the disaster shows. However, for decades, the strong focus of the police on shifting away blame precluded learning from how policing errors contributed to the disaster.

In sum, we suggest taking three points away from this example. First, even when public events occur with some regularity, the individual HOT-factors with specific crises remain important. They provide a suitable analytical lens, which focuses on why one event risk can turn into a disaster, while many others do not. Second, as the Hillsborough example shows, one of the main reasons for the preclusion of organized learning in the aftermath of event crises is the blame game, a configuration that can lead to learning in some areas, while others remain obscured by politics and vested interests. Paradoxically, the organizational defensiveness aimed at managing risks and prohibiting crises (cf. Power, 2007) can turn into a defensiveness against learning, once a risk has turned into a crisis. Third, reconstructing the facts of a crisis is a political process which might take a long time. However, it does not lose importance, as the collective memory is more prone to store neurotic experiences than success stories related to the management of event risks and crises.

Conclusion

In this final section, we draw some conclusions from the literature and illustrations presented in this chapter. We suggest that interesting and impactful research will need to engage with the fragmented and unique properties of events and their associated risks.

This chapter set out to offer a review of the fragmented literature dealing with risks and crises of public events. We started out by briefly specifying the different bodies of literature that relate to public event risks and crises, despite the absence of a field called public event studies (or something similar). We suggested first defining public events as organized mass gatherings around a specific core event. Since delineating public events from other types of events occurring in more stable organizational settings is difficult, we made our first contribution to the literature by offering a systematic definition of key features of public event risks and crises. Table 14.1 summarizes the key features in this HOT-framework, which outlines the human, organizational, technological factors in event risks and crises.

We then reviewed the literature concerned with public events. This led us to address one of the most pertinent challenges to organizing public events, namely, the barriers they pose to learning. Since public events are often organized by short-lived project organizations that are independent but operate as part of a network of organizations, learning from experience, be it disasters, near-misses, or best practices, has proven to be notoriously difficult due to communication problems and the lack of organizational learning. The second major contribution of our chapter is hence a systematic collection of the key barriers to learning for public event organizations. Table 14.2 summarizes the barriers, sub-divided into intraorganizational and extra-organizational causes.

To illustrate our review, we have briefly presented two empirical examples, the Olympic Games in 2012, and the Hillsborough disaster. While both public events were markedly different in terms of length, complexity, organization, and outcome, we could identify several common barriers to learning. Table 14.3 summarizes these features and illustrates how our suggestions can help make sense of risks and crises at public events.

We offer practical insights for those facing the challenge of organizing a public event and suggestions for future research. First, both the academic and practitioner-oriented literature and public media outlets perform a strong divide between ex-post and ex-ante analyses of event risks. As we have outlined in this chapter, ex-ante perspectives often focus on questions of financial and security risks, while ex-post perspectives are often limited to issues of preventing or recovering from disasters and are mainly concerned with questions of accountability. Again, the underlying problem of such a divide is that it complicates learning *between* events. The ex-post focus on disasters ignores the potential for learning from near-misses or successfully managed event risks. Such a feed-forward of experience and key learning could be usefully incorporated into ex-ante risk and crisis management. Equally, research on event management and "success stories" could benefit from incorporating insights from more critical literature, and vice versa.

Second, we attempt to bridge what are usually divided debates. This is not only relevant because of the different strands of research that focus on different aspects of event risks and crises. Rather, the separation of discourses in which researchers, regulators, and practitioners are involved (see, for example, Gephart, 1993) hints at a fundamental challenge for a debate on public event risks and crises. While some research is explicitly aimed at practitioners, few studies manage to simultaneously be practice-focused and theoretically sound. Insights from research on risk that is inspired by organization theory could be especially helpful for infusing discourses among practitioners and regulators with profound and relevant conceptual knowledge. Weick & Sutcliffe's (2007) work on high-reliability organizations, for example, may be a role model in this regard, as it effectively provides appeal to scholars and practitioners alike.

In sum, event risks and crises are of significant importance to scholars from diverse fields, such as organization theory, tourism research, urban studies, and risk management as well as risk and crisis management practitioners. Future research would benefit from investigating the multiplicity of public events by drawing on the wide range of theoretical perspectives we attempted to systematize in this chapter.

References

Asgary, A. (2017). World Crowd Disasters Web App V1. Retrieved from: http://yorku.maps.arcgis.com/apps/webappviewer/index.html?id=e7c52856187642e19bd227865393432c; last accessed September 30th, 2017.

Clarke, L. (1999). *Mission Improbable: Fantasy Documents to Tame Disaster.* Chicago, IL: University of Chicago Press.

Coaffee, J., & Rogers, P. (2008). Reputational Risk and Resiliency: The Branding of Security in Place-Making. *Place Branding and Public Diplomacy, 4*(3), 205–217.

Crepaz, L., Huber, C., & Scheytt, T. (2016). Governing Arts through Valuation: The Role of the State as Network Actor in the European Capital of Culture 2010. *Critical Perspectives on Accounting, 37,* 35–50.

Dempsey, J. (2010). Stampede at German Music Festival Kills 18. Retrieved from: www.nytimes.com/2010/07/25/world/europe/25germany.html; last accessed December 14th, 2017.

Easterby-Smith, M., Lyles, M. A., & Tsang, E. W. K. (2008). Inter-Organizational Knowledge Transfer: Current Themes and Future Prospects. *Journal of Management Studies, 45*(4), 677–690.

Feldman, M. S., & Pentland, B. T. (2003). Reconceptualizing Organizational Routines as a Source of Flexibility and Change. *Administrative Science Quarterly, 48*(1), 94–118.

Feldman, M. S., Pentland, B. T., D'Adderio, L., & Lazaric, N. (2016). Beyond Routines as Things: Introduction to the Special Issue on Routine Dynamics. *Organization Science, 27*(3), 505–513.

Flyvbjerg, B., Bruzelius, N., & Rothengatter, W. (2003). *Megaprojects and Risk: An Anatomy of Ambition.* Cambridge: University of Cambridge Press.

Gephart Jr., R. P. (1993). The Textual Approach: Risk and Blame in Disaster Sensemaking. *Academy of Management Journal, 36*(6), 1465–1514.

Gephart Jr., R. P. (2007). Crisis Sensemaking and the Public Inquiry. In C. M. Pearson, C. Roux-Dufort, & J. A. Clair (Eds.), *International Handbook of Organizational Crisis Management*, pp. 123–160. Thousand Oaks, CA: Sage.

Getz, D., Andersson, T., & Larson, M. (2006). Festival Stakeholder Roles: Concepts and Case Studies. *Event Management, 10*(2–3), 103–122.

Gigerenzer, G., & Gaissmaier, W. (2010). Heuristic Decision Making. *Annual Review of Psychology, 62*(1), 451–482.

Hillsborough Independent Panel. (2012). Report Summary. Retrieved from: http://hillsborough.independent.gov.uk/report/Section-1/summary/accessed February 16th, 2017.

Hood, C. (2002). The Risk Game and the Blame Game. *Government and Opposition, 37*(1), 15–37.

Hopkins, N., & Reicher, S. (2016). The Psychology of Health and Well-Being in Mass Gatherings: A Review and a Research Agenda. *Journal of Epidemiology and Global Health, 6*(2), 49–57.

Horne, J. D., & Manzenreiter, W. (2004). Accounting for Mega-Events. *International Review for the Sociology of Sport, 39*(2), 187–203.

IOC (2017). London 2012 by numbers. Retrieved from: www.olympic.org/london-2012#all-facts; last accessed December 14th, 2017.

Jennings, W. (2012). *Olympic Risks.* Basingstoke: Palgrave Macmillan.

Larsson, R., Bengtsson, L., Henriksson, K., & Sparks, J. (1998). The Interorganizational Learning Dilemma: Collective Knowledge Development in Strategic Alliances. *Organization Science, 9*(3), 285–305.

Levinthal, D., & Rerup, C. (2006). Crossing an Apparent Chasm: Bridging Mindful and Less-Mindful Perspectives on Organizational Learning. *Organization Science, 17*(4), 502–513.

Lundin, R. A., & Söderholm, A. (1995). A Theory of the Temporary Organization. *Scandinavian Journal of Management, 11*(4), 437–455.

New York Times (2000). 8 Crushed to Death at Rock Festival in Denmark (2000). Retrieved from: www.nytimes.com/2000/07/01/world/8-crushed-to-death-at-rock-festival-in-denmark.html; last accessed December 14th, 2017.

Perrow, C. (1984). *Normal Accidents: Living with High-Risk Technologies.* New York: Basic Books.

Pidgeon, N., & O'Leary, M. (2000). Man-made Disasters: Why Technology and Organizations (Sometimes) Fail. *Safety Science, 34*(1–3), 15–30.

Power, M. (2007). *Organized Uncertainty: Designing a World of Risk Management.* Oxford; New York: Oxford University Press.

Power, M. (2009). The Risk Management of Nothing. *Accounting, Organizations and Society, 34*(6–7), 849–855.

Power, M., Scheytt, T., Soin, K., & Sahlin, K. (2009). Reputational Risk as a Logic of Organizing in Late Modernity. *Organization Studies, 30*(2/3), 301–324.

Public Event Law and Legal Definition (2017). Retrieved from: https://definitions.uslegal.com/p/public-event/accessed September 20th, 2017.

Roux-Dufort, C. (2007). Is Crisis Management (Only) a Management of Exceptions? *Journal of Contingencies and Crisis Management, 15*(2), 105–114.

Scraton, P. (1999). Policing with Contempt: The Degrading of Truth and Denial of Justice in the Aftermath of the Hillsborough Disaster. *Journal of Law and Society, 26*(3), 273–297.

Scraton, P. (2004). 4 Death on the Terraces: The Contexts and Injustices of the 1989 Hillsborough Disaster. *Soccer & Society, 5*(2), 183–200.

Shrivastava, P. (1992). *Bhopal: Anatomy of a Crisis* (2nd ed.). London: Paul Chapman Publishing.

Smith, D., & Dominic, E. (2007). Exploring the Barriers to Learning from Crisis: Organizational Learning and Crisis. *Management Learning, 38*(5), 519–538.

Soomaroo, L., & Murray, V. (2012). Disasters at Mass Gatherings: Lessons from History. *PLoS Currents, 4*, RRN1301.

Still, G. K. (2017). Crowd Safety and Risk Analysis. Retrieved from: www.gkstill.com/CV/Expert Witness/CrowdDisasters.html accessed September 30th, 2017.

Sports Grounds Safety Authority (2012). All Seated Football Stadia. Retrieved from: www.safety atsportsgrounds.org.uk/regulation/all-seated-football-stadia; last accessed February 28th, 2017.

Teff, H. (1992). The Hillsborough Football Disaster and Claims for 'Nervous Shock'. *Medicine, Science and the Law, 32*(3), 251–254.

Turner, B. A. (1978/1997). *Man-Made Disasters.* New York: Pidgeon.

Tversky, A., & Kahneman, D. (1971). Belief in the Law of Small Numbers. *Psychological Bulletin, 76*(2), 105–110.

Weick, K., & Sutcliffe, K. (2007). *Managing the Unexpected* (2nd ed.). San Francisco, CA: John Wiley & Sons.

Young, K. (1986). "The Killing Field": Themes in Mass Media Responses to the Heysel Stadium Riot. *International Review for the Sociology of Sport, 21*(2–3), 253–266.

Zeitz, K. M., Tan, H. M., Grief, M., Couns, P. C., & Zeitz, C. J. (2012). Crowd Behavior at Mass Gatherings: A Literature Review. *Prehospital and Disaster Medicine, 24*(1), 32–38.

15

BERNÁCER'S TOPICAL THEORY OF CRISIS AND UNEMPLOYMENT

Henri Savall and Véronique Zardet

Introduction

The current economic crisis is part of the crisis cycle of advanced capitalism that will continue to disrupt our economic systems until the basic causes of economic and social imbalances have been treated. And given the complexity of economic problems and the lack of a viable theory to treat them, the road to durable prosperity will be long and the destination may never be reached. Yet, the ongoing economic crisis also provides an exceptional opportunity to change economic policies using new theories to overcome the limitations of crisis capitalism.

This chapter argues that economic crises are due to the fact that capital markets produce wealth based on speculative investments that involve *unearned income*. For example, the Wall Street movement in the 2010s questioned the concentration of wealth in the top 1% of income earners in this type of monopoly capitalism. Wall Street protesters argue that capital market problems are due to neoliberal economic theories that encourage unearned income as a basis for wealth. Crisis management strategies that focus on capital markets and unearned income therefore cannot address the fundamental sources of economic crisis.

The innovative theory of Spanish economist Germán Bernácer has inspired the work of Keynes (Savall, 1973, 1975) and today provides an insightful alternative explanation of recurrent crises in speculative markets. Speculative markets range from markets for property and works of art to long-term money markets and all forms of speculative commercial trading. These speculative markets, rich in financial capital, seek to accumulate additional capital that consequently becomes unavailable for use in production industries where real economic value is created. This increases the cost of productive (versus nonwork) economic activity and raises the price of money.

It is thus timely to apply the theory forged by Bernácer to develop a crisis management approach to create more radical, durable, and effective economic and financial policies. It is also important to curb the outrageous speculative activities of the financial markets. Bernácer's theory is unique and inviting because it is the only economic theory that advocates a zero rate of interest. Other economic theories view interest as an essential and unavoidable incentive needed to encourage citizens to save and invest financially, and argue that the economy cannot function with a zero rate of interest. Indeed, economists have become frightened by low interest rates. Yet, the economic situation in many Western countries in the early 2010s has demonstrated that economies can function with low interest rates (near zero). Some economists (e.g. Steven Poloz, Governor General of the Bank of Canada) have even considered mandating negative interest rates.

This chapter therefore poses and answers the following research question: *How can economic crises be better understood and prevented, or mitigated, using Bernácer's theory of economics and economic crises?* To answer this question, this chapter identifies the limits of neo-Keynesian and neoliberal theories of capital market crises. Next, the chapter explains Bernácer's theory for preventing and managing socioeconomic crises and applies the theory to important crisis events. This shows the global economic situation in the early 2010s was more consistent with Bernácer's theory than with other theories. Examples of applications of Bernácer's theory to prevent and mitigate economic crisis at the national level are provided. The conclusion explains the contributions Bernácer's theory makes to effective management of economic crises, discusses the limitations of Bernácer's theory, and notes future research that is needed.

Theories of Economic Crisis

The mainstream literature on liberal capital markets addresses financial and stock exchange practices and short-term regulations, but only rarely addresses economic crisis given that these theories were mainly inspired by Keynesian thought. Here we discuss two rare examples from contemporary authors: Paul Krugman and Thomas Piketty.

Paul Krugman: Why Do Crises Keep Coming Back?

Krugman (2014) says that an extensive study of economic and financial crisis resurgence worldwide since the second half of the 20th century has demonstrated that conventional economic remedies were ineffective, even counterproductive. The two key institutional tools for prevention of economic and financial crisis used by the Federal Reserve to stabilize firms in financial difficulty – ensuring the safety of deposits and providing bailouts to firms in financial difficulty—have failed to prevent crisis in 1930, 1990, and 2003.

Economic and financial crises since the second half of the 20th century cannot be dissociated from changes in political systems. Socialism collapsed during the 1980s and 1990s, leaving property rights and free markets – capitalism's major principles – to guide the economic and political world. Krugman ignores war but emphasizes serious economic recession as a key threat to capitalism because supply is ever-present, whereas demand is not ever-present. Economic recession thus arises when the public favors savings over consumption or investment, thus accumulating cash flow. This situation is inconsistent with the traditional remedies to recession: create and put currency into circulation to increase both consumption and investment. Consequently, many economists agree that the 1929 Great Depression was due to the collapse of demand and the failure of the Federal Reserve to increase money supply sufficiently to fight the crisis.

Globalization also plays a role in modern crises. Transfers of technologies and capital between high- and low-salary countries accelerated after the 20th century, and exports from developing countries to developed nations greatly increased in most developing nations during this time. Living conditions also improved through salary increases in South Korea, Taiwan, and Indonesia. Capitalism thus enabled poor countries to develop economically based on multinational companies' foreign investments in these countries, and local businesses that took advantage of exporting. Krugman highlights the United States' lack of sensitivity to the signals of economic and financial crisis in Latin America, in particular in Mexico and Argentina in the 1980s and 1990s, and more recently in Japan and Asia. For many generations, Latin American countries only knew monetary crises, bank bankruptcies, or inflation.

Krugman analyzes the 2008–2009 crisis in the United States and the broader world that originated in the real estate sector. Prices increased so much that real estate purchases became inaccessible for many Americans. After 2006, sales slowed and quickly collapsed in 2008, particularly where prices were very high. A tragedy occurred when homeowners found it difficult to sell their property and loans were not repaid. One important difference between the 2008 crisis and the 1930s crisis is the fact the shadow banking system was more involved than the conventional banks in 2008. Extremely complex financial instruments used to make subprime loans created legal obstacles that prevented any debt reduction. Krugman estimates that the real estate bubble destroyed €8,000 billion of wealth, including €7,000 billion due to losses to homebuyers and €1,000 billion to investors. These losses caused the collapse of the "shadow banking system" and resulted in a global financial crisis.

The world economy remains a depression economy. There is limited demand for goods, and private resources are not sufficient to fully exploit production capacities. This limits the enhancement of prosperity development in developed and developing countries. The question is how can one create sufficient demand? First, central banks must inject additional capital into local banks in the near term to restore banks' lending capacity. Second, central banks must also reduce interest rates significantly to support investment. This may require recapitalization of banks, a temporary nationalization of parts of the financial system, permitting federal officers to temporarily grant loans directly to the non-financial sector, and revitalizing the credit markets by implementing the fiscal stimuli advocated by Keynes.

To conclude, Krugman's analysis of financial crisis argues that the real problem is not insufficient resources because slack resources are available to create value. The real problem lies in the limitations of current economic theories. The important structural obstacles for economic prosperity are the obsolete models and doctrines of economics that obstruct our understanding.

Thomas Piketti's Analysis of 21st-Century Capitalism

Piketti (2013) adopts a macroeconomic approach to understanding disparities in wealth using aggregated economic measures and indicators and not the factors of production that create value. He studied the evolution of countries' and individuals' economic wealth through a historical analysis of 20th- and 21st-century macroeconomic data in the United States and Western Europe that show an increasing disparity in wealth. In the 1910s and 1920s, all Western countries were unequal. But recently in the United States, the income reported by "privileged" people increased substantially, from 9% to over 20% of total income. In Europe, the disparity increased less. Piketti stresses one key difference between capital revenue and labor revenue he considers nonreversible: the wealth disparity is much greater than revenue disparity. While the two World Wars reduced wealth disparities, new and greater forms of disparity have emerged since then.

Piketti's key thesis relies on a basic capitalist law: the return on capital (e.g. interest and dividends) is always higher than economic growth. The superiority of capital revenue relative to labor revenue benefits wealthy people and will benefit younger generations born in the 21st century even more. After the 1929 crash and World War II, the United States instituted progressive taxation to reduce wealth beyond a certain amount considered as excessive.

This is the basis for the solution proposed by Piketti: increase the tax pressure on wealthy persons to narrow the disparity and institute higher levels of taxation.

Piketti does not consider companies and organizations to be entities dedicated to creating and sharing value, and firms play a modest role in his analysis. He also fails to differentiate the types of economic actors such as the risk-taking, value-producing entrepreneur, or the annuitant who takes no risks and makes no effort to produce value. He also underestimates the essential function of *innovation* in the production of value. And his analysis provides only a limited role to human beings in value creation. People are largely absent in Piketti's analysis that focuses on dehumanized abstract categories. And although influenced by Marx's concept of *class conflict*, Piketti is unaware of the internal class conflict between employees within organizations. These significant limitations to Piketti's analysis are avoided by Bernácer.

Bernácer's Theory: An Overview

Germán Bernácer, a scholar trained in physics, developed an interest in economic crisis and published important economic research early in the 20th century. Bernácer was appointed Research Director of the Bank of Spain in 1931, during the second Spanish Republic. He held this position until 1955, and was in charge of an observatory and laboratory that was able to test, refine, and validate his theory. He continued publishing until 1965.

Bernácer published his first description of a theory of crises in 1916 (Bernácer, 1916). Later, he published an important theory of *disposable funds* that explained economic crises in relation to the social problem of unemployment (Bernácer, 1922). This article inspired work by Robertson (1926) and Keynes "*General Theory*" (1936) that laid the foundations for modern macro-economic theory. This theory provided a functional theory of money, a functional theory of the rate of interest, and a basic theory of economic crises due to the existence of *speculative markets for goods* that provide income without work, that is, *unearned income*. Unearned income does not require entrepreneurial risk, the creation of real value added, or sharing revenue from market speculation between economic and social stakeholders. Bernácer argued that the elimination of speculative markets would significantly contribute to the economic and social development necessary to overcome unemployment and help redirect resources toward activities that create value added that can be shared between all parties. The elimination of speculation would also prevent the recurring financial "bubbles" that frequently accompany global business cycles.

Bernácer (1945) proposed a general theory of employment, revenue, and double hoarding (Savall, 1973, 1975, 2012, 2018) that argues for rigorous financial management of the economy. His theory emphasizes the importance of a balanced budget and price stability as factors necessary for durable economic prosperity, safeguarding employment, and encouraging the creation of new jobs, products and wealth.

Bernácer denounced Keynes' "General Theory" (1936) that recommended increasing the money supply in times of crisis to create more demand for private enterprise since it assumed that increasing the money supply will stabilize the economy. This is problematic given the government is the only player in the economy that can create money. And it can create more money than there is value in society, and thereby produce a deficit in the economy. For example, the 1929 economic slump produced high unemployment, the collapse of financial markets, and left enterprises unable to finance their debts. This also encouraged the rise of Fascism, Nazism, and Communism in European countries. Keynes' proposals found favor because his theory enhanced the role of politicians, and his recommendations were attractive alternatives to Marxism and centrally run national economies like the USSR. But Keynesian policies produced an uneasy mix of between speculative and entrepreneurial capitalism, perverted both the speculative market and the real market, and created the chronic inflation deplored by Bernácer (1945), Perroux (1948), and Allais (1947).

This review shows the limitations of neoliberal economic theory, the importance of avoiding unproductive debates over passé ideologies and economic theories, and the value of Bernácer's pioneering theory for understanding and managing the ongoing economic crisis cycle of advanced capitalism.

Key Concepts in Bernácer's Theory

Value Creation

Bernácer (1955) theorizes about several key economic processes related to crises and provides unique definitions to common economic concepts. The first process concerns how value is created through productive activity. Capital is a corporal element that aids and increases *labor* productivity, whereas labor is a living force used in the creation of a product or service. Bernácer (1955, p. 4) says, "The capital itself is nothing but past work fixed on the matter" and "The capital, fruit of labor, is a passive instrument". Thus, labor is the only creative force in production: land and capital are passive forces.

Disposable funds, hoarding, and unearned income

Bernácer's concept of *disposable funds* (1922) refers to the money disposable in the hands of various agents, for example, *cash*. This concept is pivotal to Bernácer's analysis of economic dynamics and his fluctuation theory of *hoarding* defined as the retention of purchasing power gained by taking money out of the production circuit. Hoarding can have a fixed form (disposable cash), but can also be *in motion* (e.g. financing transactions on goods that are not currently being produced). To cover the two concepts, Savall (1975, p. 193) created the term "*double hoarding*". Hoarding is the fraction of monetary saved that is not invested in the *present* production of goods. Hoarding has a perverse effect: it is unused money that exists either in consumption or in investment that enables its possessors to live well but also reduces employment. Double hoarding refers to using money prospectively for lucrative operations and using money already in lucrative operations for investments outside of the production circuit.

Hoarding is related to non-reproducible goods and unearned income that encourage speculation. *Non-reproducible goods* were produced in past periods of economic activity and include historical artworks and objects such as antiquities. These are irreplaceable goods in relation to current production. The value of non-reproducible goods is related to their high prices and the probability the value of these goods will increase: they are speculative goods whose value is neither related to the historic cost of production or current use values, and they cannot be reproduced because they are unique. Things other than antiquities can become unearned income-yielding assets that serve speculative functions, such as real estate, drilling rights, and classic automobiles. Material debt securities can also generate unearned income. These unearned income-yielding goods that do not require the intermediary of work are *unearned income-yielding assets*.

Unearned income is an income generated without work by the asset owner. Other economic situations also produce unearned income through speculation. This unearned income becomes a parasitic cost grafted on the value of goods to satisfy the needs of production. Unearned income and speculation are the demons that tempt disposable funds holders who are sometimes distracted from their roles of consumer or investor to become hoarders and speculators pursuing unearned income. This diversion of disposable funds is significant and decreases productive activity because the disposable income is not reinvested in the production process. For Bernácer, the origin of investment interest is generalized unearned income; hence, he condemns interest because it makes investments more expensive and produces unemployment.

Profit is a residual of random and stimulating processes and has two temporal forms. Profit and value added are created in the present, but one must wait until the future to be able to spend one's income or know a corporation's profit. However, some agents can spend their anticipated future earnings in the present by obtaining a loan using income extracted from the production process in another setting. This loan must be repaid by hoarded income or future income. Thus, profit becomes a source of unearned income and involves both money creation and loans. Ultimately, all income in a given period—whether earned or unearned—is disposable at the end of the period, or, more formally, income from production completed during the period (t) will only be spent at the period (t+1).

The Key Crisis Mechanism

Money has two main functions in the economic circuit: (1) production circulation and the distribution of symbolic value, and (2) the circulation and accumulation of value outside the productive sphere. Goods and services production is the primary source of income, but an unproductive channel of monetary wealth is also created. Dialectical relations exist between the two circuits: without production, no economic activity would exist. Production is based on the premise that humans have the ability to satisfy needs, and the use value prevails in this circuit. Productive activity is restricted by the quantity of labor supply (the demographic factor), the intensity level of technology (the technical factor), and is the foundation for the second economic level: the financial market.

The financial market as a competitor of contemporary production

Double hoarding involves the creation of unearned income and the perverse effects this speculation has on unearned income. The prospect of unearned income attracts disposable funds (cash) from the production circuit. These disposable funds have two functions: a) making speculative investments outside the production circuit but within the financial circuit, and b) providing a means of payment for financial market operations. Consequently, a permanent stock of money is available for transactions outside of production that differs from the hoarded money held in expectation of advantageous opportunities. The scarcity of disposable funds in the production market thus supports a supply of money outside of the production circuit that does not perform its natural function as a basis for purchasing goods produced by current production. As Bernácer (1916, pp. 157–158) notes, "Economists have generally neglected, for simplicity, the time required for the formation of accumulations and for the implementation of all these operations that hold disposable funds on the financial market, thus fulfilling no productive work and causing no effect on the demand for real products".

Thus, unearned income is due to deviant institutions and consists of any income derived from nonwork. The immediate effect of the unearned income is hoarding: any money shifted away from product circulation is hoarded in cash form, either because of the expectation of a speculative transaction or simply because of time lags between payments. In Bernácer's theory, hoarding is the fundamental cause of interest and is related to the complex and dialectical production market-financial market system. The financial market thereby dominates the production and the employment markets, as well as investment programs, productivity growth, and therefore all economic and social progress. The instrument of this domination is the *rate of interest*.

The Causes of Market Disequilibria

Structural Causes

Structurally, creating a monopoly on consumer goods has two effects: depression and inflation. Monopolization has the immediate goal of setting a more profitable price than the perfect competition price. The immediate effects are declines in production, real income, and employment level. Constraining the entire production system to function below its actual capacity causes production factors to be underutilized and production to be insufficient. The growth of monopoly capital occurs through mergers and agreements between companies, legal monopolies, and nationalization.

Cyclical Causes

Cyclically, disequilibria depend on organizational agents' behavior in relation to the firm's internal financial situation, phase of the economic cycle (upward or downward), and professional, economic, and social environments. Companies, through agents' decisions on production, investment, employment, and income distribution, play a key role in their trading policy. Different micro-level configurations in different firms interact and cascade micro disequilibria that create a composite disequilibrium in the production market.

Labor Market

Workers have an unfavorable negotiating position in the labor market, and governments have tried to impose a fixed wage set by law, by collective agreements or through contracts with trade unions. According to Bernácer, this is expedient from an economic point of view, but not from a social point of view. As a consequence, Keynes invented the strange *unemployment equilibrium* concept that is rejected by Bernácer. The notions of unemployment and of general equilibrium are incompatible since unemployment unbalances the labor market, and hence a general equilibrium is unlikely to emerge. Bernácer adopts the semantic opposite referring to "*unemployment disequilibrium*" as an economic theory scandal given his concern for an "ethic of an Economy at the service of Mankind".

Rejection of the Classical Theory of Unemployment: Unsatisfied Needs in Abundance

Although Malthus argued that natural resources are insufficient to sustain the world, human ingenuity has so far been able to discover new resources. Bernácer thus argues that the only obstacle to growth is the amount of disposable labor, *ceteris paribus:* limitations by natural factors do not cause unemployment because needs and labor are abundant. Hence, the scarcity of money is an artificial, unnatural barrier to production. And unemployment is an institutional artifact, not a natural occurrence. Further, technical progress is not the sole cause of the sustained decline in employment levels, and there are other causes such as rising unemployment in industry due to technical progress. But when natural self-regulatory processes are working properly, labor market disequilibrium can be avoidable.

Double Hoarding Produces Limited Demand and Unemployment in the Production Market

Hoarding controls the return to equilibrium and also the employment level. Starting from a given equilibrium at the end of period 1, hoarding in period 2 of a part of period 1 savings causes aggregate demand to contract and triggers decreases in production, overall income, and employment. Unemployment becomes chronic when the salary has reached a level that no longer sustains the worker, something "which is not the result of boss or workers will, but the fate of the economic system" (Bernácer, 1945, p. 160). In Bernácer's analysis, the point of debate is not the alienation of value-added by management but the fact that lack of earnings by the worker benefits no one. This creates a process leading to collective impoverishment and the gradual "proletarianization" of all the levels of society, including small entrepreneurs. Hoarding value created in production removes it from circulation in production and alienates it from the ongoing economy.

Economic crisis is impacted more by a failure in effective demand than by an increase in the interest rate. Doubly insufficient demand can occur due to a fall in investment or consumption because of hoarding or increases in supply due to the increased productivity of new investments. So the emergence of hoarding signals the end of prosperity and the existence of over-supply in relation to current demand. Stocks (working capital) that have already risen to normal levels accumulate further and become a trigger to recession.

Economic Cycles: The Hydrodynamic Metaphor

Bernácer used a hydrodynamic metaphor to explain the mechanism underlying economic cycles. In a stable economic equilibrium model, only the circuit of production would exist and there would be only two possible choices for income expenditures: consumption or investment. The introduction of a financial market adds a third choice: demand for unearned income-yielding assets. Disequilibrium occurs when the demand for investment goods cash flow is different from the actual flow of the supply of these goods. This can be expected under the following conditions.

a   The cash flow related to the demand for investment goods is less than the actual supply and flow of these goods and the goods cannot be sold at fair price. Alternatively, disequilibrium can arise when the demand for investment goods decreases but the decrease is not accompanied by increased demand for consumer goods. Here, the market disequilibrium for the first goods is extended to the market for the second goods and can depress the overall effective demand, thereby producing a crisis.

b   The cash flow of investment goods demand is relatively higher than the actual supply due, for example, to technical innovation. Rising prices for goods can increase profits and produce increases in production and total income.

c   Since the production circuit has attracted relatively more money in (b), it creates a certain scarcity of money in the financial market that pushes up the rate of interest. This increased rate of interest can attract new disposable funds to financial markets. Meanwhile, the production capacity has increased, and consequently production and supply will rise. When disposable funds flow back from the productive circuit toward the financial circuit, supply of speculative capital will increase and become excessive compared to demand (decreased) and produces an economic depression until an exogenous event causes a significant increase in demand. The savings distribution between the demand for production and the demand for speculative earnings—investment or hoarding—is therefore of utmost importance.

Asymmetry in Trend Reversal

The crisis at the end of a boom will not be symmetrical with the end of a depression. Crisis is an endogenous element of economic systems, while a boom is caused from the outside, a premise fundamental to Bernácer's cyclical theory of economic crises that explains the various actions of the government or other agents that seek to create economic recovery.

To explain the cycle, one needs to consider the idea of asymmetry that is based on the concept of dominant structure. The financial market, through its instability and because of its function as a market that provides income without work, holds a privileged position in the production market of the economic system.

A Main Effect of the Cycle Is Universal Waste of Real Value Creation

Economic depression can grow to infinity, but prosperity has a limit: the economy therefore generally performs well below its capacity. The result is that humanity has tried in vain to discover and invent sustainable forms of progress because most forms of progress do not materialize or endure. As expressed by Bernácer,

> Humanity lived and still lives submitted to the torture of Tantalus: it sees ways to improve its fate without succeeding to achieve them; the insurance of being able to live by the sweat of its brow, following the divine sentence, is not even given to him for its spirit rest.
>
> *(Bernácer, 1916, p. 212)*

Bernácer protests against certain paradoxes that distort the economic system. For example, although work is considered noble, in actuality it is debased, depreciated, and despised in the late capitalist economic organizations. And trade, the most obvious expression of cooperation among peoples, is often thwarted when others strive to create obstacles preventing trade development. In the end, Bernácer's view accords with the views of some economists and biologists: there is a natural order of things in the world that is disturbed by artifacts such as economic models and beliefs, that is by what our species has created. Institutionalization of capital markets based on misguided analyses and political and social struggles has progressively moved the economic order that is created by humans further away from natural order. The end of this process is predicted to be a state of "very advanced and destructive barbarism" for our civilization (Bernácer, 1916, p. 215).

Contemporary Evidence Supporting Bernácer's Theory

Bernácer defended the economic regime of social capitalism or liberalism that criticizes monopoles, redefines the role of the state in the economy, and advocates for an open and regulated international opened economy. The world economic system continues to show evidence of the processes and propositions uncovered by Bernácer's analyses.

Ordoliberalism

One example of an economic system that reflects concern for social liberalism is Germany's "ordoliberalism" (Bourcier de Carbon, 1966), a form of the social capitalism that was used to reorganize the German economy after World War II. This form of capitalism differs from Anglo-Saxon capitalism in several fundamental ways: (1) banking is given a central role in the sustainable financing of industrial companies, (2) a social partnership is maintained among economic stakeholders to ensure there is a means for conflict resolution and a system of co-management of the enterprises, (3) a system of social protection has been developed, (4) a policy of monetary stability exists and is managed by a central bank, and (5) there are at minimum anti-trust and anti-monopole policies to regulate the economy.

Monopolies Restrict Fair Competition

Joseph Stieglitz (2012a, 2012b) argues that the economic activity of numerous industries (e.g. information technology, health-care, and pharmaceuticals) is inconsistent with free enterprise capitalism if one considers this economic activity from the point of view of fair competition. The dominant type of competition in the contemporary world is oligopolistic competition, not the pure and perfect competition described in economic treatises. Economic advisors to US presidents have noted the high level of concentration of activities and profits in several industries and found that the market share of bank deposits of the 10 largest US banks rose from 20% in 1980 to 50% in 2010. These values show that inequalities exist at all levels of the economy, and not simply between individuals.

Limiting State Influence

The rise of an extensive public administration is inconsistent with the needs of the social liberalist economy, and is in greater evidence in France than in Germany. There were more than 6,171,400 public administrators in France in 2014, some 500,000 more than in 2004. France has 90 state employees per 1,000 inhabitants (21.9% of the working population), whereas Germany has only 50 state employees per 1,000 inhabitants; the average for other member countries of the OECD is 15.5% (Delsol, 2017). The centralist welfare state (Olivier Babeau, 2017) aims at normalizing our behavior and seeks to change individuals, even unwillingly, to enhance common well-being. The welfare state requires the dependence of the individuals toward it while the liberal state, as underlined by Tocqueville, aims to accustom people to take control of the state themselves.

Globalization

For 20 years, globalization has taken the form of value-chain segmentation where the *production* of goods was divided between different countries. Imports rose in developed countries, and more and more components were made abroad. This fact suggests that home-based production cannot replace imports of goods or services any time soon, and hence international trade is essential to economic growth and prosperity, a point that is consistent with Bernácer's theory. Further, the monetary policy of the European Central Bank is ultra-expansionist and uses very low long-term interest rates to create economic growth. These practices are also consistent with Bernácer's theory.

Addressing Chronic Under- and Unemployment Difficulties

The Spanish government implemented measures of budgetary discipline to reduce unemployment in 2015. It experienced employment growth, unemployment fell by 8%, and three years later, job growth in Spain reached 3.2%. Overall, Spain gained about 500,000 full-time equivalent jobs, and unemployment fell from 26% to 18. 5% (Morel, 2016a, 2016b). Thus, the implementation of budget discipline advocated by Bernácer was an effective way for managing unemployment.

Deemphasize Stock Prices and Reinvest Profit in the Real Economy for Future Growth

BlackRock manages more than $5,000 billion of investment in financial markets and asks client firms to deemphasize the short-term market price of their firm's stock for the next months and reinvest this profit within the firm to finance future growth and longer-term increases in share values. Larry Fink, President of BlackRock, even favors new measures to reward companies for their long-term vision and efforts to ensure a better pension system for their staff (Coffrini, 2017): these are practices consistent with social liberalism.

Perverse Speculation

Bernácer has shown the perverse effects of hoarding that limits growth and condemns the economy to stagnation and perpetual poverty. An extreme example is the fraud committed by Bernard Madoff who swindled 20,000 investors out of their investments by promising fantastic yields. He used double hoarding to finance the process: recent payments by investors were used to pay prior investors, until a 64 billion dollar gap emerged: the swindle (Lauer, 2017).

Hoarding: A Defensive Against Future Economic Uncertainty

Robert Shiller (2015) anticipated the Internet Bubble in the early 2000s, and the American real estate crisis of 2008. He argues that many people face unprecedented economic uncertainty because of the financial crisis cycle and also because of uncertainty about the side effects that new technologies have for workers. People see new technologies replacing their work at an alarming speed and cannot anticipate their work of the future. This reduces product demand because people will amass financial assets rather than purchase products because they are saving for the future. One possible outcome consistent with Bernácer's theory is that these excessive savings will limit the money in the production economy, thereby plunging the economy into a "secular stagnation". This is worrisome because a weak economy pushes people toward more radical ideas and instigates political unrest (Lacombe & Vignon, 2016).

Poverty

Extreme poverty has returned to developing countries in the global world. One billion people were below the $1.25 income level 15 years ago. The rate of extreme poverty in East Asia fell only 4% in 2015, against 61% in 1990. One problem is that the level of employment is not developing fast enough to absorb an increasing workforce because the global economy is slowing down, wealth disparities are being accentuated, and financial disturbances such as crises are common. A total of 204 million people of working age remained unemployed in 2015. This is the source of the economic crisis most feared by Bernácer and most likely to be (re)produced by monopolistic, speculative capitalism.

Putting Bernácer's Theory to Work: Preventing and Mitigating Economic Crises

The process Bernácer recommends to attenuate financial crises and unemployment is the radical reform of financial (speculative) markets and producers of unearned income. The existence of a speculative financial market stimulates hoarding in anticipation of good investment, and it makes dishoarding possible when speculator expectations are unfavorable. Hoarding and dishoarding are bases for disequilibrium in the financial market. The best way to stabilize the system is to remove the sources of disequilibrium and, therefore, the base structure of hoarding: the financial market. The closure or elimination of financial markets first requires the establishment of the inalienability of unearned income-yielding assets. Then, it requires replacement of the structures of the financial market (mainly the stock market) with a registry of movable property similar to what is used in real estate. Further, market closure requires that all contracts relating to such property at the exception of sale (e.g. inheritance, donation, lease, mortgage, or pledge) be maintained. This financial market, as defined by Bernácer, includes real estate transactions and sources of added value.

Collecting Household Savings

Savings collection could be achieved in a way similar to how it is presently done. Households could deposit their disposable funds into bank accounts with zero interest. These deposits would be refundable on demand. To better identify the money supply needed for consumption and destined to savings, banks would open two kinds of accounts: current account and savings accounts. Withdrawals would occur only for the purposes of either consumption or real capital formation, that is, as part of the overall effective demand or for the acquisition of contemporary production assets. Fixed capital formation by companies could be achieved either by self-financing or by loan. Workers could be given the ability to place their current savings in companies for the long term.

Each bank would have a credit quota available to provide the working capital to fund projects. The bank, as a production unit, would then sell its financial intermediation services by collecting a commission to cover its business expenses, staff salaries, and possibly a profit maintained at a "normal" level obtained in the competitive marketplace.

Two Legitimate Sources of Income That Foster Full Employment: Wages and Profit

Wages are the predetermined income of productive activity. They are fixed in early period, taking into account the average productivity of the industry, the past results of production units, and the workers' individual aptitudes. It represents a kind of base pay – with rather stable characteristics—for individual effort. Profit would be shared among all workers in the enterprise as profit is a kind of extra salary created by the production unit's collective efficiency during the productive process. Profit takes account of, among other things, the firm's special ability to increase its productivity.

Transfers of income or *aids* have a peculiar status in Bernácer's theory. Sometimes, he evokes equalization procedures that provide mutual insurance which aims to share the risks inherent to particular situations or events with the community. He is hostile to government subsidies that distort market mechanisms and impose tax burdens or inflation costs to finance them. Bernácer recommended that strong financial and budgetary discipline be used for states, and also that a null interest rate policy be created. He supported this argument by demonstrating that there was a correlation between inflation rate and interest rate. Bernácer's proposition to cancel the rate of interest—the source of unearned income for speculators and bankers—was seen as utopian when he first proposed it.

Low or Null Interest Rates

Economies in the 2010s witnessed the emergence of very low interest rates. Yet, in 1998, the prospect of interest rates of zero or less was only a theoretical curiosity. So when Mario Draghi began his career as a European Central Banker (ECB), low interest rates were not a concern. By acquiring massive amounts of debt on financial markets and by also lowering their interest rates to zero, Mario Draghi and his counterparts managed to lower the cost of the money to a negative level. These unconventional policies make it possible from now on for certain states (Germany, Japan) or large companies to borrow on financial markets at negative interest rates. From now, the interest as a source of income for banking services can be replaced by the explicit sale of their services at a duly fixed price.

For example, in France, the expenses for accounting increased by 13%, on average, in 2017. Traditionally, the banking industry has found its remuneration in the spread between the interest rates charged for loans and interest rates paid on deposits to lenders: other banking services were free. In an alternative future, they could be explicitly charged as services. In real estate, rates are at the lowest level in the history. Average rate of property loan is unless 2%, something unheard of since the 1940s. Between January 2009 and March 2016, the average interest rate on property loans to private individuals declined from 4.75% to 1.97%. Banks do not hesitate to reduce their margins to obtain new customers and hold their sales objectives (*Les Échos*, April 6, 2016). Thus, Bernácer's "utopian" ideas of low or negative interest rates and service charges rather than interest have been shown to be possible and even feasible.

Conclusion: Toward a Sustainable Economic Future

Much of the liberal capital markets literature is about financial and stock exchange gaming and short-term regulation and is not focused on explaining economic crises. And mainstream current theories on crisis are mainly inspired by Keynesian thought and thus limited. We presented first a short summary of a sample of mainstream theorizing about economic crises from two renowned contemporary authors: Paul Krugman and Thomas Piketty. Then, Bernácer's theory was presented. He views crises as due to speculative markets for goods that provide incomes without work, called unearned income. So Bernácer identifies two kinds of capitalism: the entrepreneur's capitalism and the financiers' capitalism, each with differing, even opposing, effects on the economy and social welfare. The non-reproducible goods which exist before the present period of economic activity, such as historical artworks and objects, usually antiquities, have a harmful effect on the production market. Their value is related to the huge sums spent for their acquisition and the probability of their value growth: these are speculative elements that make goods and labor markets go wrong.

Four main types of income exist at the same time in the economic market: wages are generally spent by employees for buying goods from current production. Nevertheless, a fraction of wages is continually diverted from its "normal" use, because it is attracted by uses that yield income without requiring any work, that is, unearned income perceived without work or entrepreneurial risk. There are different monopoly situations in economic activity that produce such unearned income; rent, as price for using a property; interest, as price to pay to generate a "double dishoarding" from sterile savings or speculative investments; and last, profit that is stimulating ethical income. It is determined at the collective level of the enterprise and divided through a kind of wage supplement, as the entrepreneur is also a worker among others in the business. Profit is a basic element of the dynamics of production system and of economic and social welfare.

Bernácer identifies two competitive markets, which create a duality of the economy circuit and are the root cause of the chronic economic crisis. The production market where goods and services production occurs is the primary source of income and the main sustainable source of value creation. The financial market is "unproductive" of real value added. Relations between the two circuits are dialectical. In the financial market, a "double hoarding" appears: hoarding in the form of money to be prospectively used for further lucrative operations, and money already underway in lucrative operations outside of the production circuit. This financial market generates a scarcity of disposable funds on production market. Hoarding is also the fundamental cause of interest. In the labor market, Bernácer rejects the classical theory of unemployment, and considers that needs and labor are in abundance. Double hoarding reduces demand in production market and is the main factor causing unemployment.

The continuing economic situation shows numerous marks of the relevance from Bernácer's analyses and propositions. He defended the economic regime of social capitalism or liberalism, criticizing monopoles and the "Keynesian" role of the state on economy, and coming in favor of an international free opened and regulated economy. He analyzed the chronic full and under-employment difficulties we faced in the late 2010s. He also denounced the harmful effects of speculation, the destabilizing role of stock exchange terms operations, the obstacles interest rates impose on economic activity, and the sources of income used by speculators, banks, and unearned income earners. He also anticipates the perverse and noxious role of hoarding. This limits growth and condemns an economy to stagnation and perpetuate poverty. All these situations are extremely common in the 21st century.

The final part of this chapter sums up the Bernácer's propositions to prevent and mitigate economic crises. He recommends a radical reform of financial speculative markets that produce unearned income in order to stabilize the system and to remove the sources of disequilibrium and the base structure of hoarding: the so-called financial market. The closure or elimination of financial markets first requires the establishment of the property of inalienability for unearned income-yielding assets. Then, it requires replacement of the different structures of the financial market (mainly stock market) by a registry of movable property as is required for real estate. The interest rate should be decreased or very low. Further, market closure requires all contracts other than sales relating to such property—inheritance, donation, lease, mortgage, or pledge—to be maintained The financial market can be replaced by reorganizing the financial circuit of production market. The importance of financial markets in the 2010s, and the adverse impact of goods that leads to speculative bubbles, show that Bernácer's theory is more timely than ever.

Bernácer is the one scholar among non-Marxist authors who severely condemns unearned income. His major concerns have timely and ongoing significance: avoiding speculation, enhancing economic stability, and meeting socioeconomic needs through new macro-economic policies. His general philosophy suggests solutions navigate between the strictures of liberalism and Keynesianism. Bernácer deserves an important place in the history of economic thought as a founder of modern, heterodox, innovative economic theory. He also deserves an important place in current economic thought given his insights into the underlying causes and consequences of economic crises inherent in late capitalism.

References

Allais, M. (1947). *À la recherche d'une discipline économique (In search of economic discipline)*, t. 1, « Économie et Intérêt » (Economy and interest), Imprimerie nationale.

Artus, P. (2016). Vérités économiques (Economic truths), *Les Échos*, 27-12, p. 8.

Babeau, O. *L'horreur politique : l'État contre la société*. Paris: Manitoba Les Belles Lettres.

Bernácer, G. (1916). *Sociedad y felicidad - Ensayo de Mecánica Social*. Madrid: Ed. Beltrán.

Bernácer, G. (1922). La teoría de las disponibilidades como interpretación de las crisis y del problema social. *Revista nacional de economía*, (40).

Bernácer, G. (1945). *La teoría funcional del dinero*. Madrid: Consejo Superior de Investigaciones Científicas, 2nd edition, 1956.

Bernácer, G. (1955). *Una economía libre sin crisis y sin paro*. Madrid: Aguilar.

Bourcier de Carbon, L. (1966). Considérations sur l'évolution actuelle du capitalisme. *DS*, 20, 1–44.

Coffrini, F. (2017). BlackRock sermonne encore les entreprises américaines. *Le Figaro* Économie, 25–1, p. 17.

Delors J. (1975). Preface to H. Savall « *Enrichir le travail humain : l'évaluation économique* ». Paris: Dunod.

Delsol, J-P. (2017). Libéralisme économique. *Le Figaro*, 25-1, p. 16.

Gattaz, P. (2016). Plein emploi: quatre réformes en France (Full employment: four reforms in France). *Le Figaro*, 27-12, p. 18.

Gordon, R. J. (2016). *The rise and fall of American growth. The U.S. standard of living since the Civil War*. Princeton, NJ: Princeton University Press.

Guichard, G. (2016). Dette publique (Public debt). *Le Figaro Économie*, 30-12, p. 20.

Keynes, J. M. (1936). *Théorie générale de l'emploi, de l'intérêt, de la monnaie*. French translation. Paris: Payot, 1959.

Krugman, P. (2014) *Pourquoi les crises reviennent toujours?* Paris: Seuil.

Lacombe, P. & Vignon, L. (2016). Économie et politique, Les Échos, April, 13th, p. 16.

Lauer, S. (2017). Madoff continue à faire des affaires en prison. *Le Monde*, 25-1, p. 15.

Marx, K. (1962). *Le capital*. Paris: Ed Sociales.

Morel, S. (2016a). L'Espagne accélère les baisses d'impôts. *Le Monde*, 12-7, p. 15.

Morel, S. (2016b). En Espagne, moins de chômage. *Le Monde*, 6-4, p. 13.

Nême Cordebas, C. (1956). *La théorie monétaire de Sir Dennis Robertson*. PhD dissertation, Paris.

Perroux, F. (1948). *Le capitalisme*, Collection « Que sais-je ». Paris: PUF; 3rd edition, 1958.

Piketty, T. 2013. *Capital in the twenty-first century*. Boston, MA.: Harvard University Press.

Robertson, D. H. (1926). *Banking policy and the price level*. London: Augustus M. Kelley.

Robertson, D. H. (févr. 1940). "A Spanish contribution to the theory of fluctuations", *Economica*.

Robertson, D. H. (1952). *Utility and all that and other essays*. London: Allen.

Savall, H. (1973). *Germán Bernácer, économiste espagnol (1883–1965). Une théorie générale de l'emploi, de la rente et de la thésaurisation*. PhD dissertation at the University of Paris II, 602 p. mimeographed.

Savall, H. (1975). *G. Bernácer : L'hétérodoxie en science économique (G. Bernácer : The heterodoxy in Economics)*. Dalloz, Collection Les Grands Économistes.

Savall, H. (2012). *Origine radicale des crises économiques : Germán Bernácer, précurseur visionnaire*. Charlotte: Information Age Publishing.

Savall, H. (2018). *Radical origins to economic crisis: Germán Bernácer, a visionary precursor*. Preface by Robert P. Gephart. New-York: Palgrave Macmillan.

Savall, H. & Zardet, V. (2008). *Mastering hidden costs and socio-economic performance*. Charlotte: IAP.

Savall, H. & Zardet, V. (2011). *Challenges and dynamics of Tetranormalization*, 1st edition. Paris: Economica, 2005.

Savall, H. & Zardet, V. (2017). *Strategic engineering of the reed*. Charlotte: IAP.

Savall, H., Zardet, V., & Bonnet, M. (2000, 2nd ed. 2008). *Releasing the untapped potential of enterprises through socio-economic management*. Genève: ILO-BIT.

Savall, H., Peron, M., Zardet, V., & Bonnet, M. (2017). *Socially responsible capitalism and management*. New-York: Routledge.

Schumpeter, J. (1939). *Business cycles*, vol. 1. New-York: Mc Graw-Hill.

Schumpeter, J. (1965). *Capitalisme, socialisme, démocratie*. Paris: Payot.

Shiller, R.J. (2015) *Irrational exuberance*. Princeton, NJ and Oxford: Princeton University Press.

Smolar, P. (2016). L'économie israélienne est proche du plein emploi. *Le Monde*, 18–3, p. 16.

Stiglitz, (2012a). *Cost of inequality*. Luxemburg City: Babel.

Stiglitz, J.E. (2012b) Interview, Journal du Dimanche, September 2nd, p. 17.

Vignaud, M. (2016). Les nouvelles lois de l'économie. *Le Point*, 21–4, p. 27.

Visot, M. (2016). La dette française. *Le Figaro*, 24–12, p. 18.

Worley, C., Zardet, V., Bonnet, M., & Savall, A. (2015). *Becoming agile. How the SEAM approach to management builds adaptability*. Hoboken, NJ: John Wiley & Sons.

16

RISK AND HUMAN RESOURCES

Mike Annett

Introduction

Many notable disasters are linked to organizations. Recent examples include a space shuttle explosion (NASA), ship loss (Costa Cruises), building collapse (Sohel Rana, and by implication Loblaws, Walmart, Benetton, and others), and train derailment (MMA Railway). These disasters, with drastic implications for human life and the environment, manifested organizational crises – existential threats to the organizations involved (Seeger, Sellnow, & Ulmer, 1998).

Often, the accountable response involves naming a person(s) whose direct action or inaction contributed to the disaster. In the aforementioned examples, human error and action have been assigned at least partial blame. G. Madhavan Nair, former chair of the Indian Space Research Organization, attributes the Columbia space shuttle disaster to a failure of human judgment and inaction regarding repair of a known materials defect (First Post, 2017). The Costa Concordia ran aground due to unsafe sailing practices and the captain wanting to impress a crowd (Nadeau, Yan, & Bothelho, 2015). The Dhaka building in Bangladesh collapsed due to known and ignored foundation cracks (Marriot, 2013). People needlessly died as company owners reportedly gave employees false assurances of safety and threatened absent workers with pay-loss (Devnath & Srivastava, 2013). The Lac-Megantic town destruction has been attributed to a host of interconnected issues, including insufficient employee training on trains' handbrake equipment (Hopper, 2013).

Employee-involved risks do not always manifest in the destruction of life and environment, but do often jeopardize the success and capability of organizations. For example, with a simple coding typo an employee of GitLab wiped out primary server data and imperiled the operations of many organizational clients (Weinberger, 2017). The consequences are also not always 'full blown crises', and may reside further down an impact or significance scale. For example, HSBC employees were charged with currency manipulation, putting the legitimacy of the bank's operations and competitive capabilities in question (Stevenson, 2016). Coach Bill Belichick was caught violating the NFL's videotaping rules – essentially spying on the competitors, resulting in a monetary fine to himself and the team, plus the loss of a coveted draft pick (Reiss, 2007). Lastly, employees regularly fall victim to social engineering scams (Francis, 2017) that can result in varying loss levels for company finances, reputation, and competitive advantage (Goel, Williams, & Dincelli, 2017; Seidenberger, 2016). These circumstances may still be termed 'crisis' as they are times of intense difficulty, and important rapid decisions must be made in response. For the people involved in these lower-level crises, the continuation of the organization may hang in the balance.

From these examples, it is readily apparent that the actions and inactions of employees present fundamental risks for organizations, and are at the heart of many organizational crises. However, the treatment of employee-related risks in the literature, particularly the human resource management field, is relatively sparse (Becker & Smidt, 2016). This chapter brings the analysis of organizational risk and crisis down a few levels to the performance area of employees – leaders, supervisors, and frontline employees, and in doing so, brings forward, articulates, and expounds organizational risks pertaining to the employment of people.

The following risk and crisis categories addressed in the chapter are based on the examples referenced earlier; the academic work of Choi, Ye, Zhao, and Luo (2016) which identifies Human Resources as one of several enterprise risks meriting optimization; and guidance from practical consultancies such as Deloitte and Touche (2017):

- **Strategy** – Non-execution of longer-term governance and corporate direction.
- **Reputation** – Negative public attitudes and diminished respect.
- **Regulation** – Noncompliance with statutory requirements.
- **Financial** – Diminished revenue, increased costs, and/or reduced capacity to fulfill fiduciary obligations.
- **Operations** – Diminished capacity to meet production targets.

These categories help illustrate the nature of crises that may follow from certain decisions and actions regarding employees and by employees.

The focal group of this chapter is variously labeled in the management literature as 'employees', 'workers', 'staff', and 'human resources'. However, the term 'labor' is mostly used here to describe this group in a broad and flexible fashion, as well as to minimize confusion with the internal department of 'Human Resources'. Further, discussing crisis in terms of 'labor risk' also facilitates philosophical alignments to related issues of the 'labor problem'.

The chapter is organized in two major sections that offer different approaches to discussing risk and human resource management. The first section, 'Categorizing Labor Risk', presents a contingency-style table illustrating intersections of labor risk categories (Resource, System, People) and risk discourses (Directed, Normative, Calculated). This is accomplished using real-life examples of risk manifestations producing organizational crises. The second section, 'Change and Labor Risk', identifies the paradox that organizational changes, often a concerted response to global environment risk perceptions, may be thwarted by labor responding to their local environment risk perceptions. Examples pertaining to safety practices and inclusive workplaces help illustrate the role of individual attitudes and concerns impeding the fulfillment of corporate strategy. The Concerns-based Adoption Model is also suggested as a risk-relevant approach to resolving labor's reluctance to change. Together, these sections provide a broader perspective on the issues and implications of risk and human resource management.

Categorizing Labor Risk

The labor problem, described as the general struggle for control over production and distribution of income – and its industrial economy exemplars: worker soldiering, turnover, waste and inefficiency (Kaufman, 1993) – highlights the central role of resolving negative labor issues in strategies of labor management. Since the early days of focused study of the management of labor (e.g., Frederick Taylor, Henri Fayol, Elton Mayo), a clear trend has been toward positive enactment; that is, maximizing employee outputs, increasing well-being, incentivizing performance, and enhancing work clarity and employee involvement. For additional insights on this positive perspective, see Beer, Spector, Lawrence, Mills, and Walton (1984).

In as much as enhancement-oriented practices for 'maximizing gains' constitute an inherently useful and self-evident management approach, the corollary that benefits also accrue to protection-oriented practices for 'minimizing losses' is obvious but less represented in the strategy and practice literature (Boudreau & Cascio, 2014). Certainly, it is a valuable achievement for the company to not (a) experience an employee's incomplete performance of duties and perhaps loss of a prized client, as occurred when a California DMV employee accidently revealed the member names of Apple's secret team working on self-driving cars (Weinberger & Leswing, 2017); (b) suffer an abuse of trust such as employee fraud, as happened when a bank's loan officer stole money (Leitch, 2017); or (c) apologize for employee acts that are inappropriate and cause tremendous reputational harm, such as questionable air passenger deplaning practices (Podoshen, 2017).

Juxtaposing Labor Risk and Risk Perspectives

Organizations may become aware of or be affected by labor risks in any or all of the following three categories: **Resource**, **System**, and **Person**. Becker and Smidt's (2016) review of risk perspectives and human resource management articulates these categories with different labels (Integrative, Organizational/HRM Practices, and Human Resources, respectively) and comparable descriptions as below:

- **Resource:** Risks arising from the engagement of labor as a productive element in the organization (alongside capital, infrastructure, technology, raw product, etc.).
- **System:** Risks arising from the rules and processes of managing labor.
- **Person:** Risks arising from the free attitudes, decisions, and behaviors of labor.

In attending to these risk categories, the organization may adopt one or several perspectives on the risk: **Directed**, **Normative**, and **Calculated**. Debrah Lupton (1999) articulates these with different labels (Governmentality, Socio-Cultural, and Cognitive Science, respectively) and comparable descriptions as below:

- **Directed**: A decree, normally by a jurisdictional or organizational leader, that a circumstance is high or low risk, with the decree being communicated to the governed or supervised people.
- **Normative**: A view by a collective (explicitly or implicitly) that a circumstance is high or low risk, mutually reinforced by in-group members, and subject to change over time.
- **Calculated**: A factors assessments (e.g., probability and consequence) of high or low risk, and a rational assessment of harm potential.

Juxtaposing these two constructs – labor risk and risk perspective (in relation to the aforementioned forms of harm and crises) – provides an organizing framework for the risks experienced by organizations. Table 16.1 presents three exemplar labor issues (**Resource**:

Table 16.1 Matrix of Risk Categories and Perspectives

		Categories of labor risk		
		Resource	*System*	*Person*
		E.g., Humans as a productive resource	E.g., Sourcing workers	E.g., Employee behavior
Risk perspectives	Directed	Cell 1. Topic: Requirement for human labor. Risk: Organizations may be open to legal crises and harm related to ambiguous and evolving permissibility of substituting artificial intelligence for human labor.	Cell 4. Topic: National workforce and temporary foreign workers. Risk: An organization's talent sourcing approach may open it to legal crises and harm related to employing foreign workers.	Cell 7. Topic: Employee termination Risk: The organization's response to poor employee conduct may open it to legal crises and harm related to its adherence to statutory requirements.
	Normative	Cell 2. Topic: Acceptance of mechanized services. Risk: Organizations may be open to reputational and financial crises and harm if customers reject the replacement of human labor in favor of artificial intelligence, self-serve kiosks, and other mechanized services.	Cell 5. Topic: Employing foreign or guest workers Risk: An organization's talent sourcing practices may open it to reputation and revenue crises and harm related to customer views of foreign workers.	Cell 8. Topic: Off-duty conduct Risk: The organization may be open to reputational and financial crises and harm related to their non-response of publicly observed employee off-duty discreditable conduct.
	Calculated	Cell 3. Topic: Business case of automation Risk: Organizations may be open to operational and financial crises and harm if human labor is ineffectively replaced by automation and mechanized work.	Cell 6. Topic: Realized value of foreign workers Risk: An organization's talent sourcing practices may open it to operational crises and harm related to practical aspects of managing foreign workers.	Cell 9. Topic: Termination or discipline Risk: The organization's decision to terminate employees may open it to operational crises and harm related to practical aspects of completing work without the employee.

Humans as Resource; **System**: Sourcing Workers; and **Person**: Employee Behavior) and addresses them according to each risk perspective. Indicated in each cell is a representative, real-world situation.

Following the table are more fulsome descriptions.

Category of Labor Risk: Humans as a Productive Resource

The first labor issue addressed in the table is the broad question of whether the company should employ labor to perform work. Human labor has long been a given in the achievement of organizational goals. Indeed, from the monumental (e.g., pyramids, railroads) to the common (e.g., tax returns, teaching), people have held a de facto place in the planning, management, and performance of work. However, pre- and post-Industrial Revolution, and especially during the revolution, human labor has been substituted out in favor of animals, machines, and software. Sometimes, the substitution occurs because the work is dangerous to the human. More often, substitution occurs because limitations of the human are positively addressed by the other resources. Limitations may include unwillingness to comply with directions, physical or cognitive thresholds, and inconsistency of performance.

As organizations initiate, maintain, or expand their lines of business, they regularly address a fundamental question: Will they use human labor to accomplish work? Alongside the enhancement orientation toward labor, this decision calls forward views on the protection orientation toward labor. Three protection–oriented views (minimizing loss by labor) are outlined below with clarifying examples.

Cell 1) Resource & Directed. The directed perspective, based largely on the work of Foucault (1991), takes the view that state/governmental apparatus manages or regulates populations through knowledge and power relations. They do so in part by identifying activities risky to the society and protecting the society from such activities. While the directed perspective presupposes that risks are socially constructed, it argues that there exists certain expert knowledge on these risks. Such knowledge is gained through surveillance or other information acquiring practices such as the 'panoptic-gaze' that provides context for the 'truths' of that society. Foucault, like Beck (1998) and Giddens (2002), also sees the role of expert knowledge collected and analyzed via a heterogeneous network of researchers, statisticians, lawyers, and other such actors. Through these efforts, risks are problematized and rendered governable.

In this way, the rightness of nonhuman involvement in the performance of work becomes the purview of elected officials and risk assessments expressed through enabling or prohibiting legislation and regulation. In practical terms, companies such as Google, Apple, Uber, and Otto look to legislation for guidance on the permissibility (riskiness) of removing human drivers from the personal and commercial operation of motor vehicles. While Google and Apple appear more focused on personal driving circumstances, Uber and Otto clearly intend to provide commercial services with artificial intelligence control of the vehicles.

As the issue of artificial technology emerges, many governments have passed laws governing autonomous cars (Weaver, 2014). A portion of the debate pertains to vehicle, passenger, and pedestrian safety (Howard & Dai, 2013; Hsu, 2017). Another portion of the debate pertains to the employment and economic impacts that may accompany the legalization of autonomous cars (Fahey, 2016; McKinsey & Company, 2016). This is akin to economic upheaval and adjustments associated with the Industrial Revolution and the changing applications of labor (Clements & Kockelman, 2017).

A synthesis of this risk concern is: Organizations may be open to legal crises and harm related to ambiguous and evolving permissibility of substituting artificial intelligence for human labor.

Cell 2) Resource & Normative. The normative perspective draws on the work of Douglas (1966) and takes the view that notions of risk are culturally specific and help form ideas of self and others. Culture not only helps individuals understand risk but sets up a communal notion of risk: not what is risky to one person, but what is risky to us. This approach considers the boundaries between the individual and group, and conceptualizes risks as threats to the body/symbol/society. Risks are often recognized as pollutants, which if not controlled against may invade the social body and cause damage.

A normatively risky activity may be the introduction of a mechanized workforce to a function usually performed by human labor. The abovementioned driverless car is a futuristic example of this issue – that patrons may reject a driverless taxi on the premise that it is putting a fellow human out of work. Similarly, the past Luddite movement recognized the risk of mechanization to their jobs and way of life. In present day, some members of society reject efforts to automate customer service (Tuttle, 2011) and speak out against self-serve kiosks (Maras, 2016). The concerns here are not about safety or quality, but about the slippery slope of convenience automation trumping personal interactions and individual employment.

A synthesis of this risk concern is: Organizations may be open to reputational and financial crises and harm if customers reject the replacement of human labor in favor of artificial intelligence, self-serve kiosks, and other mechanized services.

Cell 3) Resource & Calculated. The calculated perspective suggests that risks can be objective and known, understood, calculated, and managed through the scientific method. Essentially, risk is a statistical description of predictable events that may be minimized through recognition, compensation, and avoidance. Questions that are important to this perspective include (1) how can risk be identified or calculated, (2) what is the accuracy of models of risk, and (3) why do risks occur? Lupton (1999) argues that the approach 'constructs individuals as calculating and emotion-free actors' (p. 22).

Underpinning the traditional risk management practice, this perspective 'is a scientific approach to dealing with pure risks by anticipating accidental losses and designing and implementing procedures that minimize the occurrence of loss or the financial impact of losses that do occur' (Vaughan 1997, p. 30). Two broad risk management tools are risk control – the minimization of costs, and risk financing – the guaranteeing of funds to meet losses.

Returning to the example of driverless vehicles, the executive of a transportation company may look at the specific pros and cons of autonomous vehicles relative to driver labor concerns. A study by ACA Research (Nuttall, 2015) reveals that fleet owners considering fully- and semi-autonomous vehicles anticipate (1) increased safety, (2) enhanced driver productivity, and (3) lower staff expenses, and believe that autonomous vehicles present a lower overall risk than human-piloted vehicles. Similarly, industrial robots are increasingly appearing in factories. RobotWorks, a company advocating for more use of independent robots (segregated) and collaborative robots (working with humans), indicates there are pros and cons of what they call the 'fourth industrial revolution' (RobotWorks, n.d.). Specifically, advantages include (a) shorter cycle times, (b) improved quality and reliability, (c) increased safety, and (d) reduced waste. Challenges involve (a) big initial investment, (b) production planning, and (c) employee training (service and interaction). Ultimately, RobotWorks advocates that the upside of industrial automation outweighs the downside.

However, not all organizations will benefit from automation. Shacklett (2015) points out that organizations with rote and repetitive tasks or those with data crunching elements (e.g., financial fraud identification) are more likely to benefit from automation than those with more intensive customer interactions or frequent non-routine decision-making. Further, economic downturns or a stagnant business environment may make it difficult to recoup the upfront costs of automation.

A synthesis of this risk concern is: Organizations may be open to operational and financial crises and harm if human labor is ineffectively replaced by automation and mechanized work.

Category of Labor Risk: Sourcing Workers

The second labor issue addressed in the table relates to the question of a company sourcing workers locally or globally. 'Locally' is the common and publicly popular answer, but also possibly problematic. What if the local labor supply does not have the required skills or abilities? Or, what if the domestic workers are expensive when compared to foreign workers? At what point of hardship does it become acceptable or wise to overlook the local talent?

As organizations search the specialized, globalized world for the right talent, at the right time, and at the right cost, it becomes increasingly likely that a fit will be found with workers that reside somewhere other than the local labor market. Again, the three risk perspectives are applied to illuminate views of labor risk from the system perspective. For parsimony, however, the introduction to each risk perspective is foregone allowing the issues to be directly presented.

Cell 4) System & Directed. 'Who is legally entitled to work?' is a direct question of this perspective and engenders the risk perspective that the employment of some workers may hamper the livelihood and safety of citizens, or otherwise imperil society. Governmental distinction between issuance of visitor and work visas illustrates this risk. However, the risk concern may also be domestic mobility. The Canadian Charter of Rights and Freedoms (Canadian Charter of Rights and Freedoms, 1982) expressly contains a mobility clause in Subsection 6(2) enshrining the right of a citizen of one province to commence work in another province without satisfying a residency requirement. Residency laws were previously enacted to address concerns that domestic aliens may flock to a location and undercut the native residents' employment opportunities (Greene, 2014). Another concern is that organizations may choose to avail themselves of a lower-cost, relocating workforce, to the detriment of the local labor market. For example, interprovincial and territorial acts include regulations for the mutual recognition of certain standards and competencies for trades designated as Red Seal (e.g., baker, carpenter), thus enabling the mobility of such workers (Red Seal, 2017) while conversely making migration more difficult for non-Red Seal trades (e.g., heavy equipment technician, locksmith).

The emergence of a migratory class of workers (Newhook et al., 2011; Sharma, 2001), plus increased governmental response to local labor market shortages (Foster & Barnetson, 2015), has resulted in the development of regulations and programs to ease the organizational burden of insufficient employees to perform work. An example of this program is Canada's Temporary Foreign Workers Program. This program is designed to permit organizations to temporarily hire foreign workers to perform work that would otherwise be done by domestic workers. As part of the process, the employer may need to obtain a Labor Market Impact Assessment from the Canadian government indicating that Canadian workers are unavailable or unlikely to fill the jobs.

A synthesis of this risk concern is: An organization's talent sourcing approach may open it to legal crises and harm related to employing foreign workers.

Cell 5) System & Normative. While organizations may become legally permitted to hire foreign workers, by allowance of the Temporary Foreign Workers Program or virtue of the worker's attainment of a work visa, there may be prevailing anti-foreigner views among key stakeholders. For example, clients/customers and current employees may hold negative views toward the practice.

In this sense, an effective human resource system for securing foreign workers may increase an organization's risk level due to (a) potential decline of customer sales revenue and (b) retaliatory sabotage by or turnover of current employees. For example, the British Columbia Federation of Labor threatened a boycott of McDonald's due to their use of the Temporary Foreign Workers Program (CBC, 2014). And, Royal Bank of Canada (RBC) was charged with wrongdoing in their transitioning of a work unit from domestic workers to a multinational outsourcing firm (Tomlinson, 2013). In that circumstance, the foreign workers did not have special skills and did require training on basic banking systems. Understandably, the RBC domestic employees were both disgruntled with their job loss and the expectation to train their replacements.

A synthesis of this risk concern is: An organization's talent sourcing practices may open it to reputation and revenue crises and harm related to customer views of foreign workers.

Cell 6) System & Calculated. Hiring foreign workers may be the only option for businesses facing an acute shortage of labor. Such workers also may be a preferred option when considering their assumed (or realized) work ethic. Dan Kelly, President of the Canadian Federation of Independent Business, states that

> I can tell you, anecdotally, I've had many, many emails from small business owners who've said that their temporary foreign workers are among the most productive employees, are doing really high quality work, have terrific customer service skills and, more than anything, are reliable.

(Gollom, 2014, para. 2)

In contrast, some employers note that employing foreign workers brings the following problems: (a) communication barriers, (b) fake resumes and falsified credentials, and (c) insulating practices/not integrating to the community (McQuillan, 2013).

A synthesis of this risk concern is: An organization's talent sourcing practices may open it to operational crises and harm related to practical aspects of managing foreign workers.

Category of Labor Risk: Employee Behavior

The final labor issue addressed in the table pertains to organizational tolerance of, and response to, employee deleterious conduct. While Western democracies advocate and provide for the employment of citizens, it is a truism that in capitalist countries people do not have a 'right to a job'. Rather, people make their own jobs (self-employment) or seek acceptance and employment in separate organizations (traditional employment). In the case of the latter, there are typically systems in place to facilitate staffing activities (e.g., selection, deployment, and retention/termination).

When employees engage in 'bad behavior', organizations may find themselves at risk and motivated to terminate the worker's employment. The three risk perspectives again form a structure for observing protection-oriented behavior.

Cell 7) Person & Directed. The customary trajectory of an employment relationship involves the organization first soliciting and selecting workers (staffing), then mutual agreements of duties and rewards are continually struck and fulfilled (performance management), and finally the organization or employee cancels the agreement (termination or resignation). The organization's termination decisions are typically dependent on business cycles, structural reorganizations, and employee nonperformance of duties (Harcourt, Hannay, & Lam, 2013; Joseph, Klingebiel, & Wilson, 2016). However, from time to time, organizations may choose to end the employment of a worker for non-work-related reasons (Malos, Haynes, & Bowal, 2003). That is, the organization may perceive some negative or imprudent attitude or action of the employee and decide that it is prudent to terminate his/her employment.

In Canada, governments have largely determined that organizations have the right to 'terminate at will' providing that certain statutory considerations are adhered to (Bird & Charters, 2004). For example, in Alberta, Division 8 of the Employment Standards Act allows for termination without cause, as long as the employee receives the designated notice, or pay in lieu of notice (Alberta Employment Standards Code, 2000). Such provisions make it possible for the organization to end the employment of one worker that simply 'gives a funny look' to the boss as easily as one that engages in patently incompetent work. The pretense is that the organization should not suffer employees that do not conform or behave as desired, regardless of their work performance.

In some contrast, the Supreme Court of Canada decided in 2016 that non-unionized employees covered by the Canada Labor Code were subject to termination without cause until their 12-month work anniversary and thereafter could only be terminated for just cause (Supreme Court of Canada, 2016). This decision reflects the idea that the character, attributes, and actions of employees can be reasonably assessed in such a period, and thereafter employees should not kowtow under the implied threat of termination without cause.

Excepting the stance taken by the Supreme Court for certain employees, a broadly applicable synthesis of this risk concern is: The organization's response to poor employee conduct may open it to legal crises and harm related to its adherence to statutory requirements.

Cell 8) Person & Normative. Off-duty conduct is an evolving normative context. In past decades, an employee's private time (non-work time) presented distinct boundaries. The organization may not have liked the attitudes or actions expressed by the worker in his/her private life, but these were outside the purview of the organization. More recently, there has been a melding of corporate and personal lives, such that, for example, employees now strive more for 'work-life integration' rather than 'work-life balance' (Westring, 2015). This newer approach creates more of a harmonious interchange and less 'equal this' and 'equal that'. Correspondingly, organizations increasingly perceive their labor as 'always on' and/or 'always representing' the organization, even while technically 'off duty'.

It is this 'always representing' aspect of the corporate-private life melding that is generating increasing employee terminations. The Millhaven Test, established in 1967 (Buntsma, 2015), sets out the following criteria for assessing validity of an off-duty action-related termination:

1   Did the employee's conduct harm the employer's reputation?
2   Did the employee's behavior render the employee unable to perform his or her duties in a satisfactory manner?
3   Did the employee's behavior lead to a refusal, or inability, of other employees to work with him/her?
4   Is the employee guilty of a serious breach of the Criminal Code, adversely affecting the reputation of the employer and its employees?
5   Did the employee's conduct hinder the employer's ability to manage its operations and direct its workforce efficiently?

The test is applicable to several recent events. For example, a CEO was terminated after being filmed kicking a dog (CTV, 2014), multiple people have been terminated for insensitive, controversial, or offensive social media posts (Workopolis, 2015), and a man was terminated for seeking a job with another company (Lublin, 2012). In some cases, it is clearer that the company's reputation could be harmed, or co-workers could be unwilling to work with the offender.

What is further interesting is that in some cases, the public leads the charge in calling for termination. In the cases of Bill O'Reilly and Jian Ghomeshi, consumers, advertisers, and pundits led the charge to call for their firing following sexual harassment allegations (Bloom, 2017; Bradshaw & McArthur, 2014). One further cogent example relates to a Vancouver company firing an employee alleged to have looted during the Vancouver hockey riots, partly because of public complaints to the company (CBC, 2011). A company may not wish to terminate such an employee, but consequences of not terminating may be too steep in terms of reputation and financial harm.

A synthesis of this risk concern is: The organization may be open to reputational and financial crises and harm related to non-response in the face of publicly observed employee off-duty discreditable conduct.

Cell 9) Person & Calculated. Organizations often engage in a calculated analysis of risk when deciding to terminate employment (Batt & Colvin, 2011) whether on the basis of conduct that is job-related, non-job-related, and/or exhibited while off-duty. Sinoway (2012) describes the 'pro and con' decision-making involved in terminating a top performer that has been hurting the company culture. In other cases, termination may be immediately satisfying to the organization, and in certain cases to the public. However, in both scenarios, it can carry significant internal costs. That is, aside from the offensive choice or conduct, the employee may be otherwise well-performing and the termination may result in overall productivity losses. As well, recruitment and selection costs will be incurred. Lastly, if the termination is not performed correctly, it may result in a lawsuit for damages.

As a further example, Hydro One terminated an employee caught on video tape affirming a reprehensible statement against a female reporter. Interestingly, Hydro One rehired the same employee after a process of arbitration and apology took place (CBC, 2015), presumably because of difficulty defending the decision in a grievance and because the employee offered unique value to the organization. In this case, the termination was determined to be an over-step and reactionary – not properly considered.

A synthesis of the risk concern is: The organization's decision to terminate employees may open it to operational crises and harm related to practical aspects of completing work without the employee.

Section Closing

Although not every labor risk pulls neatly through each of the directed, normative, and calculated perspectives, many of them do. One further issue currently being addressed in Canada is the legalization of marijuana for medicinal and recreational uses – it stands in ironic contrast to the banning of smoking in workplaces which similarly struck chords on all three perspectives of risk. Through the examples and explanations offered, it is clear that there are many forms and circumstances of labor risk that organizations must attend to. And, if not appropriately mitigated, risk may result in an organizational crisis requiring concerted management action and accountable response.

Change and Labor Risk

Crisis and risk associated with labor may be viewed from at least two perspectives. The preceding section described crises and harm stemming from organizational decisions and directions for managing labor. In this section, the focus shifts to describing crisis and risks relating to employee noncompliance with organizational decisions and directions. Together, these sections address both sides of the coin – management (in)actions and employee (in)actions, and provide insight and mitigation points for labor risks that may effectuate strategic, legal, reputational, financial, and operational crises.

Organizational and human resource strategies are developed to leverage strengths and avoid weaknesses in service of optimizing the organization's pursuit of corporate objectives (Huselid & Becker, 1997; Wright & McMahan, 1992; Youndt, Snell, Dean, & Lepack, 1996). Given the implicitly desirable alignment between strategy, policy, and practice, it follows that a change in strategy necessitates changes in practices.

It is unfortunate that a change in strategy can be thwarted by employees reluctant to en-act the practices required for the change to take place and hold (Burnes, 2005; Hope, 2010). Some of this reluctance can be attributed to disagreement with the strategy and attitudinal barriers to accept the changes (Cascio, 2002; Raelin & Cataldo, 2011). Also, employee reluc-tance may be attributed to the employees' personal and professional comfort with the status quo (Cascio, 2002; Floyd & Wooldridge, 1994; Luscher & Lewis, 2008). That is, employees may perceive risks with altering their day-to-day or regular practices that are tried, tested, and perhaps true (Higgs & Rowland, 2010). Thus, ironically, an organization's efforts to minimize risk at one level with a corporate strategy or policy change intended to avoid po-tential corporate harm may be undercut at another level because of employees' views of the change and the personal risk they associate with it.

An element of managing labor risk is addressing issues of aligned interests (willing or unwilling) (e.g., Akdere & Azevedo, 2006; Eisenhardt, 1989; Heath, 2009) and practical opportunity (able or unable) (Dobbins, Cardy, Facteau, & Miller, 1993; Griffin, Neal, & Neale, 2000). It is self-evident that an unwilling employee (misaligned attitude) is less likely to implement the changes in the practices. Furthermore, a willing employee that experiences a blockage in his or her efforts (no practical opportunity) is unable to implement changes in his or her practices. These two challenges (unwilling and unable) are further articulated with conceptual frameworks and practical examples. These are followed by a presentation of the Concerns-Based Adoption Model – a risk perception-centered approach to overcoming reluctance to changes in practice.

Unwilling to Change Practices

A person's attitude strongly influences the actions he or she performs (Eagly & Himmelfarb, 1978). Regarding organizations, employee attitudes, and the aligned practices the employ-ees engage in or refrain from, can affect the performance of the business (Lai, Saridakis, & Johnstone, 2017; Lambooij, Sanders, Koster, & Zwiers, 2006). Further, Sitkin, See, Miller, Lawless, and Carton (2011) call attention to attitudes and the achievement of leader-directed organizational change (autogenic crisis). They posit that stretch goals for organizational learning or performance improvement may be facilitated or disrupted by affective, behav-ior, and cognitive mechanisms, which are components of attitude (Hogg & Cooper, 2003). Thus, it is fair to expect that changes in corporate direction (internal or external strategy) may be inhibited by employees' unwillingness to perform the practices required to manifest that strategy.

The influence of each of the mechanisms of attitude on a person's willingness to enact change has received considerable attention (see Pardo del Val & Fuentes, 2003, for a review). As well, attention to the antecedents of each, and mediating and moderating effects of other constructs (e.g., process, rewards, self-esteem, involvement, fairness) have been explored and shown to have situational and contextual constraints (Garcia-Cabrera & Hernadez, 2014). For the purposes of this chapter, the affective, behavioral, and cognitive mechanisms are presented and treated equally while respecting that different changes in different companies and situations may evoke stronger or lesser resistances from each.

Useful and practical crisis/risk and labor-related examples of the interaction of corporate strategies and employee attitudes are found in the domain of Occupational Health and Safety (OHS). Creating a safe and healthy work environment is a joint effort, being regulated by jurisdictional authorities (e.g., federal and provincial governments), directed and resourced by organizations, and enacted by employees (Yasmin, 2014). The failure of any party to uphold its obligations and competently perform its responsibilities can result in disaster and death (Kelloway, Francis, & Gatien, 2017).

Unfortunately, fulsome leadership and corporate action toward quality OHS is often lacking (Mullen, Kelloway, & Teed, 2011). However, a change in regulation, financial incentive, or leadership, or a significant accident, may induce a demonstrably positive change in organizational strategy and direction for safety policy and practices. For example, the Government of Nova Scotia (n.d.) issued a dust explosion alert and updated regulations for mills and mines to improve their worksite safety communications, 'hot work' permitting, and general housekeeping to prevent explosions like the Westeray Mine disaster that killed 26 workers and disabled the mine. BP (British Petroleum) dramatically changed its operating management system and enhanced the corresponding safety protocols after the Texas City refinery explosion and further still after the Macondo well blowout at Deepwater Horizon (Adams & Crooks, 2015).

Sadly, the most difficult aspect of creating a safe workplace is generating a safety culture (Ali & Shariff, 2017), that is, getting employees to buy into working in a safe way, and self-sanctioning unsafe practices for themselves and peers. One explanation for why employees do not enact their organization's expressed or required safety policy and practices is that they are simply unwilling to do so (Petitta, Probst, & Barbaranelli, 2017). To clarify such situations, Table 16.2 indicates three mechanisms of attitude, corresponding corporate examples, and safety enhancement practices organizations commonly apply to remediate the risk of unwilling employees. A brief discussion of the corporate examples and unwilling attitude mechanisms is provided further below.

Affective Aspects of Unwilling Attitudes at Jayson Global. Jayson Global Roofing, Inc. is a roofing company operating in the Alberta capital region. Adrianna Barton (2014) writes in a *Globe and Mail* article that roofing is one of the ten most dangerous jobs – dangers include exposure to chemicals (e.g., asbestos and tar) and weather (e.g., sunstroke), but falls are the most significant risk. Correspondingly, roofing-related workers are one of the leading

Table 16.2 Unwilling Attitude and Safety

Aspects of unwilling attitude		Corporate examples	Safety attitude tactics
Affective	The employee does not like the presence or performance of the safety practice.	Jayson global	Motivate
Behavior	The employee has not seen positive examples of the safety practice.	PCL	Model and monitor
Cognitive	The employee does not know how the safety practice can be of benefit.	Waiward steel	Train

Workers Compensation Board premium categories in the province of Alberta (in 2017, about $5.50 per $1,000 of coverage) (WCB Alberta, 2017). Fall protection regulations are present in the Alberta Occupational Health and Safety Code (Alberta, 2009), and falls form a major portion of fatality inquiries in the province (Alberta, n.d.).

According to an Order of the Alberta Occupational Health and Safety Council (Alberta OHS Council, 2015), Jayson Global operates a health and safety program with dedicated personnel to observe its worksites and address safety concerns. However, across successive years, the government's safety officers noted repeated infractions for fall protection and issued several stop work orders. The infractions became sufficiently significant in 2014 that a government OHS director issued an administrative penalty (fine) against the company.

In the company's appeal of the fine, the company stated that

> We believe that the human factor has to be accounted for. When a worker chooses non-compliance over compliance that he has agreed upon and signed off on when not under direct supervision, that is a decision we cannot prevent unless otherwise observed.
> *(Alberta OHS Council, 2015, p. 11)*

Further, the company indicates there are many labor challenges in the industry, both in terms of labor supply (e.g., shortage, turnover) and work characteristics (e.g., personality, qualifications). Pertaining to attitudes, they describe roofing installers as being 'free-spirited, work-hard, accept risks, do not always follow directions, and work independently' (Alberta OHS Council, 2015, p. 10). The implication by Jayson Global is that their roofers did not observe safety protocols simply because the roofers did not want to – they did not feel a positive inclination toward the safety practices. This practical observation is echoed in Schwatka and Rosecrance's (2016) research on construction worker safety practices and individual and group norms.

As part of the resolution to the Order, Jayson Global agreed to explore its compensation practices as an extrinsic motivator (affective influence) to induce stronger roofer adherence to the required safety practices.

Behavioral Aspects of Unwilling Attitudes at PCL. Headquartered in Edmonton, Alberta, PCL Industrial Constructors, Inc. is a group of construction companies operating in Canada, the United States, and Australia. Construction is one of the three most deadly industries in Canada (Pinsent, 2012), with fatalities often attributed to falls and worker inattention. PCL, however, is recognized by the Alberta Government as one of the best safety performers in Alberta (2007).

To address safety risks, some government departments (e.g., Ontario Labor) and organizations (e.g., PCL, Dow Chemical, Syncrude) advocate for supervisor role modeling and behavior-based safety practices (Ontario, n.d.). In a presentation for the Construction Owners Association of Alberta, PCL (2012) indicated that observable safety performance by supervisors and supervisor monitoring/coaching of worker behaviors contributes to increases in safety practice performance by workers and a decrease in frequency of incidents. The implication is that prior to positive, legitimating examples and reinforcement, workers lacked an experiential 'safety frame of reference' to guide them during performance of construction duties.

Cognitive Aspects of Unwilling Attitudes at Waiward Steel. Based in Edmonton, Alberta, Waiward Steel is a leading and large provider of engineering, drafting, fabrication, and construction services. Recent Alberta OHS statistics (Alberta, 2016) indicate that the manufacturing, processing, and packaging industry has the highest disabling rate in the province.

Waiward Steel has many 'Canada's 50 Best Managed Companies' awards and is thus recognized by Deloitte as exemplifying innovation, responsible management, and customer orientation. However, as reported by Gary Lamphier (2016), Waiward recognized that it was not appropriately addressing its obligations for employee 'safety competency'. That is, following several incidents and one horrific injury that caused the leadership group to 'look in the mirror', Waiward Steel identified that its safety training protocols were not oriented to the learning needs and capacities of the employees, and thus corresponding safety infractions and poor practices were not necessarily the fault of employees.

After working on improved safety standards, training, and assessment, that helped employees know and understand what safety practices were expected of them, Waiward Steel reached four million hours of injury-free work hours (their previous record was less than 1 million hours) (Lamphier, 2016).

Summary Related to Unwillingness. Collectively, Jayson Global, PCL, and Waiward Steel have increased the safety of their workplace by influencing the attitudes of their workers. They accomplished this, respectively, by addressing worker motivation, behaviors, and competence. It is likely that employees would not have positively and significantly responded to each company's direction for increased safety without the corresponding interventions and thus would have implicitly or explicitly had unwilling attitudes toward the organizations' corporate directions for safety.

Unable to Change Practices

Although an employee may have a positive attitude toward an organizational strategy change, he or she may be blocked or prevented from carrying out the practices that support the change. Explanations of this contrast are often implicitly and explicitly explored through Fishbein and Ajzen's (1975) Reasoned Action Approach. A simplified description of that approach is that a person's actual behavior is preceded by an intention which is carried through into an action, unless inhibited by external forces or unexpected internal limitations.

Inclusive employment is an emerging context where an employee's intention to adhere to a policy change and his or her inability to put it into practice have been generating organizational crises. In response to legislation, social norms, and labor market conditions, some organizations have developed diversity and inclusion policies designed to provide express direction to the public and employees with regards to being an equal opportunity employer and not discriminating on protected grounds (e.g., race, gender, disability) (Casper, Wayne, & Manegold, 2013; Hirsh & Youngjoo, 2017). From an organizational perspective, employing, for example, persons with disabilities presents several positive opportunities, including:

- Incorporation of diverse perspectives (Derven, 2013).
- Access to specialized skills (The Associated Press, 2011; Schrage, 2013).
- Refinement and simplification of internal processes (Kalargyrou, 2014).
- Reduction of business costs and labor issues (Lengnick-Hall, Gaunt, & Kulkarni, 2008).

There are also national laws (e.g., Canadian Human Rights Act, Americans with Disabilities Act) and international agreements (i.e., ILO Declaration and Convention No. 159) that provide legal compulsion and jurisdictional direction toward inclusion of persons with disabilities in the common workforce. Over time, Western society's general perception of disabilities and employability of persons with disabilities has improved (Munyi, 2012). However, despite supporting corporate business cases, improving societal views, and enabling legislation, the actual employment of persons with disabilities is comparatively low (Statistics Canada, 2014, U.S. Department of Labor, 2016). Government statistics show that disparity in employment rates is consistent across industry category, and recent popular media callouts for 'where are the disabled teachers / scientists / actors?' are highlighting the prevalence of the issue (Birrell, 2012; Smith, 2012; The Guardian, 2012, Wichard-Edds, 2017).

Based on the author's own research (Annett, 2017; Annett & Mairs, 2017), frontline supervisors experience both organizational/systemic impediments and personal limitations that inhibit their actual hiring of persons with disabilities. Supervisors describe organizational/systemic impediments as conflicts between the new policy and existing policies and practices. For example, several organizations maintain a 'merit policy' which directs supervisors to hire the most qualified candidate. Such a policy is often implemented to reduce the risk of 'bad hires' due to nepotism and favoritism. However, supervisors often find that the candidates with disabilities have lower overall merit scores which require job duty accommodations. Furthermore, in their internal decision-making calculus, the supervisors weight the merit policy as a more dominant obligation and thus bypass the diversity and inclusion policy.

A second external inhibitor that prevents willing supervisors from fulfilling the diversity and inclusion policy is the absence of job candidates that would meet the criteria of the policy. That is, either due to systemic discrimination in the application process or due to a lack of relevant applicants, the candidate pool often does not include disabled candidates to be hired.

Pertaining to individual limiters, several frontline supervisors in my research unexpectedly found themselves no longer willing to hire persons with disabilities when presented with the opportunity to do so. That is, while in agreement with the policy in the abstract, they perceived clear risks in the actual application of the policy. The risks included:

- **Productivity.** The person might drag down the overall performance level of the work group.
- **Safety.** The person might hurt himself/herself or other workers through an equipment accident.
- **Personal Involvement.** The person might require a degree of personal support or relational attachment the supervisor is not willing to provide (this concern certainly can override generally positive intentions at the moment of decision).
- **Social Sanction.** The diversity and inclusion policy might be intended for lip-service and actual enactment of it would invoke displeasure from senior leadership and staff.

The first two risks were the most prominent – productivity and safety. Essentially, a number of supervisors indicated that even if they wanted to hire a person with a disability, the objective matters of running a business effectively and preventing accidents and injury trumped their personal proclivity to hire and accommodate persons with disabilities.

Concerns-based Adoption Model

The Concerns-based Adoption Model (Hall, Wallace, & Dossett, 1973) addresses employee unwillingness (attitude) and/or inability (limitations) to put into action the practice changes needed to support an organization change.

This model involves a psychological and personal approach to understanding why an individual is resistant to an innovation or alternative (Hall, 1979). The approach was developed

Table 16.3 Addressing Supervisor Concerns toward Inclusive Hiring

Stage of concern		Concern/issue	Teaching intervention	PWD employment intervention
6	Refocusing	Better way	Channel ideas and energies	Facilitate discussion and solution-pathing
5	Collaboration	Collective effort ambiguity	Form communities of practice	Share examples and practices of others
4	Consequence	End result uncertainty	Provide positive feedback and support	Safeguard against negative consequences; share positive impact information
3	Management	Enactment uncertainty	Provide delivery protocols	Buddy support; provide how-to's
2	Personal	Personal discomfort	Address concerns; Implement iteratively	Build rapport; provide encouragement
1	Informational	Superficial awareness	Provide clear information; relate changes to current practices	Share case and practice information
0	Awareness	Do not know/Do not care	Involve teachers in discussions	Share basic information

in response to teachers' reluctance to adopt new instructional methodologies and technologies in their classrooms. Although there is little evidence of efforts to translate the model to other change contexts, there does not appear to be prima facia obstacles for doing so.

The model has seven stages of concerns (Awareness, Informational, Personal, Management, Consequence, Collaboration, Refocusing) and is often accompanied by situation-specific suggestions for intervention or mitigation of each concern. The role of the change leader is to help the individual identify his or her personal concerns and accept mitigating solutions, and thus move the innovation or change forward.

To help illustrate the application of the model, Table 16.3 presents the stages of concern and intervention examples for school-based teaching and transference to addressing supervisor risk perceptions toward the employment of persons with disabilities.

Section Closing

Further research and enquiry is required to determine the efficacy of the Concerns-based Adoption Model for resolving the contradiction between organizational strategy changes and supervisor/employee reluctance to change their personal and professional practices accordingly. As the inclusive employment of persons with disabilities has impacts on the societal, organizational, and individual level (Bucher, 2000), and with noncompliance being an ongoing issue, continued attention in this area is particularly germane.

Chapter Closing

This chapter began with illustrations of organizational crises resulting from the actions or inactions of employees. Two subsequent sections work to fill-in the risk and human resource management picture by offering real-life, contemporary concerns that organizations must address by virtue of employing people. The first section on Categorizing Labor Risk leveraged existing general perspectives on risk (directed, normative, and calculated) and cross-compared them with three distinct categories of labor risk (resource, system, and people), and in doing so illustrated the breadth and depth of application of risk and crisis concepts to the field of human resource management. The second section drew attention to organization change as both a risk-mitigating and risk-inciting activity. The example of an organization's shift toward disability inclusive hiring practices illustrated this paradox and allowed for the application of the Concerns-based Adoption Model toward employees' change-based risk perceptions. In sum, the chapter makes contributions in the distinguishing and exploring phase of the HRM field's development, as advocated by Becker and Smidt (2016).

The risks and resulting crises related to the employment of people presented in this chapter represent only a minor portion of what organizations actually face. At the time of writing, the following issues were present in the news media:

- **False Alarm**: Employee mistake related to Hawaii missile emergency alert system traumatizes citizens and sparks questions of government agency credibility (Park, 2018).
- **Ransomware**: WannaCry, a ransomware virus affecting organizations (and individuals) in 100 countries and linked to (a) employee improper link clicking, and (b) IT departments failing to maintain or offer sufficient security (Sherr, 2017).
- **Border Security**: Canada's auditor general finds that border guards share passwords and do not fully vet thousands of border crossers (Meyer, 2017).
- **Corporate Espionage**: An ex-employee of Google may have stolen and transferred intellectual property that allowed Uber to revive a stalled autonomous driving program (Solomon, 2017).
- **Overtime Lawsuit**: CIBC is involved in a class action lawsuit by employees alleging the bank's system of tracking and paying overtime violated labor law (Pellegrini, 2017).
- **Pay System Failure**: Poor change and centralization activities for Canada's federal government compensation system (Phoenix) has resulted in (a) non-payments to employees, which in turn affect their daily living and credit payments, and (b) significant overrun expenditures (Scotti, 2017).

Certainly, these will not be the last issues related to the actions and inactions of employees, or poorly managed human resource systems, but awareness and mitigation strategies may work to minimize the impact and reduce the likelihood of escalation to organizational crisis.

References

Adams, C., & Crooks, E. (2015, July 09). BP: Into unchartered waters. *Financial Times*. Retrieved from www.ft.com

Akdere, M., & Azevedo, R. E. (2006). Agency theory implications for efficient contracts in organization development. *Organization Development Journal, 24*(2), 43–54.

Alberta. (n.d.). *Fatality Investigation Reports*. Retrieved from work.alberta.ca/

Alberta. (2007). Awards. *Occupational Health & Safety, 30*(3), 14–15.

Alberta. (2009). *Occupational health and safety act: Occupational health and safety code*. Alberta: Queens Printer.

Alberta. (2016). *2016 Workplace injury, disease and fatality statistics provincial summary*. Alberta: Queens Printer.

Alberta Employment Standards Code. (2000). Revised Statutes of Alberta 2000 Chapter E-9: Current as of November 1, 2014. Retrieved from www.qp.alberta.ca

Alberta OHS Council. (2015). *Order: File #1501.* Retrieved from work.alberta.ca/documents/ohsc-decisions/ohsc-jayson-global-roofing-inc-vs-ohs.pdf

Ali, S., & Shariff, A. M. (2017). Development of conceptual key factors model for safety culture. *Global Business & Management Research*, 963–972.

Annett, M. (2017). Categorizing supervisor reflections on risks of hiring persons with disabilities. *Journal of Organizational Psychology*, 14(4), 29–35.

Annett, M., & Mairs, S. (2017). Hiring persons with disabilities: Understanding the intentions and actions of hiring managers, and the influence of employment advocates. *Proceedings of the Annual Conference of the Administrative Sciences Association of Canada: Gender and Diversity in Organizations*, (38), 54–82.

Barton, A. (2014, January 15). And the top 10 most dangerous jobs are … *The Globe and Mail.* Retrieved from www.theglobeandmail.com

Batt, R. & Colvin, A. (2011). An employment systems approach to turnover: Human resources practices, quits, dismissals, and performance. *Academy of Management Journal*, 54(4), 695–717.

Beck, U. (1998). *World risk society.* Cambridge: Polity Press.

Becker, K., & Smidt. M. (2016). A risk perspective on human resource management: A review and directions for future research. *Human Resource Management Review*, 26(2), 149–165.

Beer, M., Spector, B., Lawrence, P. R., Mills, D. Q., & Walton, R. E. (1984). *Managing human assets.* New York: The Free Press.

Bird, R. C., & Charters, D. (2004). Good faith and wrongful termination in Canada and the United States: A comparative and relational inquiry. *American Business Law Journal*, 41(2/3), 205–250.

Birrell, I. (2012). Where are the disabled actors? *Independent.* Retrieved from www.independent.co.uk/voices/where-are-the-disabled-actors-a6831001.html

Bloom, I. E. (2017, April 05). Poll: Should fox news fire Bill O'reilly? *Dennis Michael Lynch.* Retrieved May 19, 2017 from http://dennismichaellynch.com

Boudreau, J. W., & Cascio, W. F. (2014). Human-capital strategy: It's time for risk optimization. *Employment Relations Today*, 33–39.

Bradshaw, J., & McArthur, G. (2014, October 31). Behind the CBC's decision to fire Jian Ghomeshi. *The Globe and Mail.* Retrieved from www.theglobeandmail.com

Bucher, R. D. (2000). *Diversity consciousness: Opening our minds to people, cultures, and opportunities.* Upper Saddle River, NJ: Prentice-Hall.

Buntsma, D. (2015, June 08). Is off-duty conduct an employer's business? *Lawrences Lawyers.* Retrieved from www.lawrences.com

Burnes, B. (2005). Complexity theories and organizational change. *International Journal of Management Review*, 7(2), 73–90.

Canadian Charter of Rights and Freedoms, s 7, Part I of the Constitution Act, 1982, being Schedule B to the Canada Act 1982 (UK), 1982, c11. Canada: Queens Printer.

Cascio, W. F. (2002). Strategies for responsible restructuring. *Academy of Management Executive*, 16(3), 80–91.

Casper, W. J., Wayne, J. H., & Manegold, J. G. (2013). Who will we recruit? Targeting deep- and surface-level diversity with human resource policy advertising. *Human Resource Management*, 52(3), 311–332.

CBC News. (2011, June 22). Alleged riot looter fired from job. *CBC News.* Retrieved from www.cbc.ca

CBC News. (2014, April 14). McDonald's boycott threatened over use of temporary foreign workers. *CBC News.* Retrieved from www.cbc.ca

CBC News. (2015, November 02). Hyrdo One rehires man fired after FHRITP incident. *CBC News.* Retrieved from www.cbc.ca

Choi, Y., Ye, X., Zhao, L., & Luo, A. (2016). Optimizing enterprise risk management: a literature review and critical analysis of the work of Wu and Olson. *Annals of Operations Research*, 237(1/2), 281–300.

Clements, L. M., & Kockelman, K. M. (2017). *Economic Effects of Automated Vehicles.* Retrieved from www.caee.utexas.edu/prof/kockelman/

CTV Vancouver. (2014, September 02). CEO caught kicking dog in elevator resigns from his job. *CTV News.* Retrieved from http://bc.ctvnews.ca

Devnath, A. & Srivastava, M. (2013, April 25). 'Suddenly the floor wasn't there', factory survivor says. *Bloomberg News.* Retrieved from www.bloomberg.com

Derven, M. (2013). The competitive advantage of diverse perspectives. *T+D*, 67(8), 44–48.

Deloitte & Touche (2017). *Risk Advisory Services: Our Common Storefront*. Retrieved from www2. deloitte.com/content/dam/Deloitte/cy/Documents/risk/CY_RiskAdvisoryServices_Noexp.pdf

Dobbins, G. H., Cardy, R. L., Facteau, J. D., & Miller, J. S. (1993). Implications of situational constraints on performance evaluation and performance management. *Human Resource Management Review*, 3(2), 105–128.

Douglas, M. (1966). *Purity and danger: An analysis of concepts of pollution and taboo*. New York: Frederick A. Praeger.

Eagly, A. H., & Himmelfarb, S. (1978). Attitudes and opinions. *Annual Review of Psychology*, 29(1), 517–554.

Eisenhardt, K. (1989). Agency theory: An assessment and review. *Academy of Management Review*, 14(1), 57–75.

Fahey, M. (2016, September 02). Driverless cars will kill the most jobs in select US states. *CNBC*. Retrieved from www.cnbc.com

First Post. (2017, February 16). Columbia space shuttle accident was human error of judgement: G Madhavan Nair. *First Post*. Retrieved from www.firstpost.com

Fishbein, M. and I. Ajzen. (1975). *Belief, attitude, intention, and behavior: An introduction to theory and research*. Reading, MA: Addison-Wesley.

Floyd, S. W., & Wooldridge, B. (1994). Dinosaurs or dynamos? Recognizing middle management's strategic role. *Academy of Management Executive*, 8(4), 47–56.

Foster, J., & Barnetson, B. (2015). The construction of migrant work and workers by Alberta legislators, 2000–2011. *Canadian Ethnic Studies*, 47(1), 107–131.

Foucault, M. (1991). *Governmentality*, trans. Rosi Braidotti and revised by Colin Gordon. In Graham Burchell, Colin Gordon and Peter Miller (eds.), *The Foucault effect: Studies in governmentality*, pp. 87–104. Chicago, IL: University of Chicago Press.

Francis, R. (2017, March 28). Social engineering fake outs: Learn how a consultant infiltrated his client's buildings and networks. *CSO*. Retrieved from www.csoonline.com

Garcia-Cabrera, A. M., & Hernandez, F. G-B. (2014). Differentiating the three components of resistance to change: The moderating effect of organization-based self-esteem on the employee involvement-resistance relation. *Human Resource Development Quarterly*, 25(4), 441–469.

Giddens, A. (2002). *Where know for new labour?* Cambridge: Polity.

Goel, S., Williams, K., & Dincelli, E. (2017). Got phished? Internet security and human vulnerability. *Journal of the Association for Information Systems*, 18(1), 22–44.

Gollom, M. (2014, May 19). Temporary foreign workers have better work ethic, some employers believe. *CBC News*. Retrieved from www.cbc.ca/

Greene, I. (2014). *The charter of rights and freedoms: 30+ years of decisions that shape Canadian life*. Toronto: James Lorimer & Company.

Griffin, M. A., Neal, A., & Neale, M. (2000). The contribution of task performance and contextual performance to effectiveness: Investigating the role of situational constraints. *Applied Psychology: An International Review*, 49(3), 517–533.

Hall, G. E. (1979). The concerns-based approach to facilitating change. *Educational Horizons*, 57(4), 202–208.

Hall, G. E., Wallace Jr, R. C., & Dossett, W. A. (1973). *A developmental conceptualization of the adoption process within educational institutions*. Austin: University of Texas Research and Development Centre.

Harcourt, M., Hannay, M., & Lam, H. (2013). Distributive justice, employment-at-will and just-cause dismissal. *Journal of Business Ethics*, 115(2), 311–325.

Heath, J. (2009). The uses and abuses of agency theory. *Business Ethics Quarterly*, 19(4), 497–528.

Higgs, M., & Rowland, D. (2010). Emperors with clothes on: The role of self-awareness in developing effective change leadership. *Journal of Change Management*, 10(4), 369–385.

Hirsh, E., & Youngjoo, C. (2017). Mandating change: The impact of court-ordered policy changes on managerial diversity. *ILR Review*, 70(1), 42–72.

Hogg, M. & Cooper, J. (2003). *The SAGE handbook of social psychology*. London: Sage Publications.

Hope, O. (2010). The politics of middle management sensemaking and sensegiving. *Journal of Change Management*, 10(2), 195–215.

Hopper, T. (2013, July 12). 'Complex' latticework of errors that caused Lac-Megantic train disaster have just begun to emerge. *National Post*. Retrieved from http://news.nationalpost.com

Howard, D., & Dai, D. (2013). Public perceptions of self-driving cars: The case of Berkeley, California. *Slate*. Retrieved from www.slate.com

Hsu, J. (2017, January 18). When it comes to safety, autonomous cars are still 'teen drivers'. *Scientific American*. Retrieved from www.scientificamerican.com

Huselid, M. A., & Becker, B. E. (1997). The impact of high performance work systems, implementation effectiveness, and alignment with strategy on shareholder wealth. *Academy of Management Proceedings*, 30, 144–149.

Joseph, J., Klingebiel, R., & Wilson, A. J. (2016). Organizational structure and performance feedback: Centralization, aspirations, and termination decisions. *Organization Science*, 27(5), 1065–1083.

Kalargyrou, V. (2014). Gaining a competitive advantage with disability inclusion initiatives. *Journal of Human Resources in Hospitality and Tourism*, 13, 120–145.

Kaufman, B. E. (1993). The origins and evolution of the field of industrial relations in the United States. Ithica, NY: ILR Press.

Kelloway, E. K., Francis, L., & Gatien, B. (2017). *Management of occupational health and safety (7th Ed.)*. Toronto: Nelson.

Lai, Y., Saridakis, G., & Johnstone, S. (2017). Human resource practices, employee attitudes and small firm performance. *International Small Business Journal*, 35(4), 470–494.

Lambooij, M., Sanders, K., Koster, F., & Zwiers, M. (2006). Human resource practices and organisational performance: Can the HRM-performance linkage be explained by the cooperative behaviours of employees? *Management Review*, 17(3), 223–240.

Lamphier, G. (2016, October 14). Devastating accidents prompts workplace revolution at Waiward Steel. *Edmonton Journal*. Retrieved from http://edmontonjournal.com

Leitch, S. (2017, May 24). Woman charged with stealing $250,000 from Alberta treasury branches. *Edmonton Journal*. Retrieved from http://edmontonjournal.com

Lengnick-Hall, M. L., Gaunt, P. M., & Kulkarni, M. (2008). Overlooked and underutilized: People with disabilities are an untapped human resource. *Human Resource Management*, 47(2), 255–273.

Lublin, D. (2012, December 07). I was fired for seeking another job. How can I get compensation? *Workopolis*. Retrieved from https://careers.workopolis.com

Lupton, D. (1999). *Risk*. London: Psychology Press.

Luscher, L. S. and Lewis, M. W. (2008). Organizational change and managerial sensemaking: Working through paradox. *Academy of Management Journal*, 51(2), 221–240

Malos, S., Haynes, P., & Bowal, P. (2003). A contingency approach to the employment relationship: Form, function, and effectiveness implications. *Employee Responsibilities & Rights Journal*, 15(3), 149–167.

Maras, E. (2016, December 14). Are restaurant kiosks taking jobs off the menu? *ICX Association*. Retrieved from https://icxa.org/2016/12/are-restaurant-kiosks-taking-jobs-off-the-menu/

Marriott, R. (2013, April 26). The house of cards: The Savar building collapse. *Libcom*. Retrieved from http://libcom.org

Meyer, C. (2017, May 16). Border guards broke rules says auditor general. *National Observer*. Retrieved from www.nationalobserver.com

McKinsey & Company. (2016). Automotive revolution - perspective towards 2030. *Advanced Industries*.

McQuillan, K. (2013). All the workers we need: Debunking Canada's labour-shortage fallacy. *SPP Research Paper No. 6–16*.

Mullen, J., Kelloway, E. K., & Teed, M. (2011). Inconsistent style of leadership as a predictor of safety behaviour. *Work & Stress*, 25(1), 41–54.

Munyi, C. W. (2012). Past and present perceptions towards disability: A historical perspective. *Disability Studies Quarterly*, 32(2).

Nadeau, B. L., Yan, H., & Botelho, G. (2015, February 11). Costa Concordia captain convicted in deadly shipwreck. *CNN World*. Retrieved from www.cnn.com

Newhook, J. T., Neis, B., Jackson, L., Roseman, S. R., Romanow, P., & Vincent, C. (2011). Employment-related mobility and the health of workers, families, and communities: The Canadian context. *Labour / Le Travail*, 67, 121–156.

Nova Scotia (n.d.). *Dust Explosion Hazard*. Retrieved from https://novascotia.ca/lae

Nuttall, S. (2015, December 17). Top 3 business benefits of autonomous vehicles for commercial fleets. *ACRA Research*. Retrieved from ww.acaresearch.com.au

Ontario. (n.d.). *Health & safety at work: Prevention starts here*. Ontario: Queens Printer.

Pardo del Val, M., & Fuentes, M. (2003). Resistance to change: A literature review and empirical study. *Management Decision*, 41, 148–155.

Park, M. (2018, January 16). Hawaii has been preparing for a missile attack; now its credibility is under fire. *CNN*. Retrieved from www.cnn.com/2018/01/15/us/hawaii-false-alarm-sirens/index.html

PCL. (2012). *Behavior Based Safety*. Retrieved from www.coaa.ab.ca

Pellegrini, C. (2017, May 20). Plaintiff takes another swing at CIBC in unpaid overtime suit. *The Globe and Mail*. Retrieved from www.theglobeandmail.com

Petitta, L., Probst, T., & Barbaranelli, C. (2017). Safety culture, moral disengagement, and accident underreporting. *Journal of Business Ethics*, 141(3), 489–504.

Pinsent, A. (2012, April 25). 3 most dangerous job sectors in Canada. *CBC News*. Retrieved from www.cbc.ca

Podoshen, J. S. (2017, April 27). After the United deplaning fiasco, airlines need some rules. *Newsweek*. Retrieved from www.newsweek.com

Raelin, J. D., & Cataldo, C. G. (2011). Whither middle management? Empowering interface and the failure of organizational change. *Journal of Change Management*, 11(4), 481–507.

Red Seal. (2017). *Red Seal Program*. Retrieved from www.red-seal.ca

Reiss, M. (2007, September 14). Big fines for Belichick, team taping also will cost Patriots a draft pick. *The Boston Globe*. Retrieved from http://archive.boston.com

RobotWorks. (n.d.). Advantages and disadvantages of automating with industrial robots. Retrieved from www.robots.com

Schrage, M. (2013, May 29). Autism's competitive advantage, and challenge, in the workplace. *Harvard Business Review*. Retrieved from https://hbr.org/2013/05/autisms-competitive-advantage.html

Schwatka, N. V., & Rosecrance, J. C. (2016). Safety climate and safety behaviors in the construction industry: The importance of co-workers commitment to safety. *Work*, 54(2), 401–413.

Scotti, M. (2017, April 27). New approach to fixing Phoenix pay system. *Global News*. Retrieved from http://globalnews.ca

Seeger, M. W., Sellnow, T. L. & Ulmer, R. R. (1998). Communication, organization, and crisis. *Communication Yearbook*, 21, 231–275.

Seidenberger, S. (2016). A new role for human resource managers: social engineering defense. *Cornell HR Review*, 1–10.

Sharma, N. (2001). On being not Canadian: The social organization of "migrant workers" in Canada. *Canadian Review of Sociology & Anthropology*, 38(4), 415–439.

Shacklett, M. (2015, August 03). Business process automation: Where it works and where it doesn't. *ZDNet*. Retrieved from www.zdnet.com

Sherr, I. (2017, May 19). WannaCry ransomware: Everything you need to know. *CNET*. Retrieved from www.cnet.com

Smith, S. E. (2012). Where are all the Disabled Scientists? *XO Jane*. Retrieved from www.xojane.com/issues/disabled-people-in-science-technology-math-engineering-fields

Sinoway, E. C. (2012). When to fire a top performer who hurts your company culture. *Harvard Business Review*. Retrieved from https://hbr.org/2012/10/beware-of-the-cultural-vampire

Sitkin, S. B., See, K. E., Miller, C. C., Lawless, M. W., & Carton, A. M. (2011). The paradox of stretch goals: Organizations in pursuit of the seemingly impossible. *Academy of Management Review*, 36(3), 544–566.

Solomon, B. (2017, March 30). Uber exec accused of stealing IP from Google will plead the fifth. Forbes. *Forbes*. Retrieved from www.forbes.com

Statistics Canada. (2014). *Insights on Canadian society: Persons with disabilities and employment*. Catalogue no. 75-006-X. Canada: Queens Printer.

Stevenson, A. (2016, July 20). HSBC bank executives face charges in $3.5 billion currency case. *The New York Times*. Retrieved from www.nytimes.com

Supreme Court of Canada. (2016). *Wilson v. Atomic Energy of Canada Ltd*. Citation: 2016 SCC 29; Case No. 36354.

The Associated Press. (2011, September 22). Adults with autism work as software testers. *CBC News*. Retrieved from www.cbc.ca

The Guardian. (2012, November 12). Where are the disabled teachers? *The Guardian*. Retrieved from www.theguardian.com/education/2012/nov/12/disabled-not-encouraged-teacher-training-costs

Tomlinson, K. (2013, April 06). RBC replaces Canadian staff with foreign workers. *CBC News*. Retrieved from www.cbc.ca

Tuttle, B. (2011, August 25). Customer service done right: When an actual human being answers the phone. *Time.* Retrieved from http://business.time.com

U.S. Department of Labor. (2016). Persons with a disability: Labour force characteristics -2015. *Economic News Release.* Retrieved from www.bls.gov

Vaughan, E. J. (1997). *Risk management.* USA: John Wiley & Sons.

WCB Alberta (2017). *Industry Rates.* Retrieved from: https://my.wcb.ab.ca

Weaver, J. F. (2014, September 12). We need to pass legislation on artificial intelligence early and often. *Slate.* Retrieved from www.slate.com

Weinberger, M. (2017, February 01). A startup with $25 million in funding is in crisis mode because an employee deleted the wrong files. *Business Insider.* Retrieved from www.businessinsider.com

Weinberger, M. & Leswing, K. (2017, April 24). A bureaucratic mistake has revealed Apple's secret team of self-driving car experts. *Business Insider.* Retrieved from www.businessinsider.com

Westring, A. F. (2015). Handbook of work-life integration among professionals: Challenges and opportunities. *Personnel Psychology*, 68(3), 697–699.

Wichard-Edds, A. (2017, August 10). Disability advocates stage Capitol Hill summit on Hollywood inclusion. *The Hollywood Reporter.* Retrieved from www.hollywoodreporter.com

Workopolis. (2015, December 07). 14 Canadians who were fired for social media posts. *Workopolis.* Retrieved from https://careers.workopolis.com

Wright, P. M., & McMahan, G. C. (1992). Theoretical perspectives for strategic human resource management. *Journal of Management*, 18(2): 295–320.

Yasmin, T. (2014). Burning death traps made in Bangladesh: Who is to blame? *Labor Law Journal*, 65(1), 51–61.

Youndt, M. A., Snell, S. A., Dean, J. W. & Lepak, D. P. (1996). Human resource management, manufacturing strategy, and firm performance. *Academy of Management Journal*, 39(4), 836–866.

PART V

International Case Studies

17

INVASIVE SPECIES, RISK MANAGEMENT, AND THE COMPLIANCE INDUSTRY

The Case of Daro Marine

Debbie Harrison, Claes-Fredrik Helgesson,
and Karin Svedberg Helgesson

Introduction

Sea freight is essential for businesses and societies across the globe. Around 90% of world trade is conducted through international shipping (International Chamber of Shipping, 2017), and vast quantities of goods thus travel across the seas. By way of illustration, there are more than 50,000 ships in the world's merchant fleets (Statista, 2018), and 3.8 billion tons of goods passed through EU ports in 2015 (Eurostat, 2017).

Though international sea freight is a necessity for upholding modern ways of life, it also contributes to the rise and spread of new risks. These are not limited to risks of shipwrecks with the possibilities of oil spills and similar extraordinary events. Rather, risks abound even when ships fare as planned under normal conditions. These "every day" risks of international shipping involve risks stemming from the movement of dangerous commodities such as drugs or toxic waste, and the risks of enabling the spread of infectious diseases and aquatic invasive species. Hence, global shipping is not only central to the sustenance of world trade, but is a source of several complex risks.

In this chapter, we will particularly focus on the management of risks related to invasive species, a risk where the associated costs are huge. For instance, it has been estimated that the annual cost of the zebra mussel, a designated invasive species, amounts to $1 billion in the United States alone (Pimentel, Zuniga, & Morrison, 2005). Paradoxically, the risk of invasive species is exacerbated by attempts to mitigate a different risk and increase safe operations in international freight – the use of ballast water as a stabilization mechanism in the hull of a ship. In international sea freight, ballast water serves several purposes related to safety and maneuverability:

> If the ship is travelling without cargo, or has discharged some cargo in one port and is on route to its next port of call, ballast may be taken on board to achieve the required safe operating conditions. This includes keeping the ship deep enough in the water to ensure efficient propeller and rudder operation and to avoid the bow emerging from the water, especially in heavy seas.
>
> *(Transport Canada, 2017)*

A side effect of the use of ballast water is that the water sourced in the vicinity of the port of departure ends up in the port of arrival. In effect, the sediments contained in the ballast water travel from place to place, and can include non-native, possibly "invasive," species hidden in their midst. Thus, whenever a ship discharges ballast water from its tanks, there is a risk that non-native aquatic species are set free in the new environs, thereby becoming aquatic invasive species. This illustrates that the "call for action" (Marx, 2006) that comes with designating something as a risk may have unintended consequences, and that risk management is itself party to the pervasiveness of risk (e.g. Maguire & Hardy, 2013).

To be sure, finding out what to do when facing a specific risk can be relatively straightforward for many organizations. Contemporary organizations often do not need to figure out all by themselves how to act upon a risk.[1] The building blocks for risk management have come to be "littered around the societal landscape" (Meyer & Rowan, 1977, p. 345), much like other generic organizational building blocks. From such a standpoint, it can be argued that the call for action implied by the identification of a new risk may be answered by simply applying designated risk management solutions that are likely scattered in the vicinity of the focal organization (compare Cohen, March, & Olsen, 1972).

On the other side, the efficacy of standardized risk management systems for the focal risk cannot simply be presumed. As Weick and Sutcliffe (2011) caution, strong faith in the merits of preemptive planning may result in "mindless" behavior, and a higher, rather than lower, probability of risk turning into disasters. Moreover, in a risk-regulation context, one needs to bear in mind that organizations face (at least) two principle risks. That is, alongside the focal risk at hand, such as the risk of invasive species, there is the risk of being deemed non-compliant[2] in relation to extant regulation aimed at reducing the focal risk. Here, previous research has shown that a strong focus on compliance may feed an obsession with creating a visible audit trail (Power, 1997, 2009) in order to ensure what Ericson (2006) has called "defendable compliance." Such engagement with the management of compliance risk may, in turn, undermine proactive engagement with mitigation of the actual focal risk, as illustrated by Favarel-Garrigues, Lascoumes, and Godefroy (2011), Amicelle (2011), and others.

In short, managing risk is a complex process. A part of the problem is that, in practice, there is often interdependence between the management of the focal risk and the management of compliance risk. Consequently, to better understand how risk management of focal risks works (or not) in organizations, it is important to understand how the systems used to manage focal risks are designed, by whom, and for what purpose.

As such, this chapter focuses on the supply side of risk management, rather than on the clients demanding and applying risk management solutions (or on the regulators obliging actors to engage in the mitigation and prevention of risks). Our interest involves probing how suppliers come up with a specific risk solution, or product,[3] for risk management, including how the focal risk is defined and concretized in that process. Our main research question is: *How do suppliers of risk management solutions strike a balance between mitigating focal risk and compliance risk?* We empirically investigate this question through a case study of Daro Marine's attempt to provide a solution for managing the risk of invasive species in international sea freight.

The chapter is structured as follows: we first outline our analytical framework with a view to discussing how organizations supplying risk management products are part of a compliance industry (see Verhage, 2009a). This section is followed by a brief summary of the methods used in our case study. In the next, and main part of the chapter, we present our empirical case on invasive species. We first outline how invasive species came to be conceptualized as a risk. We then provide an account of Daro Marine's attempts to develop a product for the management and mitigation of the risk of invasive species. In the ensuing discussion section, we conclude by summarizing some key learning points for scholars and practitioners.

Risk Management and the Compliance Industry

A risk can be positively construed as an "opportunity for gain," but in late modernity it is rather conceptualized as "a possibility of loss" (Gephart, Van Maanen, & Oberlechner, 2009, p. 141). As Marx (2006) observes, denoting something as a risk begs us to act. Where there is a risk, it should be managed and mitigated. In parallel, there is a growing faith in, and expansion of, risk-based regulation (Hood, Rothstein, & Baldwin, 2001; Black, 2005; Rothstein, Huber, & Gaskell, 2006) and risk governance (Van Asselt & Renn, 2011; Boholm, Corvellec, & Carlsson, 2012) across the public-private divide (Helgesson & Mörth, 2012), spanning a diversity of problems and harms from occupational health and safety (Hutter, 2001) to the war on terror (Amoore & de Goede, 2008). Ideas on risk have even been likened to a "logic of organizing" (Power, Scheytt, Soin, & Sahlin, 2009). Taken together, these developments feed the demand for risk management. From the perspective of Power (2004), nowadays there appears to be a demand for "the risk management of everything." And, as basic textbooks in economics tell us, where there is demand, there will be supply.

In broad terms, the supply side of risk management consists of all of those organizations that are in the business of producing and selling products aimed at risks that (prospective) clients face. In this chapter, we have chosen to employ the term "compliance industry" (Verhage, 2009a) to denote the providers on the supply side of risk management.

Verhage (2009a) introduced the concept of compliance industry to signify service providers in the context of risk management and anti-money laundering (AML) regulation. In the present context, we use compliance industry as an umbrella concept for all those organizations that have made it their business to help client organizations align with risk-based rules and regulations, and perhaps mitigate focal risks, by supplying risk management solutions. Like risks, risk management solutions come in many shapes and forms. Some seemingly entail little client effort beyond box-ticking, while others may require significant investment in specialized IT-based risk management tools and equipment, and/or rely on education of staff, or a mix of all of these.

Of particular importance for our purposes is the fact that the concept of compliance industry highlights some generic qualities[4] of the suppliers providing risk management solutions. First, the concept of compliance *industry* underscores that many suppliers of risk management solutions are in fact commercial actors with an "entrepreneurial approach" (Verhage, 2009a, p. 15) to risk and risk management. One should thus be aware that risk management solutions are products provided by the compliance industry in a business context.

Among organizations that have made it their business to help client organizations align with risk-based rules and regulations by supplying risk management solutions, we find professional services firms, such as the Big 4 accounting firms and other professional services organizations. The compliance industry further includes the specialized systems and software providers like Thompson Reuters, Akelis, and Bureau van Dijk. Relatedly, in the wake of increasing risk regulation, there are emerging new groups of compliance professionals, as analyzed by Tsingou (2017). And then there are a multitude of organizations across industries that provide risk management solutions for clients in their particular fields, such as our case organization Daro Marine.

Second, the concept of *compliance* industry underscores that suppliers are businesses active in providing "compliance services" (Verhage, 2009b, p. 372). Suppliers provide products for risk management that are designed to help clients comply with risk-based rules and regulations, and mitigate focal risk. As discussed in the Introduction, in a risk-regulation context, organizations face (at least) two principle risks: the risk of noncompliance and the focal risk itself.

We argue that the concept of the *compliance* industry emphasizes the first of these two risks. A sales pitch for the compliance product ORBIS illustrates this point: "We capture and treat private company information for better decision making and increased efficiency, so we're ideally suited to help compliance risk professionals – with both regulatory and reputational risk management" (Bureau van Dijk, 2018). Analytically, then mitigation of compliance risk, rather than "actual" risk mitigation related to focal risk, is foregrounded in the offering.

Via the provision of risk management products, the compliance industry helps organizations enact identifiable audit trails (Power, 2009) and "defendable compliance" (Ericson, 2006), thereby mitigating compliance risk. Hence, the compliance industry is purportedly instrumental in helping client organizations reduce the risk of being held to account and found wanting by the regulator, oversight bodies, and other stakeholders.

Whether the focal risks in question are actually managed in a way that mitigates them as well and prevents possible ensuing crisis is another matter. For instance, a high frequency of reports on a specific risk, which is a common benchmark for successful regulatory compliance (e.g., Financial Supervisory Authority, 2013), says little in and of itself about the quality of the risk management for companies or of the efficacy of the regulation (Levi, Reuter, & Halliday, 2017). To be sure, it is possible to be compliant with risk-based regulation while simultaneously having little knowledge of how or whether compliance actually mitigates the focal risk (Helgesson & Mörth, 2016). Moreover, a focus on mitigating compliance risks can undermine proactive mitigation of the focal risk (Amicelle, 2011; Favarel-Garrigues, Lascoumes, & Godefroy, 2011).

Consequently, we would argue that how suppliers design products for compliance with regulation aiming to mitigate specific risks will have a bearing on whether and how users will actually (also) be engaging in mitigation of the focal risk when applying these risk management products. A pertinent question, therefore, relates to how suppliers of risk management solutions attempt to strike a balance between mitigating focal risk and compliance risk in their offerings, including deliberations on how risk is defined and concretized in that process. It is against this background that we have chosen to outline and discuss the process of how one supplier, Daro Marine, attempted to come up with such a solution for managing the risk of invasive species in international sea freight.

A Note on Methods

This chapter is based on data collected for a larger project focused on technological development and market creation at a supplier of a ballast water treatment system (BWTS) (Harrison, 2010). In addition, data have been assembled from an affiliated project examining intertwined endeavors to map the spread of invasive species, regulate ballast water use, and create advancements in ballast water treatment (Harrison & Helgesson, 2017). In all, the main empirical body consists of 50 semi-structured interviews carried out by Harrison with the supplier of a BWTS, Daro Marine (a pseudonym), secondary data such as reports and presentations from the case company, news and reports from websites of industry actors and regulators including the International Maritime Organization (IMO) and the United States Coast Guard (USCG), and similar materials from the websites of several of the involved classification societies. On the topic of invasive species mapping, we have gathered and examined more than 60 documents, of which roughly 40 are articles in scientific journals in areas such as biology, ecology, and ecological economics. Taken together, these empirical materials have allowed us to get a broad understanding of how the awareness of, and action toward, the risk of invasive species in global shipping has developed, as well as a more in-depth understanding of the specific case reported here.

The Emergence of Aquatic Invasive Species as a Risk

The co-movement of species and vessels has a long history. By way of illustration, biologists have used the notion of "canoe species" to signify species introduced to Hawaii with the original Polynesian settlements (Helmreich, 2005, p. 116). Increased global shipping has perpetuated the unintended movement of aquatic species. The previous practice of using dry ballast involved, for instance, the spread of fire ants. The technological shifts in ballasting technology, from dry bulk to water, turned the ballast water into "the principal pathway of unintentional introduction for aquatic alien invasive species" (MacPhee, 2007, p. 33).

Awareness about the damages and challenges caused by invasive species traveling in ballast water rose rapidly in the late 1980s. A pivotal moment was the discovery in the summer of 1988 of the zebra mussel in the North American Great Lakes (Carlton, Reid, & van Leeuwen, 1995, p. 1). Originally from the Black Sea and the Caspian Sea, the zebra mussel had first spread to Hungary (late 18th century), and then to the Netherlands (19th century). The transatlantic move of the zebra mussel was not primarily an ecological curiosity: they attached themselves to water pipes, causing massive costs to the power industry. In 1993, the U.S. Office of Technology Assessment (OTA) published a report that estimated the zebra mussel had cost the power industry some $3.1 billion over a 10-year period (OTA, 1993, p. 68). Consequently, the discovery of the zebra mussels in the Great Lakes spurred several government initiatives in the United States, and increased efforts to map invasive species and estimate the social and economic consequences of their spread.

The year 1988 also marks the start of the international regulatory process, as both Canada and Australia raised concerns with the IMO about the risks of invasive species in relation to ballast water (Euroshore, 2000). Around the same time, the United States introduced national legislation to control the spread of invasive species, for example, the Nonindigenous Aquatic Nuisance Prevention and Control Act of 1990. After a lengthy process of negotiation, IMO agreed on the Ballast Water Management Convention in 2004. Due to a prolonged process of ratification, this convention came into force only in September 2017 (Green4sea, 2016).

There are four regulations contained within the Convention. First, there is a biological standard for ballast water to qualify as "disinfected" (a measure of the number of viable biological organisms post-treatment). Second, there are two ways to conform to the biological standard: (i) exchange at sea (until 2016) and (ii) installing a treatment system on board. The implementation timetable is the third standard. Different compliance deadlines for installations on new-build vessels compared to retrofitting existing vessels were established. The fourth standard involves a three-step type approval (TA) process, known as the IMO G8 guidelines. "Type approval or certificate of conformity is granted to a product that meets a minimum set of regulatory, technical and safety requirements" (Wikipedia). IMO requires that a BWTS be granted TA before it can be sold. Each of the 172 member states, or flag states, of IMO has the authority to test for and grant TA using the IMO G8 guidelines. Therefore, multiple flag states are involved.

In parallel, the USCG introduced its own TA process and associated implementation schedule. Any system already awarded an IMO type approval certificate – from whichever member state – was now *also* required to obtain a USCG type approval. The U.S. standard, which somewhat differs from the IMO standard, was *in force* already from June 2012. Although the separate U.S. regulation at first hand might appear to be local, it has large consequences; approximately 85% of the world's ships will call at a U.S. port during their lifetimes.

Setting the struggles to regulate aside, there have been further difficulties in developing technologies for treating ballast water to mitigate the risk of invasive aquatic species. When the early systems were installed in 2011, reports emerged that even TA or certified systems might not work in all water conditions encountered (due to different temperatures and salinities). The resulting confusion, compounded by the fact that legally the onus that installed systems actually worked fell on *ship owners* rather than on the system supplier, meant that sales were static.

Sales were further depressed by the parallel existence of the IMO and USCG standards. In essence, the key difference hinged on the appropriate testing method for one form of technology underpinning a BWTS, ultra-violet light (UV). The USCG required a test method for UV-based systems that killed species in the ballast water, whereas the IMO standard only tested for "non-viability," that is, that species were unable to reproduce after treatment. A classification organization even introduced the notion of having treatment systems with an "IMO mode" and an "USCG mode" to meet the diverging regulatory requirements (DNV GL, 2015).

The emergence of the issue of aquatic species spreading with ballast water has, in conjunction with the related regulations, outlined a new market for risk management. As such, it has created business opportunities for organizations in the compliance industry. In the following, we describe the attempts of one supplier to develop a risk management solution – a BWTS – for clients in need of managing the risk of invasive species in ballast water.

Supplying Risk Management: The Case of Daro Marine

Awareness of a New Market for Risk Management

Interest in developing a system to handle the risk of invasive species, a BWTS, began in the mid-2000s. Daro Marine was established in the existing core business of safety products, which was considered a mature market. The customer base was familiar: *"we knew all the actual and potential customers - there were no big surprises"* (Business development manager). Furthermore, the company had a stated ambition to grow in the business area of environmental solutions.

The decision to invest in development was taken a few years after the Convention had been settled in 2004, and with an anticipation that the Convention would be ratified by 2010. At the time, market estimates of a $35 billion market spurred Daro on and encouraged an entrepreneurial stance. The materializing of a mandatory regulation on the risk of invasive species was key in triggering Daro's product development efforts, because it ensured that there would be a market for a BWTS in the eyes of Daro managers.

Risk Management Product Development

A prototype treatment system was obtained from a new supplier after a search process. It combined several treatment technologies, such as filtration, within one system. With no full testing standard in place, Daro intended to work on a system that would be viable across all water types and temperatures. This was expected to result in large potential market penetration across different vessel segments.

A testing process was put in place on board a vessel. In part, this involved attempts to retrofit a system on the vessel when in dry dock. The learning involved in working out where and how the system was to "fit" or be placed on board led to ongoing modifications of the system, both at the supplier and in-house. For example, efforts were focused on optimizing the design of the system regarding how the sub-technologies worked together. There were issues in terms of how to literally fit the system on board a vessel, given its size. Interesting for our work, relatively inexperienced engineers were put in charge of this process.

The testing process was directed in part toward the three-step IMO process for obtaining TA, or the technology certification process. The first two steps included "*the suitability of the safety of the crew, vessels and environment. But they did not cover whether the product works as intended. For this, it [was the third step of] type approval*" (product manager). Daro's system supplier was heavily involved in the process of gaining the TA. Here, the focus was on mitigating the focal risk — the actual spread of invasive species. The basic question was "did the product work," that is, did it disinfect ballast water to a sufficient biological standard in accordance with the Convention.

Overall, in the first year of the process a project plan was drawn up, but as the product manager said, "*we didn't keep it...I didn't know enough about what the product was about...there have been various versions of the template, and they have not been all that successful.*" The manager also said that the "*process was not there, we had no common template,*" which was magnified by the fact that the NPD team was split over multiple locations (due to the global nature of the business). The project manager attended an in-house course that provided "*clearer ideas regarding the starting point, roles*" and established a new template as the process moved into the next phase.

Attendance at the course, general frustration within the team regarding the lack of coordination, and some additional resources being added to the team meant that a working project plan ultimately was put in place. Afterward, decisions were made within R&D to take a step-by-step approach to product development. That is, to "*do one thing at once*" (lead engineer) and develop first a standard product that would fit several applications, and then different versions of this for smaller/larger vessels later (often potential customers have multiple vessel types in their fleets). The focus was to develop a flexible system that would allow multiple customers to manage their compliance risk.

At the same time, individuals in the sales network intensified their activities to increase market awareness around the new system. The purpose was to "*cultivate the market without a finished product... to build awareness of what we were selling even if it was not 100% finished... it takes a while to get the information into the market*" (sales manager). The new system would not be a gap in a product line within an existing range. The assumption that demand was "*there*" remained, in that "*customers had to do it*" (purchase a system to manage the risk of invasive species) because of legislation (business development manager). In other words, customers had a compliance risk that had to be managed. However, one consequence of early market awareness activity was that "*the information provided to the sales network had changed repeatedly as the product design had changed...Sales thought it was finalized when it was not*" (product manager). There were, in essence, different ideas related to how ready the system was to be marketed. In addition, sales acted with more confidence in that the system would soon be approved as complying with the regulations. This unit acted in a way that downplayed the compliance risk and instead focused on getting sales.

For Daro's existing shipyard customers, the expected sales volumes of the new technology were related to existing plans for new builds (new ships). At the time, the business development manager said, "*we have an idea of the output each year…it is big.*" In addition, ship owners would require a system to be retrofitted on existing vessels (up to 40,000 vessels worldwide). However, this was considered more difficult to forecast. A sales manager said the following, as events unfolded: "*the owner market is more time consuming…there is a different buying set up and engineering requirements.*" A Customer Benefits Exercise was also established. There was disagreement in terms of how to provide quotes – by emphasizing the technical design or starting from customer needs and motivations. In other words, "*what is the product offer…we don't know*" (marketing manager). The structured process took place over several months.

Toward the end of the phase, Daro received TA. This indicated that prospective customers would be deemed compliant when using Daro's system. In other words, they were able to manage their compliance risk by purchasing an approved Daro system. Efforts within the "commercial" part of the NPD team moved toward an internal launch (to "sell" the product to the sales network), and to plan and start to execute a large-scale external launch. It was assumed at the time that compliance risk had been mitigated because the Daro system had been certified (awarded TA). It was therefore a question of achieving sales. At the same time, the relatively few people in R&D continued their efforts to fix ongoing design and development issues in order to make the product ready. This was partly an issue of working toward a second layer of approvals (for industry "class" societies) and a mentality of "*problem solving along the way*" (lead engineer). There were, hence, tensions between those on the team who equated the acquired TA with "go go go" and those who were more cautious, seeing that there remained uncertainties as to whether the current system mitigated all compliance and focal risks.

Within this time frame, individual U.S. states such as California, alongside the USCG, were creating additional noise regarding separate requirements on how to mitigate risks of invasive species (separate from those of the IMO). However, there was no clear standard or testing protocol for suppliers to relate to. This increased the uncertainty for both the supply and customer sides. Nevertheless, the awaited ratification of the Convention was expected to trigger sales. Lastly, the relevant division at Daro merged with another of the company's divisions within this phase. The merger created noise and some degree of political uncertainty within the team.

Pitching and Selling Compliance

Near the end of the external launch process, efforts were underway toward "*where we think we can get sales quickly*" (marketing manager). Target lists were already in place from the existing customer base, typically based on the size of a customer's fleet. A progression from building market awareness to "*getting as many orders as possible*" (marketing manager) was in essence a sales approach based on "*a machine gun… where does it hit the market*" (marketing manager). What is implied here is that orders can be scaled up or aggregated into segments later. There were ongoing disagreements within the team as to the important segments and vessel types. Nevertheless, the focus was on getting sales.

The new post-merger management team started to review the ongoing projects within both of the previously separate divisions. On the one hand, there was the opportunity of the ongoing market size estimated at $36 billion. On the other hand, there were problems. The marketing manager said the following at the time: sales "*are not getting any direction… we are in danger of being 'all things to all people'…what are the biggest segments where we have a product?*" One outcome was a requirement to filter the existing 100–200 "*serious enquiries*" (lead engineer) to approximately 50 whereby "*we can interact and have a real chance to get these*" (lead engineer).

The new management team viewed the ballast water/invasive species area as a commercial opportunity which needed more directing. The "machine gun" approach of trying to pick up orders incrementally, in an emergent way, was viewed as a weak commercial approach. Furthermore, because the Daro BWTS had been awarded TA, it was assumed that compliance risk had been mastered, a situation that potentially could be commercially leveraged. The filtering process was therefore based on a desire to increase sales by focusing efforts, and focal risk moved to a somewhat marginal position in the commercial agenda. It is fair to say that invasive species had been effectively black-boxed in light of the achievement of the TA certificate. This is because focal risk was assumed to be mitigated as the testing processes involved in obtaining TA had been carried out.

The need to interact to get a sale also highlighted an ongoing concern for key actors, the practicability of installing a new system on an existing vessel. A sales manager said at the time, "*we have to actively help the customer… to make an initial assessment for installation.*" However, the lack of technical sales knowledge presented both an immediate problem – "*how to help define the scope*" (sales manager) – and an issue of how to accumulate operational experience over time. Moreover, the internal capability to handle increasing numbers of orders was a source of conflict. "*There were expectations regarding the level of orders we could get in reserve… these led to expectations regarding deliveries and investment*" (lead engineer). In other words, making sales implied a capability to be able to deliver.

Managerial attention turned to building the internal capability in order to scale up to meet both existing orders and the expected jump in sales post-ratification of the Convention. The need to scale up was partially underpinned by recognition of the lack of scope reduction, even within the more filtered selling process described earlier. In addition, one consequence of the focus on scaling up was "*a need to iterate during the process, in terms of who to sell to and where to, this can change over time*" (product manager). The overall outcome was renewed focus on defining exactly what the product was and for which applications; several team members pushed for stabilizing a "*mark one*" of the new technology, arguing for "*let's go with what we have*" (lead engineer).

The Demands of Large Demand

The "*lack of readiness*" (lead engineer) was related to a changing understanding of the situation and a stark realization: "*it was beginning to sink in just how big the opportunity was*" (product manager). After the external launch, the continuing "*doing something new under time pressure*" (product manager) led to reflections that "*it is huge and that was the mistake from the beginning… we knew it was a big market … but we had no awareness as to how to meet the market … we didn't know*" (lead engineer). To some extent, the development and commercialization of the technology took place as if it were an incremental innovation within the existing product range.

The project team was reorganized in order to focus attention, increase the numbers of people involved in order to finalize the product, set up production, build the supply chain, and so forth. In other words, "*we needed awareness of the project, and the opportunity… but also the challenges*" (product manager). This was supplemented by changing the roles for both project management and ownership. This included a dedicated senior manager position. A series of workshops was set up with the purpose of completing the project in 6–8 months. In the first of these, "*we started to create a team… it was fantastic, there were lots of fights… didn't understand each other… we make plans, we do it, we report back… people… are pulling in the same direction"* (new senior manager).

Toward the end of this phase, several collisions occurred as the Daro team began to gain market feedback. For example, there were problems gaining the second-layer approvals (with class societies) due to a lack of prior testing in operational conditions. Furthermore, efforts to install a system on a customer vessel were unsuccessful, and there were also increasing numbers of difficult questions from customers regarding how the system worked in real-world conditions. Would it really manage and actually mitigate the risk of invasive species? In other words, a focus on focal risk was returning. There was a disagreement across the senior managers within the team of *"sell, sell, sell versus test, test, test"* (new senior manager). The issue was whether they should focus on selling their system or further working to assert that their system was compliant (or managing focal risk).

Verification Following Market Feedback

In this phase, Daro, just as many of its competitors, was required to verify the new product after receiving market feedback. A suggestion was that the NPD team had handled risk and maintained momentum in the innovation process via a *"problem solve as we go"* mentality (product manager). Nevertheless, *"there were too many blanks… we didn't know about the water environment, the pressure… we were starting to understand where we were in readiness and the impact on the project"* (new senior manager). A new scaled-down team of three central persons was created. The focus was on reengineering and retesting the technology. Earlier tensions were now downplayed in the face of a clear need to respond to the market feedback. At the time, the product manager said, *"the team works well… it is stable in the responsibilities… clear on roles… good at talking,"* and there was one designated leader on a day-to-day basis.

Daro planned and executed a verification program. A challenge from the company management team was in place to address exactly what the product was able to do in normal ship operating conditions. In other words, to what extent was the product able to mitigate focal and compliance risks. Over time, the verification program expanded in scope to incorporate reengineering and the essential workings of the technology. The supplier of the system was involved here.

Daro also started to use external water testing labs in order to obtain third-party verification. A realization developed within the team that the IMO type approval process was somewhat disconnected from operational conditions: *"Type approval is dangerous…it is disconnected from an understanding of ballast practices…this is our learning internally"* (lead engineer). For example, the awarding of a TA certificate is not a guarantee that a treatment solution is viable in all water conditions (fresh, etc.).

One response to the lack of understanding of the use of the new technology on both the supplier and customer sides involved the efforts of the USCG to change its vessel permit regulations vis-à-vis ballast water management. The U.S. regulations required more prescribed testing than the IMO TA process, which also led Daro and its suppliers to the independent water labs, such as DHI.

Epilogue

The confusion over the validity of the TA process and the need for Daro and its competitors to undertake further testing at water treatment laboratories to investigate the limitations of their systems continued. This was not least due to the need to meet the more prescribed requirements of the USCG in order to try to obtain USCG TA. The speed at which the ballast water treatment system industry was developed at least in part explains why many of the current systems can be considered to be prototypes. A perception started to develop that the approvals process is "*full of holes*" (e.g., it does not require a potential supplier to test its system across a range of water temperatures) (product manager).

There are continuing difficulties in gaining operational experience to fully understand ballasting practices. That the Ballast Water Convention remained unratified for so long meant that ship owners could delay a decision to invest in risk management of invasive species. For example, the limited sales that actually have materialized are mainly for new builds at the yard; few systems are in use (because they do not need to be used). However, this is starting to change. IMO has undergone a highly politicized process over the last few years in which the implementation deadlines contained within the Convention, the TA process, and the treatment standard have been debated very publically and at some considerable length.

Discussion and Conclusions

Managing risk is a difficult and seemingly never ending task. In this chapter, we have focused on the supply side of risk management, on the compliance industry. Our research question was focused on how suppliers of risk management solutions strike a balance between mitigating focal risk and compliance risk. Empirically, we focused on the case of managing risks related to the spread of aquatic invasive species via the ballast water of ships. In particular, we examined the efforts of a firm, here called Daro Marine, which developed a ballast water treatment system to manage the risk of invasive species as the issue of aquatic invasive species surfaced and as regulations were coming into play.

Our case study about the trials and tribulations of product development at Daro Marine suggests that risks in focus varied across time, and also across different parts of the organization. The emergence of the international convention with mandatory regulation was key in starting the efforts to create a system that managed the risk of invasive aquatic species, enabling Daro Marine to constitute itself as an actor within a compliance industry for the management of this risk. Activities to test the system in development in different water types indicate instances where mitigation of the focal risk, the actual spread of invasive species, was in focus. In other instances, the focus appeared to be more toward having a system that met regulations, putting compliance risk at the fore. Finally, we identified fractions where attention to both types of risk was dispersed. Specifically, when one TA had been acquired, sales focused neither on compliance nor on focal risk, but on getting sales. To answer our question, the balancing between mitigating focal risk and compliance risk in this case shifted over time, and across different parts of the organization.

The chapter also underscores the need to further probe the interplay between the regulatory environment and the actors in the compliance industry. In our case, product development of risk management solutions, and the balancing of focal and compliance risks, were intertwined with developments in the regulatory context. Like many other complex risks in modern society, the risk of aquatic invasive species in relation to global shipping is difficult to delineate spatially. The gradual emergence of parallel U.S. and international regulations is telling in this respect, and made compliance risk management a more ambiguous task. Here, our case also highlights the added complexity of managing a focal risk that is difficult to mitigate from a technical perspective: how is the risk of invasive species to be best handled? Indeed, it has proven difficult to indisputably assert that a system compliant with regulations actually mitigates the risk of aquatic species spreading via ballast water in all possible scenarios. Relatedly, it could be argued that while the USCG regulation had the focal risk at its center, the IMO regulation unwittingly had a TA process that did not sufficiently incorporate focal risk.

To conclude, we would like to caution against putting the blame on the users of extant risk management systems for engaging in "defendable compliance" (Ericson, 2006), as opposed to focusing on mitigating real risk. To be sure, there are organizations that primarily aim to tick all of the boxes in the risk regulations, just to be safe rather than sorry when the auditor calls. However, even if users of risk management products were always to do their very best to promote the mitigation of focal risk, they may not be fully successful as a result of the risk choices suppliers in the compliance industry, and the regulators, already have made for them.

Notes

1 Of course, risks may still be taken, or pursued, by actors. However, contemporary conceptualizations view risk as being less about "the opportunity for gain and more possibility of loss" (Gephart et al., 2009, p. 141).

2 Compliance risk may also be seen as part of the more all-encompassing concept of reputational risk, defined as "the purest man-made risk of organizing as such, namely the risk of how one is perceived by others" (Power, Scheytt, Soin, & Sahlin, 2009, p. 309).

3 Here, we use the term "product" in a broad sense without making a clear distinction between products and services.

4 This list is by no means exhaustive. In addition, we do not suggest that all suppliers of risk management solutions are business organizations, though many are.

References

Amicelle, A. (2011). Towards a 'new' political anatomy of financial surveillance. *Security Dialogue, 42*(2), 161–178.

Amoore, L., & De Goede, M. (Eds.). (2008). *Risk and the War on Terror.* New York: Routledge.

Black, J. (2005). The emergence of risk-based regulation and the new public risk management in the United Kingdom. *Public Law,* 512.

Bureau van Dijk, (2018). Solutions for your role. Compliance and financial crime. Available at: www.bvdinfo.com/en-gb/solutions-for-your-role/compliance-and-financial-crime (Accessed January 4, 2018).

Boholm, Å., Corvellec, H., & Karlsson, M. (2012). The practice of risk governance: Lessons from the field. *Journal of Risk Research, 15*(1), 1–20.

Carlton, J. T, Reid, D. M., & van Leeuwen, H. (1995). Shipping study: The role of shipping in the introduction of nonindigenous aquatic organisms to the coastal waters of the United States (other than the Great Lakes) and an analysis of control options. The national sea grant college program/connecticut sea grant project R/ES-6.

Cohen, M. D., March, J. G., & Olsen, J. P. (1972). A garbage can model of organizational choice. *Administrative Science Quarterly,* 1–25.

DNV GL. (2015). USCG makes decision on use of MPN method for BWMS. Available at: www.dnvgl.com/news/uscg-makes-decision-on-use-of-mpn-method-for-ballast (Accessed December 23, 2015).

Ericson, R. (2006). Ten uncertainties of risk-management approaches to security. *Canadian Journal of Criminology and Criminal Justice, 48*(3), 345–356.

Euroshore. (2000). Ballast water. Available at: https://euroshore.com/framework-imo/ballast-water (Accessed March 5, 2011).

Eurostat. (2017). Freight transport statistics. http://ec.europa.eu/eurostat/statistics-explained/index.php/Freight_transport_statistics (Accessed October 16, 2017).

Favarel-Garrigues, G., Godefroy, T., & Lascoumes, P. (2011). Reluctant partners? Banks in the fight against money laundering and terrorism financing in France. *Security Dialogue, 42*(2), 179–196.

Financial Supervisory Authority. (2013). Redovisning av uppdrag. Report Dnr 13-2864. Stockholm: Finansinspektionen.

Gephart Jr, R. P., Van Maanen, J., & Oberlechner, T. (2009). Organizations and risk in late modernity. *Organization Studies, 30*(2–3), 141–155.

Green4sea. (2016). IMO BWM Convention to enter into force in 2017. www.green4sea.com/imo-bwm-convention-enter-force-2017/ (Accessed January 23, 2018).

Harrison, D. (2010). *Invasive Species in the Shipping Industry*. Research Project, BI Norwegian Business School, Oslo, Norway.

Harrison, D., & Helgesson, C-F. (2017). When stakeholder identities are co-moving targets: The case of global shipping and 'invasive species'. Paper under preparation for review.

Helgesson, K. S., & Mörth, U. (Eds.). (2012). *Securitization, accountability and risk management: Transforming the public domain*. London: Routledge.

Helgesson, K. S., & Mörth, U. (2016). Involuntary public policy-making by for-profit professionals: European lawyers on anti-money laundering and terrorism financing. *JCMS: Journal of Common Market Studies, 54*(5), 1216–1232.

Hutter, B. M. (2001). *Regulation and risk: Occupational health and safety on the railways*. Oxford: Oxford University Press.

Levi, M., Reuter, P., & Halliday, T. (2017). Can the AML system be evaluated without better data? *Crime, Law and Social Change*, 1–22.

MacPhee, B. (2007). Hitchhikers' guide to the ballast water management convention: An analysis of legal mechanisms to address the issue of alien invasive species. *Journal of International Wildlife Law and Policy, 10*(1), 29–54.

Maguire, S., & Hardy, C. (2013). Organizing processes and the construction of risk: A discursive approach. *Academy of Management Journal, 56*(1), 231–255.

Marx, G. T. (2006). Varieties of personal information as influences on attitudes toward surveillance. In K. D. Haggerty, Kevin D. & R. V. Ericson (Eds.), *The new politics of surveillance and visibility*, 79–110.

Meyer, J. W., & Rowan, B. (1977). Institutionalized organizations: Formal structure as myth and ceremony. *American Journal of Sociology, 83*(2), 340–363.

OTA. (1993). *Harmful non-indigenous species in the United States*. Report, office of technology assessment, United States Congress, Washington, DC.

Pimentel, D., Zuniga, R., & Morrison, D. (2005). Update on the environmental and economic costs associated with alien-invasive species in the United States. *Ecological Economics, 52*(3), 273–288.

Power, M. (1997). *The audit society: Rituals of verification*. OUP Oxford.

Power, M. (2004). *The risk management of everything: Rethinking the politics of uncertainty*. London: Demos.

Power, M. (2009). The risk management of nothing. *Accounting, Organizations and Society, 34*(6), 849–855.

Power, M., Scheytt, T., Soin, K., & Sahlin, K. (2009). Reputational risk as a logic of organizing in late modernity. *Organization Studies, 30*(2–3), 301–324.

Rothstein, H., Huber, M., & Gaskell, G. (2006). A theory of risk colonization: The spiralling regulatory logics of societal and institutional risk. *Economy and Society, 35*(1), 91–112.

Statista. (2018). Number of ships in the world merchant fleet between January 1, 2008 and January 1, 2017, by type. www.statista.com/statistics/264024/number-of-merchant-ships-worldwide-by-type/ (Accessed January, 2, 2018).

Transport Canada. (2017). Ballast water defined. www.tc.gc.ca/eng/marinesafety/oep-environment-ballastwater-defined-249.htm (Accessed October 16, 2017).

Tsingou, E. (2017). New governors on the block: The rise of anti-money laundering professionals. *Crime, Law and Social Change*. https://doi.org/10.1007/s10611-017-9751-x.

Van Asselt, M. B., & Renn, O. (2011). Risk governance. *Journal of Risk Research, 14*(4), 431–449.

Verhage, A. (2009a). Between the hammer and the anvil? The anti-money laundering-complex and its interactions with the compliance industry. *Crime, Law and Social Change, 52*(1), 9–32.

Verhage, A. (2009b). Supply and demand: Anti-money laundering by the compliance industry. *Journal of Money Laundering Control, 12*(4), 371–391.

Weick, K. E., & Sutcliffe, K. M. (2011). *Managing the unexpected: Resilient performance in an age of uncertainty* (Vol. 8). Hoboken, NJ: John Wiley & Sons.

18

TENSION IN THE AIR

Behind the Scenes of Aviation Risk Management

David Passenier

Introduction

On July 25, 2015, Air Traffic Control (ATC) radio communication went viral on YouTube (ATC audio, n.d.) featuring a Dutch airline jet that encountered a wind shear—an abrupt change of wind direction. One of the pilots was heard exclaiming "Scary!" and "Speed, speed, speed!" The air traffic controller warned the pilots that they were accidentally broadcasting their private talking over the radio frequency, but for some reason the captain was heard on the radio again, coaching the copilot: "You've flown really well, I just wanted to say that." The aircraft made a go-around and then landed low on fuel, having already diverted from another airport due to bad weather. While this information might typically only have ended up in an anonymous reporting database, the cockpit scare now spread via YouTube to national news media and even debates in parliament (AD, 2015, 30 July). Despite the upheaval, the Dutch Safety Board subsequently responded that there would be no investigation, because the event was too regular to learn anything new (AD, 2015, 2 September).

The wind shear scare demonstrates common, contrasting risk perceptions. The public perceived the scary-looking event as an accident waiting to happen. The common expectation is for the authorities to take control and investigate the matter: could the incident be due to technical or human error; is anyone to blame (Dekker, 2004)? In contrast, the event may appear regular from the point of view of highly experienced safety-critical organizations, whose core operational processes are inherently hazardous. Through risk management, these organizations can reduce, but not eliminate the likelihood of damage and loss (La Porte & Consolini, 1991), so the close call might be classified as an acceptable risk (Vaughan, 1997).

The inherent social tension between safe and scary risk perceptions can have consequences when perceptions of different actors are opposed, such as directly after the reported incident. Organizational relations may be damaged when managers blame individual operators for incidents, perhaps in order to avoid legal consequences (Dekker, 2007), while safety-critical organizations rely on good internal relations to continually improve safety (Cox, Jones, & Collinson, 2006). These discussions, however, remain rather abstract while we have limited understanding of the way safety-critical organizations regularly interact with their societal contexts. Seminal empirical studies focus on incidents (Vaughan, 1997; Weick, 1990) or their aftermaths (Brown, 2000; Gephart, 1993, 1997; Maguire & Hardy, 2013), rather than any impacts that these societal interactions might have on the regular work process.

In this chapter, I therefore present empirical evidence of social tensions occurring in day-to-day operations in the Dutch commercial aviation industry. In aviation, contrasting risk perceptions might surface more sharply than in other safety-critical industries, such as oil and gas (Hudson, Parker, & van der Graaf, 2002, January), because passengers are often physically confronted with disturbances like windy weather. Thus, contrasting perceptions of aviation risk frequently emerge as these scares enter the public arena through news and social media. Yet, the impact of these media hypes on the regular work done within the privacy of the cockpit usually remains opaque to outsiders. I therefore ask: *How do contrasting risk perceptions manifest themselves in the societal context of airline risk management processes, and how do these social manifestations impact regular work in the cockpit?*

I continue this chapter by reviewing the relevant risk management literature, followed by the choice of settings and methods I used to collect, analyze, and present qualitative data from the Dutch aviation industry. I then present my findings in a series of vignettes and discuss the implications for the debate on risk perceptions.

Risk Management in a Social Context

Risk management can refer to any organized attempt to exercise control over uncertainties (Power, 2007), but I limit my discussion here to safety risks. I first describe how risk management literature depicts the way managers and government officials can design routines for operating safety-critical technologies, and coordination processes between operators. However, the operation may look messier in practice than on paper, which fuels debate between opposing perceptions of whether such messiness is risky.

Risk Management by Design

Risk management can refer to an administrative office occupation, as well as a real-time operational activity performed by operators like pilots. In the literature, the administrative occupation dominates (Maguire & Hardy, 2013). The administrative risk management process first identifies risks retrospectively by investigating reported incidents and accidents, or prospectively by projecting those risks on future operations. Second, risk managers design and implement mitigating measures. Third, risk management systems monitor and provide feedback on the effectiveness of these measures.

Risk management methods are anchored in accident models from which control systems for safe work practices are inferred (Hollnagel, 2012; Leveson, 2011; Reason, 1997). These control systems look technical, but a major concern is with human actors. Hazards originate in technical processes like flying jet aircraft, but engineering progress has made the hardware, like jet engines, highly reliable. Thus, the most unpredictable factor in risk management is the human factor (Reason, 1990) or rather its complex interaction with software and hardware (Leveson, 2011).

Two broad approaches to human factors risk management can be identified. The first reasons that human errors are sadly inevitable and sometimes cause accidents, and therefore develop organizational safeguards to contain the effects of errors and thus prevent accidents (Reason, 1990, 1997). A checklist, for example, can function as a safeguard by catching a mistake made earlier, and help the operators correct their mistake. In aircraft, the landing checklist item reminding pilots to lower their landing gear before landing is a good example.

The second approach (Woods, Johannesen, Cook, & Sarter, 1994) reasons that hazards can be managed by redesigning the socio-technical system from which errors emerge (Rasmussen, 1997). A socio-technical system represents safety-critical processes consisting of interacting human and technical elements, such as an aircraft consisting of technical elements, and a flight crew and computers controlling the aircraft. An established origin of human error lies in ergonomic design choices of the hardware. A famous example from World War II was the design solution to B-17 bombers that kept getting damaged when the landing gear was raised while the aircraft was on the ground (Stanton et al., 2010). Pilots kept making this mistake because the landing gear toggle switch looked exactly like another switch that they had to operate after landing. By differentiating the landing gear actuation design, pilots no longer made the same mistake.

The design of complex organizational systems can also create hazardous situations. The formalized coordination processes between pilots and air traffic controllers, for example, is partially automated, enabling detailed planning of aircraft movements, but occasionally complex, unforeseen interactions emerge, causing dangerous situations. Various regulatory agencies ultimately influence the design processes by which the risks of systems like global air transport are managed; Rasmussen (1997) therefore extended risk management thinking to the societal level. New risk management methods (Hollnagel, 2012; Leveson, 2011) now challenge managers and administrators to think about complex interdependencies and redesign organizational systems so that hazards do not emerge.

However, like the original design, the redesigned organization also functions differently in practice. Human operators are usually confronted with many unaccounted operational variabilities, even in routine technical operations (Orr, 1996; Suchman, 1987). Such variation requires operational personnel to respond adaptively (Weick & Sutcliffe, 2007), although it may be hard to appreciate what actions are required from them: technical work tends to look messy in practice (Schulman, 1993). Because risk management methods tend to select on the dependent variable (Dekker, 2004) and infer bad outcomes from messy-looking work, messy-looking work is often treated as an accident waiting to happen.

Normal Accidents Theory

Sociologist Charles Perrow (1984) coined the term Normal Accidents to explain why messy-looking work processes are accidents waiting to happen. Two characteristics of socio-technical systems compromise control over hazardous processes. The first characteristic is interactive complexity, which refers to the innate tendency of system elements to interact in unforeseen ways. The second characteristic is a tight coupling between these elements, denoting strong interdependencies between operational processes and little time, or few alternative courses of action, for operators to respond to unforeseen events. Thus, the messy system will inevitably produce unexpected situations where operators do not have enough time or courses of action to respond. Subsequently, because the system is tightly coupled, one small failure may immediately cause other failures, and the failure, rippling through the system, might end in catastrophe.

Despite several criticisms (Leveson, Marais, & Carroll, 2009; Weick, 2004), Normal Accidents Theory (NAT) remains popular to describe accidents waiting to happen. Although its risk predictions are not entirely accurate (Leveson et al., 2009), there is broad agreement on the following central point. However advanced professionals' abilities are to deal with messy processes, some safety issues cannot be resolved unless the socio-technical system is redesigned. When the political momentum to accomplish costly and disruptive redesigns is lacking, the prospect or actual occurrence of a catastrophic accident can amass such momentum (Turner & Pidgeon, 1997).

The Normal Accident frame is further strengthened by the influential risk theories of Dianne Vaughan's (1997) *normalization of deviance* and Scott Snook's (2000) *practical drift*. These established, influential theories point to messiness as indicating a slow process of degradation. The degradation process is hard to see while one is immersed in it because the messiness has become normalized, by way of cultural blindness or groupthink (Vaughan, 1997). The dangers only manifest themselves when the inevitable accident happens. Retrospective analyses then reveal how the purpose behind risk management systems gradually shifted, allowing deviations from standards to become the norm and blinding organizations to dangerous incompatibilities between diverse organizational units.

High Reliability Organizations

In contrast, the High Reliability Organization (HRO) concept suggests that safety-critical organizations can continually progress without accidents (La Porte & Consolini, 1991; Roberts, 1990). HROs impressed social science scholars because HROs operate inherently dangerous technologies low-risk (La Porte & Consollini, 1991). Social psychological processes contributing to this phenomenon are summarized as "chronic worries" about risks (Weick & Sutcliffe, 2007), and continuous learning, tweaking, and improvement (Roberts, 1990; Schulman, 1993; Weick & Sutcliffe, 2007). These characteristics were observed in a range of technical work contexts, such as ATC (La Porte & Consolini, 1991), nuclear power plants (Schulman, 1993), and aircraft carrier deck operations (Weick & Roberts, 1993).

The HRO perspective is further elaborated by systems theories emerging from engineering disciplines (Leveson et al., 2009), labeled Resilience Engineering (Hollnagel, Woods, & Leveson, 2007). Resilience Engineering suggests that the way in which operational variabilities are handled explains why most operational processes are performed safely (Leveson, 2004; Hollnagel, 2012; Woods et al., 1994). From a Resilience Engineering standpoint, it is impossible to design frictionless planning systems, complete system operating instructions, or unambiguously purposed management systems. These views are grounded in influential science and technologies studies such as the work of Lucy Suchman (1987) on situated action, and Susan Leigh Star's work on boundary objects (Star & Griesemer, 1989).

To handle unexpected, but systematically occurring variabilities, HRO operators develop professional, experiential expertise that entitles them to make safety-critical decisions in the daily operation (Roberts, 1990; Weick & Sutcliffe, 2007). Their knowledge and experience can make a difference between life and death, but they are not infallible (Weick & Sutcliffe, 2007). Instead, HRO members humbly accept their human limitations and make an effort to learn from failure. To accomplish this, the organization has to protect them from the age-old tendency of the society, in which they operate, to punish someone for a failure (Turner & Pidgeon, 1997). Societies confronted with catastrophe tend to seek a scapegoat to release all the public emotion and political stress.

Weick (1987) therefore argues that the precondition for a constructive organizational culture in HROs is that they are relatively secluded from their societal context. This portrays HROs as creating their own "bubble" in society, within which professionals can perform their work by their own, expert professional ethics, undisturbed by the anxieties from the surrounding society. The resulting culture of high reliability (Weick, 1987), or safety culture (Weick & Sutcliffe, 2007), is protected by translating erratic public pressures for safety into rational, incremental process improvements characterized by high levels of formalization (La Porte, 1996).

However, the inside of the bubble looks messy because HRO risk management is not strictly centralized (Schulman, 1993). In order to facilitate continuous learning, Schulman (1993) argued that HROs foster "conceptual slack," or "a divergence in analytical perspectives among members of an organization over theories, models, or causal assumptions pertaining to its technology or production processes" (Schulman, 1993, p. 364). Schulman's study of a nuclear power plant revealed how "much of the formalization at the plant is meant to document and reinforce an elaborate balance, even fractionation, of administrative power" (Schulman, 1993, p. 358). HROs thus manage risks through a negotiated order where zealous proceduralization of technical work processes and office politics come together.

Schulman's (1993) work on HROs is relevant in the context of today's globally intensifying accountability practices (Power, 1997), within which conceptual slack is often perceived as a risk and a liability (Dekker, 2011b). This trend indicates that HROs' negotiated orders involve interaction with actors in their societal contexts, which suggests that HROs are not always isolated bubbles within society. I therefore continue to show how, in the case of commercial aviation, the negotiated order of high reliability manifests itself at the societal level and how that order impacts regular, safety-critical work processes in the cockpit.

Methods

Based on seven years of research (2011–2017) in the Dutch aviation industry, I developed five vignettes that demonstrate regular social tensions in airline risk management. The vignettes, adopting three levels of Rasmussen's (1997) multi-level view of risk management, answer the central question in two main ways. First, vignettes 1 and 2 illustrate how contrasting risk perceptions manifest themselves in a negotiated order in airline's societal contexts. Vignette 1 describes a debate emerging between professional and public risk perceptions at the societal level. Vignette 2 shows how actors negotiate within this common tension at the administrative level. Second, vignettes 3 through 5 describe impacts of this negotiated order on work done in the cockpit, at the level of the safety-critical work process. I look at the impacts represented by pilots' social responses to risk management systems such as flight data monitoring, their involvement in the negotiated order that standard operating procedures (SOPs) represent, and the social influence they exert in negotiating between different planning systems.

The first two vignettes derive from data collected by investigating and participating in two interconnected aviation networks (see Table 18.1). First, I participated in an industry network consisting of a cross-section of aviation professionals. Second, I interviewed members of a governance network consisting of the aviation authorities, government, and industry management. Third, I conducted two rounds of in-depth interviews with airline pilots, who represented a subset of the industry network. In total, I participated in 9 seminars and conducted 47 interviews; I recorded and transcribed interviews or made notes in case recording was not allowed or impractical.

The last three vignettes are based on two consecutive flight observations of a flight crew flying back and forth between two European cities. I made these observations from the back seat of the cockpit, called a jump-seat. I observed the pilots at work in the middle of a regular workday; they had more flights scheduled that day that I did not observe. During the flight, I was able to engage in conversations with them about topics that came up because something happened. Meanwhile, I made notes with pen and paper and occasionally took a photo or a short video. After the flights, I wrote down and analyzed the events I had observed and checked my interpretations in two rounds with one of the observed pilots. In developing the vignettes, I compared them to the data from interviews and documents that I had collected and continued to collect for another year (see Table 18.1).

Table 18.1 Data Collection and Analysis

Timeframe	Type of do to	Data source	Content
2011–2017	Participation in nine seminars, ethnographic interviews	Aviation professional industry network: • Airlines • Maintenance • Ground services • Air traffic control • Research • Oversight • Government	Emerging risk-related topics relevant to aviation professionals
2011–2012	Twelve interviews, 1-hour long on average	Aviation professional industry network: • Airline captains, copilots • Pilot trainer, examiners, managers • Retired pilots • Human factors training entrepreneurs • Flight simulator technology entrepreneurs • Aviation contract researchers • Aviation psychologists • Aviation consultants	Contrasting risk perceptions and their implications for regular work in the cockpit
2013–2015	20 interviews, 1 hour long on average	Aviation governance network: • Safety managers • Airline officials • ATC officials • Aviation judiciary • Aviation police • Aviation inspectors • Pilot union member • Government officials • National & EU government bodies	Manifestation of contrasting risk perceptions in interactions between airline companies and their societal context
2011–2017	Fifteen in-depth 1–4-hour long interviews, of which 7 were recurrent with the same interviewee	Airline pilots: • Captains • Copilots • Trainers, examiners, managers • Retired pilots	Impacts of contrasting risk perceptions emerging as social tensions in the regular work of airline pilots

(Continued)

Timeframe	Type of do to	Data source	Content
2015–2016	Jump seat observations of 2 × 2 consecutive flights to/from European cities, about 1 hour per flight and about 1 hour turnaround time for each set of flights.	Cockpit work environment of short haul jet aircraft: • Captains • Copilots • Flight attendants • Ground services • Air traffic controllers • Aircraft systems • Weather • Traffic • Airports • Airspaces	Impacts of contrasting risk perceptions emerging as social tensions in the regular work of airline pilots
2011–2017	Various documentation	• Aircraft Operating Manuals • Navigational charts • Policy documents • Accident investigation reports • News media reports	Textual representations of contrasting risk perceptions

In the cockpit, I was able to make detailed, in-depth observations due to the extensive preparatory study of the technical and social aspects of pilot work. Earlier, I was trained as a private pilot to fly general aviation aircraft such as the popular Cessna 152. I also followed introductory aerospace engineering courses. This background allowed me to make an analytical jump to the level of large, complex, multiengine, multi-crew airline jet operations. I performed a first flight observation in which I refined the observation technique. For this flight, I prepared myself by flying for one hour in a fixed flight simulator of that aircraft type. I analyzed aircraft operating manuals and studied multi-crew coordination techniques before entering into the second flight observation reported here.

In the final analysis phase, I compared different data content thus gathered. For example, to develop the fourth vignette, I compared procedure variations reported by various interviewees. It emerged from these stories that procedure variations involved confusion, fueling industry-wide debates about contrasting risk perceptions. Thus, I was able to relate tensions I found in the societal context with subtle social expressions of humor, emotions, and stress in the regular cockpit work setting.

Tensions in Airline Risk Management

Vignette 1. An Emotional Debate about Risk

A live display of a debate between public and professional risk perceptions occurred in a seminar organized by a Dutch aviation network, exemplifying a cross-section of industry professionals. A few prominent Dutch journalists were invited to share their views on how they reported on aviation. The safety manager of a major aviation organization shared the stage to enable a debate between the media and the industry. The audience was occupied by members of the industry network and by students in journalism.

Tensions rose in the room when a journalist from the popular newspaper *Telegraaf* took the stage. He talked about an occasion when a KLM aircraft, flying across the Atlantic Ocean, had made a precautionary landing in the UK due to unexpectedly strong headwinds.

The flight crew thus managed to stay well within their safe fuel margins and there was never any danger to the passengers and crew. A *Telegraaf* journalist traveling on board, however, immediately contacted the editorial staff to report an "emergency landing" due to low fuel. As soon as this news came out, a storm erupted in the news media to which KLM had to respond.

The discussion in the room now unfolded about the question if it was right for the *Telegraaf* to use the phrase "emergency landing" if this was factually incorrect. The journalist held on to his standpoint and said that he would not hesitate to use the phrase emergency landing again. He argued that he could not expect from his readership to tell the difference between an emergency and a precautionary landing.

Tensions escalated in shouting anger amongst the aviation professionals in the audience as the journalist went on to argue that his job was to report something newsworthy. Aviation professionals in the audience charged the journalist for fabricating news, which could have negative consequences for aviation professionals, organizations, and ultimately flight safety. However, the journalist continued that his professional ethic was to report something newsworthy in a language that his readership would understand.

"I actually liked the *Telegraaf* journalist," an aviation researcher told me afterward. "At least he was honest." The researcher, an active member of the industry network that had organized the seminar, was more appalled by the story of another journalist. This journalist had spent years investigating to try and prove a pilot guilty of an accident. The researcher found this kind of investigative journalism similar to the *Telegraaf*'s example in that it fabricated aviation news, but in a more destructive way. From the industry perspective, fabricating news about guilty pilots amounted to witch hunts, or calls for justice when there is no justice to be served.

This vignette demonstrates how contrasting risk perceptions manifest themselves in emotional debate about the way unusual events are portrayed and serve vested interests. One could sense the tension in the atmosphere that the emotional disagreement caused, which could perhaps be better understood when placed into the broader societal context. These were no idle semantic games, as a horrifying case from nearby Germany demonstrated. After investigators acquitted an air traffic controller who was on duty when two aircraft crashed mid-air over Überlingen, Germany, the controller was murdered by a relative of crash victims. The relative had felt that justice had not been served, and had taken matters into his own hands. Thus, members of the authorities and the industry could sense urgency to negotiate a position in risk debates that satisfies contrasting perspectives, as is demonstrated by the next vignette.

Vignette 2. Negotiating an Emotional Disagreement

Indeed, actors in the aviation industry are aware of the contrasting risk perceptions and actively manage their differences. This is demonstrated by an event taking place in the office of a safety manager of a Dutch ATC organization, occurring as I sat down to have an interview with the manager. The phone rang; it was the aviation judiciary. A Dutch aircraft had accidentally overrun a taxiway and hit the grass while taxiing in freezing weather. Nobody was hurt, but in aviation, such a small event potentially becomes the site of an extensive investigation because it could have been worse. The airport where it happened was controlled by the safety manager's ATC organization, so they also became part of the investigation. The judiciary was at this stage judging if the incident could have been caused by someone's intention or gross negligence, which would require him to start a formal investigation.

Now on the phone with the judiciary, the manager expressed dismay with the fact that the aviation police were visiting his organization. The judiciary replied that the police were only conducting a preliminary investigation, but the manager felt that the line between preliminary evidence gathering and full-on prosecution was blurry. "Any evidence that they might gather now can be used to prosecute our employees later," he explained to me, after hanging up. From the manager's point of view, the judiciary did not live up to the kind of hesitancy to prosecute that they had mutually agreed on before.

What had happened? The reason for the incident was unclear at this stage, but it was tempting to speculate that the pilots were maybe taxying too fast; this was a pattern I had heard about from pilots. If the pilots were speeding, however, it was unclear to me how the ATC organization could be blamed. Could they be blamed for putting pressure on pilots to taxi faster than the speed limit? It seemed unlikely to me, but it was all speculation at this point—I had no access to data of the incident.

A few weeks later, I talked to the judiciary and asked him to clarify what had happened. He told me that to his mind, there was no direct cause for worry for the ATC organization. Instead, his perception was that air traffic controllers were overly sensitive to the prospect of prosecution; more so than airline pilots. He said that members of the ATC organization would still reference a 1990s case where a Dutch air traffic controller had been prosecuted. The judiciary found it hard to understand why the case resonated so strongly that, in 2015, it still caused hostile sentiments amongst Dutch air traffic controllers toward the judiciary. The judiciary pursued a policy of hesitancy to prosecute (see Dekker, 2007; EESC, n.d.; & ICAO, 2016, 25 August, for elaborations on this policy of "Just Culture"), enabled by maintaining rapport with various crucial industry officials like the ATC safety manager. By keeping in touch on a regular basis, the judiciary cultivated a knowledge basis to judge if a reported incident could be left to an organization's own investigative process.

The vignette exemplifies how emotional disagreements emerge in daily risk management activities, and that considerable energy is spent to maintain a dynamic, negotiated order. The tensions erupting in the phone call between the safety manager and the judiciary illustrate the tensions arising in this work. The judiciary and the safety manager did not give any impression that the incident, and the disagreement it had caused between them, seriously threatened their relationship. These tensions seemed to be part of the game.

The negotiated order may also impact the regular safety-critical work processes in airlines. In the following vignettes, I focus on the airline cockpit work process and a selection of events and conversations unfolding there on a regular working day. The first impact is a social response of pilots to their company's risk management systems.

Vignette 3. Ironic and Laconic Talking about Risk Management

On a routine flight between two European cities, risks of speeding in the air came up as a topic of conversation. While climbing out and passing around 3,000 feet altitude, I noticed that the speed indicator read 270 knots, instead of the 250 knots I expected. The copilot, as if anticipating my question, explained that: "Nine out of ten times we will fly maximum 250 knots [463 km/h] below Flight Level 100 [an altitude of 10,000 feet or 3 km]. However, when the captain agrees, we might go faster."

Speeding below 10,000 feet was deemed to be one of the "gray areas" where, according to some pilots whom I interviewed, the rules are not as fixed as they look on paper. This gray area differs from speeding on the taxiways of airports, which I allowed myself to speculate about in the previous vignette. Speed limits exist in certain parts of the airspace. Pilots I interviewed said that speeding often happens in the airspace between the ground and 10,000 feet, where a 250 knots speed limit applies. In this airspace, aircraft usually are either climbing away or descending on approach to airports. The reason for the speed limit is to keep these dynamic traffic flows manageable and prevent mid-air collisions between aircraft. However, pilots argued, sometimes exceeding the limit by 20 or 30 knots (37–55 km/h), would not endanger flight safety and could help. Speeding could sometimes straighten out the flow of traffic or simply help a flight catch up from an earlier delay, so that it could be on time for an arrival slot.

Back to the cockpit. Shortly after the copilot clarified the current speed—by now, reading 280 knots—an unusual warning popped up on one of the computer screens. "Speed limit exceeded." We were now passing through 6,500 feet, and both pilots said they had never seen this computer warning before. The copilot quickly canceled the warning, joking that he did not want to be summoned to the office. The captain added that the office would probably get this message, in view of their extensive flight data monitoring. "You don't want to know what they are checking. The reversers you were pulling on landing, your flaps settings, everything."

It sounded like the pilots felt uneasy about being monitored, so I asked if there was any truth in the copilot's joke. The captain replied that they did not have to fear being summoned because that only happened if one "experienced something," some kind of incident. The current situation would not qualify: "Flying 30 knots faster won't matter if you hit someone." Perhaps to make sure that I would not misunderstand his joke, the copilot concluded the conversation by stating that he had "complete confidence in the reporting culture of the company. It's really all about learning."

This vignette illustrates how pilots may respond to the negotiated order embodied by their risk management system. The impact described here is subtle and of no direct consequence for the flight I observed, but it illustrates how pilots may respond socially to technical risk management systems. The social response here consisted of ironic and laconic talking about the system, revealing some ambiguity in the company management's perceived intentions behind the system.

Vignette 4. *Shocked and Confused by Variations on SOPs*

Besides variations on air traffic rules like speed limits, I also found that routine variations on technical systems operating procedures sometimes surface in regular work. The topic of performing variations on system operating procedures arose when one of the covers of the emergency rope, above the captain's head, suddenly fell open mid-flight. The emergency rope is intended for escaping out of the cockpit after a crash. The before start-up checklist required checking the rope on every flight, as I had seen the captain perform on the ground. Evidently, the captain suggested while closing the cover again, opening and closing the cover regularly had weakened the closing mechanism.

A conversation then arose about how in aircraft little things tend to break, and how the formal procedure for dealing with small system failures may differ from the informal norm. The copilot then shared his experience of becoming socialized in the culture of pilots flying the current aircraft type. In his initial training, he learned to strictly revert to the books whenever a failure occurred. Then, as he began participating in the operation, he was a little shocked to find that for many failures, the only accepted response was a simple, "quick reset." That is, many failures would be remedied by simply turning the failed system off and on again. The copilot learned that the informal norm for a quick reset was more authoritative in practice than the formal procedure to which he was accustomed.

The background of the quick reset practice was that earlier generations of pilots were routinely faced with small system failures. They had learned that the formal procedure for many failures—taking out the Quick Reference Handbook and following the checklist—was unnecessarily cumbersome. Pilots found that in many cases a quick reset did the trick, and they began spreading this practice informally. The practice thus spread as seniors conveyed operational experience to juniors. Eventually, the quick reset practice found its way to "the office," which decreed through an email communication that resets were allowed under certain conditions. The copilot added that he had missed the email, which was sent after he had already gotten used to the informal practice. Later on, he had heard about the formal change from a colleague.

This vignette thus illustrates how pilots socially participate in the negotiated order represented by SOPs. Pilots participate in creative socialization processes by which informal operational norms are created and maintained. A new member's experience of slight shock and confusion demonstrates the process when he gets exposed to the social norm that the informal routine prevails over the formal procedure. The differences between formal and informal practices may cause confusion at first, for how does one know which parts of the books are authoritative, and which are not? When the informal norm is adopted in an amendment of the SOP, it turns out that pilots are not merely recipients of the negotiated order but also, as a collective, participate in the process of negotiation.

Vignette 5. Angry and Frustrated Negotiation in Contingent Planning

The regular flight that I observed was planned in detail but also encountered contingencies to which the pilots had to respond in a coordinated manner. Whereas coordination may sound like a neat, technical process, it can look tense, even angry, in practice. The following vignette illustrates coordination between air traffic controllers and the flight crew, taking the point of view of the latter. Even on a short flight in Europe, flight crews may pass through several, slightly differently organized ATC planning systems, with different customs and accents in English. The pilots on this flight had already spent some time talking about the annoyances that the different airport planning systems caused, before the following events happened.

When it was time to depart for the return flight, everything looked well. The weather was perfect and the passengers had boarded without incident. The ground crew had put some fuel in the wrong tank but it would be possible to correct this in-flight. While taxying out from the gate, the flight crew was confident that they would arrive on time at the destination, until they spotted an ominous row of waiting aircraft. The captain requested an expected take-off time and the air traffic controller replied: "We will call you back." The captain cursed, sensing trouble. "How do they not know yet?"

A few minutes later, the ground controller returned on the frequency and politely informed the flight crew that "delay is one-niner minutes." The captain replied with a neutral "roger" but the mood in the cockpit instantly flipped to anger. The captain had just promised the passengers that they would be on time; now, they might have suddenly incurred about twenty minutes delay. "Ridiculous," the copilot exclaimed. "Why not let us wait at the gate so we don't have to stand here burning fuel?" In addition to the expected delay, the fuel management situation had suddenly changed. The copilot quickly calculated that their fuel reserve could now get below their expected Take Off Fuel (TOF). The number was written on a piece of paper clipped to the inside of the cockpit. Would they even have enough fuel to depart, by the time they would be allowed to take off?

The pilots continued to decompose the TOF-number to arrive at the minimally required amount of fuel to arrive safely at the destination. With a delay of about 20 minutes, they concluded, there would still be enough fuel to arrive at the destination well above minimum fuel required by law. There might, however, not be enough fuel left to divert without issue to another airport, in case of bad weather or a runway obstruction at the destination, for example. Even if they would have to divert, there would still be plenty of nearby airports in range, but the flight crew might have to declare an emergency. Declaring an emergency is legally required below 30 minutes of fuel remaining. Once an emergency is declared, a formal investigative process will start and the event will be thrust into the public arena.

Diverting was an unlikely scenario, because the weather was good and the destination was unlikely to get unexpectedly closed at arrival. Talking it through, the captain reasoned that if something unforeseeable happened, they could "commit" to the destination. Confronted with this phrase, an air traffic controller could become more willing to find a way and let an aircraft land on a closed airport. "Committed" would essentially communicate the impeding need to declare an emergency, thus preventing the situation where one has to come out and actually do it. Having calculated and reasoned it through, the pilots felt reassured. They continued to wait in line for take-off and the rest of the flight proved to be routine. Flying a bit over the speed limit, the pilots later even managed to catch up some of the delay and got their passengers to the destination on time.

The vignette demonstrates how anger and frustration can mark pilots' preparation to negotiate contingent planning with ATC. Anger and frustration emerged first from the pilots' lack of influence on the ATC planning system in which they operated, which pushed them toward the limits of their fuel planning. They responded by reasserting their fuel planning and reevaluating the safety and accountability risks associated with the landing phase of the flight, preparing a way to implicitly negotiate with ATC on arrival. Since the flight continued without incident, they did not need to exert this influence and their efforts never escaped the confines of the cockpit.

Discussion

The five vignettes I presented in this chapter show what dynamic risk management looks like as a socio-technical phenomenon, embedded in a social context where contrasting risk perceptions exist. Contrasting risk perceptions manifest themselves in a negotiated order in airline's societal contexts. I described a debate emerging between professional and public risk perceptions at the societal level, and subsequently showed how risk management actors negotiate contingent positions within this common tension at the administrative level. These observations demonstrate the interaction between aviation HROs and their societal context. The actors invest in negotiation because failing to do justice to either of the contrasting risk perceptions can have damaging consequences to aviation organizations.

I subsequently demonstrated how the impacts of the negotiated order of aviation HROs are visible at the level of the safety-critical work process. I looked at three manifestations of the negotiated order in HROs: the application of risk management systems in regular flight operations, social norms guiding variations on SOPs, and formal jargon used to negotiate contingent planning. The impacts of these manifestations of the negotiated order were visible, first, in how pilots responded socially to ambiguity in technical risk management systems by laconic and ironic talking. Second, I showed pilots' feelings of shock and confusion when getting involved in the negotiated order through socialization and learning how to perform variations on SOPs. Third, I highlighted pilots' anger and frustration when they were facing frictions in the negotiated order represented by different planning systems, and engaged in contingent planning to reassert their position toward ATC.

Social Tensions: Precipitating Normal Accidents or Indicating HRO?

This empirically rich description of the social tensions marking HROs' interactions with their societal contexts could further the debate about the meaning and consequences of these tensions. The observations reveal social tensions between actors engaging in risk management at different levels—society, administration, and hazardous work process—in the form of disagreement, ambiguity, and strains in the relationships between them. These social tensions become visible in emotions, humor, and stress, and provide a window into the regular irregularities, or the negotiated orders, that characterize HROs on a daily basis. What the consequences of these social tensions are is a complex matter and subject to debate.

Going back to the wind shear scare described in the Introduction, it seems obvious that the emotion of fear is an indication of danger and therefore demands action from actors who share some responsibility for the HRO risk management process. However, in light of the evidence presented in this chapter, the reader might appreciate the complexity of interpreting the risks associated with emotions like fear, and of arriving at a proportionate response. I demonstrated shared responsibilities between authorities, administrators, and operational personnel, and showed how they interact to subtly negotiate and renegotiate an order that works. Much of their investments in this process may never be seen by higher authorities or outsiders to the professional community or even the single work space. For example, the efforts of the observed flight crew, to prepare for the highly unlikely prospect of negotiating with ATC, would never have escaped the cockpit if I had not been there to write about it here.

Social tensions can add depth to the debate about how HROs usually manage to perform safely. Should the social tensions observed here be interpreted as demonstrations of safety, or of hazard—as accidents waiting to happen? NAT suggests that operational tensions are accidents waiting to happen. Social tensions indicate competitive strains on safety-critical organizations with complex interdependencies that, due to tight coupling of system elements such as in fuel planning, will inevitably lead to disaster. In contrast, from a HRO perspective, the observed tensions could mark resilient responses to normal variabilities. Since there are no frictionless planning systems, complete SOPs, or unambiguously purposed management systems; the social tensions that I observed could simply be what handling normal variabilities looks and feels like. After all, is there such a thing as human involvement in technical systems without humor, emotion, and stress?

Socializing the Risk Management Debate

Airline captain Sullenberger makes an important point, as quoted in the movie *Sully*: "[If] you are looking for human error, make it human." Dekker (2004) furthermore argues that we should not be looking for error, but a more neutral vocabulary about operational variabilities. He argues that human error is a concept that fails to do justice to the equivocality of human actions, due to the psychological mechanism of hindsight bias. The effect of hindsight bias can be summarized as an innate tendency to look back at the evidence and read the outcome as inevitable. Seeing human error in an action is, therefore, more about looking for explanations for a failure, than appreciating human action for what it is (Dekker, Cilliers, & Hofmeyr, 2011). The same could be said for the accident analyses that support the NAT-frame of mind. Notwithstanding the subtleties of Snook's (2000) and Vaughan's (1997) analyses, they lend their strength from the apparent inevitability of the accident (Dekker, 2011a). Subsequently, in the face of technological accidents, human action, in all its variability and equivocality, looks weak, fallible, and unreliable.

Adding to Sullenberger and Dekker, I argue that since human action is social, we should add social texture to the risk debate. In this chapter, I therefore offer the idea that social tensions might indicate how HROs continuously renegotiate order to control inherently hazardous processes. Looking at social tensions adds useful texture in the debate between the opposing HRO and NAT viewpoints, which tend to get stuck in caricatures (Leveson et al., 2009; Rijpma, 1997, 2003; Shrivastava, Sonpar & Pazzaglia, 2009). The caricatures are as follows: if a safety-critical organization is successful, we perceive an HRO; if the organization is involved in an accident, we see evidence of a Normal Accident (Rijpma, 2003). Getting stuck in these opposing frames of mind does not lead to new insights about risk management. Instead, studying the social interactions of HROs in their societal contexts opens up the debate between NAT and HRO scholarship because, rather than debating how observed human action is evidence of either a Normal Accident or an HRO, we can debate what constitutes a range of vulnerable HROs.

Studying the range of social tensions found in HROs could be a fruitful direction for research into HROs' vulnerabilities. An example of such work is found in Atak and Kingma's (2011) longitudinal, auto-ethnographic study of an aircraft maintenance organization's negotiated order. When the organization experienced rapid growth, the competitive strain was reflected in heightened social tensions between technicians, client pilots, and managers of the company. In this phase, Atak and Kingma (2011) argue, the aircraft maintenance company was more vulnerable to failure, because managers pushed technicians to compromise safety margins. With such an analysis it becomes possible to debate under what conditions HROs become vulnerable, without needing to jump immediately to the inevitable accident waiting to happen.

Furthering the risk debate in this manner is a cross-disciplinary challenge, because different scientific disciplines specialize in different levels of the risk management process (Rasmussen, 1997, p. 185). An example can be found in the attempt of Passenier, Mols, Bím, and Sharpanskykh (2016) to translate Atak and Kingma's (2011) qualitative explanation of social tensions into a formal agent-based model. Applying the approach in a ground service organization (Passenier, Sharpanskykh, & de Boer, 2015), this cross-disciplinary research led to new insights in the negotiated order at the work process level (Sharpanskykh & Haest, 2017).

Conclusion

I presented a study of the airline risk management including how actors in the societal context invest in a negotiated order to satisfy contrasting risk perceptions, and how these negotiations impact the regular work process of airline pilots. Despite available methods, it remains hard to judge if regular but messy or odd-looking events should be seen as risky, and what organizations should do about these risks. Further, cross-disciplinary research on the social conditions under which tensions emerge and modify the negotiated orders in regular technical work could move this debate forward.

References

Algemeen Dagblad. (2015, 30 July). Tweede Kamer onthutst over weigering Transavia-vlucht. URL: www.ad.nl/binnenland/tweede-kamer-onthutst-over-weigering-transavia-vlucht~a924aaee/

Algemeen Dagblad. (2015, 2 September). Weigering Transavia-vlucht op Eindhoven niet onder zocht. URL: www.ad.nl/binnenland/weigering-transavia-vlucht-op-eindhoven-niet-onderzocht~ae6753ed/

Atak, A., & Kingma, S. (2011). Safety culture in an aircraft maintenance organisation: A view from the inside. *Safety Science, 49*(2), 268–278.

ATC Audio: Transavia 737 in Heavy Wind Shear Trouble! [25–7–2015, Subtitles Included] URL: www.youtube.com/watch?v=F9LruOa-hzA&t=1s

Brown, A. D. (2000). Making sense of inquiry sensemaking. *Journal of management studies, 37*(1).

Cox, S., Jones, B., & Collinson, D. (2006). Trust relations in high-reliability organizations. *Risk Analysis, 26*(5), 1123–1138.

Dekker, S. (2004). *Ten questions about human error: A new view of human factors and system safety.* CRC Press.

Dekker, S. (2007). *Just culture: Balancing safety and accountability.* Aldershot, UK: Ashgate Publishing, Ltd.

Dekker, S. (2011a). *Drift into failure: From hunting broken components to understanding complex systems.* Farnham, UK: Ashgate.

Dekker, S. (2011b). The criminalization of human error in aviation and healthcare: A review. *Safety science, 49*(2), 121–127.

Dekker, S., Cilliers, P., & Hofmeyr, J. H. (2011). The complexity of failure: Implications of complexity theory for safety investigations. *Safety Science, 49*(6), 939–945.

EESC (n.d.).Open reporting in civil aviation - Assessment of the EESC's prospective in designing a "European Just Culture charter". Accessed on 13 October 2017 via www.eesc.europa.eu/sites/default/files/resources/docs/qe-02-13-501-en-c.pdf

Gephart, R. P. (1993). The textual approach: Risk and blame in disaster sensemaking. *Academy of Management Journal, 36*(6), 1465–1514.

Gephart, R. (1997). Hazardous measures: An interpretive textual analysis of quantitative sensemaking during crises. *Journal of Organizational Behavior, 18*(S1), 583–622.

Hollnagel, E. (2012). *FRAM, the functional resonance analysis method: Modelling complex socio-technical systems.* Boca Raton, FL: CRC Press.

Hollnagel, E., Woods, D. D., & Leveson, N. (2007). *Resilience engineering: Concepts and precepts.* Aldershot, UK: Ashgate Publishing, Ltd.

Hudson, P. T., Parker, D., & van der Graaf, G. C. (2002, January). The hearts and minds program: Understanding HSE culture. In *SPE International Conference on Health,* Safety and Environment in Oil and Gas Exploration and Production. Society of Petroleum Engineers.

ICAO (2016, 25 August). *Improving just culture.* Working paper presented by the civil air navigation services organisation. Accessed on 13 October 2017 via www.icao.int/Meetings/a39/Documents/WP/wp_193_en.pdf

La Porte, T. R. (1996). High reliability organizations: Unlikely, demanding and at risk. *Journal of Contingencies and Crisis Management, 4*(2), 60–71.

La Porte, T. R., & Consolini, P. M. (1991). *Working in practice but not in theory: Theoretical challenges of "high-reliability organizations".* Institute of Governmental Studies, University of California, Berkeley.

Leveson, N. (2011). *Engineering a safer world.* Cambridge, MA: The MIT Press.

Leveson, N., Dulac, N., Marais, K., & Carroll, J. (2009). Moving beyond normal accidents and high reliability organizations: A systems approach to safety in complex systems. *Organization Studies, 30*(2–3), 227–249.

Maguire, S., & Hardy, C. (2013). Organizing processes and the construction of risk: A discursive approach. *Academy of Management Journal, 56*(1), 231–255.

Orr, J. E. (1996). *Talking about machines: An ethnography of a modern job.* Ithaca, NY: Cornell University Press.

Passenier, D., Mols, C., Bím, J., & Sharpanskykh, A. (2016). Modeling safety culture as a socially emergent phenomenon: A case study in aircraft maintenance. *Computational and Mathematical Organization Theory, 22*(4), 487–520.

Passenier, D., Sharpanskykh, A., & de Boer, R. J. (2015). When to STAMP? A case study in aircraft ground handling services. *Procedia Engineering, 128*, 35–43.

Perrow, C. (1984). *Normal accidents: Living with high risk technologies.* New York: Basic Books.

Power, M. (1997). *The audit society: Rituals of verification.* OUP Oxford.

Power, M. (2007). Organized uncertainty. *Designing a world of risk management.* Oxford: Oxford University Press.

Rasmussen, J. (1997). Risk management in a dynamic society: a modelling problem. *Safety Science, 27*(2), 183–213.

Reason, J. T. (1990). *Human Error.* Cambridge: Cambridge University Press.

Reason, J. (1997). *Managing the risks of organizational accidents.* Aldershot: Ashgate.

Rijpma, J. A. (1997). Complexity, tight–coupling and reliability: Connecting normal accidents theory and high reliability theory. *Journal of Contingencies and Crisis Management, 5*(1), 15–23.

Rijpma, J. A. (2003). From deadlock to dead end: The normal accidents-high reliability debate revisited. *Journal of Contingencies and Crisis Management, 11*(1), 37–45.

Roberts, K. H. (1990). Some characteristics of one type of high reliability organization. *Organization Science, 1*(2), 160–176.

Schulman, P. R. (1993). The negotiated order of organizational reliability. *Administration & Society, 25*(3), 353–372.

Sharpanskykh, A., & Haest, R. (2017). Understanding and predicting compliance with safety regulations at an airline ground service organization. In *Advances in social simulation 2015* (pp. 379–392). Cham: Springer.

Shrivastava, S., Sonpar, K., & Pazzaglia, F. (2009). Normal accident theory versus high reliability theory: A resolution and call for an open systems view of accidents. *Human Relations, 62*(9), 1357–1390.

Snook, S. A. (2000). *Friendly fire: The accidental shootdown of US Black Hawks over northern Iraq.* Princeton, NJ: Princeton University Press.

Stanton, N. A., Harris, D., Salmon, P. M., Demagalski, J., Marshall, A., Waldmann, T.,... & Young, M. S. (2010). Predicting design-induced error in the cockpit. *Journal of Aeronautics,* Astronautics and Aviation*, 42*(1), 1–10.

Star, S. L., & Griesemer, J. R. (1989). Institutional ecology, translations' and boundary objects: Amateurs and professionals in Berkeley's Museum of Vertebrate Zoology, 1907–1939. *Social Studies of Science, 19*(3), 387–420.

Suchman, L. A. (1987). *Plans and situated actions: The problem of human-machine communication.* Cambridge: Cambridge university press.

Turner, B. A., & Pidgeon, N. F. (1997). *Man-made disasters.* Oxford: Butterworth-Heinemann.

Vaughan, D. (1997). *The Challenger launch decision: Risky technology, culture, and deviance at NASA.* Chicago, IL: University of Chicago Press.

Weick, K. E. (1987). Organizational culture as a source of high reliability. *California Management Review, 29*(2), 112–127.

Weick, K. E. (1990). The vulnerable system: An analysis of the Tenerife air disaster. *Journal of Management, 16*(3), 571–593.

Weick, K. E. (2004). Normal accident theory as frame, link, and provocation. *Organization & Environment, 17*(1), 27–31.

Weick, K. E., & Roberts, K. H. (1993). Collective mind in organizations: Heedful interrelating on flight decks. *Administrative Science Quarterly*, 357–381.

Weick, K. E., & Sutcliffe, K. M. (2007). *Managing the unexpected: Resilient performance in an age of uncertainty.* San Francisco, CA: John Wiley & Sons.

Woods, D., Johannesen, L. J., Cook, R. I., & Sarter, N. B. (1994). *Behind human error: Cognitive systems, computers and hindsight.* Dayton, OH: Crew Systems Ergonomic Information and Analysis Center, Wright Patterson Air Force Base.

19

THE RISKS OF FINANCIAL RISK MANAGEMENT

The Case of Lehmann Brothers

Henrik Dosdall and Rolf Nichelmann

This article offers a risk sociological perspective on the risk management during – and its consequences for the course of – the subprime crisis. Building upon previous work (Dosdall & Rom-Jensen, 2017), we use the example of the non-rescue of the US-American investment bank Lehman Brothers in September 2008, to demonstrate that the regulatory interventions during the subprime crisis created new risks for the regulators. These risks led the regulators to make decisions exacerbating instead of containing the crisis. Accordingly, we aim to specify the notion that risk management presents itself as an inescapably risky operation (Japp, 1996; Luhmann, 1993) for the course of the subprime crisis. In doing so, we follow risk sociological approaches that emphasize that risk reduction and risk escalation often go hand in hand (Wildavsky, 1979, p. 34). Numerous works have demonstrated this connection within internal control systems (Power, 2004, p. 28) or redundant safety systems (Perrow, 1984, p. 53, 1999, 151f.; Sagan, 1993, 1994, p. 232, 2004). However, while this risk sociological insight has received widespread attention with regard to technical systems, it has not yet been applied with regard to the subprime crisis. Thus, the aim of this article is to further our understanding of crisis dynamics by pointing out the fruitfulness of such an analytical angle.

To contextualize our approach, we first turn to Turner's (1976, 1978) model of crisis trajectories. According to Turner, crises usually consist of six stages. In the first stage, everything seems to function according to culturally inscribed and "accepted beliefs about the world and its hazards". In the second stage, this normality is undermined by an incubating catastrophe not yet visible to those affected in the future. This veil of invisibility is subsequently lifted in the third stage when a "precipitating event" ushers in the perception of a crisis, only to be followed by its actual onset in the fourth stage. This stage, then, is followed closely by the fifth stage consisting of attempts to salvage and rescue. Finally, "cultural readjustment" – the adaption to a world in which the heretofore impossible catastrophe is now possible – takes place in the sixth stage (Turner, 1976, p. 381, 1978, p. 85), often through the establishment of government inquiries (Turner, 1978, p. 201) which make sense of the focal crisis (Gephart, 1992, 2007).

This pattern can easily be mapped onto the financial crisis of 2007, as a short glance at two central US inquiry reports – the report by the Financial Crisis Inquiry Commission (FCIC, 2011) and the report by the Permanent Subcommittee of Investigations

(PSI, 2011) – reveals. Both reports show that strong beliefs about perpetually rising housing prices and the efficiency of a self-regulating market (Orléan, 2009) were deeply ingrained in the financial system's institutional order (cf. Abolafia, 2010). Contradicting to these beliefs, though, a crisis incubated that threatened the survival of the financial system. This crisis was rooted in the increasing risk and complexity of financial products that consisted, to a great extent, of risky mortgages to subprime borrowers; that is, to borrowers with poor creditworthiness. This incubation period came to an end once subprime-related products started to default on a large scale by the end of 2006. In July 2007, the credit rating agencies ultimately responded to these developments by implementing sharp downgrades of the very products that were considered to be as safe as Treasury bonds or Bundesanleihen shortly before. The resulting loss spiral was further aggravated when two Bear Stearns hedge funds filed for bankruptcy following subprime-related losses at the end of July. This bankruptcy was the first time the big US investment banks had become affected by the deteriorating market. Together, both incidents marked the onset of the financial crisis that only abated late in 2009, after the exhaustive attempts to calm the market had culminated in the ratification of the $700 billion Troubled Asset Relief Program (TARP) in October 2008. With the crisis receding, inquiry commissions (FCIC, 2011; PSI, 2011), bankruptcy lawyers (Valukas, 2010), economists (Brunnermeier, 2009; Gorton, 2008, 2010), journalists (Lewis, 2011; Lowenstein, 2010; Tett, 2010), sociologists (Lounsbury & Hirsch, 2010a, 2010b; MacKenzie, 2011), and former decision-makers (Bernanke, 2015; Geithner, 2014; Paulson, 2013) took up their work by setting forth their respective lessons to be learned from the financial crisis.

The aforementioned reconstruction should have made clear that Turner's categories are a powerful sensemaking tool to conceive of crises in general, and the subprime crisis in particular. At the same time, though, a reconstruction of the progression of the crisis along the lines of such a model has a serious analytical blind spot as it suggests *that the crisis progresses linearly from its inception to its eventual termination due to risk management actions which steadily curb the crisis until complete containment.* While this estimation certainly is correct from a global point of view – the crisis, after all, did end as a result of the massive regulatory interventions – a linear interpretation nonetheless misses the reflexive character and thus the complexity and messiness inherent within the risk management endeavors of the subprime crisis. In fact, risk management is by no means a tool that necessarily contributes to ending crises – it can also cause new escalation points exacerbating a crisis, as the next sections will show.

To expound the argument, we will first contextualize our approach by reviewing the existing literature on the subprime crisis, before turning to a risk sociological interpretation of the relationship between the financial system and political risk management. This discussion will provide the theoretical ground upon which we present our risk sociological analysis of the non-rescue of Lehman Brothers and its consequences. Subsequently, we sum up our argument and provide further research perspectives.

Risk Sociological Approaches to the Subprime Crisis

Reviewing the literature on the subprime crisis is an undertaking in dire need of constraints due to the sheer amount of interdisciplinary research contributing to our understanding of the crisis (some of which are quoted earlier in the chapter). As we would like to set forth an argument about the fruitfulness of risk sociological approaches to the subprime crisis, it seems appropriate to confine our presentation of the state of research primarily to other risk sociological approaches to the subprime crisis.

Important contributions to our understanding of the subprime crisis were stimulated by normal accident theory (NAT). NAT, as developed by Charles Perrow (1981, 1984, 1994, 1999), holds as one of its main tenets that tightly coupled systems, which produce complex interactions among its components, display a high vulnerability to catastrophic incidents.[1] This is due to the fact that, by definition, tightly coupled systems possess only limited slack to buffer the interactions between their components (Perrow, 1984, p. 89). If these disturbances are, in addition, not linear but complex in nature so that they unfold in leaps and bounds instead of progressing in an orderly manner, the risk of a system accident further increases as occurring damages tend to reinforce each other in unforeseeable feedback loops. The limited slack available in combination with the unpredictable reactions of the components usually deprives operators of any opportunity to implement corrective action to countervail disturbances. As a result, it is increasingly difficult to stop the impending catastrophe once a chain of failures is set in motion.

Building on this argument, Palmer and Maher (2010) argue that the financial system before the mortgage crisis resembled a tightly coupled and complex system in many ways. As one of the main sources of the system's complexity, the authors identify the securitization of mortgages (Palmer & Maher, 2010, 224ff.). Securitization means that banks and bank-like financial corporations pooled mortgages and subsequently sold claims on the income stream these mortgages generated to investors in the form of the so-called structured financial products, that is, mortgage-backed securities or (synthetic) collateralized debt obligations. Fundamental characteristics of these products were their complexity and opaqueness, characteristics that made the financial system more vulnerable to complex interactions. This vulnerability was further reinforced by credit default swaps, which likewise created an opaque system of mutual dependencies by allowing market participants to mutually act as insurance givers and holders at the same time, increasing both tight coupling and complexity (Palmer & Maher, 2010, p. 233). Once the crisis struck, the different components of the financial system interacted in unpredictable ways due to their complexity and tight coupling, leading to the unraveling of the financial system. Accordingly, Palmer and Maher conceive of the subprime crisis as a "normal accident," that is, an accident mainly due to the system's characteristics. This view is also shared by Guillen and Suarez (2010) who emphasize the role of financial innovations (Guillen & Suarez, 2010, 262f.) as well as the role of deregulation as causes for this tight coupling (Guillen & Suarez, 2010, 269f.). Building upon this argument, the authors discuss ways of reducing the complexity (by restricting mergers between banks) and the tight coupling (by reducing banks equity-to-debt ratios) in the financial system (Guillen & Suarez, 2010, 276f.). Questions of regulatory actions aimed at rendering the financial system less vulnerable also underlie the work of Schneiberg and Bartley (2010). To attain this goal, the authors, also coming from a NAT perspective, suggest simplifying financial products and implementing further redundancies as ways to increase the financial systems resilience against catastrophic vulnerabilities (Schneiberg & Bartley, 2010, p. 283).

Ironically enough, it is Charles Perrow (2010) who calls into question the accuracy of a NAT account of the financial crisis of 2007. His reticence is due to NAT's emphasis on complexity as the main source of a system's vulnerability which, effectively, renders NAT a non-agentic theory (Perrow, 2010, p. 311): "no one tries to bring down the system; the system has an inherent vulnerability because nothing is perfect, and rarely, but occasionally, no matter how hard one may try, the unanticipated interaction of errors will defeat the safety systems" (Perrow, 1999, p. 150). It is this emphasis on complexity over agency that leads Perrow to not accept NAT as an explanation with regard to a crisis which was, from his perspective, caused by the willful wrongdoing on the side of financial actors and not by the system's complexity (Perrow, 2010, p. 310). This argument falls in line with other works, at times explicitly renouncing a NAT-perspective (Abolafia, 2010), which focus on the role of actors during the crisis (Davis, 2010; Mizruchi, 2010) by, for example, addressing how their actions were shaped by institutional orders (Pozner, Stimmler, & Hirsch, 2010).

While we cannot discuss these analyses in detail, the aforementioned reconstruction has shown that most of risk sociological works regarding the financial crisis of 2007 focus on matters of system complexity and attempts to render this complexity less harmful. Seen through the angle of Turner's six-step model, one can furthermore recognize that these risk sociological approaches either concentrate upon the incubation and onset period of the crisis or on the policy lessons to be learned to prevent the recurrence of such a crisis. However, a discussion of the actual risk management during the crisis – the salvage and rescue period in Turner's model – is absent. In the next sections, we will show why such a discussion is nonetheless crucial for our understanding of the subprime crisis.

Risk Transformation in the Subprime Crisis

It is a staple of economic sociology that the economy is embedded in social structures (e.g., institutions or cultures) that influence economic action (Granovetter, 1985; Smelser & Swedberg, 2005). Undoubtedly, the political system plays a special role in this regard, as its policies and institutions do not just influence economic action but also contribute to the functioning of the overall economy (Fligstein, 2001). From a risk sociological perspective, one crucial contribution of the political system in this regard is the reduction of economic uncertainties by political means, for example, by enacting laws that render contracts enforceable or prevent the cartelization of market segments. In so doing, the political system relieves economic actors from having to worry about fundamental questions that would otherwise become obstructive to economic action. Instead, by absorbing these fundamental risks, the political system fosters the emergence of system trust, that is, an impersonal trust in the overall functioning of the system (cf. Luhmann, 1979). In what follows, we will refer to this as "risk transformation" (Japp, 1996, Chapter 3; Luhmann, 1982, 1993, Chapter 8) because risks that develop in the economic system and threaten the functioning of this very system are transferred to the political realm where they are more or less successfully absorbed.

In the case of the financial system, one central mechanism of risk transformation is the too-big-to-fail doctrine. This doctrine expresses the regulatory principle that "the authorities have strong incentives to prevent the failure of a large, highly interconnected financial firm, because of the risks such a failure would pose to the financial system and the broader economy" (Bernanke, 2009). Accordingly, the risk of the default of such highly interconnected firms is transferred to the political system in that the regulatory authorities – more or less openly – promise to prevent such defaults.[2] For the regulators, too-big-to-fail thus presents a disaster threshold, that is, a threshold separating acceptable from unacceptable damage events (Japp, 1997; Rescher, 1983, 70ff.). While the default of small- or medium-sized banks clearly does not present an unacceptable risk, the default of a bank deemed too-big-to-fail does. Consequentially, the potential default of such a bank triggers actions aimed at preventing the default of too-big-to-fail firms (cf. Dosdall & Rom-Jensen, 2017). Usually, this action assumes the form of government bail-outs, with the regulators acting as the lender of last resort or the provision of credit lines to keep banks afloat. Designed to prevent the worst of shocks, the too-big-to-fail decision rule presents one crucial tool of regulatory risk management in the case of financial crises.[3]

The prominence of this risk management tool was clearly visible during the subprime crisis. With the onset of the crisis in the summer of 2007, more and more financial institutions became affected by the crisis. However, at first, the regulators did not intervene in favor of financial firms, since those firms initially affected by the crisis were considered to be second-tier corporations not relevant to the stability of the financial system. This was the case, for example, when the New Century Financial Corporation, the second largest subprime lender at that time, with approximately 7,200 employees in the United States, faced financial troubles in the beginning of 2007. As the firm was not deemed crucial to the stability of the financial system, no regulatory efforts were undertaken to rescue it. A wholly different case presented itself to the regulators once the US investment bank Bear Stearns started to go at the beginning of 2008. As we have noted in the Introduction, Bear Stearns had to liquidate two of its hedge funds in the summer of 2007 due to subprime-related losses. While these bankruptcies had no immediate effect on the solvency of the bank, they forced the bank to accept nearly $1.6 billion dollars in subprime assets onto its books. This came in addition to a $1.9 billion write-down that Bear Stearns had to make public later in 2007 (FCIC, 2011, p. 280). These developments culminated in the near-collapse of the bank in March 2008. To prevent its default, the Federal Reserve violated its long-standing policy to lend only to those banks it also supervised by setting up a limited liability company named Maiden Lane that provided Bear Stearns with new liquidity in March 2008 (FCIC, 2011, p. 290; Wessel, 2009, p. 147). This rescue was made possible by section 13(3) of the Federal Reserve Act, which was evoked for the first time since the Great Depression (FCIC, 2011, p. 287).

The rescue of Bear Stearns was by no means the only case where the regulatory authorities, including the U.S. Treasury and the Federal Reserve Bank of New York in addition to the already mentioned U.S. Federal Reserve, intervened in favor of banks deemed too-big-to-fail. After the Bear Stearns rescue failed to calm the markets, the two government-sponsored entities Fannie Mae and Freddie Mac found themselves on the brink of collapse when their subprime-related losses reached new heights in the summer of 2008. In December 2007, the banks already had been forced to make public losses amounting to several billion US dollars (FCIC, 2011, p. 312). The situation worsened as both banks could hardly stop investing in the housing market because such a withdrawal would have meant the utter collapse of this already dried-up market segment, as falling home prices and increasing foreclosure rates would have followed (Geithner, 2014, p. 170). In other words, Fannie and Freddie were "the only game in town" (FCIC, 2011, 311f.), that is, the only institutions keeping the housing market at least marginally alive. Of course, this meant both banks had to take on higher risks as they kept purchasing mortgages and guarantying risky mortgage-backed securities. The result of this development was that Fannie and Freddie were in dire need of government support in late summer 2008. The regulators, making good on the implicit promise that the mortgage giants had the full faith of the US government, came to rescue by taking both banks into conservatorship, effectively taking them over.

So far, we have argued that the risk of the default of financial firms considered either too-big or too-interconnected-to-fail is effectively absorbed by regulatory authorities, which, in this way, ensures that the system is spared the economic ramifications of such defaults and thus can operate with a basic certainty. During the subprime crisis, this risk transformation was exemplified by the regulatory actions regarding Bear Stearns and Fannie and Freddie. Risk management by risk transformation, though, is by no means a one-way action. Instead, this kind of regulatory risk management tends to create feedback loops for the regulators as the *absorption of economic risks* for the financial system by means of market intervention *creates political risks*. Put differently, by absorbing economic risks, regulators trade higher stability of the financial system for a higher political vulnerability.[4] In what follows, we will substantiate this argument with regard to the subprime crisis. To this end, we will draw on the account provided by Dosdall and Rom-Jensen (2017) who examine in greater detail the reactions of public opinion to the rescues during the subprime crisis and its impact on the regulators' decision-making.

The political vulnerability of too-big-to-fail interventions is caused by the political and media backlash that accompanies such regulatory action. Thus, interventions in distressed financial markets are a politically risky undertaking due to their critique-generating character. This criticism has three main sources. First, and maybe most important, regulators by definition rely on taxpayer money to save privately run banks. Usually, this prompts the critique that "profits are privatized while losses are socialized". Second, fears of moral hazard can be problematic, which entail concerns that banks are encouraged to act in riskier ways in anticipation of government bailouts, relative to how they would act without a safety net. Third, in the US-American institutional context that promotes the idea of self-regulating markets, interventions in favor of banks visibly decouple this institutional belief from regulatory action, thereby rendering regulators vulnerable to charges of hypocrisy (cf. Brunsson, 1989). Together, these aspects guarantee that regulators, when intervening, find themselves confronted with considerable criticism leveled at the legitimacy of their actions. Under normal circumstances, however, these criticisms will have only small effects as the regulators can justify their actions with regard to the necessity of preventing the harm caused by a collapsing too-big-to-fail firm. The political vulnerability of the regulators is further reduced when there are no upcoming elections as there is a good chance that, in the long run, interventions will not last in the public memory, thus not affecting voter behavior.

During the subprime crisis, though, the regulators were confronted with a situation that differed considerably from such a scenario. To begin with, the regulators had to intervene multiple times in relatively short intervals: hardly six months passed between the rescue of Bear Stearns and the subsequent rescues of Fannie and Freddie. In addition, there was little hope that no further interventions would be necessary. In fact, after Bear Stearns was rescued, the regulators unanimously perceived Lehman would be the next bank to go (FCIC, 2011, p. 324; Valukas, 2010, p. 631). Yet, while Lehman managed to outlive Fannie and Freddie, losses in the banking sector continued to spiral upward, threatening the survival of more and more banks. This became manifest when, during the Lehman negotiations in September 2008, the regulators realized that the insurance-giant AIG and the US investment bank Merrill Lynch were on the brink of collapse (Paulson, 2013, p. 217). Put succinctly, there was no end in sight that would have allowed regulators to quell criticism by pointing to the foreseeable end of interventions. This was further aggravated by the fact that every rescue mission set new records in terms of the required money. While the regulators had to spend almost $30 billion dollars to rescue Bear Stearns (FCIC, 2011, p. 290), the bailout of Fannie and Freddie incurred costs of around $200 billion dollars (FCIC, 2011, 320f.). Worse still for the regulators, their interventions increasingly became the subject of political attacks, with no party willing to sacrifice their chances for the election in November 2008. This held especially true for Hank Paulson, the Republican Treasury Secretary, who increasingly came under pressure from his own party members to cease using taxpayers' money to bail out banks (Sorkin, 2009, p. 199). This criticism came on top of criticism from media outlets, which often referred to him as "Mr. Bailout" (Sorkin, 2009, p. 284).

In sum, the interventions during the subprime crisis created a goal conflict for the regulators in that the regulators increasingly had to make a choice between political and economic expediency regarding further bailouts. Theoretically, it is important to note that this goal conflict cannot be conceived of as an unintended consequence (Merton, 1936) of regulatory action, but instead possesses a distinct process quality. In other words, the goal conflict was not the result of a single intervention but the result of the repeated interventions of 2008, which accumulated high political risks. Once Lehman started to go in September 2008, this conflict was again cast into sharp relief for the regulators. Consequently, the regulators, having little doubt about the catastrophic consequences of a Lehman default, tried to avoid this conflict by orchestrating a private rescue of Lehman Brothers. While these efforts initially seemed to lead to a successful solution when the British Bank Barclays emerged as a serious buyer of Lehman Brothers, the desired deal fell apart when the British regulators, who had to approve of the deal, rescinded their support for fears of importing the crisis. Deprived of a private solution, the US-American regulators were confronted with the decision of whether or not to rescue Lehman Brothers. In the face of the "bitter criticism" (Bernanke, 2015, 260f.) regarding potential interventions, the regulators decided to let Lehman go.[5]

Uncertainty

The bankruptcy of Lehman Brothers considerably aggravated the subprime crisis on at least three interrelated levels. On a first and very immediate level, this aggravation was due to the huge financial losses caused by the insolvency of the fourth largest US investment bank (cf. FCIC, 2011, p. 340). A major consequence that followed these losses was that Lehman's insolvency affected a large mutual fund called Reserve Primary Fund whose fate became a crucial factor in the unfolding of the crisis. Founded in 1971, this money-market fund was known for its conservative investment strategy. However, after it failed to meet the expectations of its investors in 2006, it started to invest more aggressively in commercial paper, that is, in unsecured and riskier short-term debt issued by corporations which promised higher returns. In so doing, the fund invested more than $785 million of the $65 billion under its management in Lehman's commercial paper (FCIC, 2011, p. 357; Kacperczyk & Schnabl, 2010, p. 40). After the exposure to Lehman's commercial paper and the concomitant losses became public in the wake of the bank's insolvency, investors flooded the fund with redemption requests. On the day of the bankruptcy alone, these requests amounted to $10.8 billion dollars. As a result, the mutual fund "broke the buck" which means that its net asset value dropped below $1 per share. Mutual funds, though, are by definition very conservative investment vehicles trying to avoid losses by maintaining an even balance at all costs. Investors, thus, interpreted the breaking of the buck of the Primary Reserve Fund as a signal that money-market mutual funds with high concentrations of commercial paper were not safe, because commercial paper itself was not safe. Consequentially, they pulled their money out of such funds, and out of commercial paper more generally, instead investing directly in Treasury bonds. This flight to safety meant that the commercial paper market came to a standstill as investments in this market segment came close to zero. The drying up of the commercial paper market deprived many companies in the real economy of an essential means of refinancing, thereby creating shock waves that reverberated throughout the global economy. The near-collapse of some of the biggest companies in the US automobile industry that followed these events is a case in point. Hence, it can be said that the generalized distrust the insolvency of Lehman Brothers triggered with regard to the commercial paper market presented, in addition to the losses caused by the banks demise, a second crucial factor that exacerbated the subprime crisis as it created those self-validating distrust spirals typical for financial crises (cf. Merton, 1948). A third aspect of the escalation dynamic set in motion by Lehman Brothers can be identified with regard to the risk transformation expectation on the side of the financial system, that is, the expectation that the big US investment banks were eligible for government support in times of crisis. As we have argued earlier, this expectation is a stabilizing factor as it absorbs the uncertainty the financial system has to deal with in case one of the banks at the system's center moves toward failure. Allowing Lehman Brothers to fail, though, disrupted this expectation, thereby creating a source of overwhelming uncertainty about which banks would still possess a government guarantee. Stiglitz (2010, p. 324) notes in this regard: "the financial disturbances that followed Lehman Brothers collapse were, in part, a result of the increased uncertainty about the scope of the government guarantee". In September 2008, the uncertainty of such defaults was especially worrisome with financial behemoths like AIG and shortly thereafter Goldman Sachs on the brink of collapse. At the same time, the Lehman disturbance was so profound that not even the unconditioned government support for these and further ailing banks later in 2008 could reestablish the expectation that the US government would step in as a stabilizing factor. Effectively, "the Lehman decision abruptly and surprisingly tore the perceived rule book into pieces and tossed it out the window" (Stewart & Eavis, 2014). The alleged inconsistency of the regulatory behavior became a driving factor of the subprime crisis.

In sum, the financial crisis gained significant downward momentum after Lehman Brothers was let go in September 2008. The primary reason for this momentum was that most lending activities froze as banks and other financial actors focused almost exclusively on shoring up their positions instead of lending out new money and thereby keeping the system afloat. The resulting liquidity crunch no longer affected only financial institutions, but increasingly took its toll on the global real economy as well. Responding to these developments, the United States ratified the TARP in October 2008 which provided an initial $700 billion rescue package to calm the markets by way of purchasing toxic assets.[6] Clearly, TARP was in part enabled as well as necessitated by the fallout of Lehman Brothers. In other words, the fallout of Lehman Brothers created a situation where it was, once again, legitimate to follow an economic rationality which prioritized the prevention of further economic destabilization over political considerations.[7] Still, despite these efforts of the US authorities, and the parallel efforts of other countries, the containment of the acute crisis was not accomplished before mid–2009.

Conclusion

The aim of this article has been to highlight the ambivalent character of regulatory risk management during the subprime crisis. To this end, we started off by pointing to the risk transformation that takes place between the political and the financial system. By risk transformation, we refer to the transfer of economic risks that have the potential to threaten the integrity of the financial sector to the political realm where these risks are absorbed by regulatory actions. In so doing, regulators contribute to the stability of the financial system. As a crucial example of this risk transformation, we discussed the too-big-to-fail premise which stipulates that those banks considered too-big-to-fail are rescued by the regulators, thereby relieving the financial system of having to deal with the uncertainty that would follow the demise of these banks.

In a second step, we argued that this clear-cut regulatory goal to maintain economic stability became increasingly muddier during the subprime crisis. While economic stability was initially the sole reference point of the regulators' actions – a reference point that allowed them to take the unfavorable decisions to rescue banks – the regulatory decision-making became increasingly infused with political considerations as the public pressure on the regulators accumulated further with every new intervention. In other words, the regulatory decision-making became highly politicized with this process of politicization creating a goal conflict between politically favorable but economically detrimental and economically helpful but politically unfavorable decisions. This goal conflict then became a dominant factor in the political opportune yet economically detrimental decision to let Lehman go.

The constraints regarding an economic solution to the Lehman crisis imposed on the regulators were predictable given the condition that a regulatory logic like "too-big-to-fail" had necessitated multiple interventions in a short time span.[8] In such a case, risk management endeavors are almost certain to create political risks that bear upon future regulatory decision-making. While we refrain from a definitive attempt to judge whether the non-rescue of Lehman Brothers was a right or wrong decision overall, the non-rescue was certainly a *likely* decision given the enormous political criticism the regulators faced in September 2008 in view of the upcoming elections and the fact that Lehman's competitors managed to survive long enough to have the grave economic situation following Lehman's demise legitimize their rescue.

From this perspective, it becomes clear that the regulatory risk management during the subprime crisis by no means led linearly toward the containment of the crisis; instead, it became itself an escalating factor when Lehman Brothers was let go as a response to the feedback engendered by previous regulatory interventions. Returning to Turner's model of different crisis stages, we thus argue that our understanding of the subprime crisis can be enriched by focusing not only on the incubation period and the different crisis triggers, but also on the ambivalent role risk management plays for the course of the crisis. For the subprime crisis, such a focus reveals that the crisis cannot be sufficiently explained with reference to its preconditions or its manifold triggers alone, as such a perspective is almost certain to miss the actual crisis dynamic. Consider the following – no matter whether one stresses the complexity of the financial system or the wrongdoing of financial actors as the main cause of the crisis, one can hardly doubt that the financial system in the run-up to the outbreak of the subprime crisis resembled a tightly coupled system prone to complex interactions. However, this feature of the financial system alone hardly provides an answer to the crucial question why the regulators decided to let the fourth biggest US investment bank go into bankruptcy in a highly destabilized market environment. To answer this question, it is instead necessary to analyze the rescue and salvage stage by focusing on the political constraints the regulatory risk management produced in its attempts to contain the crisis.

At the same time, an analytical focus on the regulatory risks of the rescue and salvage stage can easily be transferred to other cases of regulatory risk and crisis management in financial markets. The current monetary policy of quantitative easing pursued by the European Central Bank (ECB) should prove a fruitful – and so far, sociologically neglected – example in this regard. Aimed at correcting the Europe-wide inflation rate in the wake of the European debt crisis, the strategy to purchase euro-area bonds on a massive scale immediately fed the critique that such a policy was nothing but the first step toward the introduction of the highly controversial Euro-Bonds (cf. Brunnermeier, James, & Landau, 2016). Analyzing the impact of this political backlash on further regulatory decision-making by the ECB thus seems to be an instructive research program, since it stands to reason that, in this case too, the political risks created by the regulatory approach will itself influence future ECB decisions.

In concluding, we would like to draw attention to another side effect of the regulatory risk management during the subprime crisis. To do so, we return to the insight that regulatory decision-making regarding potential interventions in favor of banks usually is confronted with conflicting goals due to the stark disparity between political (non-rescue) and economically opportune (rescue) decisions. As we have argued, this goal conflict is negligible in the case of a one-time intervention while recurrent interventions render it an essential factor in regulatory decision-making. As a consequence, the regulators in the subprime crisis often tried to avoid this goal conflict altogether by pushing or at least encouraging banks to merge with their competitors – a strategy also followed, although unsuccessfully, in the case of Lehman Brothers over the summer of 2008 (cf. Valukas, 2010). As a result, many ailing banks merged, creating ever-bigger financial institutions. For example, after JP Morgan bought Bear Stearns in March 2008, the bank bought Washington Mutual, another bank formerly belonging to the set of 20 biggest US banks. Another case in point is Bank of America (BofA), which, during the negotiations about Lehman's fate, bought its competitor Merrill Lynch – a purchase that effectively made BofA one of the biggest institutions in the financial sector. While further examples are abundant, we would like to stress that another crucial effect of regulatory risk management during the subprime crisis was the facilitation of bigger and bigger financial institutions. This casts into sharp relief that, opposite to the trend among classical corporations to increasingly dissolve into new and smaller organizational forms (cf. Davis, 2013), the financial sector is still dominated by large organizations. Thus, a critical stance toward the emergence of such large organizations (Perrow, 1991), for example by asking how these organizations come into existence (Perrow, 2000, p. 469), offers plentiful analytic opportunities for risk sociologists interested in the risks of risk management during the financial crisis of 2007.

Notes

1 It should be noted that tightly coupled systems do not necessarily produce complex interactions. Instead, the kind of coupling (tight vs. loose) and the kind of interactions characteristic for a system are independent variables (cf. Perrow, 1984, 96ff.). For example, opposite to tightly coupled systems defined by complex interactions, loosely coupled systems characterized by linear interactions provide operators with "time, resources, and alternative paths to cope with the disturbance and limits its impact" (Perrow, 1984, p. 332) as disturbances unfold in an orderly and often isolated manner.

2 It should be noted that the need for transferring these economic risks to the political system arises from the fact that the economy as a decentralized system possesses no agency and thus is not able to implement remedial actions.

3 Further tools include short selling bans, the provision of liquidity by virtue of lending programs for ailing banks, or the conducting of stress tests that help to convince markets that the important financial institutions are healthy.

4 One could object that central banks are, by design, politically independent. While we would not challenge such an argument, one would nonetheless be hard-pressed not to acknowledge that the behavior of the central banks – the New York Fed as well as the Fed – was responsive to the political pressure during the subprime crisis. Kindleberger and Aliber (2005, p. 237), for example, state that the notion that "central banks are immune from political pressure seems naïve".

5 A more detailed and thorough depiction of this argument, including a discussion of alternative accounts, can once again be found in Dosdall and Rom-Jensen (2017).

6 This sum was later reduced to $475 billion.

7 In this regard, the non-rescue of Lehman Brothers could be interpreted as motivated by the intention to create a situation which allowed the regulators to get the financial means they deemed necessary to rescue the ailing US economy. However, while there is little doubt that the ramifications of Lehman's demise helped to push the highly controversial TARP through the U.S. Congress, such a pure functional perspective has little empirical support as the regulators did try to rescue Lehman Brothers, although without government support and thus with little success.

8 It goes without saying that alternative regulatory approaches like "letting it burn out" (cf. Kindleberger & Aliber, 2005, Chapter 10) likewise produce political risks – in such a scenario, the critique that regulatory inaction worsened the crisis is a distinct possibility.

References

Abolafia, M. Y. (2010). The institutional embeddedness of market failure: Why speculative bubbles still occur. In M. Lounsbury & P. M. Hirsch (Eds.), *Research in the sociology of organizations: Vol. 30. Markets on trial: The economic sociology of the U.S. financial crisis: Part B* (pp. 177–200). Bingley, England: Emerald.

Bernanke, B. (2009). *Financial reform to address systemic risk*. Speech at the Council on Foreign Relations, Washington, DC. Retrieved from https://www.federalreserve.gov/newsevents/speech/bernanke 20090310a.htm

Bernanke, B. (2015). *The courage to act: A memoir of a crisis and its aftermath*. New York, NY: W.W. Norton.

Brunnermeier, M. K. (2009). Deciphering the liquidity and credit crunch 2007–2008. *Journal of Economic Perspectives, 23*(1), 77–100.

Brunnermeier, M. K., James, H., & Landau, J.-P. (2016). *The Euro and the battle of ideas*. Princeton, NJ: Princeton University Press.

Brunsson, N. (1989). *The organization of hypocrisy: Talk, decisions, and actions in organizations*. Chichester, England: Wiley.

Davis, G. F. (2010). After the ownership society: Another world is possible. In M. Lounsbury & P. M. Hirsch (Eds.), *Research in the Sociology of Organizations: Vol. 30. Markets on Trial: The economic sociology of the U.S. financial crisis: Part B* (pp. 331–356). Bingley, England: Emerald.

Davis, G. F. (2013). After the corporation. *Politics & Society, 41*(2), 283–308.

Dosdall, H., & Rom-Jensen, B. (2017). Letting Lehman go: Critique, social change and the demise of Lehman Brothers. *Historical Social Research, 42*(3), 196–217.

FCIC (Financial Crisis Inquiry Commission). (2011). *The financial crisis inquiry report: Final report of the national commission on the causes of the financial and economic crisis in the United States* (Official Government ed.). Washington, DC: U.S. Government Printing Office.

Fligstein, N. (2001). *The architecture of markets: An economic sociology of twenty-first-century capitalist societies*. Princeton; NJ: Princeton University Press.

Geithner, T. F. (2014). *Stress test: Reflections on financial crises*. New York, NY: Crown.

Gephart, R. P., Jr. (1992). Sensemaking, communicative distortion and the logic of public inquiry legitimation. *Industrial Crisis Quarterly, 6*(2), 115–135.

Gephart, R. P., Jr. (2007). Crisis sensemaking and the public inquiry. In C. M. Pearson, C. Roux-Dufort, & J. Clair (Eds.), *International handbook of organizational crisis management* (pp. 123–160). Los Angeles, CA: Sage.

Gorton, G. B. (2008). *The panic of 2007*. Cambridge, MA: National Bureau of Economic Research.

Gorton, G. B. (2010). *Slapped by the invisible hand: The panic of 2007*. Oxford, England: Oxford University Press.

Granovetter, M. S. (1985). Economic action and social structure: The problem of embeddedness. *The American Journal of Sociology, 91*(3), 481–510.

Guillen, M. F., & Suarez, S. L. (2010). The global crisis of 2007–2009: Markets, politics, and organizations. In M. Lounsbury & P. M. Hirsch (Eds.), *Research in the sociology of organizations: Vol. 30. Markets on trial. The economic sociology of the U.S. financial crisis: Part A* (pp. 257–279). Bingley, England: Emerald.

Japp, K. P. (1996). *Soziologische Risikotheorie: Funktionale Differenzierung, Politisierung und Reflexion*. Weinheim, Germany: Juventa.

Japp, K. P. (1997). Die Beobachtung von Nichtwissen. *Soziale Systeme, 3*(2), 289–312.

Kacperczyk, M., & Schnabl, P. (2010). When safe proved risky: Commercial paper during the financial crisis of 2007–2009. *Journal of Economic Perspectives, 24*(1), 29–50.

Kindleberger, C. P., & Aliber, R. Z. (2005). *Manias, panics, and crashes: A history of financial crises* (5th ed.). Hoboken, NJ: Wiley.

Lewis, M. (2011). *The big short: Inside the doomsday machine*. New York, NY: W.W. Norton.

Lounsbury, M., & Hirsch, P. M. (Eds.). (2010a). *Research in the sociology of organizations: Vol. 30. Markets on trial: The economic sociology of the U.S. financial crisis: Part A*. Bingley, England: Emerald.

Lounsbury, M., & Hirsch, P. M. (Eds.). (2010b). *Research in the sociology of organizations: Vol. 30. Markets on trial: The economic sociology of the U.S. financial crisis: Part B*. Bingley, England: Emerald.

Lowenstein, R. (2010). *The end of wall street*. New York: Penguin.

Luhmann, N. (1979). *Trust and power*. Chichester, England: Wiley.

Luhmann, N. (1982). The economy as a social system. In N. Luhmann (Ed.), *European perspectives. The differentiation of society.* (S. Holmes & C. Larmore, Trans.) (pp. 190–225). New York, NY: Columbia University Press.

Luhmann, N. (Ed.). (1993). *Risk: A sociological theory* (R. Barrett, Trans.). New York, NY: de Gruyter.

MacKenzie, D. A. (2011). The credit crisis as a problem in the sociology of knowledge. *The American Journal of Sociology, 116*(6), 1778–1841.

Merton, R. K. (1936). The unanticipated consequences of purposive social action. *American Sociological Review, 1*(6), 894–904.

Merton, R. K. (1948). The self-fulfilling prophecy. *The Antioch Review, 8*(2), 193–210.

Mizruchi, M. S. (2010). The American corporate elite and the historical roots of the financial crisis of 2008. In M. Lounsbury & P. M. Hirsch (Eds.), *Research in the sociology of organizations: Vol. 30. Markets on trial: The economic sociology of the U.S. financial crisis: Part B* (pp. 103–139). Bingley, England: Emerald.

Orléan, A. (2009). *De l'euphorie à la panique: Penser la crise financière.* Paris, France: Éditions Rue d'Ulm.

Palmer, D., & Maher, M. (2010). A normal accident analysis of the mortgage meltdown. In M. Lounsbury & P. M. Hirsch (Eds.), *Research in the sociology of organizations: Vol. 30. Markets on trial. The economic sociology of the U.S. financial crisis: Part A.* Bingley, England: Emerald.

Paulson, H. M. (2013). *On the brink: Inside the race to stop the collapse of the global financial system* (3rd.ed.). New York, NY: Business Plus/Grand Central Publishing.

Perrow, C. (1981). Normal accident at three mile Island. *Society, 18*(July), 17–26.

Perrow, C. (1984). *Normal accidents: Living with high-risk technologies.* New York, NY: Basic Books.

Perrow, C. (1991). A society of organizations. *Theory and Society, 20*(6), 725–762.

Perrow, C. (1994). The limits of safety: The enhancement of a theory of accidents. *Journal of Contingencies and Crisis Management, 2*(4), 212–220.

Perrow, C. (1999). Organizing to reduce the vulnerabilities of complexity. *Journal of Contingencies and Crisis Management, 7*(3), 150–155.

Perrow, C. (2000). An organizational analysis of organizational theory. *Contemporary Sociology, 29*(3), 469–476.

Power, M. (2004). *The risk management of everything: Rethinking the politics of uncertainty.* London, England: Demos.

Perrow, C. (2010). The meltdown was not an accident. In M. Lounsbury & P. M. Hirsch (Eds.), *Research in the sociology of organizations: Vol. 30. Markets on trial. The economic sociology of the U.S. financial crisis: Part A* (pp. 309–330). Bingley, England: Emerald.

Pozner, J. E., Stimmler, M. K., & Hirsch, P. M. (2010). Terminal isomorphism and the self-destructive potential of success: Lessons from subprime mortgage origination and securitization. In M. Lounsbury & P. M. Hirsch (Eds.), *Research in the sociology of organizations: Vol. 30. Markets on trial. The economic sociology of the U.S. financial crisis: Part A* (pp. 183–219). Bingley, England: Emerald.

PSI (U.S. Senate Permanent Subcommittee on Investigations) (2011). *Wall Street and the Financial Crisis: Anatomy of a financial collapse.* Washington, DC: U.S. Government Printing Office.

Rescher, N. (1983). *A philosophical introduction to the theory of risk evaluation and management.* Washington, DC: University Press of America.

Sagan, S. D. (1993). *The limits of safety: Organizations, accidents, and nuclear weapons.* Princeton, NJ: Princeton University Press

Sagan, S. D. (1994). Toward a political theory of organizational reliability. *Journal of Contingencies and Crisis Management, 2*(4), 228–240.

Sagan, S. D. (2004). The problem of redundancy problem: Why more nuclear security forces may produce less nuclear security. *Risk Analysis, 24*(4), 935–946.

Schneiberg, M., & Bartley, T. (2010). Regulating or redesigning finance? Market architectures, normal accidents, and dilemmas of regulatory reform. In M. Lounsbury & P. M. Hirsch (Eds.), *Research in the sociology of organizations: Vol. 30. Markets on trial. The economic sociology of the U.S. financial crisis: Part A* (pp. 281–307). Bingley: Emerald.

Smelser, N. J., & Swedberg, R. (Eds.). (2005). *The handbook of economic sociology* (2nd ed.). Princeton, NJ: Princeton University Press.

Sorkin, R. (2009). *Too big to fail: The inside story of how wall street and Washington fought to save the financial system from crisis and themselves.* New York, NY: Viking.

Stewart, J. B., & Eavis, P. (2014). Revisiting the Lehman Brothers bailout that never was. *New York Times*. Retrieved from http://www.nytimes.com/2014/09/30/business/revisiting-the-lehman-brothers-bailout-that-never-was.html

Stiglitz, J. E. (2010). *Freefall: America, free markets, and the sinking of the World Economy*. New York, NY: Penguin.

Tett, G. (2010). *Fool's gold: How unrestrained greed corrupted a dream, shattered global markets and unleashed a catastrophe* (updated ed.). London: Abacus.

Turner, B. A. (1976). The organizational and interorganizational development of disaster. *Administrative Science Quarterly, 21*(3), 378–397.

Turner, B. A. (1978). *Man-made disasters*. London, England: Wykeham.

Valukas, A. R. (2010). *Report of Anton R. Valukas: Lehman Brothers Holdings Inc. Chapter 11 Proceedings Examiner Report*. Retrieved from United States Bankruptcy Court Southern District of New York website: https://jenner.com/lehman

Wessel, D. (2009). *In fed we trust: Ben Bernanke's war on the great panic*. New York, NY: Crown Business.

Wildavsky, A. (1979). No Risk is the highest risk of all: A leading political scientist postulates that an overcautious attitude toward new technological developments may paralyze scientific endeavor and end up leaving us less safe than we were before. *American Scientist, 67*(1), 32–37.

20

BLAME AND LITIGATION AS CORPORATE STRATEGIES IN THE CONTEXT OF ENVIRONMENTAL DISASTERS

Shell in Brazil

*Mário Aquino Alves, Maria Paola Ometto,
and Paulo Cesar Vaz Guimarães*

Introduction

On April 8, 2013, in the small industrial city of Paulínia an hour from São Paulo, a judge awarded 1,058 workers indemnities of R\$ 400 million (Brazilian currency, approximately US\$ 115 million) for their exposure to toxic substances while working in a pesticide factory belonging to Shell Brasil and Basf. The lawsuit producing this settlement began in 2007, seeking compensation for workers suffering from pesticide factory contamination between 1974 and 2002. The judge found Shell liable for about R\$ 1.1 billion (approximately US\$ 320 million) in damages to society—then the highest compensation in Brazilian history for an environmental accident.

Another case of similar proportions had significantly less dramatic results. In March 2002, the State Prosecutor (MPE) of São Paulo, Brazil, initiated a public civil action, in which Shell was the defendant for contaminating São Paulo's Vila Carioca neighborhood with pesticide. Experts estimated that 30,000 people living in the area may have been exposed to the pollution Shell generated there. Unlike the previous case, the court has yet to pass a definitive judgment, and the residents have not received any compensation for environmental damages.

In both cases, Shell's industrial activities contaminated groundwater for decades, causing health problems for employees, their families, livestock, and communities around the plants, forcing people to leave devaluated properties. Shell preferred to engage in litigation instead of negotiating an agreement between parties. Shell tried to downplay its liability in each case, mostly through blame-shifting and juridical strategies, obstruction, and adjournment. The "blame-shifting" strategy further aggravated the plights of those affected in both cases, turning the situations into "permanent disasters." This chapter aims to investigate *how corporations enact blame-shifting strategies through lengthy litigation to localize and minimize liability for organizationally based environmental disasters (OBEDs)* (Gephart, 1984). Specifically, we analyze how social actors engaged in the two disputes, which narratives they constructed, similarities and differences between those narratives, and the impact on the corporation and communities. Therefore, we consider the following research question: *how do corporations transform critical events into disasters through strategies of blame shifting and litigation?*

We organize this chapter in five sections. After this introduction, we present a literature review on blame shifting and litigation. In the following section, we report our research design, data collection, and methodology for analyzing both cases' antenarratives (Boje, 2001), extracted from media, company, and NGO websites, and the testimonies from public inquiries (CPIs) into the critical events resulting in the two litigations. Later, we offer narratives of the two disasters, trying to compare the narratives against Shell's major policies on corporate, social, and environmental responsibilities. Next, we analyze both cases through three dimensions that emerge from our theoretical framework: blame shifting and litigation, time, and stakeholder power.

Disasters, Blame Shifting, and Litigation

The extensive literature defining disaster from various fields suggests that disaster constitutes a research field on its own (Perry, 2007). A crisis is an event that urgently threatens the core functions of a social system, while a disaster is a crisis with a "dreadful ending," that is, with severe and irreversible consequences for individuals, society, and the environment (Freudenburg, 1997; Quarantelli, Lagadec, & Boin, 2007).

Natural or human hazards may cause disasters (Gephart, 1984; Freudenburg, 1997; Quarantelli et al., 2007). To differentiate them, we need to examine whether the triggering event would have occurred even if no humans were present. If so, then the disaster was natural. In some disasters, a more direct connection to human activity may be easily identifiable and should be analyzed separately. According to the effects, such disasters can be labeled natural or man-made disasters (Turner, 1978; Gephart, 1984; Beamish, 2000).

Disasters with human origins rarely happen suddenly, rather developing through a long "incubation period" (Turner, 1978); these can be identified from their beginning. Some theorists argue that such disasters are not accidents; instead, they are "socio-technical problems that involve social, organizational, and technical processes that, together, produce devastating consequences" (Beamish, 2000, p. 473).

Evidence points to more severe and enduring social, economic, cultural, and psychological negative impacts from man-made disasters than natural ones (Freudenburg, 1997) for three main reasons: indeterminacy or ambiguity of harm, development of corrosive communities (Freudenburg, 1997), and sociocultural disruption (Hirschman, 1994). The harm from technological disasters is difficult to measure due to the difficulty of setting the amplitude and ending point of the effects leading to negative psychological consequences for individuals from a disrupted community. Sociocultural disruption can occur when people perceive the problem as a non-divisible conflict, that is, compromise is never reached, even if there are temporary agreements that are "tied to the particular circumstances in which they were made, and can be reopened at the next opportunity" (Hirschman, 1994, p. 214). Among man-made disasters, there is a specific type: OBEDs. An OBED occurs when an organization triggers critical events with severe social effects through "exploitation of ecosystem resources [with] potentially adverse effects on the ecosystem" (Gephart, 1984, p. 206).

OBEDs are political phenomena (Gephart, 1984), involving the power of corporations, governments, and society. If the institutional environment is lenient, governments lack the capability or will to exert regulatory constraints. Communities that are economically dependent on the exploitation of natural resources where they settled may become vulnerable to corporate power.

In contrast to natural disasters that trigger human altruistic feelings to help others and cooperate against "the destructiveness of mother nature," technological disasters lead to legal discussions, with lawyers trying to protect their clients' interests. Victims of man-made disasters face the anxiety of responsible parties disavowing blame, often "finding that they become the victims of blame themselves" (Freudenburg, 1997, p. 31). Inconclusive or conflicting scientific findings and ineffective government response often impede efforts to identify the responsible actors (Picou, Marshall, & Gill, 2004), while ambiguous or nonresponsive authorities impede prosecution of those responsible. Moreover, politicians and corporations try to control public opinion to deflect blame (Tsoukas, 1999; Hargie, Stapleton, & Tourish, 2010). In doing so, they enact strategies of blame-shifting (Hood, 2002; Catino, 2008; Jerome & Rowland, 2009).

When an accident occurs, corporations often try to isolate the event to reduce liability (Gephart, 1984, 1988) and disclaim blame for the harm. Social movements and civil society organizations engage in protests and other activities to expose the situation, stop destructive corporation practices, and demand compensations. However, not all such responses succeed. In the aftermath of accidents and disasters, social actors mobilize legal and political rhetoric to define the nature of the event, identify the causes, and, most importantly, to assign blame (Edelman, 1964).

Blaming

Blame is part of social behavior of any society. Any time something goes wrong, people assign blame to others (Tilly, 2008). Mary Douglas (1966, 1992) explores three different types of blaming communities enact: the *moralistic,* in which something wrong happened due to the individuals' moral faults; the *adversarial,* which blames enemies inside the community; and the *outsider,* which blames enemies who are not members of the community. These types of blaming influence a community's organization and justice system (Douglas, 1992).

The conflicting features of blame lead political scientists and commentators to talk about "blame games," such as strategies politicians deploy to manage blame from the public (Hood, 2002). Impression management strategies (i.e. selecting arguments to avoid blame), policy choices (i.e. choosing positions that avoid blaming), and institutional arrangements that lower liability describe three strategies politicians enact to maneuver away from blame. Some of these strategies may result in blame shifting, especially through delegation (Hood, 2002).

Corporations also enact forms of blame management—especially when they are under public scrutiny for crises, accidents, and disasters—and engage in discursive disputes to win arguments (Tsoukas, 1999). Following an accident, organizations often take one of two approaches to explain the accident's origin and dynamics: they may try to find the guilty individuals or investigate organizational factors prompting the accident (Catino, 2008). In spite of the reason or the goal of identifying organizational factors that might contribute to accidents in order to avoid other calamities, organizations tend to search for individuals responsible (Catino, 2008). Blame shifting becomes the preferred crisis solution whenever the crisis involves significant public harm or the perceived organizational responsibility is high (Jerome & Rowland, 2009).

Organizational crisis management usually involves applying certain communication strategies such as argumentation, denial, blame, and manipulation (Hargie, Stapleton, & Tourish, 2010). Rhetoric and narrative are important to the processes of blame shifting (Herrick, 2009; Mortensen, 2016).

Blame Shifting and Litigation

Disasters involving blame shifting and litigation have far more detrimental consequences. The most essential social structural characteristic leading to negative effects is being a litigant (Picou et al., 2004). Litigation generates "conflict over equitable damage payments, stress from protracted legal procedures, and uncertainty about litigation outcomes" (Picou et al., 2004, p. 1497). These results added significant time spent with lawyers trying to apprehend complex litigation matters and repeatedly having to recall the disaster, causing stress that is higher than when the disaster occurred (Picou et al., 2004). Especially following disasters, companies have difficulty accepting their legal and moral responsibilities (Freudenberg, 1997), but once they do, they might need to compensate people properly to restore their reputation.

It's important to remember that contamination, "while often far less dramatic than natural disasters in physical terms, may nevertheless also be far more severe in socioeconomic impacts" (Freudenburg, 1997, p. 20). This happens because disproportionately severe impacts result from ambiguity and conflict regarding a disaster's damage, the responsible actors, and how to repair damages (Freudenburg, 1997; Picou et al., 2004). Specifically, disasters involving litigation cause higher stress for the litigants than others the disaster affected, and the litigants' stress increases with time (Picou et al., 2004). In fact, as John Dewey (1922, p. 320) points out, "judgment in which the emphasis falls upon blame and approbation has more heat than light. It is more emotional than intellectual."

Finally, man-made disasters disrupt a community's sociocultural health, because when actors responsible for a disaster lose the community's trust, they "can undermine or destroy accepted social patterns and understandings" (Freudenburg, 1997, p. 32). This is the case when disaster victims form groups providing social support to understand and respond to nonresponsive or hostile "established" leaders.

Research Design and Method

We gathered data for both cases from various sources, using various strategies, to capture a 20-year period (1993–2013). We collected Shell's annual reports (2003, 2004, 2005, 2006, 2007, 2008), documents from environmental nongovernmental organizations (Friends of the Earth, 2003, 2004; Greenpeace, 2002), and records from trade unions (Observatório Social, 2003).

Most of the data were collected through the Câmara Municipal de São Paulo (Local Chamber of Representatives) search engine, which compiles documents from various legislative bodies, reaching more than 40,000 pages. We obtained further litigation documents from the Tribunal Superior do Trabalho (Labor Higher Court) and Ministério Público do Trabalho (Labor Public Attorney) search engines. These documents were essential for accessing not only the litigation processes but also the Terms of Conduct Adjustment (TAC) that Shell signed in the two cases. News about the Vila Carioca and Paulínia cases was collected from the most important Brazilian newspapers (*Folha de São Paulo*, *Estado de São Paulo*, and *Jornal da Tarde*).

A combination of narrative and antenarrative analysis was necessary for analyzing these data. Alves and Blikstein (2006, p. 407) argue that a narrative of the discourse of past events can follow a chronological or causal order. Narratives lack explicit subject-emitters, allowing them to appear naturalized, although individuals construct narratives in a particular space and time to serve specific ideologies. Narratives contain contradictions, revealing how organizations select, legitimize, codify, and institutionalize meanings (Patriotta, 2003). So, audiences can accept stories as a means for interpreting events and imbuing those stories with meaning (Rhodes & Brown, 2005).

Whereas narrative analysis focuses on fully formed stories instead of discursive fragments (Vaara & Tienari, 2011), antenarratives are "fragments of organizational discourse that construct identities and interests in time and space" (Vaara & Tienari, 2011, p. 370). Most fragments are antenarratives that contribute to forming a final narrative (Boje, 2001). An antenarrative provides flexible retrospective information about recent events that reveal unusual, unexpected patterns. In this case, the research constructs a narrative after the cases, using texts as short and fragmented as messages from social media.

Drawing on this bibliography, we delineated some questions: Which voices (actors) shaped the narrative? What elements of which narrative did each actor construct? Which voices received credit? How did these actors develop a successful argument? How did the various actors' narratives interact? How did each actor assume liability or enter into blame-shifting or blame-game strategies?

In this case, we focus the analysis on Shell's antenarratives, thereby conducting a theory-informed narrative (Langley, 1999) to show two main processes: (a) Shell created a Corporate Social Responsibility discourse as a nonmarket strategy, and (b) Shell utilized a blame-shifting strategy to evade responsibility for their soil contamination at both Vila Carioca and Paulínia. The findings section includes a narrative depicting how these processes rely on discourse framing. The discussion tries to relate these findings to the theoretical framework, showing how corporations may transform critical events into disasters through strategies of blame shifting and litigation.

Findings

We took a comparative look at the cases of Vila Carioca and Paulínia to understand how corporations enact blame-shifting strategies to localize and minimize liability in organizationally based environmental disaster. In the next section, we briefly explain Royal Dutch Shell's overall Corporate Social Responsibility (CSR) strategy and then we focus on each OBED.

Shell's CSR as Strategy: "The Best Thing that has Ever Happened to Us"

In the 1990s, Shell developed a strategy that stresses the importance of being defensive against societal criticism. Especially after Shell faced denunciation from social and environmental groups (e.g. the 1995 Brent Spar incident with Greenpeace and criticism in 1996 of Shell's nonintervention in Nigeria's execution of eight Ogoni activists), the company focused on sustainable development. For instance, the company published, "Profit and Principles: does there have to be a choice? The Shell Report," Shell's first CSR report, which was a statement of business principles outlining the company's core values of "honesty, integrity, and respect for people" (Shell, 1998). By the way, Livesey (2002) affirms that this report has been regarded as extending beyond mere public relations strategy, to generate transformative effects on the company and stakeholders treatment. Corporate social responsibility and sustainability clearly became Shell's core nonmarket strategy. What is less clear is whether Shell has thoroughly incorporated this discourse when it refers to the treatment of two organizationally based environmental disasters that occurred in Brazil.

Producing DDT in Brazil

Shell entered Brazil in 1931 but did not start manufacturing pesticides in Vila Carioca until some point in the 1960s or 1970s, without officially informing the government. The government learned about this production in the 1990s, when the Environmental Company of São Paulo (Cetesb), the governmental agency responsible for pollution prevention, monitoring, and control, investigated contamination at the site. Cetesb found substances unrelated to Shell's purported activities, notably DDT, which only Shell synthesized it in Brazil.[1] In the absence of records, former employees' testimonies explained the existence of the laboratory operating there until its 1977 deactivation, when Shell transferred the equipment to a plant in Paulínia, in the state of São Paulo (Câmara Municipal de São Paulo, 2006). This chapter explains how these two plants caused environmental disasters in Brazil, though with divergent outcomes.

Vila Carioca Case

The Nature of the Disaster Phase 1: Ambiguous Health Effects, Undeniable Adverse Environmental Outcomes

Shell arrived in Vila Carioca in the 1940s, storing fuel and other chemical products on two estates (BIP I and BIP II) in an area close to two rivers and subject to constant flooding. There was then neither national nor local legislation requiring enterprises to secure environmental licenses for pollution, nor to conduct environmental impact or similar technical evaluations.

Shell used BIP I, a 180,000 square meter lot, for fuel storage. Over three decades, Shell buried the oil sludge from tank cleaning directly in the soil, a common practice at the time that contaminated soil and water (Câmara Municipal de São Paulo, 2006, p. 124). In the 1940s and 1950s, Shell used BIP II, a 24,000 square meter lot, as a service area for pipelines supplying the fuel storage base (BIP I). From 1958 to 1978, Shell used part of the site for producing organochloride and organophosphate pesticides. After that, Shell used the lot to deal with bulk petrochemical products, store canned products, produce industrial detergents, and stock lubricants (Valentim, 2007. pp. 118–119).

Despite Shell conducting many soil-contaminating activities since the beginning, only in 1993 Greenpeace, Coletivo Alternativa Verde (Green Alternative Collective – an NGO) and the Sindicato dos Trabalhadores no Comércio de Minérios e Derivados de Petróleo de São Paulo (Union of Workers in Mining, Petroleum, and Related Industries of the state of São Paulo) made a complaint in court.

For decades, the residents of Vila Carioca have been drinking water that the nearby joint Shell facility contaminated. The Institute of Technological Research of the State of São Paulo conducted technical analysis and detected lead in the soil. The same year, sludge from oil derivatives was found, evidence that the company had buried effluents there. The MPE set up a public inquiry to investigate the case. The investigations indicated that contaminants such as BTX (benzene, toluene, and xylene) and heavy metals were buried in the area the company occupied in Vila Carioca (Valentim, 2007). Between 1993 and 1999, initiatives were carried out to remediate the situation, including removing primary sources of these substances in the soil. In 1999 and 2000, new sources of contamination were detected (Marcatto, 2005).

In 2002, the MPE opened a public civil lawsuit against Shell for environmental problems at the location (Câmara Municipal de São Paulo, 2006), and Greenpeace Brazil included Shell among its Corporative Environmental Crimes in Brazil, naming the Vila Carioca contamination (Greenpeace, 2002). Environmentalists' debates on contamination in Vila Carioca reached international audiences when the Friends of Earth organization detailed the case in reports on environmental problems relating to Shell's global activities.

This first period (1993–2003) saw no legal repercussions for Shell despite evidence of Shell's wrongdoing. Though the company received numerous fines—from São Paulo City Hall for infractions and operating without a license, and from Cetesb for water contamination and delays in reporting water and soil conditions—the company appealed and escaped the fines.

The Nature of the Disaster Phase 2: Undeniable Adverse Environmental and Health Effects

In 2002, the Federal Chamber of Representatives held a public hearing to debate soil and water contamination from chemical products in the Vila Carioca neighborhood (Câmara dos Deputados, 2002). In São Paulo Chamber of Representatives, four sequential public hearings (CPIs) investigated: irregularities in gas station construction (2002); environmental contamination and liabilities (2003); noise, atmosphere, water, soil, and subsoil pollution with environmental liabilities (2006); and environmental damage with respective liabilities, due to inadequate, irregular, and illegal industrial and economic activities (2010). All hearings showed that Shell's activities created environmental and health effects for the surrounding communities.

Blame-Shifting Phase 3: From Shell to the Victims

The first two CPIs revealed Shell's many wrongdoings, with Shell assuming the most aggressive posture to halt investigations and deny participation in the contamination. According to Shell, the population should be held responsible for any vestiges of "drins" in the Vila Carioca soil, because the levels of contaminants indicated, "that drins were used (sic) by local people in the past, probably [for] agriculture, for ants, for other types of use" (Shell Representative 04 June 2003, CPI do Passivo Ambiental, 2003, p. 3.767).

Blame-Shifting Phase 3: From Shell to the National Oil Regulatory Agency (ANP)

Shell further blamed governmental agencies. For example, in 2004, the São Paulo Federal Attorney's Office complemented the judicial initiatives by filing criminal procedures against Shell and the National Oil Regulatory Agency (ANP) for non-compliance with legal obligations to monitor the area Shell occupied in Vila Carioca. They also sued two Bureau Brasileiro S/C Ltda employees who ANP hired for the Shell case, for inserting false declarations in their report.

Blame-Shifting Phase 3: From Shell to the Brazilian State

Investigations halted for a while the CPI resumed in 2006. This CPI confirmed the negative impact on local inhabitants, calling attention to over 6,000 local people exposed to risks, stating:

"Shell Brasil has proceeded, with reprehensible conduct, to bury highly pollutant, toxic, and carcinogenic products over an undetermined period, contaminating the soil, subsoil, surface and underground water. By means of its contaminants it has penetrated the other proprieties, violating the private lives of inhabitants, making it difficult for them to exercise their citizenship rights, altering the area and its inhabitants, setting obstacles for their property rights, causing illness and health problems" (Câmara Municipal de São Paulo, 2006).

The same report compiled relevant data from various technical reports relating to contamination in Vila Carioca. The soil contamination derived from the burial of oil sludge, toxic detergents, and organochlorides; fuel derivatives and pesticides contaminated the water table; and imperceptible odorless fuel vapors and organochlorides contaminated the air. The mortality rate in Vila Carioca was twice that of the surrounding Ipiranga district (Câmara Municipal de São Paulo, 2006).

The evidence against Shell was again clear, but Shell started to redirect blame onto the Brazilian state's inefficiency in conducting the investigation, diagnosis, and treatment of citizens exposed and areas contaminated by the environmental damage Shell caused in Vila Carioca. Shell also blamed the government for failing to implement measures to contain, intervene, and cleanse the contaminated area and its surroundings (Câmara Municipal de São Paulo, 2010, pp. 102–103).

Blame-Shifting Phase 3: From Shell to Environmental Agency Cetesb

The 2006 CPI highlighted that Shell had not yet concluded the identification of the boundaries of the contaminated area, despite the long period since the first accusations, and that the remediation work in the contaminated area had remained almost at a standstill since 2003. Shell's lack of action entailed blame of Cetesb for adopting negligent and imprecise conduct regarding the risks to which Shell exposed locals and workers. Both Shell and Cetesb underestimated the existing contamination.

Despite mounting evidence against Shell, the 2010 CPI once again showed that Shell had hardly resolved the contamination effects. According to Municipal Health Department estimates, 6,538 out of 28,072 current inhabitants of Vila Carioca were exposed to Shell's contamination, although necessary specific toxicological exams have not been carried out. The local population complained about being excluded from decision-making processes related to the case, Cetesb and the State and Municipal Health Department's conduct, and real estate devaluation from environmental liabilities (Câmara Municipal de São Paulo, 2010, pp. 8, 11, 13).

Shell is still using Vila Carioca to store anhydrous and hydrated alcohol, diesel oil, automotive gasoline, and organic solvents. Throughout the Vila Carioca case, blame for the environmental disaster shifted so much that the problem became diffuse, allowing Shell to avoid reputation damages and heavy fines.

Paulínia Case

Shell installed its plant on river-bordered rural land it acquired in 1974, with various small farms and industries. The goal was to produce pesticides, which started in 1977, after receiving a license from Cetesb.

Blame Shifting Phase 1: From Shell to Previous Residents

In spite of Shell's license and new equipment (although Shell also recycled old equipment from Vila Carioca), in 1978, the neighbors complained about odors the site emitted. Inspections found pollution levels surpassing legal standards, which resulted in fines. Still, complaints about the strong odor persisted. In 1991, facing overwhelming complaints, Shell argued that the chemical odors likely derived from the land's former owner's use. The local population did not accept the justification, and the problem persisted until 1999 (Ministério Público do Trabalho, 2007).

Incidentally, the industrial facilities had various problems throughout Shell's activities. Two incinerators malfunctioned, which compromised the incineration quality and occasioned the emission of pollutants beyond legal standards. Since the company could not normalize the situation, after twenty years of fierce exchanges with Cetesb, Shell disabled the devices. Another controversial point was the recurring clash over waste disposal; Shell received fines and public admonitions for directly releasing effluents into the water and depositing contaminated material in the soil (Rezende, 2004).

Blame Shifting Phase 1: Shell's Secret Self-Denunciation

In 1994, Shell denounced its own environmental malpractices to the State Prosecutor (MPE). Their motivation was the intention to sell their assets in Paulínia to the Canadian company Cyanamid, which had required clarification of any liabilities, including environmental issues. The previous year, Shell had hired an audit company that had identified three non-reported environmental accidents, highlighting the misconduct of incorrect effluent release. The audit pointed to soil contamination due to improper disposal without mentioning the air pollution, or questions of worker health and safety (Ministério Público do Trabalho, 2007).

With this document, the MPE filed a civil lawsuit resulting in Shell signing a TAC committed to recovering the aquifer and controlling possible leakage into neighboring properties. Regardless of Shell's actions, the population could not use farm wells. It´s important to register that the negotiation progress had unusual features. First, Cetesb was not involved in the TAC from the beginning, but rather integrated later. Second, and more complexly, Shell committed the self-denunciation in secrecy, concealing the events from any other organizations (e.g. unions, NGOs), preventing them from questioning the terms, such as the audit report, omission of soil and air quality concerns, or worker health issues. Shortly thereafter, the MPE concluded that Shell's measures were consistent with and appropriate for correcting the situation. Consequently, Cyanamid acquired the facilities (Ministério Público do Trabalho, 2007). The asset transfer did not relieve Shell of environmental liability. Shell remained liable, and Cyanamid, despite the contractual clauses delimiting liability role, assumed the risk of being co-responsible for any environmental damage.

The mitigating measures Shell adopted in 1996 to undergo the TAC included hiring two laboratories, one Brazilian and one American, to evaluate water quality. The first found nothing, while the second identified several pollutants, including drins. At the time, Shell only released the favorable report. The same year, Shell began to distribute drinking water to some households, without justifying the reasons for alternative drinking water (Câmara dos Deputados, 2002).

Blaming Exposed Phase 2: Facts Became Public

The situation only became public in 1999, causing discomfort among people who became increasingly concerned after noticing that Cetesb had penalized the company on several occasions, mostly due to failure to follow some TAC clauses, without informing potentially affected populations. Therefore, in 2000, people started to mobilize, camping in front of the gates of facilities to protest and pressure Shell (Rezende, 2004).

Meanwhile, Basf acquired Cyanamid International. The German company assumed the stance that it was not part of the dispute, subsequently denying any liability. Furthermore, the new management of the facilities began to face problems meeting regulatory provisions; when they presented their Environmental Risk Prevention program, they omitted the presence of dangerous products on the premises that a commissioned study had found (Sabino, 2009).

Shifting the Issue Phase 3: Environmental but not Health Blame

At a 2001 public hearing on the Paulínia situation at the Federal House of Representatives, Shell assumed a pro-environment discourse, minimizing labor concerns and denying any health risk, based on their risk assessment model. Seeking shelter in legislation and public agency reports, Shell argued that it operated within the regulatory framework context. Cetesb, in turn, affirmed that Shell strictly followed protocols (even though, Cetesb acknowledged, Shell left incinerators operating in unsuitable conditions for 20 years). Cetesb's director admitted to contamination and risk to the public, but only on a small scale (Câmara dos Deputados, 2002).

It is noteworthy that the same year, in a new self-denunciation on contamination, Shell acknowledged the possibility of health risks for the surrounding population, based on results of the inquiry that the American laboratory prepared four years earlier, and on the 1993 environmental audit that was the basis of their first self-denunciation. Shell started to buy surrounding land, supply water to the local population, and purchase the vegetable production from the surrounding contaminated farms (Justiça do Trabalho, 2008). Subsequently, Shell negotiated with Cetesb to design a recovery plan for the area.

Pressuring Blame Phase 4: Former Employees Protest and Fight Against Shell

Alienated from negotiations and angry about Shell's negligence in dealing with their demands, former employees established a committee to defend their rights in 2001. Already, the Paulínia City Hall and the Labor Attorney (MPT) had decided to conduct health examinations of the population. The results indicated that, 156 of 181 area residents had at least one type of toxic waste in their body. Of these, 88 had chronic intoxication, 59 had liver and thyroid tumors, and 72 suffered drins contamination. Of the 50 area children under 15 years old, over half had chronic contamination. Among the pollutants detected were aldrin, dieldrin, and endrin, which increase the incidence of liver cancer, gallbladder cancer, and breast cancer (Prefeitura Municipal de Paulínia, 2003).

Shell has always denied the validity of those examinations and demanded to conduct their own exams. After the release of the examination results, Shell filed a lawsuit against the doctors who conducted the examination, at the same time as it hired a clinic to examine the claimants. According to the former employees' representatives, the clinic's service was not adequate. The matter became the subject of a second public hearing in the Federal House of Representatives in 2002. The exams that the clinic Shell hired had conducted found no evidence of contamination in the former employees (Câmara dos Deputados, 2002).

One of the most dramatic moments took place in 2002, when both the Labor Attorney auditors decided to preclude utilization of the facilities, and City Hall declared a state of emergency in the area, resulting in the removal of residents from their homes (Prefeitura Municipal de Paulínia, 2003). Negotiations were not prospering in the environmental sphere, since only 25% of the recovery plan had advanced.

Pressuring Blame Phase 4: Denying Blame and Playing with Words, "Intoxication is not Contamination"

The Labor Attorney managed to obtain from the Ministry of Health funding for another study to focus on former employees rather than the entire population. The study's conclusion was not definitive because the information collected on health was limited. The authors asserted that it was impossible to establish the correlation between employee health and occupational exposure; yet, it was not possible to proclaim that there had been no exposure. They found credible evidence that this sample of people presented changes in their bodies that were compatible with exposition to hazardous conditions in their work environment (Ambios Engenharia, 2005).

Apparently, the data were enough for the Labor Attorney to propose a public civil action against BASF and Shell in 2007, to guarantee the rights of former employees. The Labor Justice Court tried three times to achieve reconciliation between the parties, and achieved nothing. In 2008, the Labor Justice Court decided to approve the employees' demands that the companies should pay their medical costs (Justiça do Trabalho, 2008). The companies appealed the decision. Shell argued that their studies found no cases of contamination among former employees. In one of Shell's appeals, the company denies that they intoxicated their employees or neighbors:

> Intoxication, incidentally, is not, in any way, contamination. This confusion permeates from the beginning of these proceedings, and needs to be eradicated. Contamination is the mere presence of a toxic substance in the human body at tolerable levels, not harmful to health. Intoxication, in turn, is the presence of the toxic substance at levels harmful to health. And the fact is that the tests performed on the former employees demonstrate that the substances identified were within normal limits, detected in large urban and industrial centers, at levels therefore tolerable to the human organism.
>
> *(Shell Final Defense Statement, Tribunal Regional do Trabalho, 2011)*

Shell stressed that the problems arose from contamination of the natural rather than work environment, arguing the Labor Justice Court's jurisdictional incompetence to judge the matter, which postponed a decision. It also denounced the technical foundations (no causation) and other formal aspects of the process that would jeopardize the case's legality. BASF followed the same logic, arguing that it was not a legitimate part of the trial, since it did not handle the denounced product and was only Shell's successor. After Shell repurchased the area in 2008, Basf insisted that it had occupied the premises only from 2000 (acquisition) to 2002 (preclusion), and that Basf no longer held proprietary rights. Basf's appeals did not succeed (Tribunal Regional do Trabalho, 2009).

Pressuring Blame Phase 4: Asserting Blame—Former Employees Focus Complaints and Win the Most Significant Labor Cause in Brazil

Considering the case's impact, the state agency's had been ephemeral. Cetesb did nothing to deal with Shell's procrastination, not even entering further litigation. The State Prosecutor who had drafted the TAC with Shell did not follow up on events.

In August 2010, the Labor Justice Court decided that the employees' plea was fair (Sandes, 2011), leading to the biggest labor cause in Brazilian court history. The final decision held that employees were exposed to harmful substances in various phases of the production process, either due to inadequate procedures or due to equipment malfunction. Since there were organochloride samples found in their bodies, there was significant possibility of an elevated incidence of cancer and dysfunction of their nervous, reproductive, and immune systems, among other conditions.

Between 2010 and 2013, the companies challenged the decision. Overall, they simply reenacted the same arguments that they used earlier. Additionally, apart from procedural aspects, they questioned the immediate payment of indemnities. The Regional Labor Court upheld only this last item in 2011 (Tribunal Regional do Trabalho, 2011). Appeals sent the case to the Superior Labor Court (TST), Brazil's highest appellate court.

In a April 2013 conciliation hearing in TST, the parties agreed to end the process. The 1,058 former employees had confirmed their rights to health care for life, compensation for moral and material damage (totaling US$ 83.5 million), and compensation for the absence of health care coverage throughout the process (US$ 87.3 million). The companies also disbursed US$ 200 million covering collective damages, to be transferred to legal organizations MPT appointed, and Shell was fined US$ 390 million in compensation for moral damages caused to Brazilian society (Tribunal Superior do Trabalho, 2013). Unlike the Vila Carioca case, in the Paulínia case, blame shifting was less prominent and the complaints were more focused. These differences may account for some of the reasons the justice system remediated this disaster.

Discussion

This chapter investigated how the two environmental accidents' stakeholders constructed judgments to identify which elements characterize the roles Shell assumed to manage its responsibility. We sought to assess whether a predominant blame-shifting strategy could generate communication that evolved while preserving the community fabric. Or, in another way, whether blame shifting could turn a critical event into a disaster.

Table 1 summarizes the similarities and differences in Shell's litigation in the two analyzed cases, Vila Carioca and Paulínia.

The two cases demonstrate litigation processes taking distinct paths. Through comparative analysis of the two cases, we conclude that, despite severe effects at both sites, different approaches to solving the situations yielded completely different outcomes. In Vila Carioca, the litigation occurred under civil law, Shell did not assume blame, and blame shifting led to a sparser litigation process. In Paulínia, the litigation occurred under labor law, with a strategy focused on workers' health effects. Working together and focusing on a single issue strengthened the community and unions. Whereas in the Paulínia case, Shell had to resolve the dispute and pay damages, the Vila Carioca case has not been resolved (as of the time of publication).

Contrasting those outcomes with the theoretical framework of blame shifting and litigation in environmental disasters allowed us to highlight three important dimensions to consider: *a) litigation is an essential part of blame shifting, b) time is crucial to either mobilizing or demobilizing affected communities and c) confrontation by collective powerful opponents mitigates corporate litigation and blame-shifting strategies.*

Our case shows what the theory emphasizes: that blame shifting is an intrinsic feature of litigation in disaster situations (Tsoukas, 1999; Picou et al., 2004). When litigation is involved, the OBED perpetrator is very likely to deploy the blame-shifting strategy to avoid sanctions. In a sense, in Vila Carioca, blame shifting created a situation precluding the

Table 20.1 Comparison between the Two Cases

Key points	Vila Carioca	Paulínia
Legal action jurisdiction	No decisive administrative or legal action until the indictment by a labor union and environmental NGOs (1993) under civil law.	Shell's public self-denunciation in the civil law sphere. Labor Union and associations sue Shell (and Basf) under labor law.
Triggering litigation	The indictment from the labor union did not motivate public agencies (including the MPE) to act until a 2001 public civil action and a Municipal Parliamentary Commission of Inquiry. However, civil litigation did not develop, due to many judiciary setbacks.	In 1994, Shell made a self-denunciation, probably due to contractual requirements of a sale-taking place. The action resulted in a Public Civil Inquiry ending in a "TAC." Afterward, continuing civil public litigation began.
Levering the public agenda	MPE and City Hall put the subject on the agenda.	A labor union and the Labor Public Attorney (MPT) put the subject on the agenda.
Community voice	The community has little voice and few alternatives.	The community has more alternatives. Many residents (mostly individually) sold land to Shell.
Blame-shifting strategy	Continuous blame shifting to various actors.	Shell assumes blame for environmental but not health damage. The community focuses on health effects.
Time	A lengthy blame-shifting period; slow mobilization.	A short blame-shifting period; quick collective mobilization.
Powerful actors involved	Many non-profits, without any taking the lead or exercising powerful voice.	The union did the most work, taking the lead as a powerful actor in the region.

Source: The authors.

possibility of reaching a final court ruling, while Shell has suffered no significant setbacks apart from litigation costs. In contrast, in Paulínia, despite early attempts, Shell did not fully deploy the blame-shifting strategy. Shell anticipated environmental litigation through a process of self-denunciation, which Basf required as a precondition of purchasing the plant. Nonetheless, Shell's blame-shifting strategy was less successful than in Vila Carioca; the community and workers achieved a significant victory.

Our case foregrounds the role of litigation time, which influences affected communities' mobilization capacity. In both cases, lawsuits took a long time. In Paulínia, the first denunciations to the final decision spanned almost 20 years, which was perfect timing for the community and labor union to create strong bonds with the Labor Public Attorney. However, in the Vila Carioca case, the longer the community took to organize, the harder it became for the community to form a robust litigation strategy. The delay allowed Shell to continue the blame-shifting strategy, achieving success in casting blame on other possible actors, reducing the possibility of any outcome.

Lastly, we demonstrate the importance of collective action when facing corporations attempting to avoid liability in OBEDs. Collective action enables community resilience as dominant opponents of litigating corporations, especially when blame shifting is prone to occur (Morello-Frosch et al., 2011). In Paulínia, a strong labor union's presence was fundamental to dismantling Shell's blame-shifting strategies. The labor union not only persistently fought for justice, it also deployed tactics to mobilize people for their cause, such as organizing demonstrations in front of the court, producing a short documentary for dissemination. However, many strong NGOs like Greenpeace and Friends of the Earth were involved in the Vila Carioca case. Though none of them became prominent actors, the NGOs could neither mobilize nor organize the community. Ultimately, the community could not demonstrate resilience, despite various forums to voice their case, such as the four Parliamentary Commissions of Inquiry. Our evidence shows that civil society organizations' involvement is crucial to litigation, and those organizations' power relationships may deflate corporate strategies of blame shifting and litigation in OBEDs.

Final Considerations

Shell has been involved in several disputes since its founding in 1907 over its environmental record, "dangerous liaisons" with governments, and poor transparency with its stakeholders. Shell's problems reached an apex in the 1990s when social movements and environmental organizations campaigned against the company, forcing it to change its approach toward stakeholders.

Through a massive public relations campaign, combined with a shift toward a business model based on sustainability and transparent dialogue with multiple stakeholders, Shell has crafted an image as a company "walking the talk" (Holliday et al., 2002). However, legal suits brought the validity of such claims into question. In our two cases, Shell representatives were authoritarian, denying any form of liability for their employees or surrounding neighborhoods. In both cases, representatives and lawyers enacted a precise survival strategy: to generate ambiguity and contradiction. Concurrently, Shell recognized that it had caused environmental impacts, and tried to anticipate statutory persecution consequences by settling a TCA with the public attorney, in which Shell promised to correct negative externalities. Meanwhile, Shell procrastinated on every serious decision to mitigate the consequences of their production and dumping drins at both sites. Moreover, Shell abandoned a softer demeanor, adopting a rude approach to their antagonists, denying any liability, and engaging in time-consuming litigation that only aggravated the disasters' effects.

We conclude that while litigation may dilute liability and minimize reputation risks for a corporation involved in a disaster, it has catastrophic effects on individuals, communities, and the environment, which, over time, transform the critical event into a disaster. Constant blame shifting diffuses complaints and the collective action, impeding effective results that might mitigate the disaster that company caused. In spite of this powerful social phenomenon, there is evidences that a robust mobilization of civil society organizations and communities can counterbalance those effects.

Note

1 In the 1970s, the United States banned the production and use of organochlorines (DDT in 1972, and dieldrin in 1974). Brazil total banned only in 2009.

References

Alves, M. A. & Blikstein, I. (2006). Análise de narrativas. In: Godoi, C. K., Bandeira-de-Melo, R., Silva, A. B. (Org.). *Pesquisa qualitativa em estudos organizacionais:* Paradigmas, estratégias e métodos. São Paulo: Editora Saraiva, 403–428.

Ambios Engenharia. (2005). Avaliação das informações sobre a exposição dos trabalhadores das empresas Shell, Cyanamid e Basf a compostos químicos – Paulínia. Disponível em portal.saude.gov.br.

Beamish, T. D. (2000). Accumulating trouble: Complex organization, a culture of silence, and a secret spill. *Social Problems, 47*(4): 473–498.

Boje, D. M. (2001). *Narrative methods for organizational & communication research*. London and Thousand Oaks CA, New Delhi: Sage Publications.

Câmara dos Deputados. (2002). Audiência pública sobre os trabalhadores de Paulínia. Brasília. Retrieved from www.camara.gov.br.

Câmara Municipal de São Paulo. (2006). CPI da Poluição. Autos do Processo. Retrieved from www.camara.sp.gov.br.

Câmara Municipal de São Paulo. (2010). CPI dos Danos Ambientais. Retrieved from www.camara.sp.gov.br.

Catino, M. (2008). A review of literature: Individual blame vs. organizational function logics in accident analysis. *Journal of Contingencies and Crisis Management, 16*(1): 53–62.

Dewey, J. (1922). *Human nature and conduct*. New York: Henri Holt and Company.

Douglas, M. (1966). *Purity and danger: An analysis of concepts of pollution and taboo*. London and New York: Routledge & Kegan Paul.

Douglas, M. (1992). *Risk and blame: Essays in cultural theory*. London, Routledge.

Edelman, M. (1964). *The symbolic uses of politics*. Urbana: Illinois University Press.

Freudenburg, W. R. (1997). Contamination, corrosion and the social order: An overview. *Current Sociology, 45*(3): 19–39.

Friends of the Earth. (2003). Behind the shine: The other Shell report 2003. Retrieved from www.foe.co.uk.

Friends of the Earth. (2004). Lessons not learned: The other Shell report. Retrieved from www.foe.co.uk.

Gephart, R. (1984). Making sense of organizationally-based environmental disasters. *Journal of Management 10*(2): 205–225.

Gephart, R. (1988). Managing the meaning of a sour gas well blowout: The public culture of organization disasters. *Organization and Environment, 2*(1): 17–32.

GREENPEACE. (2002). Crimes ambientais corporativos no Brasil. Retrieved from www.greenpeace.org.br.

Hargie, O., Stapleton, K., & Tourish, D. (2010). Interpretations of CEO public apologies for the banking crisis: Attributions of blame and avoidance of responsibility. *Organization, 17*(6): 721–742.

Herrick, C. (2009). Shifting blame/selling health: Corporate social responsibility in the age of obesity. *Sociology of Health & Illness, 31*(1): 51–65.

Hirschman, A. (1994). Social conflicts as pillars of democratic market society. *Political Theory, 22*(2): 203–218.

Holliday, C. O., Schmidheiny, S., & Watts, P. (2002). *Walking the talk: The business case for sustainable development*. Sheffield, UK: Greenleaf Publishing Limited.

Hood, C. (2002). The risk game and the blame game. *Government and Opposition, 37*(1): 15–37.

Jerome, A. M., & Rowland, R. C. (2009). The rhetoric of interorganizational conflict: A subgenre of organizational apologia. *Western Journal of Communication, 73*(4): 395–417.

Justiça do Trabalho. (2008). Decisão sobre ação civil pública nº 00222-2007-126-15-00-6. Retrieved from www.trt15.jus.br.

Langley, A. (1999). Strategies for theorizing from process data. *Academy of Management Review*, 24(4): 691–710

Livesey, S. M. (2002). The discourse of the middle ground: Citizen Shell commits to sustainable development. *Management Communication Quarterly, 15*(3): 313–349

Marcatto, F. (2005). *A participação pública na gestão de área contaminada: Uma análise de caso baseada na Convenção de Aarhus*. Dissertação de Mestrado. Universidade de São Paulo.

Ministério Público do Trabalho. (2007). Ação civil pública nº 00222-2007-126-15-00-6. Retrieved from www.trt15.jus.br.

Morello-Frosch, R., Brown, P., Lyson, M., Cohen, A., & Krupa, K. (2011). Community voice, vision, and resilience in post-Hurricane Katrina recovery. *Environmental Justice, 4*(1): 71–80.

Mortensen, P. (2016). Agencification and blame shifting: Evaluating a neglected side of public sector reforms. *Public Administration, 94*(3): 630–646.

Observatório Social. (2003). Comportamento social e trabalhista: mapa da empresa Shell. Retrieved from www.os.org.br.

Patriotta, G. (2003). Sensemaking on the shop floor: Narratives of knowledge in organizations. *Journal of Management Studies, 40*(2): 349–375.

Perry, R. W. (2007). What is a disaster? In: Dynes, R., Quarantelli, E., Rodriguez, H. (Eds.), *Handbook of disaster research*. New York: Springer, pp. 1–15.

Picou, J. S., Marshall, B. K., & Gill, D. A. (2004). Disaster, litigation, and the corrosive community. *Social Forces, 82*(4): 1493–1522.

Prefeitura Municipal de Paulínia. (2003). Avaliação do impacto na saúde dos moradores do Bairro Recanto dos Pássaros. Retrieved from www.acpo.org.br.

Quarantelli, E. L., Lagadec, P., & Boin, A. (2007). A heuristic approach to future disasters and crises: New, old and in-between types. In: Dynes, R., Quarantelli, E., & Rodriguez, H. (Eds.), *Handbook of disaster research*. New York: Springer, pp. 16–41.

Rezende, J. (2004). Caso shell, cyanamid, basf: Epidemiologoa e informação para o resgate de uma precaução negada. Tese de Doutorado. Universidade de Campinas.

Rhodes & Brown. (2005). Narrative, organizations and research. *International Journal of Management Reviews, 7*(3): 167–188.

Sabino, M. (2009). Reconstrução de coortes: Métodos, técnicas e interfaces com a vigilância em saúde do trabalhador. Dissertação de Mestrado. Universidade de Campinas.

Sandes, B. (2011). Ação civil pública: O caso de contaminação em Paulínia/SP. Monografia Final. Centro Universitário de Brasília.

SHELL. (1998) The Shell Report 1998. Profits and Principles – does there have to be a choice? Retrieved from www.shell.com.

SHELL. (2003). Relatório Shell na sociedade brasileira. Retrieved from www.shell.com.

SHELL. (2004). Relatório Shell na sociedade brasileira. Retrieved from www.shell.com.

SHELL. (2005). Relatório Shell na sociedade brasileira. Retrieved from www.shell.com.

SHELL. (2006). Relatório Shell na sociedade brasileira. Retrieved from www.shell.com.

SHELL. (2007). Relatório Shell na sociedade brasileira. Retrieved from www.shell.com.

SHELL. (2008). Relatório Shell na sociedade brasileira. Retrieved from www.shell.com.

Tilly, C. (2008). *Credit and blame*. Princeton, NJ: Princeton University Press.

Tribunal Regional do Trabalho. (2009). Decisão sobre ação civil pública n° 00222–2007–126-15-00–6. Retrieved from www.trt15.jus.br.

Tribunal Regional do Trabalho. (2011). Decisão sobre ação civil pública n° 00222–2007–126-15-00–6. Disponível em www.trt15.jus.br.

Tribunal Superior do Trabalho. (2013). Decisão sobre ação civil pública n° 00222–2007-126-15-00–6. Retrieved from www.tst.gov.br.

Tsoukas, H. (1999). David and Goliath in the risk society: making sense of the conflict between Shell and Greenpeace in the North Sea. *Organization, 6*(3): 499–528.

Turner, B. A. (1978). *Man-made disasters*. London: Wykeham Publications.

Vaara, E. and Tienari, J. (2011). On the narrative construction of multinational corporations: An antenarrative analysis of legitimation and resistance in a cross-border merger. *Organization Science, 22*(2): 370–390.

Valentim, L. (2007). *Requalificação urbana, contaminação do solo e riscos à saúde: Um caso na cidade de São Paulo*. São Paulo: Annablume.

21

FAMILY FIRMS AND STAKEHOLDER MANAGEMENT

Crisis at Blue Bell Ice Cream

Cyrus B. Parks and Laura B. Cardinal

The purpose of this study is to analyze the 2015 product contamination crisis at Blue Bell Creameries, a crisis that was caused by the shipment and consumption of *listeria*-tainted ice cream products. We focus on two key questions – why do organizations (in this case family firms) take production risks after receiving signals of problems? And how do these organizations respond and recover from the resulting crises and prevent future events? As an introduction to the case study, we review Blue Bell and its managers, employees, and customers in the context of the focal event.

The Event

For decades, Blue Bell Creameries, a large ice cream and frozen novelties manufacturer, has been a part of celebrations as well as normal family life in the southern U.S.A. (Carper, 2015). The firm has enjoyed strong growth (>11%) in an industry that generally moves with GDP (MarketLine, 2014), and it recently has become one of the largest frozen dessert brands while only being available in less than half of the U.S. market. Throughout its history, Blue Bell has been largely reliant on employees' and customers' word-of-mouth for advertising and organic growth, leveraging a simple folksy branding approach and a reputation for high quality (Apple, 2006). A common activity when driving through Brenham, Texas (population 16,101 – halfway between Austin and Houston), has been to visit Blue Bell headquarters and witness the large-scale ice cream manufacturing facility in operation while sampling the finished product. Approximately 120,000 tourists visited Blue Bell in 2014, suggesting many families treat this less as a stopover and more as a destination. No visits occurred, however, in the summer of 2015, when the plants were closed, the tours canceled, and no ice cream was to be had.

Starting in February 2015, widespread cases of illness stemming from *listeria monocytogenes* began to be reported and associated with Blue Bell products. *Listeria* is a robust and ubiquitous microorganism, and the illness it causes usually brings only mild symptoms of headache, nausea, or diarrhea – a typical stomach bug. It, however, can be fatal in the very young, very old, and the infirm. Strong effects are rare, but *listeria* is a known threat to dairy plant operations because it thrives in cold, damp environments, and can live in freezers for months. Ten hospitalizations and three deaths were genetically traced by the Centers for Disease Control

(CDC) and eventually attributed to Blue Bell products using state-of-the-art DNA tests (FDA, 2015). By mid-March 2015, Blue Bell had instituted a partial recall of frozen desserts, but subsequent sampling showed widespread contamination. In April, the firm bowed to regulatory agency pressure and "voluntarily" shut down one production line after another,[1] first at their two expansion manufacturing facilities in Oklahoma and Alabama, and then at the home plant in Texas. An FDA inspection of a Blue Bell facility – done on April 20th, the day the company announced the full recall and two months after first learning about the problem – showed a firm seemingly unaware of the severity of its situation. The following examples illustrate problematic practices:

• The (equipment) used in the chocolate blending room was stored in an unclean metal milk can between uses.
• A space heater was observed fastened to the production equipment with duct tape directly under the chocolate tray during production.
• A maintenance employee, with visibly soiled arms and shirt, was observed leaning on a package machine during production … extending over exposed product and open packaging.
• Several pieces of production equipment … were (stored) in an employee hand sink immediately following the disassembly of the line after production.

After one month of recall and shutdown, Blue Bell voluntarily entered into compliance agreements with the various agencies, which allowed resumption of production after meeting promised improvements in operations and facilities. Blue Bell products did not return to grocery shelves until August 31, 2015, amid much fanfare and celebration. (A full timeline of the contamination event is available from the authors.)

Overall, Blue Bell was out of the marketplace for over four and a half months, thus missing the summer ice cream season. By the end of May, the company had laid off or furloughed two-thirds of its workforce, and it stopped giving interviews, statements, or information to the public until production resumed in August. During this downtime, public inspection reports and media investigations revealed that Blue Bell had failed multiple inspections due to *listeria* contamination for several years prior to the recall event, going back to 2008. FDA inspection reports and root cause investigations confirmed earlier rumors of inadequate materials handling, improper disinfection procedures, and mixing of debris and condensation in the ice cream process (FDA, 2015). Multiple lines of evidence showed frequent contamination problems in manufacturing areas and in food processing equipment. The historically positive public relations gave way to withering criticism of the firm and its management (e.g., Collette, 2015a, 2015b, 2015c).

Puzzling Management Behaviors

Illness from *listeria*-laced ice cream is not common, but it is not rare either. Blue Bell was not the only ice cream manufacturer to be cited for *listeria* contamination in 2015; two other (much smaller) firms in New York and Washington suffered limited, temporary impacts. The popular fast-casual restaurant Chipotle also had waged a battle against *listeria*, with many stores on the West coast shut down for weeks due to contaminated produce received from suppliers. In each of these cases, the firm and its products were noted to be of the highest quality and freshest available ingredients, much like Blue Bell. For these other firms, the *listeria* problems were found to be short-term issues caused by hidden gaps in their product quality assurance plans. But according to the government report, Blue Bell had been aware of *listeria* contamination in its facilities for several years prior and had taken no special action nor warned the public (FDA, 2015). Many blamed Blue Bell for seemingly gross negligence (Collette, 2015a). Possible gross negligence aside, the managerial actions simply seem to have been bizarre. Why would a growing, respected firm take inordinate risks to their reputation and the public health? Had Blue Bell been taking calculated, disjunctive production risks, concluding that despite the presence of *listeria* in its equipment and products, public sickness was highly unlikely or even impossible? Probably not – the firm had not tried to exercise best practices or maintain appearances of doing so, actions that could have been used to avoid any claims of misconduct or malfeasance if/when its bet on *listeria* did not work out. In fact, contamination was found throughout all of Blue Bell's manufacturing facilities, even the show-case production lines visible during tours and to visitors via overhead observation galleries. In essence, contamination issues and evidence were frequent and evident, yet there were no covers-ups or actions to keep bad practices hidden from anyone – regulators, customers, or employees (potential whistleblowers).

Additionally, the strategic decisions made during the event appeared exceptionally irrational. After dismissal of contamination evidence for years and reluctance to warn the public or recall product, management took a 180-degree turn, issuing a complete voluntary shutdown of all production and a massive overhaul of all production assets and procedures. They did not fight the government agencies, seek to avoid responsibility, or challenge the data. They suddenly stopped all production, fixed their assets, and installed new quality control procedures. They went from denial of the issue to acceptance, with little media engagement or any effort to maintain production. They sharply and completely left the market with only a promise to one day return.

The Special Case of Family Firms

Blue Bell is a family firm, and that seems important in the present case. Such a firm can be defined as "a business governed and/or managed with the intention to shape and pursue the vision of the business held by a dominant coalition that is controlled by members of the same family (or small number of families) in a manner that is potentially sustainable across generations" (Chua, Chrisman, & Bergiel, 2009; Zellweger & Nason, 2008). Family firms are dominant in small- and medium-sized businesses in the U.S.A., and across the globe they are the largest fraction of private enterprise (La Porta, Lopez-De-Silanes, & Shleifer, 1999). Although they are ubiquitous in the post-modern economy, they receive less scholarly attention compared to public firms, and dedicated theory regarding family firms is less developed. Family firms and the rationality of their owner-managers (cf. Cyert & March, 1963) are less easily compartmentalized for analysis, making them more difficult to explain and easier to ignore; they are dismissed by many scholars as seemingly idiosyncratic or arbitrary in nature. Theoretical views related to how owner-managers view and interact with their environment, understand risk, and run their firms are mixed and often contradictory.

Speaking generally, theory regarding how family firms are governed is largely based on the public firm, one that has dispersed ownership, professional managers, and overarching economic goals (Berle & Means, 1991, 1932). Scholars typically have treated family firms as a special case with reduced agency risk (Jensen & Meckling, 1976) because the owner and manager roles are blended (Gomez-Mejia, Nunez-Nickel, & Gutierrez, 2001). Yet, these roles are still subject to opportunism and are affected by non-business ties (Schulze, Lubatkin, Dino, & Buchholtz, 2001). Interestingly, owner-managers are often seen as both more risk-averse and more risk-seeking, and family firm goals have been demonstrated to not always be economic but "socio-emotional," with special attention to personal relationships, reputation, and trans-generational family control (Chua et al., 2009; Luis R Gomez-Mejia, Haynes, Nunez-Nickel, Jacobson, & Moyano-Fuentes, 2007). Important for our purposes, the amassed literature on family firms speaks little to how owner-managers make decisions, respond during a crisis, or demonstrate resilience.

In order to make sense of the *listeria* crisis in the context of a family firm, this case study employs an interpretive deep dive to understand an endogenous shock (i.e., the contamination event) (Bettis, Gambardella, Helfat, & Mitchell, 2015; Farjoun & Starbuck, 2007; Siggelkow, 2007). First, the literature on family firm governance is used to frame the case analysis (Eisenhardt, 1989). Second, the methods and raw data are presented as a foundation for interpretation of events and behaviors (Taylor, 1971). Third, the results of the case study are presented using two themes: (1) complete control – where management seeks to internalize and control all processes seen as important, and (2) stakeholder coupling – in which management selects loosely or tightly coupled relationships with stakeholders according to their saliency. Finally, these themes, which helped us to better understand the why and how of the crisis, are used to frame a clearer understanding of owner-manager actions and behaviors, augment family firm theory, and reframe the crisis and resulting solutions, thus completing the hermeneutical circle (Geertz, 1972).

Failed Theoretical Storylines

In order to sort out the puzzling behaviors exhibited by Blue Bell management during the contamination event, we considered Blue Bell as an archetypical family firm. We initially visited extant theories regarding family firm governance, notably agency theory and stakeholder theory (Boyd & Solarino, 2016; Parmar et al., 2010), along with a behavioral extension of these theories toward goal orientation and sensemaking (Le Breton-Miller & Miller, 2011).

Family Firm Governance

According to recent interpretations of agency theory, managers in family firms are expected to act in the economic best interest of the owners due to reduced agency risk (Boyd & Solarino, 2016), but manager motivations and behaviors are still expected to be steered by a complex array of incentives (Jensen & Meckling, 1976). Owner and manager roles may be blended and subject to non-business ties (Luis R. Gomez-Mejia et al., 2001), and their behaviors may not always be purely economic (Chua et al., 2009). Owner-managers may instead focus on altruism (Schulze et al., 2001) or function on a different time horizon, typically taking a longer-term view of strategic choices (Le Breton-Miller & Miller, 2011). Economic opportunism is still considered a relevant factor in family firm management behavior, but perhaps with less of the negative stigma typically attached to it (Schulze et al., 2001). The manager may pursue noble or selfish goals that are outside the firm's economic interests but without the criticism of acting outside the owner's interests.

Blue Bell has been managed for several generations by the Kruse family, which has owned the majority of the company and recently celebrated its 100th anniversary (MacInerney, 2007). At the time of the event, the top management team had family members in the two most powerful roles – the CEO and the VP of Operations – and the board of directors had several extended family members (Kruse, 2004). Furthermore, the Kruse family is noted to have specific and generous altruistic behaviors toward their local community. For their Brenham headquarters, Swartz (2015) has stated,

The town and the company have a symbiotic relationship, both capitalizing on the safe, sweet, old-timey identity of the other. You can, for instance, take Blue Bell Road around town, and you can swim at the Blue Bell Aquatic Center. Locals have benefited enormously and routinely from the company's largesse in scholarships, charitable donations, and the like.

These noted efforts in local philanthropy and political activity align well with the concept of socio-emotional goals (Gomez-Mejia, Cruz, Berrone, & De Castro, 2011), but they do not explain management behaviors surrounding the contamination event. Increased altruism suggests closer ties with communities and sincere efforts to protect those communities from all harm; if anything, a higher level of care and concern for the well-being of their communities and customers can be expected from family firms.

Goals and Multi-Temporal Orientation

Family firm management is theorized to align long-term success with a multi-temporal orientation that is reflected in strategic plans (Le Breton-Miller & Miller, 2011). Financial success is considered vital in both the near-term and the long-term, just as it is for firms with dispersed ownership. However, family firms are expected to value long-term success over the short-term, so as to preserve family dynastic control (Chrisman, Chua, & Steier, 2011; Chrisman & Patel, 2011). This translates to an overall willingness to make sacrifices in the short-term for long-term success and to adopt a relatively conservative stance toward risk and growth (Boyd & Solarino, 2016; Cruz, Gomez-Mejia, & Becerra, 2010; Luis R Gomez-Mejia et al., 2007). Long-term goals are theorized to be related to socio-emotional ends (Chrisman & Patel, 2011; Gomez-Mejia et al., 2001) that are broader in scope and perhaps in conflict with profit-taking (Schulze et al., 2001). This strategic orientation toward a long-run view bridges an agency perspective with a stakeholder perspective, suggesting that family firms are more cognizant of their embedded context in society and especially their local communities (Zellweger & Nason, 2008; Zellweger, Nason, Nordqvist, & Brush, 2013). Limited empirical research (e.g., Gomez-Mejia et al., 2007) generally supports this view of outside connections and close personal relationships over long periods of time, reflecting the legitimacy and influence of the family firm.

Throughout its existence, Blue Bell appears to have preferred long-term success and growth over short-term gains. When challenged for their relatively slow geographic growth over the decades, the folksy retort by managers has often been, "It's a cinch by the inch, but it's hard by the yard." And Blue Bell has been known to prefer slow change that preserves product quality and firm reputation. CEO Paul Kruse opined in 2004,

> Candidly, I like it when things stay the same. But when you step back and take a good look, few things really do. In the area of principles, however, they should stay fixed. Why be in business if we can't be honest and fair in our approach and look for mutually beneficial solutions? I can tell you that, at Blue Bell, such practices have become second nature. It's simply our way of life. And it's the only way that a company will last.

Overall, we might expect that Blue Bell would be more likely to protect the health of its customers in order to maintain long-term loyalty and less likely to make cost-cutting or other strategic decisions that would risk the long-term viability of the firm or loss of family control. During the focal event, however, the firm appeared to knowingly ship potentially tainted product and responded minimally when presented with evidence. Then, after being convinced that there was a larger contamination issue, management reversed course and completely halted all production for several months, with little explanation or transparency. Both of these decisions may be viewed as risky, harmful, and costly to the long-term prospects of the firm and damaging to the reputation of the family and its business. An agency/stakeholder view does a poor job of explaining these exposed behaviors.

Owner-Manager Sensemaking

Behavioral theory suggests that owner-managers will engage outside authorities and external institutions differently than other stakeholders (Verbeke & Kano, 2010). Family firms desire strong ties to external stakeholders in order to build and maintain reputation and legitimacy, but governmental agencies and rule-giving external institutions are likely to be distrusted and held in low esteem by the firm and its managers. Such distrust may manifest in a breakdown in interpretation of the environment and a discounting of legitimate, external data and signals in favor of internal signals originating from trusted family and employees (Westrum, 1978). If external signals are discounted incorrectly, perhaps due to excessive trust in internal capabilities or an urgency to maintain reputation, the family firm may be more likely to suffer from a crisis such as a product contamination event.

Counter to this perspective, there were no conflicting signals regarding contamination at Blue Bell. Internal sampling results suggested *listeria* was a common and recurrent presence in manufacturing operations. Data suggesting a severe contamination problem were common and ignored by operations and management, and employee routines were far out of line with safe standards, much less best practices. The FDA findings suggest clan behaviors contributed to the event: a general lack of written procedures and a strong reliance on tacit routines performed by long-tenure employees. Prior to the event, high employee participation in manufacturing was professed as a virtue by one senior manager:

> We're in a semi-rural area, away from the big cities, so people tend to want to stay around. We have a good number of employees who have been with us for 20 to 25 years. We have the same access to technology as all of our competitors (but) we're a lot less automated on the production side than we are downstream. And the best way to ensure quality is to have a hands-on approach… We consider our operators and packagers to be the final QC inspectors.

External agencies were not notified by Blue Bell managers regarding the apparent contamination, and the firm failed to report the positive *listeria* findings over several years. Said one expert in comparing Blue Bell's response to another firm's responses to *listeria* contamination:

> (The other company) immediately took the tainted ice cream off the shelves. (The CEO) focused on both his customers and his employees and voiced concern over anyone potentially becoming sick from his ice cream. The last thing he talked about was his company, which is the right approach… Then they shut down their plant, invited in the health department, the FDA, everybody, and asked them to tell them what they needed to do to fix this. Blue Bell didn't do that.

Blue Bell appeared to discount external data and reject agency authority, despite the fact that their own internal data supported the findings. But the owner-managers also may have simply suffered from a disjunctive bias, dismissing any chance of public harm from their actions. Or they may have told themselves a lie. Regardless of reasoning, and given the lack of evidence of a cover-up or self-deception, the observed behaviors do not support what is theoretically expected regarding the character of the family firm. An interpretation of the contexts, communications, and patterns of strategic behaviors of the firm may provide additional insight.

Methodology for Better Understanding the Contamination Event

Blue Bell and the contamination event were approached interpretively using case study methods (Yin, 2014), which are invaluable for understanding catastrophic errors in context (Reason, 1990; Wolf & Sampson, 2007), gaining insight into a contemporary phenomenon (Farquhar, 2012), and/or answering questions of "when, how and why" in situations where the researcher has little control over events (Eisenhardt, 1989). Approaching behaviors in light of the entire phenomenon and the history of the firm helps make sense of individual actions and decisions (Reason, 1990; Weick, 1979). An interpretive case study is particularly appropriate for this case, as it is allows close examination of the unique relational aspects of family firms (Dawson & Hjorth, 2012) and the inclusion of language, images, and artifacts (Bansal & Corley, 2011; Wadham & Warren, 2013).

The sources of evidence for this case study were almost entirely archival records, with a few supporting first-person interviews and observations. The data corpus contained 77 archival sources pertinent to Blue Bell, its strategic plans, the contamination event, and subsequent recovery (a full catalog of sources is available from the authors). Most archival sources were newspaper or online articles, but also included inspection reports, opinion pieces, editorials, in-depth commentaries, trade publications, industry news pieces, market analyses, firm histories, blogs, and a first-person piece on the company written by the CEO (Kruse, 2004). Photographs and digital media from the firm's website were included in the study, as was a company-sponsored historical biopic commemorating the firm's first century (MacInerney, 2007). These data were assembled and categorized according to their temporality: before the event (prior to February 2015), during the event and subsequent shutdown (approximately February to August 2015), and after the event (post-September 2015). In all, there were 14 texts collected from before the event, 48 during the event, and 15 after the event. The character of the texts was noticeably different from phase to phase, with the pre-event texts largely extolling the firm, its management, and its history. After the recall and before the restart of production, the texts were mostly news items covering progress in the event and speculation on root causes. Opinions and investigative pieces were mostly critical in tone, with strong blame placed on the management and its unwillingness to share information or allow interviews. Despite the critical press, Blue Bell restarted production with much fanfare. Television station helicopters were deployed to track shipments of ice cream to distribution centers, and for several days store shelves were sold out within minutes of re-stocking. Blue Bell's re-introduction to the market quieted much of the news coverage and criticism, but at that time many of the details of the official root cause analyses and the federal investigation into Blue Bell's actions became public. In the months following restart, Blue Bell kept a very low profile, with minimal advertising and little press coverage. In December 2015, the federal Department of Justice began an inquiry into the contamination event.[2] One year later in December 2016, the firm requested a reprieve from the meticulous sampling and analysis requirements specified in the compliance agreements and to be allowed to return to the previous quality assurance practices used by the industry (i.e., no product sampling).

The archival data were supplemented with a theoretical sampling of customers using interviews and marketplace observations (Eisenhardt, Graebner, & Sonenshein, 2016). During the summer of 2015, several customers were approached regarding their overtly public support of the firm during its crisis. Two individuals were specifically chosen for in-depth one-on-one interviews on the basis of their local public display of loyalty toward Blue Bell during the recall period and their full consent and willingness to discuss what Blue Bell meant to them. Such focused selections were viewed as appropriate for this case study in order to understand deviant behavior patterns (Huberman & Miles, 1994). Observations of purchasing behaviors were made in August and September 2015, at a large regional supermarket in the Houston, Texas area, where Blue Bell first reentered the market. The observations occurred over several weeks: the week before Blue Bell products returned to the store, the day of return, and a week later. These first-hand data were helpful in triangulating interpretations of behaviors and actions, providing richer descriptions and developing more meaningful theoretical discussions.

Interpretation as Scientific Process

Using conventional theories, puzzling management behaviors are often described as "path-dependent" or "idiosyncratic;" under (boundedly) rationalistic economic views they may be described as "myopic" (Cyert & March, 1963) or even "opportunistic" (Williamson, 1991). Such dismissal or attribution to limited cognition may be convenient, but any theory that offers limited explanations of undesirable or irrational behaviors is itself undesirable or irrational, as it is not sufficient for fully understanding the behaviors. By contrast, the interpretive approach isolates the most puzzling actions or behaviors in order to extract meaning. Taylor (1971) describes the interpretive epistemology as one that employs a deep inquiry into the context of a situation in order to make sense of socially constructed behaviors (see Figure 21.1). The researcher becomes the instrument of measurement for thematic analysis (Braun & Clarke, 2006) and provides rich description based in the texts/behaviors to allow a re-framing of the behavior such that it is no longer puzzling. The researcher remains reflexively open to alternative arguments and continually refines the themes based on available data. Finally, after the puzzling behaviors are rendered more understandable, the themes are

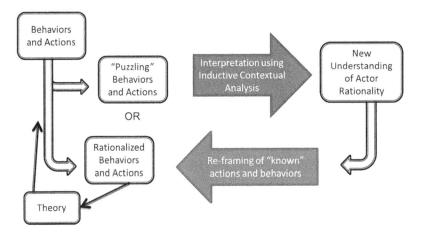

Figure 21.1 Interpretive Scientific Inquiry and the Hermeneutical Circle (after Taylor, 1971)

used to re-examine what was thought to be understood or previously settled, thus completing the hermeneutical circle. Like throwing a rock into a pond, the rippling effects of the interpretation support or question theoretical foundations, or perhaps new questions may evolve regarding actions and behaviors that were previously considered understood, thus perpetuating the cycle.

Data Analysis

After sorting the data corpus according to the timeline of the contamination event, the texts were coded to elicit emergent themes for conceptual analysis and abstraction. This inductive approach toward theme construction allowed for themes to be strongly grounded in the data, resulting in richer description (Braun & Clarke, 2006). The primary codes were then arranged axially for secondary coding, and memos were constructed as intermediate tools to collect meaning and begin interpretation. For example, in a memo excerpt entitled, "*Listeria* wipes in the wrong places," the essences of the texts were rearranged, summarized, and questioned:

> The *listeria* testing is symbolic of the firm's actions leading up to the crisis. Looking in the wrong places – of little consequence; Finding what you want to find – acceptance. Bad numbers cause re-iteration of inadequate tasks to fix the problem. Wash up again and retest. Turns out the wipes were not useful – much more complex testing needed. When they started looking, they were overwhelmed by what they found – too much signal to determine root causes.

The coding process and thematic structure are outlined in Table 21.1. During the creation of the themes, the coding structures and the data were revisited again and again according to the questions and conclusions being drawn from the analysis, until internal consistency was obtained (Huberman & Miles, 1994).

First Theme: Complete Control

Blue Bell has always been privately held, and for most of its existence it grew slowly using an inkblot approach, spreading geographically only after the existing territories were saturated and a foothold of demand was present in the new territory. The company preferred in nearly all matters to establish and maintain operations internal to the hierarchical control of the firm, resulting in near-complete vertical integration.[3] Controlling a company is a natural and necessary component of management, but complete control is typically elusive; for example, the boundaries of the firm will usually be defined by a number of arms-length relationships based on economic efficiency. Not so much with Blue Bell. The firm does not allow others to manufacture its products, and it does not toll its manufacturing assets to other ice cream makers, as is common in the industry. Blue Bell distribution centers are strategically placed no further than 75 miles from points of retail sale; supermarkets outside those limits are simply not serviced. The centers act as intermediate freezer-inventory locations and are designed, built, owned, and operated by the firm, using only its own employees or Brenham-centered nested contractors. Freezer space is never shared with other firms, and Blue Bell never stores its product with other brands (again, common storage is prevalent in the industry). Similarly for distribution, Blue Bell uses its own trucks to supply local supermarkets and points of sale and never uses third-party delivery. This is a special source of pride

Table 21.1 Thematic Analysis and Coding[†]

Themes	Secondary coding/Memos*	Primary coding categories
Complete control	Blue Bell Creameries strategy	CEO succession – family, Howard Kruse
	Complete control	Facilities – assets
	Crisis and response	Growth plans
	Family succession	Industry profile
	Strategies for growth	Company history – Myth
	Symbols of control – distribution	
	Listeria science	Illness stories
		Industry stance on listeria
	Other company impacts	Jeni's ice cream
Stakeholder coupling	Institutional romance	A past together
	Firm going through radical change	Admiration of the other
	FDA as customer proxy	Professed fealty
	Root causes	Sadness at time apart
		Defense of honor
	Enactment of Myth in the Marketplace	Symbols of customer loyalty
	Blue Bell Creameries strategy	Moving forward – restarting production
		Public relations
	Changing regulatory environment	CDC technology
		DOJ action
	Listeria science	Illness stories
	Listeria wipes in the wrong places	Quality control
Frames for actor behaviors	Opinion and input	Paul Kruse statements
		Critical opinion – commentary
		Customer behavior
	Timeline	Blue Bell recall
	Time Frames are distorted	Layoffs
		Recovery efforts – current
		Years before
	Changing regulatory environment	FDA-CDC actions
		Root causes
		Prescribed actions

* Titles of memos are shown in italics in the second column and reflect elements of interpretation. Some secondary coding schemes were factual and did not require memos for interpretation of meaning.

† This table summarizes the construction of themes. First, primary coding categories were developed from the text material. These primary codes were then arranged axially for secondary coding and abstracted or interpreted for the creation of memos. These memos and abstractions were assembled as textual themes, as noted in the first column. The third noted theme ("Frames for Actor Behaviors") was not presented as a theme per se, as it had been assigned codes and memos that did not fit the other two themes; it was used primarily for analysis of individual actions and criticism of theory.

for the company, where the distribution trucks have become a symbol of continuation, firm values, and quality.

The need for complete control extends to dedicated partner businesses that supply Blue Bell with seasonal ice cream additives such as berries and candy (but they bake their own cookies for use in the ice cream). Blue Bell's distribution systems rely on pallets for raw and finished material shipments. Decades ago, management opted to move a pallet manufacturing company from Dallas to Brenham to make pallets only for Blue Bell, eventually folding these operations into the firm.[4] All of this is done in the name of quality, but as *Dairy Foods* (an industry trade publication) noted in 2005, this desire for control borders on compulsive:

> Blue Bell drivers ensure that the ice cream remains at a constant temperature throughout the process, eliminating the chance of heat shock. This allows Blue Bell to protect the integrity of the product so that the consumer can be assured of consistency and quality. At Brenham there is a company-owned shop for truck repair and maintenance and a dedicated shop for repair and maintenance of the fleet's refrigeration equipment. Blue Bell even applies its own truck decals. But then, what would you expect from a company that makes ice cream and builds pallets?

When they enter an area as a growth move, they buy or construct their own distribution freezers and import new trucks with seasoned driver-stockers. Such an initiative is led by existing staff members who are promoted up from within the organization. They never hire for experience, preferring to grow it organically. This is continually justified by the senior management as necessary to maintain quality, as "a home-grown employee knows Blue Bell's products and story inside and out."

Blue Bell never negotiates incentives with supermarkets or retail stores. If retailers do not like the proffered terms (openly available to each retailer), they are reminded of the competitive advantage to be gained by competing stores. This practice is recognized and respected by many retailers as more above-board than typical supply agreements, most of which are complex with payments moving in both directions, including payments by retailers for stocking. Blue Bell truck drivers are also its stockers, and they provide product at the same price for all of their customers and stock (usually on a daily basis) their products in cases separate from other brands. This creates a shopping experience whereby the customer sees Blue Bell ice cream as a (continually) featured product and the other brands in smaller quantities sharing a separate case together. For smaller sellers, Blue Bell will often supply on a handshake at the discretion of the truck driver. All are welcome to sell and serve Blue Bell as long as Blue Bell's business norms are followed and Blue Bell controls the customer experience.

All of this might suggest that the firm values its control of all relevant processes as a unique competency that supplies additional economic rents, but such an understanding assumes that securing these rents is the objective of the firm, and the evidence suggests this is not the case. The high degree of control at Blue Bell instead seems to involve control itself being the objective. If the asset or process is perceived as controllable, then it is controlled. Conversely, where control is not observed, one may deduce that the process has been considered by the owner-managers as not readily controllable. For example, product sampling for *listeria* was not done at all, as it was considered to be a needle-in-a-haystack approach. Interestingly, this lack of sampling was (and is) accepted as legitimate industry practice, and the FDA (still) does not require it. Says one industry expert, "People have sought to completely eradicate [*listeria*] from their facilities. I, for one, don't think that is possible… I really do believe it's in every operation, somewhere." Martin Wiedmann, professor of food science at Cornell University, takes this concept of ubiquitous *listeria* even further, suggesting there is nothing that can be done as "*listeria* will get into a plant no matter how well it's run." When state agencies brought evidence of *listeria* contamination to Blue Bell managers in February

2015, no immediate actions were taken by those managers as the occurrence of *listeria* in the product was simply seen as unimportant and uncontrollable.

Second Theme: Stakeholder Coupling

Coupled organizations or networks imply a connection or linkage of events and actions, such that one party's actions explain and/or determine the other's behavior (Meyer & Rowan, 1977; Weick, 1976). Beyond this connection, the degree of coupling also implies the degree of dependence or separateness of identity, in which tightly coupled systems are explicit, more or less fully determined, and mutually dependent (Danneels, 2003), while loosely coupled systems allow tacitness and impermanence in the relationship (Weick, 1976). This theme of stakeholder coupling brings insight to the decisions made by the firm during the event of 2015 and is discussed from two perspectives: (1) that of customers, who contributed to a mutually dependent, enacted system (tight coupling), and (2) that of non-customer stakeholders, who were deemed to be less salient to the firm (loose coupling).

Customer Tight-Coupling

Danneels (2003) discusses customer tight-coupling as an enacted relationship: one that leads to a "better understanding of customers' needs, closer tailoring of products and services, higher customer satisfaction, easier forecasting of demand, and closer relationships" (p. 560). Through positive feedback loops of identity creation based on product purchases, this tight-coupling results in strong, mutually dependent, determinative relationships, described by Prahalad and Ramaswamy (2004) as "co-creation of value." For Blue Bell, the enactment of ice cream purchases and consumption was found to enhance customer identity and loyalty, and as stressed in numerous company communications, Blue Bell highly values its customers and their loyalty. The contamination event highlighted this tightly coupled relationship between the firm and its customers. A loosely coupled customer base would have shrugged off the event, moved on to another brand, and perhaps held the company accountable for the contamination. Instead, the loyal customer base was found to support the firm and Kruse family control during the contamination event without the availability of the ice cream.

When the *listeria* contamination was first discovered to have caused death and illness, and the firm issued limited recalls, the media attention was slim (as it is with most product recalls) and barely noticed or acted on. As a result, when the full recall and halt to production was announced, customers were caught off-guard despite two months of coverage. All other news events became trivial, and runs were made on the local grocery stores to stock up on Blue Bell products before they were removed from the shelves. Almost immediately, a campaign was started to support Blue Bell in its time of need. Thousands of yard signs were distributed and displayed outside Texas homes for months with the Blue Bell company logo, and un-coordinated grass-roots customer networks shared Internet memes and Facebook posts in enthusiastic and emotional demonstrations of loyalty.

This support was not generated overnight but rather was the result of decades of courtship and social exchange along two major paths: territorial growth and R&D. In the 1960s and 1970s, when the firm was expanding into and beyond the Houston area, customers were encouraged to ask their grocers to stock Blue Bell, and requests for specific flavors were honored, if possible.[5] As the populace generally migrated from rural communities to the suburbs of large cities, former Brenham residents were directly engaged by the firm to frequent those stores that stocked Blue Bell products (MacInerney, 2007). Similarly, Blue Bell's R&D

efforts had been focused on seeking out new ice cream formulations to fit customer identities. For example, Blue Bell offered regional favorites such as *Banana Split* for New Orleans, *Pistachio-Almond* for El Paso, and *Black Walnut* for the Midwest. Said one customer, who had moved from Michigan to Texas much earlier:

> I tried Black Walnut and I just loved it as it reminded me of back in Detroit [60 years ago]… So I wrote to the company and said, "when I tasted that ice cream, I thought I'd died and gone to heaven…" It's always been the first thing I'll buy instead of other kinds of brands, and I eat it most every day.

Blue Bell customers were found to prefer the firm to the exclusion of others, and the product differentiation that tailored the firm's product directly to the customers' needs created a positive feedback loop – and a lens through which the firm interpreted its environment.

Loyal customers largely eschewed other ice cream brands and consumption while Blue Bell was out of the market during the summer of 2015. One widely circulated posting on social media summed up the loyal customer mindset:

> Let me break this down for Northerners who can't understand the tragedy of recent events: The Blue Bell recall doesn't mean we're down a brand of ice cream. We don't BUY other brands of ice cream. The Blue Bell recall means WE ARE OUT OF ICE CREAM.

These loyal behaviors stretched what might have been expected of rational (or even boundedly rational) customers, suggesting the behaviors did not represent a simple propensity for "looking the other way" whenever the firm engaged in misconduct (Barnett, 2014). Rather, they seem to have reflected identities that were very strongly tied to the company. Personal experiences of loss shared on social media further enhanced the tight-coupling, as customer identity was enhanced by the public displays of loyalty.

Under normal circumstances, these experiences would have resulted in ongoing "co-creation of value" (Prahalad & Ramaswamy, 2004), but the situation was complicated in the case of Blue Bell. In essence, the customer tight-coupling seems to have acted as a deterrent to needed changes in internal processes, as Blue Bell leadership was unwilling to disrupt the supply of ice cream to its loyal customer base, even with the knowledge of contamination problems. Such disruption would have been an unacceptable breach of faith.

In March 2015, one day after the firm learned of customer illnesses attributed to their products, it issued its first-ever product recall. Later in the same week, Paul Kruse released an official company apology but avoided mentioning those who had died or had been harmed by sickness. His irrational apology expressed regret only for the disruption in providing ice cream to the loyal customers, with promises to return as soon as possible. Regulatory agency warnings, *listeria* sampling results, and media coverage of the outbreak were of little consequence compared to maintenance of the tight-coupling with the customer base. The dramatic change in approach to the agencies from one of dismissal or disdain to one of agreement and cooperation came not because of overwhelming agency pressure or because management was caught doing something illegal, but because tight-coupling with customers was ultimately threatened.

Stakeholder Loose-Coupling

According to stakeholder theory (Barnett, 2014; Coff, 1999; Freeman, 2010), many stakeholders have a vested interest in the firm, contribute to its success, and share in its rewards according to their saliency, which is defined in terms of managerial perceptions of legitimacy, power, and urgency (Clement, 2005; Windsor, 2011). For a family firm such as Blue Bell, stakeholders include not only customers but also employees, government agencies, local communities, competitors, and the media (Zellweger & Nason, 2008). Scholars have generally advanced the view that stakeholders offer rewards and punishments to firms, thus conditioning firms to become good corporate citizens (Parmar et al., 2010). But beyond customers, this influence has been muted at Blue Bell, and perhaps inconsequential to firm strategy. Noncustomer stakeholders seem to have been only loosely coupled with Blue Bell strategic actions and appear to have been managed only to the point at which they were mollified in their expectations or needs (Meyer & Rowan, 1977). Loosely coupled systems are described by Weick (1976) as those relationships that are fluid in participation, with the outcomes and actions taken by the actors and organizations appearing as responsive to each other but preserving the identity and separateness of the individual entities. The coupling interactions between the entities revolve around events or patterns of behavior that create consistency in the relationship and re-establish lines of authority, but these events also prevent the growth of mutually dependent relationships and seldom result in shared outcomes. Weick's example of the university classroom as a loosely coupled system shows the students and professor tied together for a class, but each has separate goals, and they hold few objectives in common. Their identity and success are only slightly tied to each other, but each party is satisfied with their situation, and the work in the class enacts the tie without altering the parties.

During the contamination crisis, employees constituted the most significant loosely coupled stakeholder group, and they took the brunt of the consequences from the event. The day after the complete recall, the company announced with much fanfare that, "We haven't laid off anyone in 100 years, and we won't do it now." Employees were touted as a valuable human capital resource, much as they had been before the event; however, within three weeks, the firm announced every employee would be affected by a layoff, furlough, or pay cut. The employees had seen (and had been encouraged by management to see) the relationship as mutually dependent and permanent, but the contamination event exposed the loose coupling. This exposure resulted in individual and mass confusion on the part of the employees, resembling what Weick labeled "vu jàdé – the opposite of déjà vu: I've never been here before, I have no idea where I am, and I have no idea who can help me" (Weick, 1993, pp. 633–634). With large concentrations of employees in small, rural towns, most Blue Bell employees knew no other lines of work and had no other means for employment. One observer at a local church noted,

> Faith Mission immediately set up outreach programs to get in touch with those furloughed or out of work… many still stunned. One man had worked at Blue Bell since high school and had never missed a day, but he was laid off. (Said the charity director), "These are folks who are not breaking down the door looking for a handout. These are people who don't know how to do this."

Loyal customers irrationally supported this action, believing the contamination issue was blown out of proportion and that others were to be blamed instead of the management:

> Well, you know, it makes you sad to hear of people getting sick and dying, um, so that just makes you sad… I think our media is basically worthless… and portray just enough to um, to voice whatever um, bias. I'm sorry somebody died. I have a certain acceptance of life and death and risks of life… So I don't mean any of that to be callous. It's hard to

blame a company… Is it the management? Is it somebody who had a hot date who didn't run the right degree of, of whatever they were supposed to do to clean the lines? You know there are just so many factors, but I would come close to attributing it to human error than company issue. The company takes the heat. The humans that make up the, uh executive branch make the decisions… And when you have um, employees that need to be fired, you fire 'em.

Employees also appeared to suffer a lack of appropriation due to management decisions during the event. The latest available data (from 2004) showed employees owned roughly 40% of the firm. Their shares were diluted by the issuance of preferred shares to Sid Bass, a colorful oil tycoon, in return for $125M in emergency funding in the summer of 2015. His convertible preferred shares granted ownership of 33% of the firm but allowed the Kruse family to maintain control.

Other stakeholders also seem to have suffered due to their loosely coupled relationship with Blue Bell. Local community stakeholders had been quick to praise the largess of Blue Bell in its altruism and donations toward public infrastructure and charities, but Blue Bell was and is among the lowest paying firms in the dairy industry, and certainly among ice cream manufacturers. Thus, Blue Bell seems to have been burnishing the family image while at the same time making the community more reliant on its philanthropy. Despite the suffering in the community as a result of the event, Brenham residents continued to support the firm and its owners:

> People are tolerant of Blue Bell and the Kruse family because of the role both entities play in the community. "The owners are real people here and they give a lot of scholarships and things and they show up for everything. They've been in business for more than 100 years and people know they weren't planning on this happening," said (one local college student). Blue Bell believes in supporting communities but the company doesn't track how much money it donates each year. Kruse sponsors the church singing scholarship that helps (students) pay for college, and a lot of people have similar ties. In return, the company seems to get unquestioning loyalty. "It'll take five years, maybe, to get back to where they were, but it'll happen," said one furloughed employee.
>
> "I know Paul Kruse and I know he did his best," the owner of (a local hotel) says. (He) pulled the ice cream out of the little mini-fridges in each hotel room after the final recall, but ate the ice cream himself rather than throw it out.

The media stakeholder group also did not escape the implications of loose coupling, as Freedom of Information requests regarding the contamination event were needed at every turn to access public information regarding the contamination. As the event unfolded, very little communication came from the firm's management (and what did come was mostly focused on their customer base), and no interviews were given. These actions did not help relations with the media. Overall, events and patterns during 2015 upset loosely coupled ties between Blue Bell and multiple stakeholder groups, and dissonance was created by the chasm between expressed firm values (family, honesty, altruism) and actions (firings, lack of transparency).

Discussion

One of the advantages of an interpretive case study involves the completion of the hermeneutical circle (Geertz, 1972; Taylor, 1971): upon better understanding of the puzzling aspects of behavior, a research team can return to the "known" or "understood" aspects and specify needed changes to these previous understandings. Well-worn theories of family firm governance were used to frame the Blue Bell case but were found to be inadequate for explaining actions taken by the owner-managers. Having better understood these actions in the themes of complete control and stakeholder coupling, we now seek to: (1) contribute to existing theory, and (2) re-examine and theoretically reframe the contamination event in order to inform future research and practice.

Family Firm Governance and Stakeholder Management

In most existing family-firm research, conventional management theories are coupled with an assumption of socio-emotional goal-setting in order to understand firm governance, which creates a specific lens through which all owner-manager actions can be interpreted (Gomez-Mejia et al., 2011). Agency theory applied to family firms results in a view of owner-managers as perhaps less selfishly opportunistic but more limited in perspective as they pursue socio-emotional ends that can display as altruism (Gomez-Mejia et al., 2001). Similarly, stakeholder theorists suggest family firms create healthier and stronger stakeholder ties than nonfamily firms due to their long-range goals and connections to their communities (Le Breton-Miller & Miller, 2011). As part of that approach, family firms might take better care of their employees and form deeper relationships with their employees than do nonfamily firms (Miller, Lee, Chang, and Le Breton-Miller (2009). Each of these theoretical views is challenged and informed by our case study.

Our work suggests that the socio-emotional lens is insufficient for explaining difficult strategic situations in family firms and perhaps is better suited for describing more stable equilibrium conditions and periods of relative inaction. Behaviors at Blue Bell during the contamination event indicate that desires of owner-managers for complete control and for tight-coupling with select stakeholders can outweigh broader concerns, including altruism. While such control and tight coupling might not hinder a firm's ability to appear altruistic under benign conditions of equilibrium (e.g., Barnard's (1968) "zone of indifference"), they occasionally could extinguish such appearances as family firms are pulled away from equilibrium by crisis events. Relatedly, family firm managers appear to evaluate the saliency of stakeholders more critically than nonfamily firms, as the controlling owner-managers require fewer stakeholders to meet their goals. For Blue Bell, customers were found to be the only stakeholder group worthy of direct and tangible influence. On the other hand, Blue Bell owner-manager behaviors toward employees suggest that apparently close ties with employees were artifacts of equilibrium conditions and low stress. During periods of crisis or intense change, loosely coupled relationships tend to be revealed as ceremonial in substance (Meyer & Rowan, 1977), and less salient stakeholders are cut off, ignored, or even blamed for management shortcomings.

In essence, our work with the Blue Bell case suggests that owner-managers frame their decisions according to their view of power and control, and under pressure they take decisive action to preserve tightly coupled relationships while hoping to not overly damage loosely coupled ones. Tightly coupled relationships, such as Blue Bell had and still has with its customers, are relied upon for firm protection and resiliency under pressure. Loosely coupled relationships are maintained with ceremonial or symbolic actions that usually appear to be value-driven or altruistic, but under pressure the relationships are discounted further and often sacrificed.

The Contamination Event as a Normal Accident

The preceding interpretations of Blue Bell's situation and actions seem credible, but there is another set of ideas to consider with regards to the underlying cause of the crisis. In this next section, we engage our themes with normal accident theory in order to obtain further insights into the driving forces for the crisis and to theorize on how complete control and stakeholder coupling suggest concepts for crisis mitigation and prevention.

Blue Bell's *listeria* problem can be seen as a system-wide failure of the entire organization that manifested in many aspects, such as management, employees, manufacturing, and quality control (Reason, 1990). This is related to what Farjoun and Starbuck (2007) in their discussion of the Columbia disaster call "an organization exceeding its limits." To examine an organizational system-wide failure that occurred under "normal" conditions, we look to normal accident theory as a guiding framework (Perrow, 1984). According to normal accident theory, accidents in some systems are inevitable, with traditional organizational improvements and technological innovations not being sufficient to prevent them (Rijpma, 1997). In addition, human interactions and interventions are largely ineffective when "warnings are ignored (and) unnecessary risks taken," both of which can be compounded by "sloppy work done, deception and downright lying" (Perrow, 1984, p. 10). From an organizational perspective, any fixes and repairs put in place might not be sufficient to prevent catastrophes if they do not fundamentally address the interactive complexity and internal tight coupling that are inherent in high-risk organizational systems.

The *listeria* contamination event at Blue Bell seems to meet the definition of a systems failure or "normal accident," but the pertinent theory must be cautiously applied to the failure of quality management systems in the low-technology field of ice cream manufacturing, given the more typical applications to failures of high-technology control systems (e.g., nuclear reactors, spacecraft). There is nothing inherently complex in the production, shipment, or consumption of ice cream that suggests an imminent risk is present; however, the biology involved with ice cream contamination is very complex, and this can lead to actions, events, or factors interacting in unexpected ways. There are no known ways to prevent *listeria* contamination in ice cream aside from preparatory cleaning and follow-up testing for effectiveness. Contamination cannot be removed from the ice cream product after the fact, such as pasteurization does for milk. As explained earlier, freezing temperatures preserve existing conditions, nothing more. *Listeria* thrives in the cold, damp environment of an ice cream process, and once established, it is exceptionally difficult to remove from equipment and facilities (CDC, 2015; Finkel, 2015; Murphy, 2015). Understanding how and where *listeria* may be growing is almost impossible, so managers and employees must assume it may grow anywhere and not focus cleaning activities solely on process surfaces. The FDA report (2015) states *listeria* was found nearly everywhere at the Blue Bell plants, including the floor drains and deep inside process machinery.

The tight-coupling among internal system elements that might lead to a normal accident describes a situation in which there is no space between cause and effect for intervention. Blue Bell took great pains not only to include the fresh seasonal ingredients desired by customers but to get the ice cream to the customer as quickly as possible. Company literature often bragged that their product was "so fresh it was grass only yesterday." Little to no contamination testing of ingredients was done, and little intermediate inventory was maintained. The untested final product was palletized and shipped as soon as it was frozen for the purposes of maintaining the highest quality. The inherent problem with *listeria* does not manifest in the manufacture of the product or in the customers use of the product; it manifests *inside* the customer, typically impacting only the sick or infirm. There was no effort made to test the final product for contamination (this was beyond control), and sampling protocol required days to report findings, with results being available about the time customers were consuming the product. In this way, any product contamination resulting from unclean process equipment would be "instantly" transmitted to customers. Any risks taken by the firm with regard to product contamination were instantly transferred into consequences felt by the customers. The conditions required for a normal accident were met.

Perrow (1984) proposed that, given the interactive complexity and coupling of many critical systems, normal accidents were unavoidable. Many scholars object to this idea (Le Coze, 2015; Weick & Sutcliffe, 2001; Wolf & Sampson, 2007), but they do not disagree with Perrow's general assertion that tight systems coupling can advance small issues into potential disasters. Le Coze (2015) analyzed 30 years of normal accidents and found that disasters are "just waiting to happen," mostly due to extreme production pressures, and this is consistent with the Blue Bell story. As Blue Bell grew its operations continually for decades, the evidence of production pressures can be seen as increasingly pronounced. Over the past 13 years, Blue Bell more than doubled its production and number of product offerings without adding any additional production facilities. In 2005, the Blue Bell VP for Operations (then Gene Supak) stated the following: "We don't run around the clock. We shoot for about 12 hours maximum… we want our employees to have quality time at home too." By 2015, many of the facilities had converted to 24-hour operations, and this led to extraordinary pressures on production:

> One machine in Brenham was running virtually 24-7, employees said. That made it hard to clean. "It was run, run, run," said one worker, who understood that the plant had to keep churning. "But if something's not working right, take the time to fix it." There was one hot water source for washup, and the heat went to whoever started cleaning first. "If it ran out, it ran out," he said. "It became a race for time.".… If their lines processed all of their mix early, supervisors would instruct them to add additional mix and produce more, even if it delayed wash-up.

These production pressures led to employee complaints, but these complaints eventually stopped as they were regularly ignored. Additionally, as Blue Bell increased the number of flavors and products (many of them seasonal), the complexity of the processes increased as well, requiring more frequent product line changes and faster wash-ups. In their discussion of a failure in the control system of a moving company, Cardinal, Sitkin, and Long (2004) similarly found that extreme production pressure and additional complexity pushed the organization to exceed its limits, nearly resulting in firm collapse. The constant pressure on production at Blue Bell can be seen to foster a climate that discounted findings of contamination and accelerated consequences, thus increasing the likelihood for the normal accident of product contamination.

Conclusions and Recommendations

Our case study provides a close examination of a family firm as it experienced a crisis, and the findings from the study challenge conventional wisdom and theories regarding family firms. Because of the privacy afforded to private firms (often owned by families) and the lack of easy-to-obtain data, scholars are less likely to engage in empirical studies of family firms in the U.S.A. Our findings, however, suggest there is a rich landscape to explore at the junction of family control and modern firm management. To complement recent theoretical attention, topics such as governance, decision-making, and risk-taking in family firms deserve more empirical attention as well.

Turning directly to matters of practice and application, there are several noteworthy implications of our work. As food contamination data and regulatory processes have become more reliable and precise (CDC, 2015), food-borne illnesses have become easier to detect and trace. With better data being available and with food supply networks becoming more interdependent than ever before, companies, trade groups, and regulators must gain a better understanding of these complex networks. At the same time, additional safeguards are needed to protect companies. Consider the following: in a small recall event for Blue Bell in 2016 (after improvements and sampling protocols were put in place), a few batches of Chocolate Chip Cookie-Dough ice cream were pulled back before customer exposure to *listeria*, demonstrating a loosening of coupling mechanisms. This permitted an internal root-cause investigation that revealed the *listeria* contamination originated with previously non-sampled inventories of raw cookie dough. New testing procedures, however, are too frequently resulting in false-positive tests during the test-and-hold procedure. After one year under the new quality plan, Blue Bell has had to destroy several million dollars' worth of product on the basis of positive screening results for *listeria* that were later disconfirmed. Following the pharmaceutical and chemical manufacturing industries, better and more reliable quality assurance protocols are needed for food manufacturers.

Notes

1   The CDC and the U.S. Food and Drug Administration (FDA) are not authorized to close facilities due to food contamination. They must publicize any problems and inform the public of risks. The authority to close facilities resides with the states.
2   At the time of this writing, no charges have been pressed, and the inquiry is ongoing.
3   Blue Bell does not own the product supply (cows, milk, additives), but it sources only from local, dedicated dairies and co-ops. This is the only observed instance of production-based alliances or partnerships for the firm; all other aspects are completely firm controlled.
4   Interestingly, the root cause investigation that followed the contamination event found pallets to be among the most contaminated assets, as they were re-used until failure. Their wood was a perfectly (slightly) porous texture for culture growth, and they passed through several quality control points in the plant uninspected.
5   Blue Bell typically manufactures 60–80 different flavors in a given year from a menu of over 200.

References

Apple, R. W. (2006, 5-31-2006). Making Texas cows proud. *New York Times*. Retrieved from http://www.nytimes.com/2006/05/31/dining/31blue.html?_r=0&ei=5088&en=b7553f0857e63d71&ex=1306728000&partner=rssnyt&emc=rss&pagewanted=all

Bansal, P., & Corley, K. G. (2011). The coming of age for qualitative research: Embracing the diversity of qualitative methods. *Academy of Management Journal, 54*(2), 233–237. doi:10.5465/amj.2011.60262792

Barnard, C. I. (1968). *The functions of the executive*. Cambridge, MA: Harvard university press.

Barnett, M. L. (2014). Why stakeholders ignore firm misconduct: A cognitive view. *Journal of Management, 40*(3), 676–702. doi:10.1177/0149206311433854

Berle, A. A., & Means, G. C. (1991). *The modern corporation and private property*. New Brunswick, NJ: Transaction Publishers.

Bettis, R. A., Gambardella, A., Helfat, C., & Mitchell, W. (2015). Qualitative empirical research in strategic management. *Strategic Management Journal, 36*(5), 637–639. doi:10.1002/smj.2317

Boyd, B. K., & Solarino, A. M. (2016). Ownership of corporations: A review, synthesis, and research agenda. *Journal of Management, 42*(5), 1282–1314. doi:10.1177/0149206316633746

Braun, V., & Clarke, V. (2006). Using thematic analysis in psychology. *Qualitative Research in Psychology, 3*(2), 77–101. doi:10.1191/1478088706qp063oa

Cardinal, L. B., Sitkin, S. B., & Long, C. P. (2004). Balancing and rebalancing in the creation and Evolution of organizational control. *Organization Science, 15*(4), 411–431. doi:10.1287/orsc.1040.0084

Carper, J. (2015). Blue bell blossoms across the nation. *Dairy Foods,* 42–46.

CDC (Ed.) (2015). *Multistate outbreak of listeriosis linked to blue bell (Final Update).* Center for Disease Control and Prevention.

Chrisman, J. J., Chua, J. H., & Steier, L. P. (2011). Resilience of family firms: An introduction. *Entrepreneurship Theory and Practice, 35*(6), 1107–1119. doi:10.1111/j.1540-6520.2011.00493.x

Chrisman, J. J., & Patel, P. C. (2011). Variations in R&D investments of family and nonfamily firms: Behavioral agency and myopic loss aversion perspectives. *Academy of Management Journal, 55*(4), 976–997. doi:10.5465/amj.2011.0211

Chua, J. H., Chrisman, J. J., & Bergiel, E. B. (2009). An agency theoretic analysis of the professionalized family firm. *Entrepreneurship Theory and Practice, 33*(2), 355–372. doi:10.1111/j.1540-6520.2009.00294.x

Clement, R. W. (2005). The lessons from stakeholder theory for U.S. business leaders. *Business Horizons, 48*(3), 255–264. doi:10.1016/j.bushor.2004.11.003

Coff, R. W. (1999). When competitive advantage doesn't lead to performance: The resource-based view and stakeholder bargaining power. *Organization Science, 10*(2), 119–133. doi:10.1287/orsc.10.2.119

Collette, M. (2015a, 7-19-2015). Blue Bell contamination exposes public health flaw. *Houston Chronicle.*

Collette, M. (2015b, 5-7-2015). Blue Bell knew about listeria contamination, feds say. *Houston Chronicle.*

Collette, M. (2015c, 6-21-2015). Blue Bell, industry, flout listeria guidelines. *Houston Chronicle.*

Cruz, C. C., Gomez-Mejia, L. R., & Becerra, M. (2010). Perceptions of benevolence and the design of agency contracts: CEO-TMT relationships in family firms. *Academy of Management Journal, 53*(1), 69–89.

Cyert, R. M., & March, J. G. (1963). *A behavioral theory of the firm.* Englewood Cliffs, NJ: Prentice-Hall.

Danneels, E. (2003). Tight-loose coupling with customers: The enactment of customer orientation. *Strategic Management Journal, 24*(6), 559–576. doi:10.1002/smj.319

Dawson, A., & Hjorth, D. (2012). Advancing family business research through narrative analysis. *Family Business Review, 25*(3), 339–355. doi:10.1177/0894486511421487

Eisenhardt, K. M. (1989). Building theories from case study research. *Academy of Management Review, 14*(4), 532–550.

Eisenhardt, K. M., Graebner, M. E., & Sonenshein, S. (2016). Grand challenges and inductive methods: Rigor without rigor mortis. *Academy of Management Journal, 59*(4), 1113–1123. doi:10.5465/amj.2016.4004

Farjoun, M., & Starbuck, W. H. (2007). Organizing at and beyond the limits. *Organization Studies, 28*(4), 541–566. doi:10.1177/0170840607076584

Farquhar, J. D. (2012). *Case study research for business.* Thousand Oaks, CA: Sage.

FDA. (2015). FDA Investigates literia monocytogenes in ice cream products from Blue Bell creameries. Retrieved from www.fda.gov

Finkel, E. (2015). Respond to listeria threat with GMPs, vigilance. *Dairy Foods,* 12–15.

Freeman, R. E. (2010). *Strategic management: A stakeholder approach.* New York: Cambridge University Press.

Geertz, C. (1972). Deep play: Notes on the Balinese cockfight. *Daedalus, 101*(1), 1–37.

Gomez-Mejia, L. R., Cruz, C., Berrone, P., & De Castro, J. (2011). The bind that ties: Socioemotional wealth preservation in family firms. *The Academy of Management Annals, 5*(1), 653–707. doi:10.1080/19416520.2011.593320

Gomez-Mejia, L. R., Haynes, K. T., Nunez-Nickel, M., Jacobson, K. J., & Moyano-Fuentes, J. (2007). Socioemotional wealth and business risks in family-controlled firms: Evidence from Spanish olive oil mills. *Administrative Science Quarterly, 52*(1), 106–137.

Gomez-Mejia, L. R., Nunez-Nickel, M., & Gutierrez, I. (2001). The role of family ties in agency contracts. *Academy of Management Journal, 44*(1), 81–95. doi:10.2307/3069338

Huberman, A. M., & Miles, M. B. (1994). Data management and analysis methods. In N. K. Denzin & Y. S. Lincoln (Eds.), *Handbook of qualitative research* (pp. 428–444). Thousand Oaks, CA: Sage.

Jensen, M. C., & Meckling, W. H. (1976). Theory of the firm: Managerial behavior, agency costs and ownership structure. *Journal of Financial Economics, 3*(4), 305–360. doi:10.1016/0304-405x(76)90026-x

Kruse, P. (2004). Change a la mode. *Baylor Business Review, 22*(1), 18–23.

La Porta, R., Lopez-De-Silanes, F., & Shleifer, A. (1999). Corporate ownership around the world. *The Journal of Finance, 54*(2), 471–517. doi:10.1111/0022-1082.00115

Le Breton-Miller, I., & Miller, D. (2011). Commentary: Family firms and the advantage of multitemporality. *Entrepreneurship Theory and Practice, 35*(6), 1171–1177. doi:10.1111/j.1540-6520.2011.00496.x

Le Coze, J.-C. (2015). 1984–2014. Normal accidents. Was Charles Perrow right for the wrong reasons? *Journal of Contingencies and Crisis Management, 23*(4), 275–286. doi:10.1111/1468-5973.12090

MacInerney, D. M. (2007). *Blue bell ice cream: A century at the little creamery in Brenham, Texas, 1907–2007.* Austin, TX: TM Custom Publishing.

MarketLine. (2014). Ice cream in the United States. *MarketLine industry profile* (October 2014 ed.): MarketLine.

Meyer, J. W., & Rowan, B. (1977). Institutionalized organizations: Formal structure as myth and ceremony. *American Journal of Sociology, 83*(2), 340–363.

Miller, D., Lee, J., Chang, S., & Le Breton-Miller, I. (2009). Filling the institutional void: The social behavior and performance of family vs non-family technology firms in emerging markets. *Journal of International Business Studies, 40*(5), 802–817. doi:10.1057/jibs.2009.11

Murphy, K. (Ed.) (2015). The New York times. 5-9-2015.

Parmar, B. L., Freeman, R. E., Harrison, J. S., Wicks, A. C., Purnell, L., & de Colle, S. (2010). Stakeholder theory: The state of the art. *The Academy of Management Annals, 4*(1), 403–445. doi:10.1080/19416520.2010.495581

Perrow, C. (1984). *Normal accidents: Living with high risk technologies.* New York: Basic Books, Inc.

Prahalad, C. K., & Ramaswamy, V. (2004). *The future of competition: Co-creating unique value with customers.* Boston, MA: Harvard Business School Press.

Reason, J. (1990). *Human error.* New York: Cambridge University Press.

Rijpma, J. A. (1997). Complexity, tight-coupling and reliability: Connecting normal accidents theory and high reliability theory. *Journal of Contingencies and Crisis Management, 5*(1), 15–23. doi:10.1111/1468–5973.00033

Schulze, W. S., Lubatkin, M. H., Dino, R. N., & Buchholtz, A. K. (2001). Agency relationships in family firms: Theory and evidence. *Organization Science, 12*(2), 99–116. doi:10.1287/orsc.12.2.99.10114

Siggelkow, N. (2007). Persuasion with case studies. *Academy of Management Journal, 50*(1), 20–24. doi:10.5465/amj.2007.24160882

Swartz, M. (2015). Rocky road. *Texas Monthly, 43*(6), 100–103, 186–187.

Taylor, C. (1971). Interpretation and the sciences of man. *The review of metaphysics, 25*(1), 3–51.

Verbeke, A., & Kano, L. (2010). Transaction cost economics (TCE) and the family firm. *Entrepreneurship Theory and Practice, 34*(6), 1173–1182. doi:10.1111/j.1540–6520.2010.00419.x

Wadham, H., & Warren, R. C. (2013). Telling organizational tales: The extended case method in practice. *Organizational Research Methods, 17*(1), 5–22. doi:10.1177/1094428113513619

Weick, K. E. (1976). Educational organizations as loosely coupled systems. *Administrative Science Quarterly, 21*(1), 1. doi:10.2307/2391875

Weick, K. E. (1979). *The social psychology of organizing.* New York: Random House.

Weick, K. E. (1993). The collapse of sensemaking in organizations: The Mann Gulch disaster. *Administrative Science Quarterly, 38*(4), 628–652. doi:10.2307/2393339

Weick, K. E., & Sutcliffe, K. (2001). *Managing the unexpected: Assuring high performance in an age of complexity.* San Francisco, CA: Jossey-Bass.

Westrum, R. (1978). Science and social intelligence about anomalies: The case of meteorites. *Social Studies of Science, 8*(4), 461–493. doi:10.1177/030631277800800403

Williamson, O. E. (1991). Strategizing, economizing, and economic organization. *Strategic Management Journal, 12*(S2), 75–94. doi:10.1002/smj.4250121007

Windsor, D. (2011). The role of dynamics in stakeholder thinking. *Journal of Business Ethics, 96*(S1), 79–87. doi:10.1007/s10551-011-0937-3

Wolf, F., & Sampson, P. (2007). Evidence of an interaction involving complexity and coupling as predicted by normal accident theory. *Journal of Contingencies and Crisis Management, 15*(3), 123–133. doi:10.1111/j.1468–5973.2007.00514.x

Wowak, A. J., Mannor, M. J., & Wowak, K. D. (2015). Throwing caution to the wind: The effect of CEO stock option pay on the incidence of product safety problems. *Strategic Management Journal, 36*(7), 1082–1092. doi:10.1002/smj.2277

Yin, R. K. (2014). *Case study research: Design and methods* (5th Ed.). Thousand Oaks, CA: Sage.

Zellweger, T. M., & Nason, R. S. (2008). A stakeholder perspective on family firm performance. *Family Business Review, 21*(3), 203–216. doi:10.1177/08944865080210030103

Zellweger, T. M., Nason, R. S., Nordqvist, M., & Brush, C. G. (2013). Why do family firms strive for nonfinancial goals? An organizational identity perspective. *Entrepreneurship Theory and Practice, 37*(2), 229–248. doi:10.1111/j.1540–6520.2011.00466.x

22

RISKY DOUBLE-SPIRAL SENSEMAKING OF ACADEMIC CAPITALISM

David M. Boje

Introduction

How *can Deleuzian-Double-Spiral-Antenarrative Theory be used to understand–and to mitigate– recurring crisis facing the public university*? Public universities, worldwide, are in a downward spiral, without a countervailing upward spiral to keep them from descending into the abyss of abandoned projects.

This is an autoethnography of my own situation. My brain is like *Velcro* to the negative news coming out day after day about downsizing the university, increasing workloads, complying with more surveillance routines, more reports on my every action. These changes are accelerating. It's difficult to forget how privileged I am: white, male, tenured, had most awards at my university, including regents professorship. I wonder, will our department be fodder for the next round of downsizing. Will I be pushed aside, so cheaper and younger contract-faculty can be hired? At my university, tenured professors have been released. "The Las Cruces campus will lose 126 positions—89 that are vacant and 37 that are filled—and engineering surveying and the equestrian team are planned for elimination" (Willis, 2016). My response to all this has been to write about it (Hillon & Boje, 2017; Boje, Hillon, & Mele, 2017).

I have noticed the more I resist and rebel against the downward spiral of the downsizing, the more it seems to get worse for me. I need to be able to, in the eye of the storm, watch the reorganizing pass without becoming fearful, anxious, or worried. I keep waiting for the storm to pass, and reach a calm and peaceful state of mind.

I am experiencing reverberations at my own university, which I interpret as "TamaraLand" institutional theater (Schneider, 2017; Boje, 1995; Hitchin, 2014). In TamaraLand, many actors are telling stories simultaneously in different rooms, and moving between rooms, in acts of moving sensemaking. My performances moving between rooms at my university replay and counter conditions of subjugation to academic capitalism that is radically transforming many public universities around the world into the neoliberal image of public education driven by market forces.

My theoretical approach is to extend sensemaking with a Deleuzian-double-spiral to make sense of recurring crises facing the public university, in monstrous admixtures of difference and repetition. The financial crisis of 2008 was not our first one. When I arrived at this university in 1996, there was a financial crisis through 1998, then another in the 2008 mortgage crisis, and now the 2016 crisis that continues to escalate. What is interesting, the powers that be, those strategic central administration planners, in all three crises, decided to merge our management department with marketing, and each time, threatened to put the Ph.D. student program on the chopping block (or under close scrutiny or suspended funding of assistantships till further notice, and so on).

In Part 1 of the chapter, I introduce double-spiral antenarrative theory. In Part 2, I apply the theory to the situation of risk to universities of current neoliberal ideology and the practices of downsizing happening worldwide to most public universities. In Part 3, I examine some alternatives to downsizing and reengineering university academic capitalism processes.

Part 1: Deleuzian-Double-Spiral Antenarrative Theory

I will begin with a basic discussion of retrospective sensemaking, drawing on Weick and on Gephart, and key concepts in this tradition. I will then introduce the concept of antenarratives from my own work, and explain what antenarrative theory is, and how it works and principally differs from/adds to retrospective sensemaking. And then when that is laid out, I will add the additional complexity of spiraling multiplicity.

Retrospective Sensemaking: Weick (1995: 14, 588) argues that sensemaking is an invention process that precedes the interpretation process of giving retrospective accounts of past events and actions meaning to the collective audience. I will assert that more is going on in sensemaking than Weick's (1995: 5) process of environmental scanning, interpretation, and responses. In the "retrospective sensemaking" of events, sudden interruptions or crises to the day-to-day trigger sensemaking and a change in cognition, because the expected event did not occur. This leads to further sensemaking. There is a creation of ideological meaning, ways of framing the crisis, and the necessary responses, as the only possible responses. This, I argue, occurs by staging a crisis inquiry that does not have the kind of wide participation and accountability that one expects of public institutions.

"Sensemaking thus involves constructing features of the world that then become available to perception" (Gephart, 1997: 588, 2007: 124). Crisis is defined by Robert Gephart (2007: 125) as, "a major, unpredictable event that may produce negative outcomes including substantial damage to an organization and its employees." Our universities, our schools of business, are in unpredictable crises resulting in risk of substantial negative outcomes, that is damage to higher education and its faculty, staff, and students. Following Gephart (2007: 123), I contend that sensemaking about the latest financial crisis of a university and its colleges is an important feature of inquiry discourse and documents (such as master plan, AACSB reaccreditation, minutes of meetings). I ask, why such an inquiry is not taking place, and why input becomes simulacra, rituals of sense, after the fact? Gephart defines sensemaking as a process by which people construct sense out of shared meaning for society and its key institutions (Gephart, 1993: 1469, 2007: 123). Some of this is simulacrum.

Antenarrative Theory: Antenarrative as a kind of sensemaking began with a double meaning: *before* narrative (first meaning of antenarrative) and what are *bets on the future* (second meaning of antenarrative) (Boje, 2001). Two additional meanings of antenarrative were devised after the antenarrative handbook (Boje, 2011). The of *between* living story relations and dominant narratives (third meaning) and finally the *beneath* in deeper structures of conception and context (fourth meaning) (Boje, 2014; Boje, Haley & Saylors, 2016). Together these three realms of storytelling are mixtures of regimes of signs and nonsense that have pragmatic importance.

For most of its history, organizational sensemaking has been looking retrospectively backward upon experience, unable to make prospective sensemaking bets on the future (i.e. antes). Retrospective sensemaking narratives (Weick, 1995; Czarniawska, 1997, 1998, 2004) have been unwilling, until quite recently, to address antenarrative notions. The exception is Weick (2012: 145): "This is a minimalist account of organizing, which, minimal though it is, includes story (in Boje's sense of antenarrative), ordering, action, sensemaking, and stabilizing, in the context of the impermanent and the temporary."

I would like to develop a more ontological understanding of prospective sensemaking processes with antenarrative. As Weick (2012: 145) puts it, "To talk about antenarrative as a bet is also to invoke an important structure in sensemaking; namely, the presumption of logic." Weick (2012: 145) continues,

> Antenarratives set up a similar dynamic. The transition from story to narrative is fostered by the belief that the fragments will have made sense although at the moment that is little more than a promise.

Spiraling Multiplicity: My main thesis is that Deleuzian spirals are antenarratives radically different from Weickian retrospective sensemaking. Further, the two kinds of sensemaking (retrospective and prospective) are mixing together. Besides retrospective narrative sensemaking, Deleuze adds a focus on multiplicity that spirals. In antenarrative theory, there is a forecaring for the future, that happens as a process before narrative coherence, and involves making "bets" or "antes" on the future, bringing one potential future into being, rather than multitude of potential futures that could be cultivated and attended to (Boje, 2001; Boje, Svane, & Gergerich, in press).

Semiotic Systems: Storytelling is theorized here as a semiotic system (Deleuze & Guattari, 1987: 111). Storytelling semiotic systems have forms of content that are inseparable and at the same time independent of forms of expression (linguistic, body language, dramaturgical, graphical, numeric interpretation, sociomaterial, and so forth). This "storytelling semiotic system" (see Figure 22.1) is dynamic diversity of mixing formalized narrative (and counternarrative), living story webs (of one story resulting in telling another, and more after), and antenarrative processes of forecaring (forehaving, foreconception, forestructuring, and foresight) (Boje, 2014; Boje, Haley, & Saylors, 2016; Boje, Svane, Henderson, & Strevel, in press; Boje, Svane, & Gergerich, in press). There are different dramatizations, immanence enunciations, and repetition regimes in these "triadic storytelling semiotic systems."

Crisis leadership initiated post-crisis consultancy, setting up task forces, and enacting changes in the budget and personnel assignments. The triggering event of this financial crisis was a drop in the gas and oil prices, resulting in a dip in revenues to the state, which, a decade earlier, made gas and oil severance taxes (collections from extraction) the major source of funding of K–12 and higher education in the state. Here, I will apply four key factors that define crises (adapted by Gephart, 2007: 125–126):

1 What type of crisis is this?
2 What are the signals of the crisis?
3 What crisis systems and organizational structures get implemented?
4 Who are the crises stakeholders, including groups and institutions affected by crisis?

What type of crisis is this? It is more than the most recent of a long line of financial crises. The crisis leadership was initiated to do budget (pre-crisis) audits of the university before the

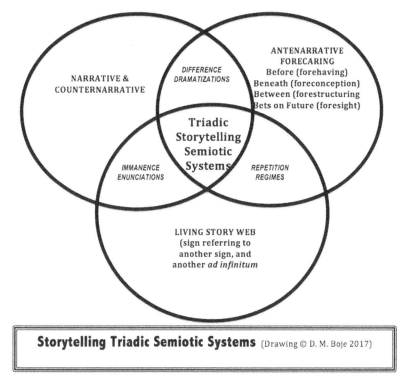

Figure 22.1 Storytelling Triadic Semiotic Systems

legislature finalized its state budget for higher education. The budgets were reassessed during the latest crisis, which as yet has not ended.

It is about ways neoliberal ideology has seeped into the administrative order of the university, as a phantasm of madness, a monster arising from the deep abyss. Can I remain calm in this storm, finding contentment in my teaching, my writing, and so on? I began to study how the public university is changing and transforming, and critiquing our university strategy of downsizing and reengineering (Hillon & Boje, 2017; Boje, Hillon, & Mele, 2017).

The storytelling semiotic systems is a triadic of three sign regimes (narratives and counternarratives, living story webs, antenarratives of forecaring in advance). I will provide an example.

Narrative and Counternarrative: A narrative we are told repeatedly is "there is no alternative" (TINA is its abbreviation). As estimates of economic downturn emerged, what I will call the "*TINA* narrative" became constructed. In the TINA narrative, there is no alternative but to cut back on faculty, graduate student, and staff positions, freeze hiring of any replacements, and engage in the kinds of business process reengineering (BPR) the Deloitte consultants recommended to the administration. This included forming six task forces to reorganize the university, cut positions, combine units or departments with fewer remaining positions, so as to save money on department/unit heads and eliminate redundant administrative assistant (and secretarial and work study) positions.

There is a strong and widespread TINA narrative, our New Mexico discussion of the necessity of implementing neoliberal idea systems and policies, to respond to the New Mexico drop in oil and gas prices. In the state of New Mexico, gas and oil prices have fallen. Since the severance tax from gas and oil is what funds K–12 and university education, when prices fall, there is no money left to fund education. The counternarrative is that a decade ago the state legislature did change the foundation of education from other sorts of taxes to just severance taxes. The triggering events (drop in gas and oil severance tax base, governor's vetoes of the higher education budget, and so on) became a pretext for university administration (board of regents, chancellor, provost, VPs) to make preemptive moves.

The problem with the assumption is that the private market (e.g. oil and gas) cannot support the legislative revenue needs for K–12 or higher education. The policy change to put New Mexico on just the oil and gas revenue standard was implemented by the legislature, under former Governor Richardson. The result is at NMSU, all colleges and administrative units are making budget cuts between 5% and 6.2%, and eliminating jobs (and benefits), outsourcing programs (e.g. Health Center outsourced to Memorial Medical Hospital), and defunding programs (e.g. Equestrian program) to cover the shortfall.

Our current round of downsizing and reorganization after financial crisis has everything to do with neoliberal significations and enunciations of common sense. The basic idea of neoliberalism ideology is to let "free market" economic have material consequence, forcing a downsizing of the funding of K–12 and higher education (i.e. public universities in New Mexico, in Illinois, and nationally, and moving globally). Such neoliberalism "free market" ideas are being used in the state of New Mexico to justify budget cuts to its public universities.

The counternarrative is the legislature could change its tax policy to other revenues. Another counternarrative is states such as Alaska and Texas have rainy day funds, collected during boom years, and set aside for leaner years.

Living Story Webwork: I experience and make sense of my own living story of the situation. And each living story has its place, its time, and what Kaylynn Twotrees (1997) calls the "mind" of the living story. The "mind" here refers to the communal or tribal context, to a web work of living stories. A living story is never alone, always referring to more than one. A sign referring to another sign *ad infinitum*. We are half the faculty size we were a decade ago (from 14 to now 7). The college responded by increasing the workload of the tenured faculty by one extra course. Courses that I have taught, about once a year, for 20 years, have been decommissioned. We are no longer recruiting doctoral candidates, since the university has no funds now, but perhaps in 2019, it will. In the interplay between the TINA narrative (and counternarratives) and my own living story, I don't accept that there are no alternatives. I also seek to disclose what is behind all the destruction of the public university. I also participated in marches and wrote blogs (Boje blog, 2017).

Difference Dramatizations: I joined and led some dramatizations of the differences. On one occasion, I held a wake for the doctoral program in my department, and invited current faculty, students, and alumni to attend. The dean was less than pleased, and at a specially called meeting, I was blamed for a doctoral student not getting a job. The faculty of the hiring university heard that the doctoral program had ceased to be funded in two departments of our college. I think, it's more likely someone read the department's website and drew their own conclusion: "We are no longer accepting applications for Fall 2018 admissions" (Management Department, 2017).

Antenarrative Process: Antenarrative processes are before-narrative (and story) form, below in pre-conceptions, between living stories and narrative, and bets made on potential futures to bring into being, while letting other wane. And some of these are spirals, others more rhizomatic. One of the antenarrative processes is called "starving the beast" (Wexler, 2016). Neoliberalism politicians wanted to "starve the beast" lowering taxes in time period one, so when the beast is starving in budget deficit in time period two, then force it to cut spending and into downsizing of faculty and staff and programs in time period three. It's an intentional process to starve the University-Beast, force it into budget deficit, and then declare gross performance deficits. This justifies more academic capitalism (Slaughter & Leslie, 1997).

Repetition Regimes: Antenarratives exhibit in the presignifying semiotic regimes in acts of forecaring that both deterritorialize and territorialize and reterritorialize in advance preparations to downsize the number of faculty and staff, while increasing the administrative order and the technical automation (digital measures, online curriculum, outcomes assessment technologies).

Part 2: Deleuzian Double-Spirals of Academic Capitalism

Here, I develop how not only retrospective sensemaking narratives but also prospective sensemaking "antenarratives" before-narratives, beneath, and between narratives, and living stories play a role in the crisis-management process. I will review key features of public documents sent around by administrators, and others posted on websites, to account for crisis-team deliberations (see online documents at https://transforming.nmsu.edu/team-6/). There are many untold stories, many fragments and snippets of antenarrative sense-nonsense circulating in the crisis. This relation between retrospective and prospective sensemaking, and the ways of centralized control over participation to control and administer, steer, and shape the official narrative.

Narratives (and counternarratives) are paradigmatic-signifying semiotic regimes of the state (by defunding much of it), its governor, university regents, and media in a deterritorialization of higher education. There are *countersignifying semantic regimes* of how syntagmatic-numbers (measures, metrics, rankings) are used as enunciation expression by war machine to effect actual destruction and abolition of university disciplines and functions in that manner of deterritorialization in numbers games. There is a postsignifying semiotic regime of redundancy of consciousness, a kind of subjectification of storytelling enunciation (narrative) in passional lines of organization of power, a deterritorialization to absolute negation.

Many regimes of signs co-constellate the upward and downward double-spiral semiotic storytelling system. The downward spiral extends into the abyss of nothingness, out of which upward spiral formations are possible, as entities and interpretations arise from the depth, because spirals must keep producing more whorls, generatively, or face the risks of entropy. The downward spiral, in this case a university and its school of business, has despotic politics, lots of reorganization by central administration to enact downsizing, lots of bureaucratic standardization and reaccreditation isomorphic mimicry (especially AACSB, which is explored in next section), and purging faculty at every turning whorl (by encouraging retirement, or scapegoating). I, of course, am rebellious and produce chapters and articles, like this one, as form of resistance to nonsense changes (Hillon & Boje, 2017; Boje, Hillon, & Mele, 2017).

Our chancellor keeps putting out spin on (countersignifying) numerical narratives. On October 16, 2017, he announced we were one of the world's top universities. While there is that one statistics of 2.3% in one category (worldwide), if you look at all the numbers, a counternarrative tells a different numbers game ranking result. Out of 311 universities ranked by the report, NMSU falls in the bottom tiers in five categories (198 in National Universities, 209 in High School Counselor Rankings, 106 in Top Public Schools, 2,016 in Business Programs, and 125 in Engineering at schools with a doctoral program (U.S. News & World Report, 2017)).

Our universities are caught in a double-spiral: a downward spiral, with one financial crisis after another, and the upward spiral phantasm of neoliberal nonsense to explain strategic downsizing, reengineering, outsourcing of academic capital (Hillon & Boje, 2017; Boje, Hillon, & Mele, 2017). I will diagram the main themes of the paper in this double-spiral that draws on the work of Deleuze (1990, 1994), and Deleuze and Guattari (1987).

In a double-spiral storytelling semiotic system, there are always multiple regimes of signs, among others. Narrative, living story, and antenarrative are mixing forms of expression constitutive of semiotic storytelling systems. Each of the regimes of signs (narrative, living story, and antenarrative) has pragmatic importance in the upward and downward, left and right, inward and outward signifying forces and countersignifying forces of semiotic storytelling systems. The double-spiral storytelling system is rhizomatic in several ways: (1) multiplicities of movement, (2) deterritorializing and reterritorializing transformations, (3) polymorphous ways of passing through many phases and stages, and (4) nomadic assemblages (offshoots, breakouts, roots).

The two spirals move about a double axis of paradigmatic and syntagmatic (Deleuze & Guattari, 1987: 131). Paradigmatic is defined as a socioeconomy of two or more persons in an organization of power relations (subordination of faculty to deans and deans to provost and chancellor, departmentalization, college assemblages of department curriculum, state's budget power over public universities). "Capital is a point of subjugation par excellence" (Deleuze & Guattai, 1987: 130). Syntagmatic is defined as how signs relate to other self-consciousness signs, making signs signifiers to other signified (courses to majors, degrees to career entry, publications to tenure and promotion, journal or college rankings to university legitimacy). Those spiral loops assembling around double axes are called "whorls." The upward spiral has to keep producing more whorls to avert entropy collapse. The downward spiral generates its whorls and must create more of them to sustain its own entropy. The double spiral semiotic system has upward and downward forces (down to abyss in death spiral, and upward to uplift to higher freedoms of movement). The orange dotted lines assemble storytelling interpretative development in both up and down spiral directions, telling interpretations between whorls, linking whorls. Blue dotted lines connect signs referring to other signs within and between spiral whorls. One can take a line of flight out of a university (jump to another university, or retire). Sometimes that line of flight is scapegoating, and the sins of the university leave with the designated, signified goat. There are four signifying semiotic regimes (presignifying, countersignifying, signifying, and postsignifying). Antenarratives are for me, *presignifying semiotic regimes* in acts of forecaring that both deterritorialize and territorialize and reterritorialize in advance preparations.

Risky Impacts: The lower-class student finds university education farther away in possibility. The upper-class family sends its children to top-tier universities (Stanford, Carnegie, Harvard, and so on). These have tuition of $50,000 or more per year for an undergraduate degree (e.g. Stanford charges $62,000). NMSU charged residents $6,729 a year for an undergraduate course before the most recent tuition hike. You get what you pay for. Stanford, for example, has a 95% graduation rate, while our university graduates 46%. Main campus enrolment at NMSU decreased by 8.2% over the previous year, and has been decreasing year by year for the past five years. NMSU administration put one million dollars into billboard and movie theater ads. There is some good news. Marketing expenditures of one million dollars has resulted in a 22% increase in freshman numbers for Spring (Sun News, 2017). Public universities in New Mexico trap students in tuition fee increase and higher loan debt, while delivering careers at low wages to work off the student loan debt.

New Mexico higher education has undergone three economic crises during my 20 years. First, the financial collapse in 1997 when I was department head. Second, the 2008–2009 bank and mortgage crisis. Third, the oil and gas revenue funding crisis expected to last at least three years.

My analysis is this is an ideological fight in the political economy, with dramatic consequences for higher education. These are competing ideologies in which disadvantaged and marginalized are deeply impacted.

Phantasm of Reengineering Academia

These are "event crises" of sense, "public sector crises" of loss of state funding, and financial crisis management by the university to construct sensible narratives out of nonsense. Therefore, this is an autoethnographic study, a crisis management consulting and reorganization used at a large southwestern university in the United States, in the form of business process reengineering, and my own paranoid storytelling of its turbulence and chaotic nonsense. What happened to our university? Answer: nonsense. On the one hand, state gives the university millions to build the physical plant of a university, refurbish dorms, build new dorms and new building for our college, and is adding a shopping mall and extending the golf course to 27 holes. On the other hand, all the while, faculty salaries are frozen and college budget is swept into central administration. Board of regents paid $622,700 to business process reengineering consultants, Deloitte Consultancy, to provide the board of regents a PowerPoint event, to legitimate paradigmatic axis (see Figure 22.2), a neoliberal (right-turning) narrative of how to reorganize (left-leaning) academic units, combine smaller units, downsize the remaining faculty, drive resisting-change faculty into jumping ship or to retiring, all the while increasing the work load of survivors. This is an example of a semiotic storytelling system, a double-spiral with upward and downward, left and right moving signification and reparadigmatic shuffling. If this was an isolated case, I would keep quiet, but colleagues around the world work in similar infernos of sense-nonsense, such as Copenhagen Business School and other universities in Denmark, and the purge of humanities (Bülow & Boje, 2015).

My assessment is this has accelerated risk of displacing tenured faculty, created the lowest moral in university history, forced out higher-paid tenured faculty to make room for lesser-paid college and adjunct faculty, and completely overworked the staff, jeopardizing the efficacy of research and teaching in one of the poorest states of all. It also legitimated higher state investments in buildings, landscaping, including a change to the universities "master plan" document, expanding the golf course from 18 to 27 holes, building a hotel and shopping mall, and increasing the investment in the center for patenting and selling faculty inventions (NMSU Materplan, 2017).

Team 6 has some distorted numbers, an untold story, and some interpretations of interest (Team 6; Minutes, 2017). See this "untold story," in the spreadsheet, that shows none of the peer universities have combined management and marketing (as we are being encouraged to do); some put supply chain in marketing, while others have organization studies and management department (Team 6; Spreadsheet, 2017). Second untold story: There are no data on doctoral programs. Some numbers are not current, such as this one that shows the NMSU management department has 14 faculty, which I think is a bit of an exaggerated number (we have no more than eight, plus an interim department head) (Team 6; Study Document, 2017). The March 6 meeting notes have a counternarrative to what the Provost shared with faculty on October 12, that paints a far less rosy picture of NMSU mimetic modeling of ASU than the Provost statement to faculty (Team 6; Minutes, 2017).

Provost puts the narrative this way "Arizona State University has become known as the most innovative university in the United States and proudly touts its academic reorganization,

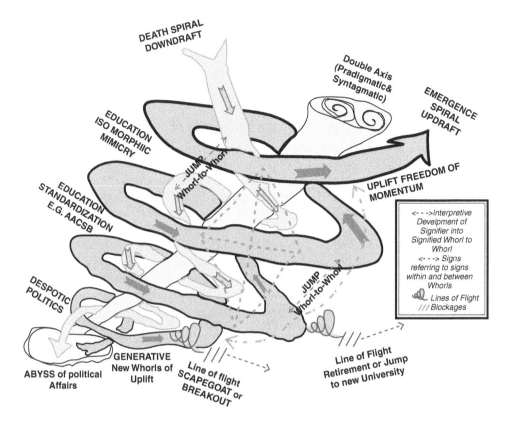

Figure 22.2 Double-Spiral Semiotic Storytelling System

which it claims has broken down silos, encouraged collaboration, and served as a catalyst for interdisciplinary research."

Then, if you look at the proposal I made, and so did Grace Ann, separately, to create "ensemble" leadership and organization (see Rosile, Boje, & Claw, 2016), this matches what ASU is doing, after doing their second reorganization. As Provost Howard put it, "Another distinguishing characteristic is joint appointments. Senior faculty members are expected to have affiliations with more than one department, which breaks down silos, encourages interactions, and leads to novel partnerships and research programs" (Team 6; Minutes, 2017).

Phantasm of AACSB

What makes our business schools so uniform? Business schools are subject to strong institutional mimetic (isomorphism-conformity) pressures (Wilson & McKiernan, 2011). Scott (1995: 3) defines institutions as "cognitive, normative and regulative structures and activities that provide stability and meaning to social behavior." The process of institutionalization happens over time, in history of people and groups with vested interests (Scott, 1995: 18). I contend that institutional effects spread through an organizational field by three isomorphism (similarity) mechanisms: coercive isomorphism, mimetic isomorphism, and normative isomorphism. Business schools, for example, have all three isomorphic mechanisms imposed upon them, promoting repetition of institutional life and belief systems and cultural mores and maxims (unquestioned ways of doing things) present in their institutional macro-environment of business schools.

One environmental factor is the decrease in state and federal funding of higher education in the United States, which makes the cost of AACSB accreditation in hiring extra staff, taking up more time of existing faculty and staff time, increasingly high during budget cutting. AACSB isomorphic pressures result in business schools adopting mechanisms of conformity to all other schools in institutional field (of the United States), rendering attainment of any strategic differentiation problematic both in United States and internationally. We as faculty follow the AACSB rules, norms, and maxims about outcomes assessments, and "jump through the AACSB hoops" without actually believing they make sense, result in quality improvements, or that the process of AACSB measurement is scientific or is not utter nonsense, and do it anyway, in order to sustain the mantle of legitimacy. Worse, institutionalized isomorphism (conformity) may actually make an accredited business school weaker and the cost of the AACSB hoop jumping.

As I write this chapter, we are coming up on reaccreditation by AACSB visiting team. My read of the official college narrative is it reports management graduates, including Ph.D. graduates, but does not deal with the issues of the attrition of faculty, the non-decision to continue funding doctoral students at this point (and this used as leverage to get us to conform), the in-group-out-group divisive style of leadership, the workload expansion for tenured professors (unlike any peer institution), the fact that doctoral courses have too many students in them, every week more advisees are added to my workload, and so on. The narrative account deals with the surface numbers and qualitative success points, but not the deeper historical issues, and avoids the issues of leadership.

Universities around the world have experienced a series of financial market crises in mortgage and real estate that are entangled with Wall Street speculative markets and government economic policies (mark-to-market accounting rules, interest rates, etc.) that resulted in less state monies to allocate to public university funding. Academic capitalism is producing models of reality, refiguring higher education, always incomplete and partial, done again and again, the sociomaterial relationships, changing the sociomateriality, bridging university people and things differently. There is lots of turnover, lots of adjuncts and temporary contractors moving in to displace senior full-time professors. The ethic of care is shifting in relation to the sociomaterial reconfiguring. There are a myriad of living stories intraactive with the new sociomateriality entanglement, with social changes and material changes rocking back and forth, tacking back and forth, reconfiguration of higher education reality.

My gestures at work travel through spaces and times that are inflected by a spectrum of political economy agendas (Schneider, 1997, 2017). Academic capitalism restructures work in public university in ways that mirror corporation, as higher education is being corporatized in the "new" economy. Academic capitalism means universities applying for patent, trademark, and copyright for intellectual property developed by faculty (Slaughter & Rhoades, 2004: 91). Money from privatizing dining services, book stores, adding shopping mall, hotel, golf course, and so on can be shifted from instructional to non-structural areas. Meanwhile, the infrastructure and administrative order swells to handle the "administrative academic capitalism" (Slaughter & Rhoades, 2004: 32).

Academic capitalism itself was spotted in the 1970s in policies among state systems of higher education, to generate patent, copyright, and trademarks from appropriations of faculty intellectual property rights. Instead of free flow of knowledge in the knowledge society, the new knowledge regime of academic capitalism was that of the knowledge economy, and ways to commodify knowledge in learning and research regimes. As state support for public universities declined, tuition fee was increased, and a host of auxiliary enterprises called revenue-generating operations (Slaughter & Rhoades, 2004: 299) were added. This is not just about economic crisis. It is also about the battle between socialist (or progressive) and neoliberal ideologies (that took shape with Thatcher in United Kingdom and Reagan in United States in the late 1970s and early 1980s). In sum, academic capitalism is a new knowledge/learning regime where president of the university becomes CEO, provost becomes human resource officer, the board of regents (or trustees) becomes the board of directors, students become customers, and knowledge becomes a commodity. Our university installed academic capitalism that has turned the university into a business model of efficiency. The university is being deskilled (displacing professional staff and faculty with lower paid people) in a relentlessly and ruthlessly administered entrepreneurial model of competitive individualism. As our university deskills its faculty and staff and lowers the quality of its university education, while promoting the business model of power over hierarchy, what is sacrificed is participative democracy, shared governance, equal citizenship, and civil rights.

TINA Phantasm

I participated in generating (critical) counternarratives to the administrative order's TINA narrative. There are several counternarratives members of student and faculty, and your truly circulated in emails, blog posts, news interviews, YouTube videos, meetings, academic publications, and speeches at marches. While providing important places and times of sensemaking, the counternarrative work was not powerful enough to mitigate belief in the TINA narrative, or stop the implementation of BPR and reorganization. In the TINA narrative, this reengineering and reorganization was the only alternative considered by the administration. There was no call for participation, no shared faculty (or staff or student) governance. The hazard of the emergence of the financial crisis had to be dealt with by swift and decisive action of the central administration. Formal participation (according to Team 6 member in our college) would be arranged in 2018, after the crisis. There were emails, briefings by the chancellor and provost to the faculty senate, student senate, and the staff union and its members, inviting participation in Team 6; however, there are costs of bringing critique of the dominant reorganization approach to college administration or central administration attention. With resistance comes retaliation (increased course load being investigated), bullying and shaming (in three-hour session by an administrator), and demonizing me as primary whistle-blower. In this state, bullying is annoying but not illegal; retaliation against a whistle-blower is illegal. I was labeled a troublemaker, a rebel, malcontent, a member of the department of insurrection, and a social pariah.

Some administrators resisted. At my own university in September 2017, the chancellor went against the governor's strategy (starving higher education by vetoing all state higher education budgets) in order to downsize it. And the chancellor's contract was not renewed, after regents, appointed by the governor took a vote and there were media stories the governor wanted his job: "… given that NMSU's chancellor is the highest paid position at the institution (Carruthers contract is for $385,000 per year), even at a portion of that, Martinez would stand to boost her overall average income by a significant margin" (Progress Now NM, 2017).

My day-to-day footsteps in the university replay (and respond to) the standard pose of surrender among colleagues in the face of the administrative order and their dominant narrative, a call for a future that is different from the path I have been on for 35 years. While narratives and counternarratives are dialectic retrospective sensemaking, antenarratives are about what comes before narrative (and counternarrative) and various bets on the future in varied and multiple prospective sensemaking processes.

Part 3: What Might Be Done?

Here I want to develop socioeconomic approach to management (SEAM) (Savall & Zardet, 2008). I will assert that Taylor-Fayol-Weber (TFW) virus has become a monster arising from the depth of financial crises, cracking the surface of fragile sense of public universities, and the SEAM approach is a way to counter the death spiral. In SEAM approach, there is first-phase analysis of the particular conditions and situation leading to downward performance.

The organization's "death spiral" happens as the socioeconomic situation is no longer being managed effectively, the dysfunctions (working conditions, work organization, communication-coordination-cooperation, training, time management, and strategic implementation) go unattended, and the "hidden costs" become critical financial sources of disaster.

These dysfunctions result in "hidden costs" because they are not being picked up in the regular accounting reports management receives, and without heavy investment in activity-based accounting, you don't know what hit you. You can also assess the "downward" or "death spiral."

When we don't buy into to the TINA narrative, it is possible to be more positive, to be prospective in our sensemaking, and bring potential solutions into being. This involves acts of forecaring. Upward spiral momentum is generated and accelerated by doing successive Diagnosis-Project-Implementation-Evaluation (DPIEs), one after the other, building upon one another, using widespread democratic forms of participation. I proposed this be applied to the university's downward spiral; however, with the Deloitte consultancy, downsizing, reengineering strategy already approved by the board of regents, chancellor, provost, and so on, there was no interest shown by the administration. In the socioeconomic approach, there is a process for becoming more agile (Worley, Zardet, Bonnet, & Savall, 2015):

1   Most change models use traditional design principles that assume stability and do not have upward spiral expectations. Instead, they turn in place without changing and growing.
2   Most organizational change system models are inefficient, have static representations, and cannot achieve more than average socioeconomic performance because they do not address upward momentum and hidden costs conversion into greater human potential for creative expression (Worley, Zardet, Bonnet, & Savall, 2015: 23). SEAM, by contrast, makes improvements in low-value-added tasks by transmuting dysfunctions and hidden costs of managing them into revenue-generating economic performance.
3   SEAM argues "that systems infected with the TFW virus cannot develop the ability to spontaneously adapt to their environment" (Worley, Zardet, Bonnet, & Savall, 2015: 29).

In sum, SEAM is an open system that includes not just sociotechnical-system, but the economic and accounting open system ways of "converting dysfunctions resulting from the TFW virus into value-added work of transforming low-value-added activities into high value-added activity, and of liberation of socioeconomic performance" (Worley, Zardet, Bonnet, & Savall, 2015: 31). While I support this sort of bottom up initiative, it is clearly not happening, so I will stop here.

Conclusions

The financial crises facing public universities are of sufficient magnitude that it takes time to comprehend the implications for faculty, staff, students, and administrators, as well as the community and the state. At the same time, crisis sensemaking can be manipulated such that non-administrators cannot comprehend the seriousness of malfunctions and dysfunctions among people, organizations, and the environment. A crisis system of select stakeholders (institutions, groups, individuals) and a crisis leadership begin to address the situation before, during, and after crises.

Why should the public university be run by a privileged power elite installing academic capitalism, replacing full-time tenured faculty with adjunct faculty, cutting off admittance of doctoral students to our Ph.D. granting department, installing college leaders who are in-civil and practice non-democracy, increasing teaching loads of the full-time tenured faculty, when no other peer institution does that?

There is very little research examining organizational crisis spirals, and far less address-ing how sensemaking is related to spiral dynamics (Boje & Strevel, 2016; Boje, Baca-Greif, Intindola, & Elias, (2017, *in press*). This is because organizational spiral research requires lon-gitudinal designs. The research designs have to collect data at the intervals (lags: minutes, or days, or months, or years, or decades, or centuries) that is appropriate to the scale dynamics of intervals of self-sameness and difference in processes. Spiraling involves an accumulation effect. For example, research gain and resource loss spiral studies have focused on mean-changes in resources without accounting for the accumulation effects implied by the spiraling. To address this, latent change score modeling techniques (McArdle, 2009) have been attempted to see if cycles recur in varying durations (Hobfoll, 2011).

I suggest spiral antenarratives are an improvement over linear-antenarratives and cy-clic antenarrative processes. Spiral antenarrative is a trajectory of organizing that curves around a central axis. A single (upward or downward) spiral is overly simplistic, as if only one trajectory at a time, in one direction at a time (upward or downward), is spi-raling around an axis. In short, a double (helix) spiral analysis sociomaterial process has upward and downward forces. There can also be triple-helix-spirals, quadruple-helix-spirals, penta-helix-spiral-fractals, and so on (Lindberg, Lindgren, & Packendorff, 2014). For example, in a quadruple-helix-spiral there is higher education, military-industrial complex, government funding, media, and natural environment that form helices. And instead of one axis, the complex reconfiguring can be polycentered (many centers) of poly-vocality (many voices) with polysemous (many meanings). Moving and morphing from linear or cyclical into spiral processes ways of organizations spacetimemattering has an upper limit of spiraling losing any sense of symmetry, and becoming thoroughly rhizom-atic directional unfolding (Deleuze & Guattari, 1987; Boje, 2011). In spiral and rhizomatic antenarrative patterns, steps pursue difference, and are not worked out in advance, as in linear and cyclic antenarrative-sameness.

My contention is that (too) many public university administrators are using financial crises as a pretext to legitimatize and rationalize the installation of academic capitalism. At the same time, this is an example of the TFW virus, ways in which Taylorism in the form of BPR combines with Fayolism in its span of control interventions, and Weberian bureaucratic initiatives. It is also what Savall and Peron (2018) theorize as speculative capitalism, which lessens the opportunities for productive capitalism. I propose that a study be done to ascer-tain if there are actual monetary savings from these current privatizations, similar to those done in previous years (e.g. Barnes and Noble book store).

What solutions can be implemented other than to fall into the neoliberal TINA (There is no alternative) syndrome? With regard to NMSU transparency, I recommend that the budget books be put on the web, and that comprehensive analyses be done by third parties. For example, below, there is a need to explain, with only a cut of 3.8% in I & G, why higher percentage cuts are being made at a rate of 5%–6.2%, and what terms such as public service, net transfers, and "Other" mean to the budget and program cut strategies?

We need a more complex and rigorous theory of private markets than neoliberal free market forces (see work by Steve Keen in slide presentation). We need to be more critical of how neoliberal agenda is implementing changes to public university faculty governance and student debt.

1 We need to snap out of the TINA syndrome and come up with revenue creating strategies
2 Aggie Experience has had a 50% drop in parents and potential students visiting the NMSU campus.
3 Parents share their concerns: "nobody wants to get on board a sinking ship."
4 People are reading about the cuts in programs, staff, and faculty, and deciding NMSU is not the place to go.
5 It was suggested that NMSU needs to change its marketing and its budget control tactics

We, the faculty, need to defend university from further implosion. Parents and students are not choosing university as much as before. The explanation is that the parents and students have read the news and are not interested in getting on board a "sinking ship." That is, with such low graduation rates, with positions cuts, with programs cut, there is anxiety in parents and their children as to the long-term viability of investing in university education.

We have to admit that public universities face a crisis that goes far beyond a drop in oil and gas prices. The subsidization of football and other sports programs is an issue. It is a matter of state-side public policy. There needs to be more transparency, and more faculty governance and control of the curriculum, for the research, teaching, and service cannot be downsized.

Perhaps we need more Mary Parker Follett, and less Taylorism. Fayol, in the 1920s, suggested that Frederick Taylor's scientific efficiency ideas were quite incomplete and did not attend to the democratic potential of organizations.

References

AACSB. (2005). The business school rankings dilemma. A report from a task force of AACSB International's committee on issues in management education. Accessed February 20, 2018 at www.aacsb.edu/~/media/AACSB/Publications/research-reports/business-school-rankings-dilemma.ashx

Boje, D. M. (2016). *Organizational Change and Global Standardization: Solutions to the Standards and Norms Overwhelming Organizations.* London and New York: Routledge.

Boje, D. M. (1995). Stories of the storytelling organization: A postmodern analysis of Disney as 'Tamara-land.' *Academy of Management Journal, 38*(4): 997–1035.

Boje, D. M. (2014). *Storytelling Organizational Practices: Managing in the Quantum Age.* London and New York: Routledge.

Boje, D. M. (2008). *Storytelling Organizations.* London and Thousand Oaks, CA: Sage.

Boje, D. M. (2011). *Storytelling and the Future of Organizations: An Antenarrative Handbook.* London: Routledge Studies in Management, Organizations and Society.

Boje, D. M. (2017). Blog, October 12, "We Can Challenge the TINA-Narrative with Untold Stories to Reverse the Downward Spiral of New Mexico's Public Universities and K-12. https://davidboje.wordpress.com

Boje, D. M., Baca-Greif, H., Intindola, M., & Elias, S. (in press). The episodic spiral model: A new approach to organizational processes. *Journal of Organizational Change Management.*

Boje, D. M., Haley, U. C., & Saylors, R. (2016). Antenarratives of organizational change: The microstoria of Burger King's storytelling in space, time and strategic context. *Human Relations, 69*(2): 391–418.

Boje, D. M., Hillon, Y., & Mele, T. M. (2017). 21st Century University and the Failure of Business Process Reengineering. Accessed February 20, 2018 at http://davidboje.com/vita/paper_pdfs/21st Century University and BPR Failure_BHM.pdf

Boje, D. M., Svane, M., Henderson, T. L., & Strevel, H. B. (in press). Critical corporate social responsibility in Tamara-land: The role of tetranormalizing fractals. In R. Ocler (Ed.), *Book Chapter for a Springer Collection.*

Boje, D. M., & Strevel, H. (2016). Using quantum storytelling to bridge appreciative inquiry to socio-economic approach to intervention research. *AI Practitioner: International Journal of Appreciative Inquiry, 18*(# 3): 79–89.

Boje, D. M., Svane, M., & Gergerich, E. (*in press*). Counternarrative and Antenarrative Inquiry in Two Cross-Cultural Contexts. *Cross Cultural Management.*

Bülow, A. M., & Boje, D. M. (2015). The antenarrative of negotiation. *Journal of Strategic Contracting and Negotiation, 1*: 200–213.

Brewer, J., & Dourish, P. (2008). Storied spaces: Cultural accounts of mobility, technology, and environmental knowing. *International Journal of Human-Computer Studies, 66*(12): 963–976.

Deleuze, G. (1990). *The Logic of Sense,* trans. Mark Lester with Charles Stivale. London and New York: Continuum Press.

Deleuze, G. (1994). *Difference and Repetition.* Columbia University Press.

Deleuze, G., & Félix G. (1983). *Anti-Oedipus,* trans. Robert Hurley, Mark Seem, and Helen R. Lane. Minneapolis: University of Minnesota Press.

Deleuze, G., & Félix G. (1987) *A Thousand Plateaus,* tans. Brian Massumi. Minneapolis: The University of Minnesota Press..

DiMaggio, P., & Powell, W. W. (1983). The iron cage revisited: Collective rationality and institutional isomorphism in organizational fields. *American Sociological Review, 48*(2): 147–160.

Gephart, R. P. Jr. (2007). Crisis sensemaking and the public inquiry, pp. 123–160. In Pearson, C. M., Roux-Dufort, C., & Clair, J. A. (Eds.), *International Handbook of Organizational Crisis Management.* Thousand Oaks, CA: Sage Publications.

Hillon, Y. C., & Boje, D. M. (2017). The dialectical development of "storytelling" learning organizations: a case study of a public research university. *The Learning Organization, 24*(4). On line version available www.emeraldinsight.com/doi/abs/10.1108/TLO-02-2017-0010

Hitchin, L. (2014). Method and story fragments, pp. 213–238. In Izak, M., Hitchin, L., & Anderson, D. (Eds.), *Untold Stories in Organizations.* London: Routledge

Hultin, L., & Mähring, M. (2017). How practice makes sense in healthcare operations: Studying sensemaking as performative, material-discursive practice. *Human Relations, 70*(5): 566–590.

Izak, M., Hitchin, L., & Anderson, D. (Eds.). (2014). *Untold Stories in Organizations.* London: Routledge.

Lindberg, M., Lindgren, M., & Packendorff, J. (2014). Quadruple Helix as a way to bridge the gender gap in entrepreneurship: The case of an innovation system project in the Baltic Sea region. *Journal of the Knowledge Economy, 5*(1): 94–113.

Management department (2018). Website accessed January 16, 2018, red letters in the original. https://business.nmsu.edu/academics/graduate-programs/mgt-phd/

Mazmanian, M., Cohn, M., & Dourish, P. (2014). Dynamic reconfiguration in planetary exploration: A sociomaterial ethnography. *Mis Quarterly, 38*(3): 831–848.

McKee, M. C., Mills, A. J., & Weatherbee, T. (2005). Exploring the AACSB and the New Legitimacy of Canadian Business Schools. *Revue canadienne des Sciences de l'administration, 22*(4): 288–301.

Meyer, J. W., & Rowan, B. (1977). Institutionalized organizations: Formal structure as myth and ceremony. *American Journal of Sociology, 83*(2): 340–363.

Nicklaus, D. (2017). Budget impasse puts Illinois economy in downward spiral. St. Louis Post-Dispatch. Downloadedfromwww.stltoday.com/business/columns/david-nicklaus/budget-impasse-puts-illinois-economy-in-downward-spiral/article_13b2ffb2-f3e0-5851-9242-4d5b20eb0841.html on January 30, 2018.

NMSU (2017) Master Plans, old and new, are online. Accessed October 19, 2017 at http://architect.nmsu.edu/masterplan/

Payscale.com website and data of NMSU. Accessed October 18, 2017 at www.payscale.com/research/US/School=New_Mexico_State_University_-_Main_Campus/Salary

Pearson, C. M., Roux-Dufort, C., & Clair, J. A. (2007). *International Handbook of Organizational Crisis Management.* Thousand Oaks, CA: Sage Publications.

Porter, L. W, McKibbin, L. E. (1988). *Management Education and Development: Drift or Trust into the 21st Century?* NY: McGraw-Hill Book Co.

Progressnow N. M. (2017). NMSU regents reject Carruthers, could Gov. Martinez be the next Chancellor? (August 30). Accessed October 18, 2017 at http://progressnownm.org/2017/08/30/breaking-nmsu-regents-reject-carruthers-could-gov-martinez-be-the-next-chancellor/

Rosile, G. A., Boje, D. M., Nez, C. C. (2016). Ensemble leadership theory: Collectivist, relational, and heterarchical roots from indigenous contexts. *Leadership Journal.*

Savall, H., & Zardet, V. (2008). *Mastering Hidden Costs and Socio-Economic Performance.* Charlotte, NC: Information Age Press

Schneider, R. (2017). In our hands: An ethics gestural response-ability. In Lucia Ruprecht. *Performance Philosophy Journal, 3* (1), Online. Accessed February 20, 2018 at www.performancephilosophy.org/journal/article/view/161/172

Scott, W. R. (1995). *Institutions and Organizations.* Thousand Oaks, CA: Sage.

Slaughter, S., & Leslie, L. L. (1997). *Academic Capitalism: Politics, Policies, and the Entrepreneurial University.* Baltimore, MD: The Johns Hopkins University Press.

Sun News (2017). Editorial April 17. Accessed September 15, 2017 at www.lcsun-news.com/story/opinion/editorial/2017/04/17/marketing-effort-pays-nmsu/100570976/

Team 6 (2017). Minutes and summary reports, March 6. Accessed October 19, 2017 at https://transforming.nmsu.edu/team-6/; Team 6, on transforming NMSU into a model university, such as Arizona State University. Accessed October 19, 2017 at https://hr.nmsu.edu/transforming/wp-content/uploads/sites/80/2017/02/TEAM-SIX-Minutes-March-6.pdf

Team 6 (2017). Spreadsheet. Accessed October 19, 2017 at https://transforming.nmsu.edu/wp-content/uploads/sites/80/2017/07/NMSUPeerStructure.xlsx

Teams 6 (2017). Study Document. Accessed October 19, October 2017 at https://transforming.nmsu.edu/wp-content/uploads/sites/80/2017/07/scanned-document-updated.pdf

Twotrees, K. (1997). Presentation at the Organizational Behavior Teaching conference, meeting at Case Western Reserve, Ohio.

US News and World Report (2017). Rankings of universities. Accessed October 16, 2017 www.usnews.com/best-colleges/new-mexico-state-university-2657

Weick, K. E. (2012). Organized sensemaking: A commentary on processes of interpretive work. *Human Relations, 65*(1): 141–153.

Wexler, E. (2016). Starving the beast. Chronicle of Higher Education. March 22. Accessed February 20, 2018 at www.insidehighered.com/news/2016/03/22/starving-beast-examines-ideological-shifts-funding-higher-education

Willis, D. (2016). NMSU budget cuts target academic, athletic program. Las Cruces Sun-News July 13. Accessed October 18, 2017, www.lcsun-news.com/story/news/education/nmsu/2016/07/13/nmsu-plans-cut-positions-well-surveying-equestrian/87045282/

Wilson, D., & McKiernan, P. (2011). Global mimicry: Putting strategic choice back on the business school agenda. *British Journal of Management, 22*(3): 457–469.

Worley, C. G., Zardet, V., Bonnet, M., & Savall, A. (2015). *Becoming Agile: How the SEAM Approach to Management Builds Adaptability.* John Wiley & Sons.

23

MANAGING RISK IN HEALTHCARE SETTINGS

Agnieszka Latuszynska, Trish Reay, and Eivor Oborn

The provision of healthcare holds inherent risk: the right patient needs to get the right treatment at the right time, and any deviations from this might result in serious consequences. But does "right" have the same meaning for patients, nurses, doctors, healthcare managers, and government? And how do their different approaches to risk intersect in healthcare settings? In this chapter we address these questions.

The issue of risk in healthcare is situated within a context of socioeconomic changes throughout the last century leading to continually increasing preoccupation with risk and uncertainty for individuals, as well as for organizations. The risk of developing a health condition, being affected by a highly contagious disease, or losing professional healthcare reputation differs in terms of the nature of the risk, how it is perceived, and how accurately the risk can be calculated or how efficiently prevented. For a company or a public organization, other risks also become apparent – the development of disruptive new technologies, the evolution of patient preferences, and/or a shortage of required professionals all can influence perceptions of risk and thus organizational activities.

Healthcare is one context in which a multiplicity of risks and views on risk come together. So how do different parties involved in public healthcare, such as physicians, nurses, healthcare managers, or the government, consider risk? How are the concepts of risk different for these different parties? What do they do to mitigate risks? The healthcare system is under constant pressure to change and improve, and there are always new challenges. How do the risk roles evolve over time? In this chapter, we start from the premise that healthcare stakeholders differ fundamentally in their conceptualization of risk and normative control, and then consider how these differences translate into interactions with each other. In addition, we consider how the healthcare system as a whole is affected by this coexistence of different risk views. Our views are grounded in our own studies of publicly funded healthcare systems, but we believe that most of our ideas are also relevant in other systems.

An important issue involves what happens when stakeholders interact in cooperation or competition regarding risk, and how their differing risk regimes can coexist. We develop an approach based on stakeholder theory (Freeman, 2010) and stakeholder value perceptions to consider the potential impact of coexisting risk regimes on healthcare organizations. We argue that organizational stakeholders are impacted when different perceptions of value are created. Hence, in the context of risk, we consider how the different risk regimes and their interplay affect stakeholder views on value creation, in this case within the healthcare system.

Risk Regulatory Regimes

A risk regulatory regime can be defined as "the complex of institutional geography, rules, practice, and animating ideas that are associated with the regulation of a particular risk or hazard" (Hood, Rothstein, & Baldwin, 2001, p. 9). Such a regime can be discussed at a general level, from a system perspective, but is more often discussed in a narrower sense, for a subset of broader risk. Based on Hood et al. (2001), we briefly outline important aspects of the risk regime **context** as well as themes that characterize **risk regulatory regimes**, with the healthcare industry as backdrop.

Type of Risk

An important aspect of the risk context is the nature and type of risk being considered. This includes understanding inherent features of the risk, such as source or cause of risk, how familiar it is to the main actors, how easily the risk can be quantified, how severe the consequences are, and how likely the risk is to occur. A key aspect to consider is often the difference in severity of the risk (understood through the combination of consequence and likelihood) without regulation, and with regulation. Regulation is here understood broadly and can refer to market processes, legal regulations, or social processes. Commonly faced types of risk in healthcare include the risk of treatment side effects, hospital-acquired infections, hacked computers containing sensitive patient information, and poor quality service provision.

Preferences and Attitudes Regarding the Risk

Preferences and attitudes of different stakeholders regarding risk is another important contextual aspect that requires attention. Thus, risk domains can vary in terms of the *anxiety* they generate, or the *level of consensus* in public opinions, as evidenced, for example, by discussions and media coverage. High or low anxiety, as well as consensus or conflicting opinions, results in very different policy contexts for conducting regulation. The issue of waiting times in hospital emergency departments, which we discuss in the penultimate section, is an example where high public anxiety has pushed healthcare regulators in the UK to introducing an arbitrary four-hour maximum waiting target for patients.

Ways of Gathering Information

Information gathering techniques are central to all risk regulation, and if disagreements regarding risk regulation arise, information gathering is often in contention. Information about risk can be gathered in numerous ways including experiments, expert knowledge, voluntary or compulsory reports, and data gathering devices, such as computer search engine histories or monitoring and tracking equipment. In the healthcare context, views on and the practice of gathering information are often central to risk management, as are how such views differ between stakeholders and how they change over time. For example, clinicians may support evidence-based medicine clinical trials as the preferred approach to identifying best clinical practices, while government departments may support population level benchmarking to determine areas of best clinical practice.

Ways of Setting Standards, Goals, and Targets

In some cases, numerical or qualitative standards or targets may be plucked out of the air by regulators (Hood et al., 2001, p. 25), or set by direct judgments without following a rigorous analysis. Such cases are referred to as *simple steering*. However, in the majority of situations, homeostatic or collibrational approaches are chosen. In the *homeostatic approach*, one sets an acceptable maximum level of risk (defined qualitatively or quantitatively) and aims to keep the risk at or below that maximum level. In the *collibrational approach*, some contradictory aims are weighed and balanced, such as risk against cost, or risk against convenience. While the collibrational approach appears to be more thoughtful, the merit of the homeostatic approach is that it doesn't suffer from design issues around balancing and optimization of contradictory goals. For example, the UK's National Institute for Health and Care Excellence (NICE) follows the collibrational approach in its recommendations for medical procedures by taking into account desired medical outcomes as well as their cost effectiveness, whereas the UK government target of a maximum wait time of four hours in emergency departments is based on a simple steering approach.

Ways of Changing Behavior to Meet the Standards or Targets

An important component of risk regulation involves changing the behavior of individuals or organizations so that certain risks are mitigated. This, however, often turns out to be a problematic issue that depends on compliance – not only of patients, but also whether health professionals follow practices associated with best available evidence, and the cultural norms of those concerned. For example, performance appraisals of senior medical professionals (e.g., consultants in UK) often reveal a significant lack of behavior change (McGivern & Ferlie, 2007).

Healthcare Stakeholders and Their Risk Perceptions

Over the last three decades, stakeholder theory (Freeman, 2010) has become one of the standard tools in the managerial toolbox for gaining perspective and insight on group or organizational interactions in both the private and public sectors. The core principle of stakeholder theory is that entities such as businesses and organizations should be understood through relationships with and between stakeholders, that is, groups of people that can affect, or be affected by, activities of the focal entity (Freeman, Harrison, & Wicks, 2007). Applications of stakeholder theory to healthcare management are frequent in research projects (see, for example, Chapter 6 of Freeman, Harrison, Wicks, Parmar, & De Colle, 2010). Here, we draw on stakeholder theory to examine different perceptions of risk, as it is layered and managed in the healthcare system. We identify four key stakeholders commonly engaged in the provision of healthcare services: (1) government, (2) healthcare managers, (3) frontline physicians and other health professionals, and (4) members of the public who are always potential patients. For each stakeholder, we explain, based on established literature, the types of risk commonly faced, their attitudes and preferences concerning risk, usual ways of gathering information to determine risk, and ways of setting targets or changing behavior to manage risk. These ideas are summarized in Table 23.1 and described in more detail below. Although there are many types of risk in healthcare contexts, our approach to thinking about the issues is in terms of healthcare management programs (Carroll, 2009) that serve to protect against harm.

Table 23.1 How Stakeholders Manage Risk

Stakeholder	Government	Healthcare managers	Frontline physicians and other professionals	Public/patients
Types of risk faced	Harm to population if appropriate policy not developed or resources provided	Harm to organization if resources (budget, staff, and equipment) not managed appropriately	Harm to patient if not able to deliver the right treatment to the right person at the right time	Harm to selves or family if unable to find right providers for information and required services
Preferences, attitudes about risk	Risk is evaluated at population level, including population satisfaction with government policies	Risk is evaluated at organizational and patient group level Risk to staff and organizational survival are important considerations	Risk is evaluated for each patient – one patient at a time Each professional bears responsibility for quality of care provided.	Risk is evaluated in terms of health vs. illness for self or family
Ways of gathering info to determine risk	Statistics, public feedback, cost evaluations, benchmarking against others	Organizational/unit outcome measures, including error rates	Personal review of research findings Review of clinical practice guidelines/professional standards	Advice from professionals Internet sources Social media Friends and family stories
Ways of setting targets or changing behavior to manage risk	Regulation change (government legislation)	Organizational policies and procedures	Protocols or clinical practice guidelines	Personal choice regarding individual behavior Access to information may not lead to behavior change

Government

Governments hold responsibility for the overall welfare of citizens, and thus face risk associated with the overall provision of healthcare, such as inadequate access for eligible citizens, economic loss through excessive costs, and operational risks of providing health services. In addition, they must continuously manage reputational or political risk that is related to public perception about how well the healthcare system is performing and to what extent the government is managing it well.

Governments must be concerned with the potential for harm to the population if appropriate healthcare policies are not in place, or if appropriate resources are not made available. These risks are critical from a societal perspective (Beck, 1992). Citizens increasingly expect their government to be part of supporting positive trends in socioeconomic development such as increasing life expectancy, an improving healthcare system, enhanced medical knowledge alongside increased expectations from the public, an expectation of comfort in everyday life, the reduction of poverty, and the satisfaction of basic needs in the society. As a result, the public tends to hold government accountable for a lack of progress, or failure to keep up with medical advances. The overarching risk for government politicians is failure to be re-elected if citizens are dissatisfied.

This type of risk is increasingly prominent in many Western countries because of aging populations. For example, an aging society implies increasing burdens on the healthcare system in terms of public spending and resource allocation because healthcare costs rise in concert with age (Bös & von Weizsäcker, 1989; OECD, 1988). Further, delivering procedural justice is also important so that all those who engage with the health system perceive the processes to be equitable to all users. Pickard (2010) shows that in their efforts to manage the risks that an aging population have for the efficiency of the healthcare system, governments have supported the development of geriatric medicine, despite opposition from rival specialists. Overall, we see that governments are in the delicate position of needing to assess and manage a wide distribution of risks associated with the provision of healthcare. It is a case of balancing the needs of different population segments (e.g., the elderly) with the needs of others, and with concern for total costs that are continually increasing.

Governments must evaluate risk at the population level because they are responsible to the public. As a result, they must take a relatively risk-averse position in order to satisfy the majority of citizens. For example, most governments engage in continual assessment of population satisfaction with policies and legislation. This process is also highly intertwined and often amplified by media and other social mechanisms, so that negative events attract disproportionate attention (Kasperson et al., 1988), create anxiety, and therefore are of special concern. In their attempts to avoid negative events, governments must work with regulatory professional associations to collectively determine quality and variability levels and boundaries of practice (Abbot, 1988; Audit Commission, 2001) in an effort to assure the population that the healthcare system is functioning effectively and safely.

Governments are continuously engaged in gathering information about how to assess and manage their risks associated with the provision of healthcare. They typically seek regulatory transparency in relation to service provision as one way of addressing public demands. As part of engaging in regulatory transparency, governments often rely on collecting information from the public regarding satisfaction with services provided by healthcare professionals. In addition, governments gather and analyze data on outcome measures associated with particular treatments, facilities, and provider groups. Such information can be used in setting minimum standards and developing statements outlining patient rights in specific treatment situations. These measures are a form of governmentality, and are put in place to minimize or at least clarify risk. In addition, governments may create financial and reputational incentives to heighten attention, so that clinicians and managers take the information and standards seriously.

In setting up targets, governments also focus on collecting relevant information in relation to performance in meeting these targets, benchmarking across regions. Collecting these aggregated forms of population level information can inform governments about the actual goods and services that are being provided, and thereby demonstrate value to the public. Further, by publishing compliance with best practice standards, such as NICE guidance in the UK, organizations can achieve value through positive affiliation with esteemed scientific authorities.

In terms of managing risk, governments typically act through the development of legislation or policies. In this way, they can set targets or benchmarks to assess overall performance in relation to risk. For example, in the UK, the Darzi report (Darzi, 2008) advocates new targets in regional spending that will shift more care into the community. Such policies are designed to encourage the replacement of hospital care with home care for long-term conditions, as well as enable patients to obtain end-of-life care at home, supported by their family doctors, rather than being admitted to hospitals – satisfying public demand for these services in ways that improve quality while reducing costs, or at least holding costs stable.

Benchmarking strategies are also used by governments in order to ensure a fair distribution of services and costs so that risk of inadequate access is mitigated. For example, in the UK, NICE has been set up to provide guidance and quality standards for the National Health Service (NHS) based on rigorous assessment of scientific evidence as well as cost effectiveness. Its recommendations and approvals are based on data obtained from medical research, including clinical trials and expert knowledge, often from independent, global academic centers. NICE-approved drugs, clinical practices, and health technologies are set using the collibrational approach that balances medical effectiveness and cost efficiency. In so doing, NICE also adds value by mitigating against procedural unfairness given the systematic assessments that can span across service types – such as pediatric versus cancer treatments.

Developing meaningful targets is an important means of achieving behavior change to manage risk among healthcare provider organizations and associated stakeholders (Sausman, Oborn, & Barrett, 2016). However, behavior can also be influenced by governments through positive incentive schemes, such as funding sources geared to new services, including genetic counseling and gene therapy. By retaining control of grant revenue schemes and research centers (e.g., Swan, Bresnen, Robertson, Newell, & Dopson, 2010), new services can be directed toward proactive prediction and prevention of diseases using new technologically intensive branches of medicine, such as genomics and neurosciences, and relying on ever increasing evidence-based understanding of determinants of physical and mental health (Darzi, 2008).

While such strategies are elements of more general long-term policies and trends of changing the public healthcare organization, such as the New Public Management or Anglo-governmentality (Ferlie & McGivern, 2013; Miller & Rose, 2008), their implementation is in the hands of the local healthcare managers. We primarily focus on public healthcare systems where the managers are representatives of government; however, most of our ideas about government responsibilities and concerns regarding risk are also relevant in at least segments of the US healthcare context (e.g., Veterans Administration and Medicare programs) where government is a key stakeholder. In the next section, we shift to discuss such managers' risk perception and collaboration with medical professionals.

Healthcare Managers

Healthcare managers hold responsibility for the safe and effective provision of services within their organizations. In public healthcare systems, healthcare managers are agents of the government and must implement locally determined policies (Sausman et al., 2016). They set objectives for organizations and create routes toward reaching these goals. Overall, they plan and implement change. They are responsible for the successful delivery of services. For example, NHS commissioners are held to account for quality of health outcomes in the populations they serve (Darzi, 2008).

Healthcare managers deal indirectly with risks related to patient safety by requiring conformance with standards of best practice. In addition, they are associated with reputational risks through their responsibilities to ensure that transparency measures are implemented, patient satisfaction is monitored, and incentives are put in place to keep healthcare professionals engaged in delivering high-quality services. Failure to manage risk adequately at the hospital level can be seen by the recent scandal linked to unnecessary deaths examined in the Francis Inquiry (2013). As hospital managers sought to bring their budget into financial control, cuts in nursing staff increased until basic nursing care was lacking. Lack of nursing oversight in Staffordshire Hospital led to the dismissal of senior managers and board members.

Healthcare managers must assess risk in two key ways. As employees of an organization, they are responsible for the way in which services are provided and often held accountable for errors that are committed. It is therefore important that they evaluate risk at both the organizational level in terms of ensuring that established organizational procedures and policies are followed, and also at the patient level because it is the interaction between providers and patients where errors are most likely to occur. Managers must be concerned about potential risk to staff and organizational survival, as well as risks of harm to patients.

Managers gather information about risk as part of their responsibility to collect outcome measures, including error rates for their areas. These data are compiled by organizations and governments to support auditability of healthcare services and individual providers. Such outcome measures are typically published in government reports that may or may not be publicly accessible. Information about treatment success rates, error rates, or patient satisfaction scores can be used to determine risk of harm and help with the development of strategies to reduce risks. Such practices, as can be explained through governmentality, typically shift responsibility for risks associated with consistency of patient treatment and satisfaction outcomes toward individual clinicians and practices. At the same time, by making these risk-related data publicly available, it enables more informed risk-related decisions to be made by patients.

Healthcare managers must rely on the consistent implementation of organizational policies and procedures to minimize risks associated with the provision of services. Patient safety and clinical error is a recurring theme of risk in healthcare services, and although managers hold responsibility, a critical component in managing risk occurs at the interface between managers and medical professionals. Waring's (2007) study shows some of the dynamics that occurred during the UK patient safety reforms of the late 1990s and early 2000s. These reforms were wide-reaching and led to the creation of the National Patient Safety Agency (NPSA) and the National Reporting and Learning System (NRLS). The underlying aim was to ensure that the lessons of service failure were learned through the sharing of knowledge across organizational and occupational boundaries (Department of Health, 2001). This particular reform was, among others, fueled by the principles of Human Factors coming from safety sciences to medical sciences. The Human Factors approach contributes the understanding that human error depends on the wider environment of behavior, and in particular that latent factors like poor communication, mismanagement of resources, or insufficient warning systems, amplify the potential for errors (Reason, 2016). Waring (2007, p. 164) observed that this discourse of safety coming from safety science, and not from the medical sciences that normally underpin the regulation of medical performance, empowered the managers to "engage in the regulation of medical work and quality through a bureaucratic panopticon of surveillance." The study conducted by Waring (2007) showed that in order to manage risks related to patient safety, managers initiated hospital-wide procedures for incident reporting, identifying possible latent factors and making decisions about service improvement locally and across the hospital. However, in none of the observed hospital departments did the doctors accept these new procedures, and by not reporting incidents effectively disabled the new system. Taking the risk standpoint of this chapter, their unwillingness to cooperate can be traced back and interpreted as preventing the risk of blame (see also Waring, 2005), the risk of inappropriate and illegitimate risk reporting, as well as the risk of losing professional authority in clinical audit and complaints handling. It is remarkable that in the observed clinical setting, the doctors in several departments were

> drawing on the emerging safety discourse either to justify the existence and exclusive use of their internal risk management procedures, or alternatively, to strategically modify and expand their pre-existing regulatory practices in order to better address the issue of risk and safety.
>
> *(Waring, 2007, p. 175)*

A similar tension was exposed by Currie, Humpreys, Waring, and Rowley (2009) where, in the context of patient safety, precisely in the area of single-use medical devices in anesthesia, the doctors authored a narrative that privileged clinical judgment over managerial control, and it was adopted by other health professionals.

We now turn our attention to physicians and other health professionals who interact directly with patients.

Physicians and Other Health Professionals

Physicians and other health professionals work at the front line of both public and private healthcare organizations, delivering services directly to patients. Collectively they diagnose and treat illnesses or injuries in hospitals or other healthcare settings. They work in many specialties focusing on the type of illness (primary healthcare, surgery, medicine, mental health, etc.) and the type of patient (e.g., children or the elderly). Health professionals' rights to practice are regulated by the government and normally mediated through professional associations. Established criteria for minimal standards of training and experience are developed and maintained by and for each profession. This means that risk is assessed as part of the interaction between a patient and health professional, and professional associations also engage in assessing risk as they determine whether individuals are safe to provide services. The key risk is whether there will be harm to the patient because of services provided or the lack of services. Healthcare professionals are thus trained to deliver the right treatment to the right person at the right time.

Risk must be evaluated for each patient – one patient at a time. Every health professional bears the responsibility for the quality and appropriateness of care he/she provides. It is the responsibility of these professionals to maintain and consistently update their own knowledge. Most professional associations require that their members engage in continuing education to minimize the risk of healthcare providers engaging in outdated or inappropriate treatments. These standards are set up as bargaining devices with governments in exchange for greater autonomy and control over jurisdictions in practice (Abbot, 1988; Reay & Hinings, 2009)

The coexistence of state- and management-imposed strategies to mitigate risks, and of traditional medical practice approved by medical professional bodies, has been recently investigated in several studies. McGivern and Ferlie (2007) examined the effects of introducing a new appraisal system for consultants (specialist physicians) by the NHS. One of the motivations behind introducing consultant appraisal (CA) was to demonstrate adequate regulation of doctors following a number of scandals that caught public attention (Donaldson, 2006). CA was both an assessment and development exercise and was linked to the revalidation of medical licenses. Consultants were supposed to provide evidence of good clinical practice through their appraisal forms, and hence, from a risk management perspective, CA was conceived as a risk prevention measure. However, McGivern and Ferlie (2007, p. 1380) revealed that most consultants treated CA as a mock ritual that provided the impression of regulation, playing "tick-box games to create the impression of accountability, while continuing to practice in a traditional professional way." Furthermore, "legitimacy provided through the impression of audit was more important than professional development" (McGivern & Ferlie, 2007, p. 1380). Deriving from the Greco-Roman ethical perspective that errors are not wrongdoings, but inevitable in the process of formative learning (Kosmala & McKernan, 2011), some consultants were concerned with the risk that CA might fail to prevent adverse clinical incidents while regulators still could use them to blame professionals for not following rules and justify even tighter controls, if something went wrong (McGivern & Ferlie, 2007, p. 1381).

McGivern and Fischer (2012) explored how regulatory transparency affected the work and practice of doctors (psychotherapists and counselors). This study showed that physicians tended to perceive regulatory transparency "as an attack based upon exaggerated risks and misunderstanding of their complex practices" (McGivern & Fischer, 2012, p. 295). Consequently, the doctors focused on their own liability risks, producing evidence of good practice more than on treatment itself. This view suggests that regulatory transparency is driven by risk preferences and attitudes of the public, fueled by anxiety, rather than by expert medical knowledge or reliable medical data on which clinicians base their recommendations. A related line of research by McGivern and Fischer (2010) investigated the views of general practitioners and psychiatrists focused on transparent forms of medical regulations. Doctors reported feeling "guilty until proven innocent" and consequently were practicing medicine more defensively. At the same time, the transparency arrangements supported the "blame business" played by the regulators, the media, and lawyers.

The Public/Patients

The potential risk for patients involves experiencing harm to themselves or family if they do not receive appropriate services. In the not so distant past, a typical patient would see a doctor about a medical issue and let him/her make all the decisions about treatment, essentially transferring the whole risk associated with the condition onto the medical professional. Patients did not have access to relevant data about diseases, treatment options, or reputations of healthcare providers.

However, the ways of gathering risk-related information and knowledge, and generating expertise, have changed. This is partly due to systemic policy evolutions (NICE being an example of a body that manages and verifies great amounts of risk-related data and knowledge), regulatory transparency and the resulting public availability of outcome measures data, and technological changes that dramatically speed up and facilitate information exchange and information search—these technological changes perhaps being most important (Oborn & Barrett, 2016).

Consequently, the perception of risk in healthcare by the public and readiness to play an active role have been changing dynamically over the last few decades, evolving from a passive stance to active participation in decision-making. Risk is evaluated as the difference between health and illness. Patients' experience of risk remains located at the point of care, and typically focused on the exchange between a health professional and the patient. Patients expect to receive the right treatment at the right time, but many are becoming increasingly aware of the risks associated with finding and choosing a healthcare provider, and choosing among different treatment options.

In terms of gathering information in order to improve their ability to assess risk, patients continue to rely on advice and information from health professionals; however, they also typically seek out other information sources such as websites and social media. Online platforms, such as PatientsLikeMe or Health Unlocked, continue to broaden the volume and scope of information available. Barrett, Oborn, and Orlikowski (2016) investigated an online health community and the value for consumers that it created over time. Information available included member assessments of health services and providers visible to the community. The platform facilitated the sharing of specific experiences and opinions in multiple disease areas, and included knowledge about diseases, drugs, and treatments. Finally, the platform provided opportunities for specific patients to link with health providers. PatientsLikeMe is a similar online platform that facilitates information exchange among patients (Frost & Massagli, 2008). The impact on patient decision-making of having such information available has been investigated in Frost and Massagli (2008) and Wicks et al. (2010). These studies suggest that patients become better informed, and become better able to assess risk as follows: "Given my status, what is the best outcome I can hope to achieve, and how do I get there?" More specifically, users of such platforms reported that they learned more about their symptoms, understood the side effects of their treatments, and increased their knowledge of alternative treatments. A significant proportion of patients found the site helpful in making decisions to start (37%), stop (22%), or change (27%) medications. Moreover, 12% of the patients changed their physicians as a result of using the site.

These changes in how patients take and participate in risk decisions are reflected in a significant shift in characteristics of the risk regime (Oborn, Barrett, & Exworthy, 2011). With access to relevant information, better-informed patients are able to better assess their own healthcare risks and engage in decision-making regarding appropriate treatment goals and targets. The way in which the public experiences risk has changed significantly in that people no longer consider themselves to be the subject of medical risks; instead, patients more actively manage such risks together with health providers. This means not only changes in preferences and attitudes regarding risk, but also changes in how mobilized the public is as a stakeholder. Overall, patients can better protect their interests through market-like choices while influencing the reputations of healthcare providers and individual healthcare professionals.

Interactions among Stakeholders with Different Perceptions of Risk

We have provided some examples regarding situations where different assessments of risk by different stakeholders resulted in confusion, misplaced resources, or professional actions that were counter to policy objectives. Each of the stakeholders discussed so far is important to the healthcare system. Each is in a position to determine, legitimize, and protect its view of risk. However, stakeholders interact with one another in the normal course of providing services, and it is in these interactions that different perceptions of risk bring interesting issues to the fore.

Communication and cooperation regarding risk may be hindered among stakeholders when they hold differing perceptions of risk. Ceci (2004) presented a case where registered nurses made sustained efforts to communicate their safety concerns regarding a cardiac surgery program, but were ignored. This system failure was linked to the power/knowledge nexus rendering nurses' evaluation of risk less valuable than that of surgeons, with the devastating result of 12 children dying during or shortly after cardiac surgery. Ceci (2004) argued that similar unequal relations between/among stakeholders are typical rather than unique and may often lead to compromises or even errors in healthcare delivery.

Another example of how uneven power relations among health professionals may affect managing risks, or create new risks, is presented in Barrett, Oborn, Orlikowski, and Yates (2012), where the introduction of pharmaceutical-dispensing robots in two hospital pharmacies was studied. As part of strategies to reduce risk associated with medication errors, robots were introduced; evaluations suggested that robots would reduce errors in the dispensing of medicine, increase cost-effectiveness, and increase overall efficiency. However, introduction of robots impacted all stakeholders, redefining their responsibilities and work relations. Especially in the early stages of implementation, the software and mechanics of the robots required close attention from pharmacy staff, and as a result the more powerful of these groups, pharmacists, managed to take over control of the robots and tune them to their needs. By assessing themselves as best able to manage risks associated with ongoing maintenance and upgrading of robots, pharmacists and some technicians benefited by developing new skills, carving out new roles for themselves, and increasing their legitimacy and profile among stakeholders. At the same time, assistants were burdened with new (mundane) tasks related to loading the robots with medicines, queuing to wait while the robots delivered prioritized medicine to pharmacists, and waiting for technicians to deal with malfunction issues when they occurred. Thus, assistants' work became more interdependent and multitasking than before, and they lost significant autonomy in performing their tasks.

In addition, several new risks emerged, some of which related to loading and dispensing delays. More importantly, robots sometimes dispensed the wrong medicine, but the technicians and pharmacists insisted the problem had to be human in origin and therefore increased surveillance and scrutiny of assistants. The assistants' perceptions of risk, and their view of the source of potentially harmful activities, were not initially considered because they lacked the organization and authority to meaningfully report their concerns. When the source of problems eventually became apparent, one pharmacy manager remarked, "I could not believe that they were there suffering in silence."

Another example showing how different perceptions of risk by different stakeholders can impact the healthcare system is the "4-hour target" that was imposed on England's emergency departments (ED) in 2005. This rule, developed by government to reduce patient wait times, requires that 98% of patients must be treated and discharged home or placed in a hospital bed within four hours of arrival in the ED (Department of Health, 2000). This rule is now well entrenched in the UK, and in other countries such as Australia. The rule is mandatory and healthcare facilities that do not meet the target face financial penalties.

The 4-hour rule is an example of regulation brought in by government to improve public perceptions of healthcare services. No medical or empirical evidence has been provided to justify fixing the waiting time threshold at this particular level (Mason, Weber, Coster, Freeman, & Locker, 2012). The rule was officially introduced as one of the key targets in reforming emergency care and improving safety; however, others suggest that it was designed to address public anxiety following press reports of such extreme cases as a 94-year-old patient remaining in an emergency department for three days in 2002 (Firth, 2002). Thus, the government may have been trying to reduce the risk of further reputational damage to the NHS.

The UK government has imposed financial incentives to meet and financial penalties for not meeting this target, attempting to motivate NHS Trusts running ED to find ways to adapt to the new regulation. This has resulted in anomalies of ED waiting time distributions that have been investigated in several quantitative studies. In particular, Mason et al. (2012) analyzed 2003–2006 data before and after introducing the reform confirming similar aggregatory statistics of the waiting time distribution. This study revealed a very significant spike in activity in the last 20 minutes before the 4-hour threshold suggesting that decision-makers at the organizational level may be managing the risk of financial penalties, rather than focusing on risks associated with the delivery of services for each patient. Physicians and other health professionals may face pressure to quickly discharge or admit patients close to the 4-hour time limit, thus overriding their usual approach to risk of managing each patient one at a time with equal care and consideration. Indeed, there have been confirmed cases (Healthcare Commission, 2009) where patients were rushed from ED into acute units without proper assessment, or were regularly admitted to inappropriate wards just to meet targets (RCN, 2007). More generally, several qualitative studies revealed that ED staff expressed concerns that safety and quality of care has been compromised. Weber, Mason, Carter, and Hew (2011) reached this conclusion and suggested that the "most critically ill are at particular risk." Hughes (2006) also revealed that staff in the majority of EDs believed efforts to meet government targets distorted clinical priorities and reported their concerns about threats to patient safety from the pressure to meet the 4-hour target.

Another side effect of the 4-hour rule was observed by Mason et al. (2012) where the pressure to meet the threshold had negative consequences on training of junior physicians, who had decisions taken out of their hands in the interest of time. Furthermore, a 2007 British Medical Association (BMA) report states that among nurses, almost all respondents (91%) reported direct or indirect pressure to meet the target, often from nonclinical managers. These pressures included bullying of nurses, repetitive phone calls about decisions as the 4-hour mark was approaching, and also being asked to go against their clinical judgments, indicating an overt conflict between managerial and clinical risk perceptions.

Conclusions

Provision of healthcare services is critical for modern societies, and it has been attracting ever increasing attention and an ever increasing proportion of societal, economic, and organizational resources. Health service entities are under constant pressure to improve: to keep up with the developments of medicine, to be timely and equally accessible for all social groups, to facilitate increasingly comfortable life, and to adapt to demographic evolution of societies. Given these pressures and limited resources, organizational tensions inevitably arise and, indeed, they have been investigated from different perspectives (see, e.g., Flynn, 2002, or Waring, 2007).

In this chapter, we have shown that the provision of healthcare services can be viewed as a large-scale, multilayered risk management process with multiple stakeholders involved. Stakeholders differ fundamentally in their risk perceptions. They focus on different risks, have different preferences and attitudes regarding risk, and engage in different ways of gathering information, setting standards, and changing behavior regarding risk. These different risk regimes coexist but affect the provision of healthcare when stakeholders interact. The tensions that arise in managing risk may be amplified by uneven power relations among stakeholders. In some cases, the different risk regimes of stakeholders working together may lead to difficulties in determining appropriate models of care, as exemplified by the 4-hour target in UK emergency departments. We hope that the ideas set out in this chapter will encourage other scholars to engage in research that further investigates the multi-layered and dynamic nature of risk in healthcare delivery.

References

Audit Commission. (2001). *A spoonful of sugar: Medicines management in NHS hospitals*. London: Audit Commission for Local Authorities in England and Wales.

Barrett, M., Oborn, E., & Orlikowski, W. (2016). Creating value in online communities: The sociomaterial configuring of strategy, platform, and stakeholder engagement. *Information Systems Research, 27*(4), 704–723.

Barrett, M., Oborn, E., Orlikowski, W., & Yates, J. (2012). Reconfiguring boundary relations: Robotic innovations in pharmacy work. *Organization Science, 23*(5), 1448–1466.

Beck, U. (1992). *Risk society: Towards a new modernity*. London: Sage.

4BMA. (2007). *Report of national survey of emergency medicine*. British Medical Association.

Bös, D., & von Weizsäcker, R. K. (1989). Economic consequences of an aging population. *European Economic Review, 33*(2–3), 345–354.

Carroll, R. (Ed.) (2009). *Risk management handbook for health care organizations*. San Francisco, CA: Jossey-Bass.

Ceci, C. (2004). Nursing, knowledge and power: A case analysis. *Social Science & Medicine, 59*(9), 1879–1889.

Currie, G., Humpreys, M., Waring, J., & Rowley, E. (2009). Narratives of professional regulation and patient safety: The case of medical devices in anaesthetics. *Health, Risk & Society, 11*(2), 117–135.

Darzi, A. (2008). *High quality care for all: NHS next stage review final report*. London: National Health Service.

Department of Health. (2000). *The NHS plan: A plan for investment, a plan for reform*. London: The Stationery Office.

Department of Health. (2001). *Building a safe NHS for patients*. London: The Stationery Office.

Donaldson, L. (2006). *Good doctors, safer patients*. London: Department of Health.

Ferlie, E., & McGivern, G. (2013). Bringing anglo-governmentality into public management scholarship: The case of evidence-based medicine in UK health care. *Journal of Public Administration Research and Theory, 1*(1), 59–83.

Flynn, R. (2002). Clinical governance and governmentality. *Health, Risk & Society, 4*(2), 155–173.

Francis, R. (2013). *Report of the mid Staffordshire NHS foundation trust public inquiry: Executive summary (HC 947)*. London: The Stationery Office.

Freeman, R. E. (2010). *Strategic management: A stakeholder approach*. Cambridge, UK: Cambridge University Press.

Freeman, R. E., Harrison, J. S., & Wicks, A. C. (2007). *Managing for stakeholders: Survival, reputation, and success*. London: Yale University Press.

Freeman, R. E., Harrison, J. S., Wicks, A. C., Parmar, B. L., & De Colle, S. (2010). *Stakeholder theory: The state of the art*. Cambridge, UK: Cambridge University Press.

Frost, J., & Massagli, M. (2008). Social uses of personal health information within PatientsLike Me, an online patient community: What can happen when patients have access to one another's data. *Journal of Medical Internet Research, 10*(3), e15.

Healthcare Commission. (2009). Investigation into Mid Staffordshire NHS foundation trust (Summary Report). Commission for healthcare audit and inspection. Retrieved from: www.nhshistory. net/midstaffs.pdf

Hood, C., Rothstein, H., & Baldwin, R. (2001). *The government of risk: Understanding risk regulation regimes*. Oxford, UK: Oxford University Press.

Hughes, G. (2006). The four hour target; problems ahead (Editorial). *Emergency Medicine Journal, 23*(1), 2.

Kasperson, R. E., Renn, O., Slovic, P., Brown, H. S., Emel, J., Goble, R., Kasperson, J. X., & Ratick, S. (1988). The social amplification of risk: A conceptual framework. *Risk Analysis, 8*(2), 177–187.

Kosmala, K., & McKernan, J. F. (2011). From care of the self to care for the other: Neglected aspects of Foucault's late work. *Accounting, Auditing & Accountability Journal, 24*(3), 377–402.

Mason, S., Weber, E. J., Coster, J., Freeman, J., & Locker, T. (2012). Time patients spend in the emergency department: England's 4-hour rule—A case of hitting the target but missing the point? *Annals of Emergency Medicine, 59*(5), 341–349.

McGivern, G., & Ferlie, E. (2007). Playing tick-box games: Interrelating defences in professional appraisal. *Human Relations, 60*(9), 1361–1385.

McGivern, G., & Fischer, M. (2010). Medical regulation, spectacular transparency and the blame business. *Journal of Health Organization and Management, 24*(6), 597–610.

McGivern, G., & Fischer, M. (2012). Reactivity and reactions to regulatory transparency in medicine, psychotherapy and counselling. *Social Science & Medicine, 74*(3), 289–296.

Miller, P., & Rose, N. (2008). *Governing the present: Administering economic, social and personal life.* Cambridge, UK: Polity Press.

OECD. (1988). *Ageing population: The social policy implications.* Paris: Organization for Economic Co-operation and Development.

Oborn, E., & Barrett, S. K. (2016). Digital health and citizen engagement: Changing the face of health service delivery. *Health Services Management Research, 29*(1–2), 16–20.

Oborn, E., Barrett, M., & Exworthy, M. (2011). Policy entrepreneurship in the development of public sector strategy. *Public Administration, 89*(2), 325–344.

Pickard, S. (2010). The role of governmentality in the establishment, maintenance and demise of professional jurisdictions: The case of geriatric medicine. *Sociology of Health & Illness, 32*(7), 1072–1086.

Reason, J. (2016). *Managing the risks of organizational accidents.* London: Routledge.

Reay, T., & Hinings, C. R. (2009). Managing the rivalry of competing institutional logics. *Organization Studies, 30*(6), 629–652.

RCN. (2007). *A&E nurses under pressure of emergency medicine.* Royal College of Nursing.

Sausman, C., Oborn, E., & Barrett, M. (2016). Policy translation through localisation: Implementing national policy in the UK. *Policy and Politics, 44*(4), 563–589.

Swan, J., Bresnen, M., Robertson, M., Newell, S., & Dopson, S. (2010). When policy meets practice: Colliding logics and the challenges of 'Mode 2' initiatives in the translation of academic knowledge. *Organization Studies, 31*(9–10), 1311–1340.

Waring, J. (2005). Beyond blame: Cultural barriers to medical incident reporting. *Social Science & Medicine, 60*(9), 1927–1935.

Waring, J. (2007). Adaptive regulation or governmentality: Patient safety and the changing regulation of medicine. *Sociology of Health & Illness, 29*(2), 163–179.

Weber, E. J., Mason, S., Carter, A., & Hew, R. L. (2011). Emptying the corridors of shame: Organizational lessons from England's 4-hour emergency throughput target. *Annals of Emergency Medicine, 57*(2), 79–88.

Wicks, P., Massagli, M., Frost, J., Brownstein, C., Okun, S., Vaughan, T., B., Bradley, R., & Heywood, J. (2010). Sharing health data for better outcomes on PatientsLikeMe. *Journal of Medical Internet Research, 12*(2), e19.

24

BUNCEFIELD STORIES

Organizational Learning and Remembering for Crisis Prevention

Jan Hayes and Sarah Maslen

Many investigations find that those who deal with hazardous technologies need to be aware of the potential consequences of their actions to inform their risk decision-making; that is they need a good safety imagination. Safety imagination is not fostered by changes to technical standards and the like but rather requires lessons to be integrated into professional practice. Scholarship on professional learning emphasizes the social nature of learning, including the sharing of stories.

This chapter draws on accounts of the Buncefield UK fuel terminal explosion to examine the link between incident investigations and production of stories that are useful for learning to improve safety imagination and so contribute to effective risk management and crisis prevention. Since learning depends on having the right stories to draw on, we also address the implications for incident investigation. We argue that while stories are often overlooked in incident investigations, they link the everyday to the disastrous and are therefore a critical ingredient for safety imagination.

Introduction

Major disasters due to failures of sociotechnical systems are mercifully rare. In the wake of an aircraft crash, chemical plant fire or explosion, pipeline rupture, or oil well blowout, major investigations are undertaken, often with a focus on who was at fault and should therefore be held responsible (Dekker, 2007). More useful for ongoing crisis prevention, significant resources are also invested in determining the factors that contributed to accident causation (Carroll, Rudolph, Hatakenaka, Wiederhold, & Boldrini, 2001; Cedergren & Petersen, 2011). Such findings are documented in publications released into the public domain by standing investigating agencies (e.g. National Transportation Safety Board, 2011) and especially appointed commissions (e.g. Baker et al., 2007) as well as academic publications (e.g. Hopkins, 2008, 2012; Snook, 2000; Vaughan, 1996). Recommendations typically lead to updates to procedures, standards and training, but to assume that this is all that is required to improve risk management and prevent further crises is to severely limit learning opportunities.

In recent decades, researchers have come to understand that accidents happen to organizations rather than individuals (Reason, 1997), and so recommendations for change must also address organizational factors. Some lessons from organizational analysis can be enacted through changes to organizational structures (Hopkins, 2008). Other organizational lessons relate to professional practice and are much harder to embed in structures and systems, such as the need to seek out weak signals of trouble (Haddon-Cave, 2009), to be aware that personal and process safety require different solutions (Hopkins, 2012) and mindfulness of potential consequences when making decisions (Hayes, 2012). The challenge for safety researchers is to determine how we can ensure that these types of lessons are remembered and actively considered in future risk-related decision-making.

Research into sensemaking provides insight into the link between remembering and action. Sensemaking is literally about the sense we make of situations. Sensemaking researchers (Helms Mills et al., 2010; Weick, 1995) emphasize the retrospective nature of our interpretations. We see our current surroundings and choices through the lens of our past experience so we are primed to make use of lessons from disasters, if only we are aware of them in the moment an important choice needs to be made. Critically, sensemaking is a social process and relies on construction of shared stories (Weick, 1995). As argued by Adorisio (2014, p. 466), "corporate narratives, working life stories, anecdotes and instructions become the tapestry that arises from interaction at different organizational levels, becoming the frame within which organizational members negotiate their organizational everyday life". Hayes and Maslen (2015) have shown that stories or narratives are used by experienced operating professionals to retain a sense of danger when it comes to dealing with hazardous technology. Whilst the general benefits of story-based learning are well established, little research has studied this practice specifically in the context of crisis prevention.

This chapter begins to address this research gap through analysis of stories and accounts generated in relation to the Buncefield fuel terminal explosion and fire in the UK in 2005. We analyze the narrative form of the various accounts of the incident and how this links to the requirements for a good story. We also consider the implications of a need for stories to use as the basis for learning for the conduct of major accident investigations. We argue that while stories are often overlooked in incident investigations, they link the everyday to the disastrous. As such, they are a critical ingredient in learning and generation of a safety imagination for better risk management.

Remembering, Narrative, and Sensemaking in Hazardous Industry

Despite the industry and regulatory focus on learning lessons after major crises, investigations find the same causal factors again and again (Quinlan, 2014). Some researchers have gone so far as to say that we have failed to learn the lessons of the past (Hopkins, 2008; Pidgeon & O'Leary, 2000). Many decades ago, Turner (1978) raised the idea of crises being the result of a failure of foresight. More recently, Taleb (2007) has argued that crises result from limitations to knowledge held by a specific individual or group who have the power to change outcomes (so-called 'black swan' events), an idea that has been taken up by many risk scholars (Aven, 2013; Murphy & Conner 2014; Paté-Cornell, 2012). These scholarly conversations point us toward a gap in strategies for learning. We suggest that the missing link perhaps lies in the narrow way in which memory has been conceptualized when it comes to technical attempts to manage risk and prevent crises.

Seeking to embed lessons from past crises in procedures and standards is a common learning strategy in hazardous industry. Underpinned by a conceptulization of organizational memory as "stored information" (Walsh & Ungson, 1991, p. 61), procedures and standards are seen as "experience carriers" (Hale, Kirwan, & Kjellén, 2007, p. 321). While compliance with rules is no doubt an important risk management strategy, the idea that lessons from crises are learned simply via system updates is misleading (Maslen & Hayes, 2016). As research within the interpretivist tradition emphasizes, formalized forms of knowledge do not capture knowing in its entirety (Klein, 1998; Knorr-Cetina, 1999; Wenger, 1998). Rather, codified knowledge such as that captured in procedures and standards "rests on an uncodifiable substrate that tells us how to use the code" (Duguid, 2005, p. 111). Given this, in complex hazardous systems rules do not completely specify necessary actions to effectively control risk in every case. This raises a major question about how to best support tacit, informal and practical forms of knowledge that underpin professional judgments for crisis prevention (Maslen, 2014, 2015).

The design of hazardous industry systems presents a second challenge to learning about risk. Crises are not the result of a single failure, but rather the accumulation of a series of small faults and errors (Reason, 1997). Given this, systems are designed with many layers of protection in place. While there are clear benefits to this strategy, it comes at a cost. Given that failure of any individual risk control can have no apparent consequences, the result can be an accumulation of latent failures that are not revealed until the last control fails. Fostering a safety imagination – an ability to link one's actions to the potential consequences (Pidgeon & O'Leary, 2000) – then becomes vital because it allows decision makers to make the link between the small, even banal, things that happen in every workplace and the potentially disastrous cumulative consequences of failed risk controls that are not addressed. As Gephart (1993, p. 1510) reminds us, "dangers are a fundamental outcome of a disorderly world" in which meanings are driven by sensemaking and not necessarily shared.

If procedures and standards alone are insufficient, and crisis prevention requires a safety imagination, how else can we support recall of safety lessons? Feldman and Feldman (2006) argue that collective knowledge is not an object, but a practice. A reorientation of research focus from the object of memory to the practice of remembering draws attention to theories of sensemaking (Helms Mills et al., 2010; Weick, 1995, 2001) as a way of understanding how experience links to action and so choices that impact risk. Of particular relevance is the notion that sensemaking is retrospective. As Helms Mills et al. (2010, p. 184) describe "we rely on past experiences to interpret current events". These past experiences take the form of stories. As Polkinghorne (1988, p. 13) argues, narrative is "the fundamental scheme for linking individual human actions and events into interrelated aspects of an understandable composite". In this way, a story about a major crisis is much more than simply the compilation of a set of facts. It provides an interpretation of "the significance that events have for one another" (Polkinghorne, 1988, p. 13). Memorable lessons from past crises are therefore likely to be the result of accounts in a narrative form.

Researchers in the field of narrative have studied the ingredients of a "good" story. In Klein's (1998, p. 181) view, good stories are packages of causal relationships: "what factors resulted in what effects". Specifically relevant to the case of hazardous industry is that in the scientific method researchers would run experiments with controls to establish this result. The status of these causal relationships in the case of stories is different. Stories are powerful because, as Klein (1998, p. 182) puts it, "they are like reports of research projects, only easier to understand, remember and use". Good stories are dramatic; they have an element of surprise. These qualities are important to making them have a "point."

When it comes to conversion of such narrative accounts into expert practices that reduce risk, studies have identified stories as an effective knowledge source for decision-making because they are a powerful tool in pattern matching and mental simulation (see Klein, 1998). They convert experiences into memorable, meaningful lessons by drawing out the significance and implications of individual actions and events (Klein, 1998; Polkinghorne, 1988). Experts understand the stakes with which they are working significantly because of their understanding of things that have gone wrong and the stories they tell about these events (Hayes & Maslen, 2015). When faced with relatively minor operating anomalies, they are able to draw connections to past major events and so dig deeper into the state of the system (Macrae, 2009). The empirical evidence of continuing crises suggests that there is a long way to go in fully understanding how past accidents are best understood and remembered.

To date, only limited attention has been devoted to incident investigations in the context of story-based learning. Investigations can be seen as a meta-story in that they are the source of the initial stories that are taken up by various experts and used in collective professional practice. This gives incident investigation reports enormous power over learning. As Dekker (2015, pp. 204–205) argues,

> When we choose words and construct plots to order an accident history, we give the crowded past and disordered chronology an order and a unity that neither the 'facts' nor the past possessed … our choices of where to look and what to call it *create* the epistemological world; the object of our accident investigation.

This reminds us that the stories that are produced by incident investigations are the source of ongoing experiences of any major disaster and so are critical for future crisis prevention. This chapter aims to advance inquiry on this vital issue.

Sources and Methods

We have chosen to examine accounts of the Buncefield disaster through a narrative lens because of its iconic status in the process industries. As a result of the impact of the event, both industry and regulators articulated intentions to learn as much as possible. Two major reports were produced by statutory investigations into the incident, and these form the basis of our analysis:

- The Buncefield Incident, December 11, 2005: The final report of the Major Incident Investigation Board (MIIB) (Vols. 1–2) (produced in 2008 and referred to from here on as the main MIIB report).
- Buncefield: Why did it happen? The underlying causes of the explosion and fire at the Buncefield oil storage depot, Hemel Hempstead, Hertfordshire, on December 11, 2005, produced by the Competent Authority for Control of Major Accident Hazards (produced in 2011 and referred to from here on as the COMAH Report).

In addition, we draw on other material about Buncefield published in academic journals, by industry groups, and in the general media on the ten-year anniversary.

We do not seek to systematically review the incident investigation overall or its recommendations, but rather to consider both the reports themselves and their recommendations through a lens of story-based learning to draw conclusions regarding the likely effectiveness of the material for supporting remembering and safety imagination. In analyzing these accounts, we have drawn on the ingredients of a good story, and so sought to distinguish accounts that are based on human actors with casual relationships between actions and outcomes rather than simple accounts of a sequence of facts.

The broad theoretical argument is also informed by over 90 qualitative interviews with engineers and senior operations experts in hazardous industries that focused on issues of professionalism, expertise and major hazard risk management (Hayes, 2013, 2015; Hayes & Maslen, 2015; Hopkins & Maslen, 2015; Maslen, 2014, 2015). Participants in these studies were practicing engineers and operating professionals in the gas pipeline, chemicals, aviation and nuclear sectors. Interviews were transcribed and thematically analyzed in the context of their original research questions. This research did not set out to examine directly the use or role of stories in learning. Nevertheless, our data are full of narratives used by interviewees to explain their actions.

The Hunt for Lessons about Buncefield

The Initial Investigation and Recommendations

The Buncefield fire was investigated by a formally constituted MIIB which operated for three years following the incident. As recounted in the main MIIB report (Major Incident Investigation Board, 2008), the immediate trigger for the catastrophe at the oil storage depot was a large petrol storage tank which overflowed whilst it was being filled from a pipeline. The magnitude of the resultant vapor explosion was much greater than anyone knew was possible. Houses close to the terminal were destroyed, and buildings as far as 8 km away had windows broken. There were no fatalities, but 43 people received minor injuries. Over 20 large storage tanks on the site were destroyed in the subsequent fire which burned for five days. There was also significant damage to the adjacent industrial estate and interruption to aviation fuel supplies in the UK. The response involved over 1,000 emergency services personnel.

The MIIB report describes events leading up to the incident as follows:

> Late on Saturday 10 December 2005 a delivery of unleaded petrol from the T/K pipeline started to arrive at Tank 912 in bund A at about 05:30 on 11 December. The safety systems in place to shut off the supply of petrol to the tank to prevent overfilling failed to operate. Petrol cascaded down the side of the tank, collecting at first in bund A. As overfilling continued, the vapour cloud formed by the mixture of petrol and air flowed over the bund wall, dispersed and flowed west off site towards the Maylands Industrial Estate… At 06:01 on Sunday 11 December 2005, the first of a series of explosions took place. The main explosion was massive and appears to have been centred on the Maylands Estate car parks just west of the HOSL [Hertfordshire Oil Storage Ltd, the operators of the site] West site.

Figure 24.1   Excerpt from Buncefield MIIB Report (Major Incident Investigation Board, 2008, p. 7)

Putting aside that the first sentence seems confused about timing, the most startling feature of this description is that there are no people involved. Reading this, one might think that the site was not staffed. This quote includes all that the report says about the events leading to the overflow of the first tank. The report goes into significant detail as to how the leaking petrol spread, what caused it to ignite, the emergency response arrangements and the ultimate impact of the event on the environment, surrounding houses and on business, and yet it provides no explanation as to why these impacts occurred. Technical lessons are addressed in detail, but lessons that have the potential to change the behavior of those who design, operate or manage similar facilities are missing. There is little in this account to capture the imagination of readers so they can see themselves as possible actors in a similar story.

Similarly, research publications have also focused on the engineering details at Buncefield including better instrumentation to prevent tank overfilling (Summers & Hearn, 2010), understanding of vapor cloud generation (Atkinson, Coldrick, Gant, & Cusco, 2015), why the overpressure was so much higher than expected (Bakke, van Wingerden, Hoorelbeke, & Brewerton, 2010; Gray, 2012), improvements to bund design (Whitfield & Nicholas, 2009), improvements to risk assessment practices (Paltrinieri, Dechy, Salzano, Wardman, & Cozzani, 2012) and the importance of managing worker fatigue (Wilkinson, 2013). However, beyond these technical lessons, there are deeper questions regarding why the technical failures occurred at all, that is, the organizational causes of the event including such questions as: What were the work practices and work pressures in play for the people involved? What can workers at all levels from frontline operations to management take from these circumstances?

The MIIB itself also issued several engineering-based reports on various aspects of the impact of and responses to the fire (Major Incident Investigation Board, 2008). This material also gives many insights into technical aspects of the event but is limited when it comes to providing insights for broader organizational learning as it says almost nothing about the circumstances leading up to the event. The reason for this is made clear in their final report. The MIIB's work was conducted in parallel with criminal investigations. As they report, "The major constraint on ... openness has been the need to avoid prejudice to the criminal investigation ... We have published information on what happened and how but have been cautiously circumspect in suggesting why the incident occurred" (Major Incident Investigation Board, 2008, p. 31). Without any engagement with cause and effect, there is no story to tell.

The Narrative Emerges in the COMAH Report

Five years after the accident when criminal proceedings were concluded, another official report, this time from the relevant regulatory agencies, filled the cause and effect gap by recounting events anew and critically including people and the choices they made (Competent Authority for Control of Major Accident Hazards, 2011). This new report detailing the underlying causes of the events was published with the view that "everyone in major hazard industries ... can learn from this incident, understand what went wrong, and take away lessons that are relevant to them" (Competent Authority for Control of Major Accident Hazards, 2011, p. 3). Whereas the MIIB report is an exclusively technical account light on narrative, this second report finally tells the story of Buncefield. A tank does not spontaneously overflow, but it is an event with narrative including human actors. The report contains no new recommendations, but it brings to life the working relationships of the various people involved in the design and operation of the systems that ultimately failed. An example of this is shown in Figure 24.2.

The Independent High-level Switch

20 Tank 912 was fitted with a new independent high-level switch on 1 July 2004. This had been designed, manufactured and supplied by TAV Engineering Ltd. TAV had designed the switch so that some of its functionality could be routinely tested. Unfortunately, the way the switch was designed, installed and maintained gave a false sense of security. Because those who installed and operated the switch did not fully understand the way it worked, or the crucial role played by a padlock, the switch was left effectively inoperable after the test.

21 The design fault could have been eradicated at an early stage if the design changes had been subjected to a rigorous review process. In any event, clear guidance, including instructions about the safety criticality of the padlock, should have been passed on to installers and users.

22 TAV was aware that its switches were used in high-hazard installations and therefore were likely to be safety critical.

23 The impact of these defects in switch design, and the failure to inform users and suppliers of the change in criticality of the padlock, could have been reduced by those further down the supply chain. Motherwell Control Systems 2003 Ltd ordered the IHLS from TAV but the ordering process by both parties fell short of what would be expected for safety critical equipment intended for such a high-hazard environment. The information TAV provided did not give sufficient clarity about the key aspects of the IHLS design and use, and TAV should have enquired as to the intended purpose of the switch and formed a view as to its suitability – in this case for a high-level only application. Motherwell staff were highly experienced in this field although the company itself had only recently come into existence as the result of a management buy-out. However, their systems for checking and understanding equipment again fell short of the mark.

Figure 24.2 Excerpt from Buncefield COMAH Report (Competent Authority for Control of Major Accident Hazards, 2011, p. 13)

In contrast to the MIIB report, in the COMAH report the story begins years before the 2005 explosion in the detailed work practices of several different groups. Experienced equipment suppliers made critical assumptions about equipment their sub-contractors had supplied. Busy maintenance people made assumptions about how equipment operated. Supervisors made the best of working with faulty equipment without appreciating the broader implications. Overworked engineers from head office did not ensure that the terminal was operated in accordance with safety documentation. It is stories such as these that have the potential to impact the safety imagination of other hazardous industry workers by linking routine actions to the possibility of a crisis.

Tenth Anniversary Narratives

The most striking narratives of Buncefield linked to the ten-year anniversary are those contained in the media, mainly stories of nearby residents and emergency services personnel.

They are compelling because readers are transported back to the Buncefield area at the time of the incident, making it easy to imagine being there and experiencing similar emotions. Critically, there is an absence in these ten-year anniversary accounts of the re-memberings of engineers. We can only speculate that this represents a response to concerns regarding liability.

In the accounts of residents of Buncefield, we can see stories that can help decision-makers understand the potential consequences of their choices. Some nearby residents have been reminded of the fragility of life and the consequences of living close to a major industrial facility. As one resident said to a reporter, "the thing that really got to me was how close to death my children came … that was something that was very, very difficult to come to terms with." Another resident said, "it doesn't take much to start the imagination going, thinking about what would happen if it exploded a second time." Others have learned different lessons. The social media editor for (BBC News, 2015) is reported as saying:

> Buncefield helped shape our thinking around safety. To what extent should we be encouraging members of the public to send us footage in an uncertain and potential dangerous situation? We needed to adapt our 'calls to action' to discourage risk and underline our duty of care.

This person is drawing lessons for their own professional practice in the media linked to the consequences of decisions made.

The link between actions and consequences is also an important lesson for those who design, operate and manage hazardous facilities that would be made much more vivid if more first-hand accounts were available from members of these professional communities. We have found one example where this type of account has been used to grab attention of process engineers. An article in *The Chemical Engineer* (the professional magazine of the Institution of Chemical Engineers), which is primarily about tank overfill protection, begins like this:

> Picture the scene, early on a Winter Sunday morning. Calm and serene, you and your family are tucked up in bed at home. Suddenly, you're awakened abruptly by an ear-splitting noise followed by your room shaking around you. Your home and life as you know it has been shattered, and so the nightmare begins. This was the scenario for many residents of Hemel Hempstead, UK, on 11 Dec 2005. A shock wave, measuring 2.4 on the Richter scale, ripped through their homes.
>
> *(Joseph, 2015, p. 26)*

The article continues in a much more technical style once readers are "hooked" by this direct appeal to their imagination.

These are the ten-year narratives in the trade and general press, but there was one other significant publication for the 10th anniversary. To mark that milestone, the regulators again published a new report. On the subject of lessons, the Report of the COMAH Strategic Forum (Competent Authority for Control of Major Accident Hazards, 2015, p. 12) on the 10th anniversary says,

> The Buncefield explosion and fire highlighted major deficiencies that resulted in appropriate enforcement by the regulators. The investigation of the incident illustrated the need for lessons to be shared and implemented more widely … The legacy of Buncefield

remains with us and in the way we work … The lessons learned are now having a far reaching impact on other industries, and as such our knowledge of safety, the standards which we use and our understanding of risks are continually improving.

Yet again, there is an emphasis here on learning lessons, but the question of how such learning is to occur remains open as is the case in all previous formal publications from the MIIB and COMAH.

Over time, accounts of Buncefield have changed from a focus on recommendations without providing cause and effect links, to a focus on the circumstances that led to the disaster. At the ten-year anniversary, there have been stories from local residents. It is conspicuous that what starts as a technical account of the events is ultimately remembered by people affected as a story. This has implications for learning, as we discuss in the following section.

Implications for Learning

Based on the key qualities of a good story, at one level the extract from the MIIB main report in Figure 24.1 qualifies as a story of what happened after the first tank at Buncefield overflowed. It describes a sequence of interrelated events – overflow, cloud formation, explosion – and it is somewhat dramatic. Professionals hearing and reading this story can no doubt see that the consequences of the tank overflow were severe. However, this is not sufficient if we are seeking to impact safety imagination. To have such an impact, professionals need to be able to link this consequence to their day-to-day work experience – the small things that happen that could contribute to disaster years down the track. The MIIB report narrative is not a story of causation that allows professionals whose work can contribute to such outcomes to easily see themselves on the page.

In contrast to this, the excerpt in Figure 24.2 from the COMAH report takes a different view of events. It tells the story of the design, manufacture and installation of the independent high-level switch (IHLS). Failure of this switch was a key cause of the catastrophic events of December 2005, but the story of the IHLS as told here starts much earlier. This is emphasized by the opening sentence that immediately places readers in July 2004 when the switch was installed. The narrative then moves even further back in time to the story of how the switch came to be designed, manufactured and supplied. These activities are described in some detail, and people playing various roles are included. The story describes the actions they took and how alternative actions would have resulted in a different outcome. It passes the test of being a story with a clear narrative, protagonists and causal relationships.

In the end, protagonists are defeated by a series of organizational and technical failures. The most striking aspect of this narrative is the relative banality of the actions described. Designers, installers, maintainers and suppliers all go about their day-to-day activities apparently without any sense of the latent failures (Reason, 1997) that they were introducing into the system. Above all, the account is plausible in its description of engineering workplaces. In contrast to the MIIB report narrative, professionals who work in similar roles can see themselves in these paragraphs. Fundamentally, this is a story of why a critical risk control failed and how such a failure might have been prevented. It links engineers and technicians going about their day-to-day work with the potential for catastrophe literally years later. The drama in the story comes from the sense of impending disaster that we can feel in hindsight but was missing at the time. It is exactly the type of story that is needed for learning lessons linked to safety imagination, and yet it took almost six years to be told.

To date, we have focused on learning from the crisis at Buncefield itself, but this major failure is simply an accumulation of smaller failures. Such failures are far more common, and so provide more material for learning if only they can be effectively captured. The recommendations from Buncefield address this issue stating:

> The sector should set up arrangements to collate incident data on high potential incidents ... The arrangements ... should include, but not be limited to, the following:
>
> - thorough investigation of root causes of failures and malfunctions of safety and environmental protection critical elements ...;
> - developing incident databases that can be shared across the entire sector, subject to data protection and other legal requirements ...;
> - collaboration between the workforce and its representatives, dutyholders and regulators to ensure lessons are learned from incidents, and best practices are shared.
>
> *(Major Incident Investigation Board, 2008, p. 49)*

These issues were also taken up by the process safety leadership group which was formed following the Buncefield incident with membership from industry, trade unions and regulators (Process Safety Leadership Group, 2009).

As the high-reliability researchers highlighted some decades ago, mindful organizations are "preoccupied with failure" (Weick & Sutcliffe, 2001; Weick, Sutcliffe, & Obstfeld, 1999). Industry has taken this on board with gusto as these recommendations illustrate, and yet research into incident databases has highlighted the ways in which these systems tend not to deliver an elegant solution to risk management including the following issues:

- databases are infrequently designed to collect the information pertinent to catastrophic risk management (Phimister, Okte, Kleindorfer, & Kunreuther, 2003);
- the abundance of data dilutes core lessons for catastrophic risk management (Maslen & Hayes, 2016);
- lack of reporting due to difficulty with the reporting process, lack of clarity over what should be reported, fear of disciplinary action and a sense that reporting is not worthwhile (Dekker, 2007; Hopkins, 2009; Phimister et al. 2003; Wahlström, 2011); and
- lack of analysis of reports and actions to prevent recurrence including identification of organizational causes (Hopkins, 2009; Hovden, Størseth, & Tinmannsvik, 2011; Jacobsson, Sales, & Mushtaq, 2009; Phimister et al. 2003; Reason, 1997).

The excessive focus on factual data held in formal databases has in many ways masked important possibilities for learning. The assumption seems to be that information stored in a database is equivalent to embedding lessons into the decision-making practices of key staff, although critical scholarship has illustrated how this process does not lead directly to learning (Hecker, 2012; Maslen & Hayes, 2016). Previous research has identified stories of near misses, small failures and crises as powerful knowledge sources (Hayes, 2013; Hayes & Maslen, 2015; Maslen, 2015). Common across this research was the finding that storytelling is valuable for developing values and practices that work to prevent crises. Storytelling does not preclude the use of incident databases, but equally, incident databases are not a replacement for stories.

When it comes to impacting professional practice, we need stories that link the banality of everyday working life to the sheer terror that can result in hazardous industry when things go wrong badly. Inspiring safety imagination requires a good story with drama and protagonists. We could think of the requirements of a good story in terms of questions professionals might ask themselves:

- What did those people do that contributed to the accident?
- In what ways does that resemble what I might do in similar circumstances and so what should I do differently from now on?
- Might I have already done similar things that have led to latent problems that need to be investigated and fixed?

Such questions are relevant to people at all levels of the organization and in all professional groups. Stories may be light on technical details, but transfer of technical facts is not their key function. As Rae (2016, p. 6) argues: "Stories … have little scientific weight … but they have a lot of emotional pull". This "emotional pull" has value that can be tapped in the interests of improved safety imagination. In this sense, stories of crises do not replace technical accounts of failures, but they are a vital ingredient in efforts to share industry's collective experience to ensure that future disaster is prevented.

Implications for Effective Investigations

Generation of stories from major accidents is part of the broader process of accident investigation, so we turn our attention here to the implications for the scope and structure of such investigations when story-based learning is a desired outcome. The first consideration is the purpose of investigation and the impact that different investigation foci have on successful ongoing story-based learning. The second related issue is the model of accident causation that is inherent in investigation.

The discussion so far has been predicated on the assumption that an accident investigation is seeking to determine the causes of what occurred with a primary view to prevent recurrence. As Dechy et al. (2012) discuss, this is far from the only reason for examining what has occurred. A major accident can lead to many investigations with a diversity of contexts and frameworks including engineering, safety, economic/contractual, managerial and legal. Any investigation that is primarily focused on finding fault takes a normative view of actions taken. In such a legal view, people are free agents and so responsible for any deviations of their actions from the prescribed course. This is substantially different to seeking an explanation as to why people acted in a particular way. Such differences are not simply a matter of the scope of investigation as written but rather a different psychological approach to investigation. Dekker (2015) describes four psychological purposes of accident investigations: epistemological (establishing what happened), preventative (identifying pathways to avoidance), moral (tracing the transgressions that were committed and reinforcing moral and regulatory boundaries) and existential (finding an explanation for the suffering that occurred). These different orientations to an investigation result in different stories as shown by Gephart (1993) in his detailed analysis of a Canadian pipeline failure.

As described earlier, the Buncefield MIIB report was constrained in its ability to support story-based learning as a result of the parallel legal processes. The MIIB report is significantly grounded in an epistemological viewpoint when it comes to establishing what happened after the tank overflow. It tries to take a preventative orientation by making wide-ranging recommendations, but the extreme lengths that the report goes to in order to avoid any suggestion of making moral judgments related to actions and possible transgressions limits its value as we have already described. A much more complete explanation of who did what and why was not available until all legal proceedings were completed.

A related issue is that the conduct of any investigation is based on assumptions regarding accident causation that may not be explicit. An organizational view of accidents which sees workers' actions as determined by their organizational circumstances is essential to prevent recurrence. However, investigations often focus on the actions of individuals, and in this we can expect such investigations to find individuals at fault. Hollnagel (2008, p. 260) summarizes this idea as "what you look for is what you find". Despite the significant impact of assumptions regarding accident causation on investigation findings, several empirical studies of accident investigation reports in the transport and industrial sectors have found that most do not explicitly state the model of investigation or assumptions regarding accident causation that underpin their work (Cedergren & Petersen, 2011; Lundberg, Rollenhagen, & Hollnagel, 2009; Okstad, Jersin, & Tinmannsvik, 2012). Despite this, narratives of accident causation will also be constructed based on such assumptions, critically impacting what readers learn and remember.

A major review of European accident investigation practices found that few adopt an organizational paradigm in their search for understanding of accident causation. Rather, an engineering paradigm – sometimes, with the addition of a human error approach – dominates (Dechy et al., 2012). The primary exception is investigation boards into major disasters. Such investigations have significant resources allocated and often also have access to more senior levels of management providing important evidence for organizational analysis. As the COMAH report regarding Buncefield notes, "a detailed investigation into a major incident provides a unique opportunity for the regulator to assess the full managerial processes involved at a particular site" (Competent Authority for Control of Major Accident Hazards, 2011, p. 30). Crises are mercifully rare, but when they do occur there is the potential to learn about how organizations function beyond the immediate site of the accident and especially at the highest levels. It is critical that investigations are consciously constructed to make the most of these opportunities in order to prevent recurrence.

One way to address this challenge is to separate investigations focused on learning, from investigations for other reasons. Various authors (Cedergren & Petersen, 2011; Dechy et al., 2012; Vuorio, Rantonen, Johnson, Ollila, Salminen, & Braithwaite, 2014) have highlighted the benefits of a standing investigation capacity independent of criminal investigation to ensure that a deep understanding of accidents is generated and made available for learning. Focusing on the benefits of story-based learning only serves to support such an argument. The work of such inquiries often includes protection of witnesses so that testimony of witnesses and findings of inquiries cannot be used for legal prosecution. One well-known example of such an organization is the US Chemical Safety Board. In addition to formal reports, their outputs include a wide range of video training materials. Also worthy of note is the emerging popularity of theatrical productions which draw on inquiry testimony to dramatically bring to life the stories of significant crises. Again, these stories move well away from technical details but provide the links between the everyday and the catastrophic that make safety imagination possible.

Conclusion

The term "lessons learned" is used to describe many publications about industrial crises. This implies that experience of an event (either directly or at a company or industry level) results in an enduring lesson that permanently changes how risks are understood and managed, but one only needs to look at recent crises to see how organizations can *fail* to learn lessons (Hopkins, 2008, 2012). Technical changes such as updating standards and codes are not, on their own, sufficient to prevent recurrence. The Buncefield case gives us a clue as to what more is required. As the COMAH report explains,

> when passing sentence on the defendants … the Judge … commented that cost cutting *per se* was not put forward as a major feature of the prosecution case, but the failings had more to do with slackness, inefficiency and a more-or-less complacent approach to matters of safety.
>
> *(Competent Authority for Control of Major Accident Hazards, 2011, p. 3)*

Drawing on theories of sensemaking, narrative and organizational memory, we have shown that sharing stories provides a foundation for remembering that is critical in linking the everyday to the disastrous. Stories act as an antidote to the complacency seen at Buncefield that can so easily be engendered by an apparent lack of safety problems. Multiple risk controls in place mean that even in poor performing systems, crises are relatively rare. Stories remind us that there may be evidence of problems if only we look for it through the lens of past failings. As Adorisio (2014, p. 463) says, "narrative represents a way to organize the selection and interpretation of the past". Our analysis of the Buncefield case has shown how poorly the link between accident investigation and story-based learning appears to be understood. If we truly wish to prevent further crises, more effort should be directed to developing ways in which to share the experiences of disasters and to foster organizational remembering as well as retaining technical lessons in standards and procedures.

The Buncefield investigation also recommended improved processes for learning from small incidents linked to use of databases for reporting and recording. Collecting factual information is important for trend analysis and to understand technical matters, but such data collection alone is insufficient for learning (Maslen & Hayes, 2016). Sharing stories of day-to-day incidents supports improved professional practice and better safety imagination. It translates information into collective knowledge. Collecting and writing effective stories is a specialized task, and yet it is rarely treated as such. In light of this, methods for investigating story collection and dissemination in hazardous industry warrant further inquiry.

The perspective of story-based learning also strengthens the case for a standing investigation capacity for major accidents as exists in some jurisdictions and some industries. Separation of investigations aimed at explanation and so future prevention, from those focused on legality and blame, is critical if the stories necessary for learning are to be generated and shared. This makes learning more timely, and it also introduces the possibility that the stories themselves will be of a higher quality.

References

Adorisio, A. L. M. (2014). Organizational remembering as narrative: 'Storying' the past in banking. *Organization, 21*, 463–476.

Atkinson, G., Coldrick, S., Gant, S., & Cusco, L. (2015). Flammable vapor cloud generation from overfilling tanks: Learning the lessons from Buncefield. *Journal of Loss Prevention in the Process Industries, 35*(35), 329–338.

Aven, T. (2013). On the meaning of a black swan in a risk context. *Safety Science, 57*, 44–51.

Baker, J. A., Bowman, F. L., Erwin, G., Gorton, S., Hendershot, D., Leveson, N., …, Wilson, L. D. (2007). The report of the BP US Refineries Independent Safety Review Panel. Retrieved from www.propublica.org/documents/item/the-bp-us-refineries-independent-safety-review-panel-report

Bakke, J. R., van Wingerden, K., Hoorelbeke, P., & Brewerton, B. (2010). A study on the effect of trees on gas explosions. *Journal of Loss Prevention in the Process Industries, 23*, 878–884.

BBC News. (2015). Buncefield explosion: 'I thought a plane landed on us'. Retrieved from www.bbc. com/news/uk-england-beds-bucks-herts-34919922

Carroll, J. S., Rudolph, J., Hatakenaka, S., Wiederhold, T., & Boldrini, M. (2001). Learning in the context of incident investigation: Team diagnoses and organizational decisions at four nuclear power plants. In E. Salas & G. Klein (Eds.), *Linking expertise and naturalistic decision making*. Mahwah, NJ: Lawrence Erbaum Associates.

Cedergren, A., & Petersen, K. (2011). Prerequisites for learning from accident investigations— A cross-country comparison of national accident investigation boards. *Safety Science, 49*, 1238–1245.

Competent Authority for Control of Major Accident Hazards. (2011). Buncefield: Why did it happen? The underlying causes of the explosion and fire at the Buncefield oil storage depot, Hemel Hempstead, Hertfordshire on 11 December 2005. Retrieved from www.hse.gov.uk/comah/buncefield/buncefield-report.pdf

Competent Authority for Control of Major Accident Hazards. (2015). The Buncefield major incident 11 December 2005: Ten years on – a report by the COMAH Strategic Forum. Retrieved from www.hse.gov.uk/comah/buncefield/buncefield-10-years-on.pdf

Dechy, N., Dien, Y., Funnemark, E., Roed-Larsen, S., Stoop, J., Valvisto, T., & Arellano, A. L. V. (2012). Results and lessons learned from the ESReDA's Accident Investigation Working Group. *Safety Science, 50*, 1380–1391.

Dekker, S. (2007). *Just culture: Balancing safety and accountability*. Aldershot, UK: Ashgate.

Dekker, S. (2015). The psychology of accident investigation: Epistemological, preventive, moral and existential meaning-making. *Theoretical Issues in Ergonomics Science, 16*, 202–213.

Duguid, P. (2005). "The art of knowing": Social and tacit dimensions of knowledge and the limits of the community of practice. *The Information Society, 21*, 109–118.

Feldman, R., & Feldman, S. (2006). What links the chain: An essay on organizational remembering as practice. *Organization, 13*(6), 861–887.

Gephart, R. P. (1993). The textual approach: Risk and blame in disaster sensemaking. *The Academy of Management Journal, 36*(6), 1465–1514.

Gray, W. (2012). The impossible explosion. *New Scientist, 213*(2858), 44–47.

Haddon-Cave, C. (2009). *The Nimrod review: An independent review into the broader issues surrounding the loss of the RAF Nimrod MR2 Aircraft XV230 in Afghanistan in 2006*. London, UK: House of Commons.

Hale, A., Kirwan, B., & Kjellén, U. (2007). Safe by design: Where are we now? *Safety Science, 45*, 305–327.

Hayes, J. (2012). Operator competence and capacity—Lessons from the Montara blowout. *Safety Science, 50*, 563–574.

Hayes, J. (2013). *Operational decision-making in high-hazard organizations: Drawing a line in the sand*. Farnham, UK: Ashgate.

Hayes, J. (2015). Investigating design office dynamics that support safe design. *Safety Science, 78*, 25–34.

Hayes, J., & Maslen, S. (2015). Knowing stories that matter: Learning for effective safety decision-making. *Journal of Risk Research, 18*(6), 714–726.

Hecker, A. (2012). Knowledge beyond the individual? Making sense of a notion of collective knowledge in organization theory. *Organization Studies, 33*, 423–445.

Helms Mills, J., Thurlow, A., & Mills, A. J. (2010). Making sense of sensemaking: The critical sensemaking approach. *Qualitative Research in Organizations and Management: An International Journal, 5*, 182–195.

Hollnagel, E. (2008). Investigation as an impediment to learning. In E. Hollnagel, C. P. Nemeth, & S. Dekker (Eds.), *Remaining sensitive to the possibility of failure*. Aldershot, UK: Ashgate.

Hopkins, A. (2008). *Failure to learn: The BP Texas City Refinery disaster*. Sydney, NSW: CCH.

Hopkins, A. (2009). Identifying and responding to warnings. In A. Hopkins (Ed.), *Learning from high reliability organisations*. Sydney, NSW: CCH.

Hopkins, A. (2012). *Disastrous decisions: The human and organizational causes of the Gulf of Mexico blowout*. Sydney, NSW: CCH.

Hopkins, A., & Maslen, S. (2015). *Risky rewards: How company bonuses affect safety*. Farnham, UK: Ashgate.

Hovden, J., Størseth, F., & Tinmannsvik, R. K. (2011). Multilevel learning from accidents—Case studies in transport. *Safety Science, 49*(1), 98–105.

Jacobsson, A., Sales, J., & Mushtaq, F. (2009). A sequential method to identify underlying causes from industrial accidents reported to the MARS database. *Journal of Loss Prevention in the Process Industries, 22*(2), 197–203.

Joseph, M. (2015). *Buncefield: A decade on, the chemical engineer.* Rugby, UK: Institution of Chemical Engineers, 26–29.

Klein, G. (1998). *Sources of power: How people make decisions.* Cambridge, MA: MIT Press.

Knorr-Cetina, K. (1999). *Epistemic cultures: How the sciences make knowledge.* London, UK: Harvard University Press.

Lundberg, J., Rollenhagen, C., & Hollnagel, E. (2009). What-you-look-for-is-what-you-find—The consequences of underlying accident models in eight accident investigation manuals. *Safety Science, 47,* 1297–1311.

Macrae, C. (2009). From risk to resilience: Assessing flight safety incidents in airlines. In A. Hopkins (Ed.), *Learning from high reliability organisations.* Sydney, NSW: CCH.

Major Incident Investigation Board. (2008). *The Buncefield incident 11 December 2005: The final report of the Major Incident Investigation Board* (Vols. 1–2). Richmond, UK: Crown.

Maslen, S. (2014). Learning to prevent disaster: An investigation into methods for building safety knowledge among new engineers to the Australian gas pipeline industry. *Safety Science, 64,* 82–89.

Maslen, S. (2015). Organizational factors for learning in the Australian gas pipeline industry. *Journal of Risk Research, 18*(7), 896–909.

Maslen, S., & Hayes, J. (2016). Preventing black swans: Incident reporting systems as collective knowledge management. *Journal of Risk Research, 19*(10), 1246–1260.

Murphy, J. F., & Conner, J. (2014). Black swans, white swans, and 50 shades of grey: Remembering the lessons learned from catastrophic process safety incidents. *Process Safety Progress, 33*(2), 110–114.

National Transportation Safety Board. (2011). *Pipeline accident report: Pacific Gas and Electric Company natural gas transmission pipeline rupture and fire, San Bruno, CA, September 9, 2010.* Washington, WA: National Transportation Safety Board.

Okstad, E., Jersin, E., & Tinmannsvik, R. K. (2012). Accident investigation in the Norwegian petroleum industry—Common features and future challenges. *Safety Science, 50,* 1408–1414.

Paltrinieri, N., Dechy, N., Salzano, E., Wardman, M., & Cozzani, V. (2012). Lessons learned from Toulouse and Buncefield disasters: From risk analysis failures to the identification of atypical scenarios through a better knowledge management. *Risk Analysis, 32,* 1404–1419.

Paté-Cornell, E. (2012). On 'black swans' and 'perfect storms': Risk analysis and management when statistics are not enough. *Risk Analysis, 32*(11), 1823–1833.

Phimister, J. R., Okte, U., Kleindorfer, P. R., & Kunreuther, H. (2003). Near-miss incident management in the chemical process industry. *Risk Analysis, 23*(3), 445–459.

Pidgeon, N., & O'Leary, M. (2000). Man-made disasters: Why technology and organizations (sometimes) fail. *Safety Science, 34,* 15–30.

Polkinghorne, D. E. (1988). *Narrative knowing and the human sciences.* Albany, NY: State University of New York Press.

Process Safety Leadership Group. (2009). Safety and environmental standards for fuel storage sites: Process Safety Leadership Group final report. Retrieved from www.hse.gov.uk/comah/buncefield/fuel-storage-sites.pdf

Quinlan, M. (2014). *Ten pathways to death and disaster: Learning from fatal incidents in mines and other high hazard workplaces.* Sydney, NSW: The Federation Press.

Rae, A. (2016). Tales of disaster: The role of accident storytelling in safety teaching. *Cognition, Technology and Work, 18,* 1–10.

Reason, J. (1997). *Managing the risks of organizational accidents.* Aldershot, UK: Ashgate.

Snook, S. A. (2000). *Friendly fire: The accidental shootdown of US black hawks over Northern Iraq.* Princeton, NJ: Princeton University Press.

Summers, A. E., & Hearn, W. (2010). Overfill protective systems—Complex problem, simple solution. *Journal of Loss Prevention in the Process Industries, 23,* 781–783.

Taleb, N. N. (2007). *The black swan: The impact of the highly improbable.* New York, NY: Random House.

Turner, B. A. (1978). *Man-made disasters.* London, UK: Wykeham Publications (London) Ltd.

Vaughan, D. (1996). *The challenger launch decision: Risky technology, culture and deviance at NASA.* Chicago, IL: University of Chicago Press.

Vuorio, A., Rantonen, J., Johnson, C., Ollila, T., Salminen, S., & Braithwaite, G. (2014). What fatal occupational accident investigators can learn from fatal aircraft accident investigations. *Safety Science, 62,* 366–369.

Wahlström, B. (2011). Organizational learning—Reflections from the nuclear industry. *Safety Science, 49*(1), 65–74.

Walsh, J., & Ungson, G. (1991). Organizational memory. *Academy of Management Review, 16*(1), 57–91.

Weick, K. E. (1995). *Sensemaking in organizations*. Thousand Oaks, CA: Sage Publications.

Weick, K. E. (2001). *Making sense of the organization*. Oxford, UK: Blackwell Business.

Weick, K. E., & Sutcliffe, K. M. (2001). *Managing the unexpected: Assuring high performance in an age of complexity*. San Francisco, CA: Jossey-Bass.

Weick, K. E., Sutcliffe, K. M., & Obstfeld, D. (1999). Organizing for high reliability: Processes of collective mindfulness. In R. I. Sutton & B. M. Staw (Eds.), *Research in organizational behavior* (Vol. 21). Stanford, CT: JAI Press.

Wenger, E. (1998). *Communities of practice: Learning, meaning, and identity*. Cambridge: UK, Cambridge University Press.

Whitfield, A., & Nicholas, M. (2009). Bunding at Buncefield: Successes, failures and lessons learned. *Loss Prevention Bulletin, 205*, 19–25.

Wilkinson, J. (2013). Shift work and fatigue – and the possible consequences. *Occupational Health Nov, 65*, 27–30.

PART VI

Current Issues

25

SPATIAL AND TEMPORAL PATTERNS IN GLOBAL ENTERPRISE RISK

Yossi Sheffi

> The world is so connected that the feedback loops are more intense. Our supply chains are global. Our financial markets are global. So uncertainty in one part of the world infiltrates all parts of the world. These days, there are things that just come shooting across the bow – economic volatility and the impact of natural events, like the Japanese earthquake and tsunami – at much greater frequency than we've ever seen, said Ellen Kullman, CEO of DuPont.
>
> *(Kirkland, 2012)*

A leading driver of this growing vulnerability is the rapid growth of global trade. Global merchandise exports surged from \$7.38 trillion in 2003 to \$18.49 trillion in 2014, implying that more companies are dependent on geographically distant suppliers and customers (World Trade Organization [WTO], 2015). Rapidly declining costs of communications and the growing efficiency of logistics are enabling all this trade, with the resulting spatial spreading of supply chains. With digital communications, companies can more readily work with geographically dispersed facilities, suppliers, and distribution centers on the other side of the world.

A second driver of this global risk lies in the growing complexity of products. For example, automobiles now contain between 30 and 100 microprocessors (Turley, 1999), with each subsystem of the car having its own controller and software (Charlotte, 2009). Increasing use of technology includes reliance on an expanding variety of engineered materials, additives, pigments, and treatments that enable high efficiencies, performance, and market acceptance. With product complexity comes the need to use more suppliers, who, in turn, may use more suppliers, leading to more complex supply chains.

Finally, business imperatives for cost-efficiency in a dynamic environment have induced the growing use of lean or just-in-time manufacturing strategies. These strategies use Internet-enabled coordination of activities in supply chains and reduce the volume of costly and obsolescence-prone inventory. The result is tighter supply chains with lower costs, higher quality, and better responsiveness in the face of innovation and demand uncertainty. Yet the lack of inventory and spare resources in the supply chains makes them more prone to disruption and makes disruptions in one part of the economy more likely to propagate to distant parts.

In the end, the rise of global trade and global competition means that companies have more moving pieces stretched over greater distances and with less slack in the system. That is, each company has a geographic risk footprint that extends beyond its own facilities to encompass the facilities of distributors and customers downstream in the supply chain, as well as suppliers at multiple tiers upstream. Thus, when an earthquake hits Japan or anywhere else, the companies of the global economy find themselves shaking, too. The spatial properties of the geographic risk footprint, in turn, create a temporal element of disruption in terms of detecting disruptive events in time, with their concomitant propagation of disruption to companies and to their customers.

More than two decades of research – culminating in two books: *The Resilient Enterprise* (Sheffi, 2005) and *The Power of Resilience* (Sheffi, 2015) – have traced companies' growing adoption and maturity of enterprise risk management practices. This chapter uses case examples to illustrate these spatial and temporal issues in enterprise risk.

Commercial Connectivity and Spatial Business Risks

Supply chain risks arise from a company's dependence on commercial partners, namely upstream suppliers and their sub-suppliers, and downstream distributors, retailers, and business customers. Disruptions to commercial partners can disrupt a firm's operations, sales, or assets through shortages of critical parts, blockage of freight movement, damage to inventory, or disruption of sales channels in proportion to the firm's share of production, revenues, or profit linked to the disrupted partner. These risks have both spatial and temporal aspects created by the *geographic risk footprint* of a company's supply chain, which encompasses all the locations and interconnecting routes of these commercial partners.

As with risks to the company's own facilities, these supply chain risks vary with the geographic pattern of the locations of the partners' facilities. Many types of natural disaster risks follow reasonably well-understood geographic patterns of likelihood and severity. For any given business location, data and models regarding seismic activities, hurricanes, tornadoes, wind, and floods can be used to estimate a statistical distribution of frequency and severities of natural disasters for that location. Such estimates are typically based on power law distributions. Actuarial models of fires, accidents, crime, and other damage claims offer insight into the diverse risks to property and equipment in different geographies. Analysis of political, social, and economic risks can elucidate some of the relative risks of supply chain partner operations in different locations. Overall, these spatial models of risk can help estimate the chance of particular facilities in particular locations being damaged or impaired by any of a wide range of natural or man-made hazards. These location-based risk estimates underpin the organization's geographic risk footprint.

These risks have other spatial aspects defined by the physical and commercial distances between nodes in the supply chain which, in turn, affect the temporal dynamics of disruptions. Within a normally functioning supply chain, goods may be traveling hundreds or thousands of miles as they move down the chain and on to the final customer. At the time of a disruption in one portion of the supply chain, goods downstream of the disruption will continue to flow for a period of time that is a function of spatial distances, the velocities of the flow, and latencies in business operations in intermediate nodes in the chain. Similarly, recovery from a disruption will renew the flow of goods, but it may take some time to refill the supply chain pipeline and to reach end customers.

Commercial distances – defined by the number of intermediate businesses between the firm and the disruption – create a second geographic and temporal phenomena. Commercial distances modulate delays in propagation of information about both risks and disruptions. With few exceptions, enterprises have little knowledge or visibility onto the companies deep in their supply chains. They know the identities of direct suppliers but rarely know all the suppliers to their suppliers, and so on, down the chain. As such, they do not know the full geographic risk footprint of their supply chain. Thus, they may not even know that some disaster in some region will be disrupting their operations until their suppliers or suppliers' suppliers detect the disruption and send notification of the impending problems up the chain.

A company's total exposure to risks of natural and human-made disasters – its geographic risk footprint – extends far beyond the direct risks to its own facilities and personnel. The geographic extent of a company's risk footprint encompasses those of its commercial partners, including both suppliers and customers. Whereas companies may know the locations of their direct suppliers, companies often have little knowledge of these deep-tier suppliers. A recent case example shows that these risks may be more pervasive than they appear.

Suppliers of Parts, Suppliers of Risk

The case of General Motors (GM) and the 2011 Japan earthquake illustrates the point. The March 11, 2011, magnitude 9 earthquake, tsunami, and Fukushima reactor disaster devastated the northeastern regions of the Japanese mainland. Although no GM facility was directly affected by the quake, the company was immediately concerned about disruptions to its 25 Japanese suppliers (out of a total of 18,500 Tier 1 suppliers). GM's first task, starting on the day of the quake, was to identify all of the affected parts and their impact on GM operations. At the first crisis management meeting, the team had a list of 390 affected parts.

The deeper the team dug, however, the bigger the problems they found. After only an hour following the first meeting, the team found another 100 disrupted parts from other suppliers (Thom, 2012), because some of GM's non-Japanese suppliers had Japanese suppliers. And some of GM's non-Japanese suppliers had other non-Japanese suppliers who had Japanese suppliers. And so on. "The list kept growing. And every day, it went up. It was a moving target for us," said Rob Thom (2012), manager, Global Vehicle Engineering Operations at GM. From the known 390 affected parts on March 14, the number grew to 1,551 parts on March 24, to 1,889 on March 29, and to a staggering 5,329 on April 13. During the month after the quake, GM discovered an average of 160 disrupted parts each day.

The extensive use of electronics – sensors, microprocessors, displays, and actuators – in modern-day cars, made GM dependent on Japan's extensive electronics industry. Although a dashboard assembly or anti-lock brake module might be made in America by an American Tier 1 supplier, some of the components on the circuit board may have come from Japan. All of GM's cars had computer chips, sensors, displays, radios, and navigation systems made with parts from Japan.

Yet electronics weren't the only items containing "made in Japan" components or materials. GM soon discovered that almost every type of part on many different vehicles required something from Japan. Xirallic, a sparkly additive in the paint used on the Corvette, came from Japan. Special plastics for the body trim came from Japan. Rubber seals and gaskets came from Japan. High-tech chrome plating on turbochargers came from Japan. Cooling fans, radiator caps, air conditioner compressors, and many more parts had some tie to Japanese suppliers. And each missing part raised the specter of halting production somewhere in GM's system.

The Geography of Reputation Risks

Vendors along the supply chain supply a second kind of risk that is independent of obvious natural disasters. That second category of disruptive risk hits companies on the demand side more so than the supply side. Social and environmental activists target reputation-sensitive brand name companies in an effort to force them to change ingredient, labor, and sourcing practices. In 2007, Greenpeace attacked Unilever, Nestle, Kraft, and others over the use of palm oil linked to deforestation and loss of habitat for orangutans in Indonesia and Malaysia (The Economist, 2012). In 2010, ForestEthics began a campaign against US brand-name retailers and consumer goods companies, to pressure them to boycott fossil fuels derived from Canadian tar sands or oil sands (McDonnell, 2011). After the collapse of the Rana Plaza garment factory that killed 1,130 workers in Bangladesh in 2013, labor activists and NGOs renewed criticisms of Western apparel makers and retailers over suppliers' labor practices (Ross, 2015).

Supply disruption risks and demand-threatening reputation risks differ in the effect of diversification on risk. Supply risks can be mitigated by diversifying the numbers of suppliers and geographies that contribute to the company's base of production so that a single disrupted supplier cannot imperil production. In contrast, reputation risks are worsened by diversifying the numbers of suppliers and geographies that contribute to the company's base of production because a single "bad apple" supplier might commit egregious transgressions (child labor, slaughtering endangered species, animal cruelty, etc.) that are then widely publicized by journalists or activists and taint the company. This last issue may be especially difficult for food companies, who often rely on very large numbers of smallholder producers such as the 120,000 coffee farms in Starbucks' supply chain, which the company is trying to map and certify (Starbucks Coffee Company, [n.d.]). A further challenge is that the risky actors are often obscured by layers of intermediaries and long-distance relationships with suppliers in countries with looser regulatory oversight.

Industrial Clusters as Spatial Risk Concentrators

Many companies use second-sourcing or multisourcing to diffuse risk. Computer hard disks would seem to be extremely easy items to procure and to second-source. They adhere to well-known mechanical, electrical, and software standards. Although drives do vary somewhat in performance and reliability, they are generally interchangeable for all but the most demanding applications. Moreover, in 2011, the hard disk industry had five large competitive suppliers to handle the volume (Hachman, 2011). But then torrential rains hit Thailand.

Above-normal monsoons, plus five tropical cyclones, sent run-off totaling more than a billion cubic meters toward the lowlands of central Thailand. Over a period of weeks during the fall of 2011, the waters rose, displacing more than two million people, flooding 7,510 factories, and damaging 1,700 roads, highways, and bridges. Some factories were underwater for more than five weeks (Impact Forecasting & Aon Benfield, 2012).

The disaster proved that second sourcing doesn't always mitigate risks. The industrial parks in central Thailand had become an economic cluster for making hard disks and their components. Four of the five top suppliers of drives (Western Digital, Seagate Technologies, Hitachi Global Storage Technologies, and Toshiba) all had facilities or key suppliers in Thailand. And all four suffered substantial decreases in production capacity after the Thai floods (Arthur, 2011). In aggregate, Thailand provided 45% of worldwide hard-drive production, and the 2011 floods disrupted much of that production (Shah, 2011). As a result, the global PC industry faced a 35% shortfall in disk supplies in the fourth quarter of 2011 (Digitimes, 2011).

Similarly, a 40-mile stretch of Taiwan – from Hsinchu to Taipei – designs and fabricates almost a quarter of the world's integrated circuits (ICs). "Why do we put all our suppliers on a little island in the Pacific where it rains and floods nine months of the year?" asked a representative of a technology company at a supply chain risk management conference. Taiwan is also home to almost 70% of the world's IC foundry capacity as well as most of the global capacity for packaging and testing ICs. A 1999 earthquake gave a taste of the effects of a disruption in this key region: the spot-price of computer memory climbed fivefold all over the world, disrupting operations at many electronic suppliers and hampering the launch of certain Apple laptops. The World Bank rated Taiwan as the most vulnerable place for natural hazards, with 73% of its land and population exposed to three or more hazards (Columbia Earth Institute, 2005).

Central Thailand's disk drive manufacturing industry and northern Taiwan's chip fabrication industry are examples of economic clusters, in which firms in a given industry co-locate in order to harvest the effects of a positive feedback loop. The feedback loop is rooted in the fact that the bigger the cluster becomes (i.e., if more companies of the same industry agglomerate in a certain geography), the more attractive the cluster becomes to even more suppliers, manufacturers, labor, and specialty service providers, which spurs further growth. Moreover, governments have been pursuing industrial cluster strategies, seeding certain industries and fomenting this self-reinforcing positive feedback loop of industrial agglomeration in order to grow these economic clusters. The mechanisms and impacts of industrial clusters are described in my 2012 book, *Logistics Clusters* (Sheffi, 2012).

Clustering increases the vulnerability of companies that rely on cluster members as suppliers or customers. The reason is that a disruption that affects a cluster – such as an earthquake, flood, labor unrest, or political instability – hits many suppliers in the same industry at once, making it more difficult to find alternative sources of supply when all the industry players are scouring the globe looking for the same things. "The floods in Thailand in the fall of 2011 showed us how dangerous it is when a component that is needed at manufacturing facilities around the world is mainly procured from only one region," said Martin Bellhäuser, Head of Governance Framework at Siemens (Ehrenberg, 2012, p. 22).

Yet, the economic feedback loops of clustering and the success of governments' cluster strategies are likely to lead to further geographic concentration of supply sources, thereby leading to possible future vulnerabilities (Managing Disruptions, 2012). "Many organizations are more or less forced to put all eggs in one basket because of the clusters of suppliers for various goods around the globe," said Damien Pang, Regional Manager, Claims, at Allianz Global Corporate & Specialty Asia/Pacific (Managing Disruptions, 2012). North Korea's belligerent stance toward South Korea threatens 78.5% of the global DRAM market (Eadiciccio, 2013). Similarly, Japan makes 100% of the world's supply of protective polarizer film for LCD displays, 89% of aluminum capacitors, and 72% of silicon wafers (March, 2011). Four companies in Japan have a near-monopoly on digital compasses – the tiny magnetic field sensors that sit inside almost every new phone, tablet, laptop, and navigation system device (EMS Now, 2011).

Diamonds in the Supply Chain

That a disaster the magnitude of the 2011 Japan quake had such far-reaching indirect disruptive effects is not surprising. Clearly, a great many companies depended on many different Japanese suppliers for a great many components. Yet some supply chains contain deeply hidden indirect risks. On March 31, 2012, a tank filled with highly flammable butadiene exploded in Evonik Industries' cyclododecatriene (CDT) plant in Marl, Germany, killing two workers. Firefighters prevented the spread of the fire and extinguished the blaze, although it took them 15 hours (Reisch, 2012).

CDT sounds like an obscure chemical and the fact that it's used to synthesize cyclodo-decane, dodecanoic acid, and laurolactam may mean nothing to most readers. But CDT is a key ingredient in making PA-12, also known as nylon-12, that is especially prized for its chemical resistance, abrasion resistance, and fatigue resistance. PA-12 is used for automotive parts, solar panels, athletic shoes, ski boots, optical fibers, cable conduits, and flame-retardant insulation for copper wire. CDT is also key precursor for making many other chemical in-gredients, such as brominated flame retardants, fragrances, hot-melt adhesives, and corrosion inhibitors.

Whereas Japan's 2011 earthquake, tsunami, and nuclear reactor disaster devastated a re-gion, directly impacted thousands of businesses, and dragged on for weeks, the Evonik fire was tiny and strictly localized by comparison. One part of one factory in one town had a fire. Half a day later, the fire was out. But the explosion and fire destroyed almost half the world's production capacity for CDT. Worse, at the time of the explosion, CDT supplies were already tight due to its use in the booming solar panel industry.

Because Evonik was so deep in the supply chain, many users of PA-12, such as auto-makers, weren't initially aware of the event. A maker of fuel lines and brake lines raised the alarm about the dire implications of the Evonik fire for automakers, which triggered an industry-wide coordinated effort to address the disruption. The effect of the Evonik fire would prove to be very large – at GM, for example, supplies of 2,000 parts were jeopardized, which was one-third the number of parts that were disrupted by the far larger Japanese di-saster. The impact of Evonik was so large because every car made by GM and every other automaker required PA-12 plastic for a wide range of parts such as fuel lines, brake lines, plastic gears, and housings. The average light vehicle in 2011 used over 46 pounds of nylon (Plastics and Polymer Composites in Light Vehicles, 2016), up from just seven pounds in 1990 (Carlson & Nelson, 2003).

The typical diagram (see Figure 25.1) of a supply chain based on the bill-of-materials shows OEMs at the top of a pyramid supported by a fan of suppliers with a reassuring broad base at the bottom. Yet the Evonik example and preceding economic clusters risk examples show that although companies may have many redundant suppliers, some parts of the supply base may converge to a single key supplier or single geographic location at a deeper layer – forming a diamond-shaped supply chain pattern (See Figure 25.2.).

The 2011 Japan quake revealed many of these supply chain diamonds. Much of the world's supply of bismaleimide triazine (BT), an epoxy resin crucial to the production of many semiconductor chips, came from Mitsubishi Gas Chemical's (MGC) Fukushima facility in Japan (Walsh, 2011). All of the supplies of a sparkly pigment used in certain col-ors of luxury cars at Toyota Motors, Chrysler LLC, GM, Ford Motor, BMW, VW, Audi,

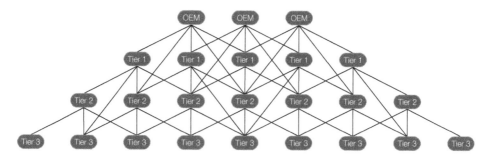

Figure 25.1 A Supply Chain Structure for a Given Industry

Figure 25.2 A "Diamond" Structure Demonstrating the Dependence on a Single Supplier

and other car makers came from one Merck plant in Japan (Seetharaman, 2011). Lithium ion batteries require PVDF (polyvinylidene fluoride), and 70% of the global supply came from one factory in Fukushima province. Although the plant survived the quake, the tsunami devastated the nearby port that was critical to supplying raw materials to the plant (Sanchanta, 2011). Other supply chain diamonds in Japan included high-purity hydrogen peroxide used in chip making, and EPDM (ethylene propylene diene monomer) used by car makers in rubber gaskets and seals (Bunkley, 2011). "What we've found is that in Tiers 3 and 4, the convergence of underlying raw material supply starts to become really significant," said Jackie Sturm (2012), Intel's Vice President and General Manager of Global Sourcing and Procurement.

Diamond structures can also create widespread quality risks. In 2005, contaminated Teflon made by DuPont was coated on sockets supplied by Federal Mogul and assembled into diesel injection pumps produced by automotive Tier 1 supplier Robert Bosch. Automakers including Audi, BMW, and DaimlerChrysler had to stop their assembly lines and recall vehicles when the defect came to light (Wagner & Bode, 2006). When Takata, the world's third largest automotive airbag manufacturer, had a problem with improperly manufactured airbags in 2013, the result was a recall of more than three million vehicles worldwide by Toyota, Honda, Nissan, and Mazda (Kubota & Klayman, 2013). In 2014, the US National Highway Traffic Safety Administration forced an expansion of the Takata airbag recall to include 15 automobile manufacturers, and some US lawmakers called for a criminal investigation by the US Department of Justice (US Senate, Blumenthal, R., & Connecticut, 2014).

Resource Concentrations

A company's deep commercial connections – and thus its spatial distribution of risk – extend to the producers of all the raw natural resources required for the production and delivery of that company's goods and services. Thus, the spatial pattern of a company's potential geographic risk exposure is linked to the geographic distribution of these natural resources, such as minerals, agricultural products, and fossil fuels. These risks have become potentially stronger through the growing sophistication of the materials used in products. "Twenty or thirty years ago electronics were being made with 11 different elements. Today's computers and smartphones use something like 63 different elements," explained Thomas Gradael, a professor of geology and geophysics at the Yale School of Forestry & Environmental Studies (Paramaguru, 2013).

Many materials come from a wide range of geographic locations, diffusing the impact of disruptions in one particular location. For these widely sourced global commodities, disruptions in production in one region (e.g., a drought in Brazil affecting coffee production or tension in the Mideast affecting crude oil) tend to induce price volatility more so than supply disruption. Yet some key materials are not so widely sourced.

For example, rare earth elements (REE) are a set of 17 metals that play a crucial role in innumerable automotive, electronic, and high-tech applications. Rare earths go into iPhones, electric cars, wind turbines, solar cells, jet engines, fiber optics, hard disk drives, compact fluorescent bulbs, and many other products (Cho, 2012). China produces 95% of these elements, and in July 2010, the country restricted exports of them, which cut off many companies that make products using these materials (Congressional Research Service, 2012).

China's rare earth export policy was but one of many examples of resource nationalism, in which governments restricted the availability of commodities produced within their borders. Besides export restrictions, special taxes on mining are another kind of resource nationalism. Countries that announced or enacted increases to taxes or royalties during 2011 and 2012 include major producers such as Australia, China, Democratic Republic of Congo, Indonesia, Ghana, Mongolia, Peru, Poland, South Africa, and the United States (Gambogi, 2011). Governments' rationale for these actions include Australia's desire to reap higher tax revenues from surging commodities prices (BBC, 2012), Indonesia's strategic intentions to move the country up the value chain (Vaswani, 2012), and China's desire to ensure that its local industries have access to sufficient supplies (Congressional Research Service, 2012). An analysis of risks in the mining industry ranked "resource nationalism" as the #1 risk in both 2011 and 2012 (Congressional Research Service). Some 33% of companies in a 2011 World Economic Forum survey ranked "export/import restrictions" as "most likely to provoke significant and systemic effects on supply chain or transport networks" (World Economic Forum, 2012).

Although the scarcity of rare earths or precious metals may not be surprising, other base metals such as aluminum, titanium, manganese, cobalt, and others could see worsening imbalances of supply and demand in the future (Kirchain, 2012). Such imbalances may create disruptions because some countries' supply chains can be heavily dependent on imports. For example, the United States is more than 90% import-reliant for many minerals such as: manganese (100%), bauxite for aluminum (100%), platinum (94%), and uranium (90%) (Congressional Research Service, 2013). Other material scarcity stress points in global supply chains include indium (used in computer display panels), silicon (chips and solar power), and wood fiber (paper, furniture, biofuel) (Kirchain, 2010).

From Eruption to Disruption: Europe Gets Grounded

Another geographic risk for global supply chains occurs in the connections between geographically dispersed nodes. Although, in theory, shipments between any two points in the world could take any of a large number of routes — creating a risk-reducing diversity of options — the economics of conveyances and distribution activities favor hub-and-spoke topologies. The effects of an April 2010 eruption of a modest-sized, ice-capped volcano named Eyjafjallajökull in southern Iceland illustrate the diverse effects of logistical disruptions. The eruption's resulting ash cloud forced the closure of major air freight hubs such as Heathrow, Amsterdam, Paris, and Frankfurt for up to five days (Wikipedia, 2017). In the UK alone, air freight provides 25% of all imports (Wray & Wearden, 2010) and 55% of exports to non-EU countries (Lee & Preston, 2012).

The disruption of these logistical linkages propagated to both suppliers and customers dependent on EU air freight. In Kenya, during the six days of airport closures, thousands of tons of fresh flowers rotted in storage units and warehouses, representing a loss to the Kenyan economy of $3.8 million per day (BBC, 2010a), which represented about 3% of Kenya's daily GDP (CIA, 2017). Italian exporters of mozzarella and fresh fruits lost about $14 million each day that flights were grounded (CBS News & CBS/AP, 2010). The Federation of Hong Kong Industries said hotels and restaurants in Hong Kong had shortages of French cheese, Belgian chocolates, and Dutch fresh-cut flowers (BBC, 2010a). Migros, the Swiss supermarket chain, noted disruptions in inbound supplies from the United States (green asparagus), Iceland (cod), and Southeast Asia (tuna). UK grocery stores ran out of pre-sliced fruit and tropical fruits like pineapple (Wray & Wearden, 2010).

In many cases, the declared value of the air freight belied the importance of the shipments to the recipient. Nissan's inability to fly $30 air pressure sensors from Ireland to Japan kept the car maker from producing $30,000 Nissan Murano SUVs (BBC, 2010b). Three BMW plants in Germany couldn't get inbound parts from Asia (BBC, 2010b). And an inability to ship transmissions out of Europe disrupted production at BMW's US factory (Bell, 2010). For lean manufacturers as well as producers and retailers of perishable goods, air freight to or from Europe was a diamond in their supply chain structure – a chokepoint in transportation that impacted all of them.

Air freight isn't the only vulnerable mode, and volcanoes aren't the only risk that can disrupt bottleneck transportation hubs or routes. The Rhine River carries 16% of Germany's trade (Germany's Transportation Systems, n.d.). Recurring droughts (Aepli, 2009; Agence France-Presse, 2015), an overturned barge in 2011 (Associated Press, 2011), and finding unexploded bombs from World War II (Day, 2011) have all created constrictions in freight volume on the river. In the United States, a quarter of all rail traffic and half of all intermodal rail traffic pass through Chicago, which ground to a standstill during a 1999 blizzard. "We basically waited for the spring thaw," said David Grewe, a supervisor for Union Pacific Railroad (Schwartz, 2012). Similarly, an eight-day strike by 400 unionized shipping clerks at the Ports of LA and Long Beach in November 2012 held up an estimated $6 billion in shipments and threatened 20,000 jobs (White, 2012).

The Timing of Disruption: Detection

Although the rise of 24-hour news, ubiquitous smartphones, and computer networks would seem to give companies instant awareness of disruptive events, analyzing case studies of actual incidents including earthquakes, hurricanes, industrial fires, and major quality control failures show that the time lag between the event and the company's awareness of it can vary greatly. Even in the case of extremely public events such as the 2011 Japan quake, companies needed days or weeks to detect the quake's disruptive effect on suppliers with deeply indirect connections to Japan's industrial base. GM needed more than two months to know how many parts were impacted. With commercial distance comes delay and uncertainty about whether and how the supply chain might be disrupted by any given event.

Thus, the first temporal variable associated with disruptive events is detection time, which is defined by the difference between the time the disruption hits and the moment when the company realizes a disruption is coming. Note that the detectability of an event can be positive (detection *before* the impact), zero (realization at the instant of occurrence), or even negative (detection *after* the disruption has taken place).

1   Forewarned is Forearmed: Positive Detection Lead-Time

When Hurricane Katrina formed in 2005, The Procter & Gamble Company started tracking the potential threat to its coastal facilities and millions of customers in the region.

When Katrina turned north toward Louisiana, the storm became a serious threat to the company because half of P&G's coffee production and 20% of all coffee drunk in American homes was roasted, ground, and canned in Folgers' plant in Gentilly, Louisiana, just east of New Orleans. P&G responded to Katrina four days before it hit Louisiana – moving inventory out of the region, getting backup data tapes, and preparing for a shutdown (Masleed, 2006).

Hurricanes, many floods, and winter storms can be forecasted hours or days before they occur. Even earthquakes can be detected as they start, enabling early warnings to those more distant from the epicenter. Businesses and residents of Tokyo knew the 2011 quake was coming about 80 seconds before it struck and had up to 40 minutes warning on the tsunami's arrival in Tokyo Bay. The dates for labor contract renewals, congestion-created special events (e.g., the Olympics), and the phase-in dates of major regulatory changes (e.g., regarding toxic chemicals) can likewise have months or years of lead time. Forewarning lets a company initiate impact-avoidance and recovery efforts.

2   BANG! Hit in an Instant: Zero Detection Lead-Time

On December 8, 2010, a power glitch lasting a 0.07 second hit Toshiba's Yokkaichi memory-chip plant in Japan, causing the factory's equipment to reboot, which ruined all the wafers in production. At the time, Toshiba provided 35.4% of the world's NAND[1] flash chips to fast-growing product categories such as smartphones, tablets, digital cameras, and music players (Clark & Osawa, 2010). The failure affected 20% of Toshiba's production and created a two-month disruption in production of NAND flash memory (Clark & Osawa).

No one could have forecast the event. Toshiba had no warning of the disruption, but it did know in an instant that disruption had struck. Some events strike with little or no warning, like a technology outage, an explosion in a factory, or a terrorist attack. One minute, everything is running smoothly and, the next second, chaos ensues.

Lurking Dangers in Hidden Events: Negative Detection Lead-Time

In early 2007, a long-time paint supplier to Mattel ran short of colorants and could not get more from its primary supplier. The supplier quickly found a backup supplier via the Internet, who claimed its colorants were certified as lead-free. To avoid delays in production, the paint supplier didn't test the new colorant, although paint workers noted that the new paint smelled differently than the usual formulation (Kenney, 2007). For two and a half months, Mattel's contract manufacturer made and shipped some one million toys of 83 different types painted with the substitute colorants. Not until early July 2007 did testing by a European retailer reveal prohibited levels of lead in the paint and coatings on these toys – leading to a massive recall (Story & Barboza, 2007) and fines (Kavilanz, 2009).

Whereas everyone knows when an earthquake hits, some disasters have a hidden start. Food contamination incidents can take weeks to surface due to delays in the food reaching consumers, the incubation time of the food-borne pathogens, and the time required to trace the illness back to particular types and brands of food. Usually, the greater the delay in detecting a hidden problem, the greater the impact and the resulting damage. Product defects – due to design errors or material quality issues – may not surface until long after the goods are in customers' hands and in use. In some cases, such as industrial espionage or cybersecurity breaches, the event might never be detected.

Mapping and Going on Alert

Recognizing the extended geographic risks coming from the supply chain, companies have begun mapping the locations of their suppliers' facilities. Yet often companies have limited visibility on the specific locations of all their suppliers' facilities – the address for the supplier might be an administrative location. A new category of service providers such as Resilinc, Inc. (n.d.) and MetricStream (n.d.) have arisen to help companies survey suppliers and manage dynamic data about which supplier facilities may be important to the continuity of the company's business.

Rather than attempt to monitor all possible events worldwide, many companies subscribe to event monitoring services that collect incident data, analyze the severity, and then relay selected, relevant alerts to their clients. In a representative week, a service such as NC4 might issue 1,700 alert messages covering 650 events around the world. Supply chain alert software tools offer customization, allowing companies to specify alert thresholds for each type of facility based on event severity and distance from the facility (NC4, n.d.). More importantly, the tools follow the bill of material and can determine quickly which products use what parts from a disrupted facility, thus letting the company prioritize response (including allocations, pricing, alternatives, etc.).

Different alert services might focus on different types of threats, from travelers' security (ANVIL Group, n.d.) to sociopolitical threats (OSAC, n.d.) to cargo security (CargoNet, n.d.). Thus, many companies subscribe to more than one service. Companies including Walmart, Intel, and Cisco noted that multiple functional groups in the organization share incident-monitoring data feeds to monitor respective risks to the supply chain, overseas personnel, and finances.

Cisco, for example, uses NC4 and then overlays event data on a Google Earth map to visually highlight the Cisco nodes that are within affected areas. Rather than wait for executives to hear the news on the morning drive to work, Cisco's incident monitoring process runs 24 × 7, with personnel around the world in different time zones. Cisco combines monitoring with an escalation process that guarantees a two-hour response time. During the 2011 Japan earthquake that occurred at 9:46 p.m., Cisco headquarters' local time, the company detected and understood the significance of the event within 40 minutes and had escalated it to senior management 17 minutes later (O'Connor, Steele, & Scott, 2011).

Higher-Density and Higher-Frequency Data Sources

The declining cost and growing use of technology in the supply chain enables a much higher spatial and temporal density of detection and monitoring of events and processes. For example, FedEx's SenseAware (n.d.) is a flat, hand-sized, red-and-white device that shippers can slip into a box, pallet, or container. The device contains a battery-powered GPS receiver, temperature monitor, pressure monitor, and light sensor. A cellular data network circuit periodically "phones home" over the same ubiquitous cellphone networks used by mobile phones. With this data, the shipper, carrier, and customer can detect problems (misrouting, theft, tampering) with a package while in transit. SenseAware is but one example of a broad trend of the "Internet of Things" (Chui, Löffler, & Roberts, 2010) which refers to a growing use of low-cost computing, sensors, wireless data, and Internet connectivity to provide enhanced situational awareness and control. Cloud-based platforms enable global uploading of sensor data and global monitoring of systems.

"Every citizen is a sensor," said Brian Humphrey of the Los Angeles Fire Department. Six billion people (out of the estimated seven billion people in the world) have access to a mobile phone (Wang, 2013). Smartphones typically include a GPS, compass, and a camera (Google, 2017) which let in-the-field supply chain workers or ordinary citizens document and transmit geotagged pictures and data about facilities and events. During Superstorm Sandy, people posted as many as 36,000 storm-related photos per hour (Agence France-Presse, 2012). Real-time damage reports accelerate detection of the extent of disruptions as well as help assess response needs (Eng, 2011).

The USGS (United States Geological Survey) now monitors Twitter to detect earthquakes. "In some cases, it gives us a heads up that it happened before it can be detected by a seismic wave," said Paul Earle, a USGS seismologist (Macmillan, 2012). Dell created a Social Media Listening Command Center to track the 22,000 mentions of Dell each day as a means to detect and respond to problems big and small (Swallow, 2010). Social media can be used to detect product quality issues and threats to the company's reputation.

Speed of Information Flows: From Blackouts to Transparency

Within the limits of the availability of telecommunications infrastructure, companies can know what is going on (and going wrong). Yet serious disasters often create a literal communications blackout due to physical damage to power and telecommunications infrastructure. Superstorm Sandy took out power to more than 7.9 million people (CBS, 2012) and damaged one quarter of cell towers in the storm-affected areas of 10 states (Gryta, 2012). After the 2011 Japan quake, some suppliers were entirely unreachable for as long as five days. Although companies such as GM and Intel immediately learned of the 2011 Japan earthquake, detecting the disruptive effects on the business depended on reaching suppliers in the affected area.

Even if the infrastructure is not damaged physically, disasters can disrupt communications due to congestion at two levels in the system. First, the high volume of attempted communications clogs the telecommunications infrastructure. Technology can help alleviate this congestion by using SMS (short message service, also known as "texting") and email, both of which use much less of the scarce bandwidth than voice communications.

Second, the volume of demands for information overwhelms the people and companies in the affected area with every customer calling, calling, calling to get updates. During case study interviews, Intel, GM, Delphi, Flextronics, and others all mentioned the problem of disruption-affected suppliers being inundated by customer calls and specific demands. "We spent more time trying to provide them data in their format than in chasing parts," said Rick Birch (2012), Global Director, Operational Excellence at Delphi. Some companies try to reduce this. For example, contract manufacturer Jabil centralized supplier contacts in the aftermath of the Japan earthquake so that its 59 sites weren't all calling the same suppliers and creating chaos (McBeth, 2012).

The Timing of Disruption: Impact and Recovery

The duration of a disruption to the operations of a company depends on the timing of two key disruption-related events. The first is the time-to-impact (TTI): when the first shortages of crucial parts would reach the company and hamper or shut down production. The second is the time-to-recovery (TTR): when implementation of the last solution for disrupted parts enables production at the previous level. (Naturally one can alternatively define these events in terms of partial availability of parts and partial production restoration.)

To manage the aftermath of the 2011 Japan earthquake, GM used an in-house graphical framework to map the timelines of the complex impacts and recovery efforts. The visual "dashboard" showed at a glance which vehicle platforms were affected, which parts were affected, when critical parts would run out, when fresh parts or alternatives might appear, and when each one of its assembly plants might be shut down for lack of parts. The solution was a very long, room-spanning chart showing the timelines on each of GM's global assembly plants along a horizontal axis. "We call these white-space charts," said Ron Mills, director, GM Components Holding (Mills, 2012). "It helps us communicate to our leadership where we are with the problem," Mills said. The white-space marked the time during which GM would not be able to produce vehicles. A stylized version of this chart is depicted in Figure 25.3.

White-Space Left Edge = Time-to-Impact

The time axis of GM's white-space charts started with the current day and near-term weeks. These near-term weeks were shaded, marked, and annotated to show the TTI when shortages of any parts might affect that assembly plant. A circle on the timeline showed when a part would run out for some vehicle options but that GM could "build through" by continuing to produce the other variants of that vehicle or by using an existing alternative. A triangle indicated a potential problem affecting production. And a square marked a definite disruption to production. "The first couple of weeks were kind of white knuckle time," said General Motors Chairman and CEO Daniel Akerson (2012) as more and more squares peppered the left side of the chart.

In general, the earliest square was the worst because GM could not build cars if any crucial part were missing. The timing of specific marks depended on the amounts of inventory

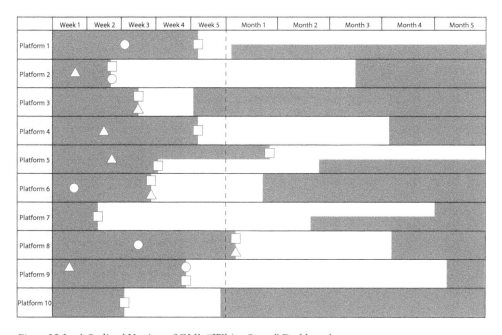

Figure 25.3   A Stylized Version of GM's "White-Space" Dashboard

in the supply chain and the speed with which these parts were shipped to GM. Although a supplier might be down, the supply chain might contain days or weeks of parts in transit, in warehouses, or in intermediate supplier sites. To help mitigate the disaster, GM's supply chain personnel worked to push out the early left-edge marks by finding hidden inventory, including spare parts held for repair and maintenance. Each added day of inventory meant one less day of lost production, sales, and profits.

These delaying tactics worked, and the left side of the white-space moved further and further into the future. The first assessment of the crisis on March 14 estimated that all plants would shut down by the end of March – only two weeks away. By March 24, the team had found enough supplies to keep all the plants running until April 11. By the end of March, the shutdown had been pushed to May 16 – providing more than six weeks of room for finding other solutions to the toughest problems.

White-Space Right Edge = Time-to-Recovery

The right-hand-side of GM's white-space chart extended out to almost a year with marks for the anticipated TTR, which is the lag between when the disruptive event occurs and when the company can restart normal production. Whereas TTI is defined by the first crucial part to be disrupted, TTR is defined by the last crucial part recovered. In general, GM's recovery options included the recovery of the original supplier, bringing alternative suppliers on line, or finding an engineering work-around. TTR also includes any transportation lead-time from recovered or second-source suppliers, which may be expedited. The chart also showed previously scheduled halts in production, such as the traditional yearly midsummer shutdown while the company did maintenance and retooling, switched over to the new model year, and gave workers a vacation. GM could also reduce or eliminate white-space by shifting the scheduled shutdown period.

Yet for GM, finding an alternative part meant more than just slapping a different part into the vehicle. Under normal circumstances, engineers take six to twelve months to qualify and validate a new part or new supplier in order to ensure the manufacturability, quality, performance, reliability, longevity, or safety of the vehicle. Validation tests or regulatory approvals take time, implying that the TTR could be very long. For example, testing nylon fuel lines for long-term reliability and safety calls for soaking the candidate plastic tubing in hot fuel for 5,000 hours (seven months) to simulate decades of exposure to fuel (Thryft, 2012). Medical products makers such as Boston Scientific face a 12- to 24-month process for regulatory approval of a supplier's manufacturing facilities. However, many companies found that internal validation processes can be accelerated during a disruption by working overtime and delaying other engineering tasks. After the 2011 quake in Japan, Cisco had to undertake over 900 new manufacturing qualifications related to disrupted parts from 65 suppliers, and it performed these activities in one-third of the usual time (O'Connor et al., 2011).

The concept of TTR raises an issue: what counts as recovery? Often, production from a restored supplier or new second source will take time to ramp from zero volume to full production. For example, Japanese automotive chip maker Renesas announced a series of expected recovery levels with different recovery times as it rebuilt after the 2011 quake: a 10% capacity resumption at 12 weeks, 35% at 16 weeks, 55% at 20 weeks, 75% at 24 weeks, and 100% at 28 weeks. Partial production of components constrains production and sales of end products.

Different companies might use different TTR thresholds to manage risks. For example, Cisco uses the 100% TTR definition, which is conservative and may overestimate the total impact because it's highly likely that a disrupted supplier would resume partial production before it recovered 100%. In contrast, Medtronic assesses the 50%, 90%, and 100% TTR points to model the ramp of the recovery. Moreover, to the extent that the affected company can prioritize the use of partial supplies, it can further reduce the financial impact by allocating the limited supplies to its most profitable or important product lines and customers – a 50% recovery in supplies is then likely to produce more than a 50% recovery in sales or profits.

White-Space

In the middle of the chart was the namesake white-space – the ominous time gap during which GM would have run out of supplies and be waiting for a solution to the disruption (see Figure 25.3). The gap between the estimated TTI (when inventories run out) and the estimated TTR (when production can resume) is the estimated customer impact time (CIT). In other words, $CIT = TTR - TTI$. For GM, this was the white-space or production down time, when GM would not be able to fulfill dealers' orders.

GM's crisis team also shaded in and color-coded the two sides of the chart to reflect progress on managing the gap. Red meant they did not yet have a plan; yellow meant they had a plan but had not implemented it yet; and green meant they were executing the plan. Because different groups were working on the two sides of the chart by extending existing supplies on the left side of the chart and resuming supplies on the right side of the chart, the two sides might have different colors. The primary goal of GM's response to the crisis was to eliminate all white-space. Moreover, as the recovery teams worked, they also aimed to make both sides of the white-space chart turn green to demonstrate confidence about parts supplies and recovery plans.

Speed-of-Impact vs. Speed-of-Recovery

A different case example from GM illustrates the relationships between commercial distance, physical distance, and the potential timelines in the impact and recovery. GM faced a potential disruption of catalytic convertors when a maker of the ceramic honeycomb substrate inside the convertor suffered severe yield problems. Some 40% of the delicate honeycombs were being scrapped, which meant that there wasn't enough supply to cover demand. This capacity bottleneck was rooted deep in a multi-tier supply chain, in which a Tier 4 supplier made the substrate, Tier 3 suppliers coated it with the catalyst, Tier 2 suppliers installed it in a metal shell, and Tier 1 suppliers assembled it into a complete exhaust system.

The TTI depended on the inventories and flows in the supply chain. Each entity in the chain held manufacturing work-in-process (WIP) inventory as well as safety stock. And each link held inventory in transit that depended on the physical shipping distances and conveyance speed. Overall, in this example, GM found there was three months of inventory in the chain, implying it would take that long for the disruption to reach GM's factories.

GM averted a disruption to car production by accelerating each stage and each shipment, thereby reducing the cycle time down to less than one month, according to Fred Brown, GM's Director of Assembly and Stamping in the global supply chain organization. Although it was more costly to run fast and lean, accelerating the cycle let GM access two months' worth of converters that were in WIP or in-transit inventories along the chain. This covered the production shortfall while the substrate maker fixed its yield problems. Once the yields improved, the substrate maker produced extra substrates to refill the buffers in the chain so that GM could return to the standard, lower-cost, three-month cycle time. This ad hoc solution suggests that the propagation of disruptive impacts and the propagation of recovery may progress at different rates, in that the propagation of disruption may be slowed by inventory and the propagation of recovery may be accelerated by expedited shipping and cycle times. Leaner supply chains that use the fastest transportation modes (i.e., air freight) would have less opportunity to avoid deep tier disruptions than would a supply chain with more inventory per tier and that uses slower modes that might be accelerated.

Conclusion

Companies enjoy tremendous access both to the fruits of human ingenuity through their global networks of suppliers and to rising billions of consumers through far-flung distribution and retailing networks. Yet the sheer number of commercial partners and the chaining of risks in both directions also bring global risk exposure and susceptibility to the myriad risks and local disasters occurring around the world. "I have 14,000 suppliers. I guarantee that with 14,000 suppliers, at least one of them is not performing well today," said Tom Linton, chief procurement and supply chain officer at contract manufacturer Flex (Linton, 2012).

Geographic models of risk intensities enable some level of supply chain risk management, but it is limited to known partners, known transportation routes, and obvious raw material commodities. The full footprint of risks goes beyond the readily mapped ones to encompass risks at greater physical and commercial distances. In expanding the horizons of risk management beyond the four walls of the organization and beyond the horizon of known partners, the spatial and temporal structure of the supply chain comes to play a major role in how companies think about risk management and crisis management.

Note

1 NAND flash is used in main memory, memory cards, USB flash drives, solid-state drives, and similar products, for general storage and transfer of data. The acronym NAND derives from "Not And," and refers to the choice of the logic gates that store the data. A NAND gate produces an output that is false only if all the incoming elements are true.

References

Aepli, N. (2009, October 4). More Misery for Rhine Shippers as Drought Continues. *Handy Shipping Guide*. Retrieved September 19, 2017, from www.handyshippingguide.com/shipping-news/more-misery-for-rhine-shippers-as-drought-continues_626

Agence France-Presse. (2012, October 30). Hurricane Sandy Pictures: Instagram Posts 10 Images per second. *The Telegraph*. Retrieved September 28, 2017, from www.telegraph.co.uk/news/world news/northamerica/usa/9644296/Hurricane-Sandy-pictures-Instagram-posts-10-images-per-second.html

Agence France-Presse. (2015, November 11). Shrinking Rhine: Shipping Scrapes by as River Stays at Lowest Level for 40 Years. *The Guardian*. Retrieved from www.theguardian.com/world/2015/nov/12/shrinking-rhine-shipping-scrapes-by-as-river-stays-at-lowest-level-for-40-years

Akerson, D. (2012, January 25). CNBC Transcript: Dan Akerson, General Motors Ceo, Speaks with CNBC'S Phil Lebeau Today on CNBC [Interview by P. LeBeau]. Retrieved September 19, 2017, from www.cnbc.com/id/46132577

ANVIL Group. (n.d.). The ANVIL Group is an Internationally Renowned Single Source Security Organisation Specialising in Travel Risk Management and Crisis Avoidance. Retrieved September 19, 2017, from www.anvilgroup.com/

Arthur, C. (2011, October 25). Thailand's Devastating Floods are Hitting PC Hard Drive Supplies, Warn Analysts. *The Guardian*. Retrieved September 28, 2017, from www.theguardian.com/technology/2011/oct/25/thailand-floods-hard-drive-shortage

Associated Press. (2011, January 13). Acid Tanker Capsizes on Rhine in Germany. *Christian Science Monitor*. Retrieved September 19, 2017, from www.csmonitor.com/World/Latest-News-Wires/2011/0113/Acid-tanker-capsizes-on-Rhine-in-Germany

BBC. (2012, March 20). Australia Passes Controversial Mining Tax into Law. *BBC Business*. Retrieved September 19, 2017, from www.bbc.com/news/business-17441170

BBC. (2010a, April 20). Iceland Volcano Cloud: The Economic Impact. *BBC News*. Retrieved September 28, 2017, from http://news.bbc.co.uk/2/hi/business/8629623.stm

BBC. (2010b, April 20). Iceland Volcano: Nissan and BMW Suspend Some Production. *BBC News*. Retrieved September 19, 2017, from http://news.bbc.co.uk/2/hi/8631676.stm

Bell, R. (2010, April 20). Volcano Disrupts BMW Supply Chain to S.C. *The State*. Retrieved September 19, 2017, from www.thestate.com/latest-news/article14383553.html

Birch, R. (2012, August). Interview with Rick Birch, Global Director of Operational Excellence at Delphi [Personal interview].

Bunkley, N. (2011, May 13). Piecing Together a Supply Chain. *New York Times*, p. B1.

CargoNet. (n.d.). The Cargo Theft Prevention and Recovery Network. Retrieved September 19, 2017, from www.cargonet.com

Carlson, E., & Nelson, K. (2003). Nylon under the Hood: A History of Innovation (Rep.). Retrieved September 29, 2017, from www2.dupont.com/Automotive/en_US/assets/downloads/nylon_under_hood.pdf

CBS News, & CBS/AP. (2010, April 20). Volcano Ash Cloud Sets Off Global Domino Effect. *CBS News*. Retrieved September 28, 2017, from www.cbsnews.com/news/volcano-ash-cloud-sets-off-global-domino-effect/

CBS. (2012, October 30). Superstorm Sandy: More Than 7 Million without Power. *CBS News*. Retrieved September 19, 2017, from www.cbsnews.com/news/superstorm-sandy-more-than-7-million-without-power/

Charlotte, R. N. (2009, February 01). This Car Runs on Code. *IEEE*. Retrieved September 19, 2017, from http://spectrum.ieee.org/green-tech/advanced-cars/this-car-runs-on-code

Cho, R. (2012, September 19). Rare Earth Metals: Will We Have Enough? *Columbia Earth Institute: State of the Planet*. Retrieved September 19, 2017, from http://blogs.ei.columbia.edu/2012/09/19/rare-earth-metals-will-we-have-enough/

Chui, M., Löffler, M., & Roberts, R. (2010, March). The Internet of Things. *McKinsey Quarterly*. Retrieved September 19, 2017, from www.mckinsey.com/insights/high_tech_telecoms_internet/the_internet_of_things

CIA. (2017, September 08). The World Factbook: KENYA. Retrieved September 19, 2017, from www.cia.gov/library/publications/the-world-factbook/geos/ke.html

Clark, D., & Osawa, J. (2010, December 10). Power Blip Jolts Supply of Gadget Chips. *Wall Street Journal*. Retrieved September 19, 2017, from www.wsj.com/articles/SB10001424052748703766704576009071694055878

Columbia Earth Institute. (2005, March 29). Risk Analysis Reports Over Half of World's Population Exposed to One or More Major Natural Hazards. *Columbia Earth Institute*. Retrieved from www.earth.columbia.edu/news/2005/story03-29-05.html

Congressional Research Service. (2012). *China's Rare Earth Industry and Export Regime: Economic and Trade Implications for the United States*, Washington. (W. M. Morrison & R. Tang, Authors) [Congress Report R42510 from 112th Congress, 2nd Session].

Congressional Research Service. (2013). *Rare Earth Elements: The Global Supply Chain* (M. Humphries, Author) [Congress Report R41347 from 113th Congress, 1st Session].

Day, M. (2011, November 23). War Bombs Cause Chaos on the Rhine. *The Telegraph*. https://www.telegraph.co.uk/history/world-war-two/8909215/War-bombs-cause-chaos-on-the-Rhine.html

Eadiciccio, L. (2013, April 16). Korean Conflict Could Nuke Your Next Phone, Experts Say. *Fox News Tech*. Retrieved September 19, 2017, from www.foxnews.com/tech/2013/04/16/korean-conflict-could-nuke-your-next-phone.html

Ehrenberg, N. (2012, Spring). Global Logistics Chains: Information Lifelines. *Pictures of the Future*, 22–25. Retrieved September 19, 2017, from www.siemens.com/content/dam/internet/siemens-com/innovation/pictures-of-the-future/pof-archive/pof-spring-2012.pdf

EMS Now. (2011, May 5). Global MEMS Industry Is Relatively Unaffected from Japan Quake Aftermath. *EMS Now*. Retrieved September 19, 2017, from www.emsnow.com/npps/story. cfm?pg=story&id=45416

Eng, P. (2011, August 29). Irene Disaster Recovery: There are Smartphone Apps for That. *Consumer Reports News*. Retrieved September 19, 2017, from www.consumerreports.org/cro/news/2011/08/ irene-disaster-recovery-there-are-smartphone-apps-for-that/index.htm

Gambogi, J. (2011). Rare Earths [Advance Release] (2011 ed., Minerals Yearbook, Rep.). Retrieved September 28, 2017, from https://minerals.usgs.gov/minerals/pubs/commodity/rare_earths/myb1-2011-raree.pdf

Germany's Transportation Systems. (n.d.). Retrieved September 19, 2017, from www.toponline.org/ books/kits/welcome%20to%20germany/WTGpdf/Handout%204.pdf

Google. (2017, July 20). Sensors Overview. Retrieved September 28, 2017, from https://developer. android.com/guide/topics/sensors/sensors_overview.html

Gryta, T. (2012, October 31). AT&T, T-Mobile, Team Up as Damaged Networks Still Strained. *Wall Street Journal*. https://www.wsj.com/articles/SB10001424052970204846304578091442059702404

Hachman, M. (2011, December 12). Intel Cuts Outlook on Disk-Drive Shortages from Thai Floods. *PCMag*. Retrieved September 20, 2017, from www.pcmag.com/article2/0,2817,2397513,00.asp

Impact Forecasting, & Aon Benfield. (2012). 2011 Thailand Floods Event Recap Report (Rep.). Retrieved September 19, 2017, from http://thoughtleadership.aonbenfield.com/Documents/20120314_ impact_forecasting_thailand_flood_event_recap.pdf

Kavilanz, P. B. (2009, June 5). Mattel Fined $2.3 Million over Lead in Toys. *CNN Money*. Retrieved September 19, 2017, from http://money.cnn.com/2009/06/05/news/companies/cpsc/

Kenney, B. (2007, September 6). How the Mattel Fiasco Really Happened. *IndustryWeek*. Retrieved September 19, 2017, from www.industryweek.com/blog/how-mattel-fiasco-really-happened

Kirchain, R. (2010, March 25). *Building Supply Chains that Deliver Sustainability*. Lecture presented at Crossroads 2010 at MIT Center for Transportation and Logistics, Cambridge, MA.

Kirchain, R. (2012, June 28). *Supply Chains in Transition*. Lecture presented at Crossroads 2012 at MIT Center for Transportation and Logistics, Cambridge, MA.

Kirkland, R. (2012, September). Leading in the 21st Century: An Interview with Ellen Kullman. Retrieved September 19, 2017, from www.mckinsey.com/global-themes/leadership/an-interview-with-ellen-kullman

Kubota, Y., & Klayman, B. (2013, April 11). Japan Carmakers Recall 3.4 Million Vehicles for Takata Airbag Flaw. *Reuters*. Retrieved September 19, 2017, from www.reuters.com/article/us-toyota-recall/ japan-carmakers-recall-3-4-million-vehicles-for-takata-airbag-flaw-idUSBRE93A04D20130411

Lee, B., Preston, F., & Green, G. (2012). Preparing for High-impact, Low-probability Events: Lessons from Eyjafjallajökull (Rep.). Retrieved September 19, 2017, from www.chathamhouse.org/ sites/files/chathamhouse/public/Research/Energy,%20Environment%20and%20Development/ r0112_highimpact.pdf

Linton, T. (2012, July 30). Interview with Tom Linton, Chief Procurement and Supply Chain Officer at Flextronics [Personal interview].

Macmillan, D. (2012, August 31). Twitter Alerts U.S. Geological Survey to Philippines Quake. *Bloomberg Technology*. Retrieved September 19, 2017, from www.bloomberg.com/news/articles/2012-08-31/ twitter-beats-u-s-geological-survey-to-philippines-quake-news

Managing Disruptions (Publication). (2012). Munich, Germany: Allianz.

March, P. (2011, April 12). Industry Left High And Dry. *The Financial Times*.

Masleed, C., Director, Coffee Supply P&G. (2006, April 11). *At the Crossroads of Supply Chain & Strategy: Simulating Disruption to Business Recovery*. Lecture presented at Crossroads 2016 at MIT Center for Transportation and Logistics, Cambridge, MA.

McBeth, J. (2012, September). Interview with Joe McBeth, Vice President of Global Supply Chain at Jabil [Personal interview].

McDonnell, T. (2011, December 15). There's No Hiding from Tar Sands Oil. *Mother Jones*. Retrieved September 19, 2017, from www.motherjones.com/environment/2011/12/theres-no-hiding-tar-sands-oil/

Mills, R. (2012, August). Interview with Ron Mills, Directs of Components Holding at GM [Personal interview].

NC4. (n.d.). Safety and Security Solutions. Retrieved September 19, 2017, from http://www.nc4.us/

O'Connor, J., Steele, J. B., & Scott, K. (2011). Supply Chain Risk Management at Cisco: Embedding End-to-End Resiliency into the Supply Chain, ISM 2012 Award for Excellence in Supply

Management Submission Category: Process. Retrieved September 19, 2017, from www.institute-forsupplymanagement.org/files/RichterAwards/CiscoSubmissionSupportDoc2012.pdf

OSAC. (n.d.). United States Department of State, Bureau of Diplomatic Security. Retrieved September 19, 2017, from www.osac.gov/Pages/Home.aspx

Paramaguru, K. (2013, December 20). Rethinking Our Risky Reliance on Rare Earth Metals. *Time*. Retrieved September 19, 2017, from http://science.time.com/2013/12/20/rare-earths-are-too-rare/

Plastics and Polymer Composites in Light Vehicles (Rep.). (2016). Retrieved September 19, 2017, from https://plastics-car.com/lightvehiclereport

Reisch, M. (2012, April 2). Explosion at German Chemical Plant Kills Two. *Chemical and Engineering News*. Retrieved from http://cen.acs.org/articles/90/web/2012/04/Explosion-German-Chemical-Plant-Kills.html

Resilinc. (n.d.). Cloud & Mobile Solution for Supply Chain Resiliency. Retrieved September 19, 2017, from www.resilinc.com/

Ross, R. J. (2015, Summer). Bringing Labor Rights Back to Bangladesh. *The American Prospect*. Retrieved September 19, 2017, from http://prospect.org/article/bringing-labor-rights-back-bangladesh

Sanchanta, M. (2011, March 29). Chemical Reaction: iPod is Short Key Material. *Wall Street Journal*. https://www.wsj.com/articles/SB10001424052748704471904576228390400576486

Schwartz, J. (2012, May 7). Freight Train Late? Blame Chicago. *New York Times*. Retrieved September 19, 2017, from https://nyti.ms/2uUdj95

Seetharaman, D. (2011, March 25). Automakers Face Paint Shortage after Japan Quake. *Reuters*. Retrieved September 28, 2017, from www.reuters.com/article/us-japan-pigment/automakers-face-paint-shortage-after-japan-quake-idUSTRE72P04B20110326

SenseAware. (n.d.). How It Works. Retrieved September 19, 2017, from www.senseaware.com/how-it-works/

Shah, A. (2011, November 23). Thailand Floods Hard-Drive Shortage Makes Small PC Makers Hike Prices. *Techworld*. Retrieved September 19, 2017, from www.techworld.com/news/apps-wearables/thailand-floods-hard-drive-shortage-makes-small-pc-makers-hike-prices-3320401/

Sheffi, Y. (2005). *The Resilient Enterprise: Overcoming Vulnerability for Competitive Advantage*. Cambridge, MA: The MIT Press.

Sheffi, Y. (2012). *Logistics Clusters: Delivering Value and Driving Growth*. Cambridge, MA: MIT Press.

Sheffi, Y. (2015). *The Power of Resilience: How the Best Companies Manage the Unexpected*. Cambridge, MA: MIT Press.

Starbucks Coffee Company. (n.d.). Retrieved September 19, 2017, from www.conservation.org/partners/Pages/starbucks.aspx

Story, L., & Barboza, D. (2007, August 15). Mattel Recalls 19 Million Toys Sent From China. *New York Times*. Retrieved September 28, 2017, from www.nytimes.com/2007/08/15/business/worldbusiness/15imports.html

Sturm, J. (2012, July 31). Interview with Jackie Sturm, VP and GM of Global Sourcing & Procurement at Intel [Personal interview].

MetricStream. (n.d.). Supply Chain Risk Management. Retrieved September 19, 2017, from www.metricstream.com/solutions/supply_chain_risk_management.htm

Swallow, E. (2010, December 8). Dell to Launch Social Media Listening Command Center. *Mashable*. Retrieved September 19, 2017, from http://mashable.com/2010/12/08/dell-social-listening-center/#NDE9.4UDVEqm

The Economist. (2010, June 24). The Other Oil Spill. *The Economist*. Retrieved September 19, 2017, from www.economist.com/node/16423833

Thom, R. (2012, August). Interview with Rob Thom, Manager, GM Global Vehicle Engineering Operations [Personal interview].

Thryft, A. R. (2012, May 14). Nylon 12 Replacements Include Bioplastics. *Design News*. Retrieved September 28, 2017, from www.designnews.com/content/nylon-12-replacements-include-bioplastics

Turley, J. (1999, May 1). Embedded Processors by the Numbers. Retrieved September 19, 2017, from www.embedded.com/print/4219542

US Senate, Blumenthal, R., & Connecticut. (2014, November 7). Blumenthal, Markey Call on Department of Justice to Open Criminal Investigation of Takata [Press release]. Retrieved September 19, 2017, from www.blumenthal.senate.gov/newsroom/press/release/blumenthal-markey-call-on-department-of-justice-to-open-criminal-investigation-of-takata-

Vaswani, R. (2012, March 13). Indonesia Trade Minister Rejects Protectionist Label. *CNBC*. Retrieved September 19, 2017, from www.cnbc.com/id/46714747

Wagner, S. M., & Bode, C. (2006). An Empirical Investigation into Supply Chain Vulnerability. *Journal of Purchasing and Supply Chain Management, 12*(6), 301–312. https://doi.org/10.1016/j.pursup.2007.01.004

Walsh, D. (2011, October 4). Quake Drying Up Supply of Flashy Pigment for Car Paint. *Crain's Detroit Business*. Retrieved September 28, 2017, from www.crainsdetroit.com/article/20110410/SUB01/304109939/quake-drying-up-supply-of-flashy-pigment-for-car-paint

Wang, Y. (2013, March 25). More People Have Cell Phones Than Toilets, U.N. Study Shows. *Time*. Retrieved September 19, 2017, from http://newsfeed.time.com/2013/03/25/more-people-have-cell-phones-than-toilets-u-n-study-shows/

White, R. D. (2012, November 30). Small Union is Causing Big Problems for Ports. *The Los Angeles Times*. Retrieved September 28, 2017, from http://articles.latimes.com/2012/nov/30/business/la-fi-ports-labor-20121130

Wikipedia. (2017, August 26). Air Travel Disruption after the 2010 Eyjafjallajökull Eruption. Retrieved September 19, 2017, from http://en.wikipedia.org/wiki/Air_travel_disruption_after_the_2010_Eyjafjallaj%C3%B6kull_eruption

World Economic Forum. (2012). New Models for Addressing Supply Chain and Transport Risk (Rep.). Retrieved September 19, 2017, from www3.weforum.org/docs/WEF_SCT_RRN_NewModelsAddressingSupplyChainTransportRisk_IndustryAgenda_2012.pdf

World Trade Organization. (2015). International Trade Statistics 2015. *World Trade Organization*. Retrieved September 19, 2017, from www.wto.org/english/res_e/statis_e/reports_newsletters_e.htm

Wray, R., & Wearden, G. (2010, April 16). Flight Ban Could Leave the UK Short of Fruit and Veg. *The Guardian*. https://amp.theguardian.com/business/2010/apr/16/flight-ban-shortages-uk-supermarkets

26

THE DEVELOPMENT OF ACTIONABLE KNOWLEDGE IN CRISIS MANAGEMENT

Carole Lalonde

Introduction

Much of crisis management research has sought guiding principles (Drabek & McEntire, 2003) to allow managers to deal more effectively with crises. Recommendations highlight the importance of good planning and of management *before* the crises occur, and the literature on crisis communication emphasizes management of the organization's image to safeguard its reputation (Alsop, 2004; Coombs & Holladay, 2006). This research provides useful lessons for crisis management, but these lessons do not always yield the desired results because managers and organizational members of organizations may not have, or implement, crisis management plans, or the defense of the organization's reputation and the search for blameworthy parties may take precedence over collective well-being. The question that arises is thus, "How can one train managers to avoid the common mistakes and dysfunctions found during crises?"

If we assume that it is possible to produce *actionable knowledge* (Argyris, 1993; Avenier & Schmidtt, 2007) that can be applied in the daily life of organizations, then crisis management researchers have much to learn from Lewin's (1951) organizational change and development (OD) intervention research . In this approach, the researcher works *with* the organization from a perspective of co-development of knowledge rather than *on* the organization from a positivist perspective of methodological individualism, characteristic of the positivist tradition in research (McArdle & Reason, 2008). Although there are several trends in scholarship that may prove helpful in better understanding and managing crises, this chapter focuses specifically on effective practices and interventions that were developed in four areas of OD – human process, technostructures, human resource management and strategy (Cummings & Worley, 2015) – and the contributions research in these areas of OD can make to the field of crisis management. This extension of OD into the field of crisis management stems from the observation that, although many organizations have incorporated advances in knowledge of crisis management into planning and practice, organizations have found it difficult to avoid the dysfunctional actions and practices that impede the efficient resolution of crises (Lalonde, 2007). Given OD's important focus on actually implementing change, this chapter proposes a framework based at the intersection of OD interventions and crisis management that can contribute to development of more effective organizational change responses to crises.

This chapter is divided into two parts. First, I will report the results of past crisis management research related to four broad themes: preparedness/planning, coordination, the social environment of crises and leadership. The use of these four dimensions of organizational configurations identified by Miller (1987) is based on the demonstrated utility in previous research (Lalonde, 2004). For each of these themes, a practical tool presents the essential questions for OD practitioners to ask in order to identify areas for improved crisis management. The second part of this chapter presents an example of an OD process using Lewin's model supporting an organization during crisis. The chapter concludes by addressing conditions to develop actionable knowledge in crisis management and the research needed to advance OD-based research-interventions in crisis management.

Organization Development and Guiding Principles of Crisis Management

Miller (1987) has proposed four dimensions of the crisis management literature that are related to the major imperatives of his model of organizational configurations: (1) *crisis preparedness/planning* are related to the strategy imperative, (2) *coordination* is related to the structure imperative, (3) *civil society* is related to the social environment imperative, and (4) *crisis leadership* is related to the leadership imperative. Given the goal of producing actionable knowledge, I first reviewed the extensive literature on crisis management and then abductively developed guiding principles for crisis management. Then, I examined the past OD interventions that are pertinent for the present case. There is a vast repertoire of methods of intervention and investigation of OD that have been developed and proven over time. This chapter will focus on the methods of intervention and investigation of OD as defined by Cummings and Worley (2015) and regrouped around four areas of intervention: (1) *human processes* (communication, decision making, leadership), (2) *technostructures* (type of organizational configuration, level of delegation and formalization), (3) *human resource management* (development of skills, modes of socialization), and (4) *strategy* (type of transactions with the environment, culture of the enterprise as leverage with stakeholders). Finally, a diagnostic tool was created for each crisis management dimensions, allowing the OD practitioners to evaluate areas for improvement and to communicate these to crisis managers and leaders.

Planning/Preparedness for Crises and OD

Many scholars (Alexander, 2005; McEntire & Myers, 2004; Perry & Lindell, 2003) have enumerated some guiding principles for planning/preparation in crisis management. While most scholars recognize the utility of plans, a number of them claim that these plans are used poorly or merely symbolically (Clarke, 1999; Ross et al., 2016). The term "fantasy document" is sometimes used to refer to some crisis management plans as they only serve to project a reassuring image to stakeholders and the general public (Birkland, 2009) and do not take sufficient stock of the inevitable contingencies that will arise on the concrete ground of the crisis (McConnell & Drennan, 2006). This type of symbolic implementation is too often mechanistic, ceremonial and disconnected from internal practices, and their application within organizations may be perfunctory and project an idealized image of planning (Lalonde & Boiral, 2012; Ross et al., 2016). Obviously, even the best crisis plans cannot predict every eventuality (Denis, 1993, 2002), and lack of plans may thus require *on the job training* in the face of adversity; in contrast, having too many plans may contribute to the risk of inertia or to a false impression that everything is under control (Rosenthal & Kouzmin, 1993; Rosenthal, Charles and Hart, 1996). In this perspective, organizations should exercise vigilance in the implementation of plans and conceive crisis preparedness as a practice-based approach, a strategy that managers *do* and not a strategy that managers *have*. They must question their own assumptions in the implementation of crisis plans. This perspective is in line with that advocated by OD practitioners.

Certain scholars advance this idea that crisis planning may necessitate a position of facilitator (Pauchant & Mitroff, 1995) or coordinator of the plans (Denis, 1993, 2002). This position would facilitate exchanges amongst the crisis stakeholders, both internally and externally, and coordinate all the necessary tasks in a crisis situation. This post should be assigned to a generalist, rather than a specialist (Denis, 1993), and to a senior executive other than the general manager. The role of facilitator could permit the organization to avoid problems associated with excessive centralization by establishing mechanisms to delegate tasks and by specifying the scope of this delegation (Denis, 1993; Kuban, 1995). Clearly, planned strategies, when well conceived, offer numerous advantages and enhance the efficacy of organizations' actions.

Therefore, in the light of these guiding principles, diverse interventions developed in OD could contribute to improve the planning/preparedness for crises. First, the organization's capacity to prepare to deal with crises can be improved, thanks to a better sharing of knowledge amongst individuals, allowing for *survey feedback*, a method that collects relevant information on a given issue, and then returns this information to the interested parties for discussion and appropriation. Second, the diagnostic model based on *open system theory*, an approach whereby organizational actors seek adaptation to external environment, might be included in the assessment of risks. Third, the updating of knowledge and the development of sharing or common vision could be achieved using *survey feedback* and methods of *teambuilding*, which have the advantage of revealing not only explicit knowledge, but also tacit knowledge. Fourth, *laboratory training sessions* based on simulations or crisis scenarios can allow individuals, employees and managers, to develop the skills required in terms of creativity, thus fostering flexible and adaptable responses to crises. Fifth, the conception of crisis management plans stems from a process in which all stakeholders participate. In this regard, OD offers interesting avenues, including *search conference, future search* and *appreciative inquiry*, interventions that bring together a group of actors with diverse perspectives and from different professional fields to reflect on the means required to collectively face the social issues confronting them. Finally, planning can be conceived as a continuous and bottom-up process of improvement through identifying a *facilitator*, a role already thoroughly delineated by OD practitioners (Schein, 2009). OD practitioners could then use the diagnostic tool presented in Table 26.1 to pinpoint the aspects on which their intervention should focus, and then present and discuss the types of collaboration required to implement this intervention.

Coordination of Crises and OD

Quarantelli (1988) provided an excellent summary of crisis coordination challenges in three main areas: communication, internal, external and with the public; the exercise of authority; and the development of cooperative structures. For each of these three areas, Quarantelli defined the central issues to consider in responding to a crisis. These propositions concern the following key topics. First, *organizational communication*, internal, external or with the general public is related to the circulation of inaccurate information, overloaded communication channels, to a public which is poorly informed or not at all informed and to difficulty in integrating the information coming from outside official channels. Second, Quarantelli also provided propositions concerning the *exercise of authority* related to the unavailability of upper management and/or managers due to an excessive workload, the absence of consensus on the

Table 26.1 Diagnosis Regarding Planning/Preparedness

Components of the diagnosis	Yes	No
Formal planning		
1 Is the plan (or are the plans) up to date?		
2 Does the plan take into account community behavior?		
3 Does the plan include the coordination of the various responders?		
4 Does the plan include personnel training?		
Risk assessment		
5 Have the risks been evaluated in advance?		
6 Does the organization have a multiple-risk plan?		
7 Has the population been informed of the potential risks?		
Capacity assessment		
8 The organization acts with diligence and purpose:		
a Have the crisis managers verified that their interventions will not harm the population?		
b Do the crisis managers regularly invest in the development of crisis intervention capabilities?		
9 The organization shows flexibility in the application of response routines:		
a Have the managers verified that responders act in a concerted manner?		
b Have the managers adapted their interventions to the contingencies?		

allocation of new tasks related to the crisis and conflicts stemming from the areas of responsibility of each organization and human resources management. Third, Quarantelli advanced general propositions regarding the development of *cooperative structures* that can address the absence of consensus on the extent and modalities of coordination, tensions resulting from the accomplishment of new tasks and blockages and dysfunctions as an effect of the convergence of too many actors claiming a particular role or a right in the management of the crisis.

The coordination of crisis management has much to do with questions related to the type of organizational alliances and configurations involved in the crisis. Webb and Chevreau (2006) note the need for flexible structural designs and loosely coupled links in dynamic and turbulent environments, and this describes crisis contexts and similar environments. OD proposals for coordination address three levels. First, in terms of intra-organizational structure, the establishment of a *collateral structure* is likely to contribute to the agility that is lacking in crises by helping the members of the organization become accustomed to functioning differently in crisis situations (Zand, 1974). Second, in terms of human resource management, the capacity to improvise could be developed within the framework of projects or scenarios that require a horizontal expansion of tasks (*job enlargement*) or a vertical expansion (*job enrichment*) (Cummings & Worley, 2015). Finally, in interorganizational terms, the establishment of crisis cells could draw on the *socio-ecological perspective of networks*, the functioning within a network allowing for the creation of links with all the external stakeholders (Trist, 1983). Clearly, the collateral structure and the socio-ecological perspective of the network constitute two interesting avenues for OD to put the major guiding principles of crisis coordination into practice.

Before proposing these avenues to leaders and managers, the OD practitioner will need to thoroughly evaluate the needs of the organization in terms of reinforcement of capacities for crisis coordination based on Table 26.2. This means exploring the three dimensions of crisis coordination identified by Quarantelli – communication, exercise of authority and the development of cooperative structures – and target the aspects on which their intervention should focus.

Table 26.2 Diagnosis Regarding Coordination

Components of the diagnosis	*Yes*	*No*
Communication		
1 Are the members of the organization skilled to create new mechanisms to facilitate internal and external information flow?		
2 Are the members of the organization skilled to provide appropriate information to the population?		
3 Are the members of the organization skilled to integrate information from outside the formal decision-making mechanisms?		
Exercising authority		
4 Do leaders authorize the delegation and decentralization of certain decisions?		
5 Do leaders demonstrate collegiality in the distribution of tasks?		
6 Are leaders skilled to resolve conflicts between organizations?		
7 Are leaders skilled to mobilize and motivate personnel and avoid burnouts?		
Developing cooperative structures		
8 Do leaders and managers work in collaboration with other leaders?		
9 Do leaders and managers integrate emerging local groups in the crisis response?		
10 Do leaders and managers maintain and strengthen harmonious relations with leaders and managers of other organizations during normal (noncrisis) periods?		

Social Environment of Crises and OD

As early as the 1960s, sociologist Allen Barton (1969) was one of the first to introduce the notion of an "emergency social system" to convey the adaptive response of communities toward crises. Far from giving rise to anti-social behavior, crises may bring about an "esprit de corps," or what Barton calls a "therapeutic community" composed of all the civic behaviors aimed at providing emergency assistance in the first moments following the destructive impact of a disaster (Drabek, 2007). Dynes (1983) uses the term "situational altruism" to characterize the expansion of civic roles in the form of mutual aid and expressions of solidarity during crises. Ultimately, the judgment of citizens may have a significant impact on leaders and managers, and may be reflected in a loss of confidence, a rejection of their proposals or fear (Taylor, 2000). Thus, according to Hart et al. (2001), citizens today have a tendency to come together in an organized fashion and make their voices heard through the intermediary of the media. Therefore, the role of such pressure groups, like that of the media, cannot be ignored, especially during and after the crisis.

The role of civil society affects a number of facets of crisis management. First, the acquisition of better knowledge of community characteristics and of civic behavior in a period of crisis is one of the guiding principles identified by a number of authors in the area of planning and preparation. *Survey feedback* allows for a sharing of knowledge among participants at this level. Moreover, the expression of altruistic gestures gives rise to emergence of more or less organized actions, an aspect which should be considered as an element of coordination in crisis management. The *socio-ecological perspective* of networks advanced by Trist (1983) allows for the integration of significant actors from civil society in coordinating the response to the crisis. The communication section has been clearly identified as a key area of competence by a number of authors, including Wooten and James (2008). *Laboratory training sessions* as well as *coaching* and *mentoring* are actions that could be conceived specifically with the goal of developing leaders' and grassroots leaders' communication skills, in order to deal with the public and media nature of the crisis.

Table 26.3 Diagnosis Regarding the Behavior of Civil Society

Components of the diagnosis	Yes	No
Civic behaviors		
1 Does the population engage in:		
a altruistic acts?		
b "normal" panic behavior?		
c delinquent acts such as looting or interference with public safety?		
d noncompliance with evacuation orders?		
e abdication of civic roles or lack of assistance to vulnerable persons?		
Emergence of grassroots leadership		
2 Does local and national actors – previously lesser known and/or less central to formal authority – act as consciousness-raisers?		
Role played by the media		
3 Do the media representatives emphasize mostly what is dysfunctional?		
4 Do the media representatives tend to focus on identifying the guilty parties?		
5 Do the media representatives communicate useful information to the population?		

On the basis of this knowledge and with the help of the diagnostic tool presented in Table 26.3, in collecting their feedback, the OD practitioner can play a role of facilitator and unifier with all the stakeholders; using *conversational approaches* of OD such as *Open Space or World Café*, the OD practitioner will create a bottom-up process for identifying what are the latent interests and motivations in large groups and help people to come to an agreement about future actions in the course of crises.

Crisis Leadership and OD

According to many authors (Boin et al., 2005; Wooten & James, 2008), managers must develop certain specific abilities required in the various phases of a crisis. Boin et al. (2005) and Stern (2013) put forward different tasks related to crisis leadership. These tasks punctuate the general process of crisis management – from the onset (in planning/preparedness, including detection of early warning signs) through the post-crisis period (when learning takes place). Wooten and James (2008) differentiate key skills for each phase – signal detection, prevention and preparation, containment and damages, business recovery, learning and reflection. Thus, the capacities to give meaning to crisis warning signs and anticipate their potential impact on others are two key skills during the detection phase. In the prevention/preparation phase, the authors suggest that the capacity to convince organizational members of the importance of investing in crisis management planning is key. They argue that an agent of change who is skilled in issue selling is essential to bringing organizational leaders to pay attention to crisis preparation. Wooten and James (2008) also suggest that two additional skills are essential during the preparation phase: *organizational agility* that involves detailed knowledge of the organization, and a systemic view of the interaction dynamics likely to be deployed to face the crisis and *creativity* (i.e., the capacity to imagine novel scenarios to deal with the contingencies of the crisis situation). At the height of the crisis, in the context of direct and active interventions, the capacity to make decisions under pressure, the ability to communicate effectively and the courage to take needed risks are critical success factors. During the phase of reconstruction, promoting organizational resilience and adopting ethical and responsible behavior are two additional skills. Finally, adopting a learning approach

Table 26.4 Diagnosis Regarding Leadership

Components of the diagnosis	Yes	No
Before the crisis		
1 Are leaders skilled in picking up on and making sense of early warning signals and the potential impacts they presage?		
2 Are leaders skilled in proposing and communicating ideas?		
3 Does the leader adopt a systemic view of the situation?		
4 Does the leader demonstrate imaginative thinking?		
During the crisis		
5 Does the leader enable good decision-making under pressure?		
6 Does the leader communicate effectively within the organizational circle?		
7 Does the leader take "calculated" risks?		
After the crisis		
8 Does the leader consolidate future interventions with a view toward resilience?		
9 Is the leader skilled in regaining the trust and confidence of other responders and employees?		
10 Does the leader adopt a learning attitude?		

encourages further reflection on improving crisis management practices outside the phases related to the crisis itself.

Given the emphasis on communication and the decision-making processes, several interventions seem particularly appropriate for the development of crisis leadership. These change tools include *executive coaching*, *programs of co-development* in which managers are encouraged to share their experiences, transformation leadership assessment such as the *Multifactor Leadership Questionnaire* proposed by Bass and Avolio (2008), cooperative investigation underlying an *appreciative inquiry* (Cooperrider et al., 2008) and *the review of critical incidents* (Flanagan, 1954; Flin, 1996). Indeed, all of these tools focus on skills considered fundamental to crisis management, including gestures showing consideration toward individuals; the capacity to articulate a vision and get others to accept it; and intellectual stimulation and positive reinforcement, which prove to be important in developing an openness to learning attitudes in the face of crises.

With the help of the diagnostic tool presented in Table 26.4, the OD practitioner will determine the most appropriate actions to develop crisis leadership. This can be done during the annual management review that takes place in most organizations, both public and private.

The OD Approach in Action: Crisis at Centre St-Charles-Borromée

This section presents an example of an organizational development intervention carried out during a reputational crisis experienced at the Centre St-Charles-Borromée in 2003, after media coverage of a case of mistreatment of a patient and her family by institutional staff. After making repeated complaints about abuse, the sisters of a patient at St-Charles-Borromée publically released a recording made on November 24, 2003, showing two employees making disrespectful and insulting comments to a 51-year-old female patient. The two sisters had long suspected that their sister, who had been handicapped since age 18 due to a serious accident, had become a victim of sexual aggression. So they hid a recording device in her hospital room and thereby confirmed repeated abuse by certain employees who dealt with her, including threats, mockery and contemptuous, violent and sexual comments.

A number of other public denunciations of the situation followed that thrust the director, Mr. Léon Lafleur, into the media spotlight. He announced a three-day suspension for the two employees concerned, but three days after the scandal broke, on November 27, 2003, the director committed suicide. This created a new public uproar as the motives and context of his suicide were never made public. Further, the director-general sent a posthumous letter to a newspaper that expressed his dismay at the lack of moral support from the Ministry of Health and implored other hospital directors to close ranks in the face of this adversity. On December 8, 2003, after an inquiry confirmed problems with personnel, the Minister of Health placed the establishment under trusteeship for 120 days, and then later extended the trusteeship to 7 months. It is in the context of this trusteeship that the author undertook an OD intervention at the St-Charles-Borromée Long-term Care Center.

Initiating the Process

The researcher-practitioner's role was clarified with the trustee of the Centre at the outset of the intervention and consisted principally of assisting him in the processes of organizational reorientation and reframing of professional practices. The goal was to establish a process to improve the organization's crisis management skills and capabilities, to restore the principles of personal responsibility for good quality practices and to develop better relations between the caregiver and resident. This role is similar to the process of *executive coaching* (Kombara-karan et al., 2008; Stern, 2004; Witherspoon & White, 1996) and is consistent with the four phases of Schein's (2009) consultation process: agreement on objectives, organizational diag-nosis, planning and implementation of the actions proposed and a conclusion marked by the withdrawal of the researcher-practitioner.

It is also important to explain the status of each person involved in this process. The director appointed by the Ministry of Health and Social Services was a former director-general with many years of experience in institutional healthcare. The researcher was myself, an academic who has previously completed numerous advisory assignments for the health and social services network and whose research focuses on managing change and crises, and organizational consulting.

Reviewing Critical Incidents

A review of critical incidents was then undertaken. Flanagan (1954) describes the critical incident technique as a collection of observations on human behavior oriented toward the resolution of practical problems that arise in modern life. The technique consists of listing certain facts in a given situation that prove determinant for the unfolding of individual and organizational activities. As the technique is grounded in shared observations, the quality of analysis is largely based on the practitioner's competence and knowledge of the current sit-uation. Second, the identification of critical incidents allows for the formulation of a certain number of inferences that could serve to improve the future course of an action. Therefore, an exercise of reviewing critical incidents was conducted in collaboration with the director, as well as on a documentary analytical basis.

Uncovering Dysfunctions

Thus, this exercise allowed the researcher-practitioner to shed some light on key shortcom-ings in the four areas of crisis management which we presented earlier. Indeed, the centre did not respect most of the guiding principles identified at each level. First, *in terms of planning*, the crisis revealed an absolute lack of any effective management plan. The sole mechanism was a management system for complaints that was not vigorously applied within the establishment. There were also flagrant shortcomings regarding the training of the personnel. For example, the trustee noticed that the clientele of this centre, who were much younger than those of other similar centers, had particular needs. More than 26% of the patients had behavioral problems, 77% had problems of incontinence and nearly 90% needed a wheelchair to move around. The complexity of the clientele would suggest the need for advanced training in terms of pathologies, something which was clearly lacking in a number of the employees. Second, *in terms of coordination*, there was no genuine partnership with representative bodies in the milieu, with other centers with similar missions. In fact, the Centre seemed to operate in a vacuum. The relations between the Ministry of Health and Social Services and the management of long-term care centers were essentially based on technical-administrative dimensions rather than on issues affecting intervention practices aiming to foster a quality institutional life for the caregivers and residents. Third, *in terms of the social environment*, the media and the public's reaction that emphasized punishment, revealed a misunderstanding of the issue of care in an institutional environment. And the centre does not effectively reflect these expressions of popular indignation. Finally, *in terms of leadership*, the centre's management has minimized the importance of warning signs indicating mistreatment of some residents by certain employees of the centre. Indeed, it was only a last resort, after family lodged a number of complaints, that centre's management chose to make public the recording of words and gestures of two employees toward at least one fragile resident of the centre. Furthermore, major flaws could also be observed in terms of communication with the public. Thus, the first response of the director-general of the establishment, like that of the union, trivialized the incident. As some journalists pointed out (Derzel & De Souza, 2004),

> A number today still have trouble explaining the remarks of Mr. Lafleur, trivializing the bad treatment of a resident, and also the minor nature of the employees' punishment (…) At a press conference, the director of the centre, Léon Lafleur, maintained that 'the employees simply wanted to have fun'.

Finally, aside from the leadership of the organization, the clinical leadership also proved deficient. Therefore, the lack of respect, intrusive language used with the residents and excessive familiarity are three of the behavioral issues noted by the trustee. While the majority of employees competently and devotedly care for the residents, the trustee confirmed that a minority failed to adopt the values promoted by the organization.

Creating a Diagnostic Tool

Next, and with the agreement of the centre's director, the researcher-practitioner initiated an in-depth analysis of principal areas of vulnerability likely to be encountered in this type of establishment. Thus, on the basis of a review of the main academic publications, the researcher was able to create a grid allowing the centre's director and, ultimately, all the centre's personnel, to determine the most sensitive areas affecting patients, with a view to acting from a perspective of organizational development. Having previously conducted an exhaustive chronological review of the main events or actions posed by the local administration and/or by the state, it was possible to observe that this chart identifying zones of vulnerability was useful for the centre's director, not only in drawing up a long-term plan to improve the situation but also in showing how to do so from a perspective of developing the organization rather than from a strictly punitive perspective.

Indeed, one observation from our review of critical incidents is the emphasis placed on the responses to the crisis in terms of greater control, more supervision and a punitive approach. For instance, in January 2004, the minister initiated an inspection process in 40 of the 500 shelters and long-term care facilities that comprise the Québec public system. With 24 hours' notice, teams of inspectors would arrive in the establishments and question administrators, residents and personnel to determine what was not working. Thus, the minister hoped to obtain, by around the beginning of May 2004, a portrait allowing him to resolve the problems permanently. Several months later, he announced that he planned to make this process permanent. "These will not be police visits but visits aiming at improving the quality of care and services," explained the minister.

Despite these claims, this punitive-authoritarian approach (Gouldner, 1954; Henry, 1987), that serves as a legitimation tool to prove to the public that the State is taking action, does not fundamentally resolve the problem at its source. This was known since the start of the century, because the system of health and social services had experienced major budgetary restrictions. The decreased number of rooms and the tightening-up of admission criteria have greatly affected, and still affect, the management of long-term care facilities. Indeed, managers and the personnel of these centers have to employ considerable imagination and make great efforts to offer quality services with limited resources to a clientele with severe health problems. According to Riendeau (2006), the current working environment – atmosphere of tension and suspicion, technocratic approach to healthcare, workload perceived as heavy, helplessness felt about the difficulties in dealing with patients – presents several barriers to the improvement in the quality of care.

In addition to being stigmatizing, this type of action completely leaves aside the dynamic management as well as the organization of work in such an establishment that is at the heart of health and social services organizations' mission. Furthermore, these actions were generally reactive and remedial rather than encouraging of proactive actions and learning attitudes. They were irrevocable and punished all the participants, including those who expressed empathy for and dedication to the patients. This may have had a deleterious effect on the employees' motivation to continue to provide a quality service and on their commitment to the work as several studies have clearly demonstrated (Cooke, 2006; Rollinson et al., 1997; Trevino, 1992).

In short, the chart identifying principal areas of vulnerability allowed the intervention team to offer a "more precise" diagnosis. The chart showed that the state's intervention to achieve greater control and supervision of the institution, while necessary, was not *a posteriori* the best or only appropriate response to managing this type of crisis. In addition, the intervention merely addressed one area of vulnerability, that of the institution, and it ignored the other three. This type of partial response does not contribute or give meaning to patients' quality of life, or to caregivers' and managers' work, or allow them to learn and consequently change their practices in a way that might restore their public reputation. Moreover, in the post-modern era, the state's interventions cannot be limited to corrective measures and attempts to punish the "guilty"; they must also educate, train, encourage and support people (Le Texier, 2011). They must be understood in conjunction with more basic interventions that address the systemic character of the provision of care in an institutional environment (the backstage drama experienced on an everyday basis by internal personnel). Certain propositions advanced in the literature, such as *good caring treatment* programs that espouse the humanist values promulgated by OD, prove to be more promising and liberating in that respect.

Adapting an OD Model to the Institutional Caregiving Context

As we have demonstrated, all the discourse on crises has been based on the prevention of risks of maltreatment and has focused on control and overseeing actions, an approach that leads to "punishments." In contrast, the current intervention proposal aimed to reverse this discourse and as an alternative to promote positive treatment was developed and submitted to the director. The basic idea of OD, with the effect of reinforcing lasting individual and organizational capacities to confront crises, is very close to the idea of implementing *good caring treatment* programs as proposed in the literature in institutional healthcare settings (Blondet, 2008). It's also a more emancipatory avenue to resolve issues regarding abusive or inappropriate behaviors toward vulnerable persons.

The researcher-practitioner stressed to the director that he needed to make his plan known to the various actors in the organization so that they could adopt it, critique it and make improvements. Furthermore, from an organizational development perspective, the director must recommend an approach to mobilize, empower and encourage the various actors in the organization to commit themselves concretely to implementing this model; rather than a punitive and disciplinary form of coercive model, this is a matter of leading the participants to better self-regulation and management of the behavior of "deviants" by a representative community of peers (Gouldner, 1954; Henry, 1987). The basic idea here is to create in this centre an environment favoring the expression of difficulties and/or dilemmas arising in the management of intervention with a clientele with demanding and complex clinical profiles and the discovery of courses of action to resolve them. In order to do so, the researcher-practitioner proposed the creation of a steering committee (Cummings & Worley, 2015; Schein, 1993) with a mandate to establish the order of priority to assign each of the sections of the proposed model (responding to the question "where do we start?"), as well as to identify those to be designated as responsible for upgrading the targeted interventions. This steering committee should come directly from the board of directors of the centre and be composed of the director general, the director of human resources, the director of professional services and at least two clinical supervisors. Within this steering committee, the members will be asked to name a president or coordinator responsible for determining the modalities of meetings and will report each year to the board of directors of the centre on progress in terms of the preventive management of crises.

Internal actors often invoke the lack of time to bring about the corrective measures necessary for a more positive development of their organization, and this is particularly true following a crisis when the eagerness to move on quickly to "something else" is often observed (Lalonde, 2007). In that regard, the researcher-practitioner recommended the director to establish the steering committee as rapidly as possible, before his departure (thus, before the end of his mandate as trustee), and, if at all possible, to call an initial meeting. The first meeting could allow for a transition from the situation of trusteeship to a "normal" situation while the board of directors was being re-established in its functions by the Ministry of Health and Social Services and a new director general was being named. With all this, the goal would be to send a signal that the prevention of crises is the responsibility of everyone within the organization, and that it is better to manage deviant behavior through mechanisms of representative bureaucracy than to have the state impose a punitive-centered bureaucratic model which would discredit the entire institution and inevitably affect the morale of employees and residents of the centre (Rollinson et al., 1997; Trevino, 1992).

Assessing and Concluding the Research-Intervention

The support work of the researcher-practitioner was completed when the mandate of the director who was the trustee expired at the end of May 2004. Both parties benefited from the research experience. Thus, the director was able to have continuous support throughout his mandate and received from the researcher various tools, charts and reviews of the literature tailored for this type of organization; this allowed him to conclude his mandate with concrete and positive proposals for managing the numerous areas of vulnerability typical of this type of establishment. For her part, the researcher was able to inform others about this experience and crisis analysis through academic publications.

Furthermore, a common finding of both parties was that the alacrity with which the Ministry of Health and Social Services brought the media crisis to an end and closed the file shortened the length of the mandate of the director who was acting as the trustee. This reduced mandate, however, was denounced by advocates defending the rights of patients. Consequently, it is difficult to confirm the extent to which the new administration that took over after the departure of the trustee actually implemented the actions proposed in the organizational development model. This fact should be added to the research observation that external parties are not systematically involved in the implementation of recommendations stemming from strategic plans (Lalonde & Adler, 2015), and, unfortunately, this is particularly true in the aftermath of a crisis (Lalonde, 2007).

Discussion

This chapter has addressed the question of "how can scholars produce actionable knowledge for crisis management?" That is, how can one derive lessons from academic research that are transferable and applicable to organizations?

First, by synthesizing principal results and findings of past research in four major spheres of crisis management, I have shown how it is possible to design practical guides and diagnostic tools that are accessible to managers, employees and OD practitioners and that embed actionable knowledge in best practices. The creation of such diagnostic tools is uncommon in OD and is one contribution of this chapter. Second, the example of a crisis in a long-term healthcare institution demonstrates how such tools can be effectively applied and adapted to particular contingencies of organizations. Third, the chapter contributes by providing a rare but important example of a successful collaboration during an OD-based crisis intervention undertaken by researchers and practitioners as there are very few concrete examples in the crisis management literature on this subject, and the few articles on actionable knowledge for crisis management remain quite theoretical. Further, by examining a crisis in a core sector of society – long-term healthcare for individuals with physical or cognitive disabilities – a sector that has experienced quite significant budget cuts in recent years – the chapter also contributes to our understanding of the experience of organizationally created harms and dangers that impact vulnerable citizens and their families.

Finally, given recent questioning of the relevance of organizational development to contemporary challenges in organizational change management, this chapter opens to opportunities development and renewal of the field of OD.

Conclusion

We conclude this chapter by addressing three final issues. The first issue is the evolution of the field of OD. The eminently humanist and liberating roots of the field of OD allow scholar practitioners to go beyond the impasses created by a positivist model of change management exclusively centered on punishment and can help to encourage the implementation of an OD model in which organizational actors themselves take charge and assume responsibility. And the current field of OD has been shown to offer many intervention strategies that support the positive development of individuals and organizations. However, this chapter has revealed two important limitations with OD as currently practiced. First, a large number of publications describing various OD interventions were done many years ago and recent works reporting on the practical efficacy of these interventions in developing individuals and organizations are limited in number. Thus, the field would benefit from revitalization and enhanced documentation of the impacts of interventions in each of the four core areas of organization: human processes, human resource management, structural configurations and strategy. This is essential for the eventual transfer of knowledge from empirical research to the practical domain and for demonstrating the capacity of OD to achieve the objectives of both enveloping individuals and organizational efficiency (Cummings & Worley, 2015).

Moreover, OD would benefit in terms of depth and realism by placing more emphasis on critical and constructivist perspectives from social sciences that highlight the mechanisms of confinement and social control that limit effective crisis responses, as was the case in the example presented. The focus on punitive and surveillance measures, especially in crisis recovery, can only exacerbate the state of actors' vulnerability and fails to shed light on the incubation process which triggered this crisis (Sementelli, 2016). Yet the field of OD has remained silent about these phenomena, an omission that limits OD's contribution to improved crisis. To address such limitations, several researchers argue for a reinvention of the OD (Bushe & Marshak, 2009; Werkman, 2010) through the development and recognition of the new "dialogic" forms of OD that anchored on discursive and conversational approaches to qualitative analysis (Bushe & Marshak, 2009), and for the adoption of new forms of OD based on a sensemaking perspective that focuses on patterns of action and mutual interactions that may lead to stagnation or deadlock (Werkman, 2010).

Second, the chapter has highlighted a number of guiding principles for crisis management that were converted into actionable knowledge. Yet, many of these principles derive from dominant trends in crisis management – planning and socio-organizational contingencies (Lalonde, 2007) – and consequently apply more readily to the so-called "conventional" or "reputational" crises (e.g. natural catastrophes, fires, and industrial accidents) and less to uncommon types of social crises that are unexpected, unconventional and intractable including social crises such as that presented in this chapter. Using crisis management strategies that apply to common crises could lead organizations to become over-prepared for conventional crises and underprepared for uncommon crises which are more difficult to resolve. Therefore, research on unconventional crises deserves greater attention from researchers. By extending the range of types of organizational crisis that are studied, crisis management scholars could increase the interest of other researchers in crisis management and encourage new collaborative efforts between organizational scholars and OD practitioners in the field of crisis management.

I conclude by offering some reflections on researcher-practitioner collaboration in crisis management. First, it is important to stress importance of temporal dimensions for research-intervention in the field of crisis management. A large proportion of crisis management research casts a *retrospective* glance at crises rather than a *prospective* look, but little research explores the preconditions for disaster. Consequently, researchers in crisis management should more extensively document the actions and efforts of organizations *prior to* crises, and should look for weak signals or emerging phenomena that anticipate crises

(Bauman et al., 2014; Costanza-Chock, 2012; Dahlgren, 2013; Dunleavy, 1994; Eijkman, 2014; Gerbaudo, 2012; Thorson et al., 2013).

Qualitative researchers using naturalist and constructivist approaches are likely better placed to gain rich details of disaster situations than scholars who use more distant research methods as they can observe what occurs throughout the entire crisis (Denyer & Tranfield, 2006). The predominance of the positivist paradigm in research, as well as the preference for publication in academic outlets, in particular scholarly journals, does not encourage a rapprochement between qualitative and quantitative scholars. Practitioners perceive a disconnection between reality as they see it and their reality as described by scholars and ultimately bypass researchers, and they turn instead to consultants to bring them actionable knowledge. To overcome this impasse, confidence in and recognition of the roles of each actor in a model of research intervention must be restored and a space for negotiated dialogue must be created if we are to produce quality research that gives rise to both actionable knowledge for practitioners and quality publications in academic journals for researchers.

References

Alexander, D. (2005), "Towards the Development of a Standard in Emergency Planning," *Disaster Prevention and Management*, 14(2), 158–175.

Alsop, R.J. (2004), "Corporate Reputation: Anything but Superficial – The Deep but Fragile Nature of Corporate Reputation," *Journal of Business Strategy*, 25(6), 21–29.

Argyris, C. (1993), *Knowledge for Action: A Guide for Overcoming Barriers to Organizational Change*. Jossey-Bass, San Francisco.

Avenier, M-J., Schmidtt, C. (2007), *La construction de savoirs pour l'action*, L'Harmattan, Paris.

Barton, A. (1969), *Communities in Disaster: A Sociological Analysis of Collective Stress Situations*, Double-Day and Company, Garden City, New York.

Bass, B.J., Avolio, B.M. (2008), *Developing the Potential Across a Full Range of Leadership. Cases on Transactional and Transformational Leadership*, Taylor & Francis, Mahwah, NJ.

Bauman, Z., Bigo, D., Esteves, P., Guild, E., Jabri, V., Lyon, D. (2014), "After Snowden: Rethinking the Impact of Surveillance," *International Politcal Sociology*, 8(2), 121–144.

Birkland, T.A. (2009), "Disasters, Lessons Learned, and Fantasy Documents," *Journal of Contingencies and Crisis Management*, 17(3), 146–156.

Blondet, E. (2008), *L'évaluation des pratiques professionnelles: un outil au service de la bientraitance*, Mémoire depose à l'École des Hautes Études en Santé Publique, Rennes (France), 50 pages.

Boin, A., Hart, P., Stern, E., Sundelius, B. (2005), *The Politics of Crisis Management. Public Leadership under Pressure*, Cambridge University Press, New York.

Bushe, G.R., Marshak, R.J. (2009), "Revisioning Organization Development. Diagnostic and Dialogic Premises and Patterns of Practice," *The Journal of Applied Behavioral Science*, 45(3), 348–368.

Clarke, L. (1999), *Mission Improbable: Using Fantasy Documents to Tame Disaster*, The University of Chicago Press, Chicago, IL.

Cooke, H. (2006), "Examining the Disciplinary Process in Nursing; A Case Study Approach," *Work, Employment and Society*, 20(4), 687–707.

Coombs, W.T., Holladay, S.L. (2006), "Unpacking the Halo Effect: Reputation and Crisis Management," *Journal of Communication Management*, 10(2), 123–137.

Cooperrider, D.L., Withney, D., Stravos, J.m. (2008), *Appreciative Inquiry Handbook. For Leaders of Change*, Berrett-Koehler, San Francico, CA.

Costanza-Chock, S. (2012), "Mic Check! Media Cultures and the Occupy Movement," *Social Movement Studies*, 11(3–4), 375–385.

Cummings, T.G., Worley, C.G. (2015), *Organization Development and Change*, Thompson South-Western, Mason, OH.

Dahlgren, P. (2013), *The Political Web: Media, Participation and Alternative Democracy*, Palgrave Macmillan, Houndsmill, Basingstoke.

Denis, H. (1993), *Gérer les catastrophes. Incertitude à apprivoiser*, Les Presses de l'Université de Montréal, Montreal.

Denis, H. (2002), *La Réponse aux Catastrophes. Quand L'impossible survient*. Presses Internationales Polytechnique, Montréal.

Denyer, D., Tranfield, D. (2006), "Using Qualitative Research Synthesis to Build an Actionnable Knowledge Base," *Management Decision*, 44(2), 213–227.

Derzel, A., De Souza, M. (2004), Report on St. Charles Borromee Portrays a Hospital in Crisis. The Gazette, May 19, 2004: A13.

Drabek, T. (2007), "Community Processes: Coordination," in Rodriguez, H., Quarantelli, E.L., Dynes, R.R. (Eds.), *Handbook of Disaster Research*, Springer, New York, 217–233.

Drabek, T., McEntire, D. (2003), "Emergent Phenomena and the Sociology of Disaster. Lessons, Trends and Opportunities from the Research Literature," *Disaster Prevention and Management*, 12(2), 97–112.

Dunleavy, P. (1994), "The Globalization of Public Services Production: Can Government be 'Best in World'?," *Public Policy and Administration*, 9(2), 36–64.

Dynes, R.R. (1983), "Problems in Emergency Planning," *Energy*, 8(8–9), 653–660.

Eijkman, Q. (2014), "Digital Security Governance and Risk Anticipation: What About the Role of Security Officials in Privacy Protection," *International Political Sociology*, 8(1), 116–119.

Flanagan, J.C. (1954), "The Critical Incident Technique," *Psychological Bulletin*, 51(4), 327–358.

Flin, R. (1996), *Sitting in the Hot Seat. Leaders and Teams for Critical Incident Management: Leadership for Critical Incidents*, John Wiley & Sons, West Sussex.

Gerbaudo, P. (2012), *Tweets and the Streets. Social Media and the Contemporary Activism*, Pluto Press, London.

Gouldner, A.W. (1954), *Patterns of Industrial Bureaucracy*, Free Press, Glencoe, IL.

Hart, P., Heyse, L., Boin, A. (2001), "Guest Editorial Introduction. New Trends in Crisis Management Practice and Crisis Management Research: Setting the Agenda," *Journal of Contingencies and Crisis Management*, 9(4), 181–188.

Henry, S. (1987), "Disciplinary Pluralism: Four Models of Private Justice in the Workplace," *Sociological Review*, 35(2), 275–319.

Kombarakaran, F.A., Baker, M.N., Yang, J.A., Fernandes, P.B. (2008), "Executive Coaching: It Works!," *Consulting Psychology Journal: Practice and Research*, 60(1), 78–90.

Kuban, R. (1995), *Crisis Management in Canada. A Study of Its Practice*, Pendragon Publishing, Calgary.

Lalonde, C. (2004), "In Search of Archetypes in Crisis Management," *Journal of Contingencies and Crisis Management*, 12(2), 76–88.

Lalonde, C. (2007), "The Potential Contribution of Organization Development to Crisis Management," *Journal of Contingencies and Crisis Management*, 15(2), 95–104.

Lalonde, C., Adler, C. (2015). "Information Asymmetry in Process Consultation: A Empirical Research on the Leader/Client and the Consultant Relationship in Healthcare Organizations," *Leadership and Organizational Development Journal*, 36(2), 177–211.

Lalonde, C., Boiral, O. (2012), "Managing Risks through ISO 31000. A Critical Analysis," *Risk Management*, 14(4), 272–300.

Le Texier, T. (2011), "Foucault, le pouvoir et l'entreprise: pour une théorie de la gouvernementalité managériale," *Revue de Philosophie Économique*, 12(2), 53–85.

Lewin, K. (1951), *Field Theory in Social Science*, Harper, New York.

McArdle, K.L., Reason, P. (2008), "Action Research and Organization Development," in Cummings, T. (Ed.), *Handbook of Organization Development*, Sage Publications, Thousand Oaks, CA, 122–136.

McConnell, A., Drennan, L. (2006), "Mission Impossible? Planning and Preparing for Crisis," *Journal of Contingencies and Crisis Management*, 14(2), 59–70.

McEntire, D., Myers, A. (2004), "Preparing Communities for Disasters: Issues and Processes for Government Readiness," *Disaster Prevention and Management*, 13(2), 140–152.

Miller, D. (1987), "The Genesis of Configuration," *Academy of Management Review*, 12(3), 686–701.

Pauchant, T.C., Mitroff, I. (1995), *La gestion des crises et des paradoxes. Prévenir les effets destructeurs de nos organisations*, Editions Québec/Amérique, Montreal.

Perry, R., Lindell, M.K. (2003), "Preparedness for Emergency Response: Guidelines for the Emergency Planning Process, *Disasters*, 27(4), 336–350.

Quarantelli, E.L. (1988), "Disaster Crisis Management: A Summary of Research Findings," *Journal of Management Studies*, 25(4), 373–385.

Riendeau, Y. (2006), La qualité des soins offerts aux personnes âgées en CHSLD: l'opinion des préposés aux bénéficiaires. Unpublished Master in Social Intervention dissertation, Université du Québec à Montréal.

Rollinson, D., Handley, J., Hook, C. (1997), "The Disciplinary Experience and Its Eggects on Behaviour," *Work, Employment and Society*, 11(2), 283–311.

Rosenthal, U., Kouzmin, A. (1993), "Globalizing an Agenda for Contingencies and Crisis Management: An Editorial Statement," *Journal of Contingencies and Crisis Management*, 1(1), 1–12.

Rosenthal, U., Charles, M.T., Hart, P.T. (1996), "Crisis Management and Institutional Resilience: An Editorial Statement," *Journal of Contingencies and Crisis Management*, 4(3), 119–124.

Ross, J.A., Deshotels, T.H., Forsyth, C.J. (2016), "Fantasy Objects: The Perception of Safety of Emergency Shelter in Place Kits," *Deviant Behavior*, 37(6), 692–708.

Schein, E.H. (2009), *Helping: How to Offer, Give and Receive Help*, Berrett-Koehler Publishers, San Francisco, CA.

Sementelli, A.J. (2016), "OD, Change Management, and the a Priori: Introducing Parrhesia," *Journal of Organizational Change Management*, 29(7), 1083–1096.

Stern, L.R. (2004), "Executive Coaching: A Working Definition," *Consulting Psychology Journal: Practice and Research*, 56(3), 154–162.

Stern, E. (2013), "Preparing: The Sixth Task of Crisis Leadership," *Journal of Leadership Studies*, 7(3), 51–56.

Taylor, M. (2000), "Cultural Variance as a Challenge to Global Public Relations: A Case Study of the Coca-Cola Scare in Europe," *Public Relations Review*, 26(3), 277–293.

Thorson, K., Driscoll, K., Ekdale, B., Edgerly, S., Gamber-Thompson, L., Schrock, A. (2013), "Youtube, Twitter and the Occupy Movement," *Information, Communication and Society*, 16(3), 421–451.

Trevino, L. (1992), "The Social Effects of Punishment in Organizations," *Academy of Management Review*, 17(4), 647–676.

Trist, E. (1983), "Referent Organizations and the Development of Inter-Organizational Domains," *Human Relations*, 36(3), 269–284.

Webb, G.R., Chevreau, F-R. (2006), "Planning to Improvise: The Importance of Creativity and Flexibility in Crisis Responses," *International Journal Emergency Management*, 3(1), 66–72.

Werkman, R. (2010), "Reinventing Organization Development: How a Sensemaking Perspective Can Enrich Theories and Interventions," *Journal of Change Management*, 10(4), 421–438.

Witherspoon, R., White, R.P. (1996), "Executive Coaching. A Continuum of Roles," *Consulting Psychology Journal: Practice and Research*, 48(2), 124–133.

Wooten, L.P. James, E.H. (2008), "Linking Crisis Management and Leadership Competencies: The Role of Human Resource Development," *Advances in Developing Human Resources*, 10(3), 352–379.

Zand, D.E. (1974), "Collateral Organization: A New Change Strategy," *Journal of Applied Behavioral Science*, 10(1), 63–89.

27

THE SOCIO-ECONOMIC APPROACH TO MANAGEMENT

Preventing Economic Crises by Harnessing Hidden Costs and Creating Sustainable Productivity

Marc Bonnet, Amandine Savall, Henri Savall and Véronique Zardet

The Socio-Economic Approach at the Organizational Level

The socioeconomic approach to management (SEAM), first disseminated in 1974, has been elaborated in recent years (Savall & Zardet, 2011a, 2011b, 2012, 2013) to better address the dynamic cycle of value creation and destruction processes in capitalist societies as well as the cyclical resurgence of these phenomena. The founding hypotheses of socioeconomic theory are:

1   Human potential is the only active factor of value-added creation, with technical and/or financial capital being precious tools but still sterile until activated by human potential.
2   Imperfections of the classical accounting model can be reduced and the relevance of decision-making improved through socioeconomic dynamic modeling.
3   Organizations create visible costs needed for production (e.g., materials, labor) of goods and services.
4   Organizational productive activities also create dysfunctions (e.g., poor working conditions) that engender hidden or implicit costs (e.g., absenteeism, staff turnover) that produce financial consequences (e.g., excess salary, overtime costs).
5   Crises emerge at all levels of analysis (unit, organization, nation) when hidden costs are high and impede effective organizational development and change.
6   Hidden costs can be harnessed and hidden human potential can be released by identifying and overcoming dysfunctions.

The principle that human potential is the only active factor in value creation, and the principle that problems with classical accounting systems that fail to account for value added can be reduced using SEAM ideas including the concepts of hidden cost and hidden performance, as well as the SEAM concept of value added on variable costs that can be used as a sustainable performance indicator. Indeed, the Malinvaud's team (Carré, Dubois & Malinvaud, 1972) demonstrated that the unexplained residual factor of the production function – the portion not explained by land, labor, and capital – represents 55% of the value measured by national income accounting. Thus, the high level of hidden costs that ISEOR researchers have measured in businesses and organizations since 1974 (Savall, 1975, 1977, 1978, 1979) can help explain the persistence of low economic performances and the large range of the residual factor.

The socioeconomic theory assumes that any organization is an intangible production system for goods and services, made up of two main, interacting elements: (1) the intensity of steering or controlling both activities and persons, and (2) hindrances to steering that result from serious dysfunctions. A key organizational illness (organizational illnesses are also called viruses at ISEOR) identified in the SEAM approach is the *TFW virus* (Taylorism, Fayolism, Weberism) that heavily impacts socioeconomic productivity. The TFW virus fragments and breaks up the organizational processes and focuses logics of actions and decision-making on biased representations of the whole organizational systems. In particular, it results in toxic management control by focusing on visible costs as opposed to hidden costs and performance. This TFW virus (Savall & Zardet, 2011b, 2012) is a metaphor for the *anachronistic* application by our contemporaries, theoreticians, and practitioners, of principles put forward a century or more ago by Taylor (1911), Fayol (1916), and Weber (1924) in a social and geopolitical economic context that is radically different from today's environment (Lussato, 1972). These authors were the instigators of maximizing the division of labor or hyper-specialization, of creating separation between design and production activities, and of the depersonalization of the organization and its main components that include operating rules, organization charts, processes, procedures, workplaces or job descriptions, and other components. These contributions were more relevant to the 19th and 20th centuries where democracy, technological innovation, and markets for capital and products existed on a different scale worldwide and that appeared to be less problematic than observed in most countries in the 21st century.

Inside organizations, the TFW virus infection is illustrated by an excessive focus on cost cutting versus business development, extensive segregation between departments and even individuals, and by the considerable difficulty employees have in communicating and co-operating, a matter that requires a high intensity of piloting (that is, launching and guiding) new practices from managers at all levels. This need increases as segregation of functions becomes more rigid (Savall & Zardet, 2011a; Heorhiadi, Conbere & Hazelbaker, 2014). In particular, one of the adverse impacts of such a virus in management practices is that it wastes intangible resources including the quality of work life by constraining individual and collective behaviors in ways that undermine the interestingness of the work content and the quality of the human environment. This in turn creates an atmosphere at work that hinders engaged activity and high-level performance. Given that these behaviors interact with a company's structures (physical, technological, organizational, demographic, mental), they can cause dysfunctions and affect the satisfaction level of the workforce along and those of external partners (customers, suppliers, institutions). ISEOR's intervention-researches in 1,854 enterprises and organizations, 72 business sectors, and 42 countries have pinpointed 4,713 generic types of dysfunction (see website www.iseor.com) that are side effects of the TFW virus and related processes. The SEAM model of the production of hidden costs is an ongoing process in all organizations and enterprises (Figure 27.1).

These dysfunctions are destroying real value by occasioning excessive costs (over-expenses) or the dysfunctions can destroy potential value in the form of opportunity costs – the missing value that would have been created without such dysfunctions (non-production). Over-expenses and non-production that do not appear in the account records have been called hidden costs. It should be mentioned that measuring hidden costs and performance has

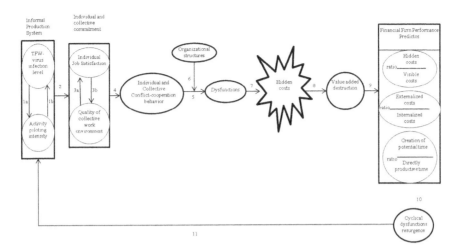

Figure 27.1 Modeling the Socioeconomic Theory of Hidden Costs

required the integration of qualitative, quantitative, and financial assessment of the impacts of dysfunctions. It could be achieved through a specific epistemological and methodological approach referred to as "qualimetrics" (Savall, 1974; Savall & Zardet, 1987, 1996, 2004, 2011; Boje, 2004).

Hidden costs and performance have an impact on financial results but are not visible in the accounts books. Their measurement by ISEOR researchers has shown that all organizations "naturally" suffer hidden costs to the tune of $ 20,000–70,000 per person per year, which represents 15%–42% of revenue (or income in the case of non-for-profit organizations).

Over a given period, these hidden costs lessen the organization's flow of added value creation. They reduce company profit levels, create financial deficits in non-for-profit organizations, and downgrade the quality of public services. Further, the everyday functioning of an organization simultaneously generates functions and dysfunctions. Functioning relies on good working practices to produce a desired performance, that is, creation of positive socio-economic value, whereas dysfunctions are deviations from this functioning that cause dissatisfaction among the internal or external stakeholders and the destruction of economic value. Following from these premises, we can now explicitly link socioeconomic productivity that is assumed to contribute to the sustainable economic development factor to economic crises. Economic crises emerge when hidden costs become significant and are not explicitly managed. By managing hidden costs, one releases significant hidden potential that reduces crisis potential, enables crisis avoidance, and facilitates economic recovery.

Conceptualizing and Measuring Socio-Economic Productivity

Socioeconomic management of organizations research has given rise to the concept of socioeconomic productivity, defined as the economic productivity compatible with an acceptable and sustainable quality of life, both at and outside work. Socioeconomic rationality (Savall 1979; Savall & Zardet, 2014) expands and enhances economic rationality by combining the dimension of social performance with that of financial performance. Socioeconomic theory defines social performance as the degree of satisfaction of people's needs involved with an organization in terms of their expectations of quality of life both at and outside work. Quality of life at work depends on six criteria or variables: working conditions, work organization, communication-coordination-cooperation, time management, integrated training, and strategic implementation. Socioeconomic theory thereby provides an expanded definition of economic performance to include two elements: immediate results and creation of potential. Immediate results are calculated using normal accounting methods and correspond to current impact in terms of income and expenditure, added value and net profits, recorded over the current accounting period. The new feature of this theory is the measurement of the flow of created potential generated alongside the immediate results over this same period. This corresponds to intangible investments that are self-financed during the current accounting period and will produce "immediate results" in following periods. The traditional accounting model neglects this created potential and seriously errs by recording these intangible investments in the expense accounts as if they were recurring costs relating only to value generated in the current period, whereas they are investments that will contribute over a longer term.

Economic productivity is the creation of tangible or financial value measured for each factor unit. Traditionally, economic productivity is measured with respect to the amount of invested capital, the payroll, the number of persons employed, or the number of hours of work. Productivity is often confused with technical output, or in other words, quantity produced per time unit, per machine, or per worker. The productivity concept has been dispraised over the years by some political and trade union figures and used to denounce certain excesses of technological development, the spread of the types of organizations characterized as having the TFW virus, and the ensuing degradation of the quality of life at work that follows. Socioeconomic theory overhauls the concept of economic productivity by giving it a new definition. Productivity thus corresponds to people's capacity to generate added value through their potential of energy, skills, and behavior, enabling them to live in a spirit of human dignity, self-respect, and be self-sufficient without depending on begging, private hand-outs from volunteers, or state charity from taxes and tax deductions. Socioeconomic productivity is the main prosperity lever for an individual, a group, a business, a public or non-profit organization, a locality, a region, a country, or a group of countries.

The Evaluation of Untapped Productivity Done with the Socio-Economic Theory

Hidden costs run at high levels as 15%–42% of business turnover or of the budgeted revenue of a public organization (Savall & Zardet, 1987). A proportion of 35%–55% of its hidden costs can be recovered by improvement actions conducted with the participation of all the people in the organization. This is equivalent to saying that economic productivity shows great elasticity depending on the organization's functional quality level, or, put differently, the quality of life and productive behavior of people involved. The existence of this deep reservoir of individual and collective human productivity enables society to absorb many of the fluctuations in activity that depend on the economic climate in the pertinent environment of the organization. Thus, a growth in activity of 10%–15% can be absorbed by existing human potential, that is, the normal workforce working normal hours if dysfunctions are reduced. The pressure from activity growth stimulates readjustments in the organization at various levels: the work team, the departments and sectors of the business or public organization. The explanation is found in the activation of human potential in the form of agility and creativity, in the quality of leadership from the supervisory staff, and in the workforce's commitment level, stimulated by the improvement in the quality of life.

The Socioeconomic Approach versus Traditional Economic and Financial Rationality

When the question "How can we attain consistency between the financial management models necessary to business development, or even survival, and the intuitive need to take account of the human and social dimension, the quality of life?" is asked, the most common answer is to propose these two apparently antagonistic factors as an answer. The juxtaposition of the different approaches implies that we simply take account of human and social problems while ignoring how to make their adoption compatible with decision models and with control featuring heavy financial pressuring. The crucial issue is indeed to demonstrate there can be compatibility between the social and the economic. As an example, current models for choosing investments based on maximum cash flow could take account of the social factor by substituting added value for cash-flow. Similarly, classifying quality of life at work improvement actions according to an economic typology (a financially advantageous, neutral, or costly solution) would enable the issue of financial planning of the quality of life improvements to be seriously addressed at company level and macro-economic level alike.

ISEOR's program of longitudinal intervention-researches (Péron & Bonnet, 2008; Savall, Zardet & Bonnet, 2009), spanning 42 years, has shown that the phenomenon of dysfunctions and hidden cost generation is cyclical and recurs "naturally" across successive periods in the history of a business or organization. This cyclical resurgence of dysfunctions and hidden costs shows that the static models frequently used in economic and management science are unsuitable for incorporating observable phenomena that have temporal dynamics. Socio-economic theory, based on analysis of temporal patterns over successive periods as created in macro-economics (Bernácer, 1922, 1945a, 1945b; Robertson, 1940), strives to put forward a dynamic model that is explanatory, prescriptive and predictive, and that can be used in the management of organizations, economic territories, and macro-economic policies.

Pinpointing resources of unexploited economic potential by measuring hidden costs also helps improve the accountant's "true and fair view." It sheds light on the organization's ability to either prepare for organization development when the cost of preventing or mending dysfunctions is less than the costs of those dysfunctions, or conversely to "mortgage" its future by accepting a heap of hidden costs that it drags around permanently like a ball and chain (Gephart, 2014).

Measuring Socio-Economic Productivity

The socioeconomic model enables measurement of the *socioeconomic productivity* at the level of an organization, a department, a workshop, an agency, or a team (Savall & Zardet, 2008) using the hourly contribution to value added on variable costs (HCVAVC) measure.

For-profit companies and small businesses measure efficiency or economic productivity by subtracting variable costs (VC) for a business unit from the revenue from the unit during a budgeting period. We call this difference the value added on variable cost (VAVC), which represents the economic performance of the set of workers who produced the activity. By dividing this value by the number of hours paid by the organization, one creates a ratio of the HCVAVC. This is also termed hourly value creation and represents the average efficiency in this organization of one hour of human activity, a measure that takes account of both the circumstances in the specific working environment and the internal strategic energy expended on that person.

Hourly value creation provides three main applications: the calculation of (a) the cost of products (i.e., overall cost, including fixed and variable costs), goods, and services; (b) the hidden cost of dysfunctions; and (c) the value of the intangible investment in qualitative development of human potential (Savall & Zardet, 1992, Zardet, 2010; Datry & Savall, 2015). This indicator is easy to calculate from accounting data, and it enables monitoring the business's "economic state of health." When hourly value creation increases, the business's state of prosperity improves in terms of market share growth, current and future competitiveness, sustainable socioeconomic productivity, added value creation, profitability, and financial results. When it decreases, this indicator raises an alert calling for stricter and more vigilant strategic and operational steering of the company or organization. According to socioeconomic theory, it is also important to ensure that the business's overall economic productivity indicator has not been produced by dysfunctional means, for example, by degradation in life and work for staff members ranging from lower level staff to the top management.

The SEAM theory also assumes that when this hourly value creation increases and there are also improved working conditions, work organization, communication-coordination-cooperation, time management, integrated training, and strategic implementation, people in the organization will see *progress* in their overall situation. These improvements will include an *improvement* of their social performance (a qualitative source of satisfaction) and an improvement in their purchasing power, both of which are financed by the recycling or transformation of hidden costs into value creation. This progress is produced through the proactive participation of staff, the level of their involvement in the organization's activities, and the development of their human potential including individual and collective energy, skills, and behaviors.

ISEOR intervention-research has measured the very high elasticity of individual and collective human productivity. And, over the long period (10–32 years), researchers have observed an ongoing improvement in this socioeconomic productivity that reveals the extensive resources that are latent in humans and that could be converted into real economic performance. Several longitudinal case studies have provided enlightening examples, corroborated by our database of 1,854 case studies (Buono & Savall, 2007; Savall, Zardet & Bonnet, 2009). These original researches have shown that all organizations have the potential capability to become self-financing in ways that foster their survival and development (Zardet & Voyant, 2003) through enhancing socioeconomic productivity, even in a context of economic crises. Substantial "deposits" of hidden costs that have accumulated due to past activities also become recyclable resources for financing innovative actions, releasing temporal resources, and assigning time and other resources to proactive strategies and practices. Thus, even without accumulating substantial debt, any company or organization can self-finance much of its investment in the development of human potential and consolidate its internal cohesion by effectively managing hidden costs and converting these into a source of sustainable performance in its relevant market and institutional environment.

Two examples can be provided of enterprises that tapped the hidden potential of employees through socioeconomic approach to management to successfully prevent organizational crises during the 2008 and subsequent economic downturn. The cases are (1) the Ninkasi company, (Savall, Zardet & Bonnet, 2009), a small firm with a brewery, a chain of restaurants, and music performance venues, and (2) the Brioche Pasquier Pastry Company (Savall & Zardet, 1995, 2017a; Pasquier, 1995–2005; and Worley, Zardet, Bonnet & Savall, 2015), a large commercial bakery and conglomerate organization with operations in several countries.

Ninkasi: Resilience in the Face of Crisis

Ninkasi is a fairly young, medium-sized company located in Lyon, France, with 260 employees. It operates three strategic units: brewery, restaurants, and music entertainment. The core of the company strategy draws on a humanistic vision that emphasizes authenticity, diversity, and friendliness. A few years after its creation, the company experienced financial difficulties, and one of the two original owners left. Facing an economic crisis, the remaining owner made the decision in 2007 to implement socioeconomic management. The goal of the SEAM intervention was to enhance management's capability to engage in active listening to employees, to improve negotiations, and to strengthen contracting. The SEAM approach enabled the company to increase by 300% its revenue and profit during the financial instability of 2008 and later to emerge from the financial crisis in strong financial shape.

Brioche Pasquier Group: Sustainable High Value-Added Creation Over Time and During Crises

The Brioche Pasquier Company, a large commercial bakery, implemented the socioeconomic approach to management starting in 1985. At this time, the firm was a medium-sized company with 260 employees on pay-roll and revenue amounted to US $37 million. Subsequently, the Brioche Pasquier Group experienced ongoing and substantial growth both through organic means and by acquiring small companies in France or abroad during several time periods where economic problems existed in France and in world markets. The company experienced a continuous increase in sales, profit, and productivity, while increases in staffing was slower. In particular, growth and productivity still increased even at lower pace during the 2007–2010 period when economic and financial crisis broke out. During this same period of crisis, BPG acquired a Californian firm in the baking industry in order to strengthen its internationalization strategy (see Worley et al., 2015, chapter 3). Between 1986 and 2013, sales increased at a rate of 12% per year and net income increased, on average, by 11.4 per year.

Transposing SEAM Concepts to the Macro-Level

The socioeconomic theory of organizations emerged by addressing macro-economic issues including economic crises and has delved down into organizations to the level of work teams. The scope of the intervention work by ISEOR, the size of the client businesses (from 1 employee up to 30,000 employees), and the trans-organizational issues that connected firm-level challenges to societal and world system challenges have led us to return to the macro-economic level. Through this process, we have identified isomorphic phenomena, such as similarities in types of dysfunctions that occur at both micro- and macro-levels, and similar ways that dysfunctions relate to hidden costs. These similarities have enabled us to identify macro-level hidden costs, including wasted medication and purchased but unused medical supplies that cost an estimated 3 billion euros a year in France (Savall & Zardet, 2005).

Socioeconomic theory considers that all geopolitical territories including boroughs, metropolitan areas, regions, countries, and groups of countries are weakly structured organizations that compose relatively loose and flexible systems with a very high number of components and countless interactions between these components. As a consequence, the number of dysfunctions are assumed to be high and hidden costs extensive. Thus, analysis of macro-level units of analysis (institutions, industries, societies, world system) are appropriate for SEAM analysis.

Macro-Social Analysis of Human Potential

Macro-human potential is an aggregate of human potential inserted in and dispersed across organizations and territories. A review of details of social crises since the 1970s reveals the existence of a growing gap between individuals' aptitudes and the place they occupy in organizations, whatever their hierarchical level (workers, employees, supervisors, managers). The cause of this gap can be attributed to the "effectiveness" of contemporary educational systems in the early 21st century that have developed general aptitudes, expectations in students for interesting and rewarding work, flexible workplaces and practices, individual discretion in performance of work tasks, and opportunities for rapid promotion. These aptitudes, expectations, and aspirations in students unfortunately are mismatches with the rigid structures and jobs often observed in companies and organizations. This results in a quality gap between job supply and demand for quality of life at and outside of work.

In a future of increased schooling, the effects of much broader access to secondary and higher education, notably in the developed countries, along with the development of ongoing training, constitute increasing factors that may extend the existing gap between the aptitudes and organizational roles of those involved (Savall, 1976). If we add to these factors the outcomes of other phenomena that have altered citizens' perception of satisfying work (Savall, Zardet & Bonnet, 2009) such as the need for more participative leadership management style, we can see that citizens in general, as employees, and also as customers, find it increasingly hard to accept being confined to the role of a production worker who holds only an impoverished and impoverishing social status in the enterprise.

ISEOR's analyses of the actual functioning of workshop and office activity (Savall Zardet & Bonnet, 2009) lead us to question the implicitly accepted and deeply anchored premise that all increases in job specialization and all technological investments do, *ipso facto*, lead to greater productivity. In the light of experiments conducted in organizations (Savall, 1974), economists must abandon the scheme in which they generally frame their analyses. Such a scheme very much inspired by "Smithian" and "Taylorist" analyses (see Adam Smith's (1759, 1776) famous example of the pin factory borrowed from the Diderot Encyclopedia that, well before Taylor's time, was given as a justification for work specialization. These experiments shed light on the considerable potential human energy and resources that are embedded in current organizations and thus cannot be released to create socioeconomic value. This observation leads to the admission that the "full use of human productive resources" (Perroux, 1972, 1973, 1975), or, to put it another way, the full employment of human potential implies recognition in organizational structures of the diversity of human abilities, the desire of people to contribute to the organization, and the existence of people's reserves of heuristic intelligence, that is, trial-and-error learning process.

Dysfunctions are an aggravating factor in an activity's production costs. The observed dysfunctions must be analyzed not only from an organizational or psychosociological point of view but also from a macro-economic perspective. Consider a hypothetical balance sheet that records the cost to society and businesses of dysfunctions including absenteeism, industrial accidents or diseases, staff turnover, scrap rates, slowdown of throughputs whether deliberate or not, strikes, and other issues. One can see that today's society as a whole, as well as its individual members, is suffering a huge opportunity loss of economic value due to macro-dysfunctions. Thus, it is essential for society to ensure that the differential explicit costs of new forms of work organization aimed at reducing dysfunctions are lower or equivalent to the reduction of hidden costs the new work forms allow, be it at micro- or macro-economic level, to maintain the firm's performance level. In this scenario, growth and quality of life will be stable and possibly based on the current resource levels. Nevertheless; another point of view is also conceivable: one can accept lower growth in order to further improve the quality of life for employees and managers. Without rejecting this second option, we assume that the struggle against recurring economic crises can be most directly explored and resolved by starting with the first of these ideas, that is, the assumption that economic growth is compatible with the improvement of living conditions.

Territorial Organizations and Socioeconomic Productivity

The first macro-level of analysis we address is the idea of a "territorial organization" – an organization with authority over a particular physical area or domain within a society. Territorial organizations are often large and complex, with many dimensions and components all in a permanent movement. As a consequence, these organizations consist of tangled sets of interconnected organizations (businesses, associations, public organizations, institutions, authorities, informal groups, families, etc.) living and functioning in territories bounded by geographical, physical, social, political, and cultural dimensions.

Territories are thus considered as weakly structured (meta-) organizations that can, according to the socioeconomic theory of organizations, be analyzed as consisting of macro-structures, functioning with collective macro-behaviors, which generate macro-dysfunctions giving rise to macro-hidden costs. These organizations do not appear in the nomenclature or entries of national accounting systems and are hidden cost centers absent from the standard national accounts records. These hidden macro-structures are made up of geographic areas and properties, the amenities and institutions installed there, the communication infrastructures, educational and cultural establishments, relatively stable components more often managed by the authorities, which make a territory more or less attractive to the eyes of citizens and economic and social stakeholders. Hidden costs identified in organizations or territories constitute reserves of productivity allowing self-financing for the development of economic and social activity.

Nations and Socioeconomic Productivity

At the country or national level of analysis, the macro-economic variables used in national income accounting are the aggregated data obtained by government statistical agencies from individual companies and organizations. Thus, the gross domestic product (GDP) of a nation is the aggregate of all added value created by all agents across the national territory that is collected by official statistical agencies. The principle of isomorphism that presided over the construction of national income accounting is applicable to dysfunctions, hidden costs, and productivity and its elasticity (Di Maggio & Powell, 1983). By applying necessary precautions when aggregating micro-economic variables, it is reasonable to argue that the macro-economic aggregation of dysfunctions, hidden costs, and the growth and recycling capacity of socioeconomic productivity enables one to define relevant concepts for the analysis of the national economy, namely, the macro-dysfunctions, the macro-hidden costs, the macro-elasticity of socioeconomic productivity, largely ignored in the usual macro-economic models (Cappelletti, 2012b).

This theory of macro-dysfunctions can be illustrated by exploring a national context characterized by emerging social issues that have enhanced citizens' expectations for a better quality of life at work. Our example involves the nation of France. During the 1970s, nongovernmental and governmental organizations took up these issues (Savall 1974, 1977a,

1977b, 1979; Savall & Zardet, 2014). Several social events, legislative and regulatory measures, and formal agreements between social organizations emerged in the decade following the "revolutionary" events of 1968 in France. This period saw the start of a general awareness of the quality of life at work as an important social issue. Recognition of trade union in companies followed in 1968. Thereafter, France witnessed the creation of ongoing training programs in 1970–1971, mandated by the inter-profession agreement of 1970 and the "1971 Act" inspired by Jacques Delors, who was then the social adviser to Prime Minister Jacques Chaban-Delmas.

By 1971, France witnessed the advent of conflicts explicitly involving working conditions in 1971. These conflicts were followed by several legislative actions including the "December 1973 Act" on working conditions, the creation of the National Agency for Improvement of Working Conditions ("ANACT"), the 1975 Sudreau report on company reform, the 1975 outline agreement on working conditions signed by a number of trade union organizations, and the 1976 introduction of a Secretary of State for manual labor working conditions (Lionel Stoléru). Eventually, the first government measures toward the revaluation of manual work were created, following the report written by Henri Savall (Savall, 1979) on the basis of the work undertaken by the commission created by Stoléru and chaired by Jacques Morin.

Just as current ecological policies have sought to base their rationales in relevant economic reasoning and implicitly consider that economic improvement will result from reducing hidden environmental costs, the development of socioeconomic policies could stimulate the development of prosperity among a large range of the citizens, organizations, and territories since this program could be self-financed through the recovery of the macro-hidden costs of dysfunctions that are overcome and not by simply passing economic value from certain economic agents to others. The reduction of macro-dysfunctions and their transformation into value-added human potential could enable extensive growth in individual and collective well-being by improving the fulfillment of societal needs (macro-social performance) along with recycling or transforming the resources wasted by macro-dysfunctions into value-added contributions (macro-economic performance). This more methodical and effective engagement of all human potentials (macro-human potential) would help increase macro-socioeconomic productivity, reduce public and private charitable transfers, and – as a side benefit – reduce mandatory deductions from pay and the syphoning of value from very active human potential to underactive or inactive human potential. Such a program would help reduce "assisted poverty" by substituting the socioeconomic approach's financial approach of integrated training and coaching that can enhance employability and productivity and hence provide more economic potential than other financial efforts such as unemployment insurance and charitable donations to the poor or unemployed. Business ethics would thus find better integration with economic rationality and could become the bedrock of a sustainably responsible capitalism (Allais, 1989, 2008; Voyant, 2003; Yunus, 2010; Davoine, 2012; Savall, Péron, Zardet & Bonnet, 2015, 2017).

Macro-dysfunctions including (1) the permanent existence in the world of hundreds of millions of unemployed persons producing little or no added value, (2) illiteracy (Bonnet, 1988, 1996) that is caused by limitations in education (schools in interaction with society), and (3) health issues (Savall, Zardet & Bonnet, 2002) such as occupational diseases and violence (Savall & Bonnet, 1996) that emerge due to workplace hazards and hidden costs all give rise to cumulative effects over time. Macro-dysfunctions display a negative or regressive spiral as they cascade in ways that create new macro-dysfunctions and macro-hidden costs in an ongoing or downward spiral.

It is this negative or regressive spiral that we are currently witnessing despite a general planet-wide rise in prosperity levels that is inconsistent and varies greatly across regions and even within countries. Intervention researches carried out by ISEOR in almost 2,000 businesses and organizations have shown that dysfunctions and hidden costs are not ineluctable. The isomorphism principle allows the hypothesis that the level of macro-dysfunctions and macro-hidden costs in territories is not a matter of fate and that the regressive spiral can be overturned into a spiral of progress, by using SEAM's rigorous research and intervention methodology.

Socio-Economic Productivity at the International Level

Dysfunctions occur at the international level and tend to stem from lack of coordination and harmonization of differing systems of norms between and among nations. In socioeconomic theory, this macro-dysfunction is also referred to as "*tetranormalization*" and it results in the growth of macro-hidden costs. Tetranormalization (Savall & Zardet, 2005, 2013; Bessire, Cappelletti & Pigé, 2010; Boje, 2015; Cappelletti, Pigé & Zardet, 2015) describes and explains the dysfunctions and hidden costs stemming from norms proliferation and contradiction between the four main categories of standards and norms: social, environment, accounting, and trade. Problems emerge because normative differences are not respected, and thus they provoke dysfunctions, create distortions in the rules of the games of markets inside both organizations and territories, and engender an extra and growing layer of hidden costs.

How Macro-Dysfunctions and Hidden Costs Create Chronic Underemployment and Crises

The history of economic thought had shed light on three main factors in economic value creation: land (natural resources), capital, and labor. Those factors are, however, all of different natures. *Natural resources* are exogenous to humanity. *Capital* is an accumulation of economic value that has in fact been created mainly by humans. As for *labor*, socioeconomic theory assumes that human potential is the only active factor in value creation (Savall, 1974, 1975b, 1977, 1979, 1981, 2003; Delors, 1975; Perroux, 1979; Ansoff, 1981; Savall & Zardet, 1987, 2008; Savall, Zardet & Bonnet, 2000, 2008; Boje & Rosile, 2003; Péron & Péron, 2003; Buono & Savall, 2007, 2015; Gephart, 2009; Sorensen et al., 2010; Conbere & Heorhiadi, 2011). Thus, labor represents those aspects of human activity that enable value production through the combined transformation of natural resources and the use of capital as an instrument of economic value creation. Certain economic theories privilege *labor value* due to an assumption that any input of labor to goods or service creates value. But SEAM notes that it is actually only the appropriate *match* between a good or service and a demand drawing on consumer *needs* that ultimately assigns value to such goods or services.

Following from this, SEAM notes that unsold or undelivered inventories have no economic value. Their cost includes work, but they have zero price, because those goods or services have not met consumers who will buy them. This is the rationale for creation of the socioeconomic concept of human potential. This concept emphasizes the specificity of humans and asserts that humans create value through their energy, skills, and behaviors. Numerous studies by researchers from ISEOR (Institut de Socio-économie des Entreprises et des Organisations) have addressed a great number and a large variety of organizations and have demonstrated that human capabilities are most often underemployed. As a result, the socioeconomic theory differs from other (classical) economic theories by giving the human factor a preeminent, determinative role in economic activity and value creation as well as in variations in economic activity and value creation over time. Although Becker (1964), the award-winning US economist (Becker, Murphy & Tamura 1990), highlighted the key role of human capital, Henri Savall (1974, 1975, 1981) has criticized the concept of human capital, because human capital is only owned by the individual and can't be alienated, as opposed to most economic and management theories assuming that talents and mandatory high involvement belong to the company and its stakeholders. Indeed, employees can either propose relevant innovations or refrain from doing so in the workplace, depending on whether value added is acknowledged or not by the management. This individual ownership of people's talents by individuals themselves can't be transferred to another company or to material capital. And there has been no market for human capital since slavery was outlawed. This is why Savall replaced the "human capital" concept with the concept of human potential (Cappelletti, 2012a).

The theory of economic crises pioneered by the Spanish economist Germán Bernácer (1922, 1945a, 1945b; Savall, 1973, 1975, 2013a, 2017), a contemporary of Keynes (1936) and Schumpeter (1942), also helps to explain the macro-economic origin of crises and underemployment. Both economic crises and underemployment arise due to the flight of capital from the real economy circuit to the confines of the more lucrative sphere of unearned income, speculation, and hoarding. Thus, socioeconomic theory has located the sources of these critical social problems as lying deep inside organizations. The dysfunctions underlying macro-problem crossing the porous boundaries of organizations, accumulate in surrounding areas, then spread locally, regionally, nationally, and internationally. Put simply, conventional capitalism emphasizes explicit costs and tries to produce profit in large part by cost minimization. In contrast, SEAM shows that activities that produce explicit costs also produce dysfunctions that create hidden costs that are typically unmeasured. The accumulation of dysfunctions that produce hidden costs thus absorbs resources that could be used to increase the size of the workforce, the level of production, and lower explicit costs. Thus, hidden costs place limits on organizational actions, restrict employment and thereby create economic problems and crises in organizations because of the proliferation of hidden costs.

Socio-Economic Theory Proposals for Preventing and Overcoming Crises

Socioeconomic theory rejects the inevitable "stagnation" of economic action ("the stationary economy") that has been prominent in certain schools of thought since the 19th century. SEAM instead advocates the development of economic activity that is correlated to individual and collective social development. The permanent existence of unfulfilled needs among countless citizen-consumers due to poverty or simply due to real or potential unassuaged desires, shows the absurdity of "stagnation" or a stationary economy.

Socioeconomic theory incorporated the concept of sustainably supported corporate responsibility from its origin to emphasize the double facet of social and economic phenomena. That is, there are both social and economic aspects to public health, food safety, job market regulation, unemployment, welfare, and for the political responsibility for matters of inequality and poverty. For example, poverty has both moral and socioeconomic facets. Thus, the transfer of wealth alone from some citizens to others cannot be a solution to poverty since it constitutes a macro-hidden cost that gives rise to lost opportunities for the full development of human potential and activities arising therefrom (Savall, Péron, Zardet & Bonnet, 2015, 2017).

In this context, we define economic crisis as an accidental situation in the normal flow of economic activity that disrupts this economic activity. This was the case in 1973 oil embargo, in the early part of the 2000s, and then much more seriously in the 2007–2008 "sub-primes" crisis that caused worldwide upheaval in financial markets. At their peaks, these crises produced imbalances in both financial and real economy markets that have had interactive effects that produce a chronic loss of economic resources that becomes worse than the crisis at its peak. One example is company restructuring of operations through mass layoffs that gives rise to recurring macro-hidden costs (e.g., unemployment) that may last for years and far outlive the "one-off" decisions that caused the layoffs. Socioeconomic theory's main interest is in these recurring cyclical crises that lead to a permanent imbalance in both the real economy and financial market spheres. Under these conditions, prosperity declines; companies go out of businesses; new businesses are created but quickly fold; workforces decline chronically; businesses, public bodies, and whole countries acquire extensive debt in real markets; financial exchange prices fluctuate heavily; unemployment is chronic; and national external trading deficits become an endemic problem.

Socioeconomic theory sheds light on the reasons for these recurring crises (e.g., accumulated hidden costs and limited development of human potential) and provides solutions for developing economic agility as a source of competitiveness and prosperity, both on a company scale and on an economic territory scale. The considerable hidden cost levels of 30% or higher of annual turnover measured by ISEOR in almost 2,000 organizations employing 110,000 people allows one to potentially estimate an aggregate value for hidden costs at business sector, local, regional, and national levels. This aggregate could be used as an indicator of macro-hidden costs inside national income accounting system. There are almost 50 countries in the world with a population of less than 110,000; hence, the statistical validity of such an aggregate estimate based on hidden cost measurements (as done by ISEOR researchers) would be no less robust than that of the aggregates in the national income accounting used as inputs to the periodic measurement of the any nation's GDP (Arkhipoff, 1985).

Thus, following well-established national income accounting principles, the GDP calculation results from the aggregation of values added in inter-company/organization transactions, that is, the total value created by a company (e.g., turnover) less the value created by its suppliers. Through this consolidated calculation, which eliminates redundancies between values created upstream of the company or organization and those it creates downstream, we reduce data aggregation errors. The calculation of added value on variable costs follows the same principle, such that the aggregate of hourly contributions to added value on variable costs is able to provide us with a macro-socioeconomic productivity figure by aggregating the hourly value creation measured at company and organization levels. Its meaning and its use in monitoring and controlling the economy would appear to be more reliable and useful than calculations made remotely without observation or verification of data in the field, as is commonly employed by the usual macro-economic models. The competitiveness of a territory, whether it be local, regional, national, or transnational (world region), could thus be measured and controlled by mixed public-private policies on added value creation.

The most dramatic crisis is not the loss of financial value in speculative markets that occurs every five or ten years and that is suffered by economic actors many of whom can afford it. Rather, the most pernicious and most harmful effects are those of a recurring crisis in which existing potential, macro-human potential, creativity, and integral innovation are undervalued and represent considerable macro-hidden costs. Through micro-level management of hidden costs and the release of hidden human potential, many macro-level economic crises can be avoided or reduced in impact.

Conclusion

The scientific objective of this chapter is to demonstrate the relativity of economic obstacles in relation to achieving social objectives. We only know information that is based on past results, or by forecasts of future results. These forecasts and past results are biased by two factors: the failure of common measurement devices to correctly assess hidden costs and hidden potential, and the absence of experimentation with alternative solutions to those that have been well-established in the field of job design. This leads us to question scientific practices and to question why scholars to not pursue the opportunity to explore utopian or imaginative ideas and practices for preventing crises into the field of investigation. To do so, one needs to provide alternative solutions to economic problems as scientific possibilities and to explore these alternatives through the use of different experimentation techniques.

Socioeconomic productivity can also be connected to the concept of socioeconomic integrated innovation. It includes all forms of innovation in the key functional areas of business: products, markets, technologies, organizations, and human potential. Indeed, a new product, the creation of a new market, or the insertion of new technologies all call for new forms of organization, fresh impetus, and new professional and managerial practices, as well as new individual and collective practices that compose the development of a permanent stream of general innovation, both within businesses or organizations and within territorial areas of economic activity, as well as at national and international levels.

Socioeconomic theory provides a way to better interpret and trace macro-economic development paths. Rather than focusing on the reduction of explicit costs as a means of enhancing profit in a zero-sum game with winners (management) and losers (workers), SEAM operates with the perspective of a non-zero-sum game, or in other words, in the development of "win-win" situations based on the growth of added value that can be shared between the parties involved – management, shareholders, and workers (Porter & Kramer, 2011).

References

Allais, M. (1989). Discours de réception du Prix Nobel d'Économie [Nobel Prize award in economics discourse], *Annales des Mines*, Mars.

Allais, M. (2008). Comment vivre ensemble: conditions économiques et sociales pour la démocratie. [How to live together: economic and social requisites for democracy], in Association François Perroux (ed.), *Comment vivre ensemble: conditions économiques de la démocratie*, 19–32. Écully: ISEOR, éditeur.

Ansoff, H.I. (1981–2009). *An Economic Evaluation of Job Enrichment*: Preface to H. Savall, *Work and People*, (Oxford University Press), 1st edition, New York. 2nd edition, Charlotte: IAP.

Arkhipoff, O. (1985). Un, deux, trois, beaucoup, ou comment l'imprécision vient aux comptables [One, two, three, many, or how imprecision comes to accountants]. *Économies et sociétés, série Sciences de gestion*, 19 (6), 185–200.

Becker, G.S. (1964). *Human capital*, 3rd edition. Chicago, IL: University of Chicago Press.

Becker, G., Murphy, K., & Tamura, R. (1990). *Human Capital Fertility and Economic Growth*, paper n°3414. Cambridge: National Bureau of Economic Research.

Bernácer, G. (1922). La teoría de las disponibilidades como interpretación de las crisis y del problema social, Revista nacional de economía [The theory of availability and interpretation of the crisis and the social problems]. *Revista Nacional de Economía*, 3 (40), 267–303.

Bernácer, G. (1945a). *La teoría funcional del dinero* [The Functional theory of Money], Madrid: Consejo Superior de Investigaciones Científicas, 2nd edition. 1956.

Bernácer, G. (1945b). *Una economía libre sin crisis y sin paro*, Madrid: Aguilar, 1955.

Bessire, D., Cappelletti, L., & Pigé, B. (2010). Normes: origines et conséquences des crises [*Standards and norms: Origin and consequence of crises*], Paris: Economica.

Boje, D. (2004). Preface, in Savall & Zardet, *Recherche en sciences de gestion: approche qualimétrique. Observer l'objet complexe*, Paris: Economica. Translated in English *Qualimetrics: Observing the complex object*, Charlotte: IAP.

Boje, D. (ed.) (2015). *Organizational change and global standardization: Solutions to standards and norms overwhelming organizations*, New York: Routledge.

Boje, D.M., & Rosile, G.A. (2003). Comparison of socio-economic and other transorganizational development methods. *Journal of Organizational Change Management*, 16 (1), 10–20.

Bonnet, M. (1988). Expériences du traitement de l'illettrisme en entreprise industrielle. Cas d'une intervention socio-économique dans une verrerie. *Actualité de la Formation Permanente*, (96), septembre-octobre, 27–29.

Bonnet, M. (1996). Entreprises et illettrisme. *Bulletin du Groupe Permanent de Lutte contre l'Illettrisme*, (34), octobre, 1–3.

Buono, A.F., & Savall, H. (eds.) (2007). *Socio-economic intervention in organizations*, Charlotte: IAP.

Buono, A.F., & Savall, H. (eds.) (2015). *The socio-economic approach to management revisited: The evolving nature of SEAM in the 21st century*, Charlotte: Information Age Publishing.

Cappelletti, L. (2012a). *Le contrôle de gestion de l'immatériel. Une nouvelle approche du capital humain* [Management control of intangibles. A new approach to human capital], Paris: Dunod.

Cappelletti, L. (2012b). La macroéconomie et l'imposture, *Les Échos*, 19 décembre.

Cappelletti, L., Pigé, B., & Zardet, V. (2015). *Dynamique normative: arbitrer et négocier la place de la norme dans l'organisation*, Paris: EMS.

Carré, J.J., Dubois, P., & Malinvaud, E. (1972). *La croissance française. Un essai d'analyse économique causale de l'après-guerre, Paris: Seuil* [French growth. A causal economic analysis test of the post-war], Paris: Édition du Seuil.

Conbere, J.P., & Heorhiadi, A. (2011). Socio-economic approach to management: A successful systemic approach to organizational change. *OD Practitioner*, 43 (1), 6–10.

Datry, F., & Savall, A. (2015). Global-local (Glocal) creation of value added, in Buono & Savall (eds.), *The socio-economic approach to management revisited: The evolving nature of SEAM in the 21st century*, Charlotte: IAP.

Davoine, L. (2012). *Économie du bonheur* [Economics of Welfare], Paris: La Découverte.

Delors, J. (1975). Preface in Savall, H., *Enrichir le travail humain : l'évaluation économique,* Paris: Dunod.

Diderot Encyclopédie. *Encyclopédie Encyclopeédie ou Dictionnaire Raisonne Des Sciences et des Metiers*. Downloaded August 19, 2018 from: https://archive.org/details/encyclopdieoudi03alemgoog

Di Maggio, P., & Powel, W. (1983). The iron cage revisited: Institutional isomorphism and collective rationality in organizational fields. *American Sociological Review*, (4) 82, 147–160.

Fayol, H. (1916). *Administration générale et industrielle* [Industrial and global administration], Paris: Gauthiers Villars.

Gephart Jr, R.P. (2009). An invitation to ethnostatistics. *Revue sciences de gestion-Management sciences-Ciencias de gestión*, 70, 85.

Gephart Jr, R.P. (2014). Using prosperity to construct an economic crisis: Alberta's "bitumen" bubble. *Recherche en sciences de gestion-Management sciences-Ciencias de gestión*, 6, 37–57.

Heorhiadi, A., Conbere, J., & Hazelbaker, C. (2014). Virtue vs. virus can OD overcome the heritage of scientific management? *Organization Development Network*. Downloaded August 18, 2018 from https://www.researchgate.net/profile/Alla_Heorhiadi/publication/265552433_Virtue_vs_Virus_Can_OD_overcome_the_heritage_of_scientific_management/links/5411f0610cf-2fa878ad3937b/Virtue-vs-Virus-Can-OD-overcome-the-heritage-of-scientific-management.pdf

Keynes, J.M. (1936). Théorie générale de l'emploi, de l'intérêt et de la monnaie, Paris: Payot. [*The general theory of employment, interest, and money*], Cambridge: Cambridge University Press.

Lussato, B. (1972). *Introduction critique aux théories d'organisation* [Critical introduction to organizational theories], Paris: Dunod.

Pasquier, S. (1995–2005). Preface, in Savall, H. & Zardet V. *Ingénierie stratégique du roseau, souple et enracinée*, Paris: Economica. Translated in English *Strategy engineering of the reed, flexible and rooted,* Charlotte: IAP, 2017.

Péron, M., & Bonnet, M. (2008). CSR in intervention-research: Example of an implementation of the SEAM model. *Revue Sciences de Gestion – Management Sciences – Ciencias de Gestión*.

Péron, M., & Péron, M. (2003). Postmodernism and the socio-economic approach to organizations. *Journal of Organizational Change Management*, 16 (1), 49–55.

Perroux, F. (1972). Économie de la ressource humaine [Human Resource economics]. *Mondes en développement*. ISMEA, 15–81.

Perroux, F. (1973). *Pouvoir et économie* [*Power and economy*], Paris: Bordas.

Perroux, F. (1975). *Unités actives et mathématiques nouvelles- Révision de la théorie de l'équilibre économique général* [Active units and new mathematics. The overall economic equilibrium theory revisited], Paris: Dunod.

Perroux, F. (1979). L'entreprise, l'équilibre rénové et les coûts 'cachés.' [The enterprise, the renovated balance and the 'hidden' costs]. Preface to Savall, H. *Reconstruire l'entreprise*, Paris: Dunod.

Porter, M.E., & Kramer, M.R. (2011). Creating shared value. *Harvard Business Review*, 89 (1/2), 62–77.

Robertson, D.H. (1940). A Spanish contribution to the theory of fluctuations. *Economica*, 7 (25), 50–65.

Savall, H. (1973, 1975, 2017). *G. Bernácer: l'hétérodoxie en science économique* [G. Bernácer: heterodoxy in economics], Paris: Dalloz, Collection Les Grands Économistes [Great economists series].

Savall, H. (1974, 1975). *Enrichir le travail humain: l'évaluation économique*, Paris: Dunod. 5th édition, Economica, 1989. Translated in English *Work and people: An economic evaluation of job enrichment*, Oxford University Press, 1981, 2nd edition; Charlotte, NC: Information Age Publishers: 2010. Translated in Spanish: Por un trabajo más humano, 1977, Madrid: Tecniban; 2nd edition, Charlotte: IAP, 2010.

Savall, H. (1976). Formation et conditions de travail, rapport au Secrétariat d'Etat à la revalorisation du travail manuel.

Savall, H. (1977). Propos d'étape sur la régulation socio-économique de l'entreprise par la recherche de la comptabilité de l'efficience économique et du développement humain [Remarks for a new stage in the socio-economic regulation of the enterprise by research on accountability of economic efficiency and human development], Paper, VIIth *Collège de France International Conference* on: *L'idée de régulation dans le mouvement des sciences* [The concept of regulation in the movement of sciences]. Paris, décembre 1977, published in *Economie Appliquée*, 1978.

Savall, H. (1978). Méthode de diagnostic socio-économique, *Revue française de gestion*.

Savall, H. (1979). *Reconstruire l'entreprise: Analyse socio-économique des conditions de travail* [*Reconstructing the enterprise: Socio-economic analysis of working conditions*], Paris: Dunod.

Savall, H. (2003). An update presentation of the socio-economic management model and international dissemination of the socio-economic model. *Journal of Organizational Change Management*, 16 (1), 33–48.

Savall, H. (2007). ISEOR's Socio-economic method: A case of scientific consultancy, pp. 1–31, in Buono & Savall (eds.), *Socio-economic intervention in organizations, the intervener-researcher and the SEAM approach to organizational analysis*, Charlotte: Information Age Publishing.

Savall, H. (2013a). *Origine radicale des crises économiques: Germán Bernácer, précurseur visionnaire,* Charlotte: IAP, États-Unis.

Savall, H. (2013b). Individu, entreprise et nation. Comment créer le PIB? in *Agir dans un nouveau monde: le développement et les coûts de l'homme*, ISEOR.

Savall, H., & Bonnet, M. (1996). Recommandations de la méthode socio-économique pour la politique de développement des entreprises d'insertion et associations intermédiaires, communication au Conseil Économique et Social, Paris, 26 p.

Savall, H., Péron, M., Zardet V., & Bonnet, M. (2015). *Le capitalisme socialement responsable existe*, Paris: EMS. Translated in English: *Socially responsible capitalism and management*, New York: Routledge, 2017.

Savall H., & Zardet V. (1987). *Maîtriser les coûts-performances cachés*, Paris: Economica. Translated in English *Mastering hidden costs and socio-economic performance*, Charlotte: IAP, 2008a.

Savall, H., & Zardet, V. (1992). *Le nouveau contrôle de gestion: Méthode des coûtsperformances cachés* [*New management control: The hidden cost-performance method*], Paris: Éditions Comptables Malesherbes-Eyrolles.

Savall, H., & Zardet, V. (1995–2005–2009–2017). *Ingénierie stratégique du roseau, souple et enracinée*, Paris: Economica. Traduit en espagnol: Ingeniería estratégica: un enfoque socioeconómico, Ed. UAM, México, 2009 et en anglais: *Strategic Engineering of the Reed, flexible and rooted*, Charlotte: IAP, 2017.

Savall, H., & Zardet, V. (1996). La dimension cognitive de la recherche-intervention: la production de connaissances par interactivité cognitive [The cognitive dimension of intervention-research: The production of knowledge through cognitive interactivity]. *Revue internationale de systémique*, 10 (1–2), 157–189.

Savall H., & Zardet V. (2004). *Recherche en Sciences de Gestion: Approche Qualimétrique : observer l'objet complexe*, Preface by David Boje, Paris: Economica. Translated in English *The qualimetrics approach, observing the complex object*, Charlotte: IAP, 2011.

Savall H., & Zardet V. (2005). *Tétranormalisation: défis et dynamiques*, Paris: Economica. Translated in English *The dynamics and challenges of tetranormalization*, Charlotte: IAP, 2013.

Savall, H., & Zardet, V. (2008). Le concept de coût-valeur des activités. Contribution de la théorie socio-économique des organisations [The concept of activity cost-value, contribution of SEAM theory]. *Revue Sciences de Gestion-Management Sciences- Ciencias de Gestión*, 64.

Savall, H., & Zardet, V. (2011a). La RSE, lien entre l'individu, l'organisation et la société: nouvel énoncé de la théorie socio-économique [CSR, link between individual, organization and society: new statement of SEAM theory]; Actes, Congrès ADERSE, Brest, mars. Publié dans la revue *Management et sciences sociales*, 2013.

Savall, H., & Zardet, V. (2011b). Linking individual, organizational and macro-economic performance levels: Hidden costs model, *Academy of Management Conference*, Orlando.

Savall, H., & Zardet, V. (2012, octobre). Nouvel énoncé de la théorie socio-économique des organisations et des territoires [New statements of the socio-economic theory of organizations and territory]. Lyon: Cahier de recherche [Working paper], ISEOR.

Savall H., & Zardet V. (2014). *Reconstruire l'entreprise. Fondements du management socio-économique*, Paris: Dunod.

Savall, H., Zardet, V., & Bonnet, M. (2000, 2008). *Libérer les performances cachées des entreprises par un management socio-économique*, Genève, BIT. Translated in English *Releasing the untapped potential of enterprises through socio-economic management*, Genève, ILO-BIT and in Spanish, *Mejorar los desempeños ocultos de las empresas a través de una gestión socioeconómica*, ILO-BIT, Genève.

Savall, H., Zardet, V., & Bonnet, M. (2002). Prévention des troubles musculo-squelettiques, Rapport à l'ANACT, décembre.

Savall H., Zardet V., & Bonnet M. (2009). *Management socio-économique: une approche innovante*, Paris: Economica.

Schumpeter, J.A. (1942). *Capitalisme, socialisme et démocratie* [Capitalism, socialism and democracy], Paris: Payot.

Smith, A. (1759). *The theory of moral sentiments*, New York: Garland, 1971.

Smith, A. (1776). *Inquiry into the nature and causes of the wealth of nations*. London: W. Strahan and T. Cadell, Londres.

Sorensen, P.F., Yaeger, T.F., Savall, H., Zardet, V., Bonnet, M., & Péron, M. (2010). A review of two major global and international approaches to organizational change: SEAM and Appreciative Inquiry. *Organization Development Journal*, 28 (4), 31–39.

Sudreau, P. (1975). Rapport pour la réforme de l'entreprise. Paris: La Documentation française. Février.

Taylor, F.W. (1911). *The principles of scientific management*, New York: Harpers and Brothers. Traduit en français *Principes d'organisation scientifique des usines*, Paris: Dunod

Voyant, O. (2003). La démocratie est un concept indissociable de l'entreprise, *AOM Conference*, Seattle.

Worley, C., Zardet, V., Bonnet M., & Savall, A. (2015). *Becoming agile. How the SEAM approach to management builds adaptability*, Hoboken, NJ: John Wiley.

Weber M. (1924). *The theory of social and economic organization*, New York: Free Press.

Yunus, M. (2010). *Building social business: The new kind of capitalism that serves humanity's most pressing needs*, Philadelphia, PA: Public Affairs.

Zardet V. (2010). Développement du potentiel humain et création de valeur économique dans l'entreprise [Human potential development and economic value creation in businesses], in Association François Perroux (ed.), *Agir dans nouveau monde: le développement et les coûts de l'Homme,* Écully: ISEOR éditeur.

Zardet, V., & Voyant, O. (2003). Organizational transformation through the socio-economic approach in an industrial context, *Journal of Organizational Change Management*, Emerald, 16 (1), 56–71.

28

WHY CRISIS MANAGEMENT MUST GO GLOBAL, AND HOW TO BEGIN

Christine M. Pearson

This chapter speaks to the issue of globalizing crisis management, an essential and complex modification that receives far too little attention, despite being needed by most organizations. My crisis management expertise evolves from action research and consulting with executives, managers, supervisors and line workers as they prepare for, contain and learn from organizational crises, as well as from traditional academic study and research. As to the acuities of my global lens, for more than a dozen years I have focused on what it takes to lead globally. I have worked with thousands of global leaders and organizations in more than two dozen countries across five continents. My orientation is always toward practice. This chapter is no different. My target audience consists of organizational leaders at all levels who have responsibility for or interest in crisis management, and for those academics and consultants who help to inform and guide them.

This Chapter Is Vital for You If …

- Your organization has crisis management strategies and approaches, but they are aligned with the cultural norms and assumptions of headquarters only, even though operations or key stakeholders are located outside the home country.
- You have operations, customers or suppliers outside your company's home country, but your organization has no overarching global crisis management strategies or approaches.
- Your organization has no overarching global crisis management strategies or approaches, and expansion outside the home country is being considered.

How Crisis Management Must Be Different If Your Company Has Operations or Stakeholders Overseas

Operating in a global environment adds extraordinary challenges to crisis management. Surprisingly, very little research touches on this fundamental complication. Few expert practitioners, in-house or external, focus specifically on global aspects of managing crises. Nonetheless, organizations with international operations or stakeholders must be prepared to encounter global spillover, which can take many forms.

Operating in multiple countries increases the number and diversity of critical stakeholders, often radically. More variables make it more difficult to predict, measure, analyze and respond to emerging problems and crises. Policies and procedures based on assumptions held at headquarters can actually harm cognizance and curiosity about organizational threats at other locations. When managed exclusively from the home office, even procedures and sign-offs that have been distributed globally may have little resemblance to the true state of readiness elsewhere.

In global business, distance presents challenges of connectivity and timing. At the extreme, if crises emerge from remote global settings or locations where your organization does not have an office or a foothold, there may be no one at hand who is qualified or willing to carry out the organization's crisis assessments and responses. If no leadership representatives are present, additional time and money may be required to formulate decisions regarding essentials, such as who will represent the organization and which additional stakeholders should be involved.

If relationship infrastructure is lacking, connecting with key individuals or accumulating essential resources at a distance may be extremely difficult. Those who will communicate about the situation, either directly or via other intermediary stakeholders (e.g., the media), may face overwhelming new challenges. Meanwhile, without local contingency plans, those on the ground in distant settings may struggle for days to understand who is in charge, what is happening, what should be reported and what types of actions they should take.

Without plans for accessing distant resources, crisis containment and business resumption may be severely stalled. Challenges in gathering information or support may be exacerbated, especially in distant time zones or secluded locations. As a simple example, product recalls may be much more challenging to execute than official internal documentation might suggest. Where manufactured batches are mingled across borders, recalls may be nearly impossible to achieve.

Where financial resources are needed to address a crisis, response efforts can be severely hampered if plans are not in place. Decision-makers may have to scramble to understand local expectations about the use and abuse of money. Precious time may be lost searching for and securing new channels to access local currencies. These delays in accessing and distributing funds can strain or disable crisis responses, which can precipitate additional delays and elevate dissatisfaction among consumers and the public.

Without translating crisis management intentions and directives into native languages and adjusting for local norms, cross-cultural differences can obstruct information flow and result in ineffective action. Verifying public records, interpreting legislation, or distinguishing the appropriate officials to contact or procedures to follow may be problematic. Cross-cultural complications can be all the more challenging when incidents or interactions call for proper tone or other nuances of communication, as is often the case in crisis.

As you consider these warnings, you may take comfort if your global organization operates in English. You may take consolation in your organization's attempts to infuse corporate values and norms cross-culturally. Nevertheless, you may learn in the thick of things that the aptitudes and culture-based behaviors you assumed would come into place in crisis have been eclipsed by local customs, attitudes and actions.

In crisis, individuals tend to revert to fundamental assumptions and values, which may vary greatly from those set out by your organization. The corporate mindset and behaviors that you rely on may be undermined by local perspectives and actions. Such a shift may catch you unaware, block essential connections and impede collaboration. Even if your organization has developed plans for managing crises, if they are not globally tailored, the preparations and responses that you are taking for granted in the event of a crisis may be wrecked by these differences.

Where the nature and depth of cross-cultural variance is unknown, even established crisis planning and preparations can go awry. False starts, unpredicted turns and missteps may occur when cross-cultural values and expectations are neglected or discounted. Executives may assume that all employees' perspectives will align with their own. Starting with an assumption that others share your worldview will lead to conceiving, creating and evaluating crisis management plans and actions strictly from this perspective. This is a precarious foundation for managing crises in a global environment.

On the bright side, adopting a global perspective for managing crises offers additional benefits beyond preventing losses of translation and adaptation. Diverse thinking enhances problem solving. Potential threats and opportunities are more readily visible from diverse perspectives. Familiarity with and ties to diverse settings can facilitate resource access. All phases of managing crises, from detecting signals to preparing and planning for and containing crises to resuming business and learning lessons, can be managed more effectively when informed by a comprehensive, global perspective of the organization, its vulnerabilities and its resources.

A Cross-Cultural Case in Point: On Time and Certainty

There is no right or wrong, or better or worse, when it comes to cultural differences. However, there are aspects of competing perspectives that can derail or boost crisis management. Managing crises globally requires understanding cultural differences and the behaviors that they may drive. Cross-cultural lessons and adjustments can facilitate and improve signal detection and preparations. Once a crisis occurs, cross-cultural understanding can retain vigilance and expedite containment. Key to global crisis management success is appreciating and planning for the cultural differences represented in your organization.

Consider, for example, the classic cultural dimensions of time and certainty. Orientations toward time and certainty are value orientations of all cultures (e.g., Hofstede, 2001; House, Hanges, Javidan, Dorfman, & Gupta, 2004; Kluckhohn & Strodtbeck, 1961). Perspectives on these dimensions vary vividly from one culture to another. In cross-cultural terms, cultures may have views toward time that vary from present orientation to future orientation. Cultural preferences also differ along the dimension of certainty. In cross-cultural terms, shared cultural perspectives exist along a continuum, from avoiding uncertainty to embracing uncertainty. Both of these fundamental cultural dimensions, time and certainty, are at the heart of crisis management practice.

Crisis management always entails calculating the appropriate tradeoff between time and certainty. To manage crises effectively, decision-makers repeatedly strike the precarious balance between moving quickly enough to contain the crisis (time) versus gathering sufficient information to feel confident in their response plans (certainty). In the global context, cultural preferences and inclinations regarding time and certainty can facilitate or stifle decision-making and action. At the extreme, in crisis, blindness toward these differences can be deadly.

Beginning with the dimension of time, people from cultures that conceive of time from a present orientation (e.g., Poland, Argentina, Italy) tend to prefer living in the moment. In present-oriented cultures, individuals favor routine and repetition over novelty and the accompanying requisite deciphering and adapting to what is new. People who prefer present orientation are more likely to attribute their futures to fate. As a consequence, they may lack a strong desire or willingness to plan. They place little value on warnings about what might happen at some unknowable time in the future, and they are less inclined to concern themselves with how their actions today might affect their tomorrows.

By contrast, people in cultures with stronger future orientation (e.g., Singapore, Sweden, the Netherlands) tend to put a great deal of value on planning. They believe that they can significantly affect their future through their own decisions and actions. Accordingly, people preferring this orientation set targets and goals for the future. They retain a readiness to be flexible, adaptable and resilient about what else might happen tomorrow so that they can adjust accordingly to optimize their futures.

Consider the impact of these competing values in the context of adopting a crisis management perspective. Individuals who are present-oriented will be reluctant to devote energy or resources to preparing for crises. They may consider any such efforts frivolous, an indulgent use of resources to prepare for something that might happen sometime in the future. Even if early signs of an actual problem emerge, they may be reluctant to act. An example of this disposition surfaced in preliminary discussions with the Italian CFO of a multinational restaurant chain who described his view of managing crises as "the ostrich approach: if I see trouble brewing, I bury my head as deeply as I can, keep at my work, and wait for the crisis to pass over."

At the same organization, the executive in charge of human resources, an American, quickly grasped the need for crisis preparations and offered his assistance in initiating new programs throughout the organization. In typical future-oriented style, he was poised for action, ready to engage even before considering the nature of prospective crises or responses that might be made by stakeholders inside or outside the organization. This can-do reaction may seem easier to mold into effective crisis management, but such responses can be rash. Even with the best of intentions, for example, individuals who prefer novel approaches may drive their organizations forward so quickly that they ignore or override standard operating procedures that already fit crisis management needs. In the worst cases, in the heat of crisis, they may feverishly attempt to invent responses when long-standing protocol could actually yield better outcomes.

Cultural preferences and dispositions toward uncertainty also hold the potential to significantly impact crisis management. In cultures where people prefer to avoid uncertainty (e.g., Germany, Switzerland, Singapore), order and clear rules prevail. To harness unpredictability, people who prefer avoiding uncertainty opt for structured guidelines and procedures, driven by the perspective that what is new and unknown is dangerous (Hofstede, 1984).

Those who prefer avoiding uncertainty tend to be reluctant to admit fault. Rather than bring forth bad news, they strive to correct problems and eliminate ambiguities before reporting them. Where uncertainty is strongly avoided, individuals do not take risks or violate rules, and they tend to be resistant to change. When innovation, risk-taking or quick decisions are required, they tend to stick to formal policies and follow established order. Where policies or procedures do not exist, individuals who are uncertainty avoidant seek confirmation of their intentions or plans in writing before they are willing to take action.

By contrast, cultures that embrace uncertainty (e.g., Brazil, Hungary, Morocco) tend to adapt to changes more quickly. In extenuating circumstances, those who embrace uncertainty may ignore norms. When pressed into action, they may pay little heed to formal policies or prescribed roles.

Cultural differences regarding uncertainty can enhance or impede crisis management. When forced to engage in crisis planning, those who are uncertainty-averse will create elaborately detailed contingency plans in attempting to precisely forestall and harness any crisis. Should a crisis hit, they follow those plans precisely. Certainly, having plans in place is essential to effective crisis management, but adaptability also is a must. Crises never unfold precisely as envisioned, so plans must always be reevaluated and honed in real time.

A challenge for cultures that embrace uncertainty relates to novel solutions being attempted in isolation by those who detect problems. In cultures where employees embrace uncertainty, individuals frequently are willing to try new measures in attempting to address dilemmas before reporting them. Very often, however, problems underlying a crisis cannot be resolved by a single individual, so precious time may be wasted and missteps taken. In the worst case, as individuals struggle to remedy dangerous situations on their own, those events flame into full-blown crises.

An example of these uncertainty differences became evident when a corporate team inspected an off-site chemical refining plant located in Hungary (where uncertainty is embraced). Luckily, before a crisis event occurred, a potentially dangerous situation was spotted and corrected. During the inspection of the facility, the corporate team, which was made up mostly of Germans (who favor avoiding uncertainty), discovered problematic placement of gauges and controls. Gauges for monitoring heat-sensitive production machinery were located two flights above the controls for adjusting temperatures of the machinery. The Hungarian employees and supervisors were aware of the awkward and potentially unsafe distances between the pieces of equipment, but they made no complaints or suggestions for improvement. Rather, they attempted to address the situation on their own, running up and down the stairs day and night to make adjustments and verify results.

Instead of evaluating and reacting based on existing guidelines, those who embrace uncertainty may sidestep preparations and take actions that escalate problems into crises. In the case of the chemical refining facility, the time wasted running up and down the stairs could have stalled emergency adjustments enough to cause an explosion. To overcome cross-cultural challenges, global crisis management efforts must be geared toward developing comprehensive and adaptable perspectives that can be customized to diverse organizational environments.

What to Do to Globalize Crisis Management

To comprehend what is needed for your organization's global crisis preparations, begin by assessing your organization's current state of global crisis readiness. Factor in and account for diverse settings and stakeholders. Compare your assessment to your organization's desirable future state for global crisis preparedness.

A fitting way to begin filling in any gaps that you detect is by differentiating crisis management guidelines and approaches that should be customized or adapted to local settings versus those that should not. In all settings, plans and actions should be embedded and aligned with your organization's fundamental values. There will always be policies that all locations and cultures must adopt identically. For example, most organizations instruct all of their employees to communicate truthfully.

Holding rigid crisis management requirements without any adjustment to local cultures can, however, undermine preparedness. Sometimes, adjusting for cultural differences is an appropriate choice, and this should be acknowledged and implemented in crisis management planning and execution. This might entail adapting spokesperson roles to fit native expectations and preferences, for example. However, a diverse perspective should never be sought at the expense of safeguards.

Recognize that policies handed down from headquarters can be very difficult to implement in other cultures. Remain alert for the possibility of transgressions driven by cultural differences. Although it may appear that policies were adapted easily, employees in foreign settings may follow some portion of what is expected simply to appear compliant. Where this occurs, crucial precautions may be disabled inadvertently because the full intent of a policy has not been embraced. To avert this dilemma, visit diverse sites from time to time to assess the quality of implementation.

Regardless of the sources of differences and adjustments to those differences, in crisis it is imperative that all resources work together. An allied front is necessary to assess and contain crises, to repair any damages and to move forward after the crisis has been resolved. Build, train and reinforce basic cross-cultural sensitivity for employees throughout the organization who span cultural boundaries. An effective place to start is by teaching why and how to get off "cultural cruise control," a term coined by Thomas and Inkson (2009), which refers to mindlessly acting and reacting based on your built-in cultural assumptions.

Surveys and other self-assessment tools can disrupt a tendency toward cultural cruise control. For example, the Cultural Orientation Inventory can be used to measure individual cultural preferences and teach basic cross-cultural insights.[1] Once employees understand their individual cultural preferences, they have a baseline for setting personal objectives for cross-cultural growth. Sharing results can build deeper awareness of similarities and differences held within teams, divisions or organizations at large.

Ground crisis preparations in an understanding of the norms and behaviors of the local workforces across organizational settings. Extend that awareness to the values and norms of local communities. Focus on locations where your organization has critical stakeholders or resources, or where there are potential sources of disruption. Integrate crisis management training across these borders and share information broadly and repeatedly. Throughout the organization, disseminate reports of crisis management best practices, as well as lessons learned from less effective actions. To maximize the reach and accuracy of communications, strive for global and local language clarity and use multiple channels (e.g., memos, video presentations, in-person meetings).

Consider putting employees through streamlined cross-cultural training and development programs that focus specifically on the most common cultural differences affecting your organization. For example, in many locations outside the U.S.A., relationship building takes a more central role for all business transactions. Americans spend far less time and attention getting acquainted than preferred in many other countries. In this example, if adjustment is warranted, development efforts might include encouraging American employees to bridge this cross-cultural difference by moving beyond business interactions, spending time sharing experiences and learning about people as individuals.

If positive interactions are built with locals across diversity in advance, it will be much easier to tap native knowledge and resources when a crisis occurs. When problems strike outside the home country, a native will often have the best understanding of typical local reactions, context and innuendos. In advance of problems, getting well acquainted and delegating or sharing responsibility and authority help set the tone for collaborative relationships needed in crisis.

Train supervisors and managers throughout the organization to be sensitive to cross-cultural differences among their subordinates, especially differences that could hinder global crisis management. For instance, focus on differences that could stifle reporting and response from frontline employees. These employees are often the first to encounter operational anomalies, customer complaints and other matters that could signal deeper trouble.

Raise awareness among supervisors and managers regarding the culturally based differences that can affect employees' willingness or reluctance to deliver negative information upward. Consider local variances in perspectives toward time and certainty, for example. Then, move toward relevant adaptive actions, such as assuring employees about the critical value of early detection or rewarding prompt warnings to avert or mitigate crises.

Where to Begin, If You Are a Leader

In many organizations, early adoption of a crisis management program or globalization of an existing program is successfully championed by an individual who holds a leadership position at some level of the organization. Taking the initiative to champion crisis management can significantly boost learning and advancement as a leader, while providing fulfillment from the crucial perspective of readying your organization to avert or mitigate crises. At the extreme, implementing an effective crisis management program can make a difference between life and death for organizations and their stakeholders. If you are a leader, muster your power to accomplish three things, as described below.

Fortify the Global Crisis Management Conviction of Senior Executives

Crisis management is only as strong as its weakest link. Therefore, the level of crisis preparations and responses must be consistent throughout an organization, which means that crisis management strategy and implementation must be driven from the very top. The power vested in senior executives is essential to lead optimal alignment of decisions, resources, actions and reputation so that preparations for and responses to crises will be unified throughout the organization. In global organizations, global adaptation also must be driven from the very top.

To uncover current convictions about global crisis management, ask senior executives about their perspectives and assess their current actions. How frequently and broadly do they interact with key stakeholders outside the organization's home culture? How meaningful to crisis readiness are the issues they discuss? What lessons have they learned from these conversations? What have they done to understand and establish links into local norms, resources and authorities in locations where vital organizational operations or resources are situated? Positive answers to these types of questions confirm a level of global crisis thinking and action.

To assess global crisis vulnerabilities, consider the following questions. Have senior executives taken into account cultural differences with regards to how they could affect crisis detection, reporting and response? Have actions taken overseas, in light of problems or crises, substantiated their expectations or created problems? As examples, how thoroughly were relevant communications before, during and after crises translated into native languages? How were varying perspectives toward time factored into plans or actions? Were actual crises or near-misses that occurred overseas handled well? Did preparations and responses reflect the organization's global realities, or were expectations and directives culturally headquarters-centric? What accounting has been done regarding the costs and benefits of perspectives and actions on overseas and organization-wide outcomes?

If senior leaders lack interest or engagement in global crisis planning, it is still possible to build internal support. Even one senior executive who recognizes the importance of improving crisis preparations globally can provide a solid base. Often, staunch support originates from individuals who have led others through crises and have experienced the consequences of doing so with or without crisis preparations. Their perspectives can ground and amplify a call for readiness.

To build a sense of urgency about preparing for crises globally, help others consider relevant dangers and costs of facing a crisis without global preparations. Bear in mind that change always succeeds one person at a time. To succeed in stimulating interest, aim to provoke support for improvements by raising genuine concern individual by individual, without causing anyone to become overwhelmed or to shut down because of the potential hazardous impacts of crises.

Conduct a Simple Crisis-Based Stakeholder Analysis

A stakeholder analysis is a collaborative, interactive discussion designed to bring to light the breadth and depth of impact that could be caused by key organizational stakeholders. The crisis-based version of this activity focuses on key stakeholders' anticipated impacts under crisis circumstances. A crisis-based stakeholder analysis hones critical perspectives on crisis preparations, resources and vulnerabilities. Participants improve their understanding of issues and relationships most in need of attention and improvement to successfully avert or mitigate crises. The approach uncovers the nature and extent of outreach, support and action necessary to effectively manage organizational crises. The description here is intended merely as an overview of the process and potential outcomes.[2]

The first step in conducting a global crisis-based stakeholder analysis involves gathering a diverse group of influential employees who represent the organization culturally. In the best cases, participants think creatively, share their viewpoints freely and listen intently, without constraining or criticizing others. Among participants, diverse views are aired and insights are learned from one another.

The question to drive a crisis-based stakeholder analysis is: *Which individuals, groups or organizations would have an interest in our organization's success or failure in the event of a crisis?* This is a broad question, fitting the goal of the activity, that is, to better understand who would be critical stakeholders in the event of a crisis and how they could affect crisis management capabilities and outcomes.

To reinforce contributions and track progress, entries to the list developed earlier should be recorded immediately for all to see. Obvious candidates for the list are usually mentioned quickly and include stakeholders fitting any organization or industry, as depicted in Figure 28.1.

Figure 28.1   Typical Crisis-Based Stakeholders

During the discussion, remind participants repeatedly to include global candidates (e.g., the local media who cover key organizational locations overseas). Continue until suggestions include creative outliers whose behaviors could significantly affect crisis management (e.g., hospital administrators near organizational sites where potentially hazardous materials are handled).

Work to generate an extensive list of potential stakeholders that exhausts participants' contributions. Then, lead the group to cluster very similar stakeholders for a shorter list that is easier to manage. Aim for about a dozen key stakeholders, including one or two outliers. The criterion for selection is the significance of the stakeholders' potential impact on crisis management efforts.

Complete the stakeholder analysis by discussing the following question in regard to each of the short-listed stakeholders: *If a crisis occurs, how would we expect each of these key stakeholder to react?* Then, consider potential outcomes and necessary crisis precautions if participants' assumptions are wrong. This activity drives an extensive consideration of the most critical stakeholders and their presumed dispositions. It helps raise shared awareness about organizational outreach to essential stakeholders, as well as the relevance of and gaps in existing crisis preparations.

Create a Global Crisis Management Team

In any organization, a crisis management team is a key resource for effective planning and response. This team is the strategic epicenter for planning, containing and learning from crises organization-wide. In the event of a crisis or near-miss, the crisis management team acts as the command center, directing all crisis-related decisions and actions.

In global organizations, this team should reflect the cultural composition of the organization, its vital locations and its key stakeholders. A crisis management team that does not yet take cross-cultural challenges and opportunities into account should be shaped to address the organization's global environment, resources and vulnerabilities. To achieve this, team members should be selected and trained to optimize access to and dissemination of their cross-cultural experiences and insights. Ideal candidates for global crisis management teams have agility in crossing cultural boundaries. For many individuals, this is rooted in multiple language competencies and experiences living and working outside their native cultures.

To create an effective global team, global crisis management goals and relevant adjustments should be set forth as early as possible. Given the gravity of the team's responsibilities, the CEO and select senior executives should be members of the team. They should designate additional members who bring distinctive competencies and cross-cultural savvy to the team.

An inaugural meeting of the global crisis management team should bring together all members to establish priorities and relationships face-to-face. The objective is to build know-how and confidence within the team so that it can handle whatever problems or crises arise. To jump-start global preparedness, the agenda should bring forth the nature and effects of diverse cultural preferences and response tendencies as related to crisis management.

The initial meeting can cover basic information regarding the nature and impact of cultural differences, as related to the organization's environments and crisis plans. Members should be encouraged to discuss specific cultural preferences of the countries or regions they represent to enhance everyone's awareness of potential impediments and boosts to cross-cultural crisis management. Discussions should begin to explore specific cultural differences held across the organization, such as perspectives of time and risk-taking, as well as the impact of those differences on crisis management.

The inaugural effort may include goals such as (1) building a shared understanding of the organization's crisis management needs, including the diverse perspectives of key stakeholders; (2) fostering trust and commitment within the global crisis management team; (3) discussing existing approaches to crises that may need realignment to fit the organization's cross-cultural environment; (4) establishing practical means for sharing best crisis management practices and emerging concerns; and (5) launching efficient channels for further communication within the global team.

Over time, the team should evolve to soliciting input, and developing, implementing and evaluating crisis management procedures and policies globally across the organization. Initially, candid discussions regarding the state of crisis preparations globally across the organization, including resources and gaps, would suffice as an early approach to building readiness. Over time, the team should progress to tabletop scenario discussions. A tabletop scenario discussion is a crisis management approach through which participants surface their individual and collective perspectives, and solidify their individual and collective readiness for crises, all in relation to the case details of hypothetical or actual crises.

These efforts will enhance insight, expertise and confidence across the team. Eventually, team representatives should engage the rest of the organization in field exercises, including the engagement of more distant, cross-cultural locations.[3] Ultimately, it is the responsibility of the global crisis management team to formulate and drive an environment throughout the organization that achieves smooth, prompt, fitting decisions and actions in the event of a crisis.

A Cautionary Closing Note

My objective here has been to differentiate global crisis management from more narrowly cast crisis management. I have attempted to raise challenges and opportunities particular to those who operate in global organizations. To complete this perspective, personally targeted advice for this extraordinary organizational charge is fitting.

Many believe that the cross-cultural expertise needed for effective crisis management is attained only by looking outward to determine how diverse others act differently. However, the starting place for crisis management success in a global environment is self-awareness. Knowing one's own preferences, values and habits constitutes the solid foundation for ongoing cross-cultural success and facilitates any type of cross-cultural crisis-related encounters.

Enhance self-awareness by contemplating your own attitudes about working cross-culturally. Reflect on the norms, values and expectations held within your own culture and by you. Build continuous learning by honing your perceptions and adjusting your behaviors based on your own cross-cultural successes and missteps, as well as those you observe. Ask others how they perceive your culture. Then, study how the various cultures with which you work perceive each other (Meyer, 2014). Understand the cultural cosmos in which you operate and determine how your thoughts, values and behaviors align or contrast with others.

Do not assume that you must attempt to align all behaviors with the norms of the new culture. This very thought can be off-putting and, for most people, the target is unattainable. Rather, aim to find a behavioral comfort zone where aspects of local customs align with your own preferences (Molinsky, 2013). Seek to identify and achieve a zone of acceptable behavior, rather than aiming for an elusive point of identical match.

For global crisis management success, it is essential to understand the world from others' viewpoints. This is exceptionally difficult. To make matters even more challenging, leadership perspectives are often blinded by hierarchical privilege. Views from the top can cloud awareness and expectations. As a result, leaders anticipate cross-cultural reactions to crises that stretch beyond realistic possibilities. They lose sight of how broad their experiences and mindset are as compared to others'. Aim for open collaboration, agility and learning by adjusting your thinking and actions for cross-cultural differences and bridge that gap for global crisis management success.

Notes

1 Information about the Cultural Orientation Index can be found at www.berlitz.com/Corporate-Solutions/Global-Leadership-Training/GLT-Web-based-Solutions/COI-Assessment/191/.
2 For a more thorough description of the crisis-based stakeholder analysis process, see I.I. Mitroff & C.M. Pearson, *Crisis Management* (San Francisco, CA: Jossey-Bass, 1993), and also see C. Pearson & I. Mitroff, "From Crisis Prone to Crisis Prepared: A Framework for Crisis Management" (*Academy of Management Executive*, 1993, 7(1), 48–59).
3 A field exercise is a simulated crisis situation designed to test and practice crisis response policies and procedures. Typically, the breadth of details and the extent of participant engagement in field exercises evolve along a continuum from single-site activities among employees to multiple-site activities that include an array of internal and external stakeholders.

References

Hofstede, G. (1984). *Culture's consequences: International differences in work-related values.* Thousand Oaks, CA: Sage.

Hofstede, G. (2001). *Cultures consequences: Comparing values, behaviors, institutions and organizations across nations.* Thousand Oaks, CA: Sage.

House, R.J., Hanges, P.J., Javidan, M., Dorfman, P.W., & Gupta, V. (2004). *Culture, leadership, and organizations: The GLOBE study of 62 societies.* Thousand Oaks, CA: Sage.

Kluckhohn, F.R., & Strodtbeck, F.L. (1961). *Variations in value orientations.* Evanston, IL: Row, Peterson.

Meyer, E. (2014). *Culture map.* New York: Public Affairs.

Molinsky, A. (2013). *Global dexterity.* Boston, MA: Harvard Business Review Press.

Thomas, D.C., & Inkson, K. (2009). *Cultural intelligence: Living and working globally.* San Francisco, CA: Barrett-Koehler.

PART VII

Dialogue and Commentary on the Future of Risk, Crisis and Emergency Management

29

MAKING MARKETS FOR UNINSURED RISK

Protection Gap Entities (PGEs) as Risk-Processing Organizations in Society

Paula Jarzabkowski and Konstantinos Chalkias

2017 has been a year of devastating natural disasters; Hurricane Harvey caused widespread flooding in Texas and Louisiana, Hurricanes Irma and Maria wreaked havoc on island states in the Caribbean and Latin America, and Mexico has suffered two high-magnitude earthquakes in quick succession that left hundreds dead and many more citizens' lives changed forever. Man-made disasters, such as terrorism, are also having devastating impact even beyond war zones. Large-scale, highly organized attacks, such as the attack on the World Trade Center, have been replaced in recent years by less sophisticated attacks using homemade bombs, guns, knives and cars in cities all over the world, from Paris, to Quetta to London.

As these natural and man-made disasters increase in frequency and severity (Allianz, 2015), they highlight a steadily widening gap between insured and actual economic losses. Some 70% of global losses from natural catastrophes are uninsured, equating to a protection gap of $1.3 trillion over the past 10 years (Swiss Re, 2015a). Indeed, the total economic loss from Hurricane Harvey is estimated at up to $90 billion, of which, at best, only $35 billion is insured (RMS, 2017). Significant gaps in protection also exist for other large-scale threats such as terrorism, cybercrime and epidemics, where the emergent or constantly evolving nature of risk makes developing adequate insurance protection difficult (Carter & Johansmeyer, 2016; Michel-Kerjan, Raschky & Kunreuther, 2015). This protection gap constitutes an economic and social problem in both developing and developed countries. Lack of insurance in developing countries means that losses from catastrophic disasters roll back development gains and exacerbate inequality (World Bank, 2014). Yet in developed countries, the protection gap is also increasing (Swiss Re, 2015b). For example, while the United States is one of the most insured countries in the world, some 50% of the natural disaster losses in 2016 remained uninsured (Aon, 2016).

Beyond Existing Organizational Responses to Risk and Disaster Management

The burden of paying for such uninsured losses falls largely on governments, individuals and aid organizations, with significant economic and social hardship for those affected. In response, governments and intergovernmental organizations around the world, often joining forces with the insurance market, have developed a range of different types of insurance schemes that attempt to close the protection gap. While these schemes differ considerably, they broadly have the same goal, which is to transform uninsured risk into insurance-based products that can be transferred into global financial markets in order to provide capital for recovery following a disaster.

We refer to the entities that convey various schemes as PGEs (Protection Gap Entities), which we define as organizations specifically set up to operate between government and market in trying to reduce some specific protection gap (Jarzabkowski, Chalkias, Cacciatori & Bednarek, 2018). Examples of PGEs include the Caribbean Catastrophe Risk Insurance Facility (CCRIF), which was set up to provide its member countries with access to rapid capital for responding to the aftermath of natural disasters, or Pool Re, a risk pool set up to support the insurance market in providing commercial terrorism cover to businesses in the United Kingdom. Such PGEs sit at the nexus of a range of critical interdependencies between market and nonmarket organizations, each with different expertise, interests and objectives that must be drawn together to address the protection gap problem. PGEs are not static organizations. Rather, their organizing practices simultaneously shape and are shaped by the pertinent interdependencies. Further, as ways are found to transform uninsured risk into insured risk, and to attract capital, these interdependencies evolve, so that PGEs themselves are dynamically evolving in tandem with the risk they process. Given the role of organizations as critical agents in "processing and handling risks" (Hutter & Power, 2005, p. 1; see also Gephart, Van Maanen, & Oberlechner, 2009; Hardy & Maguire, 2016; Maguire & Hardy, 2013; Power, 2014; Scheytt, Soin, Sahlin-Andersson, & Power, 2006), an understanding of PGEs as a particular type of risk-processing organization is critical. However, we know little of the organizational, intraorganizational, and economic and social dynamics that shape PGEs, and their respective disaster risk management responses.

Beyond Existing Understandings of Risk, Reward and Responsibility

Frank Knight's (1921) distinction between risk and uncertainty can be used as a conceptual vehicle to understand risk-taking as entrepreneurial activity for profit making (O'Malley, 2003). This is apparent in markets for large-scale risk, where insurance companies accept risk of loss and responsibility for paying claims in return for a premium that is the basis of their profit. These insurers then transfer some of this risk of large-scale loss, such as a major flood that damages many properties simultaneously, to reinsurers and other capital markets. The reinsurers and markets in turn accept this risk and the responsibility to pay for potentially disastrous losses in return for a premium which is their basis of profit (Jarzabkowski, Bednarek, & Spee, 2015). When PGEs are established, they intervene in this risk transfer value chain, acting either as insurers taking the risk directly from policyholders or as reinsurers and capital markets that accept risk from insurers. Sometimes, particularly in developing economies where the insurance market is relatively underdeveloped, they even bypass this value chain altogether, transferring risk directly from government balance sheets into the capital markets.

PGEs thus introduce a new type of actor into the value chain, with a mix of often contradictory market and nonmarket objectives (Denis, Langley, & Rouleau, 2007; Jarzabkowski, Le, & Van de Ven, 2013; Smets, Jarzabkowski, Burke, & Spee, 2015), such as a remit to protect citizens from economic disaster, rather than specifically to make a profit. The uncoupling of such market-based calculations of risk and reward may also dilute the responsibility of market players to pay claims, as this obligation shifts partially to the PGEs that negotiate the products issued against risk. Yet the implications of this intervention, in a market that so critically underpins recovery from devastating losses, are poorly understood, conceptually and empirically (Bruggeman, Faure, & Heldt, 2012; Paudel, 2012). In particular, the specific forms that PGEs take, how they share risk for public protection and private sector profit and how they coevolve alongside government policy over time are critical areas of study (Weinkle, 2015).

For example, the U.S. public-sector flood insurance scheme, the National Flood Insurance Program (NFIP), originated in response to the lack of private insurance, providing domestic insurance policies to enable householders to recover from damage following floods. However, it has run into severe problems, arguably due to a failure to share risk with the private market (Elliott, 2017) until 2015, when some risk was transferred to the reinsurance market, to offset NFIP debt. In particular, the scheme has low penetration. During the recent Hurricane Harvey, only some 20% of properties eligible for NFIP coverage actually had flood insurance, with devastating consequences for citizens and for the states of Texas and Louisiana. As Moody's Analytics noted,

> a lack of flood insurance for homeowners will prevent the type of full-scale reconstruction effort that might otherwise be expected. This could have significant long-term ramifications, weighing on household wealth and consumption, while even potentially making a dent in the region's very strong population growth.
>
> *(Evans, 2017)*

As such critical examples suggest, we need more studies that examine the use of financial tools for risk taking, while looking beyond this as primarily a matter of market actors and objectives. Rather, we need to focus on the reconfiguration of risk, reward and responsibility, in order to further existing understandings of how financial markets work in cooperation with the state, through the vehicle of specific risk-processing organizations, such as PGEs, to build economic and social resilience (e.g. Hamilton & Statman, 1993). In particular, it is necessary to generate theories of risk and risk management that explain the changing risk-reward-responsibility dynamics arising from the interplay between market and nonmarket actors and their implications on market making.

Our Research

Our response to the need for enhanced insight takes a processual approach to PGEs as risk-processing organizations that evolve over time. While PGEs are put in place to address the protection gap, they are not simply solutions to the problem. Rather, they become active participants in defining the protection gap and the potential approaches to it, through the interdependencies they establish to evaluate and trade risk, their effects on the market-based value chain, their progressive shifting of risk from uninsured to insured, and their consequences in increasing insurance penetration and in paying claims following disasters (Jarzabkowski et al., 2018). We study the processual evolution of 12 different PGEs that span different risks, from terrorism to floods, hurricanes and earthquakes. Our research, based on data across all relevant stakeholders, is designed to capture variation in relational, structural and institutional features of these PGEs, from single nation PGEs to multination risk pools, covering both developed and developing economies. Taking a comparative approach, we aim to develop two types of process theories. First, theories that explain the different paths through which particular types of PGEs evolve, and their consequences. Second, process theories that explain how PGEs as collective phenomena, through their interactions with each other, and with key multinational and interorganizational actors, shape broader global approaches to risk, the protection gap, and disaster risk management.

References

Allianz (2015). *Global claims review 2015: Business interruption in focus—Global trends and developments in business interruption claims.* Munich: Allianz Global Corporate and Specialty Report.

Aon (2016). *Global catastrophe recap: First half of 2016.* Aon Benfield Analytics, Impact Forecasting.

Bruggeman, V., Faure, M., & Heldt, T. (2012). Insurance against catastrophe: Government stimulation of insurance markets for catastrophic events. *Duke Environmental Law & Policy Forum, 23*, 185.

Carter, R. A., & Johansmeyer, T. (2016). Terror risk transfer: The evolution of the attacks and why the market needs to grow. *Artemis News.* www.artemis.bm.

Denis, J., Langley, A., & Rouleau, L. (2007). Strategizing in pluralistic contexts: Rethinking theoretical frames. *Human Relations, 60*(1), 179–215.

Elliott, R. (2017). Who pays for the next wave? The American welfare state and responsibility for flood risk. *Politics and Society, 45*(3), 415–440.

Evans, S. (2017). Harvey economic loss could be up to $75bn: Moody's analytics. *Artemis News.* www.artemis.bm.

Gephart, R., Van Maanen, J., & Oberlechner, T. (2009). Organizations and risk in late modernity. *Organization Studies, 30*(2–3), 141–155.

Hamilton, S., Jo, H. & Statman, M. (1993). Doing well while doing good? The investment performance of socially responsible mutual funds. *Financial Analysts Journal, 49*(6), 62–66.

Hardy, C., & Maguire, S. (2016). Organizing risk: Discourse, power, and "riskification". *Academy of Management Review, 41*(1), 80–108.

Hutter, B., & Power, M. (2005). Organizational encounters with risk: An introduction. In B. Hutter & M. Power (Eds.), *Organizational encounters with risk* (pp. 1–32). Cambridge: Cambridge University Press.

Jarzabkowski, P., Bednarek, R., & Spee, A. P. (2015). *Making a market for acts of god: The practice of risk trading in the global reinsurance industry.* Oxford: Oxford University Press.

Jarzabkowski, P., Chalkias, K., Cacciatori, E., Bednarek, R. (2018). *Between State and Market: Protection Gap Entities and Catastrophic Risk.* London: University of London.

Jarzabkowski, P., Lê, J. K., & Van de Ven, A. H. (2013). Responding to competing strategic demands: How organizing, belonging, and performing paradoxes coevolve. *Strategic Organization, 11*(3), 245–280.

Knight, F. H. (1921). *Risk, uncertainty and profit.* Chicago, IL: University of Chicago Press.

Maguire, S., & Hardy, C. (2013). Organizing processes and the construction of risk: A discursive approach. *Academy of Management Journal, 56*(1), 231–255.

Michel-Kerjan, E., Raschky, P. & Kunreuther, H. (2015). Corporate demand for insurance: New evidence from the U.S. terrorism and property markets. *Journal of Risk and Insurance, 82*(4), 505–530.

O'Malley, P. (2003). Governable catastrophes: A comment on Bougen. *Economy and Society, 32*(2), 275–279.

Paudel, Y. (2012). A comparative study of public-private catastrophe insurance systems: Lessons from current practices. *The Geneva Papers on Risk and Insurance Issues and Practice, 37*(2), 257–285.

Power, M. (2014). Risk, social theories and organizations. In P. Adler, P.D. Gay, G. Morgan, & M. Reed (Eds.), *The Oxford handbook of sociology, social theory, and organization studies: Contemporary currents* (pp. 370–392). Oxford: Oxford University Press.

RMS (2017). RMS estimates Hurricane Harvey insured losses from wind, storm surge and inland flood damage will be between USD $25 and $35 Billion. *RMS Newsroom.*

Scheytt, T., Soin, K., Sahlin-Andersson, K., & Power, M. (2006). Introduction: Organizations, risk and regulation. *Journal of Management Studies, 43*(6), 1331–1337.

Smets, M., Jarzabkowski, P., Burke, G. T., & Spee, P. (2015). Reinsurance trading in Lloyd's of London: Balancing conflicting-yet-complementary logics in practice. *Academy of Management Journal, 58*(3), 932–970.

Swiss Re (2015a). Underinsurance of property risks: Closing the gap. *Sigma.* No5.

Swiss Re (2015b). Natural catastrophes and man-made disasters in 2014: Convective and winter storms generate most losses. *Sigma.* No2.

Weinkle, J. (2015). A public policy evaluation of Florida's Citizens Property Insurance Corporation. *Journal of Insurance Regulation, 34*(1), 1–33.

World Bank (2014). *Bringing resilience to scale – Global facility for disaster and recovery (GFDRR),* Annual Report.

30

RISKS OF ADDRESSING VS. IGNORING OUR BIGGEST SOCIETAL PROBLEMS

When and How Moon Shots Make Sense

Sim B. Sitkin, C. Chet Miller, and Kelly E. See

Recent press reports as well as casual observations suggest we have serious societal problems, with most of them being addressed insufficiently, or even being ignored. From the almost apocalyptic problems of war and famine in the South Sudan, to the disruption of Rocky Mountain ecosystems in North America and the uncontrolled population growth in many parts of the world, large-scale problems and their associated risks are threatening human societies. In recognition of these problems, the United Nations recently has set new goals in several critical areas related to sustainability, including:

- Global poverty, health, and safety;
- Education, food, water, and energy;
- Climate sustainability;
- Equality across people and countries.

The UN's 17 specific goals in these broad areas are extraordinary in scope and purpose (see Table 30.1). In the words of UN officials, "We are setting out a supremely ambitious and transformational vision." Can the goals be attained? History suggests there is some chance of success. The Apollo 11 moon landing, the development of the Panama Canal, and the construction of the Great Wall of China and Angkor Wat in Cambodia all exemplify what is possible when there is unity and commitment to shared pursuit of societal stretch goals. On the other hand, history also suggests a non-trivial chance of failure. In the United States, President Lyndon Johnson's War on Poverty did not eliminate impoverishment, or reduce it to truly satisfactory levels. Similarly, the U.S. EPA's 13-year goal to clean up the Chesapeake Bay largely failed. Efforts to build a tolerant multicultural society largely failed in Iraq during the first part of 21st century.

Current features of the world also suggest some caution. There is distrust between regulators and regulated organizations, which has fostered polarization, secrecy, and lack of cooperation in rethinking dysfunctional regulations. Institutional trust seems to be at a low ebb because of a simultaneous lack of privacy and lack of transparency (e.g., U.S. National Security Agency, Facebook, Google). Democratic governments are experiencing difficulties

Table 30.1 United Nations' "Goals for the Planet"

1	End poverty in all its forms everywhere.
2	End hunger, achieve food security and improve nutrition, and promote sustainable agriculture.
3	Ensure healthy lives and promote well-being for all at all ages.
4	Ensure inclusive and equitable quality education and promote lifelong learning opportunities for all.
5	Achieve gender equality and empower all women and girls.
6	Ensure availability and sustainable management of water and sanitation for all.
7	Ensure access to affordable, reliable, sustainable, and modern energy for all.
8	Promote sustained, inclusive, and sustainable economic growth, full and productive employment and decent work for all.
9	Build resilient infrastructure, promote inclusive and sustainable industrialization, and foster innovation.
10	Reduce inequality within and among countries.
11	Make cities and human settlements inclusive, safe, resilient, and sustainable.
12	Ensure sustainable consumption and production patterns.
13	Take urgent action to combat climate change and its impacts.
14	Conserve and sustainably use the oceans, seas, and marine resources for sustainable development.
15	Protect, restore, and promote sustainable use of terrestrial ecosystems, sustainably manage forests, combat desertification, and halt and reverse land degradation and halt biodiversity loss.
16	Promote peaceful and inclusive societies for sustainable development, provide access to justice for all, and build effective, accountable, and inclusive institutions at all levels.
17	Strengthen the means of implementation and revitalize the Global Partnership for Sustainable Development

Adapted from Sustainable Development Goals: 17 Goals to Transform Our World, United Nations, at www.un.org/sustainabledevelopment/.

in creating enough agreement across competing groups to foster the pursuit of major, long-term policy initiatives. Low public trust in the financial sector has hampered significant financial reform. Plummeting trust in business executives has exacerbated concerns related to rising income inequality and perceived special interest influence. Creativity has faltered as large corporations have become more and more risk-averse, with attention shifting to quarterly returns and ineffective size-enhancing acquisitions.

While one might disagree with some of the individual parts of the landscape described earlier, the overall pattern raises a fundamental concern – many of our societal institutions and leaders seem to have lost the will to tackle big problems and have lost the ability to influence their followers to grow and do what is needed to address the very real and significant challenges we face as a society. Increased risk and inevitable crises are the natural result of such negligence and inertia.

Despite the difficulties, it is imperative that our organizations and leaders proactively combat the mounting problems, and it is equally imperative that researchers help them to do so. As the world becomes more complex and continues to evolve rapidly, fundamental issues need to be addressed with urgency, intelligence, and strategic nuance. In part, this demands recognition that some ambitious targets should not be pursued until the specific agencies, governments, and firms that must spearhead the efforts have been better positioned for such pursuit. In the meantime, experimenting with potential solutions (dubbed a "small losses" approach) and building momentum on incremental successes (dubbed a "small-wins" approach) might be more useful. For other ambitious targets, immediate pursuit makes more sense as the organizations that must play key roles are already well positioned for proactive behavior; their full energies should be unleashed now. In these latter cases, we must, however, understand the key elements of effective leadership and organizational capability that are most relevant to managing the risks associated with "moon shots" and for overcoming the risks of doing either too little or too much.

Understanding the Context

Our prior and ongoing research provides a set of guidelines that can help in discerning which organizations are best positioned to pursue stretch goals in the near term (Sitkin, See, Miller, Lawless, & Carton 2011; Sitkin, Miller, & See, 2017). Truly bold initiatives such as the UN's sustainability goals require organizations to pursue the seemingly impossible. This characterization of stretch goals relates to the extreme difficulty of the targeted outcomes, and the need for completely new ways of working in order to even pursue those targets.

The fundamental problem that must be considered is this: agencies, governments, and firms that are recovering from recent failures and lack excess/undeployed resources are very likely to pursue tough targets, despite not being well positioned to do so. These organizations need wins and want to put themselves on a better path, but they almost always fail when they try for goals that are simply too ambitious for their current capabilities. Our research shows that for such weakly positioned organizations, the adoption of seemingly impossible targets stimulates a problematic set of mechanisms, including fear, defensiveness, grasping for quick fixes to complex problems, increased perceptions of threats, and rigidity. Thus, after failures and when lacking excess resources, it is best to resist the urge and not pursue overly ambitious targets. It is much more viable to pursue a strategy of small wins that can build confidence and resources, or to pursue a strategy of small losses that can foster experimentation and capability development through learning.

On the other hand, agencies, governments, and firms that have the recent success and resources to take on risky, ambiguous targets instead tend to sit on their hands and play it safe because they do not need to take risks in order to prove themselves or generate positive attention. When a successful organization does break free of this tendency toward inaction, it can accomplish the seemingly impossible. Consider the following example.

In 2011, U.S. health care firm DaVita set a standard of enhancing outcomes for their dialysis patients while also increasing employee satisfaction and improving cost savings/ profitability. Any one of these aspirations would have been daunting in the very tough dialysis business, but insisting on the trio being pursued simultaneously was especially challenging. To add to the challenge, DaVita adopted the exceptionally difficult goal of saving $60–$80 million within four years through internal organizational experiments that would also immediately serve the patient-health and employee-satisfaction aspects of the company's vision. The saved money would be available in part for reinvestment in future patient initiatives. Leaders had no idea if the savings target was remotely possible, but they started by creating a "Pioneer Team" that combined front-line clinical staff, engineers, project managers, and Six Sigma experts. This team took a "community design" approach and developed a range of effective interventions that actually did result in reduced costs, improved patient outcomes, and enhanced staff satisfaction. They succeeded because they were choosing to stretch from a position of success (with growing revenues and profits and a lauded business), not to recover from failure, and because they provided adequate resources for the initiative.

Many successful organizations in DaVita's position sit on their laurels and become complacent. They shouldn't. For individual success, shareholder value, and for our society to continue to solve big problems, we need such organizations and their leaders to step forward and take a chance on doing something big.

Addressing the Trust Issue

Because tackling big problems involves significant risk and uncertainty, it requires trust in organizations and their leaders who do step forward to address the challenges. When leaders ask people to take big risks, they are asking for their trust in two ways. First, they are asking people to trust in the decision to take substantial risks inherent in tackling big, complex problems. Second, they are asking people who will do the work to experiment, be willing to fail at times, and accept on faith that failures along the way will not result in retribution (best efforts sometimes fail when very risky goals are tackled) (Sitkin, 1992; Sitkin et al., 2011; Sitkin et al., 2017). When trust erodes and even turns to active distrust, it means that our institutions and leaders have not conveyed to us that they are capable (of doing their jobs), caring (about our needs), consistent (in their words and actions), and congruent (with our values) (Sitkin & Bijlsma-Frankema, 2018). Sadly, the level of trust has eroded significantly in both our institutions and our leaders (Edelman.com, 2017). Rebuilding that trust must be an essential priority if we are to accomplish ambitious societal goals.

If we apply a systematic framework for understanding effective leadership in these challenging circumstances, we can identify four key behaviors leaders must exhibit: sensemaking, building trust through strong relational ties, inspiring high aspirations, and fostering a sense of stewardship.

- *Sensemaking*: In research that one of us has conducted with Allan Lind, the universally weakest aspect of leadership has been identified as sensemaking (Lind & Sitkin, 2015). But in a world of tough and risky goals, we must rely on our leaders to not just make the right decisions, but to make sure we understand the situation, what we can do, and how to interpret events (for related commentary, see Meschi, Métais, & Miller, 2015).
- *Building control in an uncertain world through involvement of others*: Leaders often respond to difficult conditions by tightening control rather than by building the informal relationships and enhanced decentralized capabilities needed for effective judgments. This must change. In this regard, crowd sourcing ideas might be useful as one part of overall efforts (see, for example, Afuah & Tucci, 2012).
- *Inspiring others to strive*: Supporting raised aspirations involves inspiring others to dream big and to attempt to reach the seemingly impossible (Sitkin et al., 2011; Sitkin et al., 2017). Inspirational leadership is not about creating true believers, but rather it is about creating strivers who stretch and challenge the status quo with a clear sense of why the big problem is important, while having a sense of the potential for success.
- *Creating stewardship*: Leaders in a difficult world need to encourage a sense of responsibility that pervades the organization and society; responsibility cannot reside only in the elite (Hernandez & Sitkin, 2012).

Closing

We face challenging times, and the need for well-positioned organizations and their leaders to help us meet our challenges has never been greater – the need for help in building our capacity to tackle big problems and take big risks has never been more pressing. Human societies are at stake. Furthermore, we need organizational leaders to not only help us cope with complexity and rapid change, but also to deepen our ability to acknowledge and understand what we do not yet know. Finally, we need our leaders to help rebuild trust in our societal institutions.

As we think about critically important leadership roles, we also need to extend the term "leader" beyond the very tops of our organizations. Although our focus has been on formal leaders in the upper-reaches of organizations, leadership can be shown by anyone in an organization who embraces the responsibility to act with a sense of stewardship that leads to "stepping up" to today's challenges, while helping to inform others and influence them to contribute at higher levels.

References

Afuah, A., & Tucci, C. (2012). Crowdsourcing as a solution to distant search. *Academy of Management Review, 37*(3), 355–375.

Edelman.com (2017). *The 2017 Edelman trust barometer.* Chicago, IL: Edelman, Inc.

Hernandez, M., & Sitkin, S. B. (2012). Who is leading the leader? Follower influence on leader ethicality. In D. De Cremer & A. E. Tenbrunsen (Eds.), *Behavioral Business Ethics: Shaping an Emerging Field* (pp. 81–104). New York: Routledge.

Lind, E. A., & Sitkin, S. B. (2015). *The six domains of leadership.* Detroit, MI: Learning With Leaders.

Meschi, P.-X., Métais, E., & Miller, C. C. (2015). Leader longevity, cognitive inertia, and performance in organizations with stretch goals: Evidence from "La Royale" and its ambition to gain naval supremacy between 1689 and 1783. In G. Gavetti & W. Ocasio (Eds.), *Cognition and strategy – Advances in strategic management, volume 32* (pp. 467–504). Bingley, UK: Emerald Group Publishing.

Sitkin, S.B. (1992). Learning through failure: The strategy of small losses. *Research in Organizational Behavior, 14*, 231–266.

Sitkin, S. B., & Bijlsma-Frankema, K. (2018). Distrust. In R. Searle, A. Nienhaber, & S. Sitkin, (Eds.), *The Routledge companion to trust.* New York: Routledge.

Sitkin, S. B., Miller, C. C., & See, K. E. (2017). The stretch goal paradox: Ambitious targets are widely misunderstood – and widely misused. *Harvard Business Review,* January–February, 92–99.

Sitkin, S. B., See, K. E., Miller, C. C., Lawless, M. W., & Carton, A. M. (2011). The paradox of stretch goals: Organizations in pursuit of the seemingly impossible. *Academy of Management Review, 36*(3), 544–566.

31

MANAGING FOR THE FUTURE

A Commentary on Crisis Management Research

Kathleen M. Sutcliffe

Introduction

Crisis management scholarship arguably has struggled for decades to find a central place in management and organization theory. This state of affairs belies a surge of both practical interest by executives and the popular press to better understand the origins of risk and crises and ways to better manage them (Boin, Hart, Stern, & Sundelius, 2005), and theoretical interest by scholars wanting to reinvigorate and expand research on organizational adversity and resilience (van der Vegt, Essens, Wahlström, & George, 2015). The challenges that threaten organizations and institutions continue to grow, and the types of crises and the possible sources of their origins have grown as well (Boin, Comfort, & Demchak, 2010). Yet, research has largely focused on crises that are large and highly visible (e.g., high consequence, low probability events) and has focused mostly on crisis management after the fact. Scholars have neglected incubating processes and other dynamics that precede or may lead to crises (Roux-Dufort, 2007; Williams, Gruber, Sutcliffe, Shepherd, & Zhao, 2017). It is in this domain that I urge future researchers to focus their attention.

Crisis management is often portrayed as a reactive activity directed at exceptional events or surprises that catch organizations unaware (Roux-Dufort, 2007). Fixation on events impels scholars to focus on their aftermath (Roux-Dufort, 2007). Moreover, a focus on the exceptional suggests that there is nothing that is generalizable or relevant to organizational functioning. Failure to move beyond an event-centered perspective – failure to "free crisis management from the realm of the exceptional" (Roux-Dufort, 2007: 112) – leaves little room for theoretical progress, innovation, or more generalized understanding of how organizations produce or repress their own crises (Roux-Dufort, 2007). A process-centered perspective reunites crisis management with its (somewhat) forgotten past (e.g., Barry Turner's early work showing that the seeds of crisis are sown long before turmoil arrives), and also expands and conceptually reframes the notions of crisis and crisis management to better reflect today's technological and organizational realities (Williams et al., 2017). In addition to expanding the range of interesting and important research avenues, a process-centered focus on pre-crisis organizational processes, dynamics, and mechanisms may serve to enhance the theoretical legitimacy of crisis research itself. Moreover, it may provide for a more complete understanding of the organization-adversity relationship (Williams et al., 2017).

My research program over the past two decades has sought to understand processes and dynamics relating to the sensing of risks and uncertainty and the underpinnings of organizational reliability and resilience. In the following paragraphs, I illustrate my work in the areas of organizational reliability, healthcare safety, and organizational adaptability and resilience. These works, in one way or another, are aimed at understanding how organizations produce (or avert) crises both small and large.

Underpinnings of Organizational Reliability

One domain of my work is in the area of high reliability. Weick, Sutcliffe, Obstfeld (1999) sought to explain how high reliability organizations (HROs) achieve reliable performance under conditions of risk and dynamism, and to integrate HRO research more broadly into mainstream organization and management theory. Our analysis suggested that HROs warranted closer attention both theoretically and practically because of their capabilities to adapt and to suppress inertia. In fact, the claim that *the ways in which HROs "mindfully" organize are a dormant infrastructure for performance improvement in all organizations* seems to be as true for organizations facing increasingly volatile and uncertain environments in the 21st century as it was in 1999 when we first introduced the concept of high reliability organizing. Existing theory (e.g., Hannan & Freeman, 1984) advocated that organizational reliability was a consequence of highly standardized routines. We argued that this view ignored the reality that reliable systems have to perform the same way even though working conditions fluctuate or are not known in advance. Indeed, our analysis showed that inertia is not indigenous to organizing and that routines are effective because of their variation. We proposed that reliability in dynamic contexts requires a distinctive organizing infrastructure (mindful organizing) that is grounded in a set of "metaprocesses and practices" fostering (a) a preoccupation with failure, (b) a reluctance to simplify mindsets and interpretations, (c) a sensitivity to current operations, (d) the development of resilience, and (e) underspecified (flexible) decision structures.

Existing evidence into the origins of accidents and disasters often points to patterns of missed signals or missed reactions to impending warning signs (e.g., Turner, 1976). In a study of 55 wildfire incidents that had better or worse outcomes, Michelle Barton and I (Barton & Sutcliffe, 2009) originally hypothesized that firefighting teams whose team members noticed small cues that foreshadowed dangerous complications would have better outcomes. But that hypothesis was not supported; noticing small deviations did not account for differential success in performance outcomes. Instead, we found that two social processes made the difference: giving voice to concerns and seeking alternative perspectives. Voicing concerns, even when others saw the same cue, served to make actionable that which everyone had already seen. The voiced concerns became an artifact that had to be dealt with by the group. Second, when crew leaders sought alternative perspectives, members interrupted their thought processes, reevaluated the situation, and often saw cues they had previously ignored. The key lesson is that straightforward admonitions to remain alert in changing conditions are oversimplified. Alertness becomes more complicated when actively voicing concerns and seeking alternatives are needed to make the alertness to weak signals matter. We also found that in high-risk situations, it is important to differentiate and distinguish between general expertise and situational knowledge – a distinction that is often blurred when people defer to experts (which often happens in public policy debates). The presumption is that higher-status experts have a better understanding of specific events and they see the same cues of what is unfolding as do those on the frontline. But when we differentiate status and understanding, it is easier to see that there are situational uncertainties apart from deep experience (Weick, 2016). Importantly, high-status experts might be perfectly confident in their own skills and abilities, but still maintain a belief that the task is so uncertain that no matter how skilled they are no one can be fully knowledgeable under the circumstances. We labeled this wisdom "situated humility."

Safety in Healthcare

Avoiding crises and adverse events in high-hazard, high-risk settings such as healthcare, where the strength and quality of interpersonal connections vary, where there is a constant need to re-accomplish routines, and where problems are sometimes the outcomes of attempted solutions, is critically important and difficult to achieve. In a series of two studies, Tim Vogus and I (Vogus & Sutcliffe, 2007) empirically studied the theoretical validity of mindful organizing (Weick et al., 1999) and its role in mitigating medical mishaps. The study of medical crises and adverse events has a long history in professional medicine but has gained the attention of organization theorists relatively recently. Our findings showed that fewer medication errors (and patient falls) occurred over the subsequent six months on units with higher levels of mindful organizing. Moreover, the negative association between medication errors (and patient falls) and mindful organizing was stronger when registered nurses reported higher levels of trust in their nurse managers and when units reported extensive use of standardized care protocols. Overall, the findings showed that risks were lowered through mindful organizing.

Organizational Adaptability and Resilience

Many organization theories assume that when faced with threats, individuals, units, and organizations tend to respond rigidly. In fact, images such as threat rigidity, downward spirals, vicious cycles, and tipping points have dominated the literature (Sutcliffe & Vogus, 2003). Yet, there is growing interest in factors that contribute to improvisation, coordination, flexibility, and endurance – factors that contribute to resilience.

Resilience is often used to describe adaptable organizations – organizations that are able to deal with uncertainty and risk by coping with unanticipated dangers as they become manifest (Wildavsky, 1988: 77). To understand the micro-level behaviors that underlie adaptive organizing under uncertainty, we conducted an empirical study of over 500 wildland firefighters (Barton, Sutcliffe, Vogus, & DeWitt, 2015: 75–76). Theory suggests that performance under uncertainty is a situation-specific accomplishment (Weick, 2011). Individuals and teams must actively sense and make sense in order to mitigate tendencies under pressure to normalize or overlook discrepancies that signal emerging trouble-spots or weakening. We proposed that effective performance stems from the contextualized engagement of actors at multiple organizational levels. Specifically, we hypothesized that performance is enabled when frontline employees actively strive to capture discriminatory contextual details and build coherent interpretations of them (a process we labeled anomalizing), and when leaders proactively enable sensemaking. The results affirmed our theorizing: dual sets of behaviors enacted by leaders and frontline workers were integral to effective performance under uncertainty (Barton et al., 2015: 80).

Crisis management researchers have suggested that resilience is critical to the quality of an organization's response to crisis (Williams et al., 2017: 740). Yet, studies of true resilience in crisis management are relatively sparse. Similarly, you could say that resilience research has largely been inattentive to crisis management because when organizations are resilient they may avoid major crises or may be better equipped to cope and absorb strain when they don't (Sutcliffe & Vogus, 2003). But considering these two domains of inquiry together may shed light on common mechanisms that underpin both, and may help us answer broader questions central to organizational theory – such as "why some organizations and societies successfully adjust to and even thrive amidst adversity while others fail to do so?" (van der Vegt et al., 2015: 971). In an effort to advance both streams of research, a set of colleagues and I (Williams et al., 2017) reviewed the literatures on crisis management and resilience and developed an integrative framework that suggests that crisis management and resilience are two aspects of the same challenge – the challenge of adversity.

Conclusion

The increasing complexity, dynamism, and interconnectedness of contemporary business environments coupled with technological and political volatility mean that the potential for crises, both small and large, has increased dramatically. Thus, this *Routledge Companion to Risk, Crisis and Emergency Management* could not be timelier or more important. This is not to say that fresh scholarly insights in these domains have been completely absent in the organizational literatures. In recent years, scholars have sought to examine the organizational life of risk management at the level of specific practices (e.g., Power, 2016), unpack the relational aspects of crisis management (Kahn, Barton, & Fellows, 2013), explore the role social approval plays in crisis management (Bundy & Pfarrer, 2015), and explore more mundane crises, such as crises on social media (Gruber, Smerek, Thomas-Hunt, & James, 2015). Yet, much more needs to be done. The perspective advanced here suggests that scholars studying risk, crisis, and crisis management pay more careful attention to processes, dynamics, and mechanisms that precede or may lead to crises. Small problems, mistakes, mishaps, or lapses are a natural part of organizational life, but strong tendencies to normalize, overlook, or ignore emerging conditions often means that small details don't get attention until too late – until they grow into a crisis. This doesn't have to be the case. We need to know more about it.

References

Barton, M. A., & Sutcliffe, K. M. (2009). Overcoming dysfunctional momentum: Organizational safety as a social achievement. *Human Relations, 62*(9), 1327–1356.

Barton, M. A., Sutcliffe, K. M., Vogus, T. J., & DeWitt, T. (2015). Performing under uncertainty: Contextualized engagement in wildland firefighting. *Journal of Contingencies and Crisis Management, 23*(2), 74–83.

Boin, A., Comfort, L. K., & Demchak, C. C. (2010). The rise of resilience. In L. K. Comfort, A. Boin, & C. C. Demchak (Eds.), *Designing resilience: Preparing for extreme events* (pp. 1–12). Pittsburgh, PA: University of Pittsburgh Press.

Boin, A., Hart, P., Stern, E., & Sundelius, B. (2005). *The politics of crisis management: Public leadership under pressure.* New York, NY: Cambridge University Press.

Bundy, J., & Pfarrer, M. D. (2015). A burden of responsibility: The role of social approval at the onset of a crisis. *Academy of Management Review, 40*(3), 345–369.

Gruber, D. A., Smerek, R. E., Thomas-Hunt, M. C., & James, E. H. (2015). The real-time power of Twitter: Crisis management and leadership in an age of social media. *Business Horizons, 58*(2), 163–172.

Hannan, M. T., & Freeman, J. (1984). Structural inertia and organizational change. *American Sociological Review, 49*, 149–164.

Kahn, W. A., Barton, M. A., & Fellows, S. (2013). Organizational crises and the disturbance of relational systems. *Academy of Management Review, 38*(3), 377–396. doi:10.5465/amr.2011.0363

Power, M. (Ed.). (2016). *Riskwork: Essays on the organizational life of risk management*. Oxford, UK: Oxford University Press.

Roux-Dufort, C. (2007). Is crisis management (only) a management of exceptions? *Journal of Contingencies and Crisis Management, 15*(2), 105–114.

Sutcliffe, K. M., & Vogus, T. J. (2003). Organizing for resilience. In K. S. Cameron, J. E. Dutton, & R. E. Quinn (Eds.), *Positive organizational scholarship: Foundations of a new discipline* (pp. 94–110). San Francisco, CA: Berrett-Koehler.

Turner, B. A. (1976). Organizational and interorganizational development of disasters. *Administrative Science Quarterly, 21*(3), 378–397. doi:10.2307/2391850

van der Vegt, G. S., Essens, P., Wahlström, M., & George, G. (2015). Managing risk and resilience. *Academy of Management Journal, 58*(4), 971–980.

Vogus, T. J., & Sutcliffe, K. M. (2007). The impact of safety organizing, trusted leadership, and care pathways on reported medication errors in hospital nursing units. *Medical Care, 41*(10), 992–1002.

Weick, K. E. (2011). Organizing for transient reliability: The production of dynamic non-events. *Journal of Contingencies and Crisis Management, 19*(1), 21–27.

Weick, K. E. (2016). 60th anniversary essay: Constrained comprehending: The experience of organizational inquiry. *Administrative Science Quarterly, 61*(3), 333–346.

Weick, K. E., Sutcliffe, K. M., & Obstfeld, D. (1999). Organizing for high reliability: Processes of collective mindfulness. In B. M. Staw & R. I. Sutton (Eds.), *Research in organizational behavior* (pp. 81–123). Greenwich, CT: JAI Press.

Wildavsky, A. B. (1988). *Searching for safety*. New Brunswick, NJ: USA Transaction Books.

Williams, T. A., Gruber, D. A., Sutcliffe, K. M., Shepherd, D. A., & Zhao, E. Y. (2017). Organizational response to adversity: Fusing crisis management and resilience research streams. *Academy of Management Annals, 11*(2), 733–769.

32

FROM RISK MANAGEMENT TO (CORPORATE) SOCIAL RESPONSIBILITY

Sytze F. Kingma

The following reflections stem from my personal experiences in risk research rather than from a systematic literature review. This research note therefore should be understood as personal preferences and observations that are not intended as a kind of research agenda, although they perhaps might be of some use for such an endeavor. My academic experience with risk is grounded – and on that note also biased – first by a sociological concern with risk (e.g., Douglas & Wildavsky, 1982; Beck, 1992; Luhmann, 1993; Beck, 1994; Furedi, 2002; Lyng, 2005), and second by an empirical engagement for half of my academic career with the institutional field of organized gambling (e.g., Kingma, 1991, 1993, 1996, 1997, 2004, 2008a, 2010, 2013, 2015). For instance, I quickly learned that gambling not only deals with individual risk-taking behavior but, more interesting, at the same time with risk-taking by organizations and governments who commodify, legalize and liberalize this peculiar social activity (which on closer inspection is difficult to classify as either productive or consumptive). This became particularly salient from the 1970s onward when gambling in many jurisdictions gradually transformed from an illegal and deviant activity into a more or less respectable part of the consumer society. In other words, gambling became part of our "institutionalized risk-environment" (Giddens, 1990). In this context, gambling risks such as problem gambling assume the character of "normal accidents" (Perrow, 1999), and gambling organizations, particularly casinos, develop the features of "high-reliability organizations" (Weick & Sutcliffe, 2001) with comparably high levels of risk-awareness and protective measures.

Commercial gambling activities, as they currently exist on the market, are a product of rationalized decision-making, not only by individual consumers, who have a choice in whether or not to take part in such a risky activity, but also by operators, officials and politicians, who have choices in whether or not and under which conditions to offer gambling opportunities. Social actors in all of these categories are involved in gambling ventures against the backdrop of their implicit and explicit assessment of the dangers and risks of gambling – such as problem gambling and crime – and for that reason are involved in acts of both risk-taking (Power, 2007) and organizing (Meyer & Bromley, 2013). However, similar to recreational gamblers who should not simply be regarded as reckless risk-takers because they paradoxically seek to control their individual risk-taking (Lyng, 2005), we have to acknowledge that governments and gambling operators seek to control the adverse consequences together with the exploitation of gambling risks. For these reasons, gambling also has been portrayed as a "safe risk" (Gephart, 2001).

Casinos typically fall in the category of organizations "that are both centers for processing and handling risks and potential producers and exporters of risk" (Hutter & Power, 2005). This is where the connection between risk and responsibility comes in, which I would like to highlight as an important and promising topic for the future of research on risk, organizing and crisis management. It is probably no coincidence that in the same time frame that risk became a core research theme, Corporate Social Responsibility (CSR) became an equally significant theme in organization studies (Carroll, 1999; Campbell, 2006; Pater & Lierop, 2006; Maclagan, 2008; Jackson & Apostolakou, 2010). The concept of CSR is particularly suited for addressing the productive role of risk because contemporary meanings of CSR are closely associated with the anticipation, and the mitigation and prevention of negative externalities of organization processes. Giddens (1999) even explicitly addressed the complementary role of risk and responsibility. Since the risks of the risk-society are associated with "manufactured risks," risks are based on decision-making, and "what brings into play the notion of responsibility is that someone takes a decision having discernable consequences" (Giddens, 1999: 8). This responsibility is relevant even though we can never be sure about the causality or about the actual future consequences of decisions, and whether we over- or underestimate them. Responsibility not only relates to notions of causality but also to ethical behavior and to liability. Think of Mikhail Kalasjnikov (1919–2013), the inventor of the famous automatic rifle, who was tormented by the idea that "if his gun killed thousands of people he might be responsible for their death(s)." In order to direct organizational risk-research on (corporate) responsibility, special attention should be paid to at least three themes.

1   Responsibility starts with an awareness and recognition of risks. For this, it is crucial to focus on the socially constructed nature of risks, and carefully distinguish between uncertainties and hazards on the one hand, and the risks we fabricate out of them on the other. In the risk society, science and technology and processes of globalization generate a wealth of uncertainties and unintended outcomes, but these are not the same as risks. Risks concern the understandings, representations and (probability) calculations and (estimates of) possible consequences we consciously relate to these uncertainties. This awareness of risk, and the way we relate to risk, may vary considerably in time, across cultures, organizations and social actors. Of course, Douglas and Wildavsky (1982) have long pointed out the culturally relative nature of risk and blame, but what is important here is to recognize that responsibility depends on the awareness and understanding social actors have of risks, which should thus be the focus of research and managerial concern. Social actors and organizations who are actually engaged with hazards will not adequately act upon them and take responsibility if they are unaware of the risks and the connection to their organizational practices. The downing of Malaysian Air flight MH17 over Ukraine on 14 July 2014, may illustrate the point. Globally airlines hardly reckoned with the risk of being hit by a missile high above warzones, but after this disaster the industry quickly took a range of precautionary measures, including the redistribution of responsibilities and the exchange of information concerning this risk between governments and airline companies. In this respect, we should take notice of the often unequal distribution of the responsibilities for and the adverse consequences of risks. In the field of gambling, for instance, it has been noted that responsible gambling programs have been effective in redistributing gambling risks from the state and the gambling corporations to individual consumers (Cosgrave, 2009). Another significant

area of attention and research concerning awareness involves the risks associated with the background processes and maintenance structures of our high-tech organizations (Atak & Kingma, 2011). Risk research and crisis management often focus on the immediate, manifest and obvious risks. However, the background processes and maintenance structures which sustain our complex organizations constitute equally important although often less visible and latent vulnerabilities and risks, concerning, for instance, computer networks and the supply of energy.

2   The connection between risk and responsibility is probably best served with a process view on risk. Risks are not momentary situations or fixed structures but emerge and evolve over time and are acted upon by various groups and organizational actors. For this, it is instructive to focus on processes of "risk-governance" (Renn, 2008). Such a perspective extends the notion of the organization which becomes increasingly responsive to a network of external stakeholders and internalizes unintended and adverse consequences in the organization's culture and risk-management practices. For example, it is interesting to consider what can be addressed as the "feedback-loops between risk- and crisis-management" (Kingma, 2008b). The research and management of risks on the one hand, and of crisis-management – that is, the materialization of risks – on the other, are often presented as different fields of interest. However, a standard response to crisis situations, after the recovery phase, is to learn from the accidents, failures and risks, and improve policies and organizational practices with an eye on preventing such mishaps from occurring again. With the analysis of these feedback processes, a light can also be shed on how precisely responsibility is interwoven within and between organizations. An adequate identification and evaluation of risks can hardly do without (scientific) research in the development of risk and responsibility strategies. One difficulty to take into account here is that our rationalized (scientific) representations of risk may generate a false (managerial) sense of the objectivity of risk, which may consequently also lead to illusions of control. Another significant aspect from a process view are the newly emerging objects and organizations for risk-management. One interesting example I explored concerns schools, which until a few decades ago were mainly regarded as safe havens (Binkhorst & Kingma, 2012). In contrast to the high-reliability organizations (HROs) with which much of organizational risk research is obsessed, schools can better be regarded as "low-reliability organizations" (LROs), as comparatively open organizations with a low risk awareness and low safety standards. While the concern with safety in HROs figures around the possible neglect and maintenance of high safety standards, LROs are more concerned with the inverse processes regarding the identification of risks and the introduction and justification of safety measures.

3   Further, the connections between risk-management and corporate responsibility involve the institution of new distinctions and interactions between managers and organizational actors on the one hand, and clients, officials, business professionals and other stakeholders on the other. With this, new norms and moral standards tend to be instituted in organizational fields. Desirable behaviors are more precisely defined and monitored. Awareness and attentiveness to potential problems are increased. Specialized and new roles and identities may become important in responsibilized organizations, such as "chief risk officers" (Power, 2007). Risk management may become a leading principle and integrate entire business strategies in the shape of Enterprise Risk Management (ERM), of which a concern for "reputational risk" usually constitutes an important part. In this way, business practices become redesigned and reproduce new social norms and morals, which often involve deep-rooted assumptions (embodied in prevention

practices, the monitoring instruments and the evaluation standards) concerning, for instance, values of social sensuality, the individualization of risks and responsibilities, a rational choice conception of risk and a technocratic approach to risk management. As an interesting example, I have been looking at a comparison between the risks and policies for gambling and (tobacco) smoking. What particularly intrigues me is the fact that in the same era gambling became respectable, smoking became a disrespectful and deviant activity because of its association with (lung) cancer and other diseases. As such, the negative health effects of both smoking and gambling have long been established scientifically, but while the recognition and control of the adverse consequences in the field of gambling contributed to the acceptance and liberalization of gambling, the awareness of the adverse consequences of smoking had opposite effects. How is this possible? My current ideas about this focus on the rise of public health as a dominant moral value (which is at the core of the contradictory developments). In research like this, it is important to focus on the actual responsiveness to risks by organizations and governments following from their risk perceptions and responsibility programs. It is also important to clearly distinguish between risk management as a form of problem solving and as a form of reputation management and legitimation. In the latter case, responsibilization may paradoxically even lead to an increase in risk-taking behavior.

Finally, we should realize and critically research how this complex of risks and responsibilities has evolved into an ideological structure for the efficient management and legitimation of our societies and organizations, a structure which may equally mystify and mitigate the risks.

References

Atak, A., & Kingma S. (2011). Safety culture in an aircraft maintenance organization: A view from the inside. *Safety Science, 49*, 268–278.

Beck, U. (1992). *Risk society – Towards a new modernity*. London: Sage.

Beck, U., Giddens, A., & Lash, S. (1994). *Reflexive modernization: Politics, tradition and aesthetics in the modern social order*. Cambridge: Polity.

Binkhorst, J., & Kingma, S. (2012). Safety vs. reputation: Risk controversies in emerging policy networks regarding school safety in the Netherlands. *Journal of Risk Research, 15*, 913–935.

Campbell, J. L. (2006). Institutional analysis and the paradox of corporate social responsibility. *American Behavioral Scientist, 49*, 925–938.

Carroll, A. B. (1999). Corporate social responsibility – Evolution of a definitional construct. *Business and Society, 38*, 268–294.

Cosgrave, J. F. (2009). Governing the gambling citizen: The state, consumption and risk. In J. Cosgrave & T. R. Klassen (Eds.), *Casino state. Legalized gambling in Canada* (pp. 46–68). Toronto: University of Toronto Press.

Douglas, M., & Wildavsky, A. (1982). *Risk and culture: An essay on the selection of technological and environmental dangers*. Berkeley: University of California Press.

Furedi, F. (2002). *Culture of fear: Risk-taking and the morality of low expectations (revised edition)*. New York: Walter de Gruyter.

Gephart, R. P. (2001). Safe risk in Las Vegas. *M@n@gement, 4*, 141–158.

Giddens, A. (1990). *The consequences of modernity*. Cambridge: Polity.

Giddens, A. (1999). Risk and responsibility. *Modern Law Review, 62*, 1–10.

Hutter, B., & Power, M. (2005). *Organizational encounters with risk*. Cambridge: Cambridge University Press.

Jackson, G., & Apostolakou, A. (2010). Corporate social responsibility in Western Europe: An institutional mirror or substitute? *Journal of Business Ethics, 94*, 371–394.

Kingma, S. (1991). De legitimiteit van het kienen en bingo of de smaak van de noodzaak [The legitimacy of bingo or the taste of necessity]. In D. Kalb & S. Kingma (Eds.), *Fragmenten van vermaak. Macht en plezier in moderniserend Nederland* (pp. 125–154). Amsterdam: Editions Rodopi.

Kingma, S. (1993). *Risk-analysis gambling. A research into the nature and prevalence of gambling addiction in the Netherlands.* Tilburg: Tilburg University.

Kingma, S. (1996). A sign of the times: The political culture of gaming in the Netherlands. In J. McMillen (Ed.), *Gambling cultures – Studies in history and interpretation.* London: Routledge.

Kingma, S. (1997). "Gaming is play, it should remain fun!" The gaming complex, pleasure and addiction. In P. Sulkunen, J. Holmwood, H. Radner, & G. Schulze (Eds.), *Constructing the new consumer society* (pp. 173–193). London: MacMillan.

Kingma, S. (2004). Gambling and the risk society: The liberalisation and legitimation crisis of gambling in the Netherlands. *International Gambling Studies, 4,* 47–67.

Kingma, S. (2008a). The liberalization and (re)regulation of Dutch gambling markets: National consequences of the changing European context. *Regulation & Governance, 2,* 445–458.

Kingma, S. (2008b). The risk paradigm, organizations and crisis management. *Journal of Contingencies and Crisis Management, 16,* 164–170.

Kingma, S. (2010). *Global gambling – Cultural perspectives on organized gambling.* London: Routledge.

Kingma, S. (2013). Paradoxes of risk management – Social responsibility and self-exclusion in Dutch casinos. *Culture and Organization, 19,* 1–25.

Kingma, S. (2015). Dostoevsky and Freud: Autonomy and Addiction in Gambling. *Journal of Historical Sociology, 30*(4), 891–917.

Luhmann, N. (1993). *Risk: A sociological theory.* New York: Aldine De Gruyter.

Lyng, S. (2005). *Edgework – The sociology of risk-taking.* New York: Routledge.

Maclagan, P. (2008). Organizations and responsibility: A critical overview. *Systems Research and Behavioral Science, 25,* 371–381.

Meyer, J. W., & Bromley, P. (2013). The worldwide expansion of "organization". *Sociological Theory, 31,* 366–389.

Pater, A., & Van Lierop, K. (2006). Sense and sensitivity: The roles of organisation and stakeholders in managing corporate socials responsibility. *Business Ethics: A European Review, 15*(4), 339–351.

Perrow, C. (1999). *Normal accidents – Living with high-risk technologies.* Princeton: Princeton University Press.

Power, M. (2007). *Organized uncertainty – Designing a world of risk management.* New York: Oxford University Press.

Renn, O. (2008). *Risk governance: Coping with uncertainty in a complex world.* New York: Taylor and Francis.

Weick, K. E., & Sutcliffe, K. M. (2001). *Managing the unexpected – Assuring high performance in an age of complexity.* San Francisco: Jossey-Bass.

33

WHY WE NEED TO THINK MORE ABOUT NATIONAL POLITICAL PHILOSOPHIES OF RISK MANAGEMENT

Henry Rothstein

In 2012, six Italian seismologists were found guilty of manslaughter for failing to warn the population in L'Aquila of a disastrous earthquake. Just a few months later, a French psychologist was found guilty of manslaughter because her patient murdered an elderly man. Although the seismologists were later cleared on appeal, in each case the supporters of the convicted expressed outrage with the legal system's treatment of professionals faced with risk and uncertainty. More generally, both cases were a reminder of the varied ways in which different governance cultures can respond to adverse events, and were further "grist to the mill" for a long-standing governance "movement" whose mission is to make governance more rational by making it "risk-based."

The central idea of risk-based governance is that we cannot, and should not want to, live in a risk-free world, because to do so would be disproportionately difficult or costly to achieve, distract attention from the most serious problems, and deter entrepreneurialism. Instead, advocates of risk-based governance argue that it is better to consider the *probability* as well as the *impact* of potential adverse outcomes in order to focus efforts on governing those risks deemed unacceptable. From that perspective, governance is less about avoiding all "bads" and more about a utilitarian search for "optimal" levels of risk.

The use of "probability-impact" frameworks for structuring governance problems has been advocated by many international organizations – such as the Organisation for Economic Co-operation and Development (OECD) and the World Trade Organization (WTO) – and many countries, especially in the Anglo-Saxon world (e.g. OECD, 2010). However, such approaches have by no means been universally adopted. Yet, to date, there have been few systematic attempts at explaining the noticeably different ways in which countries go about preventing harms or managing them once they have occurred.

One line of recent research suggests that such variety reflects deeply engrained national political philosophies of how the state should manage harms (Rothstein et al., 2013). That research suggests that the utilitarian conceit of risk-based governance has a very particular fit with the common law inheritance of Anglo-Saxon polities, within which consequentialist rationales for decision-making are deeply engrained (Morag-Levine, 2005). In the UK, for example, risk has emerged as central organizing idea of governance in the absence of a written constitution that accords rights to individuals that could conflict with utilitarian calculations of how to achieve optimal social welfare. Parliament is sovereign, and so in that context, the elaboration of risk-based governance principles has served the function of limiting the discretion of regulators and trying to make parliament think twice before it acts. Thus, in recent years, it is noticeable how risk ideas have become central to policy thinking in domains that range from flood protection to national security as a way of defining the limits of what the state should be expected to do.

A quick glance at other advanced European states, however, suggests that the utilitarian norms that underlie risk ideas can conflict with their deeply entrenched governance philosophies. In France, for example, the constitutional guarantee of equality works against the way in which risk-based approaches imply that some people may have to suffer for the collective good. One example was during the 2009 H1N1-flu pandemic, when the French Minister of Health decided to vaccinate everyone, rather than just a third of the population, which was all that was needed to provide herd immunity. The reason was that the minister had no legal grounds to decide which third should get preferential treatment (Assemblée Nationale, 2010). Indeed, in recent years, the French state has made much of the concept of *Sécurité Sanitaire*, invoking risk in ways that reinforce the idea of the "protective state" – that is, protecting individuals against all harms – rather than as a rationale for defining the limits of state action. But while this appears from an Anglo-Saxon perspective to be at best utopian, and at worst irrational, criticism tends to overlook the complex way in which safety is conceived in France. Safety – which translates as *sécurité* – cannot be easily disentangled in France from deeply entrenched constitutional commitments to *solidarité* and *fraternité*; concepts that focus attention more on managing the *ex post* consequences of harms that have occurred rather than on the *ex ante* prevention of those harms occurring in the first place.

In Germany, by contrast, risk-based approaches to governance are constrained by a legalistic rights-based policy culture that finds it difficult to handle risk ideas. Governance traditions that stretch back to the 19th century regarded the protection of people from "dangers" to life, freedom, and property as one of the few legitimate grounds for state action (Huber, 2009). But "dangers" were broadly dealt with in binary terms. There was either danger – in which case the state could intervene – or there was safety – in which case the state could do nothing. There was no middle ground. While the courts recognize that some small "residual risk" can be tolerated, they have struggled to reconcile historically entrenched ideas of danger and safety with the more nuanced idea of acceptable risk, particularly in the context of a post-war constitution that jealously guards the negative rights of individuals and businesses against state interference. For example, when the antinuclear movement challenged the authorities over the safety of nuclear power, the German courts found it impossible to agree on a definition of acceptable risk throughout the 1970s and 1980s, that could reconcile individuals' rights to health against business rights to economic activity (Proske, 2004: 466). One consequence is that the legitimacy of German policy-making rests much more on observing the protection of rights than the more consequentialist focus of Anglo-Saxon polities.

These contrasting political philosophies about how the state should act in the face of harms help explain the differing approaches of countries to many hazards, both old and new. Take, for example, the definitively "old" hazard of flooding, the management of which has shaped the systems of governance, and even existence, of some countries such as the Netherlands and Bangladesh. Much has been made of a new paradigm for flood management which is said to have displaced a traditional focus on absolute protection in favor of a more risk-based focus on targeting the worst adverse consequences (WMO, 2011). Yet, a look across the UK, France and Germany suggests that the extent to which risk-based approaches have penetrated flood management has been limited by national ideas of how the state should act.

The UK has been a world leader in developing a risk-based approach to flood prevention. With no constraining legal duties to keep people dry or compensate flood victims, the UK government adopted a risk-based approach to flood prevention to deliver on a political deal struck with the insurance industry following catastrophic flooding in the 1950s. That so-called "Gentleman's Agreement" guaranteed householders would have access to affordable private insurance if the state controlled flood risk through land use regulation and flood defenses; the latter posing particular resource problems for the government when it took ownership of the country's flood defense infrastructure in the 1980s. To that end, the state has made extensive use of flood risk maps and cost-benefit analysis to prioritize flood protection of those parts of the country that are most likely to suffer the worst consequences and to limit building in areas of high flood risk. This approach has been tested in recent years – not least because politicians have struggled both to explain to the public in the aftermath of floods that not everywhere can be protected, as well as ensure public access to insurance for high-risk properties – but its broad premise has remained relatively intact.

France, by contrast, has struggled to take a risk-based approach to flood prevention, not least because of a constitutional commitment to ensuring the security of flooded-out French citizens. While the state has no legal duty to prevent flooding, the 1946 Constitution's declaration of "solidarity and equality of all French people in bearing the burden resulting from national calamities" led to the creation in the 1980s of a universal national catastrophe fund to compensate flood victims. The burden of payouts from the fund did stimulate government to try to improve historically fragmented and complex flood defense and land use regulation regimes through risk-based instruments. However, these efforts have stumbled, in part because the constitutional commitment to compensating flood victims creates a moral hazard that local authorities exploit to deprioritize flood protection.

Germany too has struggled to take a risk-based approach to flood management, but in large part that is due to the character of its rights-based polity. Like the UK, Germany has no legal duties to prevent flooding or compensate flood victims, but unlike the UK, state interference in the negative rights to property and private contract is only permissible to protect the public from danger. As a consequence, prevention standards follow a binary logic of danger and safety rather than taking a more risk-based approach. For example, restrictions on development only operate in designated flood plains in the absence of constitutional grounds to prevent development in defended areas, creating classic conditions for White's (1945) "levee effect." Like the UK, Germany is committed to private funding of flood losses, but take-up of private insurance is low, not least because attempts to make insurance affordable by increasing the risk pool through mandatory coverage were regarded as unconstitutional infringements of rights to private contract by householders at low risk.

Flood management is just one example of the importance of understanding contrasting political philosophies about how the state manages harms, which, to date, have received relatively little attention. Research on occupational health and safety (Rothstein and Beaussier, 2017; Rothstein et al., 2018) reveals similar patterns albeit tempered by considerations of legal traditions and the organization of welfare states. More attention to ideas of how the state should act offers an opportunity to go beyond conventional explanations of variety that focus, for example, on divergent political agendas and economic interests, capacity problems, or crude caricatures of irrational European versus rational Anglo-Saxon behavior. In so doing, this new focus may offer a fresh perspectives on old questions, by turning them into lenses on the character of the state itself.

References

Assemblée Nationale (2010). *Rapport fait au nom de la Commission d'Enquête sur la manière dont a été pro-grammée, expliquée et gérée la campagne de vaccination contre la grippe A(H1N1)* n 2698.

Huber, P. (2009). Risk decisions in German constitutional and administrative law. In G. Woodman & D. Klippel (Eds.), *Risk and the law* (pp. 23–35). Oxford: Routledge-Cavendish.

Morag-Levine, N. (2005). *Chasing the wind: Regulating air pollution in the common law state.* Oxford: Princeton University Press.

OECD. (2010). *Risk and regulatory policy: Improving the governance of risk.* Paris: Organisation for Economic Co-operation and Development.

Proske, D. (2004). *Catalogue of risks.* Berlin: Springer Verlag.

Rothstein, H., Borraz, O. & Huber, M. (2013). Risk and the limits of governance: Exploring varied patterns of risk-based governance across Europe. *Regulation and Governance,* 7(2), 215–235.

Rothstein, H. & Beaussier, A-L. (2017). Why states think about risk differently: The case of workplace safety regulation in France and the UK. In A. Bora, M. Huber, M. Mölders, P. Münte & R. Paul (Eds.), *Society, regulation and governance: New modes of shaping social change?* Cheltenham, UK: Edward Elgar.

Rothstein, H., Demeritt, D., Paul, R., Beaussier, A-L., Wesseling, M, Howard, M., de Haan, M., Borraz, O., Huber, M., & Bouder, F. (2018). Varieties of risk regulation in Europe: Coordination, complementarity & occupational safety in capitalist welfare states. *Socio-Economic Review,* doi:10.1093/ser/mwx029.

White, G. (1945). *Human adjustment to floods.* Chicago, IL: University of Chicago.

WMO (2011). *Integrated flood management.* Geneva: World Meteorological Organization.

34

SUPPLY CHAIN RISK

Transcending Research beyond Disruptions

George A. Zsidisin

Introduction

Risk has been studied in business scholarship for quite some time now. However, within the field of supply chain management, this line of inquiry is arguably in the growth stage. Most research on supply chain risk in the prior millennium focused on providing certain service levels through inventory management (minimizing stock-outs) or determining when to use one or multiple suppliers. However, understanding and managing supply chain risk in a broader sense, and utilizing empirical approaches to do so, has only emerged with changing business practices and world events starting at the turn of the 21st century.

There are a multitude of reasons for the growing research and managerial interest in supply chain risk. One of the many reasons for its growth stems from tragedies such as 9/11, the spread of diseases such as SARS, and the effects of natural disasters. These events and others began building insight into supply chain vulnerability and its inherent risk to business performance. A second reason for increased supply chain risk awareness came from the dot-com bubble in the late 1990s through the early 2000s. Many firms failed, in part, due to their inability to fulfill increased market demand stemming from their newly created Internet platforms. A third reason for peaking interest in supply chain risk originated with firms experiencing pressure for creating leaner operations and supply chains, thereby reducing waste in the supply chain and freeing capital. As a result, the traditional buffers of safety stock inventory and the use of multiple supply sources have been going by the wayside, making supply chains even more susceptible to disruption risk.

A Focus on Supply Chain Disruptions

Most of the initial empirical work on supply chain risk focused on the straightforward threat of disruption, which entails interruptions of product flows from suppliers to customers throughout the supply chain. Much of the work I did earlier in my career, similar to other scholars, looked at how supply chain professionals define (Zsidisin, 2003a) and perceive (Zsidisin, 2003b) supply chain risk, various approaches to assess (Zsidisin, Ellram, Carter & Cavinato, 2004) and manage (Zsidisin & Ellram, 2003; Zsidisin & Smith, 2005; Swink & Zsidisin, 2006) supply chain risk, and how organizations can create supply continuity plans in preparing for disruptions (Zsidisin, Melnyk & Ragatz, 2005; Zsidisin, Ragatz & Melnyk, 2005). More recently, my research efforts have focused on examining sub-elements of supply chain risk and disruptions, such as sources of supply chain risk from quality failures (Zsidisin, Petkova, Saunders & Bisseling, 2016), global sourcing from extending supply chains (Zsidisin & Wagner, 2010), and relational risk (Jia & Zsidisin, 2014). Further, these efforts are beginning to encompass the financial effects of supply chain risk and disruptions, such as shareholder value from "glitches" in the supply chain (Zsidisin, Petkova & Dam, 2016).

The great majority of research on supply chain risk focuses narrowly on the disruption of product flows. Supply chains, however, incorporate more than product flows. Mentzer et al. (2011; p. 18) define supply chains as a "set of three or more entities (organizations or individuals) directly involved in the upstream and downstream flows of products, services, finances, and/or information from a source to a customer." I believe the next stage of new topics in supply chain risk will begin examining the under-studied flows of services, finances, and information from various business functions and organizational perspectives.

How the Study of Supply Chain Risk Is Advancing and Changing

Supply chains are complex. They are messy. What is also interesting about supply chains is they touch just about every business function in a corporation, as well as extend beyond the control of any one organization. Supply chain risk, likewise, is more intricate than just looking at product flows (which is complex in its own right). Therefore, in order to better understand supply chain risk, scholars and practitioners need to take a more holistic view of its study and interactions with business and supply chain practices, including those touching upon the service, information, and financial flows that define supply chains.

A holistic understanding of supply chain risk likewise needs to incorporate the literatures and discoveries of other business functions. Unfortunately, in my view, the academic community has a tendency to create knowledge silos. I believe the study of supply chain risk is advancing and changing through the use of cross-functional perspectives, such as from marketing, management, legal, accounting, finance, and information systems. It is with these holistic perspectives that we can begin to understand the interactions of the four supply chain flows (i.e., product, service, information, and financial) as well as the roles of the various business functions and supply chain entities (suppliers, customers, third-party providers) in how risk is viewed and studied. I was very pleased by the invitation from Professors Gephart, Miller, and Helgesson to contribute to this volume because it facilitates bringing a supply chain perspective to the discourse on risk in business practice and study.

Understanding Supply Chain Risk from a Broader Perspective

As previously described, my initial areas of inquiry into supply chain risk mostly focused on assessment and management approaches associated with preparing for or reducing the effects of product-oriented supply chain disruptions. However, during the more recent years of my academic career, I have incorporated a greater focus on financial flows, specifically with regard to commodity price volatility (CPV). The downside of CPV risk consists of paying higher prices for production inputs as a commodity buyer, or receiving lower payments if your firm is a commodity producer (e.g., steel, oil). Commodity price volatility and risk have traditionally been under the auspices of finance scholars and practitioners, primarily through the study and utilization of financial hedging instruments. However, we have seen through our research a greater involvement by supply chain professionals in creating strategies and techniques beyond financial hedging for assessing and mitigating this form of supply chain risk in their organizations (Zsidisin & Hartley, 2012; Zsidisin, Hartley & Collins, 2013; Zsidisin, Hartley, Kaufmann & Gaudenzi, 2014; Zsidisin, Hartley, Gaudenzi & Kaufmann, 2017; Gaudenzi, Zsidisin, Hartley & Kaufmann, 2017).

A second area in which we are just starting to investigate is related to another form of financial risk – foreign exchange (FX) risk (Zsidisin & Gaudenzi, 2018). This line of research is beginning to create synergies across different literatures and perspectives, such as from finance, marketing, accounting, legal, and information systems. As the field of supply chain risk continues to develop, I can envision how other flows, such as information and service flows, will be investigated by scholars from multiple business disciplines and other disciplines (i.e., engineering). For example with regard to information flows, the 2006 Taiwan earthquake caused damage to underwater cables, prolonging container wait times in the Shanghai seaport due to claim procedures relying on information systems (Tang & Musa, 2011). We need to study supply chain risk from a variety of "lenses" in order to create clearer insights for advancing theory and business practice. Supply chain risk is a cross-functional and cross-organizational challenge requiring scholars and practitioners alike to take a holistic view for its assessment and management.

Conclusions

The study of supply chain risk will continue for some time. As long as supply chains are exposed to uncertainty (which is true as well of business in general), there will be a need for determining how firms can improve performance while creating robust and flexible approaches for managing the effects of supply chain disruptions in all of its forms. With the emergence of data analytics, I envision in the very near future firms being better able to predict and offset risk in the supply chains in which they compete. However, in the end, it is leadership that makes the decisions related to how firms' supply chains are managed. By taking a holistic perspective of supply chain risk, incorporating the knowledge and skills of a myriad of business functions, firms, and perspectives, we can all take additional steps toward reducing supply chain risk exposure and improving business performance.

References

Gaudenzi, B., Zsidisin, G. A., Hartley, J. L., & Kaufmann, L. (2017). An exploration of factors influencing the choice of commodity price risk mitigation strategies. *Journal of Purchasing and Supply Management*. Advance online publication. doi:10.1016/j.pursup.2017.01.004

Jia, F., & Zsidisin, G. A. (2014). Supply relational risk: What role does guanxi play? *Journal of Business Logistics, 35*(3), 259–267.

Mentzer, J. T., DeWitt, W., Keebler, J. S., Min, S., Nix, N. W., Smith, C. D., & Zacharia, Z. G. (2011). Defining supply chain management. *Journal of Business Logistics, 22*(2), 1–25.

Swink, M., & Zsidisin, G. A. (2006). On the benefits and risks of focused commitment to suppliers. *International Journal of Production Research, 44*(20), 4223–4240.

Tang, O., & Musa, S. N. (2011). Identifying risk issues and research advancements in supply chain risk management. *International Journal of Production Economics, 133*(1), 25–34.

Zsidisin, G. A. (2003a). A grounded definition of supply risk. *Journal of Purchasing and Supply Management, 9*(5/6), 217–224.

Zsidisin, G. A. (2003b). Managerial perceptions of supply risk. *Journal of Supply Chain Management, 39*(1), 14–25.

Zsidisin, G. A., & Ellram, L. M. (2003). An agency theory investigation of supply risk management. *Journal of Supply Chain Management, 39*(3), 15–27.

Zsidisin, G. A., Ellram, L. M., Carter, J. R., & Cavinato, J. L. (2004). An analysis of supply risk assessment techniques. *International Journal of Physical Distribution & Logistics Management, 34*(5), 397–413.

Zsidisin, G. A., & Gaudenzi, B. (2018). Transcending beyond finance for managing foreign exchange risk. In K. J. Engemann (Ed.), *The Routledge companion to risk, crisis and security in business*. New York: Routledge.

Zsidisin, G. A., Hartley, J. L., & Collins, W. A. (2013). Integrating student projects with real world problems: The case of managing commodity price risk. *Supply Chain Management: An International Journal, 18*(4), 389–397.

Zsidisin, G. A., & Hartley, J. L. (2012). A strategy for managing commodity price risk. *Supply Chain Management Review, 16*(2), 46–53.

Zsidisin, G. A., Hartley, J. L., Gaudenzi, B., & Kaufmann, L. (2017). *Managing commodity price risk: A supply chain perspective*, 2nd Ed. New York: Business Expert Press Publishing.

Zsidisin, G. A., Hartley, J. L., Kaufmann, L., & Gaudenzi, B. (2014). *Managing commodity price volatility and risk*. Tempe, AZ: CAPS Research. ISBN 978-1-940404-01-1.

Zsidisin, G. A., Melnyk, S. A., & Ragatz, G. L. (2005). An institutional theory perspective of business continuity planning for purchasing and supply management. *International Journal of Production Research, 43*(16), 3401–3420.

Zsidisin, G. A., Petkova, B. N., Saunders, L. W., & Bisseling, M. (2016). Identifying and managing supply quality risk. *International Journal of Logistics Management, 27*(3), 908–930.

Zsidisin, G. A., Petkova, B. N., & Dam, L. (2016). Examining the influence of supply chain glitches on shareholder wealth: Does the reason matter? *International Journal of Production Research, 54*(1), 69–82.

Zsidisin, G. A., Ragatz, G. L., & Melnyk, S. A. (2005). The "dark side" of supply chain management. *Supply Chain Management Review, 9*(2), 46–52.

Zsidisin, G. A., & Smith, M. E. (2005). Managing supply risk with early supplier involvement: A case study and research propositions. *Journal of Supply Chain Management, 41*(4), 44–57.

Zsidisin, G. A., & Wagner, S. M. (2010). Do perceptions become reality? The moderating role of supply chain resiliency on disruption occurrence. *Journal of Business Logistics, 31*(2), 1–20.

35

THE JANUS FACES OF RISK

Cynthia Hardy and Steve Maguire

We live, as commentators are fond of saying, in a "risk society" (Beck, 1992). In contemporary organizations, risk is increasingly prominent in the managerial lexicon. Practitioners routinely cite "risk management" as the appropriate frame for a wide range of organizational activities, using technical terms such as enterprise risk management, operational risk, and risk matrix – to name but a few. "Risk talk" now permeates organizations of all descriptions (Power, 2004), and a discourse has emerged that institutionalizes a highly convergent way of thinking about risk – as the probability of a harm, hazard, or danger of some kind that can be effectively managed by accurately assessing, and then taking action to reduce, the likelihood and/or magnitude of undesirable events (Hardy & Maguire, 2016).

But is risk so straightforward? Our answer is "no," and we draw upon the image of Janus to explain why. For the Romans, Janus was the god of transitions and time – of beginnings and endings and, hence, duality. He is usually depicted with two faces looking in opposite directions, representing the past and the future. Describing someone or something as "Janus-faced" implies they have two sharply contrasting aspects, where apparent positive qualities mask more negative features. We argue that risk is Janus-faced: powerful and seductive, but also complex and potentially deceptive. Moreover, risk has *multiple* Janus faces, which we describe below.

First, just as Janus did for the Romans, risk looks both to the past and the future. Modernity's preoccupation with risk has given rise to a social order that "unlike any preceding culture lives in the future rather than the past" (Giddens & Pierson, 1998: 94). Risk management is most commonly viewed as acting on the future to thwart danger and secure safety. To do so, managers typically rely on "expert risk knowledge derived from empirical information about the past, which has been abstracted into regularities in the form of facts, correlations, and causal models and applied to a hypothetical future" (Hardy & Maguire, 2016: 94). However, insomuch as the future may not conform to the logics of the past – as is typically the case with unfamiliar hazards, low-frequency/high-impact events and systemic risks – connecting the past to the future through the calculus of risk seduces us into believing that we are masters of our destiny – that we can control the future simply by measuring it and, based on this measurement, acting upon it (Beck, 1992; Giddens, 1999).

The second Janus face of risk refers to its status as real and objective, but also constructed and subjective (e.g., Burkard, 2011). Although the realist face is the dominant one as far as the myriad techniques of risk analysis and risk management are concerned, even scientists accept that risks are not perceived the same by all stakeholders. Indeed, this "reality" forms the subject matter of the science of risk perception, which explores the so-called errors and biases of laypersons when their views diverge from those of experts. Constructionist researchers go further, pointing out that even experts cannot escape value judgments, simplifications, and assumptions. As a result, this approach can be helpful in informing risk work in situations where actors face risk controversies, such as regulatory science contexts (e.g., Jasanoff, 1998). Despite a considerable amount of work on the social construction of risk, organizations still find it difficult, however, to break away from scripted, normalized, and institutionalized ways of addressing risk that are based on realist assumptions.

A third Janus face relates to whether risk is to be avoided or embraced. While a negative view of risk often predominates in an era informed by terrorism, climate change, and the global financial crisis, risk has long been associated with opportunity. It is because risk is linked to reward that trading floors exist around the world, entrepreneurs are celebrated for their risk-taking, and particular risks are judged to be "acceptable." When controversy reigns over the question of "is it worth the risk," the discourse of risk appears to provide the answer through scientific expertise, objectivity, and neutrality but, in doing so, masks more fundamental questions. Who gets to decide whether a risk exists? Who gets to judge whether a particular distribution of benefits and harms is just? What are the differential rights to speak and act on risk of those individuals and organizations assigned clearly delineated risk identities (e.g., risk bearers, risk producers, risk assessors, risk managers)? Are there certain harms for which there is no threshold of benefits that can justify them? Such questions often fade to background, unfortunately, once risk discourse is brought to bear on a particular situation.

These Janus faces mean that, as a way to address the many undesirable side effects of modernity, risk is itself risky. It has its own unintended, negative consequences, including delusions of control, the unwarranted discipline of actors unlucky enough to be categorized in certain ways, and the transfer of responsibility for managing risks to individuals bearing them, who may be ill-equipped to do so. From a critical perspective, then, there are many sides to the Janus-faced risk coin. How can organizational researchers deal with so many dual faces of risk?

First, we argue that organizational researchers need to foreground the link between risk and power. As Beck (2006: 33) has pointed out, risk "is a socially constructed phenomenon, in which some people have a greater capacity to define risks than others." Researchers therefore need to be alert to power relations when studying how risk is organized. For maintaining sensitivity to power relations, in our own work we have found a discursive perspective invaluable. For example, in our paper on "riskification" (Hardy & Maguire, 2016), we explore the way in which the dominant discourse of risk shapes how risk is organized, both through practices that are normalizing and by rendering these practices "normal." Deviations from these practices are viewed as arbitrary, idiosyncratic, and politicized. So, even though alternative ways of organizing risk may be more effective, it is difficult for organizations to enact them because it requires resisting the dominant discourse of risk. Further, through a "second order" of critique, we illustrate how attempts to resist the dominant discourse of risk can lead to even more organizing being carried out in the name of risk and across many more realms of social life. Recognition of the uncertainty and unknowability of risk has failed to displace the dominant discourse and, instead, has been exploited by authorities as an excuse to implement draconian risk management actions. Individuals conform to organizationally produced plans, scripts, and protocols that are clearly inadequate as risks are materializing because it is less risky to comply than to improvise. The "individualization" of risk forces individuals to take more responsibility for risks they face, but, ironically, it also authorizes more organizations to intervene aggressively in some individuals' lives in the name of risk. The scope for *critical* research that examines the effects of the dominant discourse of risk on those subjected to it is, then, considerable.

Second, notwithstanding the need for more critical perspectives on risk's expanding reach, we believe that organizational researchers also need to explore ways in which organizations might act more expeditiously and effectively in assessing and managing a range of novel and systemic risks. We are, therefore, not arguing that we should reject the concept of risk; there is no doubt that risk work carried out in all kinds of organizations has saved lives, mitigated suffering, protected assets, and oriented productive entrepreneurial activity. In fact, there are times when we cry out for organizations to be *more* responsive to risk. Why do organizations not act on the risks posed by climate change? Why were the financial – and social – risks associated with the global financial crisis overlooked? Has there been adequate attention to – and action on – the risks posed by artificial intelligence or synthetic biology, to name but a few contemporary fields where humanity and life itself may be at stake?

To this end, we have explored "problematizing" practices, which emphasize "the reflexive acknowledgement of potential inadequacies in knowledge, discontinuity in organizational activities, and the use of open-ended deliberations as a basis for action" on risk (Maguire & Hardy, 2013: 240). Problematizing helps organizations to construct – and act upon – risks even where there is scientific uncertainty regarding whether they "exist" or not. Instead of demanding more data to reduce the uncertainty which, in turn, delays action, organizations that problematize make a case for special treatment, innovate, acknowledge the incompleteness of information, and involve a wider range of stakeholders than simply experts in risk assessment and management processes. In this way, they are able to construct risk objects even in situations of ambiguity. We have also explored organizational dynamics in different risk scenarios: established risks, where a risk is widely accepted by the network of organizations brought together around it; novel risks, where there is considerable controversy and conflict as to whether a risk "exists" let alone what to do about it; and the elimination of risks, where organizations seek to substitute practices or products accepted as hazardous with alternatives they believe to be nonhazardous (Maguire & Hardy, 2016). This has allowed us to distinguish forms of risk work that differ in terms of the contemporaneous discursive work they require as well as the levels of inter-organizational conflict or collaboration to which they give rise, thus providing greater insight into how organizations might act on the diverse types of risk they construct. The scope, therefore, for *practical* research that examines how organizations might organize novel and systemic risks more effectively is considerable.

In sum, we contend that the Janus faces of risk require researchers themselves to adopt a Janus-like approach, by being *both* critical and practical. Organizations construct risks when they "shouldn't" – organizing them, for example, such that some actors are silenced or responsibility for acting on risk is transferred to vulnerable individuals. So, maybe a little less organizational preoccupation with risk would be a good thing. On the other hand, however, organizations also fail to construct risks when they "should" – failing to organize novel and systemic risks, for example, even when they have significant consequences. So, maybe a little more organizational preoccupation with risk would be a good thing. The challenge for organizational researchers is then to offer insight into how our society might extricate itself from the horns of this dilemma by appreciating the Janus faces of risk.

References

Beck, U. (1992). *Risk society: Towards a new modernity*. Thousand Oaks, CA: Sage.

Beck, U. (2006). Living in the world risk society: A Hobhouse Memorial Public Lecture. *Economy and Society, 35*(3), 329–345.

Burkard, M. (2011). *Law and science: Risk assessment and risk management in the WTO agreement on the application of sanitary and phytosanitary measures*. www.boris.unibe.ch/69609/1/11burkard_m.pdf accessed August 21, 2017.

Giddens, A. (1999). Risk and responsibility. *The Modern Law Review, 62*(1), 1–10.

Giddens, A. & Pierson, C. (1998). *Making sense of modernity: Conversations with Anthony Giddens*. Stanford, CA: Stanford University Press.

Hardy, C. & Maguire, S. (2016). Organizing risk: Discourse, power and riskification. *Academy of Management Review, 41*(1), 80–108.

Jasanoff, S. (1998). The political science of risk perception. *Reliability Engineering and System Safety, 59*(1), 91–99.

Maguire, S. & Hardy, C. (2013). Organizing processes and the construction of risk: A discursive approach. *Academy of Management Journal, 56*(1), 231–255.

Maguire, S. & Hardy, C. (2016). Risk work: Three scenarios from a study of industrial chemicals in Canada. In M. Power (Ed.), *Riskwork: Essays on the organizational life of risk management* (pp. 130–149). Oxford, UK: Oxford University Press.

Power, M. 2004. *The risk management of everything: Rethinking the politics of uncertainty*. London, UK: Demos.

36

EFFECTIVENESS OF
REGULATORY AGENCIES

Charles Perrow

Since nothing is perfect in our constructed world, risks will always be with us. I am particularly concerned with those systems that can do a great deal of harm if they have accidents. Since people who build and run risky systems do not always play safe, governmental authorities seek to regulate risky systems. I will assume that practices that affect safety are the responsibility of management. If there is inadequate training of personnel, that is due to management; if corners are cut and safety provisions are ignored, that too is management's responsibility. If there are insufficient resources to play safe, organizations with catastrophic potential should be shut down by top management. If safety regulations demanded by government are ignored, that too is the responsibility of management. At the end of this essay, I will examine the present concern with "self-regulation" and the strenuous effort of the Trump administration to do away with many regulations.

There are dozens of federal regulatory agencies, and they all do some good. But what are the characteristics of effective and ineffective agencies? When do they do a good job of reducing risks and when do they not? Regulatory agencies (RAs) are concerned, of course, with more than safety; they are concerned with corruption, anti-competitive behavior, employee rights, and so on. Here we are primarily concerned with their role in preventing serious accidents and will ask four questions: How dangerous is the enterprise being examined (is effort commensurate with the risks)? How expensive would it be to increase safety (too expensive to be worth it)? How does the enterprise's technology help or hurt regulatory efforts? And, what is the connection between the enterprise and the holders of political power?

One would expect greater regulatory efforts and effectiveness in the case of nuclear power than with the chance of gas pipelines exploding. There have been an average of ten deaths per year and much physical damage associated with pipelines, and almost none associated with nuclear power, but it is the potential that we are concerned with. Because of the potential danger of a nuclear plant accident, there is a much greater regulatory effort there than in pipelines. We should also expect more effective regulatory behavior if the potential victims are elites – they fly on airplanes but are not found on marine shipping vessels. RAs presumably would be more active in chemical plants if elites rather than the poor surrounded them. The public, given its role in influencing legislation, is more likely to be concerned with dangers that affect the rich than the poor, and RAs can be expected to respond to this favoritism, as can Congress in its funding decisions. The literature on risk has not been very concerned with the distribution of risk and the finding that the poor experience greater risk than the wealthy. Sociologists, however, have done much work on the ways that risks are shifted from the rich to the poor, particularly in the prominent handbooks on climate change (Dunlap, 2015). Any work on RAs should consider the role of economic stratification in terms of who pays and who benefits, but that will not be discussed here.

Another important variable is the cost of improving safety. Regulations almost always are "expensive" for the firm or for the government enterprise – expensive in the short run even if they are economical in the long run. While we will be mainly concerned with the for-profit organizations that create the most risks, most of our comments apply as well to enterprises in the nonprofit and governmental sectors. Cutting operating costs is a sure way to increase profits (or meet budgets), and the most powerful thread that I have found in examining serious accidents is the simple one of safety being expensive. Failure to inspect, unwillingness to spend more on equipment, speed-ups and overwork, poor maintenance, and lack of proper training – all these I have found to be important in most accidents, sometimes the only really important causes. Some of this occurs because serious accidents are actually rare in most systems, while savings from cost-cutting and speed-ups are continuous, so it may be seen as worth running the risks (if one is indifferent to the human costs). But this makes such comments as the following from the Occupational Safety and Health Administration (OSHA) especially puzzling: poor safety practices that led to expensive plant disasters were repeated in other plants the company owned; no lesson was learned. Indeed, sometimes they were repeated in the same plant despite the cost. Surely this suggests a management failure and an uneconomical practice; these were expensive accidents. One is justified in showing bewilderment and noting, as many others have noted, that saving lives and saving money will often go together. Thus, it is distressing to see so many accidents in the oil and chemical refinery sector that OSHA considered. Even fines imposed by the regulatory agent had no effect and were often very small (Perrow, 2011).

The standards that RAs set and their diligence in inspecting the degree of compliance are often subject to negotiation between the agency, industry leaders, and heads of large, powerful corporations. Hard evidence of industry weakening the standards proposed by the RAs exists, but it is hard to come by. A recent study of decades of regulatory decisions in the chemical industry shows repeated and extensive modification of standards and even falsification of the evidence on behalf of the regulated companies (CMD, 2017). We should note that large corporations regularly give one or two of their top executives leave to serve in the government for two or three years, especially in regulatory matters. This gives the industry privileged access to formulating standards. There are more direct ways, of course, for reducing or eliminating standards.

For example, as a result of increasing errors and minor accidents, the Nuclear Regulatory Commission (NRC) increased the number of inspections of nuclear power plants. The plant managers objected and went to the senator that headed the committee that set the NRC's budget. The senator called in the heads of the NRC and threatened to severely cut their budget if they did not cancel the increase in plant inspections. The NRC – the organization mandated to make the plants secure and safe – gave in and reduced the number of inspections. It let the corporations decide what level of inspection is safe (Perrow, 2007). By and large, I would say that the NRC is only barely effective in its mandate. Throughout its history, it has been charged with favoring management rather than the public in some critical areas. To the alarm of experts outside of the corporations (and many of its own experts), the NRC made only minor changes concerning the safety of nuclear power plants after the Fukushima event and rejected the large changes that would have seemed appropriate and were favored by its own technical staff.

The NRC is an interesting case since nuclear power plants have the greatest lethal potential of any of our organizations; thus, this agency might be expected to be at the top of any safety ranking. It also should be safer than most since there are less than 100 plants to worry about. Finally, it is not short of money or experienced personnel. Nevertheless, the nuclear power industry keeps having serious near misses and engaging in unsafe practices despite the efforts of the regulatory agency. Unfortunately, those agency efforts have not been very strong. Three of the five members have consistently been "conservative" in their recommendations (i.e., voting for lower standards), and in two cases a more liberal chairman of the board has been forced out by the three conservative members, probably at the behest of industry elites.

Unfortunately, we do not have much information about political positions and conflicts within the boards of other regulatory agencies. Systematic inquiry here would be very valuable. What sectors appear to have the most political influence on regulatory behavior? What boards show evidence of consumer representation on the boards of risky enterprises?

An important question that is rarely systematically explored is: What technology and organizational factors make regulation easy or difficult? Here are some obvious observations. Air transport is perhaps the most successful case of regulation that we have. Despite the complexity of the system as a whole and the complexity of the aircraft that make it up, its accident rate is now extremely small. Why? There are thousands of takeoffs and landings every hour, and extensive information about all aspects of the flight is recorded and can be analyzed. This extensive trial and error operation is not available in such areas as nuclear waste disposal, chemical plant shutdowns for maintenance or new equipment, the transport of hazardous materials, the siting and the building of large dams, and so on. Changes in aircraft design are incremental. The military tests new materials and designs thoroughly before they are taken up by the commercial aviation sector. Until recently, the military also provided training for most of the pilots in the commercial sector. Accidents are thoroughly publicized, and the consequences for the particular airline company are more severe than any fines because of loss of revenue.

It would be hard to find another risky system with so many aspects that promote safety (John Downer has a splendid series of articles on airlines; e.g., Downer, 2010; 2011). Nevertheless, nothing is perfect, and there are always opportunities to save money at the expense of safety. For more than a decade, the National Transportation Safety Board (NTSB) pressured the Federal Aviation Administration (FAA) to require nonflammable materials in the cabins of the aircraft, pointing out that most deaths in airline accidents occurred because of materials in the cabin bursting into flame. Others have criticized the FAA approval of "hub and spoke" route designs, their limited attention to pilot overwork and stress, and several other areas that affect safety (Fraher, 2014). But the safety record is remarkable.

In contrast is the marine transportation system. Here the evidence is hard to examine since it may go down to the bottom of the sea. Elites are not passengers on freight ships, and since there may be dozens of companies with cargo on anyone's ship, is it is hard for them all to get together to sue the shipper for negligence. International regulations are few and often ignored; it is hard to pressure ships that are registered in small, corrupt nations, as many are. Shipping is one of the few areas that benefit from centralization rather than decentralization. If the company makes enough products that need to be shipped, it will benefit by owning its own vessel and thus have stricter control over its operation. One would expect that there are far fewer accidents with these kinds of vessels (Perrow, 1999).

Improvements in ships and navigation equipment reduce the number of accidents per ship but increase the number of ships and their speed and size; thus, losing one ship a day seems to continue to be the norm. In the crowded English Channel, where most accidents occur, the introduction of radar initially lowered the accident rate. Those with radar could safely zip through the crowded channel confident that other ships not having radar would not alter their courses. When one half of the ships had radar, the accident or collision rate climbed back up; a ship with radar could not be confident that the course of the other ship would not be altered. This increased the accident rate over the pre-radar period. Only when all ships had radar did the rate settle down to what it initially had been (but with larger volume). With more, bigger, and faster ships on the ocean, the dangers have been mitigated by changes in crew management. Following what had already occurred in air transport, many ships now distribute authority and require consultation and communication between those on the bridge. Nonetheless, in contrast to air transport, overall international safety requirements are very weak in the marine area, contributing to a poor safety rate.

In between these extreme examples of air and marine transport, we have wide variations in regulatory success. The Department of Homeland Security (DHS) seems to have successfully alerted those who run the nation's power grids to the dangers of cyber warfare, which is surprising since there have been no effective attacks upon the power grid and thus little chance for trial and error learning and "sensemaking" experience. There is much concern about accidents in the biochemical area, where there are hundreds of small startup organizations with the capacity to release pathogens that could spread widely. There does not seem to be any effective regulation in this area, and aside from alerting the firms of the dangers, not much can be done. Pharmaceutical companies can be so powerful that they continue practices that the U.S. Food and Drug Administration (FDA) tries to outlaw, despite fines. One of the largest drug companies has been fined twice for allowing suspicious shipments of opiates during the current rash of addictions and deaths. Neither of the fines appears to have changed the company's presumably very profitable but devastating behavior (Morgenson, 2017).

Currently the literature favors a "deregulated" view, with government authorities limited to making suggestions and offering help. Self-regulation is the norm that is proposed by most political scientists studying the problem (Perrow, 2015). But the limited evidence that we have suggests that at least some of the time, or perhaps most of the time, firms embraced the mantra in order to avoid inspections. Those companies that joined the nonprofit but industry-sponsored regimes advocating safety steps and processes were simply rarely inspected by the government, and they managed to, for instance, pollute more than those outside of the regimes. Regulations are almost invariably seen in this literature as reducing innovation and flexibility, and being unreasonably costly. The advocates of deregulation rarely discuss the most notable deregulation step in recent history, allowing commercial (low risk) and investment (high risk) banks to merge. The 2002 legislation is widely assumed to be the root cause of our financial turmoil.

The current efforts by the Trump administration to reduce or eliminate regulations in almost every area of activity that poses risk may give us an interesting test case. Will accidents increase over the next few years generally, and especially in systems that have catastrophic potential? It is not even clear that all firms will welcome deregulation; large firms that have made substantial investments in safety may find that smaller firms, being able to avoid this investment, become more profitable. Or firms might realize that in the long run, safety pays.

References

Center for Media and Democracy (2017). *The poison papers: Thousands of pages discovered detail the secret history of the chemical industry.* www.prwatch.org.

Downer, J. (2010). Trust and technology: The social foundations of aviation regulation. *British Journal of Sociology, 61*(1), 87–110.

Downer, J. (2011). '737-Cabriolet': The limits of knowledge and the sociology of inevitable failure. *American Journal of Sociology, 117*(3), 725–762.

Dunlap, R. E., & Brulle, R. (Eds). (2015). *Climate change and society: Sociological perspectives.* New York: Oxford University Press.

Fraher, A. L. (2014). *The next crash: How short-term profit-seeking trumps airline safety.* New York: Cornell University Press.

Morgenson, G. (2017). Hard questions for a company at the center of the opioid crises. *New York Times.*

Perrow, C. (1999). *Normal accidents: Living with high risk technologies.* Princeton, NJ: Princeton University Press.

Perrow, C. (2007, 2011). *The next catastrophe: Reducing our vulnerabilities to natural, industrial, and terrorist disasters.* Princeton, NJ: Princeton University Press.

Perrow, C. (2015). Cracks in the regulatory state. *Social Currents, 2*(3), 203–212.

INDEX